THE ART OF COMEDY
An Anthology of Plays

SECOND EDITION

Edited by Larry Eilenberg
San Francisco State University

cognella™
San Diego, CA

Bassim Hamadeh, CEO and Publisher
Christopher Foster, General Vice President
Michael Simpson, Vice President of Acquisitions
Jessica Knott, Managing Editor
Stephen Milano, Creative Director
Kevin Fahey, Cognella Marketing Program Manager
Melissa Accornero, Acquisitions Editor
Stephanie Sandler, Licensing Associate

First published in the United States of America in 2012 by Cognella, a division of University Readers, Inc.

16 15 14 13 12   1 2 3 4 5

Printed in the United States of America

ISBN: 978-1-93426-975-6

www.cognella.com 800.200.3908

CONTENTS

INTRODUCTION

By Larry Eilenberg

THIS COLLECTION OF comedies has been assembled to serve the students in "The Art of Comedy," a course I have been teaching at San Francisco State University for over 20 years. It is a class that covers a wide range of contemporary performed comedy, from standup to sitcom, film romance to television satire. But the core material for the course lies in the theater, where the art of comedy began and where it most prominently flourished until the screen-dominated 20th century. This anthology includes some landmark scripts from the history of stage comedy, chosen for their representative qualities, for their influence upon the comic form and for the considerable pleasures they offer the reader.

There is a famous saying usually credited to Robert Frost that goes: "Poetry is what gets lost in translation." For the student of comedy, a variation on this familiar maxim might be: "Comedy is what gets lost in explanation." It certainly has been my experience that the more you explain a joke, for example, the less funny it becomes. And students have routinely told me that knowing too much about how comedy works can spoil some of its fun. Yet those same students will return to say that their knowledge, finally, made them appreciate good comedy more and tolerate bad comedy less. If that is so, then for the successful course in comedy, we'll hope that comedy is what gets *found* in explanation.

Experientially, there are two ingredients in a play that signal to us that what we are experiencing is a comedy. One sign, of course, is our laughter. And the other, to put in simplest terms, is a happy ending. The scholarly literature devoted to both of these defining comic characteristics is vast, and is well represented in works explicitly concerned with criticism and theory.

This volume provides only a hint of that literature, with two extracts at the end of the collection from the works of Sigmund Freud and Henri Bergson. These two writers are among the most prominent theorists of laughter and comedy, and their ideas are foundational to its study. Freud was a psychiatrist, Bergson a philosopher. Current studies of laughter, while still amply provided by psychiatrists and philosophers, are just as apt to consider the anatomy and physiology of laughter as its psychology, the evolutionary purposes and healing qualities of comedy as much as its aesthetics. That the prestigious Sloan-Kettering Cancer Center in New York has a "Clown Care Unit," for example, is testimony to the ways in which our contemporary understanding of laughter has gone a long way to substantiate the fact that it may indeed be the proverbial "best medicine."

The happy endings of comedies are as varied as the kinds of laughter they elicit. The unbridled partying that closes Aristophanes' *Lysistrata*, for instance, is in stark tonal and thematic contrast to the family reunion feast that is promised at the end of Shakespeare's *The Comedy of Errors*. In Molière's *Tartuffe*, the jailing of the title character, a religious con man, is announced by the officer of an all-knowing and divinely inspired King, and offers a conclusion that affirms heavenly authority and good order. As such, Molière's comic universe is nearly the inverse of the one that is ruled by outrageous coincidence in Oscar Wilde's *The Importance of Being Earnest*, yet the satisfactions of their finales are surely equal. Perhaps no comic ending in this collection is more fundamental than that of Sarah Ruhl's *The Clean House*. In this highly praised contemporary comedy, the character Ana's dead body is lying on stage at the finish of the next-to-last scene of the play. Then, for the close, she rises, is transformed into Matilde's mother, and gives birth to the baby Matilde—laughing uproariously at a joke her husband tells her while she is in the midst of childbirth. The sequence serves to remind us of the essentially cyclical and affirmative nature of comedy: that life culminates not in death (the province of tragedy), but in rebirth. Whether that rebirth takes the form of a marriage, or forgiveness, or friendship restored, it can offer us a joy that transcends even the comic gift of laughter.

My teacher Erich Segal, who introduced me to the scholarly study of comedy, wrote evocatively about the origins of the word "comedy," which was coined by the ancient Greeks. The root is an etymological uncertainty, with three possibilities proposed. One is from *kōma* ("sleep"), the impulse for comedy perhaps coming from dreams, with their topsy-turvy qualities and their many wish-fulfillments. Another possible source, which Aristotle endorsed, is *kōmē* ("country village"), suggesting the birth of comedy from the elemental crudeness and vulgarities of unsophisticated rustics. The prevailing consensus today is that the word *comedy*, in which its first energy was linguistically embodied, came from the Greek *kōmos*, a wild festival, what Segal playfully called "a revel without a cause." Since the etymological mystery has not been solved, we are left free to entertain the germinal truths in all three proposed roots—that comedy, at its essence, partakes of the dreamlike, the vulgar, and the festive. The plays in this anthology are offered as evidence of all three possibilities.

* * *

This anthology, with its intention to serve as a companion "reader" to a course on comedy, does not provide the usual critical introductions to each of the collected plays. The particular approaches to these comedies that a class may wish to take are left to the instructor's judgment and presentation. Brief biographies of the playwrights follow this Introduction. More detailed biographical information on the playwrights and backgrounds to the plays, needless to say, are readily and voluminously available through the resources of any Internet search engine.

THE PLAYWRIGHTS

Aristophanes

Aristophanes (c. 448–c. 380 B.C.E.) was a writer of Greek Old and Middle Comedy. Author of approximately forty plays, his eleven surviving works are the oldest complete comedies extant. Aristophanes was an outspoken critic of the lengthy Peloponnesian War and a satirist of his contemporary Athens. Biographical information is scant, though there is a famous portrayal of the playwright in Plato's *Symposium*.

Plautus (Titus Maccius Plautus)

Plautus (c. 254–c. 184 B.C.E.) was the most popular of Roman comic playwrights. His works, twenty of which survive, are musical, farcical, and filled with wordplay. Often imitated in his own time, Plautus' comedies have been adapted throughout theatrical history. Shakespeare's *The Comedy of Errors* and Rodgers and Hart's *The Boys from Syracuse* were both drawn from *The Menaechmus Twins*, and the highly successful musical *A Funny Thing Happened on the Way to the Forum* was adapted from the Plautus comedies *Pseudolus* and *Miles Gloriosus*.

William Shakespeare

William Shakespeare (1564–1616) is widely considered to be the greatest playwright in history. Born in Stratford-upon-Avon, the son of a prosperous glover, Shakespeare made his way to London by the early 1590s, where he joined the Lord Chamberlain's Men, a leading theatrical company. Shakespeare wrote tragedies, histories, romances, and comedies, and his plays in each category are among the most famous ever written. His works have been voluminously studied, and the titles, from *Hamlet* and *Macbeth* to *Richard III* and *The Tempest*, are at the very center of the canon of world literature and drama. Shakespeare was also an actor and manager in his company, later renamed the King's Men. He retired to Stratford in 1613 and died three years later.

Molière (Jean-Baptiste Poquelin)

Molière (1622–1673) wrote the best known of French comedies and founded the theatrical company that became France's national theatre. Son of a prosperous upholsterer well connected to the French royal court, Molière was well educated and intended for court life. Instead, he changed his name, began his career as an actor, was imprisoned for debt, and then spent a decade touring the provinces. Molière turned to playwriting in the early 1650s, received a royal invitation to perform in Paris in 1658, and settled there to share a theatre with an Italian *commedia dell'arte* company. Molière's great comedies of the 1660s and 1670s included *The Misanthrope*, *The Miser*, and *The Learned Ladies*. The most controversial of his comedies was *Tartuffe*, which the playwright had to rewrite twice before it was allowed onstage. He died shortly after a performance as the title character in his last play *The Imaginary Invalid*.

Oscar Wilde

Oscar Wilde (1854–1900) was a celebrated wit and aesthete of the late nineteenth century, author of social comedies such as *Lady Windermere's Fan* and *An Ideal Husband*, as well as the novel *The Picture of Dorian Gray*. Wilde's reputation today rests principally on the continuing popularity of his subversive farce *The Importance of Being Earnest* and on his tragic prosecution and imprisonment for homosexual practices.

George Bernard Shaw

George Bernard Shaw (1856–1950) was a novelist and critic into his forties, when he began writing plays. During the next fifty years of his long life, Shaw became the most illustrious writer of comedy in the English language, winner of both the Nobel Prize in Literature and the Academy Award (for the screenplay of *Pygmalion*). Shaw was an ardent socialist, evolutionist, and vegetarian, and his plays and prefaces are full of politics and opinions. Among his best-known works are *Candida*, *Major Barbara*, *Man and Superman*, *Saint Joan*, and *Heartbreak House*. His hugely popular *Pygmalion* was adapted into the frequently revived musical *My Fair Lady*.

Luis Valdez and El Teatro Campesino

Luis Valdez (b. 1940) is the founding playwright of Chicano theatre in America, son of migrant farmworkers in California, and a graduate of San Jose State University. Briefly a member of the agitprop San Francisco Mime Troupe, Valdez formed El Teatro Campesino (The Farmworkers' Theatre) in 1965 to help unionize grape pickers and to support their strike. Valdez wrote short comic sketches for this purpose, called *actos*, among the most enduring of which were *Los Vendidos* ("The Sellouts") and *Las dos caras del patroncito* ("The Two Faces of the Boss"). Valdez wrote the hit play *Zoot Suit*, which was made into a film, and he directed the popular movie *La Bamba*. Luis Valdez has held several academic appointments in the University of California and California State University systems. El Teatro Campesino continues to produce bilingual theatre at its company home in San Juan Bautista.

Sarah Ruhl

Sarah Ruhl (b. 1974) is a poet and playwright, born and raised in Illinois and educated at Brown University, where she studied with Pulitzer Prize–winning playwright Paula Vogel. Sarah Ruhl was awarded the MacArthur "Genius" Fellowship, has been a finalist for the Pulitzer Prize, and has received wide recognition and international production for her increasingly varied body of work. Sometimes characterized as a contemporary "surrealist," she is perhaps better understood as a tragicomedian. Her best known plays are *The Clean House* and her recent success *In the Next Room (or the Vibrator Play)*, which premiered at the Berkeley Repertory Theatre before moving to Broadway.

Yasmina Reza

Yasmina Reza (b. 1959) is a French actor, playwright, novelist, and screenwriter of Hungarian-Iranian-Jewish background. Her stage comedies, especially *Art* and *The God of Carnage*, have had extraordinary international success and won the major theatre awards of France, Britain, and the United States. Yasmina Reza's screen adaptation of *The God of Carnage*, called *Carnage*, was directed by Roman Polanski, featured Jodie Foster, Kate Winslet, Christoph Waltz, and Jon C. Reilly in the leading roles, and was released in 2011.

-LE

LYSISTRATA

By Aristophanes
Translated by Sarah Ruden

CAST OF CHARACTERS

SPEAKING CHARACTERS
LYSISTRATA
CALONICE
MYRRHINE
LAMPITO
MEN'S CHORUS LEADER
CHORUS OF OLD MEN
WOMEN'S CHORUS LEADER
CHORUS OF OLD WOMEN
COUNCILOR
OLD WOMEN #1, #2 AND #3
WOMEN #1, #2 AND #3
CINESIAS
CINESIAS' BABY
SPARTAN HERALD
UNITED CHORUS
UNITED CHORUS LEADER
SPARTAN AMBASSADOR
ATHENIAN AMBASSADORS #1
  AND #2

NONSPEAKING CHARACTERS
ATHENIAN WOMEN
BOEOTIAN WOMAN
CORINTHIAN WOMAN
SPARTAN AND OTHER FOREIGN WOMEN
FEMALE SCYTHIAN GUARD
TWO SLAVES
FOUR MALE SCYTHIAN GUARDS
CINESIAS' SLAVE
ATHENIAN AMBASSADORS
SPARTAN AMBASSADORS
THE AMBASSADORS' SLAVES
RECONCILIATION
PIPER

SCENE: *A large rectangular stage behind a bare circular area with an altar in the middle. Two ramplike entrances to the circular area at the left and right. A stage building with up to three doors in front, and a hatch to allow actors onto the roof. Scene descriptions and stage directions occur nowhere in an ancient Greek dramatic text, but the context here suggests that the action begins on the lower slopes of the Acropolis or in an Athenian residential district. The action later moves to the outside of the Propylaea, or ceremonial gates leading to the top of the Acropolis, then probably to lower Athens again, and then to the outside of a banqueting hall. But the action should be considered continuous or nearly continuous: a Greek chorus remained the whole time after its entrance, and scene changes in an open-air theater with no curtain would have been sketchy.*

(Enter Lysistrata, a good-looking young matron.)

LYSISTRATA:

If I'd invited them to hoot and prance
At Bacchic rites, or at some sleazy shrine,
I would have had to crawl through tambourines
To get here. As it is, no woman's showed,
Except my neighbor Calonice. Hi.

(Enter Calonice, a middle-aged matron.)

CALONICE:

Hi, Lysistrata. Honey, what's gone wrong?
Don't spoil your pretty face with ratty snarls!
Your eyebrows look like bows to shoot me dead.

LYSISTRATA:

Oh, Calonice, this just burns me up.
Women are slacking off, can't make the grade.
Our husbands say we're cunning to the point
Of—well—depravity.

CALONICE:

                    Darn tootin' right!

LYSISTRATA:

But given word to meet me here today—

A vital matter needs our serious thought—
They're sleeping in.

CALONICE:

But sweetie, soon they'll come.
Sometimes it's quite a challenge sneaking out.
The husband might require some straightening up,
The maid a screech to get her out of bed,
The kid a bath, a nibble, or a nap.

LYSISTRATA:

But what I have to say means more than that
To women.

CALONICE:

Precious, what *is* eating you?
Why summon us in this mysterious way?
What is it? Is it... big?

LYSISTRATA:

Of course.

CALONICE:

And hard?

LYSISTRATA:

Count on it.

CALONICE:

Then how could they not have *come?*

LYSISTRATA:

Oh, shut your mouth. They *would* have flocked for that.
No, this thing I've gone through exhaustively;
I've worked it over, chewed it late at night.

CALONICE:

Pathetic if it needed that much help.

LYSISTRATA:

It's this pathetic: in the women's hands
Is the salvation of the whole of Greece.

CALONICE:

In women's hands? It's hanging by a thread.

LYSISTRATA:

We hold within our grasp the city's plight.
The Peloponnesians may be wiped out—

CALONICE:

By Zeus, that's best, as far as we're concerned—

LYSISTRATA:

And the Boeotians with them, root and branch—

CALONICE:

All of them, fine, except those gorgeous eels.

LYSISTRATA:

I won't say Athens, since the omen's bad.
Imagine if I'd said it—shocking, huh?
If all the women come together here—
Boeotians, Peloponnesians, and the rest—
And us—together we can salvage Greece.

CALONICE:

What thoughtful thing could women ever do?
What vivid venture? We just sit decked out
In saffron gowns, makeup about this thick,
Cimberian lingerie, and platform shoes.

LYSISTRATA:

It's those that I intend to save our race:
Those dresses, and perfume, and rouge, and shoes,
And little see-through numbers that we wear.

CALONICE:

> How's that?

LYSISTRATA:

> The men surviving won't lift up
> Their spears (against each other, anyway).

CALONICE:

> By the Two Gods, I've got a dress to dye!

LYSISTRATA:

> Or shields—

CALONICE:

> I've got a negligée to try!

LYSISTRATA:

> Or knives—

CALONICE:

> Ooh, ooh, and shoes! And shoes to buy!

LYSISTRATA:

> So shouldn't all the other women come?

CALONICE:

> Well, YES! With wings to boost them, hours ago!

LYSISTRATA:

> It's such a bitch assembling Attica.
> You know they'd rather die than be on time.
> Nobody even came here from the coast,
> Or out of Salamis.

CALONICE:

> I'm sure they got
> Up on those mounts of theirs at break of day.

LYSISTRATA:

I thought it would be only logical
For the Acharnians to start the crowd,
But they're not here yet.

CALONICE:

Well, Theogenes' wife
Has raised her glass to us—any excuse.
No, wait. Look thataway: here come a few.

LYSISTRATA:

And now a couple more.

(Several women straggle in, among them Myrrhine, a young
and beautiful matron.)

CALONICE:

Yuck, what a smell!
Where are they from?

LYSISTRATA:

The puke-bush swamp.

CALONICE:

By Zeus,
It must be quite a place to raise a stink.

MYRRHINE:

Ooh, Lysistrata, are we very late?
Too mad to say?

LYSISTRATA:

Why should I not be mad?
This is important! Why not come on time?

MYRRHINE:

Well, it was dark—I couldn't find my thing—
But say what's on your mind, now that we're here.

LYSISTRATA:

    No, wait a little while. The other wives,
    The Boeotians and the Peloponnesians,
    Are on the way.

MYRRHINE:

                All right, of course we'll wait.
    Look over there, though—that's not Lampito?

      (Enter Lampito, a strapping woman in a distinct, more
      revealing costume. Several others in various foreign dress
      accompany her, including a Boeotian and a Corinthian
      Woman.)

LYSISTRATA:

    Darling Laconian, Lampito, hail!
    How I admire your gleaming gorgeousness,
    Your radiant skin, your body sleek and plump.
    I bet that you could choke a bull.

LAMPITO:

                       I could.
    I'm in such shape I kick my own sweet ass.

CALONICE: *(Prodding curiously.)*
    And what a brace of boobs. How bountiful!

LAMPITO:

    What am I s'pposed to be? A pig for sale?

LYSISTRATA:

    And what's this other young thing's origin?

LAMPITO:

    Boeotia sent her as a delegate.
    She's at your service.

MYRRHINE: *(Peeking under woman's clothes.)*
                    Boeotian—sure enough:
Just look at what a broad and fertile plain.

CALONICE: *(Peeking likewise.)*
      She's even pulled the weeds. Now *that* is class.

LYSISTRATA:
      And what's the other girl?

LAMPITO:
                    Corinthian.
      Hell, ain't she fine?

LYSISTRATA:
                    Damn right she's fine … from here,
And get another angle on her—wow!

LAMPITO:
      We're like a women's army. Who put out
      The word to assemble?

LYSISTRATA:
                    That was me.

LAMPITO:
                                        How come?
      Tell us what's going on.

CALONICE:
                    Yeah, honey, what?
      What all-important burr is up your butt?

LYSISTRATA:
      The time has come. But first you answer me
      One weensy little thing.

CALONICE:
                    Okay. Just ask.

LYSISTRATA:
> I know you all have husbands far from home
> On active service. Don't you miss the men,
> The fathers of your children, all this time?

CALONICE:
> My husband's been away five months in Thrace.
> Somebody's gotta watch the general.

MYRRHINE:
> Mine's been in Pylos seven freaking months.

LAMPITO:
> Once in a while, mine's back, but then he's off.
> It's like that shield's a friggin' pair of wings.

LYSISTRATA:
> And since the Milesians deserted us
> (Along with every scrap of lover here),
> We've even lost those six-inch substitutes,
> Those dinky dildos for emergencies.
> If I could find a way to end this war,
> Would you be willing partners?

CALONICE:
> > *I* sure would.
> I'd sacrifice my nicest dress to buy
> Some wine (and sacrifice the wine to me).

MYRRHINE:
> I'd cut myself in two and donate half—
> A flat slice like a bottom-feeding fish.

LAMPITO:
> I'd hike clear up Mount Taygetus to see
> If peace is flashin' somewhere way far off.

LYSISTRATA:
> Fine. So. Here goes. You need to know the plan.

Yes, ladies. How we force the men to peace.
How are we going to do it? We must all
Hold off—

CALONICE:

        From *what?*

LYSISTRATA:

                You're positive you will?

CALONICE:

    We'll do it! Even if it costs our lives.

LYSISTRATA:

    From now on, no more penises for you.

(The women begin to disperse.)

    Wait! You can't all just turn and walk away!
    And what's this purse-lipped shaking of your heads?
    You're turning pale—is that a tear I see?
    Will you or not? You can't hold out on me!

CALONICE:

    No, I don't think so. Let the war go on.

MYRRHINE:

    Me? Not a chance in hell, so screw the war.

LYSISTRATA:

    That's it, my piscine heroine? You said
    Just now that you'd bisect yourself for peace.

CALONICE:

    ANYTHING else for me. I'd walk through fire,
    But do without a dick? Be serious!
    There's nothing, Lysistrata, like a dick.

LYSISTRATA: *(Turning to Woman #1.)*
　　And you?

WOMAN #1:
　　　　Me? Mmm, I'll take the fire, thanks.

LYSISTRATA:
　　Oh, gender fit for boning up the butt!
　　No wonder we're the stuff of tragedies:
　　Some guy, a bit of nookie, and a brat.

　　　　(To Lampito.)

　　But you, sweet foreigner, if you alone
　　Stand with me, then we still could save the day.
　　Give me your vote!

LAMPITO:
　　　　　　Shit, it's no easy thing
　　To lie in bed alone without no dong …
　　But count me in. Peace we just gotta have.

LYSISTRATA:
　　The only *woman* in this half-assed horde!

CALONICE:
　　Suppose we did—the thing you say we should—
　　Which gods forbid—what has that got to do
　　With peace?

LYSISTRATA:
　　　　　　A lot, I promise you. If we
　　Sit in our quarters, powdered daintily
　　As good as nude in those imported slips,
　　And—just—slink by with crotches nicely groomed,
　　The men will swell right up and want to boink,
　　But we won't let them near us, we'll refuse—
　　Trust me, they'll make a treaty at a dash.

LAMPITO:

> You're right! You know how Menelaus saw
> Helen's bazooms and threw his weapon down.

CALONICE:

> But what if they just shrug and walk away?

LYSISTRATA:

> For them, there's just one place a dildo fits.

CALONICE:

> As if a fake is lots of fun for us.
> Suppose they grab us, drag us into bed.
> We'll have no choice.

LYSISTRATA:

> Resist. Hang on the door.

CALONICE:

> Suppose they beat us.

LYSISTRATA:

> Yield a lousy lay.
> They force a woman, and it's no more fun.
> Plus, no more housework! They'll give up—you'll see
> How fast. No husband's going to like to screw
> Unless he knows his woman likes it too.

CALONICE:

> If that's the thing you're set on, fine—okay.

LAMPITO:

> We'll force the Spartan husbands into peace:
> No cheating, quibbling, squabbling any more.
> But what about them lowlifes in your town?
> What'll you do so they don't run amok?

LYSISTRATA:

> We'll handle things on our side. Don't you fret.

LAMPITO:

> I will. You know that god of yours has got
> An expense account for sails and all the rest.

LYSISTRATA:

> We've put aside that obstacle ourselves.
> Today we occupy the citadel.
> This is the mission of the senior squad.
> While we confer here, they've gone up to fake
> A sacrifice and storm the Acropolis.

LAMPITO:

> You *are* a clever thang. Fine all around!

LYSISTRATA:

> Let's quickly swear an oath, my friend, and set
> Our concord up unbendable as bronze.

LAMPITO:

> Give us whatever oath you wanna give.

LYSISTRATA:

> So where's the guard? (I'm talking to you! Wake up!)

> *(Enter Female Scythian Guard in an exotic uniform.)*

> Bring here your shield and set it upside down.

> *(She obeys. The women pause.)*

> Now where's the sacrifice?

CALONICE:

>   What can we find
> To swear on, Lysistrata?

LYSISTRATA:

       Aeschylus
Had people drain the blood of slaughtered sheep
Into a shield.

CALONICE:

     A shield? To swear for peace?
Excuse me, honey, but that can't be right.

LYSISTRATA:

What else, then?

CALONICE:

        We could find a giant stud,
A pure white stallion, say, and hack him up.

LYSISTRATA:

What do you mean, a horse?

CALONICE:

        We need to swear

On *something.*

LYSISTRATA:

     Listen up! I know the way:
A big black drinking bowl laid on its back;
A jar of Thasian to sacrifice;
An oath to mix no water with the wine.

LAMPITO:

Shit sakes, I like that more than I can say.

LYSISTRATA:

Somebody bring a jar out, and a bowl.

   (The items are brought.)

MYRRHINE:

Hey, sisters, that's some massive pottery!

CALONICE: *(Snatching.)*
Just fondling it, you'd start to feel real good.

LYSISTRATA:
Put the bowl down and help me hold the beast.

> *(Calonice relinquishes her hold. All the women join in lifting the jar.)*

Holy Persuasion, and our Bowl for Pals,
Be gracious toward this women's sacrifice.

> *(Lysistrata opens the jar. The women pour.)*

CALONICE:
Propitiously the gleaming blood spurts forth!

LAMPITO:
By Castor, and it smells real pretty too.

MYRRHINE:
Girls, let me be the first to swear the oath.

CALONICE:
No way, by Aphrodite. We'll draw lots.

LYSISTRATA:
Grip the bowl's rim, Lampito and the rest.

> *(They obey.)*

One of you, speak for all, repeat my words,
Then everybody else confirm the oath.
Neither my boyfriend nor my wedded spouse—

CALONICE:
Neither my boyfriend nor my wedded spouse—

LYSISTRATA:
> Shall touch me when inflated. Say it, girl!

CALONICE:
> Shall touch me when inflated. Holy hell!
> Knees—Lysistrata—wobbly. Gonna faint!

LYSISTRATA: *(Sternly, ignoring this distress.)*
> I shall stay home unhumped both night and day,

CALONICE:
> I shall stay home unhumped both night and day,

LYSISTRATA:
> While wearing makeup and a flashy dress,

CALONICE:
> While wearing makeup and a flashy dress,

LYSISTRATA:
> That I may give my man the scorching hots,

CALONICE:
> That I may give my man the scorching hots,

LYSISTRATA:
> But I will not consent to what he wants,

CALONICE:
> But I will not consent to what he wants,

LYSISTRATA:
> And if he forces me, against my will,

CALONICE:
> And if he forces me, against my will,

LYSISTRATA:
> Then I will sulk, I will not hump along;

CALONICE:

    Then I will sulk, I will not hump along;

LYSISTRATA:

    I will not point my slippers at the roof;

CALONICE:

    I will not point my slippers at the roof;

LYSISTRATA:

    Nor, like a lion knickknack, ass in air—

CALONICE:

    Nor, like a lion knickknack, ass in air—

LYSISTRATA:

    Abiding by these vows, may I drink wine;

CALONICE:

    Abiding by these vows, may I drink wine;

LYSISTRATA:

    If I transgress, let water fill the bowl.

CALONICE:

    If I transgress, let water fill the bowl.

LYSISTRATA:

    Now do you all consent?

ALL:

                By Zeus, we do.

LYSISTRATA:

    I dedicate this bowl. *(She drinks heartily.)*

CALONICE:

               Just drink your share!
We've got to work together, starting now.

(All drink. A mass ululation is heard offstage.)

LAMPITO:
Somebody's shouting.

LYSISTRATA:
                    As I said before:
It's our contingent on the citadel.
They've taken it already. Lampito,
You go arrange things back in Sparta. These

(Indicates Spartan Women.)

Will need to stay with us as hostages.
We'll join the rest of the Athenians
And help them heave the bars behind the doors.

CALONICE:
You think the men will find out right away
And all gang up on us?

LYSISTRATA:
                    The hell with them.
They can't make threats or fires fierce enough.
These doors stay shut. We only open them
On those exact conditions we've set down.

CALONICE:
So Aphrodite help us, we'll stay put,
Or not deserve the cherished title "Bitch."

(All the women exit into stage building.)

(Enter a Chorus of twelve Old Men, carrying logs, unlit torches, and pots of burning charcoal.)

MEN'S CHORUS LEADER:
Draces, lead on, ignore your throbbing back
Under the fresh, green weight of olive trunks.

CHORUS OF OLD MEN:
>A long life brings lots
>That's surprising to see.
>This, Strumodorus, is a new one on me.
>At our expense
>This pestilence
>Festered at home indoors.
>They've taken our citadel!
>Athena's image as well!
>They've barred the ceremonial gates, the whores!

MEN'S CHORUS LEADER:
>Straight ahead is the fortress, Philurgus.
>To pile up one pyre and set it afire
>For all with a hand in this wicked affair
>Can pass without debate or amendments
>Or special pleading—well, first get Lycon's wife.

CHORUS OF OLD MEN:
>Demeter's my witness, this stunt isn't cute.
>Like Cleomenes, these girls won't find it a hoot.
>Cocky Spartan! He went away,
>Dealt with efficiently, let's say,
>His arms surrendered. He wore a crappy trace
>Of the clothes that he came in.
>He was blasted with famine,
>With six hard years of beard and crud on his face.

MEN'S CHORUS LEADER:
>Fierce was the siege that we sat for the bastard,
>Camping in seventeen ranks at the bulwark.
>But the gods and Euripides both detest women.
>I'll cram their impertinence straight back inside—
>If I don't, take my Marathon monument down.

CHORUS OF OLD MEN:
>The cliff in the road
>Where I haul my load
>Is right before me, I have come so fast.

Too bad—no mule!
So much to pull.
Literally, this is a pain in the ass.
But I won't tire—
I'll puff the fire—
Won't get distracted—it's got to last!

(They blow, recoil.)

Oh shit, the smoke!
I'm going to choke!

From the basin where it slept,
Lord Hercules, how savagely it leapt,
Like a rabid bitch, to bite me in the eyes.
It's Lemnian, I think,
From the land where women stink.
It reeks of everything that I despise.
Up to the heights!
Defend our rights!
The goddess needs us, don't you realize?

(They blow, recoil.)

Oh hell, the ash!
I'm going to crash!

MEN'S CHORUS LEADER:
Gods answer our prayers and the fire rears high.
Assignment The First: put the logs on the ground.
Here are some torches to ram in the brazier.
Rush then, and batter yourselves on the gates.
Call for surrender. A slit should spread open.
Otherwise, light the gates, smoke the broads out.
Put down your logs, men. (This smoke is a hassle!)
The generals in Samos are shirking the work.

(He heaves his wood down.)

That's better—the load has stopped warping my back.
This bucket of coals has the task to provide
Me—hey, me first!—with a virulent torch.
Great goddess Victory, give me a prize
For feminine insolence valiantly squished.

(The men busy themselves with lighting torches.)

(A Chorus of twelve Old Women enter from the opposite side, carrying water jars.)

WOMEN'S CHORUS LEADER:
Women, that bright thing in a murky cloud—
Is it a fire? Quick, let's get on the scene.

CHORUS OF OLD WOMEN:
Nicodice, hurry!
Calyce's getting lit!
Critylla's getting buffeted
By blazing winds
And old men full of shit.
Oh, dear! Oh, my! Am I too late?
I went at dawn to wrangle free this water.
I struggled through the crash and screech and slaughter—
Elbows flailing, jars askew—
Scurvy maids, slaves with tattoos—
In a panic raised this urn,
Downright manic to return
To keep my friends from getting singed.
I heard the news about unhinged
Codgers who, like lumberjacks,
Dumped their logs in ten-ton stacks
And launched the most
Outrageous boasts.
They said they'd make ashes of living profanity
Help, Goddess, save women from such inhumanity,
And they will restore your dear nation to sanity.
That's why, O Golden-Helmeted One,
They dared to occupy your throne.

Oh, be their ally, Triton's daughter.
Zap every spark out with this water.
Help us haul it to the top.
What these beasts are doing must stop!

(The women notice the men and their equipment.)

WOMEN'S CHORUS LEADER:
Wait! What can this be? They've been busy pricks.
Is this the work of conscientious citizens—or dicks?

(The men notice the women.)

MEN'S CHORUS LEADER:
We didn't reckon on this other swarm
Of women, rushing toward the gates to help.

WOMEN'S CHORUS LEADER:
What are you scared of? Do we seem a throng?
You're looking at just .01 percent.

MEN'S CHORUS LEADER:
Impossible to let them blather on!
We'd better whack them with this wood instead.

WOMEN'S CHORUS LEADER:
Girls, put your pitchers down, out of the way,
So if they lift a hand, we'll be prepared.

MEN'S CHORUS LEADER:
If somebody had done a proper job
Of slapping them, they'd keep their yappers shut.

WOMEN'S CHORUS LEADER:
Fine. Try it. Here's a cheek for you to smack.
And then I'll tear your balls off like a bitch.

MEN'S CHORUS LEADER:
Shut up! I'll pound you hollow if you don't.

WOMEN'S CHORUS LEADER:
    Just put a fingertip on Stratyllis—

MEN'S CHORUS LEADER:
    And if I pummel her? What will you do?

WOMEN'S CHORUS LEADER:
    I'll gnaw your lungs and claw your entrails out.

MEN'S CHORUS LEADER:
    Euripides is my authority
    On women: "She's a creature lacking shame."

WOMEN'S CHORUS LEADER:
    Honey, we'd better lift these jars again.

MEN'S CHORUS LEADER:
    What did you bring the water for, you scum?

WOMEN'S CHORUS LEADER:
    And what's the fire for, you senile coots?
    Fogies flambés?

MEN'S CHORUS LEADER:
                    A funeral for your friends!

WOMEN'S CHORUS LEADER:
    We'll put the pyre out before it's lit.

MEN'S CHORUS LEADER:
    You'd meddle with *my* fire?

WOMEN'S CHORUS LEADER:
                    As you'll see.

MEN'S CHORUS LEADER:
    Maybe I ought to toast you with this torch.

Women's Chorus Leader:
> Have you got soap? I've got the water here.

Men's Chorus Leader:
> A bath, you rancid hag?

Women's Chorus Leader:
> Get clean, get laid.

Men's Chorus Leader:
> You hear what nerve—?

Women's Chorus Leader:
> Why not? I'm not a slave.

Men's Chorus Leader:
> I'll squelch that yelp.

Women's Chorus Leader:
> You're not the judge of me!

Men's Chorus Leader:
> Set fire to her hair!

(The men threaten with their torches.)

Women's Chorus Leader:
> Help, River God!

(The women empty one set of pitchers over the men.)

Men's Chorus Leader:
> Hell!

Women's Chorus Leader:
> Oh, was that too hot?

(The women make use of auxiliary pitchers.)

MEN'S CHORUS LEADER:

                    Hot?! Stop it, slut!

WOMEN'S CHORUS LEADER:

    I'm watering you so you'll grow nice and high.

MEN'S CHORUS LEADER:

    I'm shivering and shaking myself dry.

WOMEN'S CHORUS LEADER:

    But you've got fire to warm your footsies by.

        (Enter Councilor, accompanied by Two Slaves with crow-
        bars, and Four Male Scythian Guards.)

COUNCILOR:

    These flaming women, spoiled with kettledrums,
    And ritual howls, and this Adonis thing—
    You hear them whoop it up—they're on the *roofs*—
    Exactly like in the Assembly once.
    Demostratus—goddamn him—made the speech
    That sent us into Sicily Just then
    His dancing dame yelled, "Poor Adonis!" He
    Moved that we try Zacynthus for recruits.
    Feeling no pain, the woman on the tiles
    Burped, "Mourn Adonis!" And Demostratus
    Blasted along, that psycho. This is what
    Happens because of women on the loose.

MEN'S CHORUS LEADER:

    No kidding. What about the women here?
    They've even emptied pitchers on our heads,
    Washed us against our will. Our cloaks are drenched.
    You'd think that we were all incontinent.

COUNCILOR:

    Briny Poseidon, that's what we deserve,
    Conniving with our wives the way we do,
    Drawing them diagrams for decadence—

Of course they sprout conspiracies like this.
We stride into a jeweler's and we say,
"Goldsmith, the necklace that you made my wife—
She was, uh, dancing—hard—the other night.
The prong—you know—got jiggled and fell out.
I have to sail to Salamis today,
But if you're free this evening, go around
And put that thing back in, and screw it tight."
Or at a leather workshop someone asks
A strapping, really well-equipped young man,
"Oh, Mister Shoemaker, you know my wife's
Little toe, and how tender it can get,
Rubbed by her sandal strap? Drop by at noon
And give her hole a jimmy and a stretch."
No wonder it's resulted in *this* mess.
I AM A COUNCILOR. It is my JOB
To find the wood for oars and PAY FOR IT.
And now these WOMEN shut the gates on me!
It's no good standing here. Those crowbars, quick!
I'll separate these women from their gall.

(A slave is indecisive.)

Hey slack-jaw, move! What are you waiting for?
You're looking for a pub where you can hide?
Both of you, put these levers in the gates
From that side, and from here I'll stick mine in
And help you shove.

(Lysistrata emerges from the stage building.)

LYSISTRATA:
                    Right, you can shove those bars.
It doesn't take a tool to bring me out.
You don't need siege equipment here. Just brains.

COUNCILOR:
Really, you walking poo? Where *is* that guard?
Grab her and tie her hands behind her back.

LYSISTRATA:
> By Artemis, if that state property's
> Fingertip touches me, I'll make him wail.

> *(Guard backs away.)*

COUNCILOR:
> You're scared of her? Grab her around the waist,
> And you—look sharp and help him tie her hands.

> *(Old Woman #1 enters from door.)*

OLD WOMAN #1:
> Pandrosus[1] help me. Lay one cuticle
> On her, and I shall beat you till you shit.

> *(The two guards slink off.)*

COUNCILOR:
> Such language! Where'd the other archer go?
> Get this one first. Just hear that potty mouth!

> *(Old Woman #2 enters from door.)*

OLD WOMAN #2:
> By Phosphorus, one hangnail grazes her,
> And you'll be nursing eyes as black as tar.

> *(Third guard retreats.)*

COUNCILOR:
> What *is* this? Where's a guard? Get hold of her!
> One little expedition's at an end.

> *(Old Woman #3 enters from door.)*

---

1   An Athenian princess of myth.

OLD WOMAN #3:

> Go near her, by Tauropolus, and I
> Will give you screaming lessons on your hair.

> *(Fourth guard makes himself scarce.)*

COUNCILOR:

> Now I'm in deep. I've got no archers left.
> We can't let women have the final stomp!
> Scythians, we must form a battle line
> And march straight at them.

> *(Guards reluctantly gather together again from a distance.)*

LYSISTRATA:

> You'll find out, I swear,
> That we've got four divisions tucked away,
> Heavy-armed women itching for a fight.

COUNCILOR:

> Attendants, twist their arms behind their backs.

> *(The guards advance.)*

LYSISTRATA:

> Thunder out, allied women, from the walls!
> Sellers of garlic, gruel, and poppy seeds,
> Greengrocers, bakers, landladies—attack!
> Yank them and shove them! Sock them! Hammer them!
> Insult, belittle them—get really coarse!

> *(A mob of women enters and descends on the guards with physical and verbal abuse.)*

Fall back! To strip their dignity's enough.

> *(The women retreat. The guards lie flattened and immobile.)*

COUNCILOR:
>   My bodyguard reduced to diddly-squat!

LYSISTRATA:
>   But what were you expecting? Facing troops?
>   Or herding slaves? Apparently you don't
>   Think we have guts.

COUNCILOR:
>   The female gut's quite deep:
>   I've seen the way that you perform in bars.

MEN'S CHORUS LEADER:
>   Hey you, our Councilor: you're wasting words
>   By arguing with wild things like a fool.
>   They didn't even let us get undressed,
>   But bathed us without benefit of soap.

WOMEN'S CHORUS LEADER:
>   Well, you, sir, think your fellow citizens
>   Are fit for bullying. You *want* black eyes?
>   Given the choice, I'd play a prim, demure
>   Young girl, disturbing no one by so much
>   As blinking. I'm a hornet when I'm roused.

CHORUS OF OLD MEN:
>   O, Zeus, what shall we do with these vermin?
>   We can't just take it. Let's examine
>   How it happened, Why these women
>   Plotted to snatch the bouldered shrine,
>   Out of bounds, high in the air,
>   The Acropolis,
>   And make it theirs.

MEN'S CHORUS LEADER: *(To Councilor.)*
>   Challenge, refute! Whatever sounds right must be wrong!
>   If they shortchange us, it's the ultimate disgrace.

COUNCILOR:

>Right. Question Number One: I am anxious to hear
>Your motivation for barring the fortress doors.

LYSISTRATA:

>Keeping the money here will starve the war to death.

COUNCILOR:

>Money—and war? Huh?

LYSISTRATA:

>There's a rats' nest in this town.
>Pisander and his public office-stalking ilk
>Raised hell—it yielded marvelous chances to steal.
>Who gives a hoot what they do now? The money's safe.

COUNCILOR:

>And *your* plan is—?

LYSISTRATA:

>You have to ask? It's *management*.

COUNCILOR:

>Of public funds? By *you?*

LYSISTRATA:

>And what's so strange in that?
>You let us women do the budgeting at home.

COUNCILOR:

>It's not the same at all!

LYSISTRATA:

>Because—?

COUNCILOR:

>You don't fight wars!

LYSISTRATA:

And you don't have to either.

COUNCILOR:

                    We're in jeopardy!

LYSISTRATA:

We'll save you.

COUNCILOR:

        You?

LYSISTRATA:

            Yeah, us.

COUNCILOR:

                But that's unthinkable.

LYSISTRATA:

Think what you like.

COUNCILOR:

            Unutterable.

LYSISTRATA:

                      No, uttered.

It doesn't matter how you feel.

COUNCILOR:

              THIS ISN'T RIGHT!

LYSISTRATA:

Too bad.

COUNCILOR:

    BUT I DON'T WANT IT!

LYSISTRATA:

                                    Then you need it more.

COUNCILOR:

How can you meddle in the stern affairs of state?

LYSISTRATA:

Listen here—

COUNCILOR:

The hand may be quicker than the mouth.

LYSISTRATA:

Listen! And keep a grip on your hands.

COUNCILOR:

                                    Can't manage.

I'm furious!

WOMAN #1:

And what you're *going* to be is *sore.*

COUNCILOR:

No, *you'll* be sore, old buzzard! *(To Lysistrata.)* You, go on.

LYSISTRATA:

                                    I will.

Throughout this futile war, we women held our peace.
Propriety (and husbands) permitted no peep
To escape our mouths. But we weren't exactly pleased.
We did hear how things were going. When you had passed
Some subnormally thought-out, doom-laden decree,
We'd say, aching, but on the surface simpering,
"What rider to the treaty did you decide on
Today at the Assembly?" "That's not your affair!
Shut up." And lo, I did shut up.

OLD WOMAN #1:

                                    I wouldn't have.

COUNCILOR:
We'd have clocked you if you didn't.

LYSISTRATA:
                                        That's why I did.
Another day we'd ask, about some even more
Malignant move, "Do you *ever* think first, big boy?"
He'd glare, order me back to my wool and warn
That I could soon be wailing. "*Men* will see to the war."

COUNCILOR:
And right he was, by Zeus.

LYSISTRATA:
                                You worthless loser, why?
Because ineptitude's a shield against advice?
It got so you were yakking in the streets yourselves:
"We've got no *men* left in the country." "Yeah, no fake."
Hearing stuff like that, we decided women would
Muster and deliver Greece. Why piddle around?
We've got some useful things to tell you. If you stay
Quiet the way *we* always did, we'll set you straight.

COUNCILOR:
Insufferably presumptuous notion!

LYSISTRATA:
                                SHUT UP!!

COUNCILOR:
Shut up for you, abomination in a veil!
I'd sooner perish.

LYSISTRATA:
                        So you're hung up on the veil?

(The Councilor is mobbed and outfitted as a housewife.)

Hang one on yourself. Try mine.

Drape it around your skull.
Sit on this chair. Don't whine!

OLD WOMAN #1:
Hike up your skirt, card gobs of wool
Into a basket on the floor.

LYSISTRATA:
Look dumb. Chew gum.
The women will deal with the war.

WOMEN'S CHORUS LEADER:
Leave your pitchers, women, leap up.
Friends are struggling, we must keep up.

I will never tire of dancing.
Waking strength will move my feet.
I'll accept the worst ordeals.
What's so fine as to compete
With these women's sense and valor,
With their charm and civic zeal?

Grannies on the go, mommies with mucho macho,
The wind is behind your rage, so harden, advance!

LYSISTRATA:
If the Cyprian Goddess and sweet Eros breathe
Desire through us till our thighs and bosoms steam,
Thereby equipping men with feel-good weaponry,
The Greeks will rename us *Anti*-Battle-Axes!

COUNCILOR
What are you going to do?

LYSISTRATA:
                              Well, first of all, we'll stop
Those kooks who go shopping in battle gear.

OLD WOMAN #1:

                         Hell, yes!

LYSISTRATA:

They haul an armory among the pottery
And greens, and bash around—it's like some goddamn cult.

COUNCILOR:

They're dedicated men!

LYSISTRATA:

                   No, dedicated dweebs.
They heft their doughty Gorgon shields and buy sardines.

OLD WOMAN #1:

A captain, streaming-haired, aloft upon his steed,
Proffered a bronze hat to be shoveled full of soup.
A Thracian—just like Tereus!—clattered his shield
And downed forthwith the figs of the routed vendor.

COUNCILOR:

But there's a perfect pandemonium worldwide.
How would you cope?

LYSISTRATA:

               Without a lot of strain.

COUNCILOR:

                     What?! How?

LYSISTRATA:

Say that the wool's a mass of tangles. Take it thus,

(Miming throughout.)

Draw it apart with spindles—make some sense of it.
That's how we'll loosen up this war—if we're allowed.
Ambassadors are spindles—they can sort it out.

COUNCILOR:

Spindles and gobs of wool—it's just too fatuous.
We're in a crisis.

LYSISTRATA:

With a modicum of smarts,
You'd copy the administration of our wool.

COUNCILOR:

Do tell me how.

LYSISTRATA:

       First, give the fleece a bath to dunk
Away the sheep dung. Spread your city on a bed
Next, and beat out all the layabouts and briars.
Then card out any clumps—you know, the cliques of chumps,
Magistracy-mongers. Pluck their little heads off.
Comb what's left into a single goodwill basket.
Wad in your resident aliens and other
Nice foreigners, and don't leave out public debtors.
And heck, as for the city's scattered colonies,
I want you to construe them as neglected tufts,
Each on its lonesome. Gather them all together,
Bunch them up tight, and finally you'll have one
Big ball. Use it to weave the city something fine.

COUNCILOR:

Wads and rods and balls—the paradigm's atrocious!
What have you got to do with war?

LYSISTRATA:

         You scrap of scum,
We fight it twice: it's we who give the hoplites life,
And then we send them off, for you—

COUNCILOR:

          That spot is sore!

LYSISTRATA:
>
> Us young and frisky females, who must seize the night,
> War puts to bed beside ourselves. But screw us wives:
> I ache for the girls turned crones and never married.

COUNCILOR:
>
> Don't men get old?

LYSISTRATA:
>
> You *know* it's nothing like the same!
> Any decrepit veteran, no questions asked,
> Can get a child-bride, but a woman's chance is zip
> After her prime. She sits there maiming daisies—crap!

COUNCILOR:
>
> As long as men can get it up—

LYSISTRATA:
>
> Why don't you die and shut it up?

> *(The women mob the Councilor and dress and equip him as a corpse.)*

> We've got a plot. Just buy a box.
> And here's a wreath for you!
> A honey-cake to bribe the dog—

OLD WOMAN #1:
>
> And holy ribbons, too—

OLD WOMAN #2:
>
> A coin to get you on the boat—

LYSISTRATA:
>
> That's all—it's time to rush off.

Charon's calling. Till he's full
He's not allowed to push off.[2]

COUNCILOR:

Such disrespect for my authority!
I'll march straight to the other councilors:
My person's an indictment of your deeds.

(He exits with attendants. Lysistrata calls after him.)

LYSISTRATA:

You're angry that we didn't lay you out?
Don't worry, sir. At dawn, two days from now,
We'll come and give you the traditional rites.

(The women exit into the stage building.)

MEN'S CHORUS LEADER:

Lovers of freedom, rouse yourselves from sleep!
Strip down, my friends, and take this problem on.

(They remove their cloaks.)

CHORUS OF OLD MEN:

I've got a whiff of larger plans at work—
The reign of terror that we thought was gone!
Suppose Laconians have gathered here
With someone—oooh, with Cleisthenes, let's say—
To stir this goddamn plague of women up
And take my bare-essential jury pay.

MEN'S CHORUS LEADER:

Scandalous! Women scold us citizens
And blab about a war they've never seen:
"We'll RECONCILE you with LACONIANS."
Give me a wolf to pet—I'm just as keen.
"I'll hide my weapon under myrtle boughs."

---

2   Grave goods reflected the myth that dead souls went to the Underworld past the guard dog Cerberus, who needed to be distracted with a cake, and over the river Styx with the boatman Charon.

This plot against our precious liberty
I'll foil. On guard against a tyranny,
I'll march in armor while I shop and pose
Beside Aristogiton's statue—see!

(Strikes a pose.)

And here's a splendid opportunity
To bop this impious old troll's nose!

(His fist is raised against the Women's Chorus Leader.)

WOMEN'S CHORUS LEADER:
Your mother's going to think you're someone else.
Ladies, lay down your wraps.

(They do so.)

CHORUS OF OLD WOMEN:
We're going to tell
The city several things it needs to know.
I owe it this. It brought me up so well:
At seven as a Mystery-Carrier;
A Grinder in the holy mill at ten;
Later, at Brauron, as a bright-robed Bear;
A comely, fig-decked Basket-Bearer then.

WOMEN'S CHORUS LEADER:
That's why I'll serve my city with a chat.
So I'm a woman—why should you resent
That I come forward with the best advice?
I've done my share and more; it's men I've lent.
You wretched drool-bags, since the Persian Wars,
Just fritter our inheritance away,
No taxes to replace the cash you spend.
You're going to ruin all of us someday.
You dare to gripe? Let out one vicious word,
I'll send this slipper bashing through your beard.

(She removes a shoe and strikes a threatening pose with it.)

CHORUS OF OLD MEN:

    Isn't this too obnoxious to ignore?
    It started bad—how nasty can it get?
    Justice and Truth rely on those with balls.

MEN'S CHORUS LEADER:

    Strip off your shirts, let women smell men's sweat,
    Stride free of wrappings hampering a fight.

(They comply.)

CHORUS OF OLD MEN:

    Remember how we manned Leipsydrion?
    Shake off these rags of age and grow fresh wings!
    Swoop like the swift young eagles we were then!

MEN'S CHORUS LEADER:

    We let these wrestlers get the slightest hold,
    Their grasping handiwork will never end:
    They'll build themselves some ships, become marines,
    Like Artemisia attacking men!
    If they try horsemanship, you'd better cross
    The cavalry off your list. A woman on
    Her mount clings tight, however hard the ride.
    She won't slip off: e.g., the Amazons
    Battling in Micon's picture. No, the stocks
    Are where these girls belong, with sturdy locks!

CHORUS OF OLD WOMEN:

    Give me a prod. You'll find out soon enough
    My anger's like a savage, frothing boar.
    You'll scream for neighbors' help: "I'm getting reamed!"

WOMEN'S CHORUS LEADER:

    Quick, women, put your dresses on the floor.

(They do so.)

Let the men sniff the creature so annoyed—

CHORUS OF OLD WOMEN:
> If she just hears bad words, she'll bite men gory,
> Disqualifying them for civic tasks:
> Cf. the beetle and the eagle story.

WOMEN'S CHORUS LEADER:
> Phooey on you! Lampito's my defense,
> Ismene, too (a well-connected girl).
> Pass seven laws against me, I don't care—
> Everyone hates you, in the whole known world!
> I have a friend, the sweet Boeotian eel.
> I wanted her to come, the other day,
> To share my festive rites of Hecate.
> Her keepers told me, "No. Because *they* say."
> Either you stop it or you'll learn a trick
> You won't enjoy: to flip and break your neck.

(It is several days later. Enter Lysistrata, visibly distressed.)

WOMEN'S CHORUS LEADER:
> Our queenly leader, chief conspirator,
> Why come you forth in such a royal snit?

LYSISTRATA:
> The dastard weakness of the female mind
> Bids me to pace in fury and despair.

WOMEN'S CHORUS LEADER:
> Alas, what say you?

LYSISTRATA:
> Naught but plainest truth.

WOMEN'S CHORUS LEADER:
> What dire news? Reveal it to your friends.

LYSISTRATA:
>Shameful to speak, but heavy to withhold.

WOMEN'S CHORUS LEADER:
>Hide not from me our sore calamity.

LYSISTRATA:
>Well, in a word, our movement's getting fucked.

WOMEN'S CHORUS LEADER:
>Zeus!

LYSISTRATA:
>Why call on Zeus? Our nature's not *his* fault.
>And anyway, it's me who can't enforce
>Husband aversion. AWOL's spreading fast.
>The other day I caught one near Pan's cave,
>Making the hole a tunnel just her size.
>A second sought civilian status by
>Rappelling from a crane; another tried
>To ride a sparrow down to You-Know-Who's.
>I had to grab her hair and drag her back.
>Trying for furloughs, they evoke a vast
>Supply of fiction. Here's a sample now.

>>*(Stops Woman #1, who has entered from the stage building and is dashing off toward the side.)*

>Where are *you* running to?

WOMAN #1:
>>>>I'm going home.
>I have to rescue my—Milesian wool
>From—moths. They're going to shred it.

LYSISTRATA:
>>>>>Moths, my ass!
>Get back inside!

WOMAN #1:

By the Two Gods, I will.
I only need to spread it on the bed.

LYSISTRATA:

You'll do no spreading, 'cause you're staying put.

WOMAN #1:

I sacrifice my *wool?*

LYSISTRATA:

Yes, for the cause.

(Woman #2 enters in a tragic pose, scurrying away at the same time.)

WOMAN #2:

Pity me and my fine Amorgos flax,
At home, left on the stems!

LYSISTRATA:

Example B
Is skulking off to peel a pile of thread.
You, turn around!

WOMAN #2: *(Stopping reluctantly.)*

I swear by Hecate,
I'll only stay to give it one good—shuck.

LYSISTRATA:

No shucking way. If I give in to you,
There's going to be no end of applicants.

(Woman #3 enters, clutching a protruding stomach.)

WOMAN #3:

Goddess of Childbirth, spare me for an hour!
This place is sacrosanct—I've got to leave!

LYSISTRATA:

>What *is* this crap?

WOMAN #3:

>My baby's almost here!

LYSISTRATA:

>Yesterday you weren't pregnant.

WOMAN #3:

>Now I am!
>Please, Lysistrata, let me go. The nurse
>Is waiting for me.

LYSISTRATA:

>Sounds a lot like bull.

(She feels the front of the woman's dress.)

>There's something hard here.

WOMAN #3:

>It's a baby boy.

LYSISTRATA:

>By Aphrodite, not my guess at all.
>It's hollow metal. Let me take a peek.

(She dives under the woman's dress, emerges with a giant helmet.)

>You idiot, the holy helmet's here!
>You're pregnant, huh?

WOMAN #3:

>By Zeus, I swear I am.

LYSISTRATA:

>And what's this for?

WOMAN #3:

> If I were overcome
> On the way home, I'd have a kind of nest.
> It seems to work for doves, at any rate.

LYSISTRATA:

> No kidding. If that's your excuse, then wait
> Five days to have a party for this hat.

WOMAN #3:

> But I can't even sleep here since I saw
> The sacred snake. You gotta let me go!

WOMAN #1:

> I won't survive, I've been awake so long.
> These stupid honking owls won't take a rest.

LYSISTRATA:

> Magical stuff—shut up about it, hey?
> You want your men. You don't think they want you?
> They're spending nasty nights outside your beds.
> Dear ladies, just be patient for a bit,
> And see our project through, clear to the end.
> An oracle assures us that we'll win
> If we're united. Here, I've got the text.

WOMAN #3:

> What does it say?

LYSISTRATA:

> Be quiet and I'll read.

(She takes out a scroll.)

> Swallows will come together, huddling close—
> Fleeing hoopoes—renouncing phalluses—
> Bad things will end, when Zeus the Thunderer
> Brings low the lofty—

WOMAN #3:

> Hmm, we'll be on top?

LYSISTRATA:

> But if the bickering birds fly separate ways,
> Leaving the sacred temple, it will show
> That—swallows are the world's most shameless trash.

WOMAN #3:

> The sacred words are plain. Oh, help us, gods.

LYSISTRATA:

> We won't give in to hassles, but persist.
> Let's go inside. It would be a disgrace
> To prove unworthy of the oracle.

(The women exit into the stage building.)

CHORUS OF OLD MEN:

> When I was a boy, I heard a tale
> I'd like to share with you.
> There was a young man named Melanion.
> They told him to get married, and he said, "Pooh!"
> He fled to the mountains, where he lived,
> Hunting hares.
> He had a great dog,
> And he wove his own snares.
> He never went home. His hatred
> Continued burning bright.
> And we hate women just as much,
> Because we know what's right.

MEN'S CHORUS LEADER:

> Give me a kiss, you hag.

WOMEN'S CHORUS LEADER:

> Oh, yuck, that onion smell!

MEN'S CHORUS LEADER:
>And now a hearty kick!

(Crotch shows as he lifts leg.)

WOMEN'S CHORUS LEADER:
>Chain up your animal!

MEN'S CHORUS LEADER:
>Myronides and Phormion were formidably furred:
>Their enemies took one look at them and ran.
>A nest of black hair in the crack at the back
>Is the sign of a genuine man.

CHORUS OF OLD WOMEN:
>It's our turn to tell you a tale.
>(We don't like the Melanion one.)
>Timon once lurked in the thorns,
>A wild man, the Ghouls' foster son.
>He stayed away
>Till his dying day,
>Cursing mankind with venom.
>He loathed all of you,
>The same as we do,
>But was always a sweetie to women.

WOMEN'S CHORUS LEADER:
>Shall I bash your jaw?

MEN'S CHORUS LEADER:
>I'll be so sore!

WOMEN'S CHORUS LEADER:
>A kick at least.

(Her leg is lifted, threatening a view of crotch.)

MEN'S CHORUS LEADER:
>Talk about beasts!

WOMEN'S CHORUS LEADER:
>Fine, but I'm glad that mine
>Doesn't run wild and free.
>Though I'm not especially young,
>I groom it tenderly.

>*(The choruses step back.)*

>*(Lysistrata appears on the roof of the stage building.)*

LYSISTRATA:
>Whoopee! Get over here, you women, quick!

>*(Enter Woman #1, Myrrhine, and several other women onto the roof.)*

WOMAN #1:
>What is it? Tell me what you're squalling at.

LYSISTRATA:
>A man—he's coming in a frenzied charge,
>With Aphrodite's offering—of meat.
>Queen of Cyprus and of Cythera
>And Paphos! (Yeah, bud, come *straight up* to us!)

WOMAN #1:
>Where is our mystery man?

LYSISTRATA:
>   By Chloe's shrine.

WOMAN #1:
>No question—that thing's male. Who could he be?

LYSISTRATA:
>All of you look. Does someone know him?

MYRRHINE:

                                    Zeus!
I do. My husband—it's Cinesias.

LYSISTRATA:

Your duty is to roast him on that spit.
You will, you won't, you might—just lead him on.
Remember, though: you swore on booze—no sex!

MYRRHINE:

Leave it to me.

LYSISTRATA:

                        But I'll stay here and pull
The opening stunts and get him all worked up
For you to play with. Go back in and hide.

> *(All the women but Lysistrata exit. Enter Cinesias, with
> his Slave, who is carrying Cinesias' Baby. A giant codpiece
> hangs from Cinesias' waist. Lysistrata descends by ladder or
> through the stage building to meet Cinesias.)*

CINESIAS:

I'm screwed—I mean I'm not! I'm stretched so tight
Skilled torture couldn't do a better job.

LYSISTRATA:

Who's gotten past the sentinels?

CINESIAS:

                        It's me.

LYSISTRATA:

A man?

CINESIAS:

Yeah, can't you see?

LYSISTRATA:

                        I see. Get lost.

CINESIAS:

    Who's going to throw me out?

LYSISTRATA:

                           The lookout. Me.

CINESIAS:

    I need Myrrhine. Call her for me—please.

LYSISTRATA:

    Myrrhine? Huh? You need her? Who are you?

CINESIAS:

    Her husband. I'm Cinesias from—

LYSISTRATA:

                               Hey!
    I know *you,* or I've often heard your name.
    All of us know it. You're quite famous here.
    Your wife's mouth never takes a break from you.
    She toasts you every time she has a snack—
    Smooth eggs, or juicy apples—

CINESIAS:

                    Gods! O gods!

LYSISTRATA:

    Just Aphrodite. When we mention men,
    That wife of yours declares without delay:
    "They're all a pile of crud compared to mine."

CINESIAS:

    Call her, c'mon.

LYSISTRATA:

                And what's it worth to you?

CINESIAS:

    What have I got on me? Oh, right, there's *this*.
    It's all I have, but you can take it and—

LYSISTRATA:

    There, now. I'll call her down to you.

CINESIAS:

                                And fast.

    (Lysistrata exits into stage building.)

    There's nothing now in life to bring me joy.
    She left the house! She left me on my own!
    When I return at night, the whole place seems
    So empty, and I ache. The food has got
    No taste for me. All I can feel is dick.

    (Myrrhine appears on the roof of the stage building, calling
    behind her.)

MYRRHINE:

    I love him, oh, I do! He won't accept
    My yearning love. Don't make me go out there.

CINESIAS:

    Myrrhine, I don't get it, baby doll.
    Come down here.

MYRRHINE:

                 That event will not occur.

CINESIAS:

    I call, Myrrhine, and you won't come down?

MYRRHINE:

    What the hell for? Why are you bothering?

CINESIAS:

What *for?* To keep my prick from crushing me.

MYRRHINE:

See you around.

CINESIAS:

No—listen to your son.
(To Baby.) You little—call your Mama, or I'll—

BABY:

Waaah!

Mama! Mama! Mama!

CINESIAS:

What's wrong with you? No feeling for your child?
Six days he's gone without a bath or food.

MYRRHINE:

Poor baby. Daddy doesn't give a hoot.

CINESIAS:

Monster, at least come down and feed your whelp.

MYRRHINE:

Ah, motherhood! What choice do I have now?

(She descends and approaches him.)

CINESIAS: *(Aside.)*

Maybe my mind's just soggy, but she seems
Wonderfully young—her face has such allure.
And see that snippy way she struts along.
It's making me so horny I could croak.

MYRRHINE: *(Taking Baby.)*

My lovey-pie—too bad about your Dad.
Give Mommy kiss, my honey-dumpling-bun.

CINESIAS:

> What are you up to here? What have they done
> To lure you off? Why are you hurting me?
> You're hurting too!

(He reaches for her.)

MYRRHINE:

> Your hand can stop right there.

CINESIAS:

> My stuff at home—it's your stuff too—is shot
> Since you've been gone.

MYRRHINE:

> My, my, that's too, *too* bad.

CINESIAS:

> That nicest cloth of yours—the hens got in—
> You ought to see it.

MYRRHINE:

> Only if I cared.

CINESIAS:

> And all this time we've ditched the rituals
> Of Aphrodite. Aren't you coming back?

MYRRHINE:

> Not me, by Zeus, unless you make a deal
> To stop this war.

CINESIAS:

> If that's the way we vote,
> That's what we'll do.

MYRRHINE:

> Then you trot off and vote,
> And I'll trot home. For now, I've sworn to stay.

CINESIAS:

Then lie down here with me. It's been so long.

MYRRHINE:

No, not a chance—in spite of how I feel.

CINESIAS:

You love me? Honey, then why not lie down?

MYRRHINE:

Don't be ridiculous! The baby's here.

CINESIAS:

Right. Yeah. Okay. Boy, you can take it home.

(Slave takes Baby back and exits.)

There, do you see a baby anymore?
So if you'd just—

MYRRHINE:

                    You're crazy! Where's a spot
To do it here?

CINESIAS:

        Uh, there's the grove of Pan.

MYRRHINE:

And how am I to purify myself?

CINESIAS:

No sweat. There's the Clepsydra you can use.

MYRRHINE:

I swore an *oath*. And now I break my word?

CINESIAS:

Forget your oath. 'Cause that's my lookout, huh?

MYRRHINE:
>I'll get a cot for us.

CINESIAS:
>>No, stay right here.
>The ground is fine.

MYRRHINE:
>>Apollo help me, no!
>Stretch till you twang, before I lay you there!

>*(She exits.)*

CINESIAS:
>There's no mistaking such a doting fuss.

>*(She returns with a cot.)*

MYRRHINE:
>Hurry, lie down. I'm going to get undressed.

>*(Cinesias lies down.)*

>Now what—? I've got to drag a mattress out.

CINESIAS:
>But I don't care!

MYRRHINE:
>>By Artemis, you can't
>Think we could do it on the cords.

CINESIAS:
>>>Kiss me.

MYRRHINE:
>Okay.

>*(She kisses him.)*

CINESIAS:

Fantastic. You come back real fast.

(She exits, returns with a mattress, nudges Cinesias off the cot, and places the mattress on it.)

MYRRHINE:

Mattress. All right. Lie down.

(She rearranges him.)

I'll soon be nude!
Whoops! I forgot—something—a pillow, yes!

CINESIAS:

But I don't need one.

MYRRHINE:

That's too bad. I do.

(She exits.)

CINESIAS:

Oh, what an epic prank on my poor prick!

(She returns with a pillow.)

MYRRHINE:

Head up. *(She places the pillow under his head.)* I've got the whole collection now.

CINESIAS:

I'm sure you do. Come here, my cutie-sweet.

MYRRHINE:

Just let me get this bra off. One more time:
You wouldn't lead me on about the peace?

CINESIAS:

If I do that, Zeus strike me dead.

MYRRHINE:

A sheet!

CINESIAS:

By Zeus, forget the sheet! I want to screw!

MYRRHINE:

Don't worry, you'll get screwed. I'll be right back.

(She exits.)

CINESIAS:

She's going to decorate until I die.

(She enters with a sheet.)

MYRRHINE:

Up just a little. *(She spreads the sheet under him.)*

CINESIAS:

(Indicating penis.) How is *this* for up?

MYRRHINE:

Do you want oil?

CINESIAS:

No! By Apollo! No!

MYRRHINE:

My, looks like you don't know what's good for you.

(She exits.)

CINESIAS:

Great Zeus in heaven, make the bottle spill!

(She returns with oil bottle.)

MYRRHINE:

Hold out your hand, take some, and spread it on.

(He takes a sample.)

CINESIAS:

Yuck, I don't like it. All I smell's delay
It's got no nuance of MY WIFE and SEX.

MYRRHINE:

Well, shame on me! I brought the one from Rhodes.

CINESIAS:

No, never mind, it's perfect.

MYRRHINE:

You're a dork.

(She exits.)

CINESIAS:

Perfume's inventor ought to cram the stuff.

(She enters, offers him a bottle.)

MYRRHINE:

Take this.

CINESIAS:

I've *got* one that's about to crack!
Lie down, you tramp! Don't bring me anything!

MYRRHINE:

Okay, I'm lying down.

(She perches on edge of bed.)

I've only got
To get my shoes off. Honey don't forget:
You're voting for a treaty.

CINESIAS:

I'll assess—

(She dashes away and exits.)

Shit! Shit!! She's gone. She rubbed me out and ran.
She plucked my cock, consigning me to dust.

Oh, woe! Whom shall I screw?
The loveliest one is gone.
Who'll take this orphan on?
I need a pimp! Hey, you—
Go hire me a nanny for my dong.

CHORUS OF OLD MEN:
Misery, woe on woe!
Lo, I brim over with compassion:
You're foully swindled of your ration!
Forsooth, your guts are going to blow!
How will your nuts remain
Intact? Will you not go insane?
Your manly parts are out of luck
Without their regular morning fuck.

CINESIAS:
Great Zeus, how dreadfully I twitch!

CHORUS OF OLD MEN:
That's from the world's most evil bitch.
She tortured you, the filthy cheat.

CHORUS OF OLD WOMEN:
No, no! She's absolutely sweet.

CHORUS OF OLD MEN:
> She's a curse. She's a disease.

CINESIAS:
> She is! O Zeus, please, please!
> You know the way your whirlwind flips
> And flings the brush piles that it whips?
> And twists and loops them in a blur,
> And dumps them down? Do that to her.
> But when you let her touch the ground
> She must land tidily around
> My prong, okay? And right away?

> *(Enter Spartan Herald, bent over and holding his cloak out in front. Cinesias has recovered enough of his composure to face him.)*

SPARTAN HERALD:
> Where do you find the Elders in this town?
> No, sorry, your—Directors? I got news.

CINESIAS:
> Are you a human being or a pole?

SPARTAN HERALD:
> By the Twin Gods, I've come official-like
> From Sparta, 'cause we need to compromise.

CINESIAS:
> Then please explain that pike beneath your clothes.

SPARTAN HERALD: *(Dodging Cinesias' eyes.)*
> I swear, it's nothing.

CINESIAS:
> But you're turned away
> Your cloak is hiding something. Have you got
> Some swelling from the ride?

SPARTAN HERALD: *(Aside.)*

> His mind is gone.

CINESIAS:

> Come on, you scamming bastard, it's a bone!

SPARTAN HERALD:

> By Zeus, it ain't. Back off, you crazy fart.

CINESIAS:

> What is it, then?

SPARTAN HERALD:

> Uh, it's a Spartan staff.

CINESIAS: *(Opening cloak.)*

> Then here's a Spartan staff that's just changed sides.
> I know the whole thing. You can tell the truth
> About what Lacedaemon's going through.

SPARTAN HERALD:

> Well, us and our confederate states is stuck.
> Stuck standing up. We need to *snatch* a piece.

CINESIAS:

> And who's the source of this catastrophe?
> Pan?

SPARTAN HERALD:

> No, Lampito—I think it was her plan.
> And then all over Sparta, when they heard,
> The women thundered from the starting line—
> There went our pussy in a cloud of dust.

CINESIAS:

> How are you making out, then?

SPARTAN HERALD:
>   Hey, we're *not*.
> The whole damn town's bent double like we's kicked.
> Before we lay a finger on a twat,
> The women say we gotta all wise up
> And make a treaty with the other Greeks.

CINESIAS:
> They got together and they plotted this,
> All of the women. I can see it now.
> Quick, have the Spartans send ambassadors,
> Fully empowered to reach a settlement.
> And on the evidence of this my dick
> I'll make our Council choose some legates too.

SPARTAN HERALD:
> I'm off. You got the whole thing figured out.

(They exit.)

MEN'S CHORUS LEADER:
> To get on top of women—try a fire,
> It's easier. A leopard's got more shame.

WOMEN'S CHORUS LEADER:
> And knowing this, you won't give up this fight,
> When you can always trust me as a friend?

MEN'S CHORUS LEADER:
> Women revolt me. And it stays that way.

WOMEN'S CHORUS LEADER:
> There's lots of time. But I can't bear to see
> You standing garmentless. You look absurd.
> I'll come and put this cloak back over you.

(She drapes it around him.)

MEN'S CHORUS LEADER:

By Zeus, you've done a thing that isn't vile.
I stripped when I was raging for a fight.

WOMEN'S CHORUS LEADER:

Now you're a man again, and not a clown.
If you were nice, I might have grabbed that beast
Still lodging in your eye, and plucked him out.

MEN'S CHORUS LEADER:

So that's what's galling me. Here, take my ring.
Gouge out the critter, let me see him. Gods,
All day he's masticated in that lair.

WOMEN'S CHORUS LEADER:

For sure, here goes. But what a grouchy guy.

(Removes bug.)

Oh, Zeus, I've never seen a gnat this big.
Just look. It's like some monster from the swamp.

MEN'S CHORUS LEADER:

You helped. That thing was excavating me...
And now it's gone. There's water in my eyes.

WOMEN'S CHORUS LEADER:

I'll wipe it off, though you've been quite a pain.

(She wipes his face and kisses him.)

And here's a kiss.

MEN'S CHORUS LEADER:
                        No—

WOMEN'S CHORUS LEADER:
                        It's not up to you!

MEN'S CHORUS LEADER:

> Up your wazoo! You're born to flatter us!
> The adage says it all: that women are
> Abomination indispensable.
> But let's make peace, and in the time to come
> I'll neither dump on you nor take your crap.
> Let's all line up and dance to celebrate.

(The two choruses unite and address the audience.)

UNITED CHORUS:

> Gentlemen, I don't mean to call
> A fellow citizen a snot or blot
> Or anything like that at all.
> No, *au contraire!* I'll be much more than fair!
> Sufficient are the evils that you've got.
> Man or woman, just tell me
> If you'd like a bit—
> Two thousand, or, say, three—
> I've got so much of it.
> We'll even give you bags to haul it.
> In peaceful times we won't recall it:
> Just keep the goodies from our coffers.
> Oops: we've forgotten what we offered.
>
> We've just invited really swell
> Carystians, from overseas.
> We're going to entertain them well,
> With perfectly braised, tenderly glazed
> Piglet served with purée of peas.
> Spruce yourself up (don't leave out
> The kids!) and come today.
> March in, nothing to ask about,
> And no one in the way.
> Barge boldly to the doors.
> Pretend the place is yours.
> Don't even bother to knock—
> It's going to be locked.

(The Spartan Ambassadors approach, bent over, holding their cloaks out in front, trying to conceal massive erections. Slaves accompany them.)

UNITED CHORUS LEADER:
> Here come the Spartan legates, beards a-drag—
> In clothing that looks draped around a crate.
> Laconian gentlemen, our best to you!
> Tell us in what condition you've arrived.

SPARTAN AMBASSADOR:
> This isn't gonna take a wordy talk.

> *(Opens cloak.)*

> A look-see for yourselves should do the trick.

UNITED CHORUS LEADER:
> Oh, wow. The situation's pretty tense,
> A crisis getting more and more inflamed.

SPARTAN AMBASSADOR:
> It's crazy Anyway, what's there to say?
> We'll accept any kind of terms for peace.

> *(Enter Athenian Ambassadors, like the Spartans under obvious strain. Slaves accompany them also.)*

UNITED CHORUS LEADER:
> These natives have a tic a lot like yours,
> Of bending down like wrestlers, with a lot
> Of room for something underneath their cloaks.
> They have some hypertrophy of the groin.

ATHENIAN AMBASSADOR #1: *(To United Chorus.)*
> Where's Lysistrata? Someone's got to know.

(Pulls cloak aside to display contents, gestures toward Spartans.)

We're here, they're here, but both are way up there.

UNITED CHORUS LEADER:
I seem to see a certain parallel
Between these two diseases—cramps at dawn?

ATHENIAN AMBASSADOR #1:
Worse, we've arrived at wits' and gonads' end.
If we don't hurry and negotiate,
We'll have to make a date with Cleisthenes.

UNITED CHORUS LEADER:
If I were you, I'd cover up those things.
What if a prankster with a chisel sees?

ATHENIAN AMBASSADOR #1:
That's good advice.

(Covers himself.)

SPARTAN AMBASSADOR:
                    By the Twin Gods, it is.
We better wrap these bigger duds around.

(Covers himself likewise.)

ATHENIAN AMBASSADOR #1:
Greetings to you, dear Spartans. We've been stiffed.

SPARTAN AMBASSADOR:
And us, too, pal. Maybe the audience
Could see that we was playing with ourselves.

ATHENIAN AMBASSADOR #1:
Let's get through our agenda double-quick.
What do you want?

Spartan Ambassador:

>   We're the ambassadors.
>   We're here about a treaty.

Athenian Ambassador #1:

>   So are we.
>   But only Lysistrata's up to it.
>   Let's ask her. She can be the referee.

Spartan Ambassador:

>   Lysis or Strata—anyone who can.

>   *(Enter Lysistrata.)*

Athenian Ambassador #1:

>   It looks like there's no need for us to call.
>   She heard us. She's already coming out.

United Chorus Leader:

>   You who've got by far the biggest balls of all,
>   Show you've got the greatest tact and gall of all!
>   Be high-class, low-class, sweet, self-righteous—everything,
>   Every last minister in Greece now stumbles
>   Under your spell, surrendering his grumbles.

Lysistrata:

>   It's not hard work. You only have to swoop
>   The moment when they're bursting for a deal.
>   But here's the test. Goddess of Deals, come out!

>   *(Reconciliation, an actor in a body stocking padded to look
>   like a nude woman, enters.)*

>   To start with, take the Spartans by the hand—
>   And don't get rough, don't have it all your way;
>   Don't wreck it like our stupid husbands did.
>   Be gentle as a mother in her house—
>   But if he pulls his hand back, take his dong.
>   Lead the Athenians to center stage.

(Anything you can grab can be the leash.)
Laconian gentlemen, stand close to me,
And our guys here, and hear my reasons out.

> *(Reconciliation has arranged the Athenian and Spartan*
> *Ambassadors on either side of Lysistrata.)*

I am a woman, but I have a mind
That wasn't bad to start with, and I got
A first-class education listening
To Father and the elders year on year.
I now shall do what's right and give you hell
Together, for a single holy bowl
Sprinkles fraternal altars at the games:
Delphic, Pylaean, and Olympian.
I could go on and on and on and on!
You see barbarian armies threatening,
But you destroy the towns and lives of Greeks.
That's quite a climax to my preface, huh?

ATHENIAN AMBASSADOR #1:
What? This bald behemoth is killing me.

LYSISTRATA:
Laconians, I'm turning now to you.
Don't you remember how a suppliant
From Sparta, Pericleidas, roosted here,
Next to the altar, pale (his uniform
Bright red), and begged for troops. Messene and
Poseidon both at once had shaken you.
And Cimon took four thousand armored men
And made your territory safe again.
After this gift from the Athenians,
You come and rip their land apart as thanks?

ATHENIAN AMBASSADOR #1:
Right, Lysistrata! Bunch of criminals!

> *(Spartan Ambassador is enthralled by Reconciliation.)*

SPARTAN AMBASSADOR:
> I guess we are—that's such a gorgeous ass.

LYSISTRATA:
> You think I'm going to spare my countrymen?
>
> *(Turns to Athenians.)*
>
> Laconians once came to rescue you—
> You only had the sheepskins on your backs.
> The Spartans, marching out with you one day,
> Erased large numbers of Thessalian goons.
> A single ally made you Hippias-free:
> Denuded of the rags of refugees,
> And draped in your own polity again.

SPARTAN AMBASSADOR: *(Staring at Reconciliation.)*
> I never seen a woman so first-rate.

ATHENIAN AMBASSADOR #1: *(Staring likewise.)*
> I've never gazed on such a spiffy quim.

LYSISTRATA:
> With these good deeds already on the tab,
> Why squabble like a bunch of stupid jerks?
> Be reconciled. There's nothing in the way.
>
> *(In the following scene, Reconciliation serves as a map.)*

SPARTAN AMBASSADOR:
> Okay, if we can have this little loop,
> We're in.

ATHENIAN AMBASSADOR #1:
> What's that, my friend?

SPARTAN AMBASSADOR:
> Pylos, I mean.
> For years we've tried to get a finger in.

ATHENIAN AMBASSADOR #1:
Poseidon help me, *that* you will not do.

LYSISTRATA:
Let go.

ATHENIAN AMBASSADOR #1:
But I've got uprisings to quell!

LYSISTRATA:
Just ask them for another piece instead.

ATHENIAN AMBASSADOR #1:
Give me this thingy—this cute brushy bit,
And this deep gulf behind, which I'll explore—
And these nice legs of land: I want them too.

SPARTAN AMBASSADOR:
Buddy, you can't have every friggin' thing!

LYSISTRATA:
Hey! Make some compromise and part the legs.

ATHENIAN AMBASSADOR #1:
I'm going to strip right down and start to plow.

SPARTAN AMBASSADOR:
I'm going to spread manure on my field.

LYSISTRATA:
And you can do it when you're reconciled.
If you're quite ready for a settlement,
Then scatter and confer with your allies.

ATHENIAN AMBASSADOR #1:
Why bother? Situated in my prong,
They'll judge precisely as I do. They'll want
To screw—

SPARTAN AMBASSADOR:
>   And ours are just like yours, I swear—

ATHENIAN AMBASSADOR #1:
>   And our Carystians especially.

LYSISTRATA:
>   You're both correct! While you're still abstinent,
>   We'll have the women on the citadel
>   Open their boxes for you. You can feast
>   And then exchange your pledges of good faith.
>   Then each of you can take his wife and go
>   Straight home—

ATHENIAN AMBASSADOR #1:
>   Finally. Let's not stand around.

SPARTAN AMBASSADOR:
>   Show me—

ATHENIAN AMBASSADOR #1:
>   The fastest exit we can make.

>   *(Lysistrata and the Ambassadors exit together, leaving the*
>   *slaves, who settle down outside the stage building.)*

UNITED CHORUS:
>   Embroidered throws to beat the cold,
>   Dresses and capes—none better, a
>   Big pile of jewelry, solid gold—
>   Send kids to take the stuff away,
>   For Basket-Bearing girls, et cetera.
>   "Help yourselves," I always say,
>   "To anything you find.
>   I don't seal up the jars or check
>   What money's left behind."
>   In fact, there's nothing left at all,
>   Unless I'm going blind.

Not enough bread,
But slaves to feed,
And hosts of hungry kids?
I've got plenty of baby-fine wheat
For every citizen in need.
This dust grows into strapping loaves to eat.
Come in—bring duffel bags and sacks!
My slave will stuff them full with any
Dry goods that you lack.
Too bad my dog will fuck you up.
He's waiting at the back.

(Slaves sprawl sleepily in front of stage building. Thick-voiced Athenian Ambassador #1 pounds on the door from inside.)

ATHENIAN AMBASSADOR #1:
Open!

(Barges through, knocking slave in front of door out of the way. Ambassador is garlanded, unsteady on his feet, and carrying a torch.)

That's what you get for bein' there!

(Begins kicking and pushing dazed slaves.)

And you guys too—what if I take this torch
And carbonize you? (To audience.) What a dumb cliché.
I'm not going through with it. Okay! Calm down!
To make you happy I can play a boob.

(Athenian Ambassador #2, similar in appearance, enters from same door.)

ATHENIAN AMBASSADOR #2:
I'll help. Two boobs beat one—like this one here.

(Assaults slave.)

Haul ass! Or you'll be howling for your hair.

ATHENIAN AMBASSADOR #1:
Throw yourselves out! Our Spartan guests inside
Don't want to kick their way through piles of you.

(Slaves flee.)

ATHENIAN AMBASSADOR #2:
I've never seen a party good as this.
Those Spartans sure are fun—now who'da thought?
And we're a damn sight smarter when we're drunk.

ATHENIAN AMBASSADOR #1:
I tell ya, being sober's bad for us.
I'm gonna move that anyone we send
Anywhere to negotiate, get sloshed.
The trouble's been, we're sober when we go
To Sparta, so we're spoilers from the start.
What they *do* say, we're not prepared to hear.
And everything they *don't* say, we assume.
We've all got different versions in the end.
But now we're fine. Someone sang "Telamon"
When what we wanted was "Cleitagora":
We slapped him on the back and told him, "Great!"

(Slaves slink back onstage.)

I can't believe those slaves are comin' back.
Get out! The whip is looking for you guys.

(Slaves exit. Spartan Ambassadors enter, with a Piper.)

ATHENIAN AMBASSADOR #2:
Already we've got Spartans walking through.

SPARTAN AMBASSADOR: *(To Piper.)*
>Hey my best buddy, can we hear the pipes?
>There's something good I got to dance and sing.
>It's for our friends in Athens—and for us.

ATHENIAN AMBASSADOR #1:
>Zeus blast us if those pipes can't use a blast.
>It's wonderful to watch you Spartans dance.

(The Piper strikes up a tune.)

SPARTAN AMBASSADOR:
>Memory rouse, for my young sake,
>The Muse who knows of both our nations:
>How, godlike, the Athenians at Artemisium
>Smashed the hulls of the Medes and were victorious,
>While Leonidas led us Spartans
>Fierce as boars sharpening their tusks;
>Foam blossomed over our jaws,
>Ran down our legs.
>The Persians were as
>Many as the sand grains.
>Huntress in the wilderness,
>Come to us, O holy virgin,
>Bless our treaty
>Unite us forever.
>May our friendship
>Never be troubled.
>May our bond turn us
>From wily foxes into men.
>Come, O come,
>Maiden with your pack of hounds.

(Enter Lysistrata with the Athenian and Spartan Women.)

ATHENIAN AMBASSADOR #1:
>All but one thing is nicely put to bed.
>Reclaim your wives, Laconians, and we
>Will take our own. Each woman by her man,

And each man by his woman, celebrate,
Give thanks in joyful dances for the gods,
And vow to never go so wrong again.

(*The couples join the United Chorus, and all dance in pairs.*)

Bring on the dancers, invite the Graces,
Call Artemis and her twin, God of the joyous cry,
To lead the dance; and call the god of Nysa,
His eyes glittering, companion of the maenads;
And Zeus of the lightning bolt, and his blessed consort,
And all the spirits as witnesses
Forever mindful of gentle Peace,
Whom the goddess Cypris gave us.

UNITED CHORUS:
Shout to the gods,
Leap up, rejoice.
A victory dance,
A holy song!

ATHENIAN AMBASSADOR #1:
Add a new song to my new song.

SPARTAN AMBASSADOR:
Spartan Muse, come once more,
Leave your pretty Taygetus.
Help us hymn in fitting words Apollo in Amyclae,
And Athena of the Bronze House,
And the noble children of Tyndareos
Who play beside the Eurotas.
Start off lightly
And jump up high.
Sing for Sparta,
Where thudding feet
Worship the gods.
The girls like colts
Leap by the river.

Their steps pound.
The dust rises.
They frisk and shake their hair
Like bacchants with their wands.
And Leda's daughter leads them,
Lovely, holy patroness of the chorus.

Tie your hair back, let your footsteps fall
With the speed of a deer's, and clap your hands.
Our Goddess of the Bronze House has victory over all.

(All exit, singing and dancing.)

THE MENAECHMUS TWINS

By Plautus
Translated by Lionel Casson

DRAMATIS PERSONAE

SPONGE (PENICULUS), *hanger-on of Menaechmus of Epidamnus, who makes his way by scrounging from him and other well-to-do people*

MENAECHMUS OF EPIDAMNUS, *a well-to-do young married man, resident in Epidamnus*

LOVEY (EROTIUM), *a courtesan with whom Menaechmus of Epidamnus has been having an affair*

ROLL (CYLINDRUS), *her cook (slave)*

MENAECHMUS OF SYRACUSE, *twin brother of Menaechmus of Epidamnus, resident in Syracuse*

MESSENIO, *his servant (slave)*

MAID OF LOVEY (*slave*)

WIFE OF MENAECHMUS OF EPIDAMNUS

FATHER-IN-LAW OF MENAECHMUS OF EPIDAMNUS

A DOCTOR

[DECIO, *servant of Menaechmus' wife*]

SERVANTS

SCENE

A street in Epidamnus. Two houses front on it: stage left Menaechmus', stage right Lovey's. The exit on stage left leads downtown, that on stage right to the waterfront. The time is noon or a little after.

PROLOGUE

(The actor assigned to deliver the prologue enters, walks downstage, and addresses the audience.)

PROLOGUE: First and foremost, ladies and gentlemen, health and happiness to all of—me. And to you, too. I have Plautus here for you—not in my hands, on my tongue. Please be kind enough to take him—with your ears. Now, here's the plot. Pay attention, I'll make it as brief as I can.

Every comic playwright invariably tells you that the action of his piece takes place entirely at Athens; this is to give it that Greek touch. Well, I'm telling you the action takes place where the story says it does and nowhere else. The plot, as a matter of fact, *is* Greekish. Not Athensish, though; Sicilyish. But all this is so much preamble. Now I'll pour out your portion of plot for you. Not by the quart, not by the gallon, by the tankload. That's how big-hearted a plot-teller I am.

A certain man, a merchant, lived at Syracuse. His wife presented him with twin sons, two boys so alike that no one could tell them apart, neither the woman who nursed them, nor the mother who bore them. I got this from someone who'd seen them—I don't want you to get the idea I saw them myself; I never did.

Well, when the boys were seven years old, their father filled a fine freighter full of freight and put one twin aboard to take with him on a business trip to Tarentum. The other he left home with the mother. As it turned out, they arrived at Tarentum during a holiday, and—the usual thing during holidays—a lot of people had come to town, and son and sire got separated in the crowd. A merchant from Epidamnus, happened to be on the spot; he picked the boy up and carried him off to Epidamnus. At the lad's loss, alas, the love of life left the father; a few days later, there at Tarentum, he died of a broken heart.

A message about all this—that the boy had been carried off and the father had died at Tarentum—was brought back to Syracuse to the grandfather. When he heard the news, he changed the name of the boy who'd been left at home. The old man was so fond of the kidnaped twin that he transferred this one's name to his brother: he called the twin still left Menaechmus, the same name as the other had. (It was the old man's name too—I remember it so well because I heard it so often when his creditors dunned him.) To keep you from getting mixed up later I'm telling you now, in advance, that both twins have the same name.

Now, in order for me to make the whole story crystal clear for you, I have to retrace my steps and get back to Epidamnus. Any of you got some business you want me to take care of for you at Epidamnus? Step up, say the word, give me your orders. But don't forget the wherewithal for taking care of them. Anyone who doesn't give me some cash is wasting his time—and anyone who does is wasting a lot more. But now I'm really going back to where I started, and I'll stay put in one place.

The man from Epidamnus, the one I told you about a few seconds ago who carried off the other twin, had no children of his own—except his moneybags. He adopted the boy he had kidnaped, made him his son, found him a wife with a good dowry, and left him his whole estate when he died. You see, the old fellow happened to be going out to his country place one day after a heavy rain; a short way out of town he began fording a stream that was sweeping along, the sweeping current swept him off his feet the way he had once swept off that boy, and away to hell and gone he went.

So a handsome fortune dropped into his adopted son's lap. He—I mean the twin who was carried off—lives here (*pointing*). Now, the other, the one who lives in Syracuse, will arrive just today, along with a servant; he's searching for his twin brother. This (*gesturing toward the backdrop*) is Epidamnus—but only so long as our play is on the boards; when some other play goes on, it'll be some other city. It changes just the way the actors do—one day they're pimps, next day paupers; next youngsters, next oldsters; next beggars, kings, scroungers, cheats. ...

ACT I

(*Enter Sponge* [Peniculus, *literally "brush"*], *stage left, a man in his thirties with a protruding paunch and a general down-at-the-heels look. He is a* parasitus, *"free-loader," the character, standard in ancient comedy, who, to fill his belly, runs errands and acts as general flunky and yes-man to anyone willing to issue an invitation to a meal. He walks downstage and addresses the audience.*)

SPONGE: The boys call me Sponge. Because, when I eat, I wipe the table clean.

It's stupid to put chains on prisoners or shackles on runaway slaves, at least to my way of thinking. This misery on top of all their others just makes the poor devils more set than ever on breaking out—and breaking the peace. Prisoners get out of the chains somehow or other, and slaves saw through the shackle or smash the pin with a rock. No, bolts and bars are the bunk. If you really want to keep someone from running away, chain him with dishes and glasses. Belay him by the beak to a groaning board. You give him all he wants to eat and drink daily and, so help me, he'll never run away, not even if he's up for hanging. Holding on to him is a cinch once you chain him with *that* kind of chain. And belly bonds are so firm and flexible—the more you stretch them, the tighter they get.

For example, I'm on my way to Menaechmus' house here (*pointing*). I sentenced myself to his jail years back: I'm going now of my own free will so he can put the irons on me. This Menaechmus is a man who doesn't just feed a man; he bloats the belly for you, he restores you to life—you won't find a finer physician. He's a fellow like this: he's as big an eater as they come himself, so every meal he serves looks like a thanksgiving day banquet: he overloads the tables, he piles up the plates like pyramids; you have to stand on your chair if you want something from on top. But it's been quite a while since my last invitation. I've had to be homebound with all that's dear to me—you see, whatever I eat that I pay for is dear, very dear. And there's this: right now all that's so dear to me has broken ranks and deserted the table. So (*pointing again to Menaechmus' house*) I'm paying him a visit. Wait—the door's opening. There's Menaechmus himself; he's coming out.

(*Sponge moves off to the side. The door opens and Menaechmus of Epidamnus stomps out. He is a good-looking man in his middle twenties, whose grooming, clothes, and air all smack of a substantial income. His manifest irascibility is unusual: normally he is gay, an inveterate jokester, and always out for a good time. He is wearing a coat which he clutches tightly about him. He turns and addresses his wife who is visible in the doorway.*)

SONG

MENAECHMUS OF EPIDAMNUS: (*angrily*)
If you weren't so stupid and sour,
Such a mean-tempered bitch, such a shrew,
What you see gives your husband a pain,
You'd make sure would give *you* a pain too.
    From this moment henceforth,
    You just try this once more,
    And, a divorce in your hand,
    You go darken Dad's door.

Every time that I want to go out
I get called, I get grabbed, I get grilled:
    "Where are you going to go?"
    "Why are you going outside?"
    "What are you going to do?"
    "What are you going to get?"
    "What have you got in your hand?"
    "What were you doing downtown?"

Why, the way I declare every act of my life,

It's a customs official I wed, not a wife!
Oh, you're spoiled, and I did it myself. Listen, you—
I'll explain here and now what I'm planning to do.

> I've filled your every need:
> The clothes you've on your back,
> Your servants, food, and cash—
> There's nothing that you lack.

> If you only had some sense,
> You'd watch what you're about.
> You'd let your husband be,
> And cut the snooping out.

And what's more, so your snooping's not lost
And the time you put in not a waste,
I'll be off to go find me a girl
Who can join me for dinner someplace.

SPONGE: (*to the audience, in anguish*)
> He pretends to be hard on his wife—
> But it's *me* that he's giving the knife!
> Eating out! Do you know who he'll hurt?
> It's yours truly he'll hurt, not his wife.

MENAECHMUS OF EPIDAMNUS: (*to himself, wonderingly, as his wife disappears inside*)
> Well, I finally gave her what for—
> And I drove the old bitch from the door!

(*To the audience, triumphantly*)
What's happened to the husbands who've been keeping mistresses?
What's holding up their plaudits and their cheers for what I've done?
They *all* owe me a medal for the fight I fought and won!
(*Throws his coat open to reveal a woman's dress he has on over his clothes*)
I stole this dress from her just now—I'll bring it to my girl.
Now *that's* the way to operate—outfox a foxy guard!
A beautiful piece of work it was, a feat to shout about,
A lovely piece of work it was, superbly carried out.
(*Losing his jubilation suddenly as realization dawns*)
I snitch from the bitch at *my* expense—and my downfall gets it all.
(*Cheering up again*)
But the enemy's camp's been looted, and we've safely made our haul!

SPONGE: (*calling as Menaechmus starts marching toward Lovey's door*) Hey, mister, any share in that swag for me?

MENAECHMUS OF EPIDAMNUS: (*stopping and closing his coat, but not turning around; to himself*) Ambushed! I'm lost!

SPONGE: Saved, you mean. Don't be afraid.

MENAECHMUS OF EPIDAMNUS: (*still not turning*) Who is it?

SPONGE: Me.

MENAECHMUS OF EPIDAMNUS: (*turning*) Hi, friend-in-need and Johnny-on-the-spot.

SPONGE: Hi.

MENAECHMUS OF EPIDAMNUS: What are you doing these days?

SPONGE: (*grabbing Menaechmus' hand and pumping it*) I'm shaking the hand of my guardian angel.

MENAECHMUS OF EPIDAMNUS: You couldn't have timed it better to meet me.

SPONGE: I'm always like that—I know Johnny-on-the-spotitude down to the last dotitude.

MENAECHMUS OF EPIDAMNUS: You want to see a brilliant piece of work?

SPONGE: (*smacking his lips*) Who cooked it? One look at the leftovers and I can tell in a minute if he slipped up anywhere.

MENAECHMUS OF EPIDAMNUS: Tell me, have you ever seen those famous pictures they hang on walls? The eagle carrying off Ganymede or Venus with Adonis?

SPONGE: (*testily*) Lots of times. But what have those pictures got to do with me?

MENAECHMUS OF EPIDAMNUS: (*throwing open his coat to reveal the dress*) See this? Do I look like one?

SPONGE: (*staring*) What have you got on there, anyway?

MENAECHMUS OF EPIDAMNUS: (*slyly*) Tell me I'm the nicest guy you know.

SPONGE: (*suspiciously*) Where do we eat?

MENAECHMUS OF EPIDAMNUS: (*pretending to be annoyed*) First tell me what I told you to.

SPONGE: All right, all right. You're the nicest guy I know.

MENAECHMUS OF EPIDAMNUS: (*as before*) How about adding something on your own, please?

SPONGE: (*grudgingly*) And the most fun to be with.

MENAECHMUS OF EPIDAMNUS: Go On.

SPONGE: (*exploding*) God damn it, no going on till I know what for. You're on the outs with your wife, so I'm watching my step with you.

MENAECHMUS OF EPIDAMNUS: (*sensing his teasing has gone far enough, gaily and conspiratorially*) Let's you and I, without letting my wife know a thing, kill off this day—

SPONGE: (*interrupting*) Well, all right! That's something like! How soon shall I start the funeral? The day's already half dead, all the way down to the waist.

MENAECHMUS OF EPIDAMNUS: (*with a great show of patience*) Interrupt me, and you just hold things up for yourself.

SPONGE: (*hurriedly*) Menaechmus, poke my eye out if I utter another word. Orders from you excepted, of course.

MENAECHMUS OF EPIDAMNUS: (*tiptoeing away from his house with anxious glances over his shoulder at the door*) Come on over here. Away from that door.

SPONGE: (*following*) Sure.

MENAECHMUS OF EPIDAMNUS: (*tiptoeing farther, with more glances*) Even more.

SPONGE: (*following*) All right.

MENAECHMUS OF EPIDAMNUS: (*now far enough away to give up tiptoeing—but still glancing*) Come on, step along. Farther from that lion's den.

SPONGE: I swear, if you ask me, you'd make a wonderful jockey.

MENAECHMUS OF EPIDAMNUS: Why?

SPONGE: The way you look behind every second to make sure your wife's not catching up.

MENAECHMUS OF EPIDAMNUS: I want to ask you a question.

SPONGE: Me? The answer's Yes, if you want yes; No, if you want no.

MENAECHMUS OF EPIDAMNUS: If you smelled something, could you tell from the smell—

SPONGE: (*with one type of smell in mind, interrupting*) Better than a board of prophets.

MENAECHMUS OF EPIDAMNUS: All right, then, try this dress I have. What do you smell? (*He hands Sponge part of the skirt, Sponge sniffs, then jerks his nose away*) What did you do that for?

SPONGE: You've got to smell a woman's dress at the top. Down there there's an odor that never washes out, and it's death on the nose.

MENAECHMUS OF EPIDAMNUS: (*moving the upper part toward him*) Smell here then. (*Laughing as Sponge sniffs gingerly*) You do a wonderful job of wrinkling up your nose.

SPONGE: I had good reason.

MENAECHMUS OF EPIDAMNUS: Well? What does it smell from? Tell me.

SPONGE: Loot, lechery—and lunch.

MENAECHMUS OF EPIDAMNUS: (*clapping him on the back and leading him toward Lovey's door*) Right you are. Now it goes right to my lady friend Lovey here. And I'll have her fix up a lunch for me, you, and her.

SPONGE: (*smacking his lips*) Fine!

MENAECHMUS OF EPIDAMNUS: (*gaily*) We'll pass the bottle from now till the crack of dawn tomorrow.

SPONGE: (*as before*) Fine! Now you're talking. Should I knock on the door?

MENAECHMUS OF EPIDAMNUS: Knock away. (*As Sponge races up to Lovey's door and raises a fist to deliver a lusty bang*) No, wait!

SPONGE: (*bitterly*) You just passed that bottle back a mile.

MENAECHMUS OF EPIDAMNUS: Try a tiny tap.

SPONGE: What are you scared of? That the door's made of bone china? (*Turns to knock.*)

MENAECHMUS OF EPIDAMNUS: (*excitedly*) Wait! Wait, for god's sake! See? She's coming out. Look how the sun grows
gray 'gainst the glory of that gorgeous figure!

(*The door opens and Lovey* [Erotium, *literally "little love"*] *comes out, a good-looking girl in a brassy sort of way, flashily dressed and heavily made up.*)

LOVEY: Menaechmus, darling! How nice to see you!

SPONGE: How about me?

LOVEY: (*witheringly*) You don't count.

SPONGE: (*unruffled*) I do so. I'm in this man's army too. Rear guard.

MENAECHMUS OF EPIDAMNUS: (*seeing a chance to tease her, slyly*) Orders from head-quarters, Lovey; invite Sponge and me to your house today. For a duel.

LOVEY: All right. (*Throwing a baleful look at Sponge*) Just for today.

MENAECHMUS OF EPIDAMNUS: (*as before*) A duel of drinks to the death. Whichever's the better man with the bottle becomes your bodyguard. You be referee, you decide which you'll sleep with tonight. (*Abruptly dropping his teasing as he notices her begin to sulk*) Honey, one look at you and, oh, do I hate that wife of mine!

LOVEY: (*not yet mollified—and catching sight of the dress, frigidly*) In the meantime, you can't even keep from wearing her clothes. What is this, anyway?

MENAECHMUS OF EPIDAMNUS: (*throwing his coat open, gaily*) Embezzled from her to embellish you, my flower.

LOVEY: (*magically thawed out*) You always win out over all the other men who run after me. You have such winning ways.

SPONGE: (*aside*) That's a mistress for you: nothing but sweet talk so long as she sees something to get her hands on. If you really loved him, you'd be kissing his mouth off this minute.

MENAECHMUS OF EPIDAMNUS: (*taking off his coat*) Sponge, hold this. I want to carry out the dedication ceremony I scheduled.

SPONGE: Hand it over. (*Taking the coat and eying Menaechmus in the dress*) Since you're in costume, how about favoring us with a bit of ballet later?

MENAECHMUS OF EPIDAMNUS: Ballet? Me? Are you in your right mind?

SPONGE: You mean are *you* in your right mind. All right, if no ballet, get out of costume.

MENAECHMUS OF EPIDAMNUS: (*taking the dress off and handing it to Lovey*) I took an awful chance stealing this today. Riskier, if you ask me, than when Hercules helped himself to Hippolyta's girdle. It's all for you—because you're the only person in the whole world who's really nice to me.

LOVEY: What a lovely thought! That's the way all nice lovers should think.

SPONGE: (*aside*) You mean if they're hell-bent to get to the poorhouse.

MENAECHMUS OF EPIDAMNUS: (*to Lovey*) I paid a thousand dollars last year for that dress you have there. Got it for my wife.

SPONGE: (*aside*) Using your own figures, that works out to a thousand dollars down the drain.

MENAECHMUS OF EPIDAMNUS: (*to Lovey*) You know what I'd like you to do?

LOVEY: I know one thing: I'll do whatever you like.

MENAECHMUS OF EPIDAMNUS: Then have your cook prepare lunch for the three of us. Send him to the market for some gourmetetitious shopping. Have him bring back the pig family: the Duke of Pork, Lord Bacon, the little Trotters, and any other relatives. Things that, served roasted, reduce me to ravenousness. Right away, eh?

LOVEY: But of course!

MENAECHMUS OF EPIDAMNUS: Sponge and I are on our way downtown but we'll be back in a few minutes. We can have drinks while the things are on the fire.

LOVEY: Come back whenever you like. Everything will be ready.

MENAECHMUS OF EPIDAMNUS: Just hurry it up. (*Turning and striding off, stage left; to Sponge*) Follow me.

SPONGE: (*running after him*) I'm not only following you, I'm not letting you out of my sight. Today is the one day I wouldn't lose you for all the treasures of heaven!

(*As Menaechmus and Sponge leave, Lovey walks to the door of her house.*)

LOVEY: (*calling through the door to her maids inside*) Tell Roll, the cook, to come out here right away. (A *second later, Roll* [Cylindrus], *a roly-poly cook, races out and stands attentively in front of her.*) You'll need a shopping basket and some money. Here's fifteen dollars.

ROLL: Yes, ma'am.

LOVEY: Go do the marketing. Get just enough for three—not a bit more and not a bit less.

ROLL: What people are you having?

LOVEY: Menaechmus, his parasite, and myself.

ROLL: (*thoughtfully*) That makes ten—a parasite can do for eight. Easily.

LOVEY: Now you know who'll be there; you take care of the rest.

ROLL: (*importantly*) Right. Consider lunch cooked. Tell your guests to go in and sit down. (*Races off, stage left.*)

LOVEY: (*calling after him*) Come right back!

ROLL: (*over his shoulder*) Be back in a flash.

(*Roll dashes off, Lovey enters her house, and the stage is now empty.*)

ACT II

(*Enter, stage right, Menaechmus of Syracuse and his servant Messenio carrying a satchel; behind them, loaded down with luggage, is a pair of rowers from the skiff that brought them ashore. These two move off to the side of the stage and put their burdens down.*

In appearance Menaechmus of Syracuse is identical with his twin. But there the likeness ends. Menaechmus of Epidamnus is gay, generous, and fun loving; his brother is shrewd, calculating, and cynical. Messenio, about the same age as his master, is the long-faced type who worries easily and takes himself very seriously.)

MENAECHMUS OF SYRACUSE: Messenio, if you ask me, the greatest joy a sailor can have is to sight land from the open sea.

MESSENIO: (*pointedly*) I'll be honest with you: it's even greater when the land you come near and see is your homeland. Will you please tell me why we're here in Epidamnus? Are we going to do like sea water and go around every island there is?

MENAECHMUS OF SYRACUSE: (*grimly*) We're here to look for my brother. My twin brother.

MESSENIO: (*exasperated*) When are we going to put an end to looking for that man? We've been at it six years! Austria, Spain, France, Jugoslavia, Sicily, every part of Italy near salt water, up and down the Adriatic—we've made the rounds of all of them. Believe me, if you were looking for a needle, and it was anywhere to be found, you'd have found it long ago. We're looking for the dead among the living. Because, if he was alive to be found, you'd have found him long ago.

MENAECHMUS OF SYRACUSE: (*as before*) Then I'm looking for someone who can prove it, someone who'll tell me he knows for certain my brother is dead. Once I hear that, I'll never look for him again. But until I do, so long as I live, I'll never stop. *I* know how much he means to me.

MESSENIO: (*grumbling*) You're looking for hens' teeth. Why don't we turn around and go home? Or maybe you and I are going to write a travel book?

MENAECHMUS OF SYRACUSE: (*sharply*) You do what you're told, eat what you're given, and stay out of trouble! Don't annoy me now; we're doing things my way, not yours.

MESSENIO: (*aside*) Ho-ho! That's telling me who's the slave around here. Couldn't have put things plainer with fewer words. But I can't hold this in, I've got to speak up. (*To Menaechmus*) Listen, Menaechmus. I've been looking over our finances. So help me, we're traveling with a summer-weight wallet. If you want my opinion, either you head for home, or you'll be mourning your long-lost money while you look for your long-lost brother. Let me tell you what kind of people live in these parts. The hardest drinkers and worst rakes are right here in Epidamnus. Besides, the town's full of crooks and swindlers. And they say the prostitutes here have a smoother line of talk than anywhere else in the world. That's why this place is called Epidamnus: nobody stays here without a damned lot of damage.

MENAECHMUS OF SYRACUSE: (*unperturbed*) I'll keep my eyes open. You just hand over the wallet.

MESSENIO: (*suspiciously*) What do you want with it?

MENAECHMUS OF SYRACUSE: After what you've been telling me, I'm scared to leave it with you.

MESSENIO: Scared of what?

MENAECHMUS OF SYRACUSE: That you'll do me a damned lot of damage in Epidamnus. You're a big man with the women, Messenio, and I'm a man with a big temper, the explosive type. If I keep the money, I avoid trouble both ways: you don't lose your head and I don't lose my temper.

MESSENIO: (*handing over the wallet*) Here it is. You keep it. Glad to have you take over.

(*Enter Roll, stage left, lugging a loaded shopping basket.*)

ROLL: (*to himself*) No trouble at all with the shopping. I got just what I wanted. I'll serve the diners a delicious dinner. Hey—who's that I see there? Menaechmus! Heaven help my poor back! The guests already at the door before I'm even back from the market! Well, I'll say hello. (*Walking up to Menaechmus*) Good afternoon, Menaechmus.

MENAECHMUS OF SYRACUSE: (*surprised but cordial*) Good afternoon to you— whoever you are.

ROLL: (*taken aback*) Whoever I am? You don't know who I am?

MENAECHMUS OF SYRACUSE: Of course not.

ROLL: (*deciding to overlook the exchange as just another of Menaechmus' jokes*) Where are the rest of the guests?

MENAECHMUS OF SYRACUSE: Guests? What guests are you looking for?

ROLL: That parasite of yours.

MENAECHMUS OF SYRACUSE: (*blankly*) Parasite of mine? (*To Messenio, sotto voce*) The man's daft.

MESSENIO: (*sotto voce to Menaechmus*) Didn't I tell you the place was full of swindlers?

MENAECHMUS OF SYRACUSE: Now, mister, who is this parasite you're looking for?

ROLL: Sponge.

MESSENIO: (*digging into the satchel he is carrying*) Got it safe right here in the satchel. See?

ROLL: (*apologetically*) Menaechmus, you're too early. Lunch isn't ready. I just got back from the shopping.

MENAECHMUS OF SYRACUSE: (*with exaggerated concern*) Tell me, mister, what were fresh fish selling for today?

ROLL: Dollar apiece.

MENAECHMUS OF SYRACUSE: Here's a dollar. Buy some for yourself; it's on me. The food'll do your brains good. Because there's one thing I'm dead sure of: you're out of your senses, whoever you are. Otherwise why would you make such a nuisance of yourself to a total stranger?

ROLL: (*smiling indulgently*) You don't know *me?* You don't know Roll?

MENAECHMUS OF SYRACUSE: (*testily*) I don't care if you're roll or loaf. Go to the devil! I don't know you, and, what's more, I don't want to!

ROLL: (*with an I'll-play-along-with-your-little-joke smile*) Your name's Menaechmus, isn't it?

MENAECHMUS OF SYRACUSE: (*anger giving way to curiosity*) To the best of my knowledge. And when you call me "Menaechmus" you talk sense. Where do you know me from, anyway?

ROLL: (*chuckling*) You're carrying on an affair with my owner Lovey (*gesturing toward the house*), and you have to ask *me* where I know you from?

MENAECHMUS (*tartly*) I'm not carrying on any affairs, and I haven't the slightest idea who you are.

ROLL: (*as before*) You don't know who *I* am? Me? Your glass-filler all the times you come over to our house for drinks?

MESSENIO: (*to the world at large*) Damn! Here I am without a thing to split that skull of his in half!

MENAECHMUS OF SYRACUSE: You my glass-filler? When I've never set foot in Epidamnus, never set eyes on the place in my life till today?

ROLL: You mean you deny it?

MENAECHMUS OF SYRACUSE: I certainly do deny it!

ROLL: *pointing to the house of Menaechmus of Epidamnus*) You mean to say you don't live in that house there?

MENAECHMUS OF SYRACUSE: (*roaring*) To hell with any and everyone who lives in that house there!

ROLL: (*to the audience, smiling*) Swearing at himself. *He's* the one who's daft. (*To Menaechmus*) Listen, Menaechmus.

MENAECHMUS OF SYRACUSE: (*sourly*) What do you want?

ROLL: You know that dollar you offered to give me a minute ago? Take my advice and use it to buy fish for your own brains. You swore at your own self just now, you certainly can't be in your right mind.

MENAECHMUS OF SYRACUSE: God! Talk, talk, talk! He's getting on my nerves!

ROLL: (*to the audience*) He always kids around with me like this. He's a real card— when his wife's not around. (*To Menaechmus*) I say, Menaechmus. (*As Menaechmus stubbornly stands with his back to him*) I say there, Menaechmus! (*Menaechmus throws up his hands in despair and turns around. Roll holds out the basket.*) Take a look. You think I bought enough for you, your parasite, and your lady? Or should I go back for more?

MENAECHMUS OF SYRACUSE: (*wearily*) What lady? What parasite are you talking about?

MESSENIO: (*to Roll, truculently*) What's the matter? Something on your conscience that's driving you out of your mind? Is that why you're making a nuisance of yourself to this man?

ROLL: (*resentfully*) What are *you* butting in for? I don't know you. I'm talking to this man here. Him I know.

MESSENIO: There's one thing I know: you're stark-raving mad, you are.

ROLL: (*pointedly ignoring Messenio; to Menaechmus, reassuringly*) I'll have everything cooked in a minute. You won't have to wait. So please don't go too far from the house. (*Turning to go*) Anything I can do for you before I go in?

MENAECHMUS OF SYRACUSE: (*stalking away*) Yes. Go to hell.

ROLL: (*muttering*) No, damn it, you go—(*as Menaechmus whirls around*) and have a seat while I (*importantly*) expose all this to the flame's fiery fury. I'll go and tell my mistress you're here so she can invite you in and not leave you standing around outside. (*Goes into the house.*)

MENAECHMUS OF SYRACUSE: (*to Messenio*) Has he gone? (*Hearing the door slam*) He's gone. So help me, now I know that what you said was no lie.

MESSENIO: (*importantly*) You just watch your step. It's my theory that one of those prostitutes lives here. That's what that lunatic who just left said.

MENAECHMUS OF SYRACUSE: (*puzzled*) What amazes me is how he knew my name.

MESSENIO: (*with the air of an expert*) Nothing amazing about that. These girls have a system. They send their tricky little maids and houseboys down to the docks. Whenever a foreigner heads for a berth, they start asking the name and the home port. The next minute the girls are hanging around his neck and sticking to him like glue. And, if he once takes the bait, he goes home a goner. (*Pointing to Lovey's house*) Now, there's a privateer moored in this berth right here. My advice is, let's steer clear of her.

MENAECHMUS OF SYRACUSE: Good advice. Messenio, you're on your toes.

MESSENIO: I'll know I'm on my toes when I see you on your guard, not before.

MENAECHMUS OF SYRACUSE: Sh! Quiet a minute. I hear the door opening. Let's see who's coming out.

MESSENIO: I'll get rid of this in the meantime. (*Handing the satchel to one of the rower-porters*) Hey, oar-power, keep an eye on this, will you please?

(*Lovey appears in the doorway. She turns and addresses a maid who was about to close the door behind her.*)

SONG

LOVEY: (*adjusting the door*)
> No, not closed. Just like this, open wide.
> Now go in and get going inside.
> See that everything's set in the room.
> Spread some cushions. And lots of perfume.

(*Turns and addresses the audience*)
> Sophistication—that's the way
> To bring a lover-boy to bay.
> Plus saying Yes—to men a curse,
> To girls a way to fill a purse.

(*Looks around and, at first, doesn't see Menaechmus*)
> Now, where's he gone? My cook reports
>   He's standing by the door.
> Oh, there he is—my useful and
>   Most profitable amour.

> He's lord and master in my house.
> He's earned, the right to be,
> And so I let him. Now I'll go
> And let him talk to me.

(*Walks up to Menaechmus*)
Sweetie-pie! You surprise me, you do,
With this standing around outside here.
Why, my door's open wider to you
Than your own. This is *your* house, my dear.
Not a thing that you asked to be done

Have my servants forgotten, not one.
They're all ready inside, honeybunch,
They've made *just* what you ordered for lunch.
So, whenever you'd like to come in,
We can all take our seats and begin.

MENAECHMUS OF SYRACUSE: (to *Messenio*) Who's this woman talking to?

LOVEY: (*with a dazzling smile*) You, of course.

MENAECHMUS OF SYRACUSE: And just what have you, in the present or past, ever had to do with me?

LOVEY: (*meltingly*) So much! And just because Cupid told me to pick you out of all the men in the world and make you the most important man in my life. And it's no more than you deserve. I can't tell you how happy you've made me, just you alone, by all the nice things you've done for me.

MENAECHMUS OF SYRACUSE: (*sotto voce to Messenio*) Messenio, this woman's either drunk or daft. She treats a total stranger like a bosom friend.

MESSENIO: (*sotto voce*) Didn't I tell you? That's the land of thing that goes on around here. But this is just the leaves falling. Stay three days longer and see what you get then: a tree trunk on your head. That's what prostitutes here are like—gold diggers, every one of them. (*Tapping himself importantly on the chest*) You just let *me* talk to her. Hey, lady! (As *Lovey looks at him blankly*) Yes, you.

LOVEY: What is it?

MESSENIO: Where do you know this man from?

LOVEY: (*with a that's-a-silly-question air*) Same place he's known me from, all these years. Epidamnus.

MESSENIO: Epidamnus? When he never set foot in the place till today?

LOVEY: Tee-hee! You make such funny jokes. (*Taking Menaechmus by the arm*) Menaechmus dear, why don't you come inside? It's much nicer in here.

MENAECHMUS OF SYRACUSE: (*extricating himself; sotto voce to Messenio*) What the devil! This woman's called me by my right name. I don't get it. What's going on here?

MESSENIO: (*sotto voce*) She got a whiff of that wallet you're carrying.

MENAECHMUS OF SYRACUSE: (*sotto voce*) Darned good thing you warned me. (*Handing over the wallet*) Here, you take it. Now I'll find out whether it's me or my money she's so passionate about.

LOVEY: Let's go in and have lunch.

MENAECHMUS OF SYRACUSE: It's awfully nice of you, but, thank you, I really can't.

LOVEY: (*staring at him in amazement*) Then why did you tell me to make lunch for you a little while ago?

MENAECHMUS OF SYRACUSE: I told you to make lunch?

LOVEY: You certainly did. For you and that parasite of yours.

MENAECHMUS OF SYRACUSE: (*peevishly*) Damn it all, what parasite? (*Sotto voce to Messenio*) This woman must be out of her mind.

LOVEY: Sponge.

MENAECHMUS OF SYRACUSE: Sponge? What sponge? For cleaning shoes?

LOVEY: (*accustomed to Menaechmus' jokes, patiently*) The one who was here with you a little while ago, of course. When you brought me the dress you stole from your wife.

MENAECHMUS OF SYRACUSE: (*clutching his head*) What's this? I brought you a dress I stole from my wife? Are you crazy? (*Sotto voce to Messenio*) She's dreaming; she sure goes to sleep like a horse—standing up.

LOVEY: (*starting to sulk*) You always get such pleasure out of teasing me. Why do you say you didn't do what you definitely did do?

MENAECHMUS OF SYRACUSE: (*slowly, emphasizing each word*) Now, will you kindly tell me just what I did do that I say I didn't do?

LOVEY: Give me one of your wife's dresses today.

MENAECHMUS OF SYRACUSE: (*helplessly*) And I *still* say I didn't! Listen: I never had a wife, I don't have one now, and never, since the day I was born, have I set foot inside this city till this minute. I had lunch aboard ship, I came from there here, and I ran into you.

LOVEY: (*tearfully*) Well! Oh, this is terrible, this will be the end of me! What ship are you talking about?

MENAECHMUS OF SYRACUSE: (*glibly*) A wooden one. Been scraped, calked, and repaired time and again. More pine plugs patching the planks than pegs holding pelts at a furrier's.

LOVEY: (*pleading*) Please, dear, no more games. Come inside with me now.

MENAECHMUS OF SYRACUSE: Lady, it's not me you want. It's some other man, I haven't the slightest idea who.

LOVEY: (*with a let's-be-serious-now air*) I know perfectly well who you are. You're Menaechmus, your father's name was Moschus, and I've heard say you were born in Syracuse in Sicily. (*Like a schoolgirl reciting—and getting most of her lesson wrong*) The king of Syracuse was Agathocles, then Phint-something, then Etna, and now Hiero. Etna gave it to Hiero when he died.

MENAECHMUS OF SYRACUSE: (*amazed—and amused; dryly*) Absolutely right, lady, every word.

MESSENIO: (*sotto voce to Menaechmus*) By god, I bet she comes from there, and that's how she knows all about you.

MENAECHMUS OF SYRACUSE: (*sotto voce*) Then I really don't think I can turn down her invitation.

MESSENIO: (*sotto voce*) You do nothing of the sort! You go through that door, and you're through.

MENAECHMUS OF SYRACUSE: (*sotto voce, peevishly*) Shut up, will you? Everything's going fine. I'm going to say yes to whatever she says: maybe I can get myself some free entertainment (*To Lovey*) My dear girl, I knew what I was doing when I kept saying no to you up to now. I was afraid that fellow (*gesturing toward Messenio*) would tell my wife about the dress and our date. Since you'd like to go in now, let's.

LOVEY: You're not going to wait for your parasite?

MENAECHMUS OF SYRACUSE: (*exploding*) No, I am *not* going to wait for my parasite, I don't give a damn about my parasite, and, if he shows up, I want him kept out.

LOVEY: It'll be a pleasure, believe me. (*Going up to him and stroking his cheek*) Menaechmus, do you know what I'd like you to do for me?

MENAECHMUS OF SYRACUSE: Just say the word.

LOVEY: I'd like you to take that dress you just gave me to the dressmaker and have her make some alterations and add some touches I want.

MENAECHMUS OF SYRACUSE: (*enthusiastically*) By god, you're right! That way nobody'll recognize it, and my wife won't know you have it on if she sees you in the street.

LOVEY: Then remember to take it with you when you leave.

MENAECHMUS OF SYRACUSE: I sure will!

LOVEY: Let's go in.

MENAECHMUS OF SYRACUSE: I'll be right with you; I want to have a last word with this fellow here. (*Lovey goes into the house; he turns to Messenio.*) Hey, Messenio, come over here.

MESSENIO: (*angrily*) What's going on? What do you have to do *this* for?

MENAECHMUS OF SYRACUSE: I have to. (*As Messenio opens his mouth*) I know all about it, you can save your breath.

MESSENIO: (*bitterly*) That makes it even worse.

MENAECHMUS OF SYRACUSE: (*triumphantly*) Initial operation proceeding according to plan. I'm practically looting the enemy camp. Now, get going as fast as you can and take these fellows (*gesturing toward the rower-porters*) to the hotel this minute. Be sure you come back for me before sundown.

MESSENIO: (*pleading*) Menaechmus, listen, you don't know these girls.

MENAECHMUS OF SYRACUSE: (*sharply*) Enough talk. If I do anything stupid it'll be my neck, not yours. The stupid one's this woman. She doesn't have a brain in her head. From what I saw just now, there's rich pickings in here for us. (*Goes into the house.*)

MESSENIO: (*calling after him*) Good lord, are you really going in? (*Shaking his head, to himself*) He's a dead duck. The privateer has our rowboat in tow and is hauling it straight to hell and gone. But I'm the one without a brain in my head for thinking I can run my master. He bought me to listen to what he says, not order him around. (*To the rower-porters*) Follow me. I have orders to get back here in time, and I don't want to be late.

(*Messenio and his men file out, stage right. The stage is now empty.*)

ACT III

(*Enter Sponge, stage left, in a mad hurry. The sight of Lovey's closed door brings him to an abrupt halt. He claps a hand to his brow, then turns and walks downstage to address the audience.*)

SPONGE: I'm over thirty now, and never have I ever in all those years pulled a more damned fool stunt than the one I pulled today: there was this town meeting, and I had to dive in and come up right in the middle of it. While I'm standing there with my mouth open, Menaechmus sneaks off on me. I'll bet he's gone to his girl friend. Perfectly willing to leave me behind, too!

(*Paces up and down a few times, shaking his head bitterly. Then, in a rage*) Damn, damn, damn the fellow who first figured out town meetings! All they do is keep a busy man away from his business. Why don't people pick a panel of men of leisure for this kind of thing? Hold a roll call at each meeting and whoever doesn't answer gets fined on the spot. There are plenty of persons around who need only one meal a day; they don't have business hours to keep because they don't go after dinner invitations or give them out. They're the ones to fuss with town meetings and town elections. If that's how things were run, I wouldn't have lost my lunch today. He sure wanted me along, didn't he? I'll go in, anyway. There's still hope of leftovers to soothe my soul. (*He is about to go up to the door when it suddenly swings open and Menaechmus of Syracuse appears, standing on the threshold with a garland, a little askew, on his head; he is holding the dress and listening to Lovey who is chattering at him from inside. Sponge quickly backs off into a corner.*) What's this I see? Menaechmus—and he's leaving, garland and all! The table's been cleared! I sure came in time—in time to walk him home. Well, I'll watch what his game is, and then I'll go and have a word with him.

MENAECHMUS OF SYRACUSE: (*to Lovey inside*) Take it easy, will you! I'll have it back to you today in plenty of time, altered and trimmed to perfection. (*Slyly*) Believe me, you'll say it's not your dress; you won't know it any more.

SPONGE: (*to the audience*) He's bringing the dress to the dressmaker. The dining's done, the drinks are down—and Sponge spent the lunch hour outside. God damn it, I'm not the man I think I am if I don't get even with him for this, but really even. You just watch. I'll give it to him, I will.

MENAECHMUS OF SYRACUSE: (*closing the door and walking downstage; to the audience, jubilantly*) Good god, no one ever expected less—and got more blessings from heaven in one day than me. I dined, I wined, I wenched, and (*holding up the dress*) made off with this to which, from this moment on, she hereby forfeits all right, title, and interest.

SPONGE: (*straining his ears, to the audience*) I can't make out what he's saying from back here. Is that full-belly talking about me and my right title and interest?

MENAECHMUS OF SYRACUSE: (*to the audience*) She said I stole it from my wife and gave it to her. I saw she was mistaking me for someone else, so I promptly played it as if she and I were having a hot and heavy affair and began to yes her; I agreed right down the line to everything she said. Well, to make a long story short, I never had it so good for so little.

SPONGE: (*clenching his fists, to the audience*) I'm going up to him. I'm itching to give him the works. (*Leaves his corner and strides belligerently toward Menaechmus.*)

MENAECHMUS OF SYRACUSE: (*to the audience*) Someone coming up to me. Wonder who it is?

SPONGE: (*roaring*) Well! You featherweight, you filth, you slime, you disgrace to the human race, you double-crossing good-for-nothing! What did I ever do to you that you had to ruin my life? You sure gave me the slip downtown a little while ago! You killed off the day all right—and held the funeral feast without me. Me who was coheir under the will! Where do you come off to do a thing like that!

MENAECHMUS OF SYRACUSE: (*too pleased with life to lose his temper*) Mister, will you please tell me what business you and I have that gives you the right to use language like that to a stranger here, someone you never saw in your life? You hand me that talk and I'll hand you something you won't like.

SPONGE: (*dancing with rage*) God damn it, you already have! I know god damned well you have!

MENAECHMUS OF SYRACUSE: (*amused and curious*) What is your name, mister?

SPONGE: (*as before*) Still making jokes, eh? As if you don't know my name!

MENAECHMUS OF SYRACUSE: So help me, so far as I know, I never heard of you or saw you till this minute. But I know one thing for sure; whoever you are, you'd better behave yourself and stop bothering me.

SPONGE: (*taken aback for a minute*) Menaechmus! Wake up!

MENAECHMUS OF SYRACUSE: (*genially*) Believe me, to the best of my knowledge, I am awake.

SPONGE: You don't know me?

MENAECHMUS OF SYRACUSE: (*as before*) If I did, I wouldn't say I didn't.

SPONGE: (*incredulously*) You don't know your own parasite?

MENAECHMUS OF SYRACUSE: Mister, it looks to me as if you've got bats in your belfry.

SPONGE: (*shaken, but not convinced*) Tell me this: didn't you steal that dress there from your wife today and give it to Lovey?

MENAECHMUS OF SYRACUSE: Good god, no! I don't have a wife, I never gave anything to any Lovey, and I never stole any dress. Are you in your right mind?

SPONGE: (*aside, groaning*) A dead loss, the whole affair. (*To Menaechmus*) But you came out of your house wearing the dress! I saw you myself!

MENAECHMUS OF SYRACUSE: (*exploding*) Damn you! You think everybody's a pervert just because you are? I was wearing this dress? Is that what you're telling me?

SPONGE: I most certainly am.

MENAECHMUS OF SYRACUSE: Now you go straight to the one place fit for you! No—get yourself to the lunatic asylum; you're stark-raving mad.

SPONGE: (*venomously*) God damn it, there's one thing nobody in the world is going to stop me from doing: I'm telling the whole story, exactly what happened, to your wife this minute. All these insults are going to boomerang back on your own head. Believe you me, you'll pay for eating that whole lunch yourself. (*Dashes into the house of Menaechmus of Epidamnus.*)

MENAECHMUS OF SYRACUSE: (*throwing his arms wide, to the audience*) What's going on here? Must everyone I lay eyes on play games with me this way? Wait—I hear the door.

(*The door of Lovey's house opens, and one of her maids comes out holding a bracelet. She walks over to Menaechmus and, as he looks on blankly, hands it to him.*)

MAID: Menaechmus, Lovey says would you please do her a big favor and drop this at the jeweler's on your way? She wants you to give him an ounce of gold and have him make the whole bracelet over.

MENAECHMUS OF SYRACUSE: (*with alacrity*) Tell her I'll not only take care of this but anything else she wants taken care of. Anything at all. (*He takes the piece and examines it absorbedly.*)

MAID: (*watching him curiously, in surprise*) Don't you know what bracelet it is?

MENAECHMUS OF SYRACUSE: Frankly no—except that it's gold.

MAID: It's the one you told us you stole from your wife's jewel box when nobody was looking.

MENAECHMUS OF SYRACUSE: (*forgetting himself, in high dudgeon*) I never did anything of the kind!

MAID: You mean you don't remember it? Well, if that's the case, you give it right back!

MENAECHMUS OF SYRACUSE: (*after a few seconds of highly histrionic deep thought*) Wait a second. No, I *do* remember it. Of course—this is the one I gave her. Oh, and there's something else: where are the armlets I gave her at the same time?

MAID: (*puzzled*) You never gave her any armlets.

MENAECHMUS OF SYRACUSE: (*quickly*) Right you are. This was all I gave her.

MAID: Shall I tell her you'll take care of it?

MENAECHMUS OF SYRACUSE: By all means, tell her. I'll take care of it, all right. I'll see she gets it back the same time she gets the dress back.

MAID: (*going up to him and stroking his cheek*) Menaechmus dear, will you do me a favor too? Will you have some earrings made for me? Drop earrings, please; ten grams of gold in each. (*Meaningfully*) It'll make me so glad to see you every time you come to the house.

MENAECHMUS OF SYRACUSE: Sure. (*With elaborate carelessness*) Just give me the gold. I'll pay for the labor myself.

MAID: Please, you pay for the gold too. I'll make it up to you afterward.

MENAECHMUS OF SYRACUSE: No, you pay for the gold. I'll make it up to *you* afterward. Double.

MAID: I don't have the money.

MENAECHMUS OF SYRACUSE: (*with a great air of magnanimity*) Well, any time you get it, you just let me have it.

MAID: (*turning to go*) I'm going in now. Anything I can do for you?

MENAECHMUS OF SYRACUSE: Yes. Tell her I'll see to both things—(*sotto voce, to the audience*) that they get sold as quickly as possible for whatever they'll bring. (*As the maid starts walking toward the door*) Has she gone in yet? (*Hearing a slam*) Ah, she's in, the door's closed. (*Jubilantly*) The lord loves me! I've had a helping hand from heaven! (*Suddenly looks about warily*) But why hang around when I have the time and chance to get away from this (*jerking his thumb at Lovey's house*) pimping parlor here? Menaechmus! Get a move on, hit the road, forward march! I'll take off this garland and toss it to the left here (*doing so*). Then, if anyone tries to follow me, he'll think I went that way. Now I'll go and see if I can find my servant. I want to let him know all the blessings from heaven I've had.

(*He races off, stage right. The stage is now empty.*)

ACT IV

(*The door of Menaechmus' house flies open and his wife bursts out, shrieking, with Sponge at her heels.*)

WIFE: Am I supposed to put up with a marriage like this? Look the other way while that husband of mine sneaks off everything in the house and hands it all over to his lady friend?

SPONGE: (*looking around uneasily*) Not so loud, please! I'll see to it you catch him red-handed right now. Just follow me. (*Starting to walk off, stage left*) He was on his way to the dressmaker with that dress he stole from you today. Had a garland on his head and was dead drunk. (*Noticing the garland Menaechmus of Syracuse had thrown down*) Hey, look! The garland he had on! I wasn't lying to you, was I? There you are. That's the way he went if you want to follow his trail. (*Looking toward the wings, stage left*) Well, look at that! He's coming back. Perfect! (*Peering hard*) But he doesn't have the dress!

WIFE: (*grimly*) What should I do to him this time?

SPONGE: Same as usual; lace into him. That's what I'd vote for. (*Pulling her off to the side*) Let's go over here. Then jump on him from ambush.

(*Enter Menaechmus of Epidamnus, hot, tired, and in a foul temper. He walks downstage and addresses the audience.*)

SONG

MENAECHMUS OF EPIDAMNUS:

> What a custom we have! Bothersome, bad.
> Stupid, silly, senseless, mad!
> And practiced most by our leading lights;
> > They all adore,
> > They're passionate for
> A flock of fawning satellites.
> Whether good or bad never bothers them:
> The fawner's funds they're bothered about.
> How people regard his character—
> > They leave that out.
>
> Is he good as gold but rather poor?
> > He's a bum.
> Is he worthless but has lots of gold?
> > The best they come!
> A patron goes wild with worry and care
> > Because of his charges' acts.
> > They know no truth or law or Justice;
> They deny undeniable facts;

They're vicious, avaricious crooks
    Forever up for trial—
Through usury and perjury
    They've made their pile.

In summary, civil, or criminal court,
Whenever a case of theirs comes up,
    We patrons come up too—
Of course: we have to take the stand
    And defend what the dastards do.

(Pauses, shakes his head despondently, then continues bitterly.)

That's what I had to do just today.
One of mine simply held me at bay.
I couldn't do what I wished, nor with whom,
For he hung and he clung; it was doom.
I went up on the stand and I entered a plea
On behalf of this creature's chicanery.

I proposed the most twisted and tortuous terms;
    Here I'd skim, there go on for a while.
I was arguing to settle the case out of court;
    What does *he* do? Insist on a trial!

There were three solid citizens who'd witnessed each crime—
Most open-and-shut case since the beginning of time!

He ruined this day for me.
God damn that stupid clown!
And god damn me as well!
For setting foot downtown.
I told her to make me lunch;
She's expecting me, I know.
A perfect day set up—
And I had to ruin it so!
I left as soon as I could
And hurried back uptown.
She'll be sore at me, I'm sure—

But that dress will calm her down,
The one I sneaked today from my wife
And handed to Lovey, the light of my life!

SPONGE: (*sotto voce to the wife, triumphantly*) Well, what do you say?

WIFE: (*sotto voce*) That I'm the miserable wife of a miserable husband.

SPONGE: (*sotto voce*) You can hear what he's saying, can't you?

WIFE: (*sotto voce, grimly*) I can hear, all right.

MENAECHMUS OF EPIDAMNUS: (*to the audience, gesturing toward Lovey's door*) Now why don't I be smart and go right inside here where I can have myself a good time?

SPONGE: (*springing out of his corner, shouting*) Wait! You're going to have a bad one, instead.

WIFE: (*following him, shrieking*) You'll pay me and with interest, you burglar.

SPONGE: (*gleefully*) That's giving it to him!

WIFE: So you thought you could commit all these crimes and get away with it, eh?

MENAECHMUS OF EPIDAMNUS: (*all innocence*) My dear wife, what are you talking about?

WIFE: (*witheringly*) You ask *me*?

MENAECHMUS OF EPIDAMNUS: (*acting puzzled, and gesturing toward Sponge*) Should I ask him? (*Walks toward her as if to put an arm about her.*)

WIFE: Don't you dare touch me!

SPONGE: (*to the wife*) Keep at him!

MENAECHMUS OF EPIDAMNUS: (*switching from puzzlement back to innocence*) What are you so mad at me for?

WIFE: (*grimly*) You ought to know.

SPONGE: He knows, all right, but he's pretending he doesn't, the dirty rat!

MENAECHMUS OF EPIDAMNUS: (*to his wife, as before*) What *is* this all about?

WIFE: That dress—

MENAECHMUS OF EPIDAMNUS: (*quickly*) Dress?

WIFE: Yes, dress. Which a certain person— (*Menaechmus begins to shake. She observes him with grim satisfaction.*) What are you so scared about?

MENAECHMUS OF EPIDAMNUS: (*with a sickly attempt at nonchalance*) Me? Nothing. Nothing at all.

SPONGE: (to *Menaechmus, sneering*) With one exception—dress distress. (*As Menaechmus looks at him startled and then begins to pass frantic nods and winks*) So you *would* eat lunch behind my back, would you? (*To the wife*) Keep at him!

MENAECHMUS OF EPIDAMNUS: (*sotto voce to Sponge*) Shut up, will you!

SPONGE: (*answering Menaechmus' stage whisper in ringing tones*) I most certainly will *not* shut up. (*To the wife*) He's making signs to me not to speak.

MENAECHMUS OF EPIDAMNUS: Me? I most certainly am not! I'm not winking, I'm not nodding, I'm not doing anything of the kind.

SPONGE: (*to the wife, shaking his head incredulously*) Of all the nerve! He actually denies what you can see with your own eyes!

MENAECHMUS OF EPIDAMNUS: (*to the wife, solemnly*) My dear wife, I swear to you by all that's holy, I did *not* make any signs to (*jerking his head contemptuously in Sponge's direction*) that there. Now are you satisfied?

SPONGE: All right, she believes you about that there; now get back to the point.

MENAECHMUS OF EPIDAMNUS: (*with angelic innocence*) Get back where?

SPONGE: Get back to that dressmaker, *I* say. Go ahead. And bring back the dress.

MENAECHMUS OF EPIDAMNUS: (*as before*) What dress are you talking about?

SPONGE: It's time for me to stop doing the talking. This lady is forgetting her duty.

WIFE: (*responding promptly to the cue*) Oh, I'm a poor, unhappy woman!

MENAECHMUS OF EPIDAMNUS: (*going over to her, solicitously*) Why are you so unhappy, dear? Please tell me. Has one of the servants done something wrong? Are the maids or the houseboys answering you back? (*Switching from solicitousness to righteous indignation*) You just let me know about it. They'll pay for it, they will!

WIFE: (*witheringly*) Nonsense!

MENAECHMUS OF EPIDAMNUS: (*tenderly, to himself—but aloud*) She's so out of sorts. This distresses me.

WIFE: (*as before*) Nonsense!

MENAECHMUS OF EPIDAMNUS: (*nodding with sympathetic understanding*) Yes, you must be angry at one of the servants.

WIFE: (as *before*) Nonsense!

MENAECHMUS OF EPIDAMNUS: (*chuckling, as if what he's going to say is a great joke*) You can't be angry at *me,* at any rate.

WIFE: (*grimly*) Now you're making sense.

MENAECHMUS OF EPIDAMNUS: I certainly haven't done anything wrong.

WIFE: Hah! Back to nonsense again.

MENAECHMUS OF EPIDAMNUS: (*going up and putting his arm about her*) My dear, *please* tell me what's troubling you so much.

SPONGE: (*to the wife, sneering*) Your little bunny's buttering you up.

MENAECHMUS OF EPIDAMNUS: (*over his shoulder to Sponge, exasperated*) Can't you lay off me? Who's talking to you?

WIFE: (*suddenly screaming*) Take your hands off me! (*Menaechmus leaps back as if stunned.*)

SPONGE: (*to the wife*) That's giving it to him! (*To Menaechmus*) So you'll hurry off to eat lunch without me, will you? And then get drunk and walk out the door with a garland on your head and make fun of me, eh? (*Menaechmus grabs Sponge and yanks him over to the side.*)

MENAECHMUS OF EPIDAMNUS: (*sotto voce*) So help me, I not only haven't eaten lunch, I haven't set foot inside that house today!

SPONGE: (*sotto voce*) You mean you deny it?

MENAECHMUS OF EPIDAMNUS: (*sotto voce*) Of course I deny it.

SPONGE: (*sotto voce*) What a nerve! You mean to say I didn't see you a little while ago standing in front of the door there with a garland on your head? When you said I had bats in the belfry and that you didn't know me and that you were a stranger here?

MENAECHMUS OF EPIDAMNUS: (*sotto voce, blankly*) How could I? I just this minute came back home after you and I got separated.

SPONGE: (*sotto voce, sneering*) Oh, I know your type. Didn't think I could get even with you, did you? I told the whole story to your wife, that's what I did!

MENAECHMUS OF EPIDAMNUS: (*sotto voce, anxiously*) What did you tell her?

SPONGE: (sotto v*oce, blandly*) I don't know. Ask the lady herself.

(*Menaechmus turns on his heel and hurries to where his wife is standing.*)

MENAECHMUS OF EPIDAMNUS: (*nervously*) My dear wife, what's going on here? What sort of story did this fellow hand you? What is it? Why don't you answer me? Why don't you tell me what's the matter?

WIFE: (*witheringly*) As if you don't know! (*Slowly, emphasizing each word*) A dress was stolen from me.

MENAECHMUS OF EPIDAMNUS: (*with wide-eyed innocence*) A dress was stolen from you?

WIFE: (*as before*) Do you have to ask?

MENAECHMUS OF EPIDAMNUS: (*as before*) If I knew, I certainly wouldn't ask.

SPONGE: Damn you! What a faker! But you can't cover up any longer—she knows the whole story; I told it to her myself down to the last detail.

MENAECHMUS OF EPIDAMNUS: (*as before*) What story?

WIFE: (*grimly*) Since you have such an unmitigated gall and refuse to confess of your own free will, listen and listen hard. Believe you me, you'll find out what I'm mad about and what this fellow told me. (*Looking him straight in the eye*) A dress was stolen from me.

MENAECHMUS OF EPIDAMNUS: (*with histrionic astonishment*) A dress was stolen from me?

SPONGE: (*to the wife*) Look at that! The dirty rat's trying to fool you! (*To Menaechmus*) Stolen from *her,* not you. Damn it all, if it had been stolen from *you,* then it really would be lost.

MENAECHMUS OF EPIDAMNUS: (*to Sponge, savagely*) You keep out of this. (*To his wife*) Now, what were you saying, dear?

WIFE: (*tight-lipped*) I was saying that one of my dresses disappeared from the house.

MENAECHMUS OF EPIDAMNUS: Who could have stolen it?

WIFE: (*meaningfully*) I should think the man who made off with it knows the answer to that one.

MENAECHMUS OF EPIDAMNUS: Who is he?

WIFE: Someone named Menaechmus.

MENAECHMUS OF EPIDAMNUS: (*thundering*) God in heaven, the man's a criminal! Who is this Menaechmus?

WIFE: I'll tell you: *you.*

MENAECHMUS OF EPIDAMNUS: Me?

WIFE: You. (*They stand in silence for a few seconds, eying one another.*)

MENAECHMUS OF EPIDAMNUS: (*blustering*) Who says so?

WIFE: I do.

SPONGE: So do I. And I also say you gave it to your lady friend Lovey here.

MENAECHMUS OF EPIDAMNUS: *I* gave it?

WIFE: Yes, you. You yourself.

SPONGE: What do you want us to do? Bring an owl here to keep saying "yoo yoo" to you? We're getting hoarse, the both of us.

MENAECHMUS OF EPIDAMNUS: (*solemnly, one hand on heart, the other raised*) My dear wife, I swear to you by all that's holy, I didn't give it. Does that satisfy you?

SPONGE: And, damn it all, we take the same oath that you're lying!

(*Menaechmus looks from one to the other. They glower back. He quails visibly.*)

MENAECHMUS OF EPIDAMNUS: (*feebly*) Well, you see, I didn't *give* it away, I sort of lent it out.

WIFE: (*exploding*) Good god in heaven! I don't lend out your coats or suits, do I? If there's any lending to do, the wife will see to her things and the husband to his. Now you get that dress back into this house, do you hear?

MENAECHMUS OF EPIDAMNUS: (*meekly*) I'll see you get it back.

WIFE: (*grimly*) And my opinion is, you'd better. Because you don't enter this house unless that dress is with you. I'm going in now. (*Turns her back on him and stalks off toward the door.*)

SPONGE: (*calling after her, alarmed*) Don't I get anything for all I've done for you?

WIFE: (*pausing at the threshold, contemptuously*) I'll do the same for you when something's stolen from your house. (*Slams the door behind her.*)

SPONGE: (*to the audience, horror-stricken*) My god! That means never—I don't have anything to steal! Husband, wife—to hell with the both of you! I'm off downtown. In a hurry—one thing I know for sure: I've worn out my welcome with this household! (*Scuttles off, stage left.*)

MENAECHMUS OF EPIDAMNUS: (*to the audience, gaily*) My wife thinks she's giving me a bad time by shutting me out. As if I don't have another place to go into, lots better, (*Addressing the closed door*) You don't like me, eh? (*With a mock sigh*) I'll just have to put up with it. But Lovey here likes me. She's not going to shut me out, she's going to shut me *in*. (*Turning back to the audience*) I'll go see her and ask her to return the dress I just gave her. I'll buy her another one, even better. (*Walking up to Lovey's door and knocking*) Hey! Anybody minding this door? Open up, someone, and call Lovey out here!

LOVEY: (*from inside*) Who wants me?

MENAECHMUS OF EPIDAMNUS: Someone who'd sooner see his own self hurt than hurt you.

LOVEY: (*opening the door*) Menaechmus! Darling! What are you standing outside for? Come on in. (*Turns to go inside.*)

MENAECHMUS OF EPIDAMNUS: (*seriously*) No, wait. You don't know what I've come for.

LOVEY: (*walking up to him and stroking his cheek*) Sure I do. So you can have your fun with me.

MENAECHMUS OF EPIDAMNUS: (as *before*) Damn it all, it's not that. Would you please do me a big favor and give me back that dress I just gave you? My wife's found out everything, she knows exactly what happened. I'll buy you another that costs twice as much, any one you like.

LOVEY: (*staring at him blankly*) But I just gave it to you a few minutes ago to take to the dressmaker! Along with that bracelet you were to take to the jeweler so he could make it over.

MENAECHMUS OF EPIDAMNUS: (*staring at her blankly*) What's that? You gave *me* the dress and a bracelet? Oh, no. You never did. Figure it out. Right after I gave it to you, I went downtown, I came back from there just a few minutes ago, and this is the first I've seen of you since.

LOVEY: (*stepping back and eying him frigidly*) I see what your game is. I trusted you with the dress, and now you're looking for a way to do me out of it.

MENAECHMUS OF EPIDAMNUS: (*earnestly*) I swear I'm not asking for it to do you out of it. I tell you my wife knows everything!

LOVEY: (*building up a head of feminine steam*) *I* didn't ask you to give it to me. *You* brought it to me of your own free will. You gave it as a gift, and now you want it back. Well, I don't mind. Take it. Keep it. Let your wife wear it, wear it yourself, lock it up in a closet, for all I care. But don't you fool yourself: you're not setting foot inside this door from now on. After all I've done for you, you'll treat me like dirt under your feet, will you? Unless you come with cash in your hands, you're wasting your time, you'll get nothing out of me. Find some other girl to treat like—like a fool under your feet!

MENAECHMUS OF EPIDAMNUS: Don't carry on so, please! (*As she turns her back on him and flounces inside*) Hey, wait, I tell you! Come on back! Stop, won't you? Please, do me a favor, and come back! (*She slams the door behind her. Menaechmus turns despondently to the audience*) She's gone in and shut the door. I'm the shuttest-out man there is: my wife, my mistress—nobody believes a thing I say. Well, I'll go and talk things over with my friends and see what they think I ought to do.

(*Menaechmus leaves, stage left. The stage is now empty.*)

ACT V

(*Menaechmus of Syracuse enters, stage right, back from his search for Messenio along the waterfront. At the same moment, the door of Menaechmus of Epidamnus' house opens, and the wife comes out.*)

MENAECHMUS OF SYRACUSE: (*to himself, disgustedly*) That was a stupid stunt I pulled a little while ago, to trust the wallet with all our money to Messenio. If you ask me, he's made himself at home in some dive somewhere,

WIFE: (*to herself*) I'll keep an eye out for that husband of mine. See how soon he comes back. (*Noticing Menaechmus of Syracuse*) Well! There he is! And the day's saved—he's bringing back my dress.

MENAECHMUS OF SYRACUSE: (*to himself, testily*) I wonder where that Messenio would be wandering about now?

WIFE: (*to herself*) I'll go up to him and give him the welcome he deserves. (*Striding up to Menaechmus*) Aren't you ashamed to show yourself in front of me with that dress, you criminal!

MENAECHMUS OF SYRACUSE: (*startled*) What's the matter, madam? What's all the agitation about?

WIFE: (*shrieking*) The nerve of him! How dare you talk to me! How dare you utter a single solitary word in my presence!

MENAECHMUS OF SYRACUSE: (*in astonishment*) Will you please tell me what I did that I'm not allowed to utter a word?

WIFE: (*as before*) What a question! The unmitigated gall of this man!

MENAECHMUS OF SYRACUSE: (*tartly*) Madam, do you happen to know why the Greeks called Hecuba a bitch?

WIFE: (*huffily*) No, I don't.

MENAECHMUS OF SYRACUSE: (*as before*) Because she used to do exactly what you're doing now. Everyone she laid eyes on, she loaded with insults. And so they began to call her The Bitch—and she deserved it.

WIFE: (*after staring at him blankly for a few seconds, unable to believe her ears*) I *will* not put up with this criminal behavior! I'd sooner spend the rest of my days a divorcee than put up with this absolutely criminal behavior of yours!

MENAECHMUS OF SYRACUSE: (*shrugging*) What difference does it make to me whether you put up with your marriage or walk out on your husband? Is it the custom around here for people to talk nonsense to every stranger who comes to town?

WIFE: (*as before*) Talk nonsense? Well! I tell you I can't stand this one second longer. I'll die a divorcee rather than put up with the likes of you.

MENAECHMUS OF SYRACUSE: (*as before*) Die a divorcee or live till doomsday. Believe me, it makes no difference to me.

WIFE: A minute ago you were insisting you hadn't stolen it and now you're holding it right in front of my eyes. Aren't you ashamed of yourself?

MENAECHMUS OF SYRACUSE: (*finally needled into an angry retort*) Good god, woman, you certainly have a nerve! You're a bad one, you are! How dare you say I stole from you what another woman gave me to have trimmed and altered for her?

WIFE: (*throwing up her hands*) So help me, you know what I'm going to do? I'm going to call my father right here and now and tell him about every one of your crimes. (*Calling*) Decio! (*A scared houseboy scurries out and listens breathlessly.*) Go get my father and bring him right here; tell him he must come. (*Decio dashes off, stage left.*) In a few minutes the whole world will know all about these crimes of yours.

MENAECHMUS OF SYRACUSE: Are you in your right mind? What crimes of mine?

WIFE: That you stole dresses and jewelry from your own wife and carried them off to your lady friend. Is it the truth or isn't it?

MENAECHMUS OF SYRACUSE: (*helplessly*) Please, lady, if you know of any tranquilizer I can take to help me put up with your tantrums, for god's sake, lead me to it! I haven't the vaguest idea of who you think I am. I know you about as well as I know the man in the moon.

WIFE: (*pointing toward the wings, stage left*) You can make fun of me, all right, but, believe me, you're not going to make fun of *him*. There's my father coming this way. Turn around and look. I suppose you don't know him.

MENAECHMUS OF SYRACUSE: (*his gaze following her finger*) About as well as I know the old man of the mountain. You know when I saw him before? The same day I saw you.

WIFE: You deny that you know me? You deny that you know my father?

MENAECHMUS OF SYRACUSE: (*airily*) And the same goes for your grandfather, if you want to add him.

WIFE: (*disgustedly*) Ugh! Just what I'd expect from you!

(Menaechmus moves away, stage right, and stands moodily, looking off into the wings trying to catch the first glimpse of Messenio. A wizened graybeard emerges from the wings, stage left, leaning heavily on a stick; he makes his way at a snail's pace across the stage.)

SONG

FATHER: *(stopping to address the audience)*
> As fast as these old legs can go—
> When duty calls I can't say no—
> I'll step, I'll stride, I'll speed, I'll run.
> I'm well aware this is no fun;
> The spryness has gone out of me,
> I'm buried deep in senility,
> My body's hard to haul along,
> I've lost the strength I had when young.
>
> In getting old you don't do well;
> It's bad stuff, age. Do well? It's hell!
> Its coming brings a load of grief—
> But, to tell it all, I can't be brief.

(Totters on a few more steps, then stops abruptly and shakes his head worriedly)
> Now here's the thing that's on my mind
> And worries me to the core:
> What brought my daughter so suddenly
> To call me to her door?
> What does she want? She doesn't say!
> What is it she's called me for?

(Goes on for a few more steps, then halts again)
> I'm sure I know what it's all about:
> A fight with her husband has broken out.
> It's bound to happen to every shrew
> Who feels her dowry entitles her to
> A husband whose sole aim in life
> Is to fetch and carry for his wife.

(A few more steps, then another stop and more worried headshakings)
> Yet the men are not exactly pure.
> And there's just so much a wife can endure.
> A daughter doesn't call her dad
> Unless the insult's pretty bad,

Or else the squabbling got too rough.
Whatever it is, I'll know soon enough,
(*Turns and catches sight, finally, of his daughter and Menaechmus*)
There she is before the door
There's her husband, looking sore.
Just what I thought—a brawl once more.

FATHER: (to *himself*) I'll have a word with her.

WIFE: (*to herself*) I'll go up to him. (*Walking up to her father*) Papa! I'm *so* glad to see you!

FATHER: Glad to see you too. Well, here I am; any glad tidings? Were things glad around here when you sent for me? What are you looking so black for? (*Pointing to Menaechmus still watching out moodily for Messenio*) And what's he standing off over there in a huff for? You two have had a skirmish about something, all right. Well, speak up. Who's to blame? And make it short—no long lectures.

WIFE: I haven't done a thing wrong. Let me put your mind at ease about that first, Papa. It's simply that I can't go on living here, it's impossible, I can't stand it. So please take me away from here.

FATHER: (*wearily*) What's the trouble this time?

WIFE: Papa, he's making a fool of me.

FATHER: Who is?

WIFE: That man you trusted me to. That husband of mine.

FATHER: (*throwing up his hands*) I knew it! Another squabble. (*Peevishly*) How many times have I expressly warned you to watch out about coming to me with your complaints. Both of you.

WIFE: (*plaintively*) Watch out about *that?* How can I, Papa!

FATHER: (*snappishly*) What a question! You can if you want to. How many times have I pointed out to you that you *must* give in to your husband and not keep checking on what he does and where he goes and how he spends his time.

WIFE: (*expostulating*) But, Papa, he's passionately in love with that prostitute who lives next door!

FATHER: Very sensible of him. And, believe me, all this effort of yours will simply make him more passionate.

WIFE: (*sulking*) He goes there for drinks too.

FATHER: (*angrily*) If he likes to have a drink there—or anywhere—what's he supposed to do? Not go just to please you? You do have a devil of a nerve! By the same token you ought to stop him from accepting invitations to eat out or from bringing dinner guests to the house. If you think husbands are such slaves, why don't you hand him some wool, sit him down with the maids, and have him do a daily stint of spinning.

WIFE: (*with heavy sarcasm*) Naturally, it wasn't *me* I brought you here to defend, but my husband. You take the stand for *me*—and plead *his* case!

FATHER: (*sharply*) If he's done anything wrong, I'll go after him lots harder than I've gone after you. Since he keeps you in money and clothes, gives you maids, and pays for the household, the best thing you can do, my lady, is to start getting some sense.

WIFE: (*in desperation*) But he steals my jewelry and dresses right out of my closets, he robs me, he carries off my things behind my back and brings them to those whores of his!

FATHER: If he does that, he's to be blamed. But if he doesn't, *you're* to be blamed for blaming a blameless man.

WIFE: Papa, he's got the dress and bracelet that he gave her with him right now. I found out all about it, so he's bringing them back.

FATHER: (*shaking his head perplexedly, to himself*) I'll find out all about this right now. I'll go up and have a word with him. (*Tottering over to Menaechmus, who is still looking impatiently, stage right, for Messenio*) Tell me, Menaechmus, what have you two been—er——discussing? What are you looking so black about? What are you standing off here in a huff for?

MENAECHMUS OF SYRACUSE: My dear sir, I don't know who you are or what your name is, but I swear to you by god almighty and—

FATHER: (*interrupting in astonishment*) Swear? What in the world about?

MENAECHMUS OF SYRACUSE: (*holding up the dress*) This woman claims I stole this out of her house and made off with it. She's crazy. I swear I never did a thing wrong to her. (*Solemnly*) So help me, may I become more miserable than the most miserable specimen of humanity alive if I ever set foot in the house where she lives.

FATHER: Listen, you madman, if you take an oath like that, if you say you never set foot in your own house, you're stark-raving mad.

MENAECHMUS OF SYRACUSE: (*pointing to Menaechmus of Epidamnus' house*) My dear sir, are you telling me that I live in that house?

FATHER, Do you deny it?

MENAECHMUS OF SYRACUSE: I most certainly do deny it.

FATHER: No, you most certainly can't deny it. (*Suddenly struck by a thought*) Unless you moved out last night. (*Turning to the wife*) Daughter, come over here. What's this? You two haven't moved out of here?

WIFE: Now, just where or why would we be moving?

FATHER: Good god, I don't know.

WIFE: (*disgustedly*) It's so obvious. He's pulling your leg. Don't you get it?

FATHER: (*turning back to Menaechmus, sharply*) All right, Menaechmus, enough jokes. Now get to the point.

MENAECHMUS OF SYRACUSE (*finally losing his patience*) Please, what do you want with me? Where do you come from? Who are you? What have I got to do with you or this woman here who's pestering the life out of me?

WIFE: (*fearfully, to her father*) Look! His eyes are green! He's turning green around his temples and his forehead! Look at the glitter in his eyes!

MENAECHMUS OF SYRACUSE: (*to the audience*) They say I'm insane. Well, in that case, the best thing for me to do is act the part and scare them away.
(*Menaechmus proceeds forthwith to put on a garish performance.*)

WIFE: (*as before*) Look at the way he's throwing his arms around! Look at the faces he's making! Papa! What should I do!

FATHER: (*taking her by the arm and tottering off with her*) Come over here, daughter. As far away from him as we can get.

MENAECHMUS OF SYRACUSE: (*pretending to be calling to the God of Wine*) Yoho! Yoho! Bacchus! Where away in what wood do you call me for the hunt? I hear you—but I can't leave these parts. They've got their eyes on me—on my left that mad bitch and, behind, that old stink-goat who's perjured himself plenty of times in his day to the ruination of innocent men.

FATHER: You go to hell!

MENAECHMUS OF SYRACUSE: (*listening attentively as if to an unseen voice, and nodding briskly*) Ah! Orders from the Oracle of Apollo for me to burn her eyes out with blazing brands.

WIFE: Papa! This will be the end of me! He says he's going to burn my eyes out!

MENAECHMUS OF SYRACUSE: (*aside, chuckling*) They say *I'm* crazy. Damn it all, they're the ones who're crazy.

FATHER: Psst! Daughter!

WIFE: What is it? What are we going to do?

FATHER: Why don't I call the servants out here? I'll go get some to carry him in the house and tie him up before he causes any more commotion.

MENAECHMUS OF SYRACUSE: (*aside*) Stuck! If I don't come up with some scheme first, they're going to haul me into the house. (*Resumes his elaborate listening and nodding to celestial commands.*) Yes, Apollo: I'm not to spare the socks on the jaw unless she gets the hell out of my sight I will carry out your orders, Apollo. (*Advances menacingly toward the wife.*)

FATHER: (*frantically*) Run home as fast as you can or he'll beat you to a pulp!

WIFE: (*making for the door*) I am! Papa dear, please, please keep an eye on him and don't let him get away. (*To herself*) Oh, this is terrible! The things I have to listen to! (*Rushes into the house and slams the door behind her.*)

MENAECHMUS OF SYRACUSE: (*aside*) Not bad at all, the way I got rid of her. Now for this Titan here—a Titan with the shakes, a bearded, benighted one begat by the

Holy Swan. (*Starts listening and nodding again.*) So your orders are to grab that stick he's holding and make pulp of his arms, legs, bones, and joints?

FATHER: (*raising his stick*) You lay a hand on me or come any closer, and you're in for trouble!

MENAECHMUS OF SYRACUSE: (*as before*) I will carry out your orders, Apollo: I'm to take an ax and chip off every scrap of flesh this old boy has until I'm down to the bone.

FATHER: (*aside*) I've got to watch out and take care of myself now. These threats of his have me worried: he might hurt me.

(*Menaechmus advances, brandishing an imaginary ax, but the old man, instead of running, whirls his stick menacingly, and Menaechmus stops short before that formidable instrument. Forced to take another tack, he resumes his listening and nodding act.*)

MENAECHMUS OF SYRACUSE: That's a big order, Apollo. Now I'm to get a team of fierce wild horses, harness them to a chariot, and mount it so I can trample down this stinking, toothless, broken-down lion, eh? (*Launches into an elaborate dumb show.*) Now I'm in the chariot, I'm holding the reins, the whip's in my hand. (*Mimicking the manner of grand opera*) Come, my steeds! Let the clatter of your hoofs ring out! Bend the nimble knee in headlong haste!

FATHER: (*grimly*) Threatening me with a team of horses, eh?

(*Menaechmus gallops madly about, then, full tilt, makes for the old man, who holds his ground gamely, swinging his stick. Just before getting within range, Menaechmus prudently swerves aside, pulls up, and readies himself for another try.*)

MENAECHMUS OF SYRACUSE: Ah, Apollo, the orders are to make a second charge and wipe out this one who insists on standing his ground, eh? (*Charges down on the old man but the stick, whistling through the air, brings Menaechmus to an abrupt halt. He throws his head back and staggers backward as if irresistibly dragged against his will.*) What's this? Someone has me by the hair and is hauling me from my car! Who is it? Apollo! He's changing your direct orders!

FATHER: (*shaking his head dolefully, to the audience*) Dear, oh dear! These fits are such terrible things! Heaven help us! This fellow, for instance, was perfectly sane a minute ago and now he's completely out of his mind. And it came on him so suddenly and with such force! I'll go get a doctor as quick as I can. (*Rushes out, stage left.*)

MENAECHMUS OF SYRACUSE: (to *himself, in surprise*) Have they really gone? That pair who made a sane man insane? What am I waiting for? I should be off for the ship while the coast is clear, (*Walking downstage and addressing the audience*) Please, all of you, if the old fellow comes back, don't show him which street I took to get out of here.

(*Menaechmus of Syracuse dashes off, stage right. A second later the father re-enters, stage left, followed by a self-important little man who struts along majestically.*)

FATHER: (*to the audience, grumbling*) My seat hurts from sitting and my eyes from watching while I waited for the doctor to finish his rounds. Finally the pain-in-the-neck tore himself away from his patients and came back. "Aesculapius fractured a leg and Apollo an arm, and I was mending the breaks," he tells me. I wonder what I'm bringing, a doctor or a repairman? Look at that walk! (*Under his breath*) Shake a leg, you ant!

DOCTOR: (*in his professional manner*) What did you say his trouble is? Please describe it to me. Is it hallucinations or delirium? I'd like to know. Is he in a coma? Does he have water on the brain?

FATHER: (*testily*) Listen, that's just the reason I brought you here. To give *me* the answers—and to cure him.

DOCTOR: (*airily*) Nothing easier. He'll be a well man, I give you my word.

FATHER: I want you to be careful to take good care of him.

DOCTOR: Listen, I'll heave sixty sighs an hour for him. That's how careful I'll be to take good care of him.

FATHER: (*pointing toward the wings, stage left*) Look, there's your patient. Let's watch what he does.

(*The two back off to an unobtrusive spot. As they do, Menaechmus of Epidamnus trudges in despondently. Without noticing them, he walks downstage and addresses the audience.*)

MENAECHMUS OF EPIDAMNUS: God! What a day this one's been! Everything's gone against me. I thought I had kept what I did a secret—and my parasite spills the whole story, leaving me scared to death and in disgrace. That Ulysses of mine! The trouble he stirred up for his lord and master! (*Shaking his fist so hard his mantle slips from his shoulder*) As sure as I'm alive, I'll see to it he and his life part company. (*Snorting*) Now that's stupid of me, to call it *his* life. It's *mine*: he's stayed alive eating my food and at my expense. All right then, I'll make him part company with his soul. And that whore was every bit as bad. What else can you expect from a whore? Because I ask for the dress, so I can bring it back to my wife, she tells me she's already given it to me! Lord, oh lord, what a miserable life I lead!

FATHER: (*sotto voce to the doctor*) You hear what he's saying?

DOCTOR: (*sotto voce, with a knowing air*) Claims he's miserable.

FATHER: (*sotto voce*) I wish you'd talk with him.

DOCTOR: (*walking up to Menaechmus*) Good afternoon, Menaechmus. Will you please tell me why you have to leave your arm bare? Don't you realize the harm this can do to a man in your condition?

MENAECHMUS OF EPIDAMNUS: (*glaring*) Oh, go hang yourself.

FATHER: (*sotto voce to the doctor, anxiously*) Notice anything?

DOCTOR: (*sotto voce to the father*) Lord, yes! (*Shaking his head*) Even an acre of hellebore[1] couldn't cure this case. (*Turning back to Menaechmus*) I say, Menaechmus—

MENAECHMUS OF EPIDAMNUS: (*impatiently*) What do you want?

DOCTOR: (*assuming his professional manner*) Answer my questions, please. Do you drink white or red wine?

MENAECHMUS OF EPIDAMNUS: Why don't you go straight to hell?

DOCTOR: (*sotto voce to the father, clucking mournfully*) Beginning to show the initial symptoms of a seizure.

MENAECHMUS OF EPIDAMNUS: (*disgustedly*) Why don't you ask me whether my diet includes purple or red or yellow bread? Or birds with scales? Or fish with feathers?

FATHER: (*sotto voce to the doctor, urgently*) Good god! You hear him talk? He's delirious! What are you waiting for? Quick, give him some medicine before he goes completely insane!

DOCTOR: (*sotto voce, pontifically*) Not yet. I still have some questions to ask.

FATHER: (*to himself, between his teeth*) Your nonsense will be the death of me!

DOCTOR: (*to Menaechmus*) Tell me this: do your eyes at times become fixed and staring?

MENAECHMUS OF EPIDAMNUS: What's that? You damned fool! What do you think I am, a lobster?

DOCTOR: (*ignoring the outburst and nodding knowingly*) Now tell me this: does your stomach ever growl, so far as you've noticed?

MENAECHMUS OF EPIDAMNUS: After meals, no; when I'm hungry, yes.

DOCTOR: (*sotto voce to the father, puzzled*) So help me, there's nothing insane about that answer! (*Turning back to Menaechmus*) Do you sleep through the night? Do you have trouble falling asleep when you go to bed?

MENAECHMUS OF EPIDAMNUS: When my bills are paid, I sleep through. (*Suddenly losing his patience*) You and your questions! God damn you to hell!

DOCTOR: (*sotto voce to the father, nodding knowingly*) The start of a fit of insanity. Did you hear what he said? Watch out for him!

---

1 The standard ancient remedy for insanity.

FATHER: (*sotto voce to the doctor*) Oh no. To hear him talk now, he's Nestor himself compared with what he was before. After all, just a few minutes ago he was calling his wife a mad bitch.

MENAECHMUS OF EPIDAMNUS: (*overhearing this, roaring*) *What* did I call her?

FATHER: I was saying that, in a fit of insanity—

MENAECHMUS OF EPIDAMNUS: (*interrupting, as before*) Insanity? Me?

FATHER: (*angrily*) Yes, you. And you threatened to trample me down with a four-horse chariot. I saw you do it with my own eyes. I can prove you did it.

MENAECHMUS OF EPIDAMNUS: (*snorting*) Oh sure. And I can prove you stole the holy halo from god almighty. And that you were packed off to prison for it. And that after they let you out, you were tarred and feathered. And what's more, I can prove you killed your father and sold your mother. What do you say? Don't I swap insult for insult just like some one who's sane?

FATHER: (*to the doctor, pleading*) For god's sake, please, doctor, hurry and do whatever you're going to do! Don't you see the man's losing his mind?

DOCTOR: Do you know the best thing to do? Have him brought to my clinic.

FATHER: (*doubtfully*) You really think so?

DOCTOR: (*heartily*) Of course. I'll be able to treat him there just the way I want.

FATHER: Well, as you wish,

DOCTOR: (to *Menaechmus, cheerily*) I'll dose you with hellebore for about three weeks.

MENAECHMUS OF EPIDAMNUS: And I'll string you up and dose you with a whip for four. (*Stomps away angrily out of earshot.*)

DOCTOR: (*to the father*) Go get some men to carry him.

FATHER: How many will we need?

DOCTOR: Considering the symptoms I've observed, four would be the minimum.

FATHER: I'll have them here right away. Doctor, you keep an eye on him.

DOCTOR: (*hastily*) Oh no. I've got to get back to make ready whatever—er—has to be made ready. (*Airily, as he prudently hustles off, stage left*) You just have your servants bring him to me.

FATHER: I'll see to it. He'll be there.

DOCTOR: (*as he disappears into the wings*) I'm off now.

FATHER: (*as he limps off resignedly at his top speed after the doctor*) Good-by.

MENAECHMUS OF EPIDAMNUS: (*to the audience*) My father-in-law's left; the doctor's left; I'm alone. God almighty, what's going on? What are these men saying I'm crazy for? Why, I haven't had a sick day since the day I was born. Me insane? I don't even start fights or get into arguments! And I'm sane enough to think everyone else is sane and to recognize people and talk with them. If they can make the mistake of saying I'm crazy, maybe they're the ones who are crazy!

(Paces up and down a moment in silence. Then, shaking his head despondently)
Now what do I do? I want to go home but my wife won't let me. *(Gesturing toward Lovey's house)* And no one's going to let me in *there*. Oh, the whole thing's a mess! I'll stay right where I am. I suppose when it gets dark I'll be allowed to go inside. *(Sits down gloomily in front of the door of his house.)*

(Enter Messenio, stage right. He walks downstage and addresses the audience.)

SONG

> You know what marks the servant who's good,
> The kind that'll watch, take care, arrange,
> And plan for a master's livelihood?
> It's taking as good—or better—care
> When the master is out as when he's there.

If a slave's more concerned for his belly than back,
And his gullet than shins, then his brain's out of whack.

> He must not forget that masters pay
> The good-for-nothings in just one way:
> With shackles, whip, and mill,
> Hunger, fatigue, and chill;
> The wage of no work and all play.

So to hell with bad acting, I'll be good, I've decided,
Since I hellishly hate to get hurt or get hided.
I can stomach the curses and cries
It's the beatings and blows I despise.
And I'm many times happier having for lunch
The bread that's been browned
From what others have ground
Than grinding, myself for all others to munch.

> So I see that orders get obeyed
> With speed and skill and no fuss made.
> The system works out well for me;
> Others are free to test
> What seems for them the best,
> But *I'll* be as I have to be.

The Menaechmus Twins • 123

Be a Johnny-on-the-spot when the master commands—
If I only can keep this one worry in mind,
Not a fault will he ever be able to find.

But the day's soon to come when my worrying's done,
When he'll pay me the freedom I've worked for and won.
        So till then I'll behave
        Like a dutiful slave,
        And I'll practice my knack
        Of being kind to my back!
(*He turns and walks briskly toward Lovey's door.*)
    Well, I settled the bags and the servants in the hotel as he ordered, and now I've come to get him. I'll knock on the door so he knows I'm here. Let's see if I can spring him safe and sound from this sink of iniquity. I'm afraid, though, I may be too late; the battle may be all over.
(*Enter, stage left, the father with four husky slaves at his heels.*)

FATHER: (to *the slaves*) I'm warning you: in the name of all that's holy, make sure you use your head when you carry out my orders, the ones I gave you before and am giving you now. Unless you don't give a damn for your shins and ribs, you'll pick up that man there (*pointing to Menaechmus of Epidamnus*) and carry him to the clinic. And none of you are to pay the slightest attention to any threats he makes. Well, why are you standing there? What are you waiting for? You should have had him up on your shoulders and on his way by now! I'm off to the doctor's; I'll be waiting when you get there.

(*The old man hurries off, stage left. The four huskies make for Menaechmus, who looks up as they gallop toward him.*)

MENAECHMUS OF EPIDAMNUS: (*to himself*) This looks bad! What's going on here? God knows why, but these men are running toward me! (*To the men as they draw near*) What do you want? What are you after? (*Frantically*) Why are you surrounding me? (*With a rush they grab him and swing him on to their shoulders.*) Where are you taking me? Where am I going? Help! Murder! Save me, citizens of Epidamnus! (*To his abductors*) Let go of me!

MESSENIO: (*whirling about at the commotion*) Good god in heaven, what's this I see? Some strangers carrying off my master! This is an outrage!

MENAECHMUS OF EPIDAMNUS: (*despairingly*) Doesn't anyone have the heart to help me?

MESSENIO: (*calling*) I do, master, the heart of a hero! (*Orating at the top of his lungs, as he races to the rescue*) People of Epidamnus! This is a foul, a criminal act! In a city street, in broad daylight, in peacetime, to kidnap my poor master, a gentleman on a visit to your town! (*Tearing into the abductors*) Let go of him!

MENAECHMUS OF EPIDAMNUS: Whoever you are, for god's sake, stand by me! Don't let them get away with this flagrant miscarriage of justice!

MESSENIO: (*shouting, as he flails away*) They won't. I'll stand by you. I'll help you. I'll defend you to the death. I won't let them kill you—better I get killed myself! Master, for god's sake, the one there that's got you by the shoulder —gouge his eye out! These three here, why I'll plow their jaws and plant my fists there. (*To his opponents*) Kidnap him, will you? You'll pay for it and pay plenty! Let go of him!

MENAECHMUS OF EPIDAMNUS: (*triumphantly*) I got him by the eye!

MESSENIO: Tear it out of the socket! (*To his adversaries*) Criminals! Kidnapers! Bandits!

THE SLAVES (*shouting*) Don't kill us! Please!

MESSENIO: (*snarling*) Then let go!

MENAECHMUS OF EPIDAMNUS (*to his abductors*) What do you mean by laying hands on me! (*To Messenio*) Sock 'em on the jaw!

MESSENIO: (*as his three opponents break and run*) On your way! Go to hell, the bunch of you! (*Rushes over and lands a haymaker on Menaechmus' opponent*) And here's this from me! A bonus for being the last one out of here. (*To Menaechmus, smugly; as the four scamper off, stage left*) Well, I rearranged the geography of their faces to suit my taste. Believe me, master, I came to the rescue just in time.

MENAECHMUS OF EPIDAMNUS: (*fervently*) I don't know who you are, mister, but god's blessings on you forever. If it hadn't been for you, I wouldn't have lived to see the sun go down today.

MESSENIO: (*promptly*) Then if you want to do right by me, damn it all, you'll set me free.

MENAECHMUS OF EPIDAMNUS: Set you free? Me?

MESSENIO: Sure, master, I just saved your life, didn't I?

MENAECHMUS OF EPIDAMNUS: What are you talking about? Mister, you're making a mistake.

MESSENIO: Me making a mistake? What do you mean?

MENAECHMUS OF EPIDAMNUS: I give you my solemn oath, I'm not your master.

MESSENIO: (*taking this as a cruel joke, bitterly*) Don't give me that!

MENAECHMUS OF EPIDAMNUS: (*earnestly*) I'm not lying to you. (*Ruefully*) No servant of mine ever did as much for me as you have.

MESSENIO: (*as before*) All right. If you say I'm not your slave, why don't you let me go free?

MENAECHMUS OF EPIDAMNUS: (*smiling*) If it's up to me, by all means. Be a free man. Go where you like.

MESSENIO: (*unable to believe his ears*) You mean it? It's official?

MENAECHMUS OF EPIDAMNUS: (*as before*) If I have any official rights over you, it certainly is.

MESSENIO: (*ecstatically*) Hail, my patron! (*Menaechmus winces at the title, remembering the experience in that capacity that cost him his lunch. Messenio launches into an imaginary dialogue with his fellow slaves*) "Well, well, Messenio, so you're a free man. Congratulations!" "Thank you, thank you all." (*Turning back to Menaechmus, earnestly*) Patron, I want you to keep ordering me around the same as when I was your servant. I'll live with you, and, when you go back home, I'll go with you.

MENAECHMUS OF EPIDAMNUS: (*aside, wincing again*) Not a chance!

MESSENIO: I'll go back to the hotel now and get the bags and the money for you. The wallet with our cash is safe under lock and key in my satchel. I'll bring it to you right now.

MENAECHMUS OF EPIDAMNUS: (*promptly*) You do that. And hurry.

MESSENIO: (*over his shoulder as he rushes off, stage right*) You'll get it back just as it was when you gave it to me. Wait for me here.

MENAECHMUS OF EPIDAMNUS: (to *the audience, shaking his head in bewilderment*) Amazing, the amazing things that have happened to me! People tell me I'm not me and lock me out of the house. Then this fellow, (*grinning*) the one I just now emancipated, comes along, claims he's my slave, and tells me he's going to bring me a wallet full of cash. If he actually does, I'll tell him he's a free man and he's to leave me and go wherever he likes; I don't want him asking for the money back when he gets his sanity back. My father-in-law and the doctor say *I'm* mad. It's all a mystery to me. I must be dreaming the whole business.

Well, I'll pay a call on this whore here, even if she is sore at me. Maybe I can get her to give back the dress so I can bring it home.

(*He enters Lovey's house. A second later Menaechmus of Syracuse and Messenio enter, stage right, deep in conversation.*)

MENAECHMUS OF SYRACUSE: (*angrily*) I sent you off with orders to come back here for me. Where do you get the nerve to tell me I saw you anywhere since?

MESSENIO: (*frantically*) Just a minute ago I rescued you, right in front of this house, from four men who were carrying you off on their shoulders. You were hollering to heaven and earth for help, and I ran up and by fighting hard made them let you go. And, because I saved your life that way, you set me free. (*Bitterly*) And then, when I said I was going for the money and the bags, you ran ahead and got there first just so you could deny everything you did!

MENAECHMUS OF SYRACUSE: (*incredulously*) I set you free?

MESSENIO: You certainly did.

MENAECHMUS OF SYRACUSE: (*grimly*) I'll tell you what I certainly did: made up my mind to be a slave myself before I ever set you free. (*Starts stalking off, stage right.*)

(*The door of Lovey's house opens, and Menaechmus of Epidamnus stomps out. He turns and talks to Lovey and her maid inside.*)

MENAECHMUS OF EPIDAMNUS: (*through the doorway, excitedly*) Listen, you bitches, you can cross your heart and swear all you want but, damn it all, that's not going to change things: I did *not* walk off with that bracelet and dress.
(*Messenio glances over his shoulder at the sound of the voice—and does a double take.*)

MESSENIO: Good god in heaven! What's this I see?

MENAECHMUS OF SYRACUSE: (*sourly, and without stopping*) What?

MESSENIO: Your reflection!

MENAECHMUS OF SYRACUSE: (*stopping*) What are you talking about?

MESSENIO: (*excitedly*) He's your image! He couldn't be more like you.

MENAECHMUS OF SYRACUSE: (*following Messenio's gaze*) By god, you know, when I think about what I look like, he *does* resemble me.

MENAECHMUS OF EPIDAMNUS: (*turning from the door and noticing Messenio*) Hello there, my savior, whoever you are.

MESSENIO: (*to Menaechmus of Epidamnus, tensely*) Mister, would you please do me a favor and tell me your name, if you don't mind?

MENAECHMUS OF EPIDAMNUS: (*earnestly*) I mind any favors you ask for? I should say not. That isn't the treatment you deserve from me! The name's Menaechmus—

MENAECHMUS OF SYRACUSE: (*interrupting*) Hell, no! That's my name!

MENAECHMUS OF EPIDAMNUS: (*ignoring him*)—and I was born at Syracuse in Sicily.

MENAECHMUS OF SYRACUSE: (*resentfully*) That's *my* city and country.

MENAECHMUS OF EPIDAMNUS: (*looking at him for the first time*) What's that you say?

MENAECHMUS OF SYRACUSE: (*glowering*) Nothing but the truth.

MESSENIO: (*stares at the two in utter puzzlement. Then, to himself, uncertainly, pointing to Menaechmus of Epidamnus*) This must be the one I know; *he's* my master. I thought I was (*pointing to Menaechmus of Syracuse*) his servant, but I'm really (*pointing to Menaechmus of Epidamnus*) his. (*Addressing Menaechmus of Epidamnus*) I thought he was you; (*guiltily*) matter of fact, I gave him quite a bit of trouble. (To *Menaechmus of Syracuse*) Please forgive me if I said anything to you that sounded stupid. I didn't mean to.

MENAECHMUS OF SYRACUSE: (in *astonishment*) Are you crazy? You sound it. You and I came off the ship together today. Don't you remember?

MESSENIO: (astonished in his turn) You're absolutely right. *You're* my master. (*To Menaechmus of Epidamnus, apologetically*) You'd better find yourself another servant. (To *Menaechmus of Syracuse*) Hello. (*To Menaechmus of Epidamnus*) Good-by. Take my word—(*pointing to Menaechmus of Syracuse*) this man is Menaechmus.

MENAECHMUS OF EPIDAMNUS: No. *I* am.

MENAECHMUS OF SYRACUSE: (*to Menaechmus of Epidamnus*) What sort of nonsense is this? You're Menaechmus?

MENAECHMUS OF EPIDAMNUS: That's what I said. Son of Moschus.

MENAECHMUS OF SYRACUSE: (*bewildered*) The son of my father? You?

MENAECHMUS OF EPIDAMNUS: (*smiling*) No, mister, of *mine*. I have no intention of adopting your father or stealing him from you.

MESSENIO: (*to the audience, in great excitement*) Something just dawned on me! A hope that no one could have hoped for! God in heaven, make it come true! I tell you, unless my mind is going back on me, these two are the twin brothers! After all, they both give the same names for father and fatherland. I've got to have a word with my master in private. (*Calling out*) Menaechmus!

MENAECHMUS OF EPIDAMNUS:
MENAECHMUS OF SYRACUSE: } What do you want?

MESSENIO: I don't want you both! Which one of you was on the ship with me?

MENAECHMUS OF EPIDAMNUS: Not I.

MENAECHMUS OF SYRACUSE: I.

MESSENIO: Then you're the one I want. Step over here, will you?
(*Messenio walks a few steps off to the side, and Menaechmus of Syracuse joins him.*)

MENAECHMUS OF SYRACUSE: Here I am. What's up?

MESSENIO: (*sotto voce, excitedly*) That man there is either a swindler or your twin brother! I've never seen two people more alike. Believe me, you two are more like each other than one drop of water or one drop of milk to another. Besides, he gives the same names as you for father and fatherland. We'd better go up to him and ask him some questions.

MENAECHMUS OF SYRACUSE: (*catching Messenio's excitement*) That's a darned good idea! Thanks very much. But, please, do me a favor; you do it. (*As they walk back toward Menaechmus of Epidamnus*) Messenio, you're a free man if you can find out he's my brother.

MESSENIO: (*fervently*) I hope I can.

MENAECHMUS OF SYRACUSE: I hope so too.

MESSENIO: (*to Menaechmus of Epidamnus, drawing himself up self-importantly, like a judge questioning a party to a case*) Harrumph! (*As Menaechmus of Epidamnus looks at him inquiringly*) You stated, as I remember, that your name was Menaechmus.

MENAECHMUS OF EPIDAMNUS: That's right.

MESSENIO: (*gesturing toward Menaechmus of Syracuse*) This man's name is Menaechmus too. You stated you were born at Syracuse in Sicily; he was born there. You stated your father's name was Moschus; so was his. Now you can both help me—and yourselves at the same time.

MENAECHMUS OF EPIDAMNUS: Anything you want from me, the answer's yes; you've earned it. I'm a free man, but I'm at your service just as if you'd bought and paid for me.

MESSENIO: (*solemnly*) My hope is that the two of you will discover you are twin brothers, born the same day to the same mother and the same father.

MENAECHMUS OF EPIDAMNUS: (*wistfully*) What you're talking about is a miracle. Ah, If you could only do what you hope to!

MESSENIO: (*determinedly*) I can. But now let's start. Answer my questions, both of you.

MENAECHMUS OF EPIDAMNUS: (*promptly*) Ask away. I'll tell you everything I know.

MESSENIO: Is your name Menaechmus?

MENAECHMUS OF EPIDAMNUS: It is.

MESSENIO: (*to Menaechmus of Syracuse*) And yours too?

MENAECHMUS OF SYRACUSE: Yes.

MESSENIO: (*to Menaechmus of Epidamnus*) And you say your father's name was Moschus?

MENAECHMUS OF EPIDAMNUS: I do.

MENAECHMUS OF SYRACUSE: So do I. (*Receives a lordly look of disapproval from Messenio for anticipating the question.*)

MESSENIO: (*to Menaechmus of Epidamnus*) And you were born at Syracuse?

MENAECHMUS OF EPIDAMNUS: Absolutely.

MESSENIO: (*to Menaechmus of Syracuse*) What about you?

MENAECHMUS OF SYRACUSE: You know I was.

MESSENIO: So far everything agrees perfectly. We'll go on; your attention please. (*To Menaechmus of Epidamnus*) Tell me, what is your earliest recollection of your homeland?

MENAECHMUS OF EPIDAMNUS (*holding his forehead and closing his eyes as he struggles to remember*) Going off to Tarentum with my father on a business trip. Then wandering off in the crowd and being carried away.

MENAECHMUS OF SYRACUSE: (*exclaiming involuntarily*) God in heaven! Help me now!

MESSENIO: (*with the voice of authority*) What's the meaning of this shouting? Can't you keep quiet! (*To Menaechmus of Epidamnus*) How old were you when your father took you from your fatherland?

MENAECHMUS OF EPIDAMNUS: Seven. I remember because I was just beginning to lose my baby teeth. (*Sadly*) I never saw my father again.

MESSENIO: Answer this: how many sons were there in your family?

MENAECHMUS OF EPIDAMNUS: As best as I can remember, two.

MESSENIO: Which was the older, you or your brother?

MENAECHMUS OF EPIDAMNUS: We were the same age.

MESSENIO: How is that possible?

MENAECHMUS OF EPIDAMNUS: We were twins.

MENAECHMUS OF SYRACUSE: (*exclaiming fervently*) Heaven has come to my rescue!

MESSENIO: (*icily*) If you're going to interrupt, I'm not going to say another word!

MENAECHMUS OF SYRACUSE: (*meekly*) No, no—I won't say another word.

MESSENIO: (*to Menaechmus of Epidamnus*) Tell me: did you both have the same name?

MENAECHMUS OF EPIDAMNUS: Oh, no. You see, I was called Menaechmus, as now, but his name was Sosicles.

MENAECHMUS OF SYRACUSE: (*to himself, wildly excited*) For me the case is proved. I can't hold back, I've got to take him in my arms. (*Taking his hands*) Welcome, my brother, my twin brother! I'm Sosicles!

MENAECHMUS OF EPIDAMNUS: (*gently disengaging his hands; uncertainly*) If that's so, how come you got the name Menaechmus?

MENAECHMUS OF SYRACUSE: When the news came about you and about father's death, grandfather changed it: he gave me yours instead.

MENAECHMUS OF EPIDAMNUS: I guess it could have happened that way. But answer this question.

MENAECHMUS OF SYRACUSE: (*eagerly*) What is it?

MENAECHMUS OF EPIDAMNUS: (*intently*) What was our mother's name?

MENAECHMUS OF SYRACUSE: Teuximarcha.

MENAECHMUS OF EPIDAMNUS: (*rushing to embrace him*) Right! Welcome to you, my brother! I never expected to see you again, and now, after so many years, I have you before me.

MENAECHMUS OF SYRACUSE: And welcome to you, my brother. I searched and searched for you right up to this moment, and now, after so many trials and tribulations, I have the joy of having found you.

MESSENIO: (*to Menaechmus of Syracuse, a light dawning*) That explains it! That girl called you by your brother's name. I'm sure she thought it was he she was inviting in to lunch, not you.

MENAECHMUS OF EPIDAMNUS: (*smiling broadly*) As a matter of fact, I had told her to prepare lunch for me today. My wife wasn't to know a thing about it. I sneaked a dress of hers out of the house and gave it to the girl.

MENAECHMUS OF SYRACUSE: (*holding up the dress*) You mean the one I have here?

MENAECHMUS OF EPIDAMNUS: (*astonished*) That's it! How did it ever get to you?

MENAECHMUS OF SYRACUSE: (*laughing*) That girl who carried me off to give me lunch insisted I had given it to her. The wench wined me and dined me in style and then went to bed with me. I made off with the dress and this bracelet (*holding it up*).

MENAECHMUS OF EPIDAMNUS: Believe me, I'm delighted to hear something nice happened to you because of me. When she invited you in, she thought it was me, you know.

MESSENIO: (*breaking in, anxiously*) There's nothing to stop you now, is there, from giving me my freedom the way you promised?

MENAECHMUS OF EPIDAMNUS: A perfectly proper and fair request, my brother. Do it for my sake.

MENAECHMUS OF SYRACUSE: Messenio, you're a free man.

MENAECHMUS OF EPIDAMNUS: (*his eyes twinkling, mimicking the exact tone of voice Messenio had used a few moments ago*) Well, well, Messenio, so you're a free man. Congratulations!

MESSENIO: (*meaningfully, holding out his hand, palm upward*) But I could use a better beginning to make sure I stay free.

MENAECHMUS OF SYRACUSE: (*pointedly ignoring the hand and the remark*) Now that things have turned out just the way we wanted, my brother, let's both of us go back to our homeland.

MENAECHMUS OF EPIDAMNUS: Brother, I'll do whatever you wish. I can hold an auction and sell whatever I own around here. (*Leading him toward the door of his house*) But let's go inside for now.

MENAECHMUS OF SYRACUSE: Yes, let's.

MESSENIO: (*who had been listening avidly to the last exchange*) Do you know what favor I'd like to ask?

MENAECHMUS OF EPIDAMNUS: What?

MESSENIO: (*eagerly*) Let me run the auction.

MENAECHMUS OF EPIDAMNUS: It's all yours.

MESSENIO: (*rubbing his hands delightedly*) Then how about my announcing right now that an auction will take place?

MENAECHMUS OF EPIDAMNUS: All right. Make it a week from today. (*The two brothers enter the house.*)

MESSENIO: (*to the audience, in an auctioneer's chant*): Hear ye, hear ye! Selling at auction, one week from today, rain or shine, the property of Menaechmus. For sale: slaves, household effects, farm land, and buildings. All items to go for whatever they'll bring, and all payments strictly cash. Sale includes one wife—if anyone will bid. (*Leaning forward:, in a confidential tone*) If you ask me, the whole auction won't net fifty cents.

(*Straightening up, in ringing tones*) And now, ladies and gentlemen, good-by. Your loudest applause, please!

THE COMEDY OF ERRORS

By William Shakespeare

Dramatis Personae

SOLINUS, *Duke of Ephesus*

AEGEON, *a Merchant of Syracuse*

ANTIPHOLUS *of Ephesus, twin brothers and sons*

ANTIPHOLUS *of Syracuse, to Aegeon and Aemilia*

DROMIO *of Ephesus, twin brothers, attendants*

DROMIO *of Syracuse, on the two Antipholuses*

BALTHAZAR, *a Merchant*

ANGELO, *a Goldsmith*

FIRST MERCHANT *of Ephesus, friend to Antipholus of Syracuse*

SECOND MERCHANT *of Ephesus, to whom Angelo is a debtor*

DOCTOR PINCH, *a schoolmaster and a Conjurer*

AEMILIA, *wife to Aegeon, an Abbess at Ephesus*

ADRIANA, *wife to Antipholus of Ephesus*

LUCIANA, *her Sister*

LUCE, *servant to Adriana*

COURTEZAN

GAOLER, OFFICERS, AND OTHER ATTENDANTS

SCENE: *Ephesus*

ACT I.

Scene I. Hall in the Duke's Palace.

Enter DUKE, AEGEON, GAOLER, OFFICERS, *and other Attendants.*

AEGEON: Proceed, Solinus, to procure my fall,
 And by the doom of death end woes and all.
DUKE: Merchant of Syracusa, plead no more.
 I am not partial to infringe our laws:
 The enmity and discord which of late
 Sprung from the rancorous outrage of your duke
 To merchants, our well-dealing countrymen,
 Who, wanting guilders to redeem their lives,
 Have seal'd his rigorous statutes with their bloods,
 Excludes all pity from our threat'ning looks.
 For, since the mortal and intestine jars
 'Twixt thy seditious countrymen and us,
 It hath in solemn synods been decreed,
 Both by the Syracusians and ourselves,
 T' admit no traffic to our adverse towns:
 Nay, more, if any, born at Ephesus
 Be seen at Syracusian marts and fairs;
 Again, if any Syracusian born
 Come to the bay of Ephesus, he dies,
 His goods confiscate to the duke's dispose;
 Unless a thousand marks be levied,
 To quit the penalty and to ransom him.
 Thy substance, valu'd at the highest rate,
 Cannot amount unto a hundred marks;
 Therefore, by law thou art condemn'd to die.
AEGEON: Yet this my comfort: when your words are done,
 My woes end likewise with the evening sun.
DUKE: Well, Syracusian; say, in brief the cause
 Why thou departedst from thy native home,
 And for what cause thou cam'st to Ephesus.
AEGEON: A heavier task could not have been impos'd
 Than I to speak my griefs unspeakable;
 Yet, that the world may witness that my end
 Was wrought by nature, not by vile offence,
 I'll utter what my sorrow gives me leave.

In Syracusa was I born, and wed
Unto a woman, happy but for me,
And by me too, had not our hap been bad.
With her I liv'd in joy: our wealth increas'd
By prosperous voyages I often made
To Epidamnum; till my factor's death,
And the great care of goods at random left,
Drew me from kind embracements of my spouse:
From whom my absence was not six months old,
Before herself,—almost at fainting under
The pleasing punishment that women bear,—
Had made provision for her following me,
And soon and safe arrived where I was.
There had she not been long but she became
A joyful mother of two goodly sons;
And, which was strange, the one so like the other,
As could not be distinguish'd but by names.
That very hour, and in the self-same inn,
A meaner woman was delivered
Of such a burden, male twins, both alike.
Those,—for their parents were exceeding poor,—
I bought, and brought up to attend my sons.
My wife, not meanly proud of two such boys,
Made daily motions for our home return:
Unwilling I agreed; alas! too soon
We came aboard.
A league from Epidamnum had we sail'd,
Before the always-wind-obeying deep
Gave any tragic instance of our harm:
But longer did we not retain much hope;
For what obscured light the heavens did grant
Did but convey unto our fearful minds
A doubtful warrant of immediate death;
Which, though myself would gladly have embrac'd,
Yet the incessant weepings of my wife,
Weeping before for what she saw must come,
And piteous plainings of the pretty babes,
That moum'd for fashion, ignorant what to fear,
Forc'd me to seek delays for them and me.

And this it was, for other means was none:
The sailors sought for safety by our boat,
And left the ship, then sinking-ripe, to us:
My wife, more careful for the latter-born,
Had fasten'd him unto a small spare mast,
Such as seafaring men provide for storms;
To him one of the other twins was bound,
Whilst I had been like heedful of the other.
The children thus dispos'd, my wife and I,
Fixing our eyes on whom our care was fix'd,
Pasten'd ourselves at either end the mast;
And floating straight, obedient to the stream,
Were carried towards Corinth, as we thought.
At length the sun, gazing upon the earth,
Dispers'd those vapours that offended us,
And, by the benefit of his wished light
The seas wax'd calm, and we discovered
Two ships from far making amain to us;
Of Corinth that, of Epidaurus this:
But ere they came,—O!'let me say no more;
Gather the sequel by that went before.

DUKE: Nay, forward, old man; do not break off so;
For we may pity, though not pardon thee.

AEGEON: O! had the gods done so, I had not now
Worthily term'd them merciless to us!
For, ere the ships could meet by twice five leagues,
We were encounter'd by a mighty rock;
Which being violently borne upon,
Our helpful ship was splitted in the midst;
So that, in this unjust divorce of us
Fortune had left to both of us alike
What to delight in, what to sorrow for.
Her part, poor soul! seeming as burdened
With lesser weight, but not with lesser woe,
Was carried with more speed before the wind,
And in our sight they three were taken up
By fishermen of Corinth, as we thought.
At length, another ship had seiz'd on us;
And, knowing whom it was their hap to save,

Gave healthful welcome to their ship-wrack'd guests;
And would have reft the fishers of their prey,
Had not their bark been very slow of sail;
And therefore homeward did they bend their course.
Thus have you heard me sever'd from my bliss,
That by misfortune was my life prolong'd,
To tell sad stories of my own mishaps.

DUKE: And, for the sake of them thou sorrowest for,
Do me the favour to dilate at full
What hath befall'n of them and thee till now.

AEGEON: My youngest boy, and yet my eldest, care,
At eighteen years became inquisitive
After his brother; and importun'd me
That his attendant—for his case was like,
Reft of his brother, but retain'd his name—
Might bear him company in the quest of him;
Whom whilst I labour'd of a love to see,
I hazarded the loss of whom I lov'd.
Five summers have I spent in furthest Greece,
Roaming clean through the bounds of Asia,
And, coasting homeward, came to Ephesus,
Hopeless to find, yet loath to leave unsought
Or that or any place that harbours men.
But here must end the story of my life;
And happy were I in my timely death,
Could all my travels warrant me they live.

DUKE: Hapless Aegeon, whom the fates have mark'd
To bear the extremity of dire mishap!
Now, trust me, were it not against our laws,
Against my crown, my oath, my dignity,
Which princes, would they, may not disannul,
My soul should sue as advocate for thee.
But though thou art adjudged to the death
And passed sentence may not be recall'd
But to our honour's great disparagement,
Yet will I favour thee in what I can:
Therefore, merchant, I'll limit thee this day
To seek thy life by beneficial help.
Try all the friends thou hast in Ephesus;

Beg thou, or borrow, to make up the sum,
And live; if no, then thou art doom'd to die.
Gaoler take him to thy custody.

GAOLER: I will, my lord.

AEGEON: Hopeless and helpless doth Aegeon wend,
But to procrastinate his lifeless end. (*Exeunt.*)

Scene II.—*The Mart.*

Enter ANTIPHOLUS *of Syracuse,* DROMIO *of Syracuse, and a* MERCHANT.

MERCHANT: Therefore, give out you are of Epidamnum,
Lest that your goods too soon be confiscate.
This very day, a Syracusian merchant
Is apprehended for arrival here;
And, not being able to buy out his life,
According to the statute of the town
Dies ere the weary sun set in the west.
There is your money that I had to keep,

ANTIPHOLUS S.: Go bear it to the Centaur, where we host,
And stay there, Dromio, till I come to thee.
Within this hour it will be dinner-time:
Till that, I'll view the manners of the town,
Peruse the traders, gaze upon the buildings,
And then return and sleep within mine inn,
For with long travel I am stiff and weary.
Get thee away.

DROMIO S.: Many a man would take you at your word,
And go indeed, having so good a mean. ((*Exit.*)

ANTIPHOLUS S.: A trusty villain, sir, that very oft,
When I am dull with care and melancholy,
Lightens my humour with his merry jests.
What, will you walk with me about the town,
And then go to my inn and dine with me?

MERCHANT: I am invited, sir, to certain merchants,
Of whom I hope to make much benefit;
I crave your pardon. Soon at five o'clock,
Please you, I'll meet with you upon the mart,
And afterward consort you till bed-time:
My present business calls me from you now.

ANTIPHOLUS S.: Farewell till then: I will go lose myself,
　　And wander up and down to view the city.
MERCHANT: Sir, I commend you to your own content. (*Exit.*)
ANTIPHOLUS S.: He that commends me to mine own content,
　　Commends me to the thing I cannot get.
　　I to the world am like a drop of water
　　That in the ocean seeks another drop;
　　Who, falling there to find his fellow forth,
　　Unseen, inquisitive, confounds himself:
　　So I, to find a mother and a brother,
　　In quest of them, unhappy, lose myself.

(*Enter* DROMIO *of Ephesus.*)

　　Here comes the almanack of my true date.
　　What now? How chance thou art return'd so soon?
DROMIO E.: Return'd so soon! rather approach'd too late:
　　The capon burns, the pig falls from the spit,
　　The clock hath strucken twelve upon the bell;
　　My mistress made it one upon my cheek:
　　She is so hot because the meat is cold;
　　The meat is cold because you come not home;
　　You come not home because you have no stomach;
　　You have no stomach, having broke your fast;
　　But we, that know what 'tis to fast and pray,
　　Are penitent for your default to-day.
ANTIPHOLUS S.: Stop in your wind, sir: tell me this, I pray:
　　Where have you left the money that I gave you?
DROMIO E.: O!—sixpence, that I had o' Wednesday last
　　To pay the saddler for my mistress' crupper;
　　The saddler had it, sir; I kept it not.
ANTIPHOLUS S.: I am not in a sportive humour now.
　　Tell me, and dally not, where is the money?
　　We being strangers here, how dar'st thou trust
　　So great a charge from thine own custody?
DROMIO E.: I pray you, jest, sir, as you sit at dinner.
　　I from my mistress come to you in post;
　　If I return, I shall be post indeed,
　　For she will score your fault upon my pate.

Methinks your maw, like mine, should be your clock
And strike you home without a messenger.
ANTIPHOLUS S.: Come, Dromio, come; these jests are out of season;
Reserve them till a merrier hour than this.
Where is the gold I gave in charge to thee?
DROMIO E.: To me, sir? why, you gave no gold to me.
ANTIPHOLUS S.: Come on, sir knave, have done your foolishness,
And tell me how thou hast dispos'd thy charge.
DROMIO E.: My charge was but to fetch you, from the mart
Home to your house, the Phoenix, sir, to dinner:
My mistress and her sister stays for you.
ANTIPHOLUS S.: Now, as I am a Christian, answer me,
In what safe place you have bestow'd my money;
Or I shall break that merry sconce of yours
That stands on tricks when I am undispos'd.
Where is the thousand marks thou hadst of me?
DROMIO E.: I have some marks of yours upon my pate,
Some of my mistress' marks upon my shoulders,
But not a thousand marks between you both.
If I should pay your worship those again,
Perchance you will not bear them patiently.
ANTIPHOLUS S.: Thy mistress' marks! what mistress, slave, hast thou?
DROMIO E.: Your worship's wife, my mistress at the Phoenix;
She that doth fast till you come home to dinner,
And prays that you will hie you home to dinner.
ANTIPHOLUS S.: What! wilt thou flout me thus unto my face,
Being forbid? There, take you that, sir knave.
(*Strikes him*)
DROMIO E.: What mean you, sir? for God's sake, hold your hands!
Nay, an you will not, sir, I'll take my heels. (*Exit.*)
ANTIPHOLUS S.: Upon my life, by some device or other
The villain is o'er-raught of all my money.
They say tins town is full of cozenage;
As, nimble jugglers that deceive the eye,
Dark-working sorcerers that change the mind,
Soul-killing witches that deform the body,
Disguised cheaters, prating mountebanks,
And many such-like liberties of sin:
If it prove so, I will be gone the sooner.

I'll to the Centaur, to go seek this slave:
I greatly fear my money is not safe. (*Exit.*)

ACT II.

Scene 1. *The House of Antipholus of Ephesus.*
Enter ADRIANA *and* LUCIANA.

ADRIANA: Neither my husband, nor the slave return'd,
　　That in such haste I sent to seek his master!
　　Sure, Luciana, it is two o'clock.
LUCIANA: Perhaps some merchant hath invited him,
　　And from the mart he's somewhere gone to dinner.
　　Good sister, let us dine and never fret:
　　A man is master of his liberty:
　　Time is their master, and, when they see time,
　　They'll go or come: if so, be patient, sister.
ADRIANA: Why should their liberty than ours be more?
LUCIANA: Because their business still lies out o' door.
ADRIANA: Look, when I serve him so, he takes it ill.
LUCIANA: O! know he is the bridle of your will.
ADRIANA: There's none but asses will be bridled so.
LUCIANA: Why, headstrong liberty is lash'd with woe.
　　There's nothing situate under heaven's eye
　　But hath his bound, in earth, in sea, in sky;
　　The beasts, the fishes, and the winged fowls,
　　Are their males' subjects and at their controls.
　　Men, more divine, the masters of all these,
　　Lords of the wide world, and wild wat'ry seas,
　　Indu'd with intellectual sense and souls,
　　Of more pre-eminence than fish and fowls,
　　Are masters to their females and their lords:
　　Then, let your will attend on their accords.
ADRIANA: This servitude makes you to keep unwed.
LUCIANA: Not this, but troubles of the marriage bed.
ADRIANA: But, were you wedded, you would bear some sway.
LUCIANA: Ere I learn love, I'll practise to obey.
ADRIANA: How if your husband start some other where?
LUCIANA: Till he come home again, I would for bear.

ADRIANA: Patience unmov'd! no marvel though she pause;
  They can be meek that have no other canse.
  A wretched soul, bruised with adversity,
  We bid be quiet when we hear it cry;
  But were we burden'd with like weight of pain,
  As much, or more we should ourselves complain:
  So thou, that hast no unkind mate to grieve thee,
  With urging helpless patience wouldst relieve me:
  But if thou live to see like right bereft,
  This fool-begg'd patience in thee will be left.
LUCIANA: Well, I will marry one day, but to try.
  Here comes your man: now is your husband nigh.

(*Enter* DROMIO *of Ephesus.*)

ADRIANA: Say, is your tardy master now at hand?
DROMIO E.: Nay, he's at two hands with me, and that my two ears can witness.
ADRIANA: Say, didst thou speak with him? Know'st thou his mind?
DROMIO E.: Ay, ay, he told his mind upon mine ear.
  Beshrew his band, I scarce could understand it.
LUCIANA: Spake he so doubtfully, thou couldst not feel his meaning?
DROMIO E.: Nay, he struck so plainly, I could too well feel his blows; and withal so
      doubtfully, that
  I could scarce understand them.
ADRIANA: But say, I prithee, is he coming home?
  It seems he hath great care to please his wife.
DROMIO E.: Why, mistress, sure my master is horn-mad.
ADRIANA: Horn-mad, thou villain!
DROMIO E.: I mean not cuckold-mad; but, sure, he is stark mad.
  When I desir'd him to come home to dinner,
  He ask'd me for a thousand marks in gold:
  ' 'Tis dinner time,' quoth I;' my gold! 'quoth he:
  'Your meat doth burn,' quoth I; 'my gold!' quoth he:
  'Will you come home?' quoth I: 'my gold!' quoth he:
  'Where is the thousand marks I gave thee, villain?'
  'The pig,' quoth I, 'is burn'd; ' 'my gold!' quoth he:
  'My mistress, sir,' quoth I: ' hang up thy mistress!
  I know not thy mistress: out on thy mistress!'
LUCIANA: Quoth who?

DROMIO E.: Quoth my master:
  'I know,' quoth he, 'no house, no wife, no mistress.'
  So that my errand, due unto my tongue,
  I thank him, I bear home upon my shoulders;
  For, in conclusion, he did beat me there.
ADRIANA: Go back again, thou slave, and fetch him home?
DROMIO E.: Go back again, and be new beaten home.
  For God's sake, send some other messenger.
ADRIANA: Back, slave, or I will break thy pate across.
DROMIO E.: And he will bless that cross with other beating:
  Between you, I shall have a holy head.
ADRIANA: Hence, prating peasant! fetch thy master home.
DROMIO E.: Am I so round with you as you with me,
  That like a football you do spurn me thus?
  You spurn me hence, and he will spurn me hither:
  If I last in this service, you must case me in leather. (*Exit.*)
LUCIANA: Fie, how impatience loureth in your face'
ADRIANA: His company must do his minions grace,
  Whilst I at home starve for a merry look.
  Hath homely age the alluring beauty took
  From my poor cheek? then, he hath wasted it:
  Are my discourses dull? barren my wit?
  If voluble and sharp discourse be marr'd,
  Unkindness blunts it more than marble hard:
  Do their gay vestments his affections bait?
  That's not my fault; he's master of my state:
  What ruins are in me that can be found
  By him not ruin'd? then is he the ground
  Of my defeatures, My decayed fair
  A sunny look of his would soon repair;
  But, too unruly deer, he breaks the pale
  And feeds from home: poor I am but his stale.
LUCIANA: Self-harming jealousy! fie! beat it hence.
ADRIANA: Unfeeling fools can with such wrongs dispense.
  I know his eye doth homage otherwhere,
  Or else what lets it but he would be here?
  Sister, you know he promis'd me a chain:
  Would that alone, alone he would detain,
  So he would keep fair quarter with his bed!

I see, the jewel best enamelled
Will lose his beauty; and though gold bides still
That others touch, yet often touching will
Wear gold; and no man that hath a name,
By falsehood and corruption doth it shame.
Since that my beauty cannot please his eye,
I'll weep what's left away, and weeping die.

LUCIANA: How many fond fools serve mad jealousy! (*Exeunt.*)

Scene II.—*A public Place.*
Enter ANTIPHOLUS *of Syracuse.*

ANTIPHOLUS S.: The gold I gave to Dromio is laid up
Safe at the Centaur; and the heedful slave
Is wander'd forth, in care to seek me out.
By computation, and mine host's report,
I could not speak with Dromio since at first
I sent him from the mart. See, here he comes.

(*Enter* DROMIO *of Syracuse.*)

How now, sir! is your merry humour alter'd?
As you love strokes, so jest with me again.
You know no Centaur? You receiv'd no gold?
Your mistress sent to have me home to dinner?
My house was at the Phoenix? Wast thou mad,
That thus so madly thou didst answer me?

DROMIO S.: What answer, sir? when spake I such sword?

ANTIPHOLUS S.: Even now, even here, not half-an-hour since.

DROMIO S.: I did not see you since you sent me hence,
Home to the Centaur, with the gold you gave me.

ANTIPHOLUS S.: Villain, thou didst deny the gold's receipt,
And told'st me of a mistress and a dinner;
For which, I hope, thou felt'st I was displeas'd.

DROMIO S.: I am glad to see you in this merry vein;
What means this jest? I pray you, master, tell me.

ANTIPHOLUS S.: Yea, dost thou jeer, and flout me in the teeth?
Think'st thou I jest? Hold, take thou that, and that (*Beating him.*)

DROMIO S.: Hold, sir, for God's sake I now your jest is earnest:

Upon what bargain do you give it me?

ANTIPHOLUS S.: Because that I familiarly sometimes
    Do use you for my fool, and chat with you,
    Your sauciness will jet upon my love,
    And make a common of my serious hours.
    When the sun shines let foolish gnats make sport,
    But creep in crannies when he hides his beams.
    If you will jest with me, know my aspect,
    And fashion your demeanour to my looks,
    Or I will beat this method in your sconce.

DROMIO S.: Sconce, call you it? so you would leave battering,
    I had rather have it a head: an you use these blows long,
    I must get a sconce for my head and insconce it too; or else I shall seek my wit
        in my shoulders.
    But, I pray, sir, why am I beaten?

ANTIPHOLUS S.: Dost thou not know?

DROMIO S.: Nothing, sir, but that I am beaten.

ANTIPHOLUS S.: Shall I tell you why?

DROMIO S.: Ay, sir, and wherefore; for they say every why hath a wherefore.

ANTIPHOLUS S.: Why, first,—for flouting me; and then, wherefore,—
    For urging it the second time to me.

DROMIO S.: Was there ever any man thus beaten out of season,
    When, in the why and the wherefore is neither rime nor reason?
    Well, sir, I thank you.

ANTIPHOLUS S.: Thank me, sir I for what?

DROMIO S.: Marry, sir, for this something that you gave me for nothing.

ANTIPHOLUS S.: Ill make you amends next, to give you nothing for something.
        But say, sir, is it dinner-time?

DROMIO S.: No, sir: I think the meat wants that I have.

ANTIPHOLUS S.: In good time, sir; what's that?

DROMIO S.: Basting.

ANTIPHOLUS S.: Well, sir. then 'twill be dry.

DROMIO S.: It it be, sir, I pray you eat none of it.

ANTIPHOLUS S.: Your reason?

DROMIO S.: Lest it make you choleric, and purchase me another dry basting.

ANTIPHOLUS S.: Well, sir, learn to jest in good time: there's a time for all things.

DROMIO S.: I durst have denied that, before you were so choleric.

ANTIPHOLUS S.: By what rule, sir?

DROMIO S.: Marry, sir, by a rule as plain as the plain bald pate of Father Time himself.

ANTIPHOLUS S.: Let's hear it

DROMIO S.: There's no time for a man to recover his hair that grows bald by nature.

ANTIPHOLUS S.: May he not do It by fine and recovery?

DROMIO S.: Yes, to pay a fine for a periwig and recover the lost hair of another roan.

ANTIPHOLUS S.: Why is Time such a niggard of hair, being, as it is, so plentiful an excrement?

DROMIO S.: Because it is a blessing that he bestows on beasts: and what he hath scanted men in hair, he hath given them in wit.

ANTIPHOLUS S.: Why, but there's many a man hath more hair than wit

DROMIO S.: Not a man of those but he hath the wit to lose his hair.

ANTIPHOLUS S.: Why, thou didst conclude hairy men plain dealers without wit

DROMIO S.: The plainer dealer, the sooner lost: yet he loseth it in a kind of jollity.

ANTIPHOLUS S.: For what reason?

DROMIO S.: For two; and sound ones too.

ANTIPHOLUS S.: Nay, not sound, I pray you.

DROMIO S.: Sure ones then.

ANTIPHOLUS S.: Nay, not sure, in a thing falsing.

DROMIO S.: Certain ones, then.

ANTIPHOLUS S.: Name them.

DROMIO S.: The one, to save the money that he spends in tiring; the other, that at dinner they should not drop in his porridge.

ANTIPHOLUS S.: You would all this time have proved there is no time for all things.

DROMIO S.: Marry, and did, sir; namely, no time to recover hair lost by nature.

ANTIPHOLUS S.: But your reason was not substantial, why there is no time to recover.

DROMIO S.: Thus I mend it: Time himself is bald, and therefore to the world's end will have bald followers.

ANTIPHOLUS S.: I knew 'twould be a bald conclusion.
But soft! who wafts us yonder?

(*Enter* ADRIANA *and* LUCIANA.)

ADRIANA: Ay, ay, Antipholus, look strange, and frown:
Some other mistress hath thy sweet aspects,
I am not Adriana, nor thy wife.
The time was once when thou unurg'd wouldst vow
That never words were music to thine ear,
That never object pleasing in thine eye,

That never touch well welcome to thy hand,
That never meat sweet-savour'd In thy taste,
Unless I spake, or look'd, or touch'd, or carv'd to thee.
How comes it now, my husband, O! how comes it,
That thou art thus estranged from thyself?
Thyself I call it, being strange to me,
That, undividable, incorporate,
Am better than thy dear self's better part.
Ah! do not tear away thyself from me,
For know, my love, as easy mayst thou fall
A drop of water in the breaking gulf,
And take unmingled thence that drop again,
Without addition or diminishing,
As take from me thyself and not me too.
How dearly would it touch thee to the quick,
Shouldst thou but hear I were licentious,
And that this body, consecrate to thee,
By ruffian lust should be contaminate!
Wouldst thou not spit at me and spurn at me,
And hurl the name of husband in my face,
And tear the stain'd skin off my harlot-brow,
And from my false hand cut the wedding-ring
And break it with a deep-divorcing vow?
I know thou canst; and therefore, see thou do it.
I am possess'd with an adulterate blot;
My blood is mingled with the crime of lust:
For if we two be one and thou play false,
I do digest the poison of thy flesh,
Being strumpeted by thy contagion.
Keep then fair league and truce with thy true bed;
I live unstain'd, thou undishonoured.

ANTIPHOLUS S.: Plead you to me, fair dame? I know you not:
In Ephesus I am but two hours old,
As strange unto your town as to your talk;
Who, every word by all my wit being scann'd,
Want wit in all one word to understand.

LUCIANA: Fie, brother: how the world Is chang'd with you!
When were you wont to use my sister thus?
She sent for you by Dromio home to dinner.

ANTIPHOLUS S.: By Dromio?

DROMIO S.: By me?

ADRIANA: By thee; and this thou didst return from him,
That lie did buffet thee, and in his blows,
Denied my house for his, me for his wife.

ANTIPHOLUS S.: Did you converse, sir, with this gentle woman?
What is the course and drift of your compact?

DROMIO S.: I, sir? I never saw her till this time.

ANTIPHOLUS S.: Villain, thou liest; for even her very words
Didst thou deliver to me on the mart

DROMIO S.: I never spake with her In all my life.

ANTIPHOLUS S.: How can she thus then, call us by our names,
Unless it be by inspiration?

ADRIANA: How ill agrees it with your gravity
To counterfeit thus grossly with your slave,
Abetting him to thwart me in my mood!
Be it my wrong you are from me exempt,
But wrong not that wrong with a more contempt.
Come, I will fasten on this sleeve of thine;
Thou art an elm, my husband, I a vine,
Whose weakness, married to thy stronger state,
Makes me with thy strength to communicate:
If aught possess thee from me, it is dross,
Usurping ivy, brier, or idle moss;
Who, all for want of pruning, with intrusion
Infect thy sap and live on thy confusion.

ANTIPHOLUS S.: To me she speaks; she moves me for her theme!
What! was I married to her in my dream?
Or sleep I now and think I hear all this?
What error drives our eyes and ears amiss?
Until I know this sure uncertainty,
I'll entertain the offer'd fallacy.

LUCIANA: Dromio, go bid the servants spread for dinner.

DROMIO S.: O, for my beads! I cross me for a sinner.
This is the fairy land: O! spite of spites.
We talk with goblins, owls, and elvish sprites:
If we obey them not, this will ensue,
They'll suck our breath, or pinch us black and blue.

LUCIANA: Why prat'st thou to thyself and answer'st not?

Dromio, thou drone, thou snail, thou slug, thou sot!

DROMIO S.:   I am transformed, master, am not I?

ANTIPHOLUS S.: I think thou art, in mind, and so am I.

DROMIO S.: Nay, master, both in mind and in my shape.

ANTIPHOLUS S.: Thou hast thine own form.

DROMIO S.: No, I am an ape.

LUCIANA: If thou art chang'd to aught, 'tis to an ass.

DROMIO S.: 'Tis true; she rides me and I long for grass.
'Tis so, I am an ass; else it could never be
But I should know her as well as she knows me.

ADRIANA: Come, come; no longer will I be a fool,
To put the finger in the eye and weep,
Whilst man and master laugh my woes to scorn.
Come, sir, to dinner. Dromio, keep the gate.
Husband, I'll dine above with you to-day,
And shrive you of a thousand idle pranks.
Sirrah, if any ask you for your master,
Say he dines forth, and let no creature enter.
Come, sister. Dromio, play the porter well.

ANTIPHOLUS S.: (*Aside.*) Am I in earth, in heaven, or in hell?
Sleeping or waking? mad or well-advis'd?
Known unto these, and to myself disguis'd!
I'll say as they say, and persever so,
And in this mist at all adventures go.

DROMIO S.: Master, shall I be porter at the gate?

ADRIANA: Ay; and let none enter, lest I break your pate.

LUCIANA: Come, come, Antipholus; we dine too late. (*Exeunt.*)

ACT III.

Scene I.—Before the House of Antipholus of Ephesus.

Enter ANTIPHOLUS *of Ephesus,* DROMIO *of Ephesus,* ANGELO, *and* BALTHAZAR.

ANTIPHOLUS E.: Good Signior Angelo, you must excuse us all;
My wife is shrewish when I keep not hours;
Say that I linger'd with you at your shop
To see the making of her carkanet,
And that to-morrow you will bring it home.
But here's a villain, that would face me down

He met me on the mart, and that I beat him,
And charg'd him with a thousand marks in gold,
And that I did deny my wife and house.
Thou drunkard, thou, what didst thou mean by this?

DROMIO E.: Say what you will, sir, but I know what I know;
That you beat me at the mart, I have your hand to show:
If the skin were parchment and the blows you gave were ink,
Your own handwriting would tell you what I think.

ANTIPHOLUS E.: I think thou art an ass.

DROMIO E.: Marry, so it doth appear
By the wrongs I suffer and the blows I bear.
I should kick, being kick'd; and, being at that pass,
You would keep from my heels and beware of an ass.

ANTIPHOLUS E.: You are sad, Signior Balthazar: pray God, our cheer
May answer my good will and your good welcome here.

BALTHAZAR: I hold your dainties cheap, sir, and your welcome dear.

ANTIPHOLUS E.: O, Signior Balthazar, either at flesh or fish,
A table-full of welcome makes scarce one dainty dish.

BALTHAZAR: Good meat, sir, is common; that every churl affords.

ANTIPHOLUS E.: And welcome more common, for that's nothing but words.

BALTHAZAR: Small cheer and great welcome makes a merry feast.

ANTIPHOLUS E.: Ay, to a niggardly host and more sparing guest:
But though my cates be mean, take them in good part;
Better cheer may you have, but not with better heart.
But soft! my door is lock'd. Go bid them let us in.

DROMIO E.: Maud, Bridget, Marian, Cicely, Gillian, Ginn!

DROMIO S.: (*Within.*) Mome, malt-horse, capon, coxcomb, idiot, patch!
Either get thee from the door or sit down at the hatch.
Dost thou conjure for wenches, that thou call'st for such store,
When one is one too many? Go, get thee from the door.

DROMIO E.: What patch is made our porter?—My master stays in the street.

DROMIO S.: (*Within.*) Let him walk from whence he came, lest he catch cold on's
    feet.

ANTIPHOLUS E.: Who talks within there? ho! open the door.

DROMIO S.: (*Within.*) Bight, sir; I'll tell you when, an you'll tell me wherefore.

ANTIPHOLUS E.: Wherefore? for my dinner: I have not din'd to-day.

DROMIO S.: Nor to-day here you must not; come again when you may.

ANTIPHOLUS E.: What art thou that keep'st me out from the house I owe?

DROMIO S.: (*Within.*) The porter for this time, sir, and my name is Dromio.

DROMIO E.: O villain! thou hast stolen both mine office and my name:
   The one ne'er got me credit, the other mickle blame.
   If thou hadst been Dromio to-day in my place,
   Thou wouldst have chang'd thy face for a name, or thy name for an ass.
LUCE. (*Within.*) What a coil is there, Dromio! who are those at the gate?
DROMIO E.: Let my master in Luce.
LUCE. (*Within.*) Faith, no; he comes too late;
   And so tell your master.
DROMIO E.: O Lord! I must laugh.
   Have at you with a proverb: Shall I set in my staff?
LUCE. (*Within.*) Have at you with another: that's—when? can you tell?
DROMIO S.: (*Within.*) If thy name be called Luce,—
   Luce, thou hast answered him well.
ANTIPHOLUS E.: Do you hear, you minion? you'll let us in, I trow?
LUCE. (*Within.*) I thought to have ask'd you.
DROMIO S.: (*Within.*) And you said, no.
DROMIO E.: So come, help: well struck! there was blow for blow.
ANTIPHOLUS E.: Thou baggage, let me in.
LUCE. (*Within.*) Can you tell for whose sake?
DROMIO E.: Master, knock the door hard.
LUCE. (*Within.*) Let him knock till it ache,
ANTIPHOLUS E.: You'll cry for this, minion, if I beat the door down.
LUCE. (*Within.*) What needs all that, and a pair of stocks in the town?
ADRIANA: (*Within.*) Who is that at the door that keeps all this noise?
DROMIO S.: (*Within.*) By my troth your town is troubled with unruly boys.
ANTIPHOLUS E.: Are you there, wife? you might have come before.
ADRIANA: (*Within.*) Your wife, sir knave! go, get you from the door.
DROMIO E.: If you went in pain, master, this 'knave' would go sore.
ANGELO: Here is neither cheer, sir, nor welcome: we would fain have either.
BALTHAZAR: In debating which was best, we shall part with neither.
DROMIO E.: They stand at the door, master: bid them welcome hither.
ANTIPHOLUS E.: There is something in the wind, that we cannot get in.
DROMIO E.: You would say so, master, if your garments were thin.
   Your cake here is warm within; you stand here in the cold:
   It would make a man mad as a buck to be so bought and sold.
ANTIPHOLUS E.: Go fetch me something: I'll break open the gate.
DROMIO S.: (*Within.*) Break any breaking here, and I'll break your knave's pate.
DROMIO E.: A man may break a word with you, sir, and words are but wind:
   Ay, and break it in your face, so he break it not behind.

DROMIO S.: (*Within.*) It seems thou wantest breaking: out upon thee, hind!

DROMIO E.: Here's too much 'out upon thee!' I pray thee, let me in.

DROMIO S.: (*Within.*) Ay, when fowls have no feathers, and fish have no fin.

ANTIPHOLUS E.: Well, I'll break in. Go borrow me a crow.

DROMIO E.: A crow without feather? Master, mean you so?
    For a fish without a fin, there's a fowl without a feather:
    If a crow help us in, sirrah, we'll pluck a crow together.

ANTIPHOLUS E.: Go get thee gone: fetch me an iron crow.

BALTHAZAR: Have patience, sir; O! let it not be so;
    Herein you war against your reputation,
    And draw within the compass of suspect
    The unviolated honour of your wife.
    Once this,—your long experience of her wisdom,
    Her sober virtue, years, and modesty,
    Plead on her part some cause to you unknown;
    And doubt not, sir, but she will well excuse
    Why at this time the doors are made against you.
    Be rul'd by me: depart in patience,
    And let us to the Tiger all to dinner;
    And about evening come yourself alone,
    To know the reason of this strange restraint.
    If by strong hand you offer to break in
    Now in the stirring passage of the day,
    A vulgar comment will be made of it,
    And that supposed by the common rout
    Against your yet ungalled estimation,
    That may with foul intrusion enter in
    And dwell upon your grave when you are dead;
    For slander lives upon succession,
    For ever housed where it gets possession.

ANTIPHOLUS E.: You have prevail'd: I will depart in quiet,
    And, in despite of mirth, mean to be merry.
    I know a wench of excellent discourse,
    Pretty and witty, wild and yet, too, gentle:
    There will we dine: this woman that I mean,
    My wife,—but, I protest, without desert,—
    Hath oftentimes upbraided me withal:
    To her will we to dinner. (*To* ANGELO.) Get you home,
    And fetch the chain; by this I know 'tis-made:

Bring it, I pray you, to the Porpentine;
For there's the house: that chain will I bestow,
Be it for nothing but to spite my wife,
Upon mine hostess there. Good sir, make haste.
Since mine own doors refuse to entertain me,
I'll knock elsewhere, to see if they'll disdain me.

ANGELO: I'll meet you at that place some hour hence.

ANTIPHOLUS E.: Do so. This jest shall cost me some expense. (*Exeunt.*)

Scene II. *The same.*

Enter LUCIANA *and* ANTIPHOLUS *of Syracuse.*

LUCIANA: And may it be that you have quite forgot
    A husband's office? shall, Antipholus,
    Even in the spring of love, thy love-springs rot?
    Shall love, in building, grow so ruinous?
    If you did wed my sister for her wealth,
    Then for her wealth's sake use her with more kindness:
    Or if you like elsewhere, do it by stealth;
    Muffle your false love with some show of blindness:
    Let not my sister read it in your eye;
    Be not thy tongue thy own shame's orator;
    Look sweet, be fair, become disloyalty;
    Apparel vice like virtue's harbinger;
    Bear a fair presence, though your heart be tainted;
    Teach sin the carriage of a holy saint;
    Be secret-false: what need she be acquainted?
    What simple thief brags of his own attaint?
    'Tis double wrong, to truant with your bed
    And let her read it in thy looks at board:
    Shame hath a bastard fame, well managed;
    Ill deeds are doubled with an evil word.
    Alas, poor women! make us but believe,
    Being compact of credit, that you love us;
    Though others have the arm, show us the sleeve;
    We in your motion turn and you may move us.
    Then, gentle brother, get you in again;
    Comfort my sister, cheer her, call her wife:
    'Tis holy sport to be a little vain,

When the sweet breath of flattery conquers strife.

ANTIPHOLUS S.: Sweet mistress—what your name is else, I know not,
Nor by what wonder you do hit of mine,—
Less in your knowledge and your grace you show not
Than our earth's wonder, more than earth divine.
Teach me, dear creature, how to think and speak;
Lay open to my earthy-gross conceit,
Smother'd in errors, feeble, shallow, weak,
The folded meaning of your words' deceit.
Against my soul's pure truth why labour you
To make it wander in an unknown field?
Are you a god? would you create me new?
Transform me then, and to your power I'll yield.
But if that I am I, then well I know
Your weeping sister is no wife of mine,
Nor to her bed no homage do I owe
Far more, far more to you do I decline.
O, train me not, sweet mermaid, with thy note,
To drown me in thy sister's flood of tears:
Sing, siren, for thyself and I will dote:
Spread o'er the silver waves thy golden hairs,
And as a bed I'll take them and there lie,
And in that glorious supposition think
He gains by death that hath such means to die:
Let Love, being light, be drowned if she sink!

LUCIANA: What, are you mad, that you do reason so?

ANTIPHOLUS S.: Not mad, but mated; how, I do not know.

LUCIANA: It is a fault that springeth from your eye.

ANTIPHOLUS S.: For gazing on your beams, fair sun, being by.

LUCIANA: Gaze where you should, and that will clear your sight.

ANTIPHOLUS S.: As good to wink, sweet love, as look on night.

LUCIANA: Why call you me love? call my sister so.

ANTIPHOLUS S.: Thy sister's sister.

LUCIANA: That's my sister.

ANTIPHOLUS S.: No;
It is thyself, mine own self's better part,
Mine eye's clear eye, my dear heart's dearer heart,
My food, my fortune and my sweet hope's aim,
My sole earth's heaven and my heaven's claim.

LUCIANA: All this my sister is, or else should be.

ANTIPHOLUS S.: Call thyself sister, sweet, for I am thee.
Thee will I love and with thee lead my life:
Thou hast no husband yet nor I no wife.
Give me thy hand.

LUCIANA: O, soft, air! hold you still:
I'll fetch my sister, to get her good will. (*Exit.*)

(*Enter* DROMIO *of Syracuse.*)

ANTIPHOLUS S.: Why, how now, Dromio! Where runn'st thou so fast?

DROMIO S.: Do you know me, sir? Am I Dromio? Am I your man?
Am I myself?

ANTIPHOLUS S.: Thou art Dromio, thou art my man, thou art thyself.

DROMIO S.: I am an ass, I am a woman's man and besides myself.

ANTIPHOLUS S.: What woman's man? and how besides thyself? besides thyself?

DROMIO S.: Marry, sir, besides myself, I am due to a woman; one
that claims me, one that haunts me, one that will have me.

ANTIPHOLUS S.: What claim lays she to thee?

DROMIO S.: Marry sir, such claim as you would lay to your
horse; and she would have me as a beast: not that, I
being a beast, she would have me; but that she,
being a very beastly creature, lays claim to me.

ANTIPHOLUS S.: What is she?

DROMIO S.: A very reverent body; ay, such a one as a man may
not speak of without he say 'Sir-reverence.' I have
but lean luck in the match, and yet is she a
wondrous fat marriage.

ANTIPHOLUS S.: How dost thou mean a fat marriage?

DROMIO S.: Marry, sir, she's the kitchen wench and all grease;
and I know not what use to put her to but to make a
lamp of her and run from her by her own light. I
warrant, her rags and the tallow in them will burn a
Poland winter: if she lives till doomsday,
she'll burn a week longer than the whole world.

ANTIPHOLUS S.: What complexion is she of?

DROMIO S.: Swart, like my shoe, but her face nothing half so
clean kept: for why, she sweats; a man may go over
shoes in the grime of it.

ANTIPHOLUS S.: That's a fault that water will mend.

DROMIO S.: No, sir, 'tis in grain; Noah's flood could not do it.

ANTIPHOLUS S.: What's her name?

DROMIO S.: Nell, sir; but her name and three quarters, that's
an ell and three quarters, will not measure her from
hip to hip.

ANTIPHOLUS S.: Then she bears some breadth?

DROMIO S.: No longer from head to foot than from hip to hip:
she is spherical, like a globe; I could find out
countries in her.

ANTIPHOLUS S.: In what part of her body stands Ireland?

DROMIO S.: Marry, in her buttocks: I found it out by the bogs.

ANTIPHOLUS S.: Where Scotland?

DROMIO S.: I found it by the barrenness; hard in the palm of the hand.

ANTIPHOLUS S.: Where France?

DROMIO S.: In her forehead; armed and reverted, making war
against her heir.

ANTIPHOLUS S.: Where England?

DROMIO S.: I looked for the chalky cliffs, but I could find no
whiteness in them; but I guess it stood in her chin,
by the salt rheum that ran between France and it.

ANTIPHOLUS S.: Where Spain?

DROMIO S.: Faith, I saw it not; but I felt it hot in her breath.

ANTIPHOLUS S.: Where America, the Indies?

DROMIO S.: Oh, sir, upon her nose all o'er embellished with
rubies, carbuncles, sapphires, declining their rich
aspect to the hot breath of Spain; who sent whole
armadoes of caracks to be ballast at her nose.

ANTIPHOLUS S.: Where stood Belgia, the Netherlands?

DROMIO S.: Oh, sir, I did not look so low. To conclude, this
drudge, or diviner, laid claim to me, call'd me
DROMIO; swore I was assured to her; told me what
privy marks I had about me, as, the mark of my
shoulder, the mole in my neck, the great wart on my
left arm, that I amazed ran from her as a witch:
And, I think, if my breast had not been made of
faith and my heart of steel,
She had transform'd me to a curtal dog and made
me turn i' the wheel.

ANTIPHOLUS S.: Go hie thee presently, post to the road:
    An if the wind blow any way from shore,
    I will not harbour in this town to-night:
    If any bark put forth, come to the mart,
    Where I will walk till thou return to me.
    If every one knows us and we know none,
    'Tis time, I think, to trudge, pack and be gone.
DROMIO S.: As from a bear a man would run for life,
    So fly I from her that would be my wife. (*Exit.*)
ANTIPHOLUS S.: There's none but witches do inhabit here;
    And therefore 'tis high time that I were hence.
    She that doth call me husband, even my soul
    Doth for a wife abhor. But her fair sister,
    Possess'd with such a gentle sovereign grace,
    Of such enchanting presence and discourse,
    Hath almost made me traitor to myself:
    But, lest myself be guilty to self-wrong,
    I'll stop mine ears against the mermaid's song.

(*Enter* ANGELO *with the chain.*)

ANGELO: Master Antipholus,—
ANTIPHOLUS S.: Ay, that's my name.
ANGELO: I know it well, sir, lo, here is the chain.
    I thought to have ta'en you at the Porpentine:
    The chain unfinish'd made me stay thus long.
ANTIPHOLUS S.: What is your will that I shall do with this?
ANGELO: What please yourself, sir: I have made it for you.
ANTIPHOLUS S.: Made it for me, sir! I bespoke it not.
ANGELO: Not once, nor twice, but twenty times you have.
    Go home with it and please your wife withal;
    And soon at supper-time I'll visit you
    And then receive my money for the chain.
ANTIPHOLUS S.: I pray you, sir, receive the money now,
    For fear you ne'er see chain nor money more.
ANGELO: You are a merry man, sir: fare you well. (*Exit.*)
ANTIPHOLUS S.: What I should think of this, I cannot tell:
    But this I think, there's no man is so vain
    That would refuse so fair an offer'd chain.

I see a man here needs not live by shifts,
When in the streets he meets such golden gifts.
I'll to the mart, and there for DROMIO stay
If any ship put out, then straight away. (*Exit.*)

ACT IV.

Scene I.—A Public Place.
Enter Second MERCHANT, ANGELO, *and an* OFFICER.

MERCHANT: You know since Pentecost the sum is due,
And since I have not much importun'd you;
Nor now I had not, but that I am bound
To Persia, and want guilders for my voyage:
Therefore make present satisfaction,
Or I'll attach you by this officer.
ANGELO: Even just the sum that I do owe to you
Is growing to me by Antipholus;
And in the instant that I met with you
He had of me a chain: at five o'clock
I shall receive the money for the same.
Pleaseth you walk with me down to his house,
I will discharge my bond, and thank you too.

(*Enter* ANTIPHOLUS *of Ephesus and* DROMIO *of Ephesus from the Courtezan's.*)

OFFICER: That labour may you save: see where he comes.
ANTIPHOLUS E.: While I go to the goldsmith's house, go thou
And buy a rope's end, that I will bestow
Among my wife and her confederates,
Por locking me out of my doors by day.
But soft! I see the goldsmith. Get thee gone;
Buy thou a rope, and bring it home to me.
DROMIO E.: I buy a thousand pound a year:
I buy a rope! (*Exit.*)
ANTIPHOLUS E.: A man is well help up that trusts to you:
I promised your presence and the chain;
But neither chain nor goldsmith came to me.
Belike you thought our love would last too long,

If it were chain'd together, and therefore came not

ANGELO: Saving your merry humour, here's the note
How much your chain weighs to the utmost carat.
The fineness of the-gold, and chargeful fashion,
Which doth amount to three odd ducats more
Than I stand debted to this gentleman:
I pray you see him presently discharg'd,
For he is bound to sea and stays but for it.

ANTIPHOLUS E.: I am not furnish'd with the present money;
Besides, I have some business in the town.
Good signior, take the stranger to my house,
And with yon take the chain, and bid my wife
Disburse the sum on the receipt thereof:
Perchance I will be there as soon as you.

ANGELO: Then, you will bring the chain to her yourself?

ANTIPHOLUS E.: No; bear it with you, lest I come not time enough.

ANGELO: Well, sir, I will. Have you the chain about you?

ANTIPHOLUS E.: An if I have not, sir, I hope you have,
Or else you may return without your money.

ANGELO: Nay, come, I pray you, sir, give me the chain:
Both wind and tide stays for this gentleman,
And I, to blame, have held him here too long.

ANTIPHOLUS E.: Good Lord! you use this dalliance to excuse
Your breach of promise to the Porpentine.
I should have chid you for not bringing it,
But, like a shrew, you first begin to brawl.

MERCHANT: The hour steals on; I pray you, sir, dispatch.

ANGELO: You hear how he importunes me: the chain!

ANTIPHOLUS E.: Why, give it to my wife and fetch your money.

ANGELO: Come, come; you know I gave it you even now.
Either send the chain or send by me some token.

ANTIPHOLUS E.: Fie! now you run this humour out of breath.
Come, where's the chain? I pray you, let me see it.

MERCHANT: My business cannot brook this dalliance.
Good sir, say whe'r you'll answer me or no:
If not, I'll leave him to the officer.

ANTIPHOLUS E.: I answer you! what should I answer you?

ANGELO: The money that you owe me for the chain.

ANTIPHOLUS E.: I owe you none till I receive the chain.

ANGELO: You know I gave it you half an hour since.

ANTIPHOLUS E.: You gave me none: you wrong me much to say so.

ANGELO: You wrong me more, sir, in denying it:
Consider how it stands upon my credit.

MERCHANT: Well, officer, arrest him at my suit.

OFFICER: I do;
And charge you in the duke's name to obey me.

ANGELO: This touches me in reputation.
Either consent to pay this sum for me,
Or I attach you by this officer.

ANTIPHOLUS E.: Consent to pay thee that I never had!
Arrest me, foolish fellow, if thou dar'st.

ANGELO: Here is thy fee: arrest him, officer.
I would not spare my brother in this case,
If he should scorn me so apparently.

OFFICER: I do arrest you, sir: you hear the suit.

ANTIPHOLUS E.: I do obey thee till I give thee bail.
But, sirrah, you shall buy this sport as dear
As all the metal in your shop will answer.

ANGELO: Sir, sir, I shall have law in Ephesus,
To your notorious shame, I doubt it not.

(*Enter* DROMIO *of Syracuse.*)

DROMIO S.: Master, there is a bark of Epidamnum
That stays but till her owner comes aboard,
And then she bears away. Our fraughtage, sir,
I have convey'd aboard, and I have bought
The oil, the balsamum, and aqua-vitae.
The ship is in her trim; the merry wind
Blows fair from land; they stay for nought at all
But for their owner, master, and yourself.

ANTIPHOLUS E.: How now! a madman! Why, thou peevish sheep,
What ship of Epidamnum stays for me?

DROMIO S.: A ship you sent me to, to hire waftage.

ANTIPHOLUS E.: Thou drunken slave, I sent thee for a rope;
And told thee to what purpose, and what end.

DROMIO S.: You sent me for a rope's end as soon:
You sent me to the bay, sir, for a bark.

ANTIPHOLUS E.: I will debate this matter at more leisure,
    And teach your ears to list me with more heed.
    To Adriana, villain, hie thee straight;
    Give her this key, and tell her, in the desk
    That's cover'd o'er with Turkish tapestry,
    There is a purse of ducats: let her send it.
    Tell her I am arrested in the street,
    And that shall bail me. Hie thee, slave, be gone!
    On, officer, to prison till it come.

(*Exeunt* MERCHANT, ANGELO, OFFICER, *and* ANTIPHOLUS *of Ephesus.*)

DROMIO S.: To Adriana! that is where we din'd,
    Where Dowsabel did claim me for her husband:
    She is too big, I hope, for me to compass.
    Thither I must, although against my will,
    For servants must their masters' minds fulfil. (*Exit.*)

Scene II.—*A Room in the House of Antipholus of Ephesus.*
Enter ADRIANA *and* LUCIANA.

ADRIANA: Ah! Luciana, did he tempt thee so?
    Mightst thou perceive austerely in his eye
    That he did plead in earnest? yea or no?
    Look'd he or red or pale? or sad or merrily?
    What observation mad'st thou in this case
    Of his heart's meteors tilting in his face?
LUCIANA: First he denied you had in him no right.
ADRIANA: He meant he did me none; the more my spite.
LUCIANA: Then swore he that he was a stranger here.
ADRIANA: And true he swore, though yet forsworn he were.
LUCIANA: Then pleaded I for you.
ADRIANA: And what said he?
LUCIANA: That love I begg'd for you he begg'd of me.
ADRIANA: With what persuasion did he tempt thy love?
LUCIANA: With words that in an honest suit might move.
    First, he did praise my beauty, then my speech.
ADRIANA: Didst speak him fair?
LUCIANA: Have patience, I beseech.

ADRIANA: I cannot, nor I will not hold me still:
   My tongue, though not my heart, shall have his will.
   He is deformed, crooked, old and sere,
   Ill-fac'd, worse bodied, shapeless every where;
   Vicious, ungentle, foolish, blunt, unkind,
   Stigmatical in making, worse in mind.
LUCIANA: Who would be jealous then, of such a one?
   No evil lost is wail'd when it is gone.
ADRIANA: Ah! but I think him better than I say,
   And yet would herein others' eyes were worse.
   Far from her nest the lapwing cries away:
   My heart prays for him, though my tongue do curse.

(*Enter* DROMIO *of Syracuse.*)

DROMIO S.: Here, go: the desk! the purse! sweet, now, make haste.
LUCIANA: How hast thou lost thy breath?
DROMIO S.: By running fast.
ADRIANA: Where is thy master, Dromio? is he well?
DROMIO S.: No, he's in Tartar limbo, worse than hell.
   A devil in an everlasting garment hath him,
   One whose hard heart is button'd up with steel;
   A fiend, a fairy, pitiless and rough;
   A wolf, nay, worse, a fellow all in buff;
   A back-friend, a shoulder-clapper, one that countermands
   The passages of alleys, creeks and narrow lands;
   A hound that runs counter and yet draws dryfoot well;
   One that, before the judgment, carries poor souls to hell.
ADRIANA: Why, man, what is the matter?
DROMIO S.:   I do not know the matter: he is 'rested on the case.
ADRIANA: What, is he arrested? tell me at whose suit,
DROMIO S.: I know not at whose suit he is arrested well;
   But he's in a suit of buff which 'rested him, that can I tell.
   Will you send him, mistress, redemption, the money in his desk?
ADRIANA: Go fetch it, sister.—(*Exit* LUCIANA.)
   This I wonder at:
   That he, unknown to me, should be in debt:
   Tell me, was he arrested on a band?
DROMIO S.: Not on a band, but on a stronger thing;

A chain, a chain. Do you not hear it ring?

ADRIANA: What, the chain?

DROMIO S.: No, no, the bell: 'tis time that I were gone:
It was two ere I left him, and now the clock strikes one.

ADRIANA: The hours come back! that did I never hear,

DROMIO S.: O yes; if any hour meet a sergeant, a' turns back for very fear.

ADRIANA: As if Time were in debt! how fondly dost thou reason!

DROMIO S.: Time is a very bankrupt, and owes more than he's worth to season.
Nay, he's a thief too: have you not heard men say,
That Time comes stealing on by night and day?
If Time be in debt and theft, and a sergeant in the way,
Hath he not reason to turn back an hour in a day?

(*Re-enter* LUCIANA.)

ADRIANA: Go, Dromio: there's the money, bear it straight,
And bring thy master home immediately.
Come, sister; I am press'd down with conceit;
Conceit, my comfort and my injury. (Exeunt.

Scene III.—*A Public Place.*
Enter ANTIPHOLUS *of Syracuse.*

ANTIPHOLUS S.: There's not a man I meet but doth salute me,
As if I were their well acquainted friend;
And every one doth call me by my name.
Some tender money to me; some invite me;
Some other give me thanks for kindnesses;
Some offer me commodities to buy:
Even now a tailor call'd me in his shop
And show'd me silks that he had bought for me,
And therewithal, took measure of my body.
Sure these are but imaginary wiles,
And Lapland sorcerers inhabit here.

(*Enter* DROMIO *of Syracuse.*)

DROMIO S.: Master, here's the gold you sent me for.
What! have you got the picture of old Adam new apparelled?

ANTIPHOLUS S.: What gold is this? What Adam dost thou mean?

DROMIO S.: Not that Adam that kept the Paradise, but that Adam that keeps the prison: he that goes in the calf's skin that was killed for the Prodigal: he that came behind you, sir, like an evil angel, and bid you forsake your liberty.

ANTIPHOLUS S.: I understand thee not.

DROMIO S.: No? why, 'tis a plain case: he that went, like a base-viol, in a case of leather; the man, sir, that, when gentlemen are tired, gives them a fob, and 'rests them; he, sir, that takes pity on decayed men and gives them suits of durance; he that sets up his rest to do more exploits with his mace than a morris-pike.

ANTIPHOLUS S.: What, thou meanest an officer?

DROMIO S.: Ay, sir, the sergeant of the band; he that brings any man to answer it that breaks his band; one that thinks a man always going to bed, and says, 'God give you good rest!'

ANTIPHOLUS S.: Well, sir, there rest in your foolery.
Is there any ship puts forth to-night? may we be gone?

DROMIO S.: Why, sir, I brought you word an hour since that the bark Expedition put forth tonight; and then were you hindered by the sergeant to tarry for the hoy Delay. Here are the angels that you sent for to deliver you.

ANTIPHOLUS S.: The fellow is distract, and so am I;
And here we wander in illusions:
Some blessed power deliver us from hence!

(*Enter a* COURTEZAN.)

COURTEZAN: Well met, well met, Master Antipholus.
I see, sir, you have found the goldsmith now:
Is that the chain you promis'd me to-day?

ANTIPHOLUS S.: Satan, avoid! I charge thee tempt me not!

DROMIO S.: Master, is this Mistress Satan?

ANTIPHOLUS S.: It is the devil.

DROMIO S.: Nay, she is worse, she is the devil's dam, and here she comes in the habit of a light wench: and thereof comes that the wenches say,
'God damn me;' that's as much as to say, 'God make me a light wench.'
It is written, they appear to men like angels of light: light is an effect of fire, and fire will burn; ergo, light wenches will bum.
Come not near her.

COURTEZAN: Your man and you are marvellous merry, sir. Will you go with me? we'll mend our dinner here.

DROMIO S.: Master, if you do, expect spoon-meat, so bespeak a long spoon.

ANTIPHOLUS S.: Why, Dromio?

DROMIO S.:   Marry, he must have a long spoon that must eat with the devil.

ANTIPHOLUS S.: Avoid thee, fiend! what tell'st thou me of supping?
    Thou art, as you are all, a sorceress:
    I conjure thee to leave me and be gone.

COURTEZAN: Give me the ring of mine you had at dinner,
    Or, for my diamond, the chain you promis'd,
    And I'll be gone, sir, and not trouble you.

DROMIO S.: Some devils ask but the parings of one's nail,
    A rush, a hair, a drop of blood, a pin,
    A nut, a cherry-stone;
    But she, more covetous, would have a chain.
    Master, be wise: an if you give it her,
    The devil will shake her chain and fright us with it.

COURTEZAN: I pray you, sir, my ring, or else the chain:
    I hope you do not mean to cheat me so.

ANTIPHOLUS S.: Avaunt, thou witch! Come, Dromio, let us go.

DROMIO S.: 'Fly pride,' says the peacock: mistress, that you know.

(*Exeunt* ANTIPHOLUS *of Syracuse and* DROMIO *of Syracuse.*)

COURTEZAN: Now, out of doubt, Antipholus is mad,
    Else would he never so demean himself.
    A ring he hath of mine worth forty ducats,
    And for the same he promis'd me a chain:
    Both one and other he denies me now.
    The reason that I gather he is mad,
    Besides this present instance of his rage,
    Is a mad tale he told to-day at dinner,
    Of his own doors being shut against his entrance.
    Belike his wife, acquainted with his fits,
    On purpose shut the doors against his way.
    My way is now to hie home to his house,
    And tell his wife, that, being lunatic,
    He rush'd into my house, and took perforce
    My ring away. This course I fittest choose,
    For forty ducats is too much to lose. (*Exit.*)

Scene IV.—A Street.

Enter ANTIPHOLUS *of Ephesus and the* OFFICER.

ANTIPHOLUS E.:   Fear me not, man; I will not break away:
 I'll give thee, ere I leave thee, so much money,
 To warrant thee, as I am 'rested for.
 My wife is in a wayward mood to-day,
 And will not lightly trust the messenger.
 That I should be attach'd in Ephesus,
 I tell you, 'twill sound harshly in her ears.

(*Enter* DROMIO *of Ephesus with a rope's end.*)

 Here comes my man: I think he brings the money.
 How now, sir! have you that I sent you for?
DROMIO E.:   Here's that, I warrant you, will pay them all.
ANTIPHOLUS E.:   But where's the money?
DROMIO E.:   Why, sir, I gave the money for the rope.
ANTIPHOLUS E.:   Five hundred ducats, villain, for a rope?
DROMIO E.:   I'll serve you, sir, five hundred at the rate.
ANTIPHOLUS E.:   To what end did I bid thee hie thee home?
DROMIO E.:   To a rope's end, sir; and to that end am I return'd,
ANTIPHOLUS E.:   And to that end, sir, I will welcome you. (*Beats him.*)
OFFICER: Good sir, be patient.
DROMIO E.:   Nay, 'tis for me to be patient; I am in adversity.
OFFICER: Good now, hold thy tongue.
DROMIO E.:   Nay, rather persuade him to hold his hands.
ANTIPHOLUS E.:   Thou whoreson, senseless villain!
DROMIO E.:   I would I were senseless, sir, that I might not feel your blows.
ANTIPHOLUS E.:   Thou art sensible in nothing but blows, and so is an ass.
DROMIO E.:   I am an ass indeed; you may prove it by my long ears.
 I have served him from the hour of my nativity to this instant, and have noth-
  ing at his hands for my service but blows.
 When I am cold, he heats me with beating; when I am warm, he cools me with
  beating;
 I am waked with it when I sleep; raised with it when I sit; driven out of doors
  with it when I go from home; welcomed home with it when I return; nay,
 I bear it on my shoulders, as a beggar wont her brat; and, I think, when he hath
  lamed me, I shall beg with it from door to door.

ANTIPHOLUS E.: Come, go along; my wife is coming yonder.

(*Enter* ADRIANA, LUCIANA, *the* COURTEZAN, *and* DR. PINCH.)

DROMIO E.: Mistress, respice finem, respect your end; or rather, to prophesy like the parrot,
'Beware the rope's end.'

ANTIPHOLUS E.: Wilt thou still talk? (*Beats him.*)

COURTEZAN: How say you now? is not your husband mad?

ADRIANA: His incivility confirms no less.
Good Doctor Pinch, you are a conjurer;
Establish him in his true sense again,
And I will please you what you will demand.

LUCIANA: Alas! how fiery and how sharp he looks.

COURTEZAN: Mark how he trembles in his ecstasy!

DR. PINCH: Give me your hand and let me feel your pulse.

ANTIPHOLUS E.: There is my hand, and let it feel your ear. (*Strikes him.*)

DR. PINCH: I charge thee, Satan, housed within this man,
To yield possession to my holy prayers.
And to thy state of darkness hie thee straight:
I conjure thee by all the saints in heaven.

ANTIPHOLUS E.: Peace, doting wizard, peace! I am not mad.

ADRIANA: O! that thou wert not, poor distressed soul!

ANTIPHOLUS E.: You minion, you, are these your customers?
Did this companion with the saffron face
Revel and feast it at my house to-day,
Whilst upon me the guilty doors were shut
And I denied to enter in my house?

ADRIANA: O husband, God doth know you din'd at home;
Where would you had remain'd until this time,
Free from these slanders and this open shame!

ANTIPHOLUS E.: Din'd at home! Thou villain, what say'st thou?

DROMIO E.: Sir, sooth to say, you did not dine at home.

ANTIPHOLUS E.: Were not my doors lock'd up and I shut out?

DROMIO E.: Perdy, your doors were lock'd and you shut out.

ANTIPHOLUS E.: And did not she herself revile me there?

DROMIO E.: Sans fable, she herself revil'd you there.

ANTIPHOLUS E.: Did not her kitchen-maid rail, taunt, and scorn me?

DROMIO E.: Certes, she did; the kitchen-vestal scorn'd you.

ANTIPHOLUS E.: And did not I in rage depart from thence?

DROMIO E.: In verity you did: my bones bear witness,
That since have felt the vigour of his rage.

ADRIANA: Is't good to soothe him in these contraries?

DR. PINCH: It is no shame: the fellow finds his vein,
And, yielding to him humours well his frenzy.

ANTIPHOLUS E.: Thou hast suborn'd the goldsmith to arrest me.

ADRIANA: Alas! I sent you money to redeem you,
By Dromio here, who came in haste for it.

DROMIO E.: Money by me! heart and good will you might;
But surely, master, not a rag of money.

ANTIPHOLUS E.: Went'st not thou to her for a purse of ducats?

ADRIANA: He came to me, and I deliver'd it.

LUCIANA: And I am witness with her that she did.

DROMIO E.: God and the rope-maker bear me witness
That I was sent for nothing but a rope!
Pinch, Mistress, both man and master is possess'd:
I know it by their pale and deadly looks.
They must be bound and laid in some dark room.

ANTIPHOLUS E.: Say, wherefore didst thou lock me forth to-day?
And why dost thou deny the bag of gold?

ADRIANA: I did not, gentle husband, lock thee forth.

DROMIO E.: And, gentle master, I receiv'd no gold;
But I confess, sir, that we were lock'd out.

ADRIANA: Dissembling villain! thou speak'st false in both.

ANTIPHOLUS E.: Dissembling harlot! thou art false in all;
And art confederate with a damned pack
To make a loathsome abject scorn of me;
But with these nails I'll pluck out those false eyes
That would behold in me this shameful sport.

ADRIANA: O! bind him, bind him, let him not come near me.

DR. PINCH: More company! the fiend is strong within him.

LUCIANA: Ay me! poor man, how pale and wan he looks!

(*Enter three or four and bind* ANTIPHOLUS *of Ephesus.*)

ANTIPHOLUS E.: What, will you murder me? Thou gaoler, thou,
I am thy prisoner: wilt thou suffer them
To make a rescue?

OFFICER: Masters, let him go:

 He is my prisoner, and you shall not have him.

DR. PINCH: Go bind this man, for he is frantic too.

 (*They bind* DROMIO *of Ephesus.*)

ADRIANA: What wilt thou do, thou peevish officer?

 Hast thou delight to see a wretched man

 Do outrage and displeasure to himself?

OFFICER: He is my prisoner: if I let him go,

 The debt he owes will be requir'd of me.

ADRIANA: I will discharge thee ere I go from thee:

 Bear me forthwith unto his creditor,

 And, knowing how the debt grows, I will pay it.

 Good Master doctor, see him safe convey'd

 Home to my house. O most unhappy day!

ANTIPHOLUS E.: O most unhappy strumpet!

DROMIO E.: Master, I am here entered in bond for you.

ANTIPHOLUS E.: Out on thee, villain! wherefore dost thou mad me?

DROMIO E.: Will you be bound for nothing? be mad, good master; cry, 'the devil!'

LUCIANA: God help, poor souls! how idly do they talk.

ADRIANA: Go bear him hence. Sister, go you with me.—

(*Exeunt* DR. PINCH *and* ASSISTANTS *with* ANTIPHOLUS *of Ephesus and* DROMIO *of Ephesus.*)

 Say now, whose suit is he arrested at?

OFFICER: One Angelo, a goldsmith; do you know him?

ADRIANA: I know the man. What is the sum he owes?

OFFICER: Two hundred ducats.

ADRIANA: Say, how grows it due?

OFFICER: Due for a chain your husband had of him.

ADRIANA: He did bespeak a chain for me, but had it not.

COURTEZAN: When as your husband all in rage, to-day

 Came to my house, and took away my ring,—

 The ring I saw upon his finger now,—

 Straight after did I meet him with a chain.

ADRIANA: It may be so, but I did never see it.

 Come, gaoler, bring me where the goldsmith is;

 I long to know the truth hereof at large.

(*Enter* ANTIPHOLUS *of Syracuse and* DROMIO *of Syracuse, with rapiers drawn.*)

LUCIANA: God, for thy mercy! they are loose again.

ADRIANA: And come with naked swords. Let 's call more help
To have them bound again.

OFFICER: Away! they'll kill us.

(*Exeunt* ADRIANA, LUCIANA, *and* OFFICER.)

ANTIPHOLUS S.: I see, these witches are afraid of swords.

DROMIO S.: She that would be your wife now ran from you.

ANTIPHOLUS S.: Come to the Centaur; fetch our stuff from thence:
I long that we were safe and sound aboard.

DROMIO SYRACUSE: Faith, stay here this night, they will surely do us no harm; you
saw they speak us fair, give us gold: methinks they are such a gentle nation,
that, but for the mountain of mad flesh that claims marriage of me,
I could find in my heart to stay here still, and turn witch.

ANTIPHOLUS S.: I will not stay to-night for all the town;
Therefore away, to get our stuff aboard.
(*Exeunt*)

ACT V.

Scene I.—*A Street before an Abbey.*
Enter MERCHANT *and* ANGELO.

ANGELO: I am sorry, sir, that I have hinder'd you;
But, I protest, he had the chain of me,
Though most dishonestly he doth deny it.

MERCHANT: How is the man esteem'd here in the city?

ANGELO: Of very reverend reputation, sir,
Of credit infinite, highly belov'd,
Second to none that lives here in the city:
His word might bear my wealth at any time.

MERCHANT: Speak softly: yonder, as I think, he walks.

(*Enter* ANTIPHOLUS *of Syracuse and* DROMIO *of Syracuse.*)

ANGELO: 'Tis so; and that self chain about his neck
Which he forswore most monstrously to have.
Good sir, draw near to me, I'll speak to him.

Signior Antipholus, I wonder much
That you would put me to this shame and trouble;
And not without some scandal to yourself,
With circumstance and oaths so to deny
This chain which now you wear so openly:
Beside the charge, the shame, imprisonment,
You have done wrong to this my honest friend,
Who, but for staying on our controversy,
Had hoisted sail and put to sea to-day.
This chain you had of me; can you deny it?

ANTIPHOLUS S.: I think I had: I never did deny it.

MERCHANT: Yes, that you did, sir, and forswore it too.

ANTIPHOLUS S.: Who heard me to deny it or forswear it?

MERCHANT: These ears of mine, thou know'st, did hear thee.
Fie on thee, wretch! 'tis pity that thou liv'st
To walk where any honest men resort.

ANTIPHOLUS S.: Thou art a villain to impeach me thus:
I'll prove mine honour and mine honesty
Against thee presently, if thou dar'st stand.

MERCHANT: I dare, and do defy thee for a villain.
(*They draw.*)

(*Enter* ADRIANA, LUCIANA, COURTEZAN, *and others.*)

ADRIANA: Hold! hurt him not, for God's sake! he is mad.
Some get within him, take his sword away.
Bind Dromio too, and bear them to my house.

DROMIO S.: Run, master, run; for God's sake, take a house!
This is some priory: in, or we are spoil'd.

(*Exeunt* ANTIPHOLUS *of Syracuse and* DROMIO *of Syracuse to the Abbey. Enter the* ABBESS.)

ABBESS: Be quiet, people. Wherefore throng you hither?

ADRIANA: To fetch my poor distracted husband hence.
Let us come in, that we may bind him fast,
And bear him home for his recovery.

ANGELO: I knew he was not in his perfect wits.

MERCHANT: I am sorry now that I did draw on him.

ABBESS: How long hath this possession held the man?

ADRIANA: This week he hath been heavy, sour, sad,
    And much different from the man he was;
    But, till this afternoon his passion
    Ne'er brake into extremity of rage.
ABBESS: Hath he not lost much wealth by wrack of sea?
    Buried some dear friend? Hath not else his eye
    Stray'd his affection in unlawful love?
    A sin prevailing much in youthful men,
    Who give their eyes the liberty of gazing.
    Which of these sorrows is he subject to?
ADRIANA: To none of these, except it be the last;
    Namely, some love that drew him oft from home.
ABBESS: You should for that have reprehended him.
ADRIANA: Why, so I did.
ABBESS: Ay, but not rough enough.
ADRIANA: As roughly as my modesty would let me.
ABBESS: Haply, in private.
ADRIANA: And in assemblies too.
ABBESS: Ay, but not enough.
ADRIANA: It was the copy of our conference:
    In bed, he slept not for my urging it;
    At board, he fed not for my urging it;
    Alone, it was the subject of my theme;
    In company I often glanced it:
    Still did I tell him it was vile and bad.
ABBESS: And thereof came it that the man was mad:
    The venom clamours of a jealous woman
    Poison more deadly than a mad dog's tooth.
    It seems, his sleeps were hinder'd by thy railing,
    And thereof comes it that his head is light.
    Thou say'st his meat was sauc'd with thy upbraidings:
    Unquiet meals make ill digestions;
    Thereof the raging fire of fever bred:
    And what's a fever but a fit of madness?
    Thou say'st his sports were hinder'd by thy brawls:
    Sweet recreation barr'd, what doth ensue
    But moody moping, and dull melancholy,
    Kinsman to grim and comfortless despair,
    And at her heels a huge infectious troop

Of pale distemperatures and foes to life?
In food, in sport, and life-preserving rest
To be disturb'd, would mad or man or beast:
The consequence is then, thy jealous fits
Have scared thy husband from the use of wits.

LUCIANA: She never reprehended him but mildly
When he demean'd himself rough, rude, and wildly.
Why bear you these rebukes and answer not?

ADRIANA: She did betray me to my own reproof.
Good people, enter, and lay hold on him.

ABBESS: No; not a creature enters in my house.

ADRIANA: Then, let your servants bring my husband forth.

ABBESS: Neither; he took this place for sanctuary,
And it shall privilege him from your hands
Till I have brought him to his wits again,
Or lose my labour in assaying it.

ADRIANA: I will attend my husband, be his nurse,
Diet his sickness, for it is my office,
And will have no attorney but myself;
And therefore let me have him home with me.

ABBESS: Be patient; for I will not let him stir
Till I have us'd the approved means I have,
With wholesome syrups, drugs, and holy prayers,
To make of him a formal man again.
It is a branch and parcel of mine oath,
A charitable duty of my order;
Therefore depart and leave him here with me.

ADRIANA: I will not hence and leave my husband here;
And ill it doth beseem your holiness
To separate the husband and the wife.

ABBESS: Be quiet, and depart: thou shalt not have him. (*Exit.*)

LUCIANA: Complain unto the duke of this indignity.

ADRIANA: Come, go: I will fall prostrate at his feet,
And never rise until my tears and prayers
Have won his Grace to come in person hither,
And take perforce my husband from the abbess.

SECOND MERCHANT: By this, I think, the dial points at five:
Anon, I'm sure, the duke himself in person
Comes this way to the melancholy vale,

The place of death and sorry execution,
Behind the ditches of the abbey here.

ANGELO: Upon what cause?

SECOND MERCHANT: To see a reverend Syracusian merchant,
Who put unluckily into this bay
Against the laws and statutes of this town,
Beheaded publicly for his offence.

ANGELO: See where they come: we will behold his death.

LUCIANA: Kneel to the duke before he pass the abbey.

(*Enter* DUKE *attended;* AEGEON *bare-headed; with the headsman and other* OFFICERS.)

DUKE: Yet once again proclaim it publicly,
If any friend will pay the sum for him,
He shall not die; so much we tender him.

ADRIANA: Justice, most sacred duke, against the abbess!

DUKE: She is a virtuous and a reverend lady:
It cannot be that she hath done thee wrong.

ADRIANA: May it please your Grace, Antipholus, my husband,
Whom I made lord of me and all I had,
At your important letters, this ill day
A most outrageous fit of madness took him,
That desperately he hurried through the street,—
With him his bondman, all as mad as he,—
Doing displeasure to the citizens
By rushing in their houses, bearing thence
Rings, jewels, anything his rage did like.
Once did I get him bound and sent him home,
Whilst to take order for the wrongs I went
That here and there his fury had committed.
Anon, I wot not by what strong escape,
He broke from those that had the guard of him,
And with his mad attendant and himself,
Each one with ireful passion, with drawn swords
Met us again, and, madly bent on us
Chas'd us away, till, raising of more aid
We came again to bind them. Then they fled
Into this abbey, whither we pursued them;
And here the abbess shuts the gates on us,

And will not suffer us to fetch him out,
Nor send him forth that we may bear him hence.
Therefore, most gracious duke, with thy command
Let him be brought forth, and borne hence for help.
DUKE: Long since thy husband serv'd me in my wars,
And I to thee engag'd a prince's word,
When thou didst make him master of thy bed,
To do him all the grace and good I could.
Go, some of you, knock at the abbey gate
And bid the lady abbess come to me.
I will determine this before I stir.

(*Enter a* SERVANT.)

SERVANT: O mistress, mistress! shift and save yourself!
My master and his man are both broke loose,
Beaten the maids a-row and bound the doctor,
Whose beard they have singed off with brands of fire;
And ever as it blaz'd they threw on him
Great pails of puddled mire to quench the hair.
My master preaches patience to him, and the while
His man with scissors nicks him like a fool;
And sure, unless you send some present help,
Between them they will kill the conjurer.
ADRIANA: Peace, fool! thy master and his man are here,
And that is false thou dost report to us.
SERVANT: Mistress, upon my life, I tell you true;
I have not breath'd almost, since I did see it.
He cries for you and vows, if he can take you,
To scotch your face, and to disfigure you.
(*Cry within.*)
Hark, hark! I hear him, mistress: fly, be gone!
DUKE: Come, stand by me; fear nothing.
Guard with halberds!
ADRIANA: Ay me, it is my husband! Witness you,
That he is borne about invisible:
Even now we hous'd him in the abbey here,
And now he's here, past thought of human reason.

(*Enter* ANTIPHOLUS *of Ephesus and* DROMIO *of Ephesus*.)

ANTIPHOLUS E.: Justice, most gracious duke! O! grant me justice,
  Even for the service that long since I did thee,
  When I bestrid thee in the wars and took
  Deep scars to save thy life; even for the blood
  That then I lost for thee, now grant me justice.
AEGEON: Unless the fear of death doth make me dote,
  I see my son Antipholus and Dromio!
ANTIPHOLUS E.: Justice, sweet prince, against that woman there!
  She whom thou gav'st to me to be my wife,
  That hath abused and dishonour'd me,
  Even in the strength and height of injury!
  Beyond imagination is the wrong
  That she this day hath shameless thrown on me.
DUKE: Discover how, and thou shalt find me just.
ANTIPHOLUS E.: This day, great duke, she shut the doors upon me,
  While she with harlots feasted in my house.
DUKE: A grievous fault! Say, woman, didst thou so?
ADRIANA: No, my good lord: myself, he, and my sister
  To-day did dine together. So befall my soul
  As this is false he burdens me withal!
LUCIANA: Ne'er may I look on day, nor sleep on night,
  But she tells to your highness simple truth!
ANGELO: O perjur'd woman! They are both forsworn:
  In this the madman justly chargeth them?
ANTIPHOLUS E.: My liege, I am advised what I say:
  Neither disturb'd with the effect of wine,
  Nor heady-rash, provok'd with raging ire,
  Albeit my wrongs might make one wiser mad.
  This woman lock'd me out this day from dinner:
  That goldsmith there, were he not pack'd with her,
  Could witness it, for he was with me then;
  Who parted with me to go fetch a chain,
  Promising to bring it to the Porpentine,
  Where Balthazar and I did dine together.
  Our dinner done, and he not coming thither,
  I went to seek him: in the street I met him,
  And in his company that gentleman.

There did this perjur'd goldsmith swear me down
That I this day of him receiv'd the chain,
Which, God he knows, I saw not; for the which
He did arrest me with an officer.
I did obey. and sent my peasant home
For certain ducats: he with none return'd.
Then fairly I bespoke the officer
To go in person with me to my house.
By the way we met
My wife, her sister, and a rabble more
Of vile confederates: along with them
They brought one Pinch, a hungry lean-fac'd villain,
A mere anatomy, a mountebank,
A threadbare juggler, and a fortune-teller,
A needy, hollow-ey'd, sharp-looking wretch,
A living-dead man. This pernicious slave,
Forsooth, took on him as a conjurer,
And, gazing in mine eyes, feeling my pulse,
And with no face, as 'twere, out-facing me,
Cries out, I was possess'd. Then, altogether
They fell upon me, bound me, bore me thence,
And in a dark and dankish vault at home
There left me and my man, both bound together:
Till, gnawing with ray teeth my bonds in sunder,
I gain'd my freedom, and immediately
Ran hither to your Grace; whom I beseech
To give me ample satisfaction
For these deep shames and great indignities.
ANGELO: My lord, in truth, thus far I witness with him,
That he dined not at home, but was lock'd out.
DUKE: But had he such a chain of thee, or no?
ANGELO: He had, my lord; and when he ran in here,
These people saw the chain about his neck.
SECOND MERCHANT: Besides, I will be sworn these ears of mine
Heard you confess you had the chain of him
After you first forswore it on the mart;
And thereupon I drew my sword on you;
And then you fled into this abbey here, 264
From whence, I think, you are come by miracle.

ANTIPHOLUS E.: I never came within these abbey walls;
   Nor ever didst thou draw thy sword on me;
   I never saw the chain, so help me heaven!
   And this is false you burden me withal.
DUKE: Why, what an intricate impeach is this!
   I think you all have drunk of Circe's cup.
   If here you hous'd him, here he would have been;
   If he were mad, he would not plead so coldly;
   You say he din'd at home; the goldsmith here
   Denies that saying. Sirrah, what say you?
DROMIO E.: Sir, he dined with her there, at the Porpentine.
COURTEZAN: He did, and from my finger snatch'd that ring.
ANTIPHOLUS E.: 'Tis true, my liege; this ring I had of her.
DUKE: Saw'st thou him enter at the abbey here?
COURTEZAN: As sure, my liege, as I do see your Grace.
DUKE: Why, this is strange. Go call the abbess hither.
   (*Exit an Attendant.*)
   I think you are all mated or stark mad.
AEGEON: Most mighty duke, vouchsafe me speak a word:
   Haply I see a friend will save my life,
   And pay the sum that may deliver me.
DUKE: Speak freely Syracusian, what thou wilt.
AEGEON: Is not your name, sir, called Antipholus?
   And is not that your bondman Dromio?
DROMIO E.: Within this hour I was his bondman, sir;
   But he, I thank him, gnaw'd in two my cords:
   Now am I Dromio and his man, unbound.
AEGEON: I am sure you both of you remember me.
DROMIO E.: Ourselves we do remember, sir, by you;
   For lately we were bound, as you are now.
   You are not Pinch's patient, are you, sir?
AEGEON: Why look you strange on me? you know me well.
ANTIPHOLUS E.: I never saw you in my life till now.
AEGEON: O! grief hath chang'd me since you saw me last,
   And careful hours, with Time's deformed hand,
   Have written strange defeatures in my face:
   But tell me yet, dost thou not know my voice?
ANTIPHOLUS E.: Neither.
AEGEON: Dromio, nor thou?

DROMIO E.: No, trust me, sir, not I.

AEGEON: I am sure thou dost.

DROMIO E.: Ay, sir; but I am sure I do not; and whatsoever a man denies, you are
now bound to beheve him.

AEGEON: Not know my voice! O, time's extremity,
Hast thou so crack'd and splitted my poor tongue
In seven short years, that here my only son
Knows not my feeble key of untun'd cares?
Though now this grained face of mine be hid
In sap-consuming winter's drizzled snow,
And all the conduits of my blood froze up,
Yet hath my night of life some memory,
My wasting lamps some fading glimmer left,
My dull deaf ears a little use to hear:
All these old witnesses, I cannot err,
Tell me thou art my son Antipholus.

ANTIPHOLUS E.: I never saw my father in my life.

AEGEON: But seven years since, in Syracusa, boy,
Thou know'st we parted: but perhaps, my son,
Thou sham'st to acknowledge me in misery.

ANTIPHOLUS E.: The duke and all that know me in the city
Can witness with me that it is not so:
I ne'er saw Syracusa in my life.

DUKE: I tell thee, Syracusian, twenty years
Have I been patron to Antipholus,
During which time he ne'er saw Syracusa.
I see thy age and dangers make thee dote.

(*Re-enter* ABBESS, *with* ANTIPHOLUS *of Syracuse and* DROMIO *of Syracuse.*)

ABBESS: Most mighty duke, behold a man much wrong'd.
(*All gather to see him.*)

ADRIANA: I see two husbands, or mine eyes deceive me!

DUKE: One of these men is Genius to the other;
And so of these: which is the natural man,
And which the spirit? Who deciphers them?

DROMIO SYRACUSE: I, sir, am Dromio: command him away.

DROMIO E.: I, sir, am Dromio: pray let me stay.

ANTIPHOLUS S.: Aegeon art thou not? or else his ghost?

DROMIO SYRACUSE: O! my old master; who hath bound him here?

ABBESS: Whoever bound him, I will loose his bonds,
    And gain a husband by his liberty.
    Speak, old Aegeon, if thou be'st the man
    That hadst a wife once call'd Aemilia,
    That bore thee at a burden two fair sons.
    O! if thou be'st the same Aegeon, speak,
    And speak unto the same Aemilia!

AEGEON: If I dream not, thou art Aemilia:
    If thou art she, tell me where is that son
    That floated with thee on the fatal raft?

ABBESS: By men of Epidamnum, he and I,
    And the twin Dromio, all were taken up:
    But by and by rude fishermen of Corinth
    By force took Dromio and my son from them,
    And me they left with those of Epidamnum.
    What then became of them, I cannot tell;
    I to this fortune that you see me in.

DUKE: Why, here begins his morning story right:
    These two Antipholus', these two so like,
    And these two Dromios, one in semblance,
    Besides her urging of her wrack at sea;
    These are the parents to these children,
    Which accidentally are met together.
    Antipholus, thou cam'st from Corinth first?

ANTIPHOLUS S.: No, sir, not I; I came from Syracuse.

DUKE: Stay, stand apart; I know not which is which.

ANTIPHOLUS E.: I came from Corinth, my most gracious lord,—

DROMIO E.: And I with him.

ANTIPHOLUS E.: Brought to this town by that most famous warrior,
    Duke Menaphon, your most renowned uncle.

ADRIANA: Which of you two did dine with me to-day?

ANTIPHOLUS S.: I, gentle mistress.

ADRIANA: And are not you my husband?

ANTIPHOLUS E.: No; I say nay to that.

ANTIPHOLUS S.: And so do I; yet did she call me so;
    And this fair gentlewoman, her sister here,
    Did call me brother. (*To* LUCIANA.) What I told you then,
    I hope I shall have leisure to make good,

If this be not a dream I see and hear.

ANGELO: That is the chain, sir, which you had of me.

ANTIPHOLUS S.: I think it be, sir; I deny it not.

ANTIPHOLUS E.: And you, sir, for this chain arrested me.

ANGELO: I think I did, sir; I deny it not.

ADRIANA: I sent you money, sir, to be your bail,
    By Dromio; but I think he brought it not.

DROMIO E.: No, none by me.

ANTIPHOLUS S.: This purse of ducats I received from you,
    And Dromio, my man, did bring them me.
    I see we still did meet each other's man,
    And I was ta'en for him, and he for me,
    And thereupon these errors are arose.

ANTIPHOLUS E.: These ducats pawn I for my father here.

DUKE: It shall not need: thy father hath his life.

COURTEZAN. Sir, I must have that diamond from you.

ANTIPHOLUS E.: There, take it; and much thanks for my good cheer.

ABBESS: Renowned duke, vouchsafe to take the pains
    To go with us into the abbey here,
    And hear at large discoursed all our fortunes;
    And all that are assembled in this place,
    That by this sympathized one day's error
    Have suffer'd wrong, go keep us company,
    And we shall make full satisfaction.
    Thirty-three years have I but gone in travail
    Of you, my sons; and, till this present hour
    My heavy burdens ne'er delivered.
    The duke, my husband, and my children both,
    And you the calendars of their nativity,
    Go to a gossip's feast, and joy with me:
    After so long grief such festivity!

DUKE: With all my heart I'll gossip at this feast.

(*Exeunt* DUKE, ABBESS, AEGEON, COURTEZAN, MERCHANT, ANGELO, *and*
ATTENDANTS.)

DROMIO SYRACUSE: Master, shall I fetch your stuff from shipboard?

ANTIPHOLUS E.: Dromio, what stuff of mine hast thou embark'd?

DROMIO SYRACUSE: Your goods that lay at host, sir, in the Centaur.

ANTIPHOLUS S.: He speaks to me. I am your master, Dromio:
    Come, go with us; we'll look to that anon:
    Embrace thy brother there; rejoice with him.

(*Exeunt* ANTIPHOLUS OF SYRACUSE *and* ANTIPHOLUS *of Ephesus,* ADRIANA *and* LUCIANA.)

DROMIO S.: There is a fat friend at your master's house,
    That kitchen'd me for you to-day at dinner:
    She now shall be my sister, not my wife.
DROMIO E.: Methinks you are my glass, and not my brother:
    I see by you I am a sweet-faced youth.
Will you walk in to see their gossiping?
DROMIO S.: Not I, sir; you are my elder.
DROMIO E.: That's a question: how shall we try it?
DROMIO S.: We'll draw cuts for the senior: till then lead thou first.
DROMIO E.: Nay, then, thus:
    We came into the world like brother and brother;
    And now let's go band in hand, not one before another. (*Exeunt*)

THE TEMPEST

By William Shakespeare

NAMES OF ACTORS

ALONSO, *King of Naples*

SEBASTIAN, *his Brother*

PROSPERO, *the right Duke of Milan*

ANTONIO, *his Brother, the usurping Duke of Milan*

FERDINAND, *Son to the King of Naples*

GONZALO, *an honest old Counsellor*

ADRIAN *and* FRANCISCO, *Lords*

CALIBAN, *a savage and deformed Slave*

TRINCULO, *a Jester*

STEPHANO, *a drunken Butler*

MASTER OF A SHIP, *boatswain, Mariners*

MIRANDA, *daughter to Prospero*

ARIEL, *an airy Spirit*

IRIS

CERES

JUNO   *spirits*

NYMPHS

REAPERS

Other SPIRITS *attending on Prospero*

SCENE: *The Sea, with a Ship; afterwards an Island*

ACT I.

Scene I.—On a Ship at Sea.

A tempestuous noise of thunder and lightning heard. Enter a SHIPMASTER *and a* BOATSWAIN.

MASTER: Boatswain!

BOATSWAIN: Here, master: what cheer?

MASTER: Good, speak to the mariners; fall to't yarely, or we run ourselves aground: bestir, bestir. (*Exit.*)

(*Enter* MARINERS.)

BOATSWAIN: Heigh, my hearts! cheerly, cheerly, my hearts! yare, yare!
    Take in the topsail. Tend to the master's whistle.—
    Blow, till thou burst thy wind, if room enough!

(*Enter* ALONSO, SEBASTIAN, ANTONIO, FERDINAND, GONZALO, *and others.*)

ALONSO: Good boatswain, have care. Where's the master? Play the men.

BOATSWAIN: I pray now, keep below.

ANTONIO: Where is the master, boson?

BOATSWAIN: Do you not hear him? You mar our labour: keep your cabins: you do assist the storm.

GONZALO: Nay, good, be patient.

BOATSWAIN: When the sea is. Hence! What cares these roarers for the name of king? To cabin: silence! trouble us not.

GONZALO: Good, yet remember whom thou hast aboard.

BOATSWAIN: None that I more love than myself. You are a counsellor: if you can command these elements to silence, and work the peace of the present, we will not hand a rope more; use your authority: if you cannot, give thanks you have lived so long, and make yourself ready in your cabin for the mischance of the hour, if it so hap. Cheerly, good hearts!—Out of our way, I say. (*Exit.*)

GONZALO: I have great comfort from this fellow: methinks he hath no drowning mark upon him; his complexion is perfect gallows.
    Stand fast, good Fate, to his hanging! make the rope of his destiny our cable, for our own doth little ad vantage! If he be not born to be hanged, our case is miserable. (*Exeunt.*)

(*Re-enter* BOATSWAIN.)

BOATSWAIN: Down with the topmast! yare! lower, lower!

Bring her to try with main-course. (*A cry within.*)

A plague upon this howling! they are louder than the weather, or our office.—

(*Re-enter* SEBASTIAN, ANTONIO, *and* GONZALO.)

Yet again? what do you here? Shall we give o'er, and drown? Have you a mind to sink?

SEBASTIAN: A pox o' your throat, you bawling, blasphemous, incharitable dog!

BOATSWAIN: Work you, then.

ANTONIO: Hang, cur, hang! you whoreson, insolent noisemaker, we are less afraid to
      be drowned than thou art.

GONZALO: I'll warrant him for drowning; though the ship were no stronger than
      a nutshell, and as leaky as an unstanched wench.

BOATSWAIN: Lay her a-hold, a-hold! Set her two courses; off to sea again; lay her off.

(*Enter* MARINERS, *wet.*)

Master: All lost! to prayers, to prayers! all lost! (*Exeunt.*)

BOATSWAIN: What, must our mouths be cold?

GONZALO: The king and prince at prayers! let us assist them,
    For our case is as theirs.

SEBASTIAN: I am out of patience.

ANTONIO: We are merely cheated of our lives by drunkards.—
    This wide-chapp'd rascal,—would thou might'st lie drowning,
    The washing of ten tides!

GONZALO: He'll be hanged yet,
    Though every drop of water swear against it,
    And gape at wid'st to glut him.
    (*A confused noise within*)—' Mercy on us!'—
    'We split, we split!'—'Farewell, my wife and children!'—
    'Farewell, brother!'—'We split, we split, we split!'—

ANTONIO: Let's all sink wi' the king. (*Exit.*)

SEBASTIAN: Let's take leave of him. (*Exit.*)

GONZALO: Now would I give a thousand furlongs of sea for an acre of barren ground;
      long heath, brown furze, any thing.
    The wills above be done! but I would fain die a dry death. (*Exit.*)

Scene II.—*The Island: before the Cell of Prospero.*

Enter PROSPERO *and* MIRANDA.

MIRANDA: If by your art, my dearest father, you have
    Put the wild waters in this roar, allay them.

The sky, it seems, would pour down stinking pitch,
But that the sea, mounting to th' welkin's cheek,
Dashes the fire out. O! I have suffer'd
With those that I saw suffer: a brave vessel,
Who had, no doubt, some noble creatures in her,
Dash'd all to pieces. O! the cry did knock
Against my very heart. Poor souls, they perish'd.
Had I been any god of power, I would
Have sunk the sea within the earth, or e'er
It should the good ship so have swallow'd and
The fraughting souls within her.

PROSPERO: Be collected,
No more amazement. Tell your piteous heart
There's no harm done.

MIRANDA: O, woe the day!

PROSPERO: No harm.
I have done nothing but in care of thee,—
Of thee, my dear one! thee, my daughter!—who
Art ignorant of what thou art, nought knowing
Of whence I am: nor that I am more better
Than Prospero, master of a full poor cell,
And thy no greater father.

MIRANDA: More to know
Did never meddle with my thoughts.

PROSPERO: 'Tis time
I should inform thee further. Lend thy hand,
And pluck my magic garment from me.—So,
(*Lays down his mantle.*)
Lie there, my art.—Wipe thou thine eyes; have comfort.
The direful spectacle of the wrack, which touch'd
The very virtue of compassion in thee,
I have with such provision in mine art
So safely order'd, that there is no soul—
No, not so much perdition as an hair,
Betid to any creature in the vessel
Which thou heard'st cry, which thou saw'st sink. Sit down;
For thou must now know further.

MIRANDA: You have often
Begun to tell me what I am, but stopp'd,

And left me to a bootless inquisition,
Concluding, 'Stay; not yet.'

PROSPERO: The hour's now come,
The very minute bids thee ope thine ear;
Obey and be attentive. Canst thou remember
A time before we came unto this cell?
I do not think thou canst, for then thou wast not
Out three years old.

MIRANDA: Certainly, sir, I can.

PROSPERO: By what? by any other house or person?
Of anything the image tell me, that
Hath kept with thy remembrance.

MIRANDA: 'Tis for off;
And rather like a dream than an assurance
That my remembrance warrants. Had I not
Four or five women once that tended me?

PROSPERO: Thou hadst, and more, Miranda. But how is it
That this lives in thy mind? What seest thou else
In the dark backward and abysm of time?
If thou remember'st aught ere thou cam'st here,
How thou cam'st here, thou may'st.

MIRANDA: But that I do not.

PROSPERO: Twelve year since, Miranda, twelve year since,
Thy father was the Duke of Milan and
A prince of power.

MIRANDA: Sir, are not you my father?

PROSPERO: Thy mother was a piece of virtue, and
She said thou wast my daughter; and thy father
Was Duke of Milan, and his only heir
A princess,—no worse issued.

MIRANDA: O, the heavens!
What foul play had we that we came from thence?
Or blessed was't we did?

PROSPERO: Both, both, my girl:
By foul play, as thou say'st,were we heav'd thence;
But blessedly help hither.

MIRANDA: O! my heart bleeds
To think o' the teen that I have turn'd you to,
Which is from my remembrance. Please you, further.

PROSPERO: My brother and thy uncle, called Antonio,—
     I pray thee, mark me,—that a brother should
     Be so perfidious!—he whom next thyself,
     Of all the world I lov'd, and to him put
     The manage of my state; as at that time,
     Through all the signiories it was the first,
     And Prospero the prime duke; being so reputed
     In dignity, and for the liberal arts,
     Without a parallel: those being all my study,
     The government I cast upon my brother,
     And to my state grew stranger, being transported
     And rapt in secret studies. Thy false uncle—
     Dost thou attend me?
MIRANDA: Sir, most heedfully.
PROSPERO: Being once perfected how to grant suits,
     How to deny them, who t' advance, and who
     To trash for over-topping; new created
     The creatures that were mine, I say, or chang'd 'em,
     Or else new formed 'em: having both the key
     Of officer and office, set all hearts i' the state
     To what tune pleas'd his ear; that now he was
     The ivy which had hid my princely trunk,
     And suck'd my verdure out on't.—Thou attend'st not.
MIRANDA: O, good sir! I do.
PROSPERO: I pray thee, mark me.
     I, thus neglecting worldly ends, all dedicated
     To closeness and the bettering of my mind
     With that, which, but by being so retir'd,
     O'erpriz'd all popular rate, in my false brother
     Awak'd an evil nature; and my trust,
     Like a good parent, did beget of him
     A falsehood in its contrary as great
     As my trust was; which had, indeed no limit,
     A confidence sans bound. He being thus lorded,
     Not only with what my revenue yielded,
     But what my power might else exact,—like one,
     Who having, into truth, by telling of it,
     Made such a sinner of his memory,
     To credit his own lie,—he did believe

He was indeed the duke; out o 'the substitution,
And executing th' outward face of royalty,
With all prerogative:—Hence his ambition growing,—
Dost thou hear?

MIRANDA: Your tale, sir, would cure deafness.

PROSPERO: To have no screen between this part he play'd
And him he play'd it for, he needs will be
Absolute Milan. Me, poor man,—my library
Was dukedom large enough: of temporal royalties
He thinks me now incapable; confederates,—
So dry he was for sway,—wi' the king of Naples
To give him annual tribute, do him homage;
Subject his coronet to his crown, and bend
The dukedom, yet unbow'd,—alas, poor Milan!—
To most ignoble stooping.

MIRANDA: O the heavens!

PROSPERO: Mark his condition and the event; then tell me
If this might be a brother.

MIRANDA: I should sin
To think but nobly of my grandmother:
Good wombs have borne bad sons.

PROSPERO: Now the condition.
This King of Naples, being an enemy
To me inveterate, hearkens my brother's suit;
Which was, that he, in lieu o' the premises
Of homage and I know not how much tribute,
Should presently extirpate me and mine
Out of the dukedom, and confer fair Milan,
With all the honours on my brother; whereon,
A treacherous army levied, one midnight
Fated to the purpose did Antonio open
The gates of Milan; and, i' the dead of darkness,
The ministers for the purpose hurried thence
Me and thy crying self.

MIRANDA: Alack, for pity!
I, not rememb'ring how I cried out then,
Will cry it o'er again: it is a hint,
That wrings mine eyes to't.

PROSPERO: Hear a little further,
　　And then I'll bring thee to the present business
　　Which now's upon us; without the which this story
　　Were most impertinent.
MIRANDA: Wherefore did they not
　　That hour destroy us?
PROSPERO: Well demanded, wench:
　　My tale provokes that question. Dear, they durst not,
　　So dear the love my people bore me, nor set
　　A mark so bloody on the business; but
　　With colours fairer painted their foul ends.
　　In few, they hurried us aboard a bark,
　　Bore us some leagues to sea; where they prepaid
　　A rotten carcass of a boat, not rigg'd,
　　Nor tackle, sail, nor mast; the very rats
　　Instinctively have quit it: there they hoist us,
　　To cry to the sea that roar'd to us; to sigh
　　To the winds whose pity, sighing back again,
　　Did us but loving wrong.
MIRANDA: Alack! what trouble
　　Was I then to you!
PROSPERO: O, a cherubin
　　Thou wast, that did preserve me! Thou didst smile,
　　Infused with a fortitude from heaven,
　　When I have deck'd the sea with drops full salt,
　　Under my burden groan'd; which raised in me
　　An undergoing stomach, to bear up
　　Against what should ensue.
MIRANDA: How came we ashore?
PROSPERO: By Providence divine.
　　Some food we had and some fresh water that
　　A noble Neapolitan, Gonzalo,
　　Out of his charity,—who being then appointed
　　Master of this design,—did give us, with
　　Rich garments, linens, stuffs, and necessaries,
　　Which since have steaded much; so, of his gentleness,
　　Knowing I lov'd my books, he furnish'd me,
　　From mine own library with volumes that
　　I prize above my dukedom.

MIRANDA: Would I might
    But ever see that man!
PROSPERO: Now I arise:— (*Resumes his mantle.*)
    Sit still, and hear the last of our sea-sorrow.
    Here in this island we arriv'd; and here
    Have I, thy schoolmaster, made thee more profit
    Than other princes can, that have more time
    For vainer hours and tutors not so careful.
MIRANDA: Heavens thank you for't! And now, I pray you, sir,—
    For still 'tis' beating in my mind,—your reason
    For raising this sea-storm?
PROSPERO: Know thus far forth.
    By accident most strange, bountiful Fortune,
    Now my dear lady, hath mine enemies
    Brought to this shore; and by my prescience
    I find my zenith doth depend upon
    A most auspicious star, whose influence
    If now I court not but omit, my fortunes
    Will ever after droop. Here cease more questions;
    Thou art inclined to sleep; 'tis a good dulness,
    And give it way;—I know thou canst not choose.—
    (MIRANDA *sleeps.*)
    Come away, servant, come! I'm ready now.
    Approach, my Ariel; come!

(*Enter* ARIEL.)
ARIEL: All hail, great master! grave sir, hail! I come
    To answer thy best pleasure; be't to fly,
    To swim, to dive into the fire, to ride
    On the curl'd clouds: to thy strong bidding task
    Ariel and all his quality.
PROSPERO: Hast thou, spirit,
    Perform'd to point the tempest that I bade thee?
ARIEL: To every article.
    I boarded the king's ship; now on the beak,
    Now in the waist, the deck, in every cabin,
    I flam'd amazement: sometime I'd divide
    And burn in many places; on the topmast,
    The yards, and boresprit, would I flame distinctly,

Then meet, and join: Jove's lightnings, the precursors
O' the dreadful thunder-claps, more momentary
And sight-outrunning were not; the fire and cracks
Of sulphurous roaring the most mighty Neptune
Seem to besiege and make his bold waves tremble,
Yea, his dread trident shake.

PROSPERO: My brave spirit!
Who was so firm, so constant, that this coil
Would not infect his reason?

ARIEL: Not a soul
But felt a fever of the mad and play'd -
Some tricks of desperation. All but mariners,
Plunged in the foaming brine and quit the vessel,
Then all a-fire with me: the king's son, Ferdinand,
With hair up-staring,—then like reeds, not hair,—
Was the first man that leap'd; cried, 'Hell is empty,
And all the devils are here.'

PROSPERO: Why, that's my spirit!
But was not this nigh shore?

ARIEL: Close by, my master.

PROSPERO: But are they, Ariel, safe?

ARIEL: Not a hair perish'd;
On their sustaining garments not a blemish,
But fresher than before: and, as thou bad'st me,
In troops I have dispers'd them 'bout the isle.
The king's son have I landed by himself;
Whom I left cooling of the air with sighs
In an odd angle of the isle and sitting,
His arms in this sad knot.

PROSPERO: Of the king's ship
The mariners, say how thou hast dispos'd,
And all the rest o' the fleet.

ARIEL: Safely in harbour
Is the king's ship; in the deep nook, where once
Thou call'dst me up at midnight to fetch dew
From the still-vex'd Bermoothes; there she's hid:
The mariners all under hatches stow'd;
Who, with a charm join'd to their suffer'd labour,
I have left asleep: and for the rest o' the fleet

Which I dispers'd, they all have met again,
And are upon the Mediterranean flote,
Bound sadly home for Naples,
Supposing that they saw the king's ship wrack'd,
And his great person perish.

PROSPERO: Ariel, thy charge
Exactly is perform'd: but there's more work:
What is the time o' th' day?

ARIEL: Past the mid season.

PROSPERO: At least two glasses. The time 'twixt six and now
Must by us both be spent most preciously.

ARIEL: Is there more toil? Since thou dost give me pains,
Let me remember thee what thou hast promis'd,
Which is not yet perform'd me.

PROSPERO: How now! moody?
What is't thou canst demand?

ARIEL: My liberty.

PROSPERO: Before the time be out? no more!

ARIEL: I prithee
Remember, I have done thee worthy service;
Told thee no lies, made no mistakings, serv'd
Without or grudge or grumblings: thou didst promise
To bate me a full year.

PROSPERO: Dost thou forget
From what a torment I did free thee?

ARIEL: No.

PROSPERO: Thou dost; and think'st it much to tread the ooze
Of the salt deep,
To run upon the sharp wind of the north,
To do me business in the veins o' th' earth
When it is bak'd with frost.

ARIEL: I do not, sir.

PROSPERO: Thou liest, malignant thing! Hast thou forgot
The foul witch Sycorax, who with age and envy
Was grown into a hoop? hast thou forgot her?

ARIEL: No, sir.

PROSPERO: Thou hast. Where was she born? speak; tell me.

ARIEL: Sir, in Argier.

PROSPERO: O! was she so? I must,

Once in a month, recount what thou hast been,
Which thou forget'st. This damn'd witch, Sycorax,
For mischiefs manifold and sorceries terrible
To enter human hearing, from Argier,
Thou know'st, was banish'd: for one thing she did
They would not take her life. Is not this true?

ARIEL: Ay, sir.

PROSPERO: This blue-ey'd hag was hither brought with child
And here was left by the sailors. Thou, my slave,
As thou report'st thyself, wast then her servant:
And, for thou wast a spirit too delicate
To act her earthy and abhorr'd commands,
Refusing her grand bests, she did confine thee,
By help of her more potent ministers,
And in her most unmitigable rage,
Into a cloven pine; within which rift
Imprison'd, thou didst painfully remain
A dozen years; within which space she died
And left thee there, where thou didst vent thy groans
As fast as mill-wheels strike. Then was this island,—
Save for the son that she did litter here,
A freckled whelp hag-bom,—not honour'd with
A human shape.

ARIEL: Yes; Caliban her son.

PROSPERO: Dull thing, I say so; he that Caliban,
Whom now I keep in service. Thou best know'st
What torment I did find thee in; thy groans
Did make wolves howl and penetrate the breasts
Of ever-angry bears: it was a torment
To lay upon the damn'd, which Sycorax
Could not again undo; it was mine art,
When I arriv'd and heard thee, that made gape
The pine, and let thee out.

ARIEL: I thank thee, master.

PROSPERO: If thou more murmur'st, I will rend an oak
And peg thee in his knotty entrails till
Thou hast howl'd away twelve winters.

ARIEL: Pardon, master;
I will be correspondent to command,

And do my spiriting gently.

PROSPERO: Do so; and after two days
  I will discharge thee.

ARIEL: That's my noble master!
  What shall I do? say what? what shall I do?

PROSPERO: Go make thyself like a nymph of the sea: be subject
  To no sight but thine and mine; invisible
  To every eyeball else. Go, take this shape,
  And hither come in't: go, hence with diligence! (*Exit.* ARIEL.)
  Awake, dear heart, awake! thou hast slept well; Awake!

MIRANDA: (Waking.) The strangeness of your story put
  Heaviness in me.

PROSPERO: Shake it off. Come on;
  We'll visit Caliban my slave, who never
  Yields us kind answer.

MIRANDA: 'Tis a villain, sir,
  I do not love to look on.

PROSPERO: But, as 'tis,
  We cannot miss him: he does make our fire,
  Fetch in our wood; and serves in offices
  That profit us.—What ho! slave! Caliban!
  Thou earth, thou! speak.

CALIBAN: (Within.) There's wood enough within.

PROSPERO: Come forth, I say; there's other business for thee:
  Come, thou tortoise! when?

(*Re-enter* ARIEL, *like a water-nymph.*)
  Fine apparition! My quaint Ariel,
  Hark in thine ear.

ARIEL: My lord, it shall be done. (*Exit.*)

PROSPERO: Thou poisonous slave, got by the devil himself
  Upon thy wicked dam, come forth!

(*Enter* CALIBAN.)

CALIBAN: As wicked dew as e'er my mother brush'd
  With raven's feather from unwholesome fen
  Drop on you both! a south-west blow on ye,
  And blister you all o'er!

PROSPERO: For this, be sure, to-night thou shalt have cramps,

Side-stitches that shall pen thy breath up; urchins
Shall forth at vast of night, that they may work
All exercise on thee: thou shalt be pinch'd
As thick as honeycomb, each pinch more stinging
Than bees that made them.

CALIBAN: I must eat my dinner.
This island's mine, by Sycorax my mother,
Which thou tak'st from me. When thou earnest first,
Then strok'dst me, and mad'st much of me; wouldst give me
Water with berries in't; and teach me how
To name the bigger light, and how the less,
That burn by day and night: and then I lov'd thee
And show'd thee all the qualities o' th' isle,
The fresh springs, brine-pits, barren place, and fertile.
Cursed be I that did so!—All the charms
Of Sycorax, toads, beetles, bats, light on you!
For I am all the subjects that you have,
Which first was mine own king; and here you sty me
In this hard rock, whiles you do keep from me
The rest o' th' island.

PROSPERO: Thou most lying slave,
Whom stripes may move, not kindness! I have us'd thee,
Filth as thou art, with human care; and lodg'd thee
In mine own cell, till thou didst seek to violate
The honour of my child.

CALIBAN: Oh ho! Oh ho!—would it had been done!
Thou didst prevent me; I had peopled else
This isle with Calibans.

PROSPERO: Abhorred slave,
Which any print of goodness will not take,
Being capable of all ill! I pitied thee,
Took pains to make thee speak, taught thee each hour
One thing or other: when thou didst not, savage,
Know thine own meaning, but wouldst gabble like
A thing most brutish, I endow'd thy purposes
With words that made them known: but thy vile race,
Though thou didst learn, had that in't which good natures
Could not abide to be with; therefore wast thou
Deservedly confin'd into this rock,

Who hadst deserv'd more than a prison.

CALIBAN: You taught me language; and my profit on't
Is, I know how to curse: the red plague rid you,
For learning me your language!

PROSPERO: Hag-seed, hence!
Fetch us in fuel; and be quick, thou'rt best,
To answer other business. Shrug'st thou, malice?
If thou neglect'st, or dost unwillingly
What I command, I'll rack thee with old cramps,
Fill all thy bones with aches; make thee roar,
That beasts shall tremble at thy din.

CALIBAN: No, pray thee!—
(*Aside.*) I must obey: his art is of such power,
It would control my dam's god, Setebos,
And make a vassal of him.

PROSPERO: So, slave; hence!
(*Exit* CALIBAN.)

(*Re-enter* FERDINAND *and* ARIEL *invisible, playing and singing.*)

ARIEL'S SONG:
Come unto these yellow sands,
And then take hands;
Curtsied when you have, and kiss'd,—
The wild waves whist,—
Foot it featly here and there;
And, sweet sprites, the burden bear.
Hark, hark!
    Burden: Bow, wow, dispersedly.
The watch-dogs bark:
    Burden: Bow, wow, dispersedly.
Hark, hark! I hear
The strain of strutting Chanticleer
    Cry, Cock-a-diddle-dow.

FERDINAND: Where should this music be? i' th' air, or th' earth?
It sounds no more;—and sure, it waits upon
Some god o' th' island. Sitting on a bank,
Weeping again the king my father's wrack,
This music crept by me upon the waters,
Allaying both their fury, and my passion,

With its sweet air: thence I have follow'd it,—
Or it hath drawn me rather,—but 'tis gone.
No, it begins again.

ARIEL'S SONG.

Full fathom five thy father lies;
Of his bones are coral made:
Those are pearls that were his eyes:
Nothing of him that doth fade,
But doth suffer a sea-change
Into something rich and strange.
Sea-nymphs hourly ring his knell:
    Burden: ding-dong.
Hark! now I hear them,—ding-dong, bell.

FERDINAND: The ditty does remember my drown'd father.
This is no mortal business, nor no sound
That the earth owes:—I hear it now above me.

PROSPERO: The fringed curtains of thine eye advance,
And say what thou seest yond.

MIRANDA: What is't? a spirit?
Lord, how it looks about! Believe me, sir,
It carries a brave form:—but 'tis a spirit.

PROSPERO: No, wench; it eats and sleeps, and hath such senses
As we have, such; this gallant which thou see'st,
Was in the wrack; and, but he's something stain'd
With grief,—that beauty's canker,—thou might'st call him
A goodly person: he hath lost his fellows
And strays about to find 'em

MIRANDA: I might call him
A thing divine; for nothing natural
I ever saw so noble.

PROSPERO: (*Aside.*) It goes on, I see,
As my soul prompts it.—Spirit, fine spirit! I'll free thee
Within two days for this.

FERDINAND: Most sure, the goddess
On whom these airs attend!—Vouchsafe, my prayer
May know if you remain upon this island;
And that you will some good instruction give
How I may bear me here: my prime request,

Which I do last pronounce, is,—O you wonder!—
If you be maid or no?

MIRANDA: No wonder, sir;
But certainly a maid.

FERDINAND: My language! heavens!—
I am the best of them that speak this speech,
Were I but where 'tis spoken.

PROSPERO: How! the best?
What wert thou, if the King of Naples heard thee?

FERDINAND: A single thing, as I am now, that wonders
To hear thee speak of Naples. He does hear me;
And, that he does, I weep: myself am Naples,
Who with mine eyes,—ne'er since at ebb,—beheld
The king, my father wrack'd.

MIRANDA: Alack, for mercy!

FERDINAND: Yes, faith, and all his lords; the Duke of Milan,
And his brave son being twain.

PROSPERO: (*Aside.*) The Duke of Milan,
And his more braver daughter could control thee,
If now 'twere fit to do't.—At the first sight (*Aside.*)
They have changed eyes:—delicate Ariel,
I'll set thee free for this!—(*To* FERDINAND) A word, good sir;
I fear you have done yourself some wrong: a word.

MIRANDA: (Aside.) Why speaks my father so ungently? This
Is the third man that e'er I saw; the first
That e'er I sighed for: pity move my father
To be inclin'd my way!

FERDINAND: (*Aside.*) O: if a virgin,
And your affection not gone forth, I'll make you
The Queen of Naples.

PROSPERO: Soft, sir: one word more—
(*Aside.*) They are both in either's powers: but this swift business
I must uneasy make, lest too light winning
Make the prize light.—(*To* FERDINAND) One word more: I charge thee
That thou attend me. Thou dost here usurp
The name thou ow'st not; and hast put thyself
Upon this island as a spy, to win it
From me, the lord on't.

FERDINAND: No, as I am a man.

MIRANDA: There's nothing ill can dwell in such a temple:
    If the ill spirit have so fair a house,
    Good things will strive to dwell with 't.

PROSPERO: (*To* FERDINAND) Follow me.—
    (*To* MIRANDA) Speak not you for him; he's a traitor.—
    (*To* FERDINAND) Come;
    I'll manacle thy neck and feet together:
    Sea-water shalt thou drink; thy food shall be
    The fresh-brook muscles, wither'd roots and husks
    Wherein the acorn cradled. Follow.

FERDINAND: No;
    I will resist such entertainment till
    Mine enemy has more power.
    (*He draws, and is charmed from moving.*)

MIRANDA: O dear father!
    Make not too rash a trial of him, for
    He's gentle, and not fearful.

PROSPERO: What! I say,
    My foot my tutor?—Put thy sword up, traitor;
    Who mak'st a show, but dar'st not strike, thy conscience
    Is so possess'd with guilt: come from thy ward,
    For I can here disarm thee with this stick
    And make thy weapon drop.

MIRANDA: Beseech you, father!

PROSPERO: Hence! hang not on my garments.

MIRANDA: Sir, have pity:
    I'll be his surety.

PROSPERO: Silence! one word more
    Shall make me chide thee, if not hate thee.
    What! An advocate for an impostor? hush!
    Thou think'st there is no more such shapes as he,
    Having seen but him and Caliban: foolish wench!
    To the most of men this is a Caliban
    And they to him are angels.

MIRANDA: My affections
    Are then most humble; I have no ambition
    To see a goodlier man.

PROSPERO: (*To* FERDINAND) Come on; obey;
  Thy nerves are in their infancy again,
  And have no vigour in them.
FERDINAND: So they are:
  My spirits, as in a dream, are all bound up.
  My father's loss, the weakness which I feel,
  The wrack of all my friends, or this man's threats,
  To whom I am subdued, are but light to me,
  Might I but through my prison once a day
  Behold this maid: all corners else o' th' earth
  Let liberty make use of; space enough
  Have I in such a prison.
PROSPERO: (*Aside.*) It works.—(*To* FERDINAND)
  Come on.—Thou hast done well, fine Ariel!—
  (*To* FERDINAND) Follow me.—
  (*To* ARIEL.) Hark, what thou else shalt do me.
MIRANDA: Be of comfort;
  My father's of a better nature, sir,
  Than he appears by speech: this is unwonted,
  Which now came from him.
PROSPERO: Thou shalt be as free
  As mountain winds; but then exactly do
  All points of my command.
ARIEL: To the syllable.
PROSPERO: (*To* FERDINAND) Come, follow.—
  (*To* MIRANDA) Speak not for him. (*Exeunt.*)

ACT II.

Scene I. Another Part of the Island.

Enter ALONSO, SEBASTIAN, ANTONIO, GONZALO, ADRIAN, FRANCISCO, *and others.*

GONZALO: Beseech you, sir, be merry: you have cause,
  So have we all, of joy; for our escape
  Is much beyond our loss. Our hint of woe
  Is common: every day some sailor's wife,
  The masters of some merchant and the merchant,
  Have just our theme of woe; but for the miracle,

I mean our preservation, few in millions
Can speak like us: then wisely, good sir, weigh
Our sorrow with our comfort.

ALONSO: Prithee, peace.

SEBASTIAN: He receives comfort like cold porridge.

ANTONIO: The visitor will not give him o'er so.

SEBASTIAN: Look, he's winding up the watch of his wit; by and by it will strike.

GONZALO: Sir,—

SEBASTIAN: One: tell.

GONZALO: When every grief is entertain'd that's offer'd,
　　Comes to the entertainer—

SEBASTIAN: A dollar.

GONZALO: Dolour comes to him, indeed: you have spoken truer than you
　　purposed.

SEBASTIAN: You have taken it wiselier than I meant you should.

GONZALO: Therefore, my lord,—

ANTONIO: Fie, what a spendthrift is he of his tongue!

ALONSO: I prithee, spare.

GONZALO: Well, I have done: but yet—

SEBASTIAN: He will be talking.

ANTONIO: Which, of he or Adrian, for a good wager, first begins to crow?

SEBASTIAN: The old cock.

ANTONIO: The cockerel.

SEBASTIAN: Done. The wager?

ANTONIO: A laughter.

SEBASTIAN: A match!

ADRIAN: Though this island seem to be desert,—

SEBASTIAN: Ha, ha, ha! So you're paid.

ADRIAN: Uninhabitable, and almost inaccessible,—

SEBASTIAN: Yet—

ADRIAN: Yet—

ANTONIO: He could not miss it.

ADRIAN: It must needs be of subtle, tender, and delicate temperance.

ANTONIO: Temperance was a delicate wench.

SEBASTIAN: Ay, and a subtle; as he most learnedly delivered.

ADRIAN: The air breathes upon us here most sweetly.

SEBASTIAN: As if it had lungs, and rotten ones.-

ANTONIO: Or as 'twere perfumed by a fen.

GONZALO: Here is everything advantageous to life.

ANTONIO: True; save means to live.

SEBASTIAN: Of that there's none, or little.

GONZALO: How lush and lusty the grass looks! how green!

ANTONIO: The ground indeed is tawny.

SEBASTIAN: With an eye of green in't.

ANTONIO: He misses not much.

SEBASTIAN: No; he doth but mistake the truth totally.

GONZALO: But the rarity of it is,—which is indeed almost beyond credit,—

SEBASTIAN: As many vouch'd rarities are.

GONZALO: That our garments, being, as they were, drenched in the sea, hold notwithstanding their freshness and glosses; being rather new-dyed than stain'd with salt water.

ANTONIO: If but one of his pockets could speak, would it not say he lies?

SEBASTIAN: Ay, or very falsely pocket up his report.

GONZALO: Methinks, our garments are now as fresh as when we put them on first in Afric, at the marriage of the king's fair daughter Claribel to the King of Tunis.

SEBASTIAN: 'Twas a sweet marriage, and we prosper well in our return.

ADRIAN: Tunis was never graced before with such a paragon to their queen.

GONZALO: Not since widow Dido's time.

ANTONIO: Widow! a pox o' that! How came that widow in? Widow Dido!

SEBASTIAN: What if he had said, widower Aeneas too? Good Lord, how you take it!

ADRIAN: Widow Dido, said you? you make me study of that: she was of Carthage, not of Tunis.

GONZALO: This Tunis, sir, was Carthage.

ADRIAN: Carthage?

GONZALO: I assure you, Carthage.

ANTONIO: His word is more than the miraculous harp.

SEBASTIAN: He hath rais'd the wall, and houses too.

ANTONIO: What impossible matter will he make easy next?

SEBASTIAN: I think he will carry this island home in his pocket, and give it his son for an apple.

ANTONIO: And, sowing the kernels of it in the sea, bring forth more islands.

ALONSO: Ay?

ANTONIO: Why, in good time.

GONZALO: (*To* ALONSO.) Sir, we were talking that our garments seem now as fresh as when we were at Tunis at the marriage of your daughter, who is now queen.

ANTONIO: And the rarest that e'er came there.

SEBASTIAN: Bate, I beseech you, widow Dido.

ANTONIO: O! widow Dido; ay, widow Dido.

GONZALO: Is not, sir, my doublet as fresh as the first day I wore it? I mean, in a sort.

ANTONIO: That sort was well fish'd for.

GONZALO: When I wore it at your daughter's marriage?

ALONSO: You cram these words into mine ears, against
    The stomach of my sense. Would I had never
    Married my daughter there! for, coming thence,
    My son is lost; and, in my rate, she too,
    Who is so far from Italy remov'd,
    I ne'er again shall see her. O thou, mine heir
    Of Naples and of Milan! what strange fish
    Hath made his meal on thee?
    Fran. Sir, he may live:
    I saw him beat the surges under him,
    And ride upon their backs: he trod the water,
    Whose enmity he flung aside, and breasted
    The surge most sworn that met him: his bold head
    'Bove the contentious waves he kept, and oar'd
    Himself with his good arms in lusty stroke
    To the shore, that o'er his wave-worn basis bow'd,
    As stooping to relieve him. I not doubt
    He came alive to land.

ALONSO: No, no; he's gone,

SEBASTIAN: Sir, you may thank yourself for this great loss,
    That would not bless our Europe with your daughter,
    But rather lose her to an African;
    Where she at least is banish'd from your eye,
    Who hath cause to wet the grief on 't.

ALONSO: Prithee, peace.

SEBASTIAN: You were kneel'd to and importun'd otherwise
    By all of us; and the fair soul herself
    Weigh'd between loathness and obedience, at
    Which end o' the beam should bow. We have lost your son,
    I fear, for ever: Milan and Naples have
    More widows in them of this business' making,
    Than we bring men to comfort them: the fault's
    Your own.

ALONSO: So is the dearest of the loss.

GONZALO: My lord Sebastian,

The truth you speak doth lack some gentle
    And time to speak it in; you rub the sore,
    When you should bring the plaster.
SEBASTIAN: Very well.
ANTONIO: And most chirurgeonly.
GONZALO: It is foul weather in us all, good sir,
    When you are cloudy.
SEBASTIAN: Foul weather?
ANTONIO: Very foul.
GONZALO: Had I plantation of this isle, my lord,—
ANTONIO: He'd sow't with nettle-seed.
SEBASTIAN: Or docks, or mallows.
GONZALO: And were the king on't, what would I do?
SEBASTIAN: 'Scape being drunk for want of wine.
GONZALO: I' the commonwealth I would by contraries
    Execute all things; for no kind of traffic
    Would I admit; no name of magistrate;
    Letters should not be known; riches, poverty,
    And use of service, none; contract, succession,
    Bourn, bound of land, tilth, vineyard, none;
    No use of metal, corn, or wine, or oil;
    No occupation; all men idle, all;
    And women too, but innocent and pure;
    No sovereignty,—
SEBASTIAN: Yet he would be king on't.
ANTONIO: The latter end of his commonwealth forgets the beginning.
GONZALO: All things in common nature should produce
    Without sweat or endeavour: treason, felony,
    Sword, pike, knife, gun, or need of any engine,
    Would I not have; but nature should bring forth,
    Of its own kind, all foison, all abundance,
    To feed my innocent people.
SEBASTIAN: No marrying 'mong his subjects?
ANTONIO: None, man; all idle; whores and knaves.
GONZALO: I would with such perfection govern, sir,
    To excel the golden age.
SEBASTIAN: Save his majesty!
ANTONIO: Long live Gonzalo!
ANTONIO: And,—do you mark me, sir?

ALONSO: Prithee, no more: thou dost talk nothing to me.

GONZALO: I do well believe your highness; and did it to minister occasion to these gentlemen, who are of such sensible and nimble lungs that they always use to laugh at nothing.

ANTONIO: 'Twas you we laugh'd at.

GONZALO: Who in this kind of merry fooling am nothing to you; so you may continue and laugh at nothing still.

ANTONIO: What a blow was there given!

SEBASTIAN: An it had not fallen flat-long.

GONZALO: You are gentlemen of brave mettle: you would lift the moon out of her sphere, if she would continue in it five weeks without changing.

(*Enter* ARIEL, *invisible, playing solemn music.*)

SEBASTIAN: We would so, and then go a-bat-fowling.

ANTONIO: Nay, good my lord, be not angry.

GONZALO: No, I warrant you; I will not adventure my discretion so weakly.
Will you laugh me asleep, for I am very heavy?

ANTONIO: Go sleep, and hear us.
(*All sleep but* ALONSO, SEBASTIAN, *and* ANTONIO.)

ALONSO: What! all so soon asleep! I wish mine eyes
Would, with themselves, shut up my thoughts: I find
They are inclin'd to do so.

SEBASTIAN: Please you, sir,
Do not omit the heavy offer of it:
It seldom visits sorrow; when it doth
It is a comforter.

ANTONIO: We two, my lord,
Will guard your person while you take your rest,
And watch your safety.

ALONSO: Thank you. Wondrous heavy.
(ALONSO *sleeps. Exit* ARIEL.)

SEBASTIAN: What a strange drowsiness possesses them!

ANTONIO: It is the quality o' the climate.

SEBASTIAN: Why
Doth it not then our eyelids sink? I find not
Myself dispos'd to sleep.

ANTONIO: Nor I: my spirits are nimble.
They fell together all, as by consent;
They dropp'd, as by a thunder-stroke. What might,

Worthy Sebastian? O! what might?—No more:—
And yet methinks I see it in thy face,
What thou should'st be. The occasion speaks thee; and
My strong imagination sees a crown
Dropping upon thy head.

SEBASTIAN: What! art thou waking?

ANTONIO: Do you not hear me speak?

SEBASTIAN: I do; and surely,
It is a sleepy language, and thou speak'st
Out of thy sleep. What is it thou didst say?
This is a strange repose, to be asleep
With eyes wide open; standing, speaking, moving,
And yet so fast asleep.

ANTONIO: Noble Sebastian,
Thou let'st thy fortune sleep—die rather; wink'st
Whiles thou art waking.

SEBASTIAN: Thou dost snore distinctly:
There's meaning in thy snores.

ANTONIO: I am more serious than my custom: you
Must be so too, if heed me; which to do
Trebles thee o'er.

SEBASTIAN: Well; I am standing water.

ANTONIO: I'll teach you how to flow.

SEBASTIAN: Do so: to ebb,
Hereditary sloth instructs me.

ANTONIO: O!
If you but knew how you the purpose cherish
Whiles thus you mock it! how, in stripping it,
You more invest it! Ebbing men, indeed,
Most often do so near the bottom run
By their own fear or sloth.

SEBASTIAN: Prithee, say on:
The setting of thine eye and cheek proclaim
A matter from thee, and a birth indeed
Which throes thee much to yield.

ANTONIO: Thus, sir:
Although this lord of weak remembrance, this
Who shall be of as little memory
When he is earth'd, hath here almost persuaded,—

For he's a spirit of persuasion, only
Professes to persuade,—the king, his son's alive,
'Tis as impossible that he's undrown'd
As he that sleeps here swims.

SEBASTIAN: I have no hope
That he's undrown'd.

ANTONIO: O! out of that 'no hope,'
What great hope have you! no hope that way is
Another way so high a hope that even
Ambition cannot pierce a wink, beyond,
But doubts discovery there. Will you grant with me
That Ferdinand is drown'd?

SEBASTIAN: He's gone.

ANTONIO: Then tell me
Who's the next heir of Naples?

SEBASTIAN: Claribel.

ANTONIO: She that is Queen of Tunis; she that dwells
Ten leagues beyond man's life; she that from Naples
Can have no note, unless the sun were post—
The man i' th' moon's too slow—till new-born chins
Be rough and razorable: she that, from whom?
We all were sea-swallow'd, though some cast again,
And by that destiny to perform an act
Whereof what's past is prologue, what to come
In yours and my discharge.

SEBASTIAN: What stuff is this!—How say you?
'Tis true my brother's daughter's Queen of Tunis;
So is she heir of Naples; 'twixt which regions
There is some space.

ANTONIO: A space whose every cubit
Seems to cry out, 'How shall that Claribel
Measure us back to Naples?—Keep in Tunis,
And let Sebastian wake!'—Say, this were death
That now hath seized them; why, they were no worse
Than now they are. There be that can rule Naples
As well as he that sleeps; lords that can prate
As amply and unnecessarily
As this Gonzalo; I myself could make
A chough of as deep chat. O, that you bore

The mind that I do! what a sleep were this
For your advancement! Do you understand me?

SEBASTIAN: Methinks I do.

ANTONIO: And how does your content
Tender your own good fortune?

SEBASTIAN: I remember
You did supplant your brother Prospero.

ANTONIO: True:
And look how well my garments sit upon me;
Much feater than before; my brother's servants.
Were then my fellows; now they are my men.

SEBASTIAN: But, for your conscience,—

ANTONIO: Ay, sir; where lies that? if it were a kibe,
'T would put me to my slipper; but I feel not
This deity in my bosom: twenty consciences,
That stand 'twixt me and Milan, candied be they,
And melt ere they molest! Here lies your brother,
No better than the earth he lies upon,
If he were that which now he's like, that's dead;
Whom I, with this obedient steel,—three inches of it,—
Can lay to bed for ever; whiles you, doing thus,
To the perpetual wink for aye might put
This ancient morsel, this Sir Prudence, who
Should not upbraid our course. For all the rest,
They'll take suggestion as a cat laps milk;
They'll tell the clock to any business that
We say befits the hour.

SEBASTIAN: Thy case, dear friend,
Shall be my precedent: as thou got'st Milan,
I'll come by Naples. Draw thy sword: one stroke
Shall free thee from the tribute which thou pay'st,
And I the king shall love thee.

ANTONIO: Draw together;
And when I rear my hand, do you the like,
To fall it on Gonzalo.

SEBASTIAN: O! but one word. (*They converse apart.*)

(*Music. Re-enter* ARIEL, *invisible.*)

ARIEL: My master through his art foresees the danger
   That you, his friend, are in; and sends me forth—
   For else his project dies—to keep thee living.
   (*Sings in* GONZALO'*s ear.*)
   While you here do snoring lie,
   Open-ey'd Conspiracy
   His time doth take.
   If of life you keep a care,
   Shake off slumber, and beware:
   Awake! awake!

ANTONIO: Then let us both be sudden.

GONZALO: Now, good angels
   Preserve the king! (*They wake.*)

ALONSO: Why, how now! ho, awake! Why are you drawn?
   Wherefore this ghastly looking?

GONZALO: What's the matter?

SEBASTIAN: Whiles we stood here securing your repose,
   Even now, we heard a hollow burst of bellowing
   Like bulls, or rather lions; did't not wake you?
   It struck mine ear most terribly.

ALONSO: I heard nothing.

ANTONIO: O! 'twas a din to fright a monster's ear,
   To make an earthquake: sure it was the roar
   Of a whole herd of lions.

ALONSO: Heard you this, Gonzalo?

GONZALO: Upon mine honour, sir, I heard a humming,
   And that a strange one too, which did awake me.
   I shak'd you, sir, and cry'd; as mine eyes open'd,
   I saw their weapons drawn:—there was a noise,
   That's verily. 'Tis best we stand upon our guard,
   Or that we quit this place: let's draw our weapons.

ALONSO: Lead off this ground, and let's make further search
   For my poor son.

GONZALO: Heavens keep him from these beasts!
   For he is, sure, i' the island.

ALONSO: Lead away. (*Exit.*) with the others.

ARIEL: Prospero my lord shall know what I have done:
   So, king, go safely on to seek thy son. (*Exit.*)

Scene II. Another Part of the Island.

Enter CALIBAN, *with a burden of wood. A noise of thunder heard.*

CALIBAN: All the infections that the sun sucks up
    From bogs, fens, flats, on Prosper fall, and make him
    By inch-meal a disease! His spirits hear me,
    And yet I needs must curse. But they'll nor pinch,
    Fright me with urchin-shows, pitch me i'the mire,
    Nor lead me, like a firebrand, in the dark
    Out of my way, unless he bid 'em; but
    For every trifle are they set upon me:
    Sometime like apes, that mow and chatter at me
    And after bite me; then like hedge-hogs, which
    Lie tumbling in my bare-foot way and mount
    Their pricks at my foot-fall; sometime am I
    All wound with adders, who with cloven tongues
    Do hiss me into madness.—

(*Enter* TRINCULO.)
    Lo now! lo!
    Here comes a spirit of his, and to torment me
    For bringing wood in slowly: I'll fall flat;
    Perchance he will not mind me.

Trin; Here's neither bush nor shrub to bear off any weather at all, and another
    storm brewing; I hear it sing i' the wind: yond same black cloud, yond huge
    one, looks like a foul bombard that would shed his liquor. If it should thun-
    der as it did before, I know not where to hide my head: yond same cloud
    cannot choose but fall by pailfuls.—What have we here? a man or a fish?

'Dead or alive? A fish: he smells like a fish; a very ancient and fish-like smell; a
    kind of not of the newest Poor-John. A strange fish!

Were I in England now,—as once I was,—and had but this fish painted, not a
    holiday fool there but would give a piece of silver: there would this monster
    make a man; any strange beast there makes a man. When they will not give
    a doit to relieve a lame beggar, they will lay out ten to see a dead Indian.

Legg'd like a man! and his fins like arms! Warm, o' my troth; I do now let loose
    my opinion, hold it no longer; this is no fish, but an islander, that hath
    lately suffered by a thunderbolt. (*Thunder.*)

Alas! the storm is come again: my best way is to creep under his gaberdine; there is no other shelter hereabout: misery acquaints a man with strange bedfellows. I will here shroud till the dregs of the storm be past.

(*Enter* STEPHANO, *singing; a bottle in his hand.*)

STEPHANO: I shall no more to sea, to sea,
Here shall I die a-shore:—
This is a very scurvy tune to sing at a man's funeral:
Well, here's my comfort. (*Drinks.*)
The master, the swabber, the boatswain and I,
The gunner and his mate,
Lov'd Mall, Meg, and Marian and Margery,
But none of us car'd for Kate;
For she had a tongue with a tang,
Would cry to a sailor, 'Go hang!'
She lov'd not the savour of tar nor of pitch,
Yet a tailor might scratch her where-e'er she did itch:
Then to sea, boys, and let her go hang.
This is a scurvy tune too: but here's my comfort. (*Drinks.*)
CALIBAN: Do not torment me: O!
STEPHANO: What's the matter? Have we devils here?
Do you put tricks upon us with savages and men of Ind? Ha!
I have not 'scaped drowning, to be afeard now of your four legs; for it hath
been said, As proper a man as ever went on four legs cannot make him give
ground; and it shall be said so again while Stephano breathes at's nostrils.
CALIBAN: The spirit torments me: O!
STEPHANO: This is some monster of the isle with four legs, who hath got, as I take
it, an ague.
Where the devil should he learn our language?
I will give him some relief, if it be but for that: if I can recover him and keep
him tame and get to Naples with him, he's a present for any emperor that
ever trod on neat's-leather.
CALIBAN: Do not torment me, prithee: I'll bring my wood home faster.
STEPHANO: He's in his fit now and does not talk after the wisest.
He shall taste of my bottle: if he have never drunk wine afore it will go near to
remove his fit. If I can recover him, and keep him tame,
I will not take too much for him: he shall pay for him that hath him, and that
soundly,

CALIBAN: Thou dost me yet but little hurt; thou wilt anon,
   I know it by thy trembling: now
   Prosper works upon thee.
STEPHANO: Come on your ways: open your mouth; here is that which will
      give language to you, cat.
   Open your mouth: this will shake your shaking,
   I can tell you, and that soundly (*gives* CALIBAN *drink*):
   You cannot tell who's your friend; open your chaps again.
TRINCULO: I should know that voice: it should be—but he is drowned, and these
      are devils. O! defend me.
STEPHANO: Four legs and two voices; a most delicate monster
   His forward voice now is to speak well of his friend; his backward voice is to
      utter foul speeches, and to detract.
   If all the wine in my bottle will recover him,
   I will help his ague. Come. Amen!
   I will pour some in thy other mouth.
TRINCULO: Stephano!
STEPHANO: Doth thy other mouth call me? Mercy! mercy!
   This is a devil, and no monster: I will leave him; I have no long spoon.
TRINCULO: Stephano!—if thou beest Stephano,; touch me, and speak to me; for
      I am Trinculo: —be not afeard—thy good friend Trinculo.
STEPHANO: If thou beest Trinculo, come forth.
   I'll pull thee by the lesser legs: if any be Trinculo's legs, these are they.
   Thou art very Trinculo indeed!
   How cam'st thou to be the siege of this moon-calf?
   Can he vent Trinculos?
TRINCULO: I took him to be killed with a thunderstroke.
   But art thou not drowned, Stephano?
   I hope now thou art not drowned.
   Is the storm overblown?
   I hid me under the dead mooncalf s gaberdine for fear of the storm.
   And art thou living, Stephano? O Stephano! two Neapolitans 'scaped!
STEPHANO: Prithee, do not turn me about: my stomach is not constant.
CALIBAN: (*Aside.*) These be fine things an if they be not sprites.
   That's a brave god and bears celestial liquor:
   I will kneel to him.
STEPHANO: How didst thou 'scape?
   How cam'st thou hither? swear by this bottle, how thou cam'st hither.

I escaped upon a butt of sack, which the sailors heaved overboard, by this
bottle! which I made of the bark of a tree with mine own hands, since I was
cast ashore.

CALIBAN: I'll swear upon that bottle, to be thy true subject; for the liquor is not
earthly.

STEPHANO: Here: swear then, how thou escapedst.

TRINCULO: Swam ashore, man, like a duck: I can swim like a duck, I'll be sworn.

STEPHANO: Here, kiss the book (*gives* TRINCULO *drink*). Though thou canst swim
like a duck, thou art made like a goose.

TRINCULO: O Stephano! hast any more of this?

STEPHANO: The whole butt, man: my cellar is in a rock by the seaside, where my
wine is hid.

How now, moon-calf! how does thine ague?

CALIBAN: Hast thou not dropped from heaven?

STEPHANO: Out o' the moon, I do assure thee:

I was the man in the moon, when time was.

CALIBAN: I have seen thee in her, and I do adore thee; my mistress showed me thee,
and thy dog, and thy bush.

STEPHANO: Come, swear to that; kiss the book;

I will furnish it anon with new contents; swear.

TRINCULO: By this good light, this is a very shallow monster.—

I afeard of him!—a very weak monster.—

The man i' the moon! a most poor credulous monster!—

Well drawn, monster, in good sooth.

CALIBAN: I'll show thee every fertile inch o' the island;

And I will kiss thy foot. I prithee, be my god.

TRINCULO: By 'this light, a most perfidious and drunken monster: when his god's
asleep, he'll rob his bottle.

CALIBAN: I'll kiss thy foot: I'll swear myself thy subject.

STEPHANO: Come on then; down, and swear.

TRINCULO: I shall laugh myself to death at this puppy-headed monster.

A most scurvy monster!

I could find in my heart to beat him,—

STEPHANO: Come, kiss.

TRINCULO: But that the poor monster's in drink: an abominable monster!

CALIBAN: I'll shew thee the best springs; I'll I pluck thee berries;

I'll fish for thee, and get thee wood enough.

A plague upon the tyrant that I serve!

I'll bear him no more sticks, but follow thee,
    Thou wondrous man.
TRINCULO: A most ridiculous monster, to make a wonder of a poor drunkard!
CALIBAN: I prithee, let me bring thee where crabs grow;
    And I with my long nails will dig thee pig-nuts;
    Show thee a jay's nest and instruct thee how
    To snare the nimble marmozet; I'll bring thee
    To clust'ring filberts, and sometimes I'll get thee
    Young scamels from the rock. Wilt thou go with me?
STEPHANO: I prithee now, lead the way, without any more talking.—
    Trinculo, the king and all our company else being drowned, we will inherit
        here.—
    Here; bear my bottle.—Fellow Trinculo, we'll fill him by and by again.
CALIBAN: Farewell, master; farewell, farewell.
    (*Sings drunkenly.*)
TRINCULO: A howling monster, a drunken monster.
CALIBAN: No more dams I'll make for fish;
    Nor fetch in firing
    At requiring,
    Nor scrape trenchering, nor wash dish;
    'Ban, 'Ban, Ca—Calrban,
    Has a new master—Get a new man.
    Freedom, high-day! high-day, freedom! freedom! high-day, freedom!
STEPHANO: O brave monster! lead the way. (*Exeunt.*)

ACT III.

Scene I.—*Before Prospero's Cell.*
Enter FERDINAND, *bearing a log.*

FERDINAND: There be some sports are painful, and their labour
    Delight in them sets off: some kinds of baseness
    Are nobly undergone, and most poor matters
    Point to rich ends. This my mean task
    Would be as heavy to me as odious; but
    The mistress which I serve quickens what's dead
    And makes my labours pleasures: O! she is
    Ten times more gentle than her father's crabbed,
    And he's composed of harshness. I must remove

Some thousands of these logs and pile them up,
Upon a sore injunction: my sweet mistress
Weeps when she sees me work, and says such baseness
Had never like executor. I forget:
But these sweet thoughts do even refresh my labours,
Most busiest when I do it.

(*Enter* MIRANDA; *and* PROSPERO *behind.*)

MIRANDA: Alas! now, pray you,
Work not so hard: I would the lightning had
Burnt up those logs that you are enjoined to pile!
Pray, set it down and rest you: when this burns,
'Twill weep for having wearied you. My father
Is hard at study; pray now, rest yourself;
He's safe for these three hours.

FERDINAND: O most dear mistress,
The sun will set, before I shall discharge
What I must strive to do.

MIRANDA: If you'll sit down,
I'll bear your logs the while. Pray, give me that;
I'll carry it to the pile.

FERDINAND: No, precious creature:
I had rather crack my sinews, break my back,
Than you should such dishonour undergo,
While I sit lazy by.

MIRANDA: It would become me
As well as it does you: and I should do it
With much more ease; for my good will is to it,
And yours it is against.

PROSPERO: (*Aside.*) Poor worm! thou art infected:
This-visitation shows it.

MIRANDA: You look wearily.

FERDINAND: No, noble mistress; 'tis fresh morning with me
When you are by at night. I do beseech you—
Chiefly that I might set it in my prayers—
What is your name?

MIRANDA: Miranda.—O my father!
I have broke your best to say so.

FERDINAND: Admir'd Miranda!

Indeed, the top of admiration; worth
What's dearest to the world! Full many a lady
I have ey'd with best regard, and many a time
The harmony of their tongues hath into bondage
Brought my too diligent ear: for several virtues
Have I lik'd several women; never any
With so full soul but some defect in her
Did quarrel with the noblest grace she ow'd,
And put it to the foil: but you, O you!
So perfect and so peerless, are created
Of every creature's best.

MIRANDA: I do not know
One of my sex; no woman's face remember,
Save, from my glass, mine own; nor have I seen
More that I may call men than you, good friend,
And my dear father: how features are abroad,
I am skill-less of; but, by my modesty,—
The jewel in my dower,—I would not wish
Any companion in the world but you;
Nor can imagination form a shape,
Besides yourself, to like of. But I prattle
Something too wildly and my father's precepts
I therein do forget.

FERDINAND: I am in my condition
A prince, Miranda; I do think, a king;—
I would not so!—and would no more endure
This wooden slavery than to suffer
The flesh-fly blow my mouth.—Hear my soul speak:—
The very instant that I saw you did
My heart fly to your service; there resides,
To make me slave to it; and for your sake
Am I this patient log-man.

MIRANDA: Do you love me?

FERDINAND: O heaven! O earth! bear witness to this sound,
And crown what I profess with kind event
If I speak true: if hollowly, invert
What best is boded me to mischief! I,
Beyond all limit of what else i' the world,
Do love, prize, honour you.

MIRANDA: I am a fool
  To weep at what I am glad of.
PROSPERO: (*Aside.*) Fair encounter
  Of two most rare affections! Heavens rain grace
  On that which breeds between 'em!
FERDINAND: Wherefore weep you?
MIRANDA: At mine unworthiness, that dare not offer
  What I desire to give; and much less take
  What I shall die to want. But this is trifling;
  And all the more it seeks to hide itself
  The bigger bulk it shows. Hence, bashful cunning!
  And prompt me, plain and holy innocence!
  I am your wife, if you will marry me;
  If not, I'll die your maid: to be your fellow
  You may deny me; but I'll be your servant
  Whether you will or no.
FERDINAND: My mistress, dearest;
  And I thus humble ever.
MIRANDA: My husband then?
FERDINAND: Ay, with a heart as willing
  As bondage e'er of freedom: here's my hand.
MIRANDA: And mine, with my heart in't: and now farewell
  Till half an hour hence.
FERDINAND: A thousand thousand!
  (*Exeunt* FERDINAND *and* MIRANDA *severally.*)
PROSPERO: So glad of this as they, I cannot be,
  Who are surpris'd withal; but my rejoicing
  At nothing can be more. I'll to my book;
  For yet, ere supper time, must I perform
  Much business appertaining. (*Exit.*)

Scene II.—*Another Part of the Island.*
Enter CALIBAN, *with a bottle,* STEPHANO, *and* TRINCULO.

STEPHANO: Tell not me:—when the butt is out, we will drink water; not a drop
    before: therefore bear up, and board 'em.—
    Servant-monster, drink to me.

TRINCULO: Servant-monster! the folly of this island!

They say there's but five upon this isle: we are three of them; if th' other two
be brained like us, the state totters.

STEPHANO: Drink,-servant-monster, when I bid thee: thy eyes are almost set
in thy head.

TRINCULO: Where should they be set else? he were a brave monster indeed,
if they were set in his tail.

STEPHANO: My man-monster hath drowned his tongue in sack: for my part,
the sea cannot drown me;

I swam, ere I could recover the shore, five-and-thirty leagues, off and on,
by this light.

Thou shalt be my lieutenant, monster, or my standard.

TRINCULO: Your lieutenant, if you list; he's no standard.

STEPHANO: We'll not run. Monsieur monster.

TRINCULO: Nor go neither: but you'll lie, like dogs; and yet say nothing neither.

STEPHANO: Moon-calf, speak once in thy life, if thou beest a good moon-calf,

CALIBAN: How does thy honour? Let me lick thy shoe.

I'll not serve him, he is not valiant.

TRINCULO: Thou liest, most ignorant monster:

I am in case to justle a constable.

Why, thou deboshed fish thou, was there ever a man a coward that hath
drunk so much sack as I to-day?

Wilt thou tell a monstrous lie, being but half a fish and half a monster?

CALIBAN: Lo, how he mocks me! wilt thou let him, my lord? .

TRINCULO: 'Lord' quoth he!—that a monster

I should be such a natural!

CALIBAN: Lo, lo, again! bite him to death, I prithee.

STEPHANO: Trinculo, keep a good tongue in your

I head: if you prove a mutineer, the next tree!

The poor monster's my subject, and he shall not suffer indignity.

CALIBAN: I thank my noble lord. Wilt thou be pleas'd

To hearken once again the suit I made thee?

STEPHANO: Marry, will I; kneel, and repeat it: I will stand, and so shall Trinculo.

(*Enter* ARIEL, *invisible.*)

CALIBAN: As I told thee before, I am subject to a tyrant, a sorcerer, that by his
cunning hath cheated me of the island.

ARIEL: Thou liest.

CALIBAN: Thou liest, thou jesting monkey thou;
    I would my valiant master would destroy thee: I do not lie.
STEPHANO: Trinculo, if you trouble him any more in his tale, by this hand,
    I will supplant some of your teeth.
TRINCULO: Why, I said nothing.
STEPHANO: Mum then and no more.—
    (*To* CALIBAN.) Proceed.
CALIBAN: I say, by sorcery he got this isle;
    From me he got it: if thy greatness will,
    Revenge it on him,—for, I know, thou dar'st;
    But this thing dare not,—
STEPHANO: That's most certain.
CALIBAN: Thou shalt be lord of it and I'll serve thee.
STEPHANO: How now shall this be compassed?
    Canst thou' bring me to the party?
CALIBAN: Yea, yea, my lord: I'll yield him thee asleep,
    Where thou may'st knock a nail into his head.
ARIEL: Thou liest; thou canst not.
CALIBAN: What a pied ninny's this! Thou scurvy patch!—
    I do beseech thy greatness, give him blows,
    And take his bottle from him: when that's gone
    He shall drink nought but brine; for I'll not show him
    Where the quick freshes are.
STEPHANO: Trinculo, run into no further danger: interrupt the monster one word
    further, and, by this hand, I'll turn my mercy out o' doors and make a stock-
    fish of thee.
TRINCULO: Why, what did I? I did nothing. I'll go further off.
STEPHANO: Didst thou not say belied?
ARIEL: Thou liest.
STEPHANO: Do I so? take thou that. (*Strikes* TRINCULO)
    As you like this, give me the lie another time.
TRINCULO: I did not give thee the lie:—Out o' your wits and hearing too?—
    A pox o' your bottle! this can sack and drinking do.—
    A murrain on your monster, and the devil take your fingers!
CALIBAN: Ha, ha, ha!
STEPHANO: Now, forward with your tale.—Prithee stand further off.
CALIBAN: Beat him enough: after a little time
    I'll beat him too.
STEPHANO: Stand further.—Come, proceed.

CALIBAN: Why, as I told thee, 'tis a custom with him
    I' the afternoon to sleep: there thou may'st brain him,
    Having first seized his books; or with a log
    Batter his skull, or paunch him with a stake,
    Or cut his wezand with thy knife. Remember
    First to possess his books; for without them
    He's but a sot, as I am, nor hath not
    One spirit to command: they all do hate him
    As rootedly as I. Bum but his books;
    He has brave utensils,—for so he calls them,—
    Which, when he has a house, he'll deck withal:
    And that most deeply to consider is
    The beauty of his daughter; he himself
    Calls her a nonpareil: I never saw a woman,
    But only Sycorax my dam and she;
    But she as far surpasseth Sycorax
    As great'st does least.
STEPHANO: Is it so brave a lass?
    Col. Ay, lord; she will become thy bed, I warrant,
    And bring thee forth brave brood.
STEPHANO: Monster, I will kill this man: his daughter and I will be king and
    queen,—save our graces! and Trinculo and thyself shall be viceroys.
    Dost thou like the plot, Trinculo?
TRINCULO: Excellent.
STEPHANO: Give me thy hand: I am sorry I beat thee; but, while thou livest, keep a
    good tongue in thy head.
CALIBAN: Within this half hour will he be asleep;
    Wilt thou destroy him then?
STEPHANO: Ay, on mine honour.
ARIEL: This will I tell my master.
CALIBAN: Thou mak'st me merry: I am full of pleasure.
    Let us be jocund; will you troll the catch
    You taught me but while-ere?
STEPHANO: At thy request, monster, I will do reason, any reason: Come on, Trinculo,
    let us sing. (*Sings.*)
    Flout'em, and scout'em; and scout'em, and flout'em;
    Thought is free.
CALIBAN: That's not the tune.
    (ARIEL *plays the tune on a tabor and pipe.*)

STEPHANO: What is this same?

TRINCULO: This is the tune of our catch, played by the picture of Nobody.

STEPHANO: If thou beest a man, show thyself in thy likeness: if thou beest a devil, take't as thou list.

TRINCULO: O, forgive me my sins'

STEPHANO: He that dies pays all debts: I defy thee.—Mercy upon us!

CALIBAN: Art thou afeard?

STEPHANO: No, monster, not I.

CALIBAN: Be not afeard: the isle is full of noises,
Sounds and sweet airs, that give delight, and hurt not.
Sometimes a thousand twangling instruments
Will hum about mine ears; and sometime voices,
That, if I then had wak'd after long sleep,
Will make me sleep again: and then, in dreaming,
The clouds methought would open and show riches
Ready to drop upon me; that, when I wak'd
I cried to dream again.

STEPHANO: This will prove a brave kingdom to me, where I shall have my music for nothing.

CALIBAN: When Prospero is destroyed.

STEPHANO: That shall be by and by: I remember the story.

TRINCULO: The sound is going away: let's follow it, and after do our work.

STEPHANO: Lead, monster; we'll follow.—
I would I could see this taborer! he lays it on. Wilt come?

TRINCULO: I'll follow, Stephano. (*Exeunt.*)

Scene III. *Another part of the Island.*

Enter ALONSO, SEBASTIAN, ANTONIO, GONZALO, ADRIAN, FRANCISCO, *and others.*

GONZALO: By'r lakin, I can go no further, sir;
My old bones ache: here's a maze trod indeed,
Through forth-rights, and meanders! by your patience,
I needs must rest me.

ALONSO: Old lord, I cannot blame thee,
Who am myself attach'd with weariness,
To the dulling of my spirits: sit down, and rest.
Even here I will put off my hope, and keep it
No longer for my flatterer: he is drown'd

Whom thus we stray to find; and the sea mocks
Our frustrate search on land. Well, let him go.

ANTONIO: (*Aside to* SEBASTIAN.) I am right glad that he's so out of hope.
Do not, for one repulse, forego the purpose
That you resolv'd to effect.

SEBASTIAN: (*Aside to* ANTONIO.) The next advantage
Will we take throughly.

ANTONIO: (*Aside to* SEBASTIAN.) Let it be to-night;
For, now they are oppress'd with travel, they
Will not, nor cannot, use such vigilance
As when they are fresh.

SEBASTIAN: (*Aside to* ANTONIO.) I say to-night: no more.

(*Solemn and strange music; and* PROSPERO *above, invisible. Enter below several strange Shapes, bringing in a banquet: they dance about it with gentle actions of salutation; and, inviting the King, &c., to eat, they depart.*)

ALONSO: What harmony is this? my good friends, hark!

GONZALO: Marvellous sweet music!

ALONSO: Give us kind keepers, heavens! What were these?

SEBASTIAN: A living drollery. Now I will believe
That there are unicorns; that in Arabia
There is one tree, the phoenix' throne; one phoenix
At this hour reigning there.

ANTONIO: I'll believe both;
And what does else want credit, come to me,
And I'll be sworn 'tis true: travellers ne'er did lie,
Though fools at home condemn them.

GONZALO: If in Naples
I should report this now, would they believe me?
If I should say I saw such islanders,—
For, certes, these are people of the island,—
Who, though they are of monstrous shape, yet, note,
Their manners are more gentle-kind than of
Our human generation you shall find
Many, nay, almost any.

PROSPERO: (*Aside.*) Honest lord,
Thou hast said well; for some of you there present
Are worse than devils.

ALONSO: I cannot too much muse,
  Such shapes, such gesture, and such sound, expressing,—
  Although they want the use of tongue,—a kind
  Of excellent dumb discourse.
PROSPERO: (*Aside.*) Praise in departing.
FRANCISCO: They vanish'd strangely.
SEBASTIAN: No matter, since
  They have left their viands behind; for we have stomachs.—
  Will't please you to taste of what is here?
ALONSO: Not I.
GONZALO: Faith, sir, you need not fear. When we were boys,
  Who would believe that there were mountaineers
  Dew-lapp'd like bulls, whose throats had hanging at them
  Wallets of flesh? or that there were such men
  Whose heads stood in their breasts? which now we find
  Each putter-out of five for one will bring us
  Good warrant of.
ALONSO: I will stand to and feed,
  Although my last; no matter, since I feel
  The best is past—Brother, my lord the duke,
  Stand to and do as we.

(*Thunder and lightning. Enter* ARIEL *like a harpy; claps his wings upon the table; and, with a quaint device, the banquet vanishes.*)
ARIEL: You are three men of sin, whom Destiny—
  That hath to instrument this lower world
  And what is in't,—the never-surfeited sea
  Hath caused to belch up you; and on this island
  Where man doth not inhabit; you 'mongst men
  Being most unfit to live. I have made you mad;
  (*Seeing* ALONSO, SEBASTIAN, *&c., draw their swords.*)
  And even with such-like valour men hang and drown
  Their proper selves. You fools! I and my follows
  Are ministers of fate: the elements
  Of whom your swords are temper'd, may as well
  Wound the loud winds, or with bemock'd-at stabs
  Kill the still-closing waters, as diminish
  One dowie that's in my plume; my fellow-ministers
  Are like invulnerable. If you could hurt,

Your swords are now too massy for your strengths,
And will not be uplifted. But, remember,—
For that's my business to you,—that you three
From Milan did supplant good Prospero;
Expos'd unto the sea, which hath requit it,
Him and his innocent child: for which foul deed
The powers, delaying, not forgetting, have
Incens'd the seas and shores, yea, all the creatures,
Against your peace. Thee of thy son, Alonso,
They have bereft; and do pronounce, by me,
Lingering perdition,—worse than any death
Can be at once,—shall step by step attend
You and your ways; whose wraths to guard you from—
Which here in this most desolate isle, else falls
Upon your heads,—is nothing but heart-sorrow
And a clear life ensuing.
(*He vanishes in thunder: then, to soft music, enter the*
Shapes again, and dance with mocks and mows, and carry out the table.)

PROSPERO: (*Aside.*) Bravely the figure of this harpy hast thou
Perform'd, my Ariel; a grace it had, devouring:
Of my instruction hast thou nothing bated
In what thou hadst to say: so, with good life
And observation strange, my meaner ministers
Their several kinds have done. My high charms work,
And these mine enemies are all knit up
In their distractions: they now are in my power;
And in these fits I leave them, while I visit
Young Ferdinand,—whom they suppose is drown'd,—
And his and mine lov'd darling. (*Exit above.*)

GONZALO: I' the name of something holy, sir, why stand you
In this strange stare?

ALONSO: O, it is monstrous! monstrous!
Methought the billows spoke and told me of it;
The winds did sing it to me; and the thunder,
That deep and dreadful organ-pipe, pronounc'd
The name of Prosper: it did bass my trespass.
Therefore my son i' th' ooze is bedded; and
I'll seek him deeper than e'er plummet sounded,
And with him there lie mudded. (*Exit.*)

SEBASTIAN: But one fiend at a time,
    I'll fight their legions o'er.
ANTONIO: I'll be thy second.
    (*Exeunt* SEBASTIAN *and* ANTONIO.)
GONZALO: All three of them are desperate; their great guilt,
    Like poison given to work a great time after,
    Now 'gins to bite the spirits.—I do beseech you
    That are of suppler joints, follow them swiftly
    And hinder them from what this ecstasy
    May now provoke them to.
ADRIAN: Follow, I pray you. (*Exeunt.*)

ACT IV.

Scene I. Before Prospero's Cell.
Enter PROSPERO, FERDINAND, *and* MIRANDA.

PROSPERO: If I have too austerely punish'd you,
    Your compensation makes amends; for I
    Have given you here a thrid of mine own life,
    Or that for which I live; whom once again
    I tender to thy hand: all thy vexations
    Were but my trials of thy love, and thou
    Hast strangely stood the test: here, afore Heaven,
    I ratify this my rich gift. O Ferdinand!
    Do not smile at me that I boast her off,
    For thou shalt find she will outstrip all praise,
    And make it halt behind her.
FERDINAND: I do believe it
    Against an oracle.
PROSPERO: Then, as my gift and thine own acquisition
    Worthily purchas'd, take my daughter: but
    If thou dost break her virgin knot before
    All sanctimonious ceremonies may
    With full and holy rite be minister'd,
    No sweet aspersion shall the heavens let fall
    To make this contract grow; but barren hate,
    Sour-ey'd disdain and discord shall bestrew
    The union, of your bed with weeds so loathly

That you shall hate it both: therefore take heed,
As Hymen's lamps shall light you.

FERDINAND: As I hope
For quiet days, fair issue and long life,
With such love as 'tis now, the murkiest den,
The most opportune place, the strong'st suggestion
Our worser genius can, shall never melt
Mine honour into lust, to take away
The edge of that day's celebration
When I shall think, or Phoebus' steeds are founder'd,
Or Night kept chain'd below.

PROSPERO: Fairly spoke:
Sit then, and talk with her, she is thine own.
What, Ariel! my industrious servant Ariel!

(*Enter* ARIEL.)

ARIEL: What would my potent master? here I am.

PROSPERO: Thou and thy meaner fellows your last service
Did worthily perform; and I must use you
In such another trick. Go bring the rabble,
O'er whom I give thee power, here to this place:
Incite them to quick motion; for I must
Bestow upon the eyes of this young couple
Some vanity of mine art: it is my promise,
And they expect it from me.

ARIEL: Presently?

PROSPERO: Ay, with a twink.

ARIEL: Before you can say, 'Come,' and 'Go;
And breathe twice; and cry, 'so, so,'
Each one, tripping on his toe,
Will be here with mop and mow.
Do you love me, master? no?

PROSPERO: Dearly, my delicate Ariel. Do not approach
Till thou dost hear me call.

ARIEL: Well, I conceive. (*Exit.*)

PROSPERO: Look, thou be true; do not give dalliance
Too much the rein: the strongest oaths are straw
To the fire i' the blood: be more abstemious,
Or eise good night your vow!

FERDINAND: I warrant you, sir;
    The white-cold virgin snow upon my heart
    Abates the ardour of my liver.
PROSPERO: Well.—
    Now come, my Ariel! bring a corollary,
    Rather than want a spirit: appear, and pertly.
    No tongue! all eyes! be silent. (*Soft music.*)

(*A masque. Enter* IRIS.)
IRIS: Ceres, most bounteous lady, thy richleas
    Of wheat, rye, barley, vetches, oats, and peas;
    Thy turfy mountains, where live nibbling sheep,
    And flat meads thatch'd with stover, them to keep;
    Thy banks with pioned and twilled brims,
    Which spongy April at thy hest betrims,
    To make cold nymphs chaste crowns; and thy broom groves,
    Whose shadow the dismissed bachelor loves,
    Being lass-lorn; thy pole-dipt vineyard;
    And thy sea-marge, sterile and rocky-hard,
    Where thou thyself dost air: the queen o' the sky,
    Whose watery arch and messenger am I,
    Bids thee leave these; and with her sovereign grace,
    Here on this grass-plot, in this very place,
    To come and sport; her peacocks fly amain:
    Approach, rich Ceres, her to entertain.
    (*Enter* CERES.)
CERES: Hail, many-coloured messenger, that ne'er
    Dost disobey the wife of Jupiter;
    Who with thy saffron wings upon my flowers
    Diffusest honey-drops, refreshing showers:
    And with each end of thy blue bow dost crown
    My bosky acres, and my unshrubb'd down,
    Rich scarf to my proud earth; why hath thy queen
    Summon'd me hither, to this short-grass'd green?
IRIS: A contract of true love to celebrate,
    And some donation freely to estate
    On the bless'd lovers.
CERES: Tell me, heavenly bow,
    If Venus or her son, as thou dost know,

Do now attend the queen? since they did plot
The means that dusky Dis my daughter got,
Her and her blind boy's scandal'd company
I have forsworn.

IRIS: Of her society
Be not afraid; I met her deity
Cutting the clouds towards Paphos and her son
Dove-drawn with her. Here thought they to have done
Some wanton charm upon this man and maid,
Whose vows are, that no bed-rite shall be paid.
Till Hymen's torch be lighted; but in vain:
Mars's hot minion is return'd again;
Her waspish-headed son has broke his arrows,
Swears he will shoot no more, but play with sparrows,
And be a boy right out.

CERES: Highest queen of state,
Great Juno comes; I know her by her gait.
(*Enter* JUNO.)

JUNO: How does my bounteous sister? Go with me
To bless this twain, that they may prosperous be,
And honour'd in their issue.

SONG.

JUNO: Honour, riches, marriage-blessing,
Long continuance, and increasing,
Hourly joys be still upon you!
Juno sings her blessings on you.

CERES: Earth's increase, foison plenty,
Barns and garners never empty;
Vines,with clust'ring bunches growing;
Plants with goodly burden bowing;
Spring come to you at the farthest
In the very end of harvest!
Scarcity and want shall shun you;
Ceres' blessing so is on you.

FERDINAND: This is a most majestic vision, and
Harmonious charmingly: May I be bold
To think these spirits?

PROSPERO: Spirits, which by mine art
   I have from their confines call'd to enact
   My present fancies.
FERDINAND: Let me live here ever:
   So rare a wonder'd father and a wise,
   Makes this place Paradise.
   (JUNO *and* CERES *whisper, and send* IRIS *on employment.*)
PROSPERO: Sweet, now, silence!
   Juno and Ceres whisper seriously,
   There's something else to do: hush, and be mute,
   Or else our spell is marr'd.
IRIS: You nymphs, call'd Naiades, of the windring brooks,
   With your sedg'd crowns, and ever-harmless looks,
   Leave your crisp channels, and on this green land
   Answer your summons: Juno does command.
   Come, temperate nymphs, and help to celebrate
   A contract of true love: be not too late.

(*Enter certain* NYMPHS.)
   You sun-burn'd sicklemen, of August weary,
   Come hither from the furrow, and be merry:
   Make holiday: your rye-straw hats put on,
   And these fresh nymphs encounter every one
   In country footing.

(*Enter certain* REAPERS, *properly habited: they join with the* NYMPHS *in a graceful dance; towards the end whereof* PROSPERO *starts suddenly, and speaks; after which, to a strange, hollow, and confused noise, they heavily vanish.*)
PROSPERO: (*Aside.*) I had forgot that foul conspiracy
   Of the beast Caliban, and his confederates
   Against my life: the minute of their plot
   Is almost come.—(*To the Spirits.*) Well done! avoid; no more!
FERDINAND: This is strange: your father's in some passion
   That works him strongly.
MIRANDA: Never till this day
   Saw I him touch'd with anger so distemper'd.
PROSPERO: You do look, my son, in a mov'd sort,
   As if you were dismay'd: be cheerful, sir:
   Our revels now are ended. These our actors,

As I foretold you, were all spirits and
Are melted into air, into thin air:
And, like the baseless fabric of this vision,
The cloud-capp'd towers, the gorgeous palaces,
The solemn temples, the great globe itself,
Yea, all which it inherit, shall dissolve
And, like this insubstantial pageant faded,
Leave not a rack behind. We are such stuff
As dreams are made on, and our little life
Is rounded with a sleep.—Sir, I am vex'd:
Bear with my weakness; my old brain is troubled.
Be not disturb'd with my infirmity.
If you be pleas'd, retire into my cell
And there repose: a turn or two I'll walk,
To still my beating mind.

FERDINAND *and* MIRANDA: We wish your peace. (*Exeunt.*)

PROSPERO: Come with a thought!—(*To them.*)
I thank thee: Ariel, come!

(*Enter* ARIEL.)

ARIEL: Thy thoughts I cleave to. What's thy pleasure?

PROSPERO: Spirit,
We must prepare to meet with Caliban.

ARIEL: Ay, my commander; when I presented
Ceres, I thought to have told thee of it; but I fear'd
Lest I might anger thee.

PROSPERO: Say again, where didst thou leave these varlets?

ARIEL: I told you, sir, they were red-hot with drinking;
So full of valour that they smote the air
For breathing in their faces; beat the ground
For kissing of their feet; yet always bending
Towards their project. Then I beat my tabor;
At which, like unback'd colts, they prick'd their ears,
Advanc'd their eyelids, lifted up their noses
As they smelt music: so I charm'd their ears
That, calf-like, they my lowing follow'd through
Tooth'd briers, sharp furzes, pricking goss and thorns,
Which enter'd their frail shins: at last I left them
I' the filthy-mantled pool beyond your cell,

There dancing up to the chins, that the foul lake
    O'erstunk their feet.
PROSPERO: This was well done, my bird.
    Thy shape invisible retain thou still:
    The trumpery in my house, go bring it hither,
    For stale to catch these thieves.
ARIEL: I go, I go. (*Exit.*)
PROSPERO: A devil, a born devil, on whose nature
    Nurture can never stick; on whom my pains,
    Humanely taken, are all lost, quite lost;
    And as with age his body uglier grows,
    So his mind cankers. I will plague them all,
    Even to roaring.

(*Re-enter* ARIEL, *loaden with glistering apparel, &c.*)
    Come, hang them on this line.

(PROSPERO *and* ARIEL *remain invisible. Enter* CALIBAN, STEPHANO, *and*
TRINCULO, *all wet.*)
CALIBAN: Pray you, tread softly, that the blind mole may not
    Hear a foot fall: we now are near his cell.
STEPHANO: Monster, your fairy, which you say is a harmless fairy, has done
    little better than played the Jack with us.
TRINCULO: Monster, I do smell all horse-piss; at which my nose is in great
    indignation.
STEPHANO: So is mine.—Do you hear, monster?
    If I should take a displeasure against you, look you,—
TRINCULO: Thou wert but a lost monster.
CALIBAN: Good my lord, give me thy favour still:
    Be patient, for the prize I'll bring thee to
    Shall hoodwink this mischance: therefore speak softly;
    All's hush'd as midnight yet.
TRINCULO: Ay, but to lose our bottles in the pool,—
STEPHANO: There is not only disgrace and dishonour in that, monster,
    but an infinite loss.
TRINCULO: That's more to me than my wetting: yet this is your harmless
    fairy, monster.
STEPHANO: I will fetch off my bottle, though I be o'er ears for my labour.
CALIBAN: Prithee, my king, be quiet. Seest thou here,

This is the mouth o' the cell: no noise, and enter.
Do that good mischief, which may make this island
Thine own for ever, and I, thy Caliban,
For aye thy foot-licker.

STEPHANO: Give me thy hand: I do begin to have bloody thoughts.

TRINCULO: O king Stephano! O peer! O worthy Stephano! look,
what a wardrobe here is for thee!

CALIBAN: Let it alone, thou fool; it is but trash.

TRINCULO: O, ho, monster! we know what belongs to a frippery.—
O king Stephano!

STEPHANO: Put off that gown, Trinculo; by this hand, I'll have that gown.

TRINCULO: Thy grace shall have it.

CALIBAN: The dropsy drown this fool! what do you mean
To dote thus on such luggage? Let's along,
And do the murder first: if he awake,
From toe to crown he'll fill our skins with pinches;
Make us strange stuff.

STEPHANO: Be you quiet, monster.—
Mistress line, is not this my jerkin?
Now is the jerkin under the line: now, jerkin, you are like to lose
your hair and prove a bald jerkin.

TRINCULO: Do, do: we steal by line and level, an't like your grace.

STEPHANO: I thank thee for that jest; here's a garment for't: wit shall not
go unrewarded while I am king of this country:
'Steal by line and level/ is an excellent pass of pate; there's another
garment for't.

TRINCULO: Monster, come, put some lime upon your fingers, and away
with the rest.

CALIBAN: I will have none on't: we shall lose our time,
And all be turned to barnacles, or to apes
With foreheads villanous low.

STEPHANO: Monster, lay-to your fingers: help to bear this away where
my hogshead of wine is, or I'll turn you out of my kingdom.
Go to; carry this.

TRINCULO: And this.

STEPHANO: Ay, and this. A noise of hunters heard.

(*Enter divers* SPIRITS, *in shape of hounds, and hunt them about;* PROSPERO *and* ARIEL
setting them on.)

PROSPERO: Hey, Mountain, hey!

ARIEL: Silver! there it goes, Silver!

PROSPERO: Fury, Fury! there, Tyrant, there! hark, hark!
(CALIBAN, STEPHANO, *and* TRINCULO *are driven out.*)
Go, charge my goblins that they grind their joints
With dry convulsions; shorten up their sinews
With aged cramps, and more pinch-spotted make them
Than pard, or cat o' mountain.

ARIEL: Hark! they roar.

PROSPERO: Let them be hunted soundly. At this hour
Lie at my mercy all mine enemies:
Shortly shall all my labours end, and thou
Shalt have the air at freedom: for a little,
Follow, and do me service. (*Exeunt.*)

ACT V.

Scene I. Before the Cell of Prospero.

Enter PROSPERO *in his magic robes; and* ARIEL.

PROSPERO: Now does my project gather to a head:
My charms crack not; my spirits obey, and time
Goes upright with his carriage. How's the day?

ARIEL: On the sixth hour; at which time, my lord,
You said our work should cease.

PROSPERO: I did say so,
When first I rais'd the tempest. Say, my spirit,
How fares the king and's followers?

ARIEL: Confin'd together
In the same fashion as you gave in charge;
Just as you left them: all prisoners, sir,
In the line-grove which weather-fends your cell;
They cannot budge till your release. The king,
His brother, and yours, abide all three distracted,
And the remainder mourning over them,
Brimful of sorrow and dismay; but chiefly
Him, that you term'd, sir, 'The good old lord Gonzalo:'
His tears run down his beard, like winter's drops
From eaves of reeds; your charm so strongly works them,

That if you now beheld them, your affections
Would become tender.
PROSPERO: Dost thou think so, spirit?
ARIEL: Mine would, sir, were I human.
PROSPERO: And mine shall.
Hast thou, which art but air, a touch, a feeling
Of their afflictions, and shall not myself,
One of their kind, that relish all as sharply,
Passion as they, be kindlier mov'd than thou art?
Though with their high wrongs I am struck to the quick,
Yet with my nobler reason 'gainst my fury
Do I take part: the rarer action is
In virtue than in vengeance: they being penitent,
The sole drift of my purpose doth extend
Not a frown further. Go, release them, Ariel.
My charms I'll break, their senses I'll restore,
And they shall be themselves.
ARIEL: I'll fetch them, sir. (*Exit.*)
PROSPERO: Ye elves of hills, brooks, standing lakes, and groves;
And ye, that on the sands with printless foot
Do chase the ebbing Neptune and do fly him
When he comes back; you demi-puppets, that
By moonshine do the green sour ringlets make
Whereof the ewe not bites; and you, whose pastime
Is to make midnight mushrooms; that rejoice
To hear the solemn curfew; by whose aid,—
Weak masters though ye be—I have bedimm'd
The noontide sun, call'd forth the mutinous' winds,
And 'twixt the green sea and the azur'd vault
Set roaring war: to the dread-ratthng thunder
Have I given fire and rifted Jove's stout oak
With his own bolt: the strong-bas'd promontory
Have I made shake; and by the spurs pluck'd up
The pine and cedar: graves at my command
Have wak'd their sleepers, op'd, and let them forth
By my so potent art. But this rough magic
I here abjure; and, when I have requir'd
Some heavenly music,—which even now I do,—
To work mine end upon their senses that

This airy charm is for, I'll break my staff,
Bury it certain fathoms in the earth,
And, deeper than did ever plummet sound,
I'll drown my book. (*Solemn music.*)

(*Re-enter* ARIEL: *after him,* ALONSO, *with a frantic gesture, attended by*
GONZALO; SEBASTIAN *and* ANTONIO *in like manner, attended by* ADRIAN
and FRANCISCO: *they all enter the circle which* PROSPERO *had made, and there
stand charmed; which* PROSPERO *observing, speaks.*)
A solemn air and the best comforter
To an unsettled fancy, cure thy brains,
Now useless, boil'd within thy skull! There stand,
For you are spell-stopp'd.
Holy Gonzalo, honourable man,
Mine eyes, even sociable to the show of thine,
Fall fellowly drops. The charm dissolves apace;
And as the morning steals upon the night,
Melting the darkness, so their rising senses
Begin to chase the ignorant fumes that mantle
Their clearer reason.—O good Gonzalo!
My true preserver, and a loyal sir
To him thou follow'st, I will pay thy graces
Home, both in word and deed.—Most cruelly
Didst thou, Alonso, use me and my daughter:
Thy brother was a furtherer in the act;—
Thou'rt pinch'd for't now, Sebastian.—Flesh and blood,
You, brother mine, that entertain'd ambition,
Expell'd remorse and nature; who, with Sebastian,—
Whose inward pinches therefore are most strong,—
Would here have kill'd your king; I do forgive thee,
Unnatural though thou art!—Their understanding
Begins to swell, and the approaching tide
Will shortly fill the reasonable shores
That now lie foul and muddy. Not one of them
That yet looks on me, or would know me.—
Ariel, fetch me the hat and rapier in my cell:—
(*Exit* ARIEL.)
I will disease me, and myself present,

As I was sometime Milan.—Quickly, spirit;
Thou shalt ere long be free.

(ARIEL *re-enters, singing, and helps to attire* PROSPERO.)
ARIEL: Where the bee sucks, there suck I:
    In a cowslip's bell I lie;
    There I couch when owls do cry.
    On the bat's back I do fly
    After summer merrily:
    Merrily, merrily shall I live now
    Under the blossom that hangs on the bough.
PROSPERO: Why, that's my dainty Ariel! I shall miss thee;
    But yet thou shalt have freedom;—so, so, so.—
    To the king's ship, invisible as thou art:
    There shalt thou find the mariners asleep
    Under the hatches; the master and the boatswain
    Being awake, enforce them to this place,
    And presently, I prithee.
ARIEL: I drink the air before me, and return
    Or e'er your pulse twice beat. (*Exit.*)
GONZALO: All torment, trouble, wonder, and amazement
    Inhabits here: some heavenly power guide us
    Out of this fearful country!
PROSPERO: Behold, sir king,
    The wronged Duke of Milan, Prospero.
    For more assurance that a living prince
    Does now speak to thee, I embrace thy body;
    And to thee and thy company I bid
    A hearty welcome.
ALONSO: Whe'r thou beest he or no,
    Or some enchanted trifle to abuse me,
    As late I have been, I not know: thy pulse
    Beats, as of flesh and blood; and, since I saw thee,
    Th' affliction of my mind amends, with which,
    I fear, a madness held me: this must crave,—
    An if this be at all—a most strange story.
    Thy dukedom I resign, and do entreat
    Thou pardon me my wrongs.—But how should Prospero
    Be living, and be here?

PROSPERO: First, noble friend,
Let me embrace thine age; whose honour cannot
Be measur'd, or confin'd.

GONZALO: Whether this be,
Or be not, I'll not swear.

PROSPERO: You do yet taste
Some subtilties o' the isle, that will not let you
Believe things certain.—Welcome! my friends all—
(*Aside to* SEBASTIAN *and* ANTONIO)
But you, my brace of lords, were I so minded,
I here could pluck his highness' frown upon you,
And justify you traitors; at this time
I will tell no tales.

SEBASTIAN: (*Aside.*) The devil speaks in him.

PROSPERO: No.
For you, most wicked sir, whom to call brother
Would even infect my mouth, I do forgive
Thy rankest fault; all of them; and require
My dukedom of thee, which, perforce, I know,
Thou must restore.

ALONSO: If thou beest Prospero,
Give us particulars of thy preservation;
How thou hast met us here, who three hours since
Were wrack'd upon this shore; where I have lost,—
How sharp the point of this remembrance is!—
My dear son Ferdinand.

PROSPERO: I am woe for't, sir.

ALONSO: Irreparable is the loss, and patience
Says it is past her cure.

PROSPERO: I rather think
You have not sought her help; of whose soft grace,
For the like loss I have her sovereign aid,
And rest myself content.

ALONSO: You the like loss!

PROSPERO: As great to me, as late; and, supportable
To make the dear loss, have I means much weaker
Than you may call to comfort you, for I
Have lost my daughter.

ALONSO: A daughter?
　　O heavens! that they were living both in Naples,
　　The king and queen there! that they were, I wish
　　Myself were mudded in that oozy bed
　　Where my son lies. When did you lose your daughter?
PROSPERO: In this last tempest. I perceive, these lords
　　At this encounter do so much admire
　　That they devour their reason, and scarce think
　　Their eyes do offices of truth, their words
　　Are natural breath: but, howsoe'er you have
　　Been justled from your senses, know for certain
　　That I am Prospero and that very duke
　　Which was thrust forth of Milan; who most strangely
　　Upon this shore, where you were wrack'd, was landed,
　　To be the lord on't. No more yet of this;
　　For 'tis a chronicle of day by day,
　　Not a relation for a breakfast nor
　　Befitting this first meeting. Welcome, sir;
　　This cell's my court: here have I few attendants
　　And subjects none abroad: pray you, look in.
　　My dukedom since you have given me again,
　　I will requite you with as good a thing;
　　At least bring forth a wonder, to content ye
　　As much as me my dukedom,
　　(*The entrance of the Cell opens, and discovers*
　　FERDINAND *and* MIRANDA *playing at chess.*)
MIRANDA: Sweet lord, you play me false.
FERDINAND: No, my dearest love,
　　I would not for the world.
MIRANDA: Yes, for a score of kingdoms you should wrangle,
　　And I would call it fair play.
ALONSO: If this prove
　　A vision of the island, one dear son
　　Shall I twice lose.
SEBASTIAN: A most high miracle!
FERDINAND: Though the seas threaten, they are merciful:
　　I have curs'd them without cause.
　　(*Kneels to* ALONSO.)

ALONSO: Now, all the blessings
    Of a glad father compass thee about!
    Arise, and say how thou cam'st here.
MIRANDA: O, wonder!
    How many goodly creatures are there here!
    How beauteous mankind is! O brave new world,
    That has such people in't!
PROSPERO: 'Tis new to thee.
ALONSO: What is this maid, with whom thou wast at play?
    Your eld'st acquaintance cannot be three hours:
    Is she the goddess that hath sever'd us,
    And brought us thus together?
FERDINAND: Sir, she is mortal;
    But by immortal Providence she's mine;
    I chose her when I could not ask my father
    For his advice, nor thought I had one. She
    Is daughter to this famous Duke of Milan,
    Of whom so often I have heard renown,
    But never saw before; of whom I have
    Received a second life; and second father
    This lady makes him to me.
ALONSO: I am hers:
    But O! how oddly will it sound that I
    Must ask my child forgiveness!
PROSPERO: There, sir, stop:
    Let us not burden our remembrances
    With a heaviness that's gone.
GONZALO: I have inly wept,
    Or should have spoke ere this. Look down, you gods,
    And on this couple drop a blessed crown;
    For it is you that have chalk'd forth the way
    Which brought us hither!
ALONSO: I say, Amen, Gonzalo!
GONZALO: Was Milan thrust from Milan, that his issue
    Should become kings of Naples? O, rejoice
    Beyond a common joy, and set it down
    With gold on lasting pillars. In one voyage
    Did Claribel her husband find at Tunis,
    And Ferdinand, her brother, found a wife

Where he himself was lost; Prospero his dukedom
In a poor isle; and all of us ourselves,
When no man was his own.

ALONSO: (*To* FERDINAND *and* MIRANDA.) Give me your hands:
Let grief and sorrow still embrace his heart
That doth not wish you joy!

GONZALO: Be it so: Amen!

(*Re-enter* ARIEL, *with the* MASTER *and* BOATSWAIN *amazedly following.*)
O look, sir! look, sir! here are more of us.
I prophesied, if a gallows were on land,
This fellow could not drown.—Now, blasphemy,
That swear'st grace o'erboard, not an oath on shore?
Hast thou no mouth by land? What is the news?

BOATSWAIN: The best news is that we have safely found
Our king and company: the next, our ship,—
Which but three glasses since we gave out split,—
Is tight and yare and bravely rigg'd as when
We first put out to sea.

ARIEL: (*Aside to* PROSPERO.) Sir, all this service
Have I done since I went.

PROSPERO: (*Aside to* ARIEL.) My tricksy spirit!

ALONSO: These are not natural events; they strengthen
From strange to stranger.—Say, how came you hither?

BOATSWAIN: If I did think, sir, I were well awake,
I'd strive to tell you. We were dead of sleep,
And,—how we know not,—all clapped under hatches,
Where, but even now, with strange and several noises
Of roaring, shrieking, howling, jingling chains,
And mo diversity of sounds, all horrible,
We were awak'd; straightway, at liberty:
Where we, in all her trim, freshly beheld
Our royal, good, and gallant ship; our master
Capering to eye her: on a trice, so please you,
Even in a dream, were we divided from them,
And were brought moping hither.

ARIEL: (*Aside to* PROSPERO.) Was't well done?

PROSPERO: (*Aside to* ARIEL.) Bravely, my diligence!
Thou shalt be free.

ALONSO: This is as strange a maze as e'er men trod;
    And there is in this business more than nature
    Was ever conduct of: some oracle
    Must rectify our knowledge.
PROSPERO: Sir, my liege,
    Do not infest your mind with beating on
    The strangeness of this business: at pick'd leisure
    Which shall be shortly, single I'll resolve you,—
    Which to you shall seem probable,—of every
    These happen'd accidents; till when, be cheerful,
    And think of each thing well.—(*Aside to* ARIEL.)
    Come hither, spirit;
    Set Caliban and his companions free;
    Untie the spell. (*Exit* ARIEL.) How fares my gracious sir?
    There are yet missing of your company
    Some few odd lads that you remember not.

(*Re-enter* ARIEL, *driving in* CALIBAN, STEPHANO, *and* TRINCULO, *in their stolen apparel.*)
STEPHANO: Every man shift for all the rest, and let no man take care for himself, for
        all is but fortune.—Coragio! bully-monster, Coragio!
TRINCULO: If these be true spies which I wear in my head, here's a goodly sight.
CALIBAN: O Setebos! these be brave spirits, indeed.
    How fine my master is! I am afraid
    He will chastise me.
SEBASTIAN: Ha, ha!
    What things are these, my lord Antonio?
    Will money buy them?
ANTONIO: Very like; one of them
    Is a plain fish, and, no doubt, marketable.
PROSPERO: Mark but the badges of these men, my lords,
    Then say, if they be true.—This mis-shapen knave,—
    His mother was a witch; and one so strong
    That could control the moon, make flows and ebbs,
    And deal in her command without her power.
    These three have robb'd me; and this demi-devil,—
    For he's a bastard one,—had plotted with them
    To take my life: two of these fellows you

Must know and own; this thing of darkness I
Acknowledge mine.

CALIBAN: I shall be pinch'd to death.

ALONSO: Is not this Stephano, my drunken butler?

SEBASTIAN: He is drunk now: where had he wine?

ALONSO: And Trinculo is reeling-ripe: where should they
Find this grand liquor that hath gilded them?
How cam'st thou in this pickle?

TRINCULO: I have been in such a pickle since I saw you last that,
I fear me, will never out of my bones; I shall not fear fly-blowing.

SEBASTIAN: Why, how now, Stephano!

STEPHANO: O! touch me not: I am not Stephano, but a cramp.

PROSPERO: You'd be king of the isle, sirrah?

STEPHANO: I should have been a sore one then

ALONSO: This is a strange thing as e'er I look'd on.
    (*Pointing to* CALIBAN.)

PROSPERO: He is as disproportion'd in his manners
As in his shape,—Go, sirrah, to my cell;
Take with you your companions: as you look
To have my pardon, trim it handsomely.

CALIBAN: Ay, that I will; and I'll be wise hereafter,
And seek for grace. What a thrice-double ass
Was I, to take this drunkard for a god,
And worship this dull fool!

PROSPERO: Go to; away!

ALONSO: Hence, and bestow your luggage where you found it.

SEBASTIAN: Or stole it, rather.
    (*Exeunt* CALIBAN, STEPHANO, *and* TRINCULO.

PROSPERO: Sir, I invite your highness and your train
To my poor cell, where you shall take your rest
For this one night; which—part of it—I'll waste
With such discourse as, I not doubt, shall make it
Go quick away; the story of my life
And the particular accidents gone by
Since I came to this isle; and in the morn
I'll bring you to your ship, and so to Naples,
Where I have hope to see the nuptial
Of these our dear-beloved solemniz'd;

And thence retire me to my Milan, where
Every third thought shall be my grave.
ALONSO: I long
To hear the story of your life, which must
Take the ear strangely.
PROSPERO: I'll deliver all;
And promise you calm seas, auspicious gales
And sail so expeditious that shall catch
Your royal fleet far off.—(*Aside to* ARIEL.) My Ariel, chick,
That is thy charge: then to the elements
Be free, and fare thou well!—Please you, draw near. (*Exeunt.*)

EPILOGUE.

(*Spoken by* PROSPERO.)
Now my charms are all o'erthrown,
And what strength I have's mine own;
Which is most faint: now, 'tis true,
I must be here confin'd by you,
Or sent to Naples. Let me not,
Since I have my dukedom got
And pardon'd the deceiver, dwell
In this bare island by your spell;
But release me from my bands
With the help of your good hands.
Gentle breath of yours my sails
Must fill, or else my project fails,
Which was to please. Now I want
Spirits to enforce, art to enchant;
And my ending is despair,
Unless I be reliev'd by prayer,
Which pierces so that it assaults
Mercy itself and frees all faults.
As you from crimes would pardon'd be,
Let your indulgence set me free.

TARTUFFE

By Molière
Translated by Richard Wilbur

CHARACTERS

MADAME PERNELLE, *Orgon's mother*

ORGON, *Elmire's husband*

ELMIRE, *Orgon's wife*

DAMIS, *Orgon's son, Elmire's stepson*

MARIANE, *Orgon's daughter, Elmire's stepdaughter, in love with Valère*

VALÈRE, *in love with Mariane*

CLÉANTE, *Orgon's brother-in-law*

TARTUFFE, *a hypocrite*

DORINE, *Mariane's lady's-maid*

M. LOYAL, *a bailiff*

A POLICE OFFICER

FLIPOTE, *Madame Pernelle's maid*

THE SCENE THROUGHOUT: *Orgon's house in Paris*

Scene I

MADAME PERNELLE *and* FLIPOTE, *her maid,* ELMIRE, MARIANE, DORINE, DAMIS, CLÉANTE

MADAME PERNELLE: Come, come, Flipote; it's time I left this place.

ELMIRE: I can't keep up, you walk at such a pace.

MADAME PERNELLE: Don't trouble, child; no need to show me out.
　　It's not your manners I'm concerned about.

ELMIRE: We merely pay you the respect we owe.
　　But, Mother, why this hurry? Must you go?

MADAME PERNELLE: I must. This house appals me. No one in it
　　Will pay attention for a single minute.
　　Children, I take my leave much vexed in spirit.
　　I offer good advice, but you won't hear it.
　　You all break in and chatter on and on.
　　It's like a madhouse with the keeper gone.

DORINE: If …

MADAME PERNELLE: Girl, you talk too much, and I'm afraid
　　You're far too saucy for a lady's-maid.
　　You push in everywhere and have your say.

DAMIS: But …

MADAME PERNELLE: You, boy, grow more foolish every day.
　　To think my grandson should be such a dunce!
　　I've said a hundred times, if I've said it once,
　　That if you keep the course on which you've started,
　　You'll leave your worthy father broken-hearted.

MARIANE: I think …

MADAME PERNELLE: And you, his sister, seem so pure,
　　So shy, so innocent, and so demure.
　　But you know what they say about still waters.
　　I pity parents with secretive daughters.

ELMIRE: Now, Mother …

MADAME PERNELLE: And as for you, child, let me add
　　That your behavior is extremely bad,
　　And a poor example for these children, too.
　　Their dear, dead mother did far better than you.
　　You're much too free with money, and I'm distressed
　　To see you so elaborately dressed.

When it's one's husband that one aims to please,
One has no need of costly fripperies.
CLÉANTE: Oh, Madam, really ...
MADAME PERNELLE: You are her brother, Sir,
    And I respect and love you; yet if I were
    My son, this lady's good and pious spouse,
    I wouldn't make you welcome in my house.
    You're full of worldly counsels which, I fear,
    Aren't suitable for decent folk to hear.
    I've spoken bluntly, Sir; but it behooves us
    Not to mince words when righteous fervor moves us.
DAMIS: Your man Tartuffe is full of holy speeches ...
MADAME PERNELLE: And practises precisely what he preaches.
    He's a fine man, and should be listened to.
    I will not hear him mocked by fools like you.
DAMIS: Good God! Do you expect me to submit
    To the tyranny of that carping hypocrite?
    Must we forgo all joys and satisfactions
    Because that bigot censures all our actions?
DORINE: To hear him talk—and he talks all the time—
    There's nothing one can do that's not a crime.
    He rails at everything, your dear Tartuffe.
MADAME PERNELLE: Whatever he reproves deserves reproof.
    He's out to save your souls, and all of you
    Must love him, as my son would have you do.
DAMIS: Ah no, Grandmother, I could never take
    To such a rascal, even for my father's sake.
    That's how I feel, and I shall not dissemble.
    His every action makes me seethe and tremble
    With helpless anger, and I have no doubt
    That he and I will shortly have it out.
DORINE: Surely it is a shame and a disgrace
    To see this man usurp the master's place—
    To see this beggar who, when first he came,
    Had not a shoe or shoestring to his name
    So far forget himself that he behaves
    As if the house were his, and we his slaves.
MADAME PERNELLE: Well, mark my words, your souls would fare far better
    If you obeyed his precepts to the letter.

DORINE: You see him as a saint. I'm far less awed;
 In fact, I see right through him. He's a fraud.
MADAME PERNELLE: Nonsense!
DORINE: His man Laurent's the same, or worse;
 I'd not trust either with a penny purse.
MADAME PERNELLE: I can't say what his servant's morals may be;
 His own great goodness I can guarantee.
 You all regard him with distaste and fear
 Because he tells you what you're loath to hear,
 Condemns your sins, points out your moral flaws,
 And humbly strives to further Heaven's cause.
DORINE: If sin is all that bothers him, why is it
 He's so upset when folk drop in to visit?
 Is Heaven so outraged by a social call
 That he must prophesy against us all?
 I'll tell you what I think: if you ask me,
 He's jealous of my mistress' company.
MADAME PERNELLE: Rubbish! (*To* ELMIRE.)
 He's not alone, child, in complaining
 Of all of your promiscuous entertaining.
 Why, the whole neighborhood's upset, I know,
 By all these carriages that come and go,
 With crowds of guests parading in and out
 And noisy servants loitering about.
 In all of this, I'm sure there's nothing vicious;
 But why give people cause to be suspicious?
CLÉANTE: They need no cause; they'll talk in any case.
 Madam, this world would be a joyless place
 If, fearing what malicious tongues might say,
 We locked our doors and turned our friends away.
 And even if one did so dreary a thing,
 D'you think those tongues would cease their chattering?
 One can't fight slander; it's a losing battle;
 Let us instead ignore their tittle-tattle.
 Let's strive to live by conscience' clear decrees,
 And let the gossips gossip as they please.
DORINE: If there is talk against us, I know the source:
 It's Daphne and her little husband, of course.
 Those who have greatest cause for guilt and shame

Are quickest to besmirch a neighbor's name.
When there's a chance for libel, they never miss it;
When something can be made to seem illicit
They're off at once to spread the joyous news,
Adding to fact what fantasies they choose.
By talking up their neighbor's indiscretions
They seek to camouflage their own transgressions,
Hoping that others' innocent affairs
Will lend a hue of innocence to theirs,
Or that their own black guilt will come to seem
Part of a general shady color-scheme.

MADAME PERNELLE: All that is quite irrelevant. I doubt
That anyone's more virtuous and devout
Than dear Orante; and I'm informed that she
Condemns your mode of life most vehemently.

DORINE: Oh, yes, she's strict, devout, and has no taint
Of worldliness; in short, she seems a saint.
But it was time which taught her that disguise;
She's thus because she can't be otherwise.
So long as her attractions could enthrall,
She flounced and flirted and enjoyed it all,
But now that they're no longer what they were
She quits a world which fast is quitting her,
And wears a veil of virtue to conceal
Her bankrupt beauty and her lost appeal.
That's what becomes of old coquettes today:
Distressed when all their lovers fall away,
They see no recourse but to play the prude,
And so confer a style on solitude.
Thereafter, they're severe with everyone,
Condemning all our actions, pardoning none,
And claiming to be pure, austere, and zealous
When, if the truth were known, they're merely jealous,
And cannot bear to see another know
The pleasures time has forced them to forgo.

MADAME PERNELLE: (*Initially to* ELMIRE.)
That sort of talk is what you like to hear;
Therefore you'd have us all keep still, my dear,
While Madam rattles on the livelong day.

Nevertheless, I mean to have my say.
I tell you that you're blest to have Tartuffe
Dwelling, as my son's guest, beneath this roof;
That Heaven has sent him to forestall its wrath
By leading you, once more, to the true path;
That all he reprehends is reprehensible,
And that you'd better heed him, and be sensible.
These visits, balls, and parties in which you revel
Are nothing but inventions of the Devil.
One never hears a word that's edifying:
Nothing but chaff and foolishness and lying,
As well as vicious gossip in which one's neighbor
Is cut to bits with épée, foil, and saber.
People of sense are driven half-insane
At such affairs, where noise and folly reign
And reputations perish thick and fast.
As a wise preacher said on Sunday last,
Parties are Towers of Babylon, because
The guests all babble on with never a pause;
And then he told a story which, I think ...
(*To* CLÉANTE.)
I heard that laugh, Sir, and I saw that wink!
Go find your silly friends and laugh some more!
Enough; I'm going; don't show me to the door.
I leave this household much dismayed and vexed;
I cannot say when I shall see you next.
(*Slapping* FLIPOTE.)
Wake up, don't stand there gaping into space!
I'll slap some sense into that stupid face.
Move, move, you slut.

Scene II
CLÉANTE, DORINE

CLÉANTE: I think I'll stay behind;
    I want no further pieces of her mind.
    How that old lady ...
DORINE: Oh, what wouldn't she say
    If she could hear you speak of her that way!

She'd thank you for the lady, but I'm sure
She'd find the old a little premature.
CLÉANTE: My, what a scene she made, and what a din!
And how this man Tartuffe has taken her in!
DORINE: Yes, but her son is even worse deceived;
His folly must be seen to be believed.
In the late troubles, he played an able part
And served his king with wise and loyal heart,
But he's quite lost his senses since he fell
Beneath Tartuffe's infatuating spell.
He calls him brother, and loves him as his life,
Preferring him to mother, child, or wife.
In him and him alone will he confide;
He's made him his confessor and his guide;
He pets and pampers him with love more tender
Than any pretty mistress could engender,
Gives him the place of honor when they dine,
Delights to see him gorging like a swine,
Stuffs him with dainties till his guts distend,
And when he belches, cries "God bless you, friend!"
In short, he's mad; he worships him; he dotes;
His deeds he marvels at, his words he quotes,
Thinking each act a miracle, each word
Oracular as those that Moses heard.
Tartuffe, much pleased to find so easy a victim,
Has in a hundred ways beguiled and tricked him,
Milked him of money, and with his permission
Established here a sort of Inquisition.
Even Laurent, his lackey, dares to give
Us arrogant advice on how to live;
He sermonizes us in thundering tones
And confiscates our ribbons and colognes.
Last week he tore a kerchief into pieces
Because he found it pressed in a Life of Jesus:
He said it was a sin to juxtapose
Unholy vanities and holy prose.

Scene III

ELMIRE, MARIANE, DAMIS, CLÉANTE, DORINE

ELMIRE: (*To* CLÉANTE.) You did well not to follow; she stood in the door
    And said verbatim all she'd said before.
    I saw my husband coming. I think I'd best
    Go upstairs now, and take a little rest.
CLÉANTE: I'll wait and greet him here; then I must go.
    I've really only time to say hello.
DAMIS: Sound him about my sister's wedding, please.
    I think Tartuffe's against it, and that he's
    Been urging Father to withdraw his blessing.
    As you well know, I'd find that most distressing.
    Unless my sister and Valère can marry,
    My hopes to wed his sister will miscarry,
    And I'm determined …
DORINE: He's coming.

Scene IV

ORGON, CLÉANTE, DORINE

ORGON: Ah, Brother, good-day.
CLÉANTE: Well, welcome back. I'm sorry I can't stay.
    How was the country? Blooming, I trust, and green?
ORGON: Excuse me, Brother; just one moment.
    (*To* DORINE.)
    Dorine …
    (*To* CLÉANTE.)
    To put my mind at rest, I always learn
    The household news the moment I return.
    (*To* DORINE.)
    Has all been well, these two days I've been gone?
    How are the family? What's been going on?
DORINE: Your wife, two days ago, had a bad fever,
    And a fierce headache which refused to leave her.
ORGON: Ah. And Tartuffe?
DORINE: Tartuffe? Why, he's round and red,
    Bursting with health, and excellently fed.
ORGON: Poor fellow!

DORINE: That night, the mistress was unable
    To take a single bite at the dinner-table.
    Her headache-pains, she said, were simply hellish.
ORGON: Ah. And Tartuffe?
DORINE: He ate his meal with relish,
    And zealously devoured in her presence
    A leg of mutton and a brace of pheasants.
ORGON: Poor fellow!
DORINE: Well, the pains continued strong,
    And so she tossed and tossed the whole night long,
    Now icy-cold, now burning like a flame.
    We sat beside her bed till morning came.
ORGON: Ah. And Tartuffe?
DORINE: Why, having eaten, he rose
    And sought his room, already in a doze,
    Got into his warm bed, and snored away
    In perfect peace until the break of day.
ORGON: Poor fellow!
DORINE: After much ado, we talked her
    Into dispatching someone for the doctor.
    He bled her, and the fever quickly fell.
ORGON: Ah. And Tartuffe?
DORINE: He bore it very well.
    To keep his cheerfulness at any cost,
    And make up for the blood Madame had lost,
    He drank, at lunch, four beakers full of port.
ORGON: Poor fellow!
DORINE: Both are doing well, in short.
    I'll go and tell Madame that you've expressed
    Keen sympathy and anxious interest.

Scene V

ORGON, CLÉANTE

CLÉANTE: That girl was laughing in your face, and though
    I've no wish to offend you, even so
    I'm bound to say that she had some excuse.
    How can you possibly be such a goose?
    Are you so dazed by this man's hocus-pocus

That all the world, save him, is out of focus?
You've given him clothing, shelter, food, and care;
Why must you also ...
ORGON: Brother, stop right there.
You do not know the man of whom you speak.
CLÉANTE: I grant you that. But my judgment's not so weak
That I can't tell, by his effect on others ...
ORGON: Ah, when you meet him, you two will be like brothers!
There's been no loftier soul since time began.
He is a man who ... a man who ... an excellent man.
To keep his precepts is to be reborn,
And view this dunghill of a world with scorn.
Yes, thanks to him I'm a changed man indeed.
Under his tutelage my soul's been freed
From earthly loves, and every human tie:
My mother, children, brother, and wife could die,
And I'd not feel a single moment's pain.
CLÉANTE: That's a fine sentiment, Brother; most humane.
ORGON: Oh, had you seen Tartuffe as I first knew him,
Your heart, like mine, would have surrendered to him.
He used to come into our church each day
And humbly kneel nearby, and start to pray.
He'd draw the eyes of everybody there
By the deep fervor of his heartfelt prayer;
He'd sigh and weep, and sometimes with a sound
Of rapture he would bend and kiss the ground;
And when I rose to go, he'd run before
To offer me holy-water at the door.
His serving-man, no less devout than he,
Informed me of his master's poverty;
I gave him gifts, but in his humbleness
He'd beg me every time to give him less.
"Oh, that's too much," he'd cry, "too much by twice!
I don't deserve it. The half, Sir, would suffice."
And when I wouldn't take it back, he'd share
Half of it with the poor, right then and there.
At length, Heaven prompted me to take him in
To dwell with us, and free our souls from sin.
He guides our lives, and to protect my honor

Stays by my wife, and keeps an eye upon her;
He tells me whom she sees, and all she does,
And seems more jealous than I ever was!
And how austere he is! Why, he can detect
A mortal sin where you would least suspect;
In smallest trifles, he's extremely strict.
Last week, his conscience was severely pricked
Because, while praying, he had caught a flea
And killed it, so he felt, too wrathfully.

CLÉANTE: Good God, man! Have you lost your common sense—
Or is this all some joke at my expense?
How can you stand there and in all sobriety …

ORGON: Brother, your language savors of impiety.
Too much free-thinking's made your faith unsteady,
And as I've warned you many times already,
'Twill get you into trouble before you're through.

CLÉANTE: So I've been told before by dupes like you:
Being blind, you'd have all others blind as well;
The clear-eyed man you call an infidel,
And he who sees through humbug and pretense
Is charged, by you, with want of reverence.
Spare me your warnings, Brother; I have no fear
Of speaking out, for you and Heaven to hear,
Against affected zeal and pious knavery.
There's true and false in piety, as in bravery,
And just as those whose courage shines the most
In battle, are the least inclined to boast,
So those whose hearts are truly pure and lowly
Don't make a flashy show of being holy.
There's a vast difference, so it seems to me,
Between true piety and hypocrisy:
How do you fail to see it, may I ask?
Is not a face quite different from a mask?
Cannot sincerity and cunning art,
Reality and semblance, be told apart?
Are scarecrows just like men, and do you hold
That a false coin is just as good as gold?
Ah, Brother, man's a strangely fashioned creature
Who seldom is content to follow Nature,

But recklessly pursues his inclination
Beyond the narrow bounds of moderation,
And often, by transgressing Reason's laws,
Perverts a lofty aim or noble cause.
A passing observation, but it applies.

ORGON: I see, dear Brother, that you're profoundly wise;
You harbor all the insight of the age.
You are our one clear mind, our only sage,
The era's oracle, it's Cato too,
And all mankind are fools compared to you.

CLÉANTE: Brother, I don't pretend to be a sage,
Nor have I all the wisdom of the age.
There's just one insight I would dare to claim:
I know that true and false are not the same;
And just as there is nothing I more revere
Than a soul whose faith is steadfast and sincere,
Nothing that I more cherish and admire
Than honest zeal and true religious fire,
So there is nothing that I find more base
Than specious piety's dishonest face—
Than these bold mountebanks, these histrios
Whose impious mummeries and hollow shows
Exploit our love of Heaven, and make a jest
Of all that men think holiest and best;
These calculating souls who offer prayers
Not to their Maker, but as public wares,
And seek to buy respect and reputation
With lifted eyes and sighs of exaltation;
These charlatans, I say, whose pilgrim souls
Proceed, by way of Heaven, toward earthly goals,
Who weep and pray and swindle and extort,
Who preach the monkish life, but haunt the court,
Who make their zeal the partner of their vice—
Such men are vengeful, sly, and cold as ice,
And when there is an enemy to defame
They cloak their spite in fair religion's name,
Their private spleen and malice being made
To seem a high and virtuous crusade,
Until, to mankind's reverent applause,

They crucify their foe in Heaven's cause.
Such knaves are all too common; yet, for the wise,
True piety isn't hard to recognize,
And, happily, these present times provide us
With bright examples to instruct and guide us.
Consider Ariston and Périandre;
Look at Oronte, Alcidamas, Clitandre;
Their virtue is acknowledged; who could doubt it?
But you won't hear them beat the drum about it.
They're never ostentatious, never vain,
And their religion's moderate and humane;
It's not their way to criticize and chide:
They think censoriousness a mark of pride,
And therefore, letting others preach and rave,
They show, by deeds, how Christians should behave.
They think no evil of their fellow man,
But judge of him as kindly as they can.
They don't intrigue and wangle and conspire;
To lead a good life is their one desire;
The sinner wakes no rancorous hate in them;
It is the sin alone which they condemn;
Nor do they try to show a fiercer zeal
For Heaven's cause than Heaven itself could feel.
These men I honor, these men I advocate
As models for us all to emulate.
Your man is not their sort at all, I fear:
And, while your praise of him is quite sincere,
I think that you've been dreadfully deluded.
ORGON: Now then, dear Brother, is your speech concluded?
CLÉANTE: Why, yes.
ORGON: Your servant, Sir.

(*He turns to go.*)

CLÉANTE: No, Brother; wait.
There's one more matter. You agreed of late
That young Valère might have your daughter's hand.
ORGON: I did.
CLÉANTE: And set the date, I understand.
ORGON: Quite so.
CLÉANTE: You've now postponed it; is that true?

ORGO::N: No doubt.

CLÉANTE: The match no longer pleases you?

ORGON: Who knows?

CLÉANTE: D'you mean to go back on your word?

ORGON: I won't say that.

CLÉANTE: Has anything occurred
    Which might entitle you to break your pledge?

ORGON: Perhaps.

CLÉANTE: Why must you hem, and haw, and hedge?
    The boy asked me to sound you in this affair …

ORGON: It's been a pleasure.

CLÉANTE: But what shall I tell Valère?

ORGON: Whatever you like.

CLÉANTE: But what have you decided?
    What are your plans?

ORGON: I plan, Sir, to be guided
    By Heaven's will.

CLÉANTE: Come, Brother, don't talk rot.
    You've given Valère your word; will you keep it, or not?

ORGON: Good day.

CLÉANTE: This looks like poor Valère's undoing;
    I'll go and warn him that there's trouble brewing.

ACT II

Scene I

ORGON, MARIANE

ORGON: Mariane

MARIANE: Yes, Father?

ORGON: A word with you; come here.

MARIANE: What are you looking for?

ORGON: (*Peering into a small closet*)
    Eavesdroppers, dear.
    I'm making sure we shan't be overheard.
    Someone in there could catch our every word.
    Ah, good, we're safe. Now, Mariane, my child,
    You're a sweet girl who's tractable and mild,
    Whom I hold dear, and think most highly of.

MARIANE: I'm deeply grateful, Father, for your love.

ORGON: That's well said, Daughter; and you can repay me
    If, in all things, you'll cheerfully obey me.

MARIANE: To please you, Sir, is what delights me best.

ORGON: Good, good. Now, what d'you think of Tartuffe, our guest?

MARIANE: I, Sir?

ORGON: Yes. Weigh your answer; think it through.

MARIANE: Oh, dear. I'll say whatever you wish me to.

ORGON: That's wisely said, my Daughter. Say of him, then,
    That he's the very worthiest of men,
    And that you're fond of him, and would rejoice
    In being his wife, if that should be my choice. Well?

MARIANE: What?

ORGON: What's that?

MARIANE: I ...

ORGON: Well?

MARIANE: Forgive me, pray.

ORGON: Did you not hear me?

MARIANE: Of whom, Sir, must I say
    That I am fond of him, and would rejoice
    In being his wife, if that should be your choice?

ORGON: Why, of Tartuffe.

MARIANE: But, Father, that's false, you know.
    Why would you have me say what isn't so?

ORGON: Because I am resolved it shall be true.
    That it's my wish should be enough for you.

MARIANE: You can't mean, Father ...

ORGON: Yes, Tartuffe shall be
    Allied by marriage to this family,
    And he's to be your husband, is that clear?
    It's a father's privilege ...

Scene II

DORINE, ORGON, MARIANE

ORGON: (*To* DORINE.) What are you doing in here?
    Is curiosity so fierce a passion
    With you, that you must eavesdrop in this fashion?

DORINE: There's lately been a rumor going about—

Based on some hunch or chance remark, no doubt—
That you mean Mariane to wed Tartuffe.
I've laughed it off, of course, as just a spoof.

ORGON: You find it so incredible?

DORINE: Yes, I do.
I won't accept that story, even from you.

ORGON: Well, you'll believe it when the thing is done.

DORINE: Yes, yes, of course. Go on and have your fun.

ORGON: I've never been more serious in my life.

DORINE: Ha!

ORGON: Daughter, I mean it; you're to be his wife.

DORINE: No, don't believe your father; it's all a hoax.

ORGON: See here, young woman ...

DORINE: Come, Sir, no more jokes;
You can't fool us.

ORGON: How dare you talk that way?

DORINE: All right, then: we believe you, sad to say.
But how a man like you, who looks so wise
And wears a moustache of such splendid size,
Can be so foolish as to ...

ORGON: Silence, please!
My girl, you take too many liberties.
I'm master here, as you must not forget.

DORINE: Do let's discuss this calmly; don't be upset.
You can't be serious, Sir, about this plan.
What should that bigot want with Mariane?
Praying and fasting ought to keep him busy.
And then, in terms of wealth and rank, what is he?
Why should a man of property like you
Pick out a beggar son-in-law?

ORGON: That will do.
Speak of his poverty with reverence.
His is a pure and saintly indigence
Which far transcends all worldly pride and pelf.
He lost his fortune, as he says himself,
Because he cared for Heaven alone, and so
Was careless of his interests here below
I mean to get him out of his present straits
And help him to recover his estates—

Which, in his part of the world, have no small fame.
Poor though he is, he's a gentleman just the same.
DORINE: Yes, so he tells us; and, Sir, it seems to me
Such pride goes very ill with piety
A man whose spirit spurns this dungy earth
Ought not to brag of lands and noble birth;
Such worldly arrogance will hardly square
With meek devotion and the life of prayer.
... But this approach, I see, has drawn a blank;
Let's speak, then, of his person, not his rank.
Doesn't it seem to you a trifle grim
To give a girl like her to a man like him?
When two are so ill-suited, can't you see
What the sad consequence is bound to be?
A young girl's virtue is imperilled, Sir,
When such a marriage is imposed on her;
For if one's bridegroom isn't to one's taste,
It's hardly an inducement to be chaste,
And many a man with horns upon his brow
Has made his wife the thing that she is now.
It's hard to be a faithful wife, in short,
To certain husbands of a certain sort,
And he who gives his daughter to a man she hates
Must answer for her sins at Heaven's gates.
Think, Sir, before you play so risky a role.
ORGON: This servant-girl presumes to save my soul!
DORINE: You would do well to ponder what I've said.
ORGON: Daughter, we'll disregard this dunderhead.
Just trust your father's judgment. Oh, I'm aware
That I once promised you to young Valère;
But now I hear he gambles, which greatly shocks me;
What's more, I've doubts about his orthodoxy
His visits to church, I note, are very few.
DORINE: Would you have him go at the same hours as you,
And kneel nearby, to be sure of being seen?
ORGON: I can dispense with such remarks, Dorine.
(*To* MARIANE.)
Tartuffe, however, is sure of Heaven's blessing,
And that's the only treasure worth possessing.

This match will bring you joys beyond all measure;
Your cup will overflow with every pleasure;
You two will interchange your faithful loves
Like two sweet cherubs, or two turtle-doves.
No harsh word shall be heard, no frown be seen,
And he shall make you happy as a queen.

DORINE: And she'll make him a cuckold, just wait and see.

ORGON: What language!

DORINE: Oh, he's a man of destiny;
He's made for horns, and what the stars demand
Your daughter's virtue surely can't withstand.

ORGON: Don't interrupt me further. Why can't you learn
That certain things are none of your concern?

DORINE: It's for your own sake that I interfere.

(*She repeatedly interrupts* ORGON *just as he is turning to speak to his daughter.*)

ORGON: Most kind of you. Now, hold your tongue, d'you hear?

DORINE: If I didn't love you ...

ORGON: Spare me your affection.

DORINE: I'll love you, Sir, in spite of your objection.

ORGON: Blast!

DORINE: I can't bear, Sir, for your honor's sake,
To let you make this ludicrous mistake.

ORGON: You mean to go on talking?

DORINE: If I didn't protest
This sinful marriage, my conscience couldn't rest.

ORGON: If you don't hold your tongue, you little shrew ...

DORINE: What, lost your temper? A pious man like you?

ORGON: Yes! Yes! You talk and talk. I'm maddened by it.
Once and for all, I tell you to be quiet.

DORINE: Well, I'll be quiet. But I'll be thinking hard.

ORGON: Think all you like, but you had better guard
That saucy tongue of yours, or I'll ...
(*Turning back to* MARIANE.)
Now, child,
I've weighed this matter fully.

DORINE: (*Aside.*) It drives me wild
That I can't speak.
(ORGON *turns his head, and she is silent.*)

ORGON: Tartuffe is no young dandy,
  . But, still, his person …
DORINE: (Aside.) Is as sweet as candy.
ORGON: Is such that, even if you shouldn't care for his other merits …
  (*He turns and stands facing Dorine, arms crossed.*)
DORINE: (*Aside.*) They'll make a lovely pair.
  If I were she, no man would marry me
  Against my inclination, and go scot-free.
  He'd learn, before the wedding-day was over,
  How readily a wife can find a lover.
ORGON: (*To* DORINE.) It seems you treat my orders as a joke.
DORINE: Why, what's the matter? 'Twas not to you I spoke.
ORGON: What were you doing?
DORINE: Talking to myself, that's all.
ORGON: Ah! (*Aside.*) One more bit of impudence and gall,
  And I shall give her a good slap in the face.
  (*He puts himself in position to slap her;* DORINE, *whenever he glances at her, stands immobile and silent.*)
  Daughter, you shall accept, and with good grace,
  The husband I've selected … Your wedding-day …
  (*To* DORINE.)
  Why don't you talk to yourself?
DORINE: I've nothing to say.
ORGON: Come, just one word.
DORINE: No thank you, Sir. I pass.
ORGON: Come, speak; I'm waiting.
DORINE: I'd not be such an ass.
ORGON: (*Turning to* MARIANE.) In short, dear Daughter, I mean to be obeyed,
  And you must bow to the sound choice I've made.
DORINE: (Moving away.) I'd not wed such a monster, even in jest.
  (ORGON *attempts to slap her, but misses.*)
ORGON: Daughter, that maid of yours is a thorough pest;
  She makes me sinfully annoyed and nettled.
  I can't speak further; my nerves are too unsettled.
  She's so upset me by her insolent talk,
  I'll calm myself by going for a walk.

Scene III

DORINE, MARIANE

DORINE: (*Returning.*) Well, have you lost your tongue, girl?
Must I play
Your part, and say the lines you ought to say?
Faced with a fate so hideous and absurd,
Can you not utter one dissenting word?

MARIANE: What good would it do? A father's power is great.

DORINE: Resist him now, or it will be too late.

MARIANE: But ...

DORINE: Tell him one cannot love at a father's whim;
That you shall marry for yourself, not him;
That since it's you who are to be the bride,
It's you, not he, who must be satisfied;
And that if his Tartuffe is so sublime,
He's free to marry him at any time.

MARIANE: I've bowed so long to Father's strict control,
I couldn't oppose him now, to save my soul.

DORINE: Come, come, Mariane. Do listen to reason, won't you?
Valère has asked your hand. Do you love him, or don't you?

MARIANE: Oh, how unjust of you! What can you mean
By asking such a question, dear Dorine?
You know the depth of my affection for him;
I've told you a hundred times how I adore him.

DORINE: I don't believe in everything I hear;
who knows if your professions were sincere?

MARIANE: They were, Dorine, and you do me wrong to doubt it;
Heaven knows that I've been all too frank about it.

DORINE: You love him, then?

MARIANE: Oh, more than I can express.

DORINE: And he, I take it, cares for you no less?

MARIANE: I think so.

DORINE: And you both, with equal fire,
Burn to be married?

MARIANE: That is our one desire.

DORINE: What of Tartuffe, then? What of your father's plan?

MARIANE: I'll kill myself, if I'm forced to wed that man.

DORINE: I hadn't thought of that recourse.
    How splendid! Just die, and all your troubles will be ended!
    A fine solution. Oh, it maddens me
    To hear you talk in that self-pitying key.
MARIANE: Dorine, how harsh you are! It's most unfair.
    You have no sympathy for my despair.
DORINE: I've none at all for people who talk drivel
    And, faced with difficulties, whine and snivel.
MARIANE: No doubt I'm timid, but it would be wrong ...
DORINE: True love requires a heart that's firm and strong.
MARIANE: I'm strong in my affection for Valère,
    But coping with my father is his affair.
DORINE: But if your father's brain has grown so cracked
    Over his dear Tartuffe that he can retract
    His blessing, though your wedding-day was named,
    It's surely not Valère who's to be blamed.
MARIANE: If I defied my father, as you suggest,
    Would it not seem unmaidenly, at best?
    Shall I defend my love at the expense
    Of brazeness and disobedience?
    Shall I parade my heart's desires, and flaunt ...
DORINE: No, I ask nothing of you. Clearly you want
    To be Madame Tartuffe, and I feel bound
    Not to oppose a wish so very sound.
    What right have I to criticize the match?
    Indeed, my dear, the man's a brilliant catch.
    Monsieur Tartuffe! Now, there's a man of weight!
    Yes, yes, Monsieur Tartuffe, I'm bound to state,
    Is quite a person; that's not to be denied;
    'Twill be no little thing to be his bride.
    The world already rings with his renown;
    He's a great noble—in his native town;
    His ears are red, he has a pink complexion,
    And all in all, he'll suit you to perfection.
MARIANE: Dear God!
DORINE: Oh, how triumphant you will feel
    At having caught a husband so ideal!

MARIANE: Oh, do stop teasing, and use your cleverness
    To get me out of this appalling mess.
    Advise me, and I'll do whatever you say.
DORINE: Ah no, a dutiful daughter must obey
    Her father, even if he weds her to an ape.
    You've a bright future; why struggle to escape?
    Tartuffe will take you back where his family lives,
    To a small town aswarm with relatives—
    Uncles and cousins whom you'll be charmed to meet.
    You'll be received at once by the elite,
    Calling upon the bailiff's wife, no less—
    Even, perhaps, upon the mayoress,
    Who'll sit you down in the best kitchen chair.
    Then, once a year, you'll dance at the village fair
    To the drone of bagpipes—two of them, in fact—
    And see a puppet-show, or an animal act.
    Your husband ...
MARIANE: Oh, you turn my blood to ice!
    Stop torturing me, and give me your advice.
DORINE: (*Threatening to go.*)
    Your servant, Madam.
MARIANE: Dorine, I beg of you ...
DORINE: No, you deserve it; this marriage must go through.
MARIANE: Dorine!
DORINE: No.
MARIANE: Not Tartuffe! You know I think him ...
DORINE: Tartuffe's your cup of tea, and you shall drink him.
MARIANE: I've always told you everything, and relied ...
DORINE: No. You deserve to be tartuffified.
MARIANE: Well, since you mock me and refuse to care,
    I'll henceforth seek my solace in despair:
    Despair shall be my counsellor and friend,
    And help me bring my sorrows to an end.
    (*She starts to leave.*)
DORINE: There now, come back; my anger has subsided.
    You do deserve some pity, I've decided.
MARIANE: Dorine, if Father makes me undergo
    This dreadful martyrdom, I'll die, I know.

DORINE: Don't fret; it won't be difficult to discover
Some plan of action ... But here's Valère, your lover.

Scene IV
VALÈRE, MARIANE, DORINE

VALÈRE: Madam, I've just received some wondrous news
Regarding which I'd like to hear your views.
MARIANE: What news?
VALÈRE: You're marrying Tartuffe.
MARIANE: I find
That Father does have such a match in mind.
VALÈRE: Your father, Madam ...
MARIANE: ... has just this minute said
That it's Tartuffe he wishes me to wed.
VALÈRE: Can he be serious?
MARIANE: Oh, indeed he can;
He's clearly set his heart upon the plan.
VALÈRE: And what position do you propose to take,
Madam?
MARIANE: Why—I don't know.
VALÈRE: For heaven's sake—
You don't know?
MARIANE: No.
VALÈRE: Well, well!
MARIANE: Advise me, do.
VALÈRE: Marry the man. That's my advice to you.
MARIANE: That's your advice?
VALÈRE: Yes.
MARIANE: Truly?
VALÈRE: Oh, absolutely.
You couldn't choose more wisely, more astutely.
MARIANE: Thanks for this counsel; I'll follow it, of course.
VALÈRE: Do, do; I'm sure 'twill cost you no remorse.
MARIANE: To give it didn't cause your heart to break.
VALÈRE: I gave it, Madam, only for your sake.
MARIANE: And it's for your sake that I take it, Sir.
DORINE: (*Withdrawing to the rear of the stage.*)
Let's see which fool will prove the stubborner.

VALÈRE: So! I am nothing to you, and it was flat
    Deception when you ...
MARIANE: Please, enough of that.
    You've told me plainly that I should agree
    To wed the man my father's chosen for me,
    And since you've deigned to counsel me so wisely,
    I promise, Sir, to do as you advise me.
VALÈRE: Ah, no, 'twas not by me that you were swayed.
    No, your decision was already made;
    Though now, to save appearances, you protest
    That you're betraying me at my behest.
MARIANE: Just as you say.
VALÈRE: Quite so. And I now see
    That you were never truly in love with me.
MARIANE: Alas, you're free to think so if you choose.
VALÈRE: I choose to think so, and here's a bit of news:
    You've spurned my hand, but I know where to turn
    For kinder treatment, as you shall quickly learn.
MARIANE: I'm sure you do. Your noble qualities
    Inspire affection ...
VALÈRE: Forget my qualities, please.
    They don't inspire you overmuch, I find.
    But there's another lady I have in mind
    Whose sweet and generous nature will not scorn
    To compensate me for the loss I've borne.
MARIANE: I'm no great loss, and I'm sure that you'll transfer
    Your heart quite painlessly from me to her.
VALÈRE: I'll do my best to take it in my stride.
    The pain I feel at being cast aside.
    Time and forgetfulness may put an end to.
    Or if I can't forget, I shall pretend to.
    No self-respecting person is expected
    To go on loving once he's been rejected.
MARIANE: Now, that's a fine, high-minded sentiment.
VALÈRE: One to which any sane man would assent.
    Would you prefer it if I pined away
    In hopeless passion till my dying day?
    Am I to yield you to a rival's arms
    And not console myself with other charms?

MARIANE: Go then: console yourself; don't hesitate.
  I wish you to; indeed, I cannot wait.

VALÈRE: You wish me to?

MARIANE: Yes.

VALÈRE: That's the final straw.
  Madam, farewell. Your wish shall be my law.
  (*He starts to leave, and then returns: this repeatedly.*)

MARIANE: Splendid.

VALÈRE: (*Coming back again.*)
  This breach, remember, is of your making:
  It's you who've driven me to the step I'm taking.

MARIANE: Of course.

VALÈRE: (*Coming back again.*)
  Remember, too, that I am merely
  Following your example.

MARIANE: I see that clearly.

VALÈRE: Enough. I'll go and do your bidding, then.

MARIANE: Good.

VALÈRE: (*Coming back again.*)
  You shall never see my face again.

MARIANE: Excellent.

VALÈRE: (*Walking to the door, then turning about.*) Yes?

MARIANE: What?

VALÈRE: What's that? What did you say?

MARIANE: Nothing. You're dreaming.

VALÈRE: Ah. Well, I'm on my way.
  Farewell, Madame.
  (*He moves slowly away.*)

MARIANE: Farewell.

DORINE: (*To* MARIANE.) If you ask me,
  Both of you are as mad as mad can be.
  Do stop this nonsense, now. I've only let you
  Squabble so long to see where it would get you.
  Whoa there, Monsieur Valère!
  (*She goes and seizes* VALÈRE *by the arm; he makes a great show of resistance.*)

VALÈRE: What's this, Dorine?

DORINE: Come here.

VALÈRE: No, no, my heart's too full of spleen.
  Don't hold me back; her wish must be obeyed.

DORINE: Stop!

VALÈRE: It's too late now; my decision's made.

DORINE: Oh, pooh!

MARIANE: (*Aside.*)

   He hates the sight of me, that's plain.

   I'll go, and so deliver him from pain.

DORINE: (*Leaving* VALÈRE, *running after* MARIANE.)

   And now you run away! Come back.

MARIANE: No, no.

   Nothing you say will keep me here. Let go!

VALÈRE: (*Aside.*) She cannot bear my presence, I perceive.

   To spare her further torment, I shall leave.

DORINE: (*Leaving* MARIANE, *running after* VALÈRE.) Again!

   You'll not escape, Sir; don't you try it.

   Come here, you two. Stop fussing, and be quiet.

   (*She takes* VALÈRE *by the hand, then* MARIANE, *and draws them together.*)

VALÈRE: (*To* DORINE.)

   What do you want of me?

MARIANE: (*To* DORINE.) What is the point of this?

DORINE: We're going to have a little armistice.

   (*To* VALÈRE .)

   Now, weren't you silly to get so overheated?

VALÈRE: Didn't you see how badly I was treated?

DORINE: (*To* MARIANE.) Aren't you a simpleton, to have lost your head?

MARIANE: Didn't you hear the hateful things he said?

DORINE: (*To* VALÈRE.) You're both great fools. Her sole desire, Valère,

   Is to be yours in marriage. To that I'll swear.

   (*To* MARIANE.)

   He loves you only, and he wants no wife

   But you, Mariane. On that I'll stake my life.

MARIANE: (*To* VALÈRE.) Then why you advised me so, I cannot see.

VALÈRE: (*To* MARIANE.) On such a question, why ask advice of me?

DORINE: Oh, you're impossible. Give me your hands, you two.

   (*To* VALÈRE.)

   Yours first.

VALÈRE: (*Giving* DORINE *his hand.*)

   But why?

DORINE: (*To* MARIANE.)

   And now a hand from you.

MARIANE: (*Also giving* DORINE *her hand.*)

    What are you doing?

DORINE: There: a perfect fit.

    You suit each other better than you'll admit.

    (VALÈRE *and* MARIANE *hold hands for some time without looking at each other.*)

VALÈRE: (*Turning toward* MARIANE.) Ah, come, don't be so haughty.

    Give a man a look of kindness, won't you, Mariane?

    (MARIANE *tums toward* VALÈRE *and smiles*)

DORINE: I tell you, lovers are completely mad!

VALÈRE: (*To* MARIANE.) Now come, confess that you were very bad

    To hurt my feelings as you did just now.

    I have a just complaint, you must allow.

MARIANE: You must allow that you were most unpleasant ...

DORINE: Let's table that discussion for the present;

    Your father has a plan which must be stopped.

MARIANE: Advise us, then; what means must we adopt?

DORINE: We'll use all manner of means, and all at once.

    (*To* MARIANE.)

    Your father's addled; he's acting like a dunce.

    Therefore you'd better humor the old fossil.

    Pretend to yield to him, be sweet and docile,

    And then postpone, as often as necessary,

    The day on which you have agreed to marry.

    You'll thus gain time, and time will turn the trick.

    Sometimes, for instance, you'll be taken sick,

    And that will seem good reason for delay;

    Or some bad omen will make you change the day—

    You'll dream of muddy water, or you'll pass

    A dead man's hearse, or break a looking-glass.

    If all else fails, no man can marry you

    Unless you take his ring and say "I do."

    But now, let's separate. If they should find

    Us talking here, our plot might be divined.

    (*To* VALÈRE.)

    Go to your friends, and tell them what's occurred,

    And have them urge her father to keep his word.

    Meanwhile, we'll stir her brother into action,

    And get Elmire, as well, to join our faction.

    Good-bye.

VALÈRE: (*To* MARIANE.)
Though each of us will do his best,
It's your true heart on which my hopes shall rest.
MARIANE: (*To* VALÈRE.) Regardless of what Father may decide,
None but Valère shall claim me as his bride.
VALÈRE: Oh, how those words content me! Come what will ...
DORINE: Oh, lover, lovers! Their tongues are never still.
Be off, now.
VALÈRE: (*Turning to go, then turning back.*)
One last word ...
DORINE: No time to chat:
You leave by this door; and you leave by that.
(DORINE *pushes them, by the shoulders, toward opposing doors.*)

ACT III

Scene I
DAMIS, DORINE

DAMIS: May lightning strike me even as I speak,
May all men call me cowardly and weak,
If any fear or scruple holds me back
From settling things, at once, with that great quack!
DORINE: Now, don't give way to violent emotion.
Your father's merely talked about this notion,
And words and deeds are far from being one.
Much that is talked about is left undone.
DAMIS: No, I must stop that scoundrel's machinations;
I'll go and tell him off; I'm out of patience.
DORINE: Do calm down and be practical. I had rather
My mistress dealt with him—and with your father.
She has some influence with Tartuffe, I've noted.
He hangs upon her words, seems most devoted,
And may, indeed, be smitten by her charm.
Pray Heaven it's true! 'Twould do our cause no harm.
She sent for him, just now, to sound him out
On this affair you're so incensed about;
She'll find out where he stands, and tell him, too,

What dreadful strife and trouble will ensue
If he lends countenance to your father's plan.
I couldn't get in to see him, but his man
Says that he's almost finished with his prayers.
Go, now. I'll catch him when he comes downstairs.

DAMIS: I want to hear this conference, and I will.

DORINE: No, they must be alone.

DAMIS: Oh, I'll keep still.

DORINE: Not you. I know your temper. You'd start a brawl,
And shout and stamp your foot and spoil it all.
Go on.

DAMIS: I won't; I have a perfect right ...

DORINE: Lord, you're a nuisance! He's coming; get out of sight.
(DAMIS *conceals himself in a closet at the rear of the stage.*)

Scene II

TARTUFFE, DORINE

TARTUFFE: (*Observing* DORINE, *and calling to his manservant offstage.*)
Hang up my hair-shirt, put my scourge in place,
And pray, Laurent, for Heaven's perpetual grace.
I'm going to the prison now, to share
My last few coins with the poor wretches there.

DORINE: (*Aside.*) Dear God, what affectation! What a fake!

TARTUFFE: You wished to see me?

DORINE: Yes ...

TARTUFFE: (*Taking a handkerchief from his pocket.*)
For mercy's sake,
Please take this handkerchief, before you speak.

DORINE: What?

TARTUFFE: Cover that bosom, girl. The flesh is weak,
And unclean thoughts are difficult to control.
Such sights as that can undermine the soul.

DORINE: Your soul, it seems, has very poor defenses,
And flesh makes quite an impact on your senses.
It's strange that you're so easily excited;
My own desires are not so soon ignited,
And if I saw you naked as a beast,
Not all your hide would tempt me in the least.

TARTUFFE: Girl, speak more modestly; unless you do,
   I shall be forced to take my leave of you.
DORINE: Oh, no, it's I who must be on my way;
   I've just one little message to convey
   Madame is coming down, and begs you, Sir,
   To wait and have a word or two with her.
TARTUFFE: Gladly.
DORINE: (*Aside.*) That had a softening effect!
   I think my guess about him was correct.
TARTUFFE: Will she be long?
DORINE: No: that's her step I hear.
   Ah, here she is, and I shall disappear.

Scene III

ELMIRE, TARTUFFE

TARTUFFE: May Heaven, whose infinite goodness we adore,
   Preserve your body and soul forevermore,
   And bless your days, and answer thus the plea
   Of one who is its humblest votary.
ELMIRE: I thank you for that pious wish. But please,
   Do take a chair and let's be more at ease.
   (*They sit down.*)
TARTUFFE: I trust that you are once more well and strong?
ELMIRE: Oh, yes: the fever didn't last for long.
TARTUFFE: My prayers are too unworthy, I am sure,
   To have gained from Heaven this most gracious cure;
   But lately, Madam, my every supplication
   Has had for object your recuperation.
ELMIRE: You shouldn't have troubled so. I don't deserve it.
TARTUFFE: Your health is priceless, Madam, and to preserve it
   I'd gladly give my own, in all sincerity.
ELMIRE: Sir, you outdo us all in Christian charity.
   You've been most kind. I count myself your debtor.
TARTUFFE: 'Twas nothing, Madam. I long to serve you better.
ELMIRE: There's a private matter I'm anxious to discuss.
   I'm glad there's no one here to hinder us.
TARTUFFE: I too am glad; it floods my heart with bliss
   To find myself alone with you like this.

For just this chance I've prayed with all my power—
But prayed in vain, until this happy hour.

ELMIRE: This won't take long, Sir, and I hope you'll be
Entirely frank and unconstrained with me.

TARTUFFE: Indeed, there's nothing I had rather do
Than bare my inmost heart and soul to you.
First, let me say that what remarks I've made
About the constant visits you are paid
Were prompted not by any mean emotion,
But rather by a pure and deep devotion,
A fervent zeal …

ELMIRE: No need for explanation.
Your sole concern, I'm sure, was my salvation.

TARTUFFE: (*Taking* ELMIRE's *hand and pressing her fingertips.*)
Quite so; and such great fervor do I feel …

ELMIRE: Ooh! Please! You're pinching!

TARTUFFE: 'Twas from excess of zeal.
I never meant to cause you pain, I swear.
I'd rather …
(*He places his hand on* ELMIRE's *knee.*)

ELMIRE: What can your hand be doing there?

TARTUFFE: Feeling your gown; what soft, fine-woven stuff!

ELMIRE: Please, I'm extremely ticklish. That's enough.
(*She draws her chair away;* TARTUFFE *pulls his after her.*)

TARTUFFE: (*Fondling the lace collar of her gown.*)
My, my, what lovely lacework on your dress!
The workmanship's miraculous, no less
I've not seen anything to equal it.

ELMIRE: Yes, quite. But let's talk business for a bit.
They say my husband means to break his word
And give his daughter to you, Sir. Had you heard?

TARTUFFE: He did once mention it. But I confess
I dream of quite a different happiness.
It's elsewhere, Madam, that my eyes discern
The promise of that bliss for which I yearn.

ELMIRE: I see: you care for nothing here below.

TARTUFFE: Ah, well—my heart's not made of stone, you know.

ELMIRE: All your desires mount heavenward, I'm sure,
In scorn of all that's earthly and impure.

TARTUFFE: A love of heavenly beauty does not preclude
      A proper love for earthly pulchritude;
      Our senses are quite rightly captivated
      By perfect works our Maker has created
      Some glory clings to all that Heaven has made;
      In you, all Heaven's marvels are displayed.
      On that fair face, such beauties have been lavished,
      The eyes are dazzled and the heart is ravished;
      How could I look on you, O flawless creature,
      And not adore the Author of all Nature,
      Feeling a love both passionate and pure
      For you, his triumph of self-portraiture?
      At first, I trembled lest that love should be
      A subtle snare that Hell had laid for me;
      I vowed to flee the sight of you, eschewing
      A rapture that might prove my soul's undoing;
      But soon, fair being, I became aware
      That my deep passion could be made to square
      With rectitude, and with my bounden duty.
      I thereupon surrendered to your beauty.
      It is, I know, presumptuous on my part
      To bring you this poor offering of my heart,
      And it is not my merit, Heaven knows,
      But your compassion on which my hopes repose.
      You are my peace, my solace, my salvation;
      On you depends my bliss—or desolation;
      I bide your judgment and, as you think best,
      I shall be either miserable or blest.
ELMIRE: Your declaration is most gallant, Sir,
      But don't you think it's out of character?
      You'd have done better to restrain your passion
      And think before you spoke in such a fashion.
      It ill becomes a pious man like you ...
TARTUFFE: I may be pious, but I'm human too:
      With your celestial charms before his eyes,
      A man has not the power to be wise.
      I know such words sound strangely, coming from me,
      But I'm no angel, nor was meant to be,
      And if you blame my passion, you must needs

Reproach as well the charms on which it feeds.
Your loveliness I had no sooner seen
Than you became my soul's unrivalled queen;
Before your seraph glance, divinely sweet,
My heart's defenses crumbled in defeat,
And nothing fasting, prayer, or tears might do
Could stay my spirit from adoring you.
My eyes, my sighs have told you in the past
What now my lips make bold to say at last,
And if, in your great goodness, you will deign
To look upon your slave, and ease his pain,—
If, in compassion for my soul's distress,
You'll stoop to comfort my unworthiness,
I'll raise to you, in thanks for that sweet manna,
An endless hymn, an infinite hosanna.
With me, of course, there need be no anxiety.
No fear of scandal or of notoriety.
These young court gallants, whom all the ladies fancy,
Are vain in speech, in action rash and chancy;
When they succeed in love, the world soon knows it;
No favor's granted them but they disclose it
And by the looseness of their tongues profane
The very altar where their hearts have lain.
Men of my sort, however, love discreetly,
And one may trust our reticence completely.
My keen concern for my good name insures
The absolute security of yours;
In short, I offer you, my dear Elmire,
Love without scandal, pleasure without fear.

ELMIRE: I've heard your well-turned speeches to the end,
And what you urge I clearly apprehend.
Aren't you afraid that I may take a notion
To tell my husband of your warm devotion,
And that, supposing he were duly told,
His feelings toward you might grow rather cold?

TARTUFFE: I know, dear lady, that your exceeding charity
Will lead your heart to pardon my temerity;

That you'll excuse my violent affection
As human weakness, human imperfection;
And that—O fairest!—you will bear in mind
That I'm but flesh and blood, and am not blind.

ELMIRE: Some women might do otherwise, perhaps,
But I shall be discreet about your lapse;
I'll tell my husband nothing of what's occurred
If, in return, you'll give your solemn word
To advocate as forcefully as you can
The marriage of Valère and Mariane,
Renouncing all desire to dispossess
Another of his rightful happiness,
And ...

Scene IV

DAMIS, ELMIRE, TARTUFFE

DAMIS: (*Emerging from the closet where he has been hiding.*)
No!
We'll not hush up this vile affair;
I heard it all inside that closet there,
Where Heaven, in order to confound the pride
Of this great rascal, prompted me to hide.
Ah, now I have my long-awaited chance
To punish his deceit and arrogance,
And give my father clear and shocking proof
Of the black character of his dear Tartuffe.

ELMIRE: Ah no, Damis; I'll be content if he
Will study to deserve my leniency.
I've promised silence—don't make me break my word;
To make a scandal would be too absurd.
Good wives laugh off such trifles, and forget them;
Why should they tell their husbands, and upset them?

DAMIS: You have your reasons for taking such a course,
And I have reasons, too, of equal force.
To spare him now would be insanely wrong.
I've swallowed my just wrath for far too long
And watched this insolent bigot bringing strife
And bitterness into our family life.

Too long he's meddled in my father's affairs,
Thwarting my marriage-hopes, and poor Valère's.
It's high time that my father was undeceived,
And now I've proof that can't be disbelieved—
Proof that was furnished me by Heaven above.
It's too good not to take advantage of.
This is my chance, and I deserve to lose it
If, for one moment, I hesitate to use it.

ELMIRE: Damis ...

DAMIS: No, I must do what I think right.
Madam, my heart is bursting with delight,
And, say whatever you will, I'll not consent
To lose the sweet revenge on which I'm bent.
I'll settle matters without more ado;
And here, most opportunely, is my cue.

Scene V

ORGON, DAMIS, TARTUFFE, ELMIRE

DAMIS: Father, I'm glad you've joined us. Let us advise you
Of some fresh news which doubtless will surprise you.
You've just now been repaid with interest
For all your loving-kindness to our guest.
He's proved his warm and grateful feelings toward you;
It's with a pair of horns he would reward you.
Yes, I surprised him with your wife, and heard
His whole adulterous offer, every word.
She, with her all too gentle disposition,
Would not have told you of his proposition;
But I shall not make terms with brazen lechery,
And feel that not to tell you would be treachery.

ELMIRE: And I hold that one's husband's peace of mind
Should not be spoilt by tattle of this kind.
One's honor doesn't require it: to be proficient
In keeping men at bay is quite sufficient.
These are my sentiments, and I wish, Damis,
That you had heeded me and held your peace.

Scene VI

ORGON, DAMIS, TARTUFFE

ORGON: Can it be true, this dreadful thing I hear?
TARTUFFE: Yes, Brother, I'm a wicked man, I fear:
    A wretched sinner, all depraved and twisted,
    The greatest villain that has ever existed.
    My life's one heap of crimes, which grows each minute;
    There's naught but foulness and corruption in it;
    And I perceive that Heaven, outraged by me,
    Has chosen this occasion to mortify me.
    Charge me with any deed you wish to name;
    I'll not defend myself, but take the blame.
    Believe what you are told, and drive Tartuffe
    Like some base criminal from beneath your roof;
    Yes, drive me hence, and with a parting curse:
    I shan't protest, for I deserve far worse.
ORGON: (*To* DAMIS.) Ah, you deceitful boy, how dare you try
    To stain his purity with so foul a lie?
DAMIS: What! Are you taken in by such a bluff?
    Did you not hear ... ?
ORGON: Enough, you rogue, enough!
TARTUFFE: Ah, Brother, let him speak: you're being unjust.
    Believe his story; the boy deserves your trust.
    Why, after all, should you have faith in me?
    How can you know what I might do, or be?
    Is it on my good actions that you base
    Your favor? Do you trust my pious face?
    Ah, no, don't be deceived by hollow shows;
    I'm far, alas, from being what men suppose;
    Though the world takes me for a man of worth,
    I'm truly the most worthless man on earth.
    (*To* DAMIS.)
    Yes, my dear son, speak out now: call me the chief
    Of sinners, a wretch, a murderer, a thief;
    Load me with all the names men most abhor;
    I'll not complain; I've earned them all, and more;
    I'll kneel here while you pour them on my head
    As a just punishment for the life I've led.

ORGON: (*To* TARTUFFE.)

    This is too much, dear Brother.

    (*To* DAMIS.)

    Have you no heart?

DAMIS: Are you so hoodwinked by this rascal's art …?

ORGON: Be still, you monster.

    (*To* TARTUFFE.)

    Brother, I pray you, rise. (*To* DAMIS.)

    Villain!

DAMIS: But …

ORGON: Silence!

DAMIS: Can't you realize …?

ORGON: Just one word more, and I'll tear you limb from limb.

TARTUFFE: In God's name, Brother, don't be harsh with him.

    I'd rather far be tortured at the stake

    Than see him bear one scratch for my poor sake.

ORGON: (*To* DAMIS.)

    Ingrate!

TARTUFFE: If I must beg you, on bended knee,

    To pardon him …

ORGON: (*Falling to his knees, addressing* TARTUFFE.)

    Such goodness cannot be!

    (*To* DAMIS.)

    Now, there's true charity!

DAMIS: What, you …?

ORGON: Villain, be still!

    I know your motives; I know you wish him ill:

    Yes, all of you—wife, children, servants, all—

    Conspire against him and desire his fall,

    Employing every shameful trick you can

    To alienate me from this saintly man.

    Ah, but the more you seek to drive him away,

    The more I'll do to keep him. Without delay,

    I'll spite this household and confound its pride

    By giving him my daughter as his bride.

DAMIS: You're going to force her to accept his hand?

ORGON: Yes, and this very night, d'you understand?

    I shall defy you all, and make it clear

    That I'm the one who gives the orders here.

Come, wretch, kneel down and clasp his blessed feet,
And ask his pardon for your black deceit.

DAMIS: I ask that swindlers' pardon? Why, I'd rather …

ORGON: So! You insult him, and defy your father!
A stick! A stick! (*To* TARTUFFE.)
No, no—release me, do. (*To* DAMIS)
Out of my house this minute! Be off with you,
And never dare set foot in it again.

DAMIS: Well, I shall go, but …

ORGON: Well, go quickly, then.
I disinherit you; an empty purse
Is all you'll get from me—except my curse!

Scene VII
ORGON, TARTUFFE

ORGON: How he blasphemed your goodness! What a son!

TARTUFFE: Forgive him, Lord, as I've already done.
(*To* ORGON.)
You can't know how it hurts when someone tries
To blacken me in my dear Brother's eyes.

ORGON: Ahh!

TARTUFFE: The mere thought of such ingratitude
Plunges my soul into so dark a mood …
Such horror grips my heart … I gasp for breath,
And cannot speak, and feel myself near death.

ORGON: (*He runs, in tears, to the door through which he has just driven his son.*)
You blackguard! Why did I spare you? Why did I not
Break you in little pieces on the spot?
Compose yourself, and don't be hurt, dear friend.

TARTUFFE: These scenes, these dreadful quarrels, have got to end.
I've much upset your household, and I perceive
That the best thing will be for me to leave.

ORGON: What are you saying!

TARTUFFE: They're all against me here;
They'd have you think me false and insincere.

ORGON: Ah, what of that? Have I ceased believing in you?

TARTUFFE: Their adverse talk will certainly continue,
And charges which you now repudiate

You may find credible at a later date.

ORGON: No, Brother, never.

TARTUFFE: Brother, a wife can sway
Her husband's mind in many a subtle way.

ORGON: No, no.

TARTUFFE: To leave at once is the solution;
Thus only can I end their persecution.

ORGON: No, no, I'll not allow it; you shall remain.

TARTUFFE: Ah, well; 'twill mean much martyrdom and pain,
But if you wish it ...

ORGON: Ah!

TARTUFFE: Enough; so be it.
But one thing must be settled, as I see it.
For your dear honor, and for our friendship's sake,
There's one precaution I feel bound to take.
I shall avoid your wife, and keep away ...

ORGON: No, you shall not, whatever they may say.
It pleases me to vex them, and for spite
I'd have them see you with her day and night.
What's more, I'm going to drive them to despair
By making you my only son and heir;
This very day, I'll give to you alone
Clear deed and title to everything I own.
A dear, good friend and son-in-law-to-be
Is more than wife, or child, or kin to me.
Will you accept my offer, dearest son?

TARTUFFE: In all things, let the will of Heaven be done.

ORGON: Poor fellow! Come, we'll go draw up the deed.
Then let them burst with disappointed greed!

ACT IV

Scene I

CLÉANTE, TARTUFFE

CLÉANTE: Yes, all the town's discussing it, and truly,
Their comments do not flatter you unduly.
I'm glad we've met, Sir, and I'll give my view
Of this sad matter in a word or two.

As for who's guilty, that I shan't discuss;
Let's say it was Damis who caused the fuss;
Assuming, then, that you have been ill-used
By young Damis, and groundlessly accused,
Ought not a Christian to forgive, and ought
He not to stifle every vengeful thought?
Should you stand by and watch a father make
His only son an exile for your sake?
Again I tell you frankly, be advised:
The whole town, high and low, is scandalized;
This quarrel must be mended, and my advice is
Not to push matters to a further crisis.
No, sacrifice your wrath to God above,
And help Damis regain his father's love.

TARTUFFE: Alas, for my part I should take great joy
In doing so. I've nothing against the boy.
I pardon all, I harbor no resentment;
To serve him would afford me much contentment.
But Heaven's interest will not have it so:
If he comes back, then I shall have to go.
After his conduct—so extreme, so vicious—
Our further intercourse would look suspicious.
God knows what people would think! Why, they'd describe
My goodness to him as a sort of bribe;
They'd say that out of guilt I made pretense
Of loving-kindness and benevolence—
That, fearing my accuser's tongue, I strove
To buy his silence with a show of love.

CLÉANTE: Your reasoning is badly warped and stretched,
And these excuses, Sir, are most far-fetched.
Why put yourself in charge of Heaven's cause?
Does Heaven need our help to enforce its laws?
Leave vengeance to the Lord, Sir; while we live,
Our duty's not to punish, but forgive;
And what the Lord commands, we should obey
Without regard to what the world may say
What! Shall the fear of being misunderstood
Prevent our doing what is right and good?

No, no; let's simply do what Heaven ordains,
And let no other thoughts perplex our brains.
TARTUFFE: Again, Sir, let me say that I've forgiven Damis, and thus obeyed the
laws of Heaven;
But I am not commanded by the Bible
To live with one who smears my name with libel.
CLÉANTE: Were you commanded, Sir, to indulge the whim
Of poor Orgon, and to encourage him
In suddenly transferring to your name
A large estate to which you have no claim?
TARTUFFE: 'Twould never occur to those who know me best
To think I acted from self-interest.
The treasures of this world I quite despise;
Their specious glitter does not charm my eyes;
And if I have resigned myself to taking
The gift which my dear Brother insists on making,
I do so only, as he well understands,
Lest so much wealth fall into wicked hands,
Lest those to whom it might descend in time
Turn it to purposes of sin and crime,
And not, as I shall do, make use of it.
For Heaven's glory and mankind's benefit.
TARTUFFE: Forget these trumped-up fears. Your argument
Is one the rightful heir might well resent;
It is a moral burden to inherit
Such wealth, but give Damis a chance to bear it.
And would it not be worse to be accused
Of swindling, than to see that wealth misused?
I'm shocked that you allowed Orgon to broach
This matter, and that you feel no self-reproach;
Does true religion teach that lawful heirs
May freely be deprived of what is theirs?
And if the Lord has told you in your heart
That you and young Damis must dwell apart,
Would it not be the decent thing to beat
A generous and honorable retreat,
Rather than let the son of the house be sent,
For your convenience, into banishment?

Sir, if you wish to prove the honesty
Of your intentions ...
TARTUFFE: Sir, it is half-past three.
I've certain pious duties to attend to,
And hope my prompt departure won't offend you.
CLÉANTE: (*Alone.*) Damn.

Scene II

ELMIRE, MARIANE, CLÉANTE, DORINE

DORINE: Stay, Sir, and help Mariane, for Heaven's sake!
She's suffering so, I fear her heart will break.
Her father's plan to marry her off tonight
Has put the poor child in a desperate plight.
I hear him coming. Let's stand together, now,
And see if we can't change his mind, somehow,
About this match we all deplore and fear.

Scene III

ORGON, ELMIRE, MARIANE, CLÉANTE, DORINE

ORGON: Hah! Glad to find you all assembled here.
(*To* MARIANE.)
This contract, child, contains your happiness,
And what it says I think your heart can guess.
MARIANE: (*Falling to her knees.*)
Sir, by that Heaven which sees me here distressed,
And by whatever else can move your breast,
Do not employ a father's power, I pray you,
To crush my heart and force it to obey you,
Nor by your harsh commands oppress me so
That I'll begrudge the duty which I owe—
And do not so embitter and enslave me
That I shall hate the very life you gave me.
If my sweet hopes must perish. if you refuse
To give me to the one I've dared to choose,
Spare me at least—I beg you. I implore—
The pain of wedding one whom I abhor;

And do not, by a heartless use of force,
Drive me to contemplate some desperate course.
ORGON: (*Feeling himself touched by her*) Be firm my soul.
No human weakness, now.
MARIANE: I don't resent your love for him. Allow
Your heart free rein, Sir; give him your property,
And if that's not enough, take mine from me;
He's welcome to my money; take it, do,
But don't, I pray, include my person too.
Spare me, I beg you; and let me end the tale
Of my sad days behind a convent veil.
ORGON: A convent! Hah! When crossed in their amours,
All lovesick girls have the same thought as yours.
Get up! The more you loathe the man, and dread him,
The more ennobling it will be to wed him.
Marry Tartuffe, and mortify your flesh!
Enough; don't start that whimpering afresh.
DORINE: But why …?
ORGON: Be still, there. Speak when you're spoken to.
Not one more bit of impudence out of you.
CLÉANTE: If I may offer a word of counsel here …
ORGON: Brother, in counseling you have no peer;
All your advice is forceful, sound, and clever;
I don't propose to follow it, however.
ELMIRE: (*To* ORGON.) I am amazed and don't know what to say;
Your blindness simply takes my breath away.
You are indeed bewitched, to take no warning
From our account of what occurred this morning.
ORGON: Madam, I know a few plain facts, and one
Is that you're partial to my rascal son:
Hence, when he sought to make Tartuffe the victim
Of a base lie, you dared not contradict him.
Ah, but you underplayed your part, my pet:
You should have looked more angry, more upset.
ELMIRE: When men make overtures, must we reply
With righteous anger and a battle-cry?
Must we turn back their amorous advances
With sharp reproaches and with fiery glances?
Myself, I find such offers merely amusing,

And make no scenes and fusses in refusing;
My taste is for good-natured rectitude,
And I dislike the savage sort of prude
Who guards her virtue with her teeth and claws,
And tears men's eyes out for the slightest cause;
The Lord preserve me from such honor as that,
Which bites and scratches like an alley-cat!
I've found that a polite and cool rebuff
Discourages a lover quite enough.

ORGON: I know the facts. and I shall not be shaken.

ELMIRE: I marvel at your power to be mistaken.
Would it, I wonder, carry weight with you
If I could show you that our tale was true?

ORGON: Show me?

ELMIRE: Yes.

ORGON: Rot.

ELMIRE: Come, what if I found a way
To make you see the facts as plain as day?

ORGON: Nonsense.

ELMIRE: Do answer me; don't be absurd.
I'm not now asking you to trust our word.
Suppose that from some hiding-place in here
You learned the whole sad truth by eye and ear—
What would you say of your good friend, after that?

ORGON: Why I'd say ... nothing, by Jehoshaphat!
It can't be true.

ELMIRE: You've been too long deceived,
And I'm quite tired of being disbelieved.
Come now: let's put my statements to the test,
And you shall see the truth made manifest.

ORGON: I'll take that challenge. Now do your uttermost.
We'll see how you make good your empty boast.

ELMIRE: (*To* DORINE.)
Send him to me.

DORINE: He's crafty; it may be hard
To catch the cunning scoundrel off his guard.

ELMIRE: No, amorous men are gullible. Their conceit
So blinds them that they're never hard to cheat.
Have him come down.

(*To* CLÉANTE *and* MARIANE.)
Please leave us, for a bit.

Scene IV
ELMIRE, ORGON

ELMIRE: Pull up this table, and get under it.
ORGON: What?
ELMIRE: It's essential that you be well-hidden.
ORGON: Why there?
ELMIRE: Oh, Heavens! Just do as you are bidden
    I have my plans; we'll soon see how they fare.
    Under the table, now; and once you're there,
    Take care that you are neither seen nor heard.
ORGON: Well I'll indulge you, since I gave my word
    To see you through this infantile charade.
ELMIRE: Once it is over, you'll be glad we played.
    (*To her husband, who is now under the table.*)
    I'm going to act quite strangely, now, and you
    Must not be shocked at anything I do.
    Whatever I may say, you must excuse
    As part of that deceit I'm forced to use.
    I shall employ sweet speeches in the task
    Of making that impostor drop his mask:
    I'll give encouragement to his bold desires.
    And furnish fuel to his amorous fires.
    Since it's for your sake, and for his destruction,
    That I shall seem to yield to his seduction,
    I'll gladly stop when ever you decide
    That all your doubts are fully satisfied.
    I'll count on you, as soon as you have seen
    What sort of man he is, to intervene,
    And not expose me to his odious lust
    One moment longer than you feel you must.
    Remember: you're to save me from my plight
    Whenever … He's coming! Hush! Keep out of sight!

Scene V
TARTUFFE, ELMIRE, ORGON

TARTUFFE: You wish to have a word with me, I'm told.
ELMIRE: Yes. I've a little secret to unfold.
 Before I speak, however, it would be wise
 To close that door, and look about for spies.
 (TARTUFFE *goes to the door, closes it, and returns.*)
 The very last thing that must happen now
 Is a repetition of this morning's row.
 I've never been so badly caught off guard.
 Oh, how I feared for you! You saw how hard
 I tried to make that troublesome Damis
 Control his dreadful temper, and hold his peace.
 In my confusion, I didn't have the sense
 Simply to contradict his evidence;
 But as it happened, that was for the best,
 And all has worked out in our interest.
 This storm has only bettered your position;
 My husband doesn't have the least suspicion,
 And now, in mockery of those who do,
 He bids me be continually with you.
 And that is why, quite fearless of reproof,
 I now can be alone with my Tartuffe,
 And why my heart—perhaps too quick to yield—
 Feels free to let its passion be revealed.
TARTUFFE: Madam, your words confuse me. Not long ago,
 You spoke in quite a different style, you know.
ELMIRE: Ah, Sir, if that refusal made you smart,
 It's little that you know of woman's heart,
 Or what that heart is trying to convey
 When it resists in such a feeble way!
 Always, at first, our modesty prevents
 The frank avowal of tender sentiments;
 However high the passion which inflames us,
 Still, to confess its power somehow shames us.
 Thus we reluct, at first, yet in a tone
 Which tells you that our heart is overthrown,
 That what our lips deny, our pulse confesses,

And that, in time, all noes will turn to yesses.
I fear my words are all too frank and free,
And a poor proof of woman's modesty;
But since I'm started, tell me, if you will—
Would I have tried to make Damis be still,
Would I have listened, calm and unoffended,
Until your lengthy offer of love was ended,
And been so very mild in my reaction,
Had your sweet words not given me satisfaction?
And when I tried to force you to undo
The marriage-plans my husband has in view,
What did my urgent pleading signify
If not that I admired you, and that I
Deplored the thought that someone else might own
Part of a heart I wished for mine alone?

TARTUFFE: Madam, no happiness is so complete
As when, from lips we love, come words so sweet;
Their nectar floods my every sense, and drains
In honeyed rivulets through all my veins.
To please you is my joy, my only goal;
Your love is the restorer of my soul;
And yet I must beg leave, now, to confess
Some lingering doubts as to my happiness
Might this not be a trick? Might not the catch
Be that you wish me to break off the match
With Mariane, and so have feigned to love me?
I shan't quite trust your fond opinion of me
Until the feelings you've expressed so sweetly
Are demonstrated somewhat more concretely,
And you have shown, by certain kind concessions,
That I may put my faith in your professions.

ELMIRE: (*She coughs, to warn her husband.*)
Why be in such a hurry? Must my heart
Exhaust its bounty at the very start?
To make that sweet admission cost me dear,
But you'll not be content, it would appear,
Unless my store of favors is disbursed
To the last farthing, and at the very first.

TARTUFFE: The less we merit, the less we dare to hope,
 And with our doubts, mere words can never cope.
 We trust no promised bliss till we receive it;
 Not till a joy is ours can we believe it.
 I, who so little merit your esteem,
 Can't credit this fulfillment of my dream,
 And shan't believe it, Madam, until I savor
 Some palpable assurance of your favor.
ELMIRE: My, how tyrannical your love can be,
 And how it flusters and perplexes me!
 How furiously you take one's heart in hand,
 And make your every wish a fierce command!
 Come, must you hound and harry me to death?
 Will you not give me time to catch my breath?
 Can it be right to press me with such force,
 Give me no quarter, show me no remorse,
 And take advantage, by your stern insistence,
 Of the fond feelings which weaken my resistance?
TARTUFFE: Well, if you look with favor upon my love.
 Why, then, begrudge me some clear proof thereof?
ELMIRE: But how can I consent without offense
 To Heaven, toward which you feel such reverence?
TARTUFFE: If Heaven is all that holds you back, don't worry.
 I can remove that hindrance in a hurry
 Nothing of that sort need obstruct our path.
ELMIRE: Must one not be afraid of Heaven's wrath?
TARTUFFE: Madam, forget such fears, and be my pupil
 And I shall teach you how to conquer scruple.
 Some joys, it's true, are wrong in Heaven's eyes;
 Yet Heaven is not averse to compromise;
 There is a science, lately formulated,
 Whereby one's conscience may be liberated,
 And any wrongful act you care to mention
 May be redeemed by purity of intention.
 I'll teach you, Madam, the secrets of that science;
 Meanwhile, just place on me your full reliance.
 Assuage my keen desires, and feel no dread:
 The sin, if any, shall be on my head.

(ELMIRE *coughs, this time more loudly.*)
You've a bad cough.
ELMIRE: Yes, yes. It's bad indeed.
TARTUFFE: (*Producing a little paper bag.*)
A bit of licorice may be what you need.
ELMIRE: No, I've a stubborn cold, it seems. I'm sure it
Will take much more than licorice to cure it.
TARTUFFE: How aggravating.
ELMIRE: Oh, more than I can say
TARTUFFE: If you're still troubled, think of things this way:
No one shall know our joys, save us alone,
And there's no evil till the act is known;
It's scandal, Madam, which makes it an offense,
And it's no sin to sin in confidence.
ELMIRE: (*Having coughed once more.*)
Well, clearly I must do as you require,
And yield to your importunate desire.
It is apparent, now, that nothing less
Will satisfy you, and so I acquiesce.
To go so far is much against my will;
I'm vexed that it should come to this; but still,
Since you are so determined on it, since you
Will not allow mere language to convince you,
And since you ask for concrete evidence,
See nothing for it, now, but to comply.
If this is sinful, if I'm wrong to do it,
So much the worse for him who drove me to it.
The fault can surely not be charged to me.
TARTUFFE: Madam, the fault is mine, if fault there be,
And ...
ELMIRE: Open the door a little, and peek out;
I wouldn't want my husband poking about.
TARTUFFE: Why worry about the man?
Each day he grows
More gullible; one can lead him by the nose.
To find us here would fill him with delight,
And if he saw the worst, he'd doubt his sight.
ELMIRE: Nevertheless, do step out for a minute
Into the hall, and see that no one's in it.

Scene VI

ORGON, ELMIRE

ORGON: (*Coming out front, under the table.*)
    That man's a perfect monster, I must admit!
    I'm simply stunned. I can't get over it.
ELMIRE: What, coming out so soon? How premature!
    Get back in hiding, and wait until you're sure.
    Stay till the end, and be convinced completely;
    We mustn't stop till things are proved concretely.
ORGON: Hell never harbored anything so vicious!
ELMIRE: Tut, don't be hasty. Try to be judicious.
    Wait, and be certain that there's no mistake.
    No jumping to conclusions, for Heaven's sake!
    (*She places* ORGON *behind her, as* TARTUFFE *re-enters.*)

Scene VII

TARTUFFE, ELMIRE, ORGON

TARTUFFE: (*Not seeing* ORGON.)
    Madam, all things have worked out to perfection;
    I've given the neighboring rooms a full inspection;
    No one's about; and now I may at last …
ORGON: (*Intercepting him.*) Hold on, my passionate fellow, not so fast!
    I should advise a little more restraint.
    Well, so you thought you'd fool me, my dear saint!
    How soon you wearied of the saintly life—
    Wedding my daughter, and coveting my wife!
    I've long suspected you, and had a feeling
    That soon I'd catch you at your double-dealing.
    Just now, you've given me evidence galore;
    It's quite enough; I have no wish for more.
ELMIRE: (*To* TARTUFFE.) I'm sorry to have treated you so slyly.
    But circumstances forced me to be wily.
TARTUFFE: Brother, you can't think …
ORGON: No more talk from you;
    Just leave this household, without more ado.
TARTUFFE: What I intended …

ORGON: That seems fairly clear.
  Spare me your falsehoods and get out of here.
TARTUFFE: No, I'm the master, and you're the one to go!
  This house belongs to me, I'll have you know,
  And I shall show you that you can't hurt me
  By this contemptible conspiracy,
  That those who cross me know not what they do,
  And that I've means to expose and punish you,
  Avenge offended Heaven, and make you grieve
  That ever you dared order me to leave.

Scene VIII
ELMIRE, ORGON

ELMIRE: What was the point of all that angry chatter?
ORGON: Dear God, I'm worried. This is no laughing matter.
ELMIRE: How so?
ORGON: I fear I understood his drift.
  I'm much disturbed about that deed of gift.
ELMIRE: You gave him ...?
ORGON: Yes, it's all been drawn and signed.
  But one thing more is weighing on my mind.
ELMIRE: What's that?
ORGON: I'll tell you; but first let's see if there's
  A certain strong-box in his room upstairs.

ACT V

Scene I
ORGON, CLÉANTE

CLÉANTE: Where are you going so fast?
ORGON: God knows!
CLÉANTE: Then wait;
  Let's have a conference, and deliberate
  On how this situation's to be met.
ORGON: That strong-box has me utterly upset;
  This is the worst of many, many shocks.
CLÉANTE: Is there some fearful mystery in that box?

ORGON: My poor friend Argas brought that box to me
  With his own hands, in utmost secrecy;
  'Twas on the very morning of his flight.
  It's full of papers which, if they came to light,
  Would ruin him—or such is my impression.
CLÉANTE: Then why did you let it out of your possession?
ORGON: Those papers vexed my conscience, and it seemed best
  To ask the counsel of my pious guest.
  The cunning scoundrel got me to agree
  To leave the strong-box in his custody,
  So that, in case of an investigation,
  I could employ a slight equivocation
  And swear I didn't have it, and thereby,
  At no expense to conscience, tell a lie.
CLÉANTE: It looks to me as if you're out on a limb.
  Trusting him with that box, and offering him
  That deed of gift, were actions of a kind
  Which scarcely indicate a prudent mind.
  With two such weapons, he has the upper hand,
  And since you're vulnerable, as matters stand,
  You erred once more in bringing him to bay.
  You should have acted in some subtler way.
ORGON: Just think of it: behind that fervent face,
  A heart so wicked, and a soul so base!
  I took him in, a hungry beggar, and then ...
  Enough, by God! I'm through with pious men:
  Henceforth I'll hate the whole false brotherhood.
  And persecute them worse than Satan could.
CLÉANTE: Ah, there you go—extravagant as ever.
  Why can you not be rational? You never
  Manage to take the middle course, it seems,
  But jump, instead, between absurd extremes
  You've recognized your recent grave mistake
  In falling victim to a pious fake;
  Now, to correct that error, must you embrace
  An even greater error in its place,
  And judge our worthy neighbors as a whole
  By what you've learned of one corrupted soul?
  Come, just because one rascal made you swallow

A show of zeal which turned out to be hollow,
Shall you conclude that all men are deceivers,
And that, today, there are no true believers?
Let atheists make that foolish inference;
Learn to distinguish virtue from pretense,
Be cautious in bestowing admiration,
And cultivate a sober moderation.
Don't humor fraud, but also don't asperse
True piety; the latter fault is worse,
And it is best to err, if err one must,
As you have done, upon the side of trust.

Scene II

DAMIS, ORGON, CLÉANTE

DAMIS: Father, I hear that scoundrel's uttered threats
    Against you; that he pridefully forgets
    How, in his need, he was befriended by you,
    And means to use your gifts to crucify you.
ORGON: It's true, my boy. I'm too distressed for tears.
DAMIS: Leave it to me, Sir; let me trim his ears.
    Faced with such insolence, we must not waver.
    I shall rejoice in doing you the favor
    Of cutting short his life, and your distress.
CLÉANTE: What a display of young hotheadedness!
    Do learn to moderate your fits of rage.
    In this just kingdom, this enlightened age,
    One does not settle things by violence.

Scene III

MADAME PERNELLE, MARIANE, ELMIRE, DORINE, DAMIS, ORGON, CLÉANTE

MADAME PERNELLE: I hear strange tales of very strange events.
ORGON: Yes, strange events which these two eyes beheld.
    The man's ingratitude is unparalleled.
    I save a wretched pauper from starvation.
    House him, and treat him like a blood relation,
    Shower him every day with my largesse,
    Give him my daughter, and all that I possess;

And meanwhile the unconscionable knave
Tries to induce my wife to misbehave;
And not content with such extreme rascality,
Now threatens me with my own liberality,
And aims, by taking base advantage of
The gifts I gave him out of Christian love,
To drive me from my house, a ruined man,
And make me end a pauper, as he began.

DORINE: Poor fellow!

MADAME PERNELLE: No, my son, I'll never bring
Myself to think him guilty of such a thing.

ORGON: How's that?

MADAME PERNELLE: The righteous always were maligned.

ORGON: Speak clearly, Mother. Say what's on your mind.

MADAME PERNELLE: I mean that I can smell a rat, my dear.
You know how everybody hates him, here.

ORGON: That has no bearing on the case at all.

MADAME PERNELLE: I told you a hundred times, when you were small,
That virtue in this world is hated ever;
Malicious men may die, but malice never.

ORGON: No doubt that's true, but how does it apply?

MADAME PERNELLE: They've turned you against him by a clever lie.

ORGON: I've told you, I was there and saw it done.

MADAME PERNELLE: Ah, slanderers will stop at nothing, Son.

ORGON: Mother, I'll lose my temper ... For the last time,
I tell you I was witness to the crime.

MADAME PERNELLE: The tongues of spite are busy night and noon
And to their venom no man is immune.

ORGON: You're talking nonsense. Can't you realize
I saw it; saw it; saw it with my eyes?
Saw, do you understand me? Must I shout it
Into your ears before you'll cease to doubt it?

MADAME PERNELLE: Appearances can deceive, my son.
Dear me,
We cannot always judge by what we see.

ORGON: Drat! Drat!

MADAME PERNELLE: One often interprets things awry;
Good can seem evil to a suspicious eye.

ORGON: Was I to see his pawing at Elmire
 As an act of charity?
MADAME PERNELLE: Till his guilt is clear,
 A man deserves the benefit of the doubt.
 You should have waited, to see how things turned out.
ORGON: Great God in Heaven, what more proof did I need?
 Was I to sit there, watching, until he'd ...
 You drive me to the brink of impropriety.
MADAME PERNELLE: No, no, a man of such surpassing piety
 Could not do such a thing. You cannot shake me.
 I don't believe it, and you shall not make me.
ORGON: You vex me so that, if you weren't my mother,
 I'd say to you ... some dreadful thing or other.
DORINE: It's your turn now, Sir, not to be listened to;
 You'd not trust us, and now she won't trust you.
CLÉANTE: My friends, we're wasting time which should be spent
 In facing up to our predicament.
 I fear that scoundrel's threats weren't made in sport.
DAMIS: Do you think he'd have the nerve to go to court?
ELMIRE: I'm sure he won't: they'd find it all too crude
 A case of swindling and ingratitude.
CLÉANTE: Don't be too sure. He won't be at a loss
 To give his claims a high and righteous gloss;
 And clever rogues with far less valid cause
 Have trapped their victims in a web of laws.
 I say again that to antagonize
 A man so strongly armed was most unwise.
ORGON: I know it; but the man's appalling cheek
 Outraged me so, I couldn't control my pique.
CLÉANTE: I wish to Heaven that we could devise
 Some truce between you, or some compromise.
ELMIRE: If I had known what cards he held, I'd not
 Have roused his anger by my little plot.
ORGON: (*To* DORINE, *as* M. LOYAL *enters.*)
 What is that fellow looking for? Who is he?
 Go talk to him—and tell him that I'm busy.

Scene IV

MONSIEUR LOYAL, MADAME PERNELLE, ORGON, DAMIS,
MARIANE, DORINE, ELMIRE, CLÉANTE

MONSIEUR LOYAL: Good day, dear sister.
    Kindly let me see your master.
DORINE: He's involved with company,
    And cannot be disturbed just now, I fear.
MONSIEUR LOYAL: I hate to intrude; but what has brought me here
    Will not disturb your master, in any event.
    Indeed, my news will make him most content.
DORINE: Your name?
MONSIEUR LOYAL: Just say that I bring greetings from
    Monsieur Tartuffe, on whose behalf I've come.
DORINE: (*To* ORGON.) Sir, he's a very gracious man, and bears
    A message from Tartuffe, which, he declares,
    Will make you most content.
CLÉANTE: Upon my word,
    I think this man had best be seen, and heard.
ORGON: Perhaps he has some settlement to suggest.
    How shall I treat him? What manner would be best?
CLÉANTE: Control your anger, and if he should mention
    Some fair adjustment, give him your full attention.
MONSIEUR LOYAL: Good health to you, good Sir.
    May Heaven confound
    Your enemies, and may your joys abound.
ORGON: (*Aside, to* CLÉANTE.) A gentle salutation: it confirms
    My guess that he is here to offer terms.
MONSIEUR LOYAL: I've always held your family most dear;
    I served your father, Sir, for many a year.
ORGON: Sir, I must ask your pardon; to my shame,
    I cannot now recall your face or name.
MONSIEUR LOYAL: Loyal's my name; I come from
    Normandy,
    And I'm a bailiff, in all modesty.
    For forty years, praise God, it's been my boast
    To serve with honor in that vital post,
    And I am here, Sir, if you will permit
    The liberty, to serve you with this writ ...

ORGON: To—what?

MONSIEUR LOYAL: Now, please, Sir, let us have no friction:
    It's nothing but an order of eviction.
    You are to move your goods and family out
    And make way for new occupants, without
    Deferment or delay, and give the keys ...

ORGON: I? Leave this house?

MONSIEUR LOYAL: Why yes, Sir, if you please.
    This house, Sir, from the cellar to the roof,
    Belongs now to the good Monsieur Tartuffe,
    And he is lord and master of your estate
    By virtue of a deed of present date,
    Drawn in due form, with clearest legal phrasing ...

DAMIS: Your insolence is utterly amazing!

MONSIEUR LOYAL: Young man, my business here is not with you,
    But with your wise and temperate father, who,
    Like every worthy citizen, stands in awe
    Of justice, and would never obstruct the law

ORGON: But ...

MONSIEUR LOYAL: Not for a million, Sir, would you rebel
    Against authority; I know that well.
    You'll not make trouble, Sir, or interfere
    With the execution of my duties here.

DAMIS: Someone may execute a smart tattoo
    On that black jacket of yours, before you're through.

MONSIEUR LOYAL: Sir, bid your son be silent. I'd much regret
    Having to mention such a nasty threat
    Of violence, in writing my report.

DORINE: (*Aside.*) This man Loyal's a most disloyal sort!

MONSIEUR LOYAL: I love all men of upright character,
    And when I agreed to serve these papers, Sir,
    It was your feelings that I had in mind.
    I couldn't bear to see the case assigned
    To someone else, who might esteem you less
    And so subject you to unpleasantness.

ORGON: What's more unpleasant than telling a man to leave
    His house and home?

MONSIEUR LOYAL: You'd like a short reprieve?
    If you desire, Sir, I shall not press you,

But wait until tomorrow to dispossess you.
Splendid. I'll come and spend the night here, then,
Most quietly, with half a score of men.
For form's sake, you might bring me, just before
You go to bed, the keys to the front door.
My men, I promise, will be on their best
Behavior, and will not disturb your rest.
But bright and early, Sir, you must be quick
And move out all your furniture, every stick;
The men I've chosen are both young and strong,
And with their help it shouldn't take you long.
In short, I'll make things pleasant and convenient,
And since I'm being so extremely lenient,
Please show me, Sir, a like consideration,
And give me your entire cooperation.

ORGON: (*Aside.*) I may be all but bankrupt, but I vow
 I'd give a hundred louis, here and now,
 Just for the pleasure of landing one good clout
 Right on the end of that complacent snout.

CLÉANTE: Careful; don't make things worse.

DAMIS: My bootsole itches
 To give that beggar a good kick in the breeches.

DORINE: Monsieur Loyal, I'd love to hear the whack
 Of a stout stick across your fine broad back.

MONSIEUR LOYAL: Take care: a woman too may go to jail if
 She uses threatening language to a bailiff.

CLÉANTE: Enough, enough, Sir. This must not go on.
 Give me that paper, please, and then begone.

MONSIEUR LOYAL: Well, au revoir. God give you all good cheer!

ORGON: May God confound you, and him who sent you here!

Scene V

ORGON, CLÉANTE, MARIANE, ELMIRE, MADAME PERNELLE, DORINE, DAMIS

ORGON: Now, Mother, was I right or not? This writ
 Should change your notion of Tartuffe a bit.
 Do you perceive his villainy at last?

MADAME PERNELLE: I'm thunderstruck. I'm utterly aghast.

DORINE: Oh, come, be fair. You mustn't take offense
  At this new proof of his benevolence.
  He's acting out of selfless love, I know.
  Material things enslave the soul, and so
  He kindly has arranged your liberation
  From all that might endanger your salvation.
ORGON: Will you not ever hold your tongue, you dunce?
CLÉANTE: Come, you must take some action, and at once.
ELMIRE: Go tell the world of the low trick he's tried.
  The deed of gift is surely nullified
  By such behavior, and public rage will not
  Permit the wretch to carry out his plot.

Scene VI

VALÈRE, ORGON, CLÉANTE, ELMIRE, MARIANE, MADAME PERNELLE, DAMIS, DORINE

VALÈRE: Sir, though I hate to bring you more bad news,
  Such is the danger that I cannot choose.
  A friend who is extremely close to me
  And knows my interest in your family
  Has, for my sake, presumed to violate
  The secrecy that's due to things of state,
  And sends me word that you are in a plight
  From which your one salvation lies in flight.
  That scoundrel who's imposed upon you so
  Denounced you to the King an hour ago
  And, as supporting evidence, displayed
  The strong-box of a certain renegade
  Whose secret papers, so he testified,
  You had disloyally agreed to hide.
  I don't know just what charges may be pressed,
  But there's a warrant out for your arrest;
  Tartuffe has been instructed, furthermore,
  To guide the arresting officer to your door.
CLÉANTE: He's clearly done this to facilitate
  His seizure of your house and your estate.
ORGON: That man, I must say, is a vicious beast!
VALÈRE: Quick, Sir; you mustn't tarry in the least.
  My carriage is outside, to take you hence;

This thousand louis should cover all expense.
Let's lose no time, or you shall be undone;
The sole defense, in this case, is to run.
I shall go with you all the way, and place you
In a safe refuge to which they'll never trace you.

ORGON: Alas, dear boy, I wish that I could show you
My gratitude for everything I owe you.
But now is not the time; I pray the Lord
That I may live to give you your reward.
Farewell, my dears; be careful ...

CLÉANTE: Brother, hurry.
We shall take care of things; you needn't worry.

Scene VII

THE OFFICER, TARTUFFE, VALÈRE, ORGON, ELMIRE, MARIANE,
MADAME PERNELLE, DORINE, CLÉANTE, DAMIS

TARTUFFE: Gently, Sir, gently; stay right where you are.
No need for haste; your lodging isn't far.
You're off to prison, by order of the Prince.

ORGON: This is the crowning blow, you wretch; and since
It means my total ruin and defeat,
Your villainy is now at last complete.

TARTUFFE: You needn't try to provoke me; it's no use.
Those who serve Heaven must expect abuse.

CLÉANTE: You are indeed most patient, sweet, and blameless.

DORINE: How he exploits the name of Heaven! It's shameless.

TARTUFFE: Your taunts and mockeries are all for naught;
To do my duty is my only thought.

MARIANE: Your love of duty is more meritorious,
And what you've done is little short of glorious.

TARTUFFE: All deeds are glorious, Madam, which obey
The sovereign prince who sent me here today.

ORGON: I rescued you when you were destitute,
Have you forgotten that, you thankless brute?

TARTUFFE: No, no, I well remember everything;
But my first duty is to serve my King.
That obligation is so paramount
That other claims, beside it, do not count;

And for it I would sacrifice my wife,
My family, my friend, or my own life.

ELMIRE: Hypocrite!

DORINE: All that we most revere, he uses
To cloak his plots and camouflage his ruses.

CLÉANTE: If it is true that you are animated
By pure and loyal zeal, as you have stated,
Why was this zeal not roused until you'd sought
To make Orgon a cuckold, and been caught?
Why weren't you moved to give your evidence
Until your outraged host had driven you hence?
I shan't say that the gift of all his treasure
Ought to have damped your zeal in any measure;
But if he is a traitor, as you declare,
How could you condescend to be his heir?

TARTUFFE: (*To the* OFFICER.) Sir, spare me all this clamor; it's growing shrill.
Please carry out your orders, if you will.

OFFICER: Yes, I've delayed too long, Sir. Thank you kindly.
You're just the proper person to remind me.
Come, you are off to join the other boarders
In the King's prison, according to his orders.

TARTUFFE: Who? I, Sir?

OFFICER: Yes.

TARTUFFE: To prison? This can't be true!

OFFICER: I owe an explanation, but not to you.
(*To* ORGON.)
Sir, all is well; rest easy, and be grateful.
We serve a Prince to whom all sham is hateful,
A Prince who sees into our inmost hearts,
And can't be fooled by any trickster's arts.
His royal soul, though generous and human,
Views all things with discernment and acumen;
His sovereign reason is not lightly swayed,
And all his judgments are discreetly weighed.
He honors righteous men of every kind,
And yet his zeal for virtue is not blind,
Nor does his love of piety numb his wits
And make him tolerant of hypocrites.
'Twas hardly likely that this man could cozen

A King who's foiled such liars by the dozen.
With one keen glance, the King perceived the whole
Perverseness and corruption of his soul,
And thus high Heaven's justice was displayed:
Betraying you, the rogue stood self-betrayed.
The King soon recognized Tartuffe as one
Notorious by another name, who'd done
So many vicious crimes that one could fill
Ten volumes with them, and be writing still.
But to be brief: our sovereign was appalled
By this man's treachery toward you, which he called
The last, worst villainy of a vile career,
And bade me follow the impostor here
To see how gross his impudence could be,
And force him to restore your property.
Your private papers, by the King's command,
I hereby seize and give into your hand.
The King, by royal order, invalidates
The deed which gave this rascal your estates,
And pardons, furthermore, your grave offense
In harboring an exile's documents.
By these decrees, our Prince rewards you for
Your loyal deeds in the late civil war,
And shows how heartfelt is his satisfaction
In recompensing any worthy action,
How much he prizes merit, and how he makes
More of men's virtues than of their mistakes.

DORINE: Heaven be praised!

MADAME PERNELLE: I breathe again, at last.

ELMIRE: We're safe.

MARIANE: I can't believe the danger's past.

ORGON: (To TARTUFFE.)
Well, traitor, now you see …

CLÉANTE: Ah, Brother, please,
Let's not descend to such indignities.
Leave the poor wretch to his unhappy fate,
And don't say anything to aggravate
His present woes; but rather hope that he
Will soon embrace an honest piety,

And mend his ways, and by a true repentance
Move our just King to moderate his sentence.
Meanwhile, go kneel before your sovereign's throne
And thank him for the mercies he has shown.
ORGON: Well said: let's go at once and, gladly kneeling,
Express the gratitude which all are feeling.
Then, when that first great duty has been done,
We'll turn with pleasure to a second one,
And give Valère, whose love has proven so true,
The wedded happiness which is his due.

THE IMPORTANCE OF BEING EARNEST

By Oscar Wilde

CHARACTERS

JOHN WORTHING, J.P.
ALGERNON MONCRIEFF
REV. CANON CHASUBLE, D.D.
MERRIMAN (*Butler*)
LANE (*Manservant*)
LADY BRACKNELL
HON. GWENDOLEN FAIRFAX
CECILY CARDEW
MISS PRISM (*Governess*)

THE SCENES OF THE PLAY

ACT I.   Algernon Moncrieff's Flat in Half-Moon Street, W.
ACT II.   The Garden at the Manor House, Woolton.
ACT III.   Drawing-Room at the Manor House, Woolton.

TIME
The Present.

PLACE
London.

ACT 1

Morning room in ALGERNON'*s flat in Half-Moon Street. The room is luxuriously and artistically furnished. The sound of a piano is heard in the adjoining room.*

(LANE *is arranging afternoon tea on the table, and after the music has ceased,* ALGERNON *enters.*)

ALGERNON: Did you hear what I was playing, Lane?

LANE: I didn't think it polite to listen, sir.

ALGERNON: I'm sorry for that, for your sake. I don't play accurately—any one can play accurately—but I play with wonderful expression. As far as the piano is concerned, sentiment is my forte. I keep science for Life.

LANE: Yes, sir.

ALGERNON: And, speaking of the science of Life, have you got the cucumber sandwiches cut for Lady Bracknell?

LANE: Yes, sir. (*Hands them on a salver.*)

ALGERNON: (*Inspects them, takes two, and sits down on the sofa.*) Oh! … by the way, Lane, I see from your book that on Thursday night, when Lord Shoreman and Mr. Worthing were dining with me, eight bottles of champagne are entered as having been consumed.

LANE: Yes, sir; eight bottles and a pint.

ALGERNON: Why is it that at a bachelor's establishment the servants invariably drink the champagne? I ask merely for information.

LANE: I attribute it to the superior quality of the wine, sir. I have often observed that in married households the champagne is rarely of a first-rate brand.

ALGERNON: Good heavens! Is marriage so demoralising as that?

LANE: I believe it *is* a very pleasant state, sir. I have had very little experience of it myself up to the present. I have only been married once. That was in consequence of a misunderstanding between myself and a young person.

ALGERNON: (*Languidly.*) I don't know that I am much interested in your family life, Lane.

LANE: No, sir; it is not a very interesting subject. I never think of it myself.

ALGERNON: Very natural, I am sure. That will do, Lane, thank you.

LANE: Thank you, sir. (LANE *goes out.*)

ALGERNON: Lanes views on marriage seem somewhat lax. Really, if the lower orders don't set us a good example, what on earth is the use of them? They seem, as a class, to have absolutely no sense of moral responsibility.

(*Enter* LANE.)

LANE: Mr. Ernest Worthing.

(*Enter* JACK.)

(LANE *goes out.*)

ALGERNON: How are you, my dear Ernest? What brings you up to town?

JACK: Oh, pleasure, pleasure! What else should bring one anywhere? Eating as usual, I see, Algy!

ALGERNON: (*Stiffly.*) I believe it is customary in good society to take some slight refreshment at five o'clock. Where have you been since last Thursday?

JACK: (*Sitting down on the sofa.*) In the country.

ALGERNON: What on earth do you do there?

JACK: (*Pulling off his gloves.*) When one is in town one amuses oneself. When one is in the country one amuses other people. It is excessively boring.

ALGERNON: And who are the people you amuse?

JACK: (*Airily.*) Oh, neighbours, neighbours.

ALGERNON: Got nice neighbours in your part of Shropshire?

JACK: Perfectly horrid! Never speak to one of them.

ALGERNON: How immensely you must amuse them! (*Goes over and takes sandwich.*) By the way, Shropshire is your county, is it not?

JACK: Eh? Shropshire? Yes, of course. Hallo! Why all these cups? Why cucumber sandwiches? Why such reckless extravagance in one so young? Who is coming to tea?

ALGERNON: Oh! merely Aunt Augusta and Gwendolen.

JACK: How perfectly delightful!

ALGERNON: Yes, that is all very well; but I am afraid Aunt Augusta won't quite approve of your being here.

JACK: May I ask why?

ALGERNON: My dear fellow, the way you flirt with Gwendolen is perfectly disgraceful. It is almost as bad as the way Gwendolen flirts with you.

JACK: I am in love with Gwendolen. I have come up to town expressly to propose to her.

ALGERNON: I thought you had come up for pleasure? … I call that business.

JACK: How utterly unromantic you are!

ALGERNON: I really don't see anything romantic in proposing. It is very romantic to be in love. But there is nothing romantic about a definite proposal. Why, one may be accepted. One usually is, I believe. Then the excitement is all over. The very essence of romance is uncertainty. If ever I get married, I'll certainly try to forget the fact.

JACK: I have no doubt about that, dear Algy. The Divorce Court was specially invented for people whose memories are so curiously constituted.

ALGERNON: Oh! there is no use speculating on that subject. Divorces are made in Heaven—(JACK *puts out his hand to take a sandwich.* ALGERNON *at once interferes.*)

Please don't touch the cucumber sandwiches. They are ordered specially for Aunt Augusta. (*Takes one and eats it.*)

JACK: Well, you have been eating them all the time.

ALGERNON: That is quite a different matter. She is my aunt. (*Takes plate from below.*) Have some bread and butter. The bread and butter is for Gwendolen. Gwendolen is devoted to bread and butter.

JACK: (*Advancing to table and helping himself.*) And very good bread and butter it is too.

ALGERNON: Well, my dear fellow, you need not eat as if you were going to eat it all. You behave as if you were married to her already. You are not married to her already, and I don't think you ever will be.

JACK: Why on earth do you say that?

ALGERNON: Well, in the first place girls never marry the men they flirt with. Girls don't think it right.

JACK: Oh, that is nonsense!

ALGERNON: It isn't. It is a great truth. It accounts for the extraordinary number of bachelors that one sees all over the place. In the second place, I don't give my consent.

JACK: Your consent!

ALGERNON: My dear fellow, Gwendolen is my first cousin. And before I allow you to marry her, you will have to clear up the whole question of Cecily. (*Rings bell.*)

JACK: Cecily! What on earth do you mean? What do you mean, Algy, by Cecily!

I don't know any one of the name of Cecily.

(*Enter* LANE.)

ALGERNON: Bring me that cigarette case Mr. Worthing left in the smoking room the last time he dined here.

LANE: Yes, sir. (LANE *goes out.*)

JACK: Do you mean to say you have had my cigarette case all this time? I wish to goodness you had let me know. I have been writing frantic letters to Scotland Yard about it. I was very nearly offering a large reward.

ALGERNON: Well, I wish you would offer one. I happen to be more than usually hard up.

JACK: There is no good offering a large reward now that the thing is found.

(*Enter* LANE *with the cigarette case on a salver.* ALGERNON *takes it at once.* LANE *goes out.*)

ALGERNON: I think that is rather mean of you, Ernest, I must say. (*Opens case and examines it.*) However, it makes no matter, for, now that I look at the inscription inside, I find that the thing isn't yours after all.

JACK: Of course it's mine. (*Moving to him.*) You have seen me with it a hundred times, and you have no right whatsoever to read what is written inside. It is a very ungentlemanly thing to read a private cigarette case.

ALGERNON: Oh! it is absurd to have a hard and fast rule about what one should read and what one shouldn't. More than half of modern culture depends on what one shouldn't read.

JACK: I am quite aware of the fact, and I don't propose to discuss modern culture. It isn't the sort of thing one should talk of in private. I simply want my cigarette case back.

ALGERNON: Yes; but this isn't your cigarette case. This cigarette case is a present from some one of the name of Cecily, and you said you didn't know any one of that name.

JACK: Well, if you want to know, Cecily happens to be my aunt.

ALGERNON: Your aunt!

JACK: Yes. Charming old lady she is, too. Lives at Tunbridge Wells. Just give it back to me, Algy.

ALGERNON: (*Retreating to back of sofa.*) But why does she call herself little Cecily if she is your aunt and lives at Tunbridge Wells? (*Reading.*) 'From little Cecily with her fondest love.'

JACK: (*Moving to sofa and kneeling upon it.*) My dear fellow, what on earth is there in that? Some aunts are tall, some aunts are not tall. That is a matter that surely an aunt may be allowed to decide for herself. You seem to think that every aunt should be exactly like your aunt! That is absurd! For Heaven's sake give me back my cigarette case. (*Follows* ALGERNON *round the room.*)

ALGERNON: Yes. But why does your aunt call you her uncle? 'From little Cecily, with her fondest love to her dear Uncle Jack.' There is no objection, I admit, to an aunt being a small aunt, but why an aunt, no matter what her size may be, should call her own nephew her uncle, I can't quite make out. Besides, your name isn't Jack at all; it is Ernest.

JACK: It isn't Ernest; it's Jack.

ALGERNON: You have always told me it was Ernest. I have introduced you to every one as Ernest. You answer to the name of Ernest. You look as if your name was Ernest. You are the most earnest-looking person I ever saw in my life. It is perfectly absurd your saying that your name isn't Ernest. It's on your cards. Here is one of them. (*Taking it from case.*) 'Mr. Ernest Worthing, B. 4, The Albany.' I'll keep this as a proof that your name is Ernest if ever you attempt to deny it to me, or to Gwendolen, or to any one else. (*Puts the card in his pocket.*)

JACK: Well, my name is Ernest in town and Jack in the country, and the cigarette case was given to me in the country.

ALGERNON: Yes, but that does not account for the fact that your small Aunt Cecily, who lives at Tunbridge Wells, calls you her dear uncle. Come, old boy, you had much better have the thing out at once.

JACK: My dear Algy, you talk exactly as if you were a dentist. It is very vulgar to talk like a dentist when one isn't a dentist. It produces a false impression,

ALGERNON: Well, that is exactly what dentists always do. Now, go on! Tell me the whole thing. I may mention that I have always suspected you of being a confirmed and secret Bunburyist; and I am quite sure of it now.

JACK: Bunburyist? What on earth do you mean by a Bunburyist?

ALGERNON: I'll reveal to you the meaning of that incomparable expression as soon as you are kind enough to inform me why you are Ernest in town and Jack in the country.

JACK: Well, produce my cigarette case first.

ALGERNON: Here it is. (*Hands cigarette case.*) Now produce your explanation, and pray make it improbable. (*Sits on sofa.*)

JACK: My dear fellow, there is nothing improbable about my explanation at all. In fact it's perfectly ordinary. Old Mr. Thomas Cardew, who adopted me when I was a little boy, made me in his will guardian to his granddaughter, Miss Cecily Cardew. Cecily, who addresses me as her uncle from motives of respect that you could not possibly appreciate, lives at my place in the country under the charge of her admirable governess, Miss Prism.

ALGERNON: Where is that place in the country, by the way?

JACK: That is nothing to you, dear boy. You are not going to be invited … I may tell you candidly that the place is not in Shropshire.

ALGERNON: I suspected that, my dear fellow! I have Bunburyed all over Shropshire on two separate occasions. Now, go on. Why are you Ernest in town and Jack in the country?

JACK: My dear Algy, I don't know whether you will be able to understand my real motives. You are hardly serious enough. When one is placed in the position of guardian, one has to adopt a very high moral tone on all subjects. It's one's duty to do so. And as a high moral tone can hardly be said to conduce very much to either one's health or one's happiness, in order to get up to town I have always pretended to have a younger brother of the name of Ernest, who lives in the Albany, and gets into the most dreadful scrapes. That, my dear Algy, is the whole truth pure and simple.

ALGERNON: The truth is rarely pure and never simple. Modern life would be very tedious if it were either, and modern literature a complete impossibility!

JACK: That wouldn't be at all a bad thing.

ALGERNON: Literary criticism is not your forte, my dear fellow. Don't try it. You should leave that to people who haven't been at a University. They do it so well in the daily papers. What you really are is a Bunburyist. I was quite right in saying you were a Bunburyist. You are one of the most advanced Bunburyists I know.

JACK: What on earth do you mean?

ALGERNON: You have invented a very useful younger brother called Ernest, in order that you may be able to come up to town as often as you like. I have invented an invaluable permanent invalid called Bunbury, in order that I may be able to go down into the country whenever I choose. Bunbury is perfectly invaluable. If it wasn't for Bunbury's extraordinary bad health, for instance, I wouldn't be able to dine with you at Willis's tonight, for I have been really engaged to Aunt Augusta for more than a week.

JACK: I haven't asked you to dine with me anywhere tonight.

ALGERNON: I know. You are absurdly careless about sending out invitations. It is very foolish of you. Nothing annoys people so much as not receiving invitations.

JACK: You had much better dine with your Aunt Augusta.

ALGERNON: I haven't the smallest intention of doing anything of the kind. To begin with, I dined there on Monday, and once a week is quite enough to dine with one's own relations. In the second place, whenever I do dine there I am always treated as a member of the family, and sent down with either no woman at all, or two. In the third place, I know perfectly well whom she will place me next to, tonight. She will place me next Mary Farquhar, who always flirts with her own husband across the dinner-table. That is not very pleasant. Indeed, it is not even decent … and that sort of thing is enormously on the increase. The amount of women in London who flirt with their own husbands is perfectly scandalous. It looks so bad. It is simply washing one's clean linen in public. Besides, now that I know you to be a confirmed Bunburyist I naturally want to talk to you about Bunburying. I want to tell you the rules.

JACK: I'm not a Bunburyist at all. If Gwendolen accepts me, I am going to kill my brother, indeed I think I'll kill him in any case. Cecily is a little too much interested in him. It is rather a bore. So I am going to get rid of Ernest. And I strongly advise you to do the same with Mr … with your invalid friend who has the absurd name.

ALGERNON: Nothing will induce me to part with Bunbury, and if you ever get married, which seems to me extremely problematic, you will be very glad to know Bunbury. A man who marries without knowing Bunbury has a very tedious time of it.

JACK: That is nonsense. If I marry a charming girl like Gwendolen, and she is the only girl I ever saw in my life that I would marry, I certainly won't want to know Bunbury.

ALGERNON: Then your wife will. You don't seem to realise, that in married life three is company and two is none.

JACK: (*Sententiously.*) That, my dear young friend, is the theory that the corrupt French Drama has been propounding for the last fifty years.

ALGERNON: Yes; and that the happy English home has proved in half the time.

JACK: For heaven's sake, don't try to be cynical. It's perfectly easy to be cynical.

ALGERNON: My dear fellow, it isn't easy to be anything nowadays. There's such a lot of beastly competition about. (*The sound of an electric bell is heard.*) Ah! that must be Aunt Augusta. Only relatives, or creditors, ever ring in that Wagnerian manner. Now, if I get her out of the way for ten minutes, so that you can have an opportunity for proposing to Gwendolen, may I dine with you tonight at Willis's?

JACK: I suppose so, if you want to.

ALGERNON: Yes, but you must be serious about it. I hate people who are not serious about meals. It is so shallow of them. (*Enter* LANE.) Lady Bracknell and Miss Fairfax.

(ALGERNON *goes forward to meet them. Enter* LADY BRACKNELL *and* GWENDOLEN.)

LADY BRACKNELL: Good afternoon, dear Algernon, I hope you are behaving very well.

ALGERNON: I'm feeling very well, Aunt Augusta.

LADY BRACKNELL: That's not quite the same thing. In fact the two things rarely go together. (*Sees* JACK *and bows to him with icy coldness.*)

ALGERNON: (*To* GWENDOLEN.) Dear me, you are smart!

GWENDOLEN: I am always smart! Am I not, Mr. Worthing?

JACK: You're quite perfect, Miss Fairfax.

GWENDOLEN: Oh! I hope I am not that. It would leave no room for developments, and I intend to develop in many directions. (GWENDOLEN *and* JACK *sit down together in the corner.*)

LADY BRACKNELL: I'm sorry if we are a little late, Algernon, but I was obliged to call on dear Lady Harbury. I hadn't been there since her poor husband's death. I never saw a woman so altered; she looks quite twenty years younger. And now I'll have a cup of tea, and one of those nice cucumber sandwiches you promised me.

ALGERNON: Certainly, Aunt Augusta. (*Goes over to tea table.*)

LADY BRACKNELL: Won't you come and sit here, Gwendolen?

GWENDOLEN: Thanks, mamma, I'm quite comfortable where I am.

ALGERNON: (*Picking up empty plate in horror.*) Good heavens! Lane! Why are there no cucumber sandwiches? I ordered them specially.

LANE: (*Gravely.*) There were no cucumbers in the market this morning, sir. I went down twice.

ALGERNON: No cucumbers!

LANE: No, sir. Not even for ready money.

ALGERNON: That will do, Lane, thank you.

LANE: Thank you, sir. (*Goes out.*)

ALGERNON: I am greatly distressed, Aunt Augusta, about there being no cucumbers, not even for ready money.

LADY BRACKNELL: It really makes no matter, Algernon. I had some crumpets with Lady Harbury, who seems to me to be living entirely for pleasure now.

ALGERNON: I hear her hair has turned quite gold from grief.

LADY BRACKNELL: It certainly has changed its colour. From what cause I, of course, cannot say. (ALGERNON *crosses and hands tea.*) Thank you. I've quite a treat for you tonight, Algernon. I am going to send you down with Mary Farquhar. She is such a nice woman, and so attentive to her husband. It's delightful to watch them.

ALGERNON: I am afraid, Aunt Augusta, I shall have to give up the pleasure of dining with you tonight after all.

LADY BRACKNELL: (*Frowning.*) I hope not, Algernon. It would put my table completely out. Your uncle would have to dine upstairs. Fortunately he is accustomed to that.

ALGERNON: It is a great bore, and, I need hardly say, a terrible disappointment to me, but the fact is I have just had a telegram to say that my poor friend Bunbury is very ill again. (*Exchanges glances with* JACK.) They seem to think I should be with him.

LADY BRACKNELL: It is very strange. This Mr. Bunbury seems to suffer from curiously bad health.

ALGERNON: Yes; poor Bunbury is a dreadful invalid.

LADY BRACKNELL: Well, I must say, Algernon, that I think it is high time that Mr. Bunbury made up his mind whether he was going to live or to die. This shilly shallying with the question is absurd. Nor do I in any way approve of the modern sympathy with invalids. I consider it morbid. Illness of any kind is hardly a thing to be encouraged in others. Health is the primary duty of life. I am always telling that to your poor uncle, but he never seems to take much notice … as far as any improvement in his ailment goes. I should be much obliged if you would ask Mr. Bunbury, from me, to be kind enough not to have a relapse on Saturday, for I rely on you to arrange my music for me. It is my last reception, and one wants something that will encourage conversation, particularly at the end of the season when every one has practically said whatever they had to say, which, in most cases, was probably not much.

ALGERNON: I'll speak to Bunbury, Aunt Augusta, if he is still conscious, and I think I can promise you he'll be all right by Saturday. Of course the music is a great difficulty. You see, if one plays good music, people don't listen, and if one plays bad music people don't talk. But I'll run over the programme I've drawn out, if you will kindly come into the next room for a moment.

LADY BRACKNELL: Thank you, Algernon. It is very thoughtful of you. (*Rising, and following* ALGERNON.) I'm sure the programme will be delightful, after a few expurgations. French songs I cannot possibly allow. People always seem to think that they are improper, and either look shocked, which is vulgar, or laugh, which is worse. But German sounds a thoroughly respectable language, and indeed, I believe is so. Gwendolen, you will accompany me.

GWENDOLEN: Certainly, mamma.

(LADY BRACKNELL *and* ALGERNON *go into the music room,* GWENDOLEN *remains behind.*)

JACK: Charming day it has been, Miss Fairfax.

GWENDOLEN: Pray don't talk to me about the weather, Mr. Worthing. Whenever people talk to me about the weather, I always feel quite certain that they mean something else. And that makes me so nervous.

JACK: I do mean something else.

GWENDOLEN: I thought so. In fact, I am never wrong.

JACK: And I would like to be allowed to take advantage of Lady Bracknell's temporary absence …

GWENDOLEN: I would certainly advise you to do so. Mamma has a way of coming back suddenly into a room that I have often had to speak to her about.

JACK: (*Nervously.*) Miss Fairfax, ever since I met you I have admired you more than any girl … I have ever met since … I met you.

GWENDOLEN: Yes, I am quite well aware of the fact. And I often wish that in public, at any rate, you had been more demonstrative. For me you have always had an irresistible fascination. Even before I met you I was far from indifferent to you. (JACK *looks at her in amazement.*) We live, as I hope you know, Mr Worthing, in an age of ideals. The fact is constantly mentioned in the more expensive monthly magazines, and has reached the provincial pulpits, I am told; and my ideal has always been to love some one of the name of Ernest. There is something in that name that inspires absolute confidence. The moment Algernon first mentioned to me that he had a friend called Ernest, I knew I was destined to love you.

JACK: You really love me, Gwendolen?

GWENDOLEN: Passionately!

JACK: Darling! You don't know how happy you've made me.

GWENDOLEN: My own Ernest!

JACK: But you don't really mean to say that you couldn't love me if my name wasn't Ernest?

GWENDOLEN: But your name is Ernest.

JACK: Yes, I know it is. But supposing it was something else? Do you mean to say you couldn't love me then?

GWENDOLEN: (*Glibly.*) Ah! that is clearly a metaphysical speculation, and like most metaphysical speculations has very little reference at all to the actual facts of real life, as we know them.

JACK: Personally, darling, to speak quite candidly, I don't much care about the name of Ernest … I don't think the name suits me at all.

GWENDOLEN: It suits you perfectly. It is a divine name. It has a music of its own. It produces vibrations.

JACK: Well, really, Gwendolen, I must say that I think there are lots of other much nicer names. I think Jack, for instance, a charming name.

GWENDOLEN: Jack? … No, there is very little music in the name Jack, if any at all, indeed. It does not thrill. It produces absolutely no vibrations … I have known several Jacks, and they all, without exception, were more than usually plain. Besides, Jack is a notorious domesticity for John! And I pity any woman who is married to a man called John. She would probably never be allowed to know the entrancing pleasure of a single moment's solitude. The only really safe name is Ernest

JACK: Gwendolen, I must get christened at once—I mean we must get married at once. There is no time to be lost.

GWENDOLEN: Married, Mr. Worthing?

JACK: (*Astounded.*) Well … surely. You know that I love you, and you led me to believe, Miss Fairfax, that you were not absolutely indifferent to me.

GWENDOLEN: I adore you. But you haven't proposed to me yet. Nothing has been said at all about marriage. The subject has not even been touched on.

JACK: Well … may I propose to you now?

GWENDOLEN: I think it would be an admirable opportunity. And to spare you any possible disappointment, Mr. Worthing, I think it only fair to tell you quite frankly before hand that I am fully determined to accept you.

JACK: Gwendolen!

GWENDOLEN: Yes, Mr. Worthing, what have you got to say to me?

JACK: You know what I have got to say to you.

GWENDOLEN: Yes, but you don't say it.

JACK: Gwendolen, will you marry me? (*Goes on his knees.*)

GWENDOLEN: Of course I will, darling. How long you have been about it! I am afraid you have had very little experience in how to propose.

JACK: My own one, I have never loved any one in the world but you.

GWENDOLEN: Yes, but men often propose for practice. I know my brother Gerald does. All my girlfriends tell me so. What wonderfully blue eyes you have, Ernest! They are quite, quite, blue. I hope you will always look at me just like that, especially when there are other people present. (*Enter* LADY BRACKNELL.)

LADY BRACKNELL: Mr. Worthing! Rise, sir, from this semi-recumbent posture. It is most indecorous.

GWENDOLEN: Mamma! (*He tries to rise; she restrains him.*) I must beg you to retire. This is no place for you. Besides, Mr. Worthing has not quite finished yet.

LADY BRACKNELL: Finished what, may I ask?

GWENDOLEN: I am engaged to Mr. Worthing, mamma. (*They rise together.*)

LADY BRACKNELL: Pardon me, you are not engaged to any one. When you do become engaged to some one, I, or your father, should his health permit him, will inform you of the fact. An engagement should come on a young girl as a surprise, pleasant or unpleasant, as the case may be. It is hardly a matter that she could be allowed to arrange for herself … And now I have a few questions to put to you, Mr. Worthing. While I am making these inquiries, you, Gwendolen, will wait for me below in the carriage.

GWENDOLEN: (*Reproachfully.*) Mamma!

LADY BRACKNELL: In the carriage, Gwendolen! (GWENDOLEN *goes to the door. She and* JACK *blow kisses to each other behind* LADY BRACKNELL'*s back.* LADY BRACKNELL *looks vaguely about as if she could not understand what the noise was. Finally turns round.*) Gwendolen, the carriage!

GWENDOLEN: Yes, mamma. (*Goes out, looking back at* JACK.)

LADY BRACKNELL: (*Sitting down.*) You can take a seat, Mr. Worthing.

(*Looks in her pocket for notebook and pencil.*)

JACK: Thank you, Lady Bracknell, I prefer standing.

LADY BRACKNELL: (*Pencil and notebook in hand.*) I feel bound to tell you that you are not down on my list of eligible young men, although I have the same list as the dear Duchess of Bolton has. We work together, in fact. However, I am quite ready to enter your name, should your answers be what a really affectionate mother requires. Do you smoke?

JACK: Well, yes, I must admit I smoke.

LADY BRACKNELL: I am glad to hear it. A man should always have an occupation of some kind. There are far too many idle men in London as it is. How old are you?

JACK: Twenty-nine.

LADY BRACKNELL: A very good age to be married at. I have always been of opinion that a man who desires to get married should know either everything or nothing. Which do you know?

JACK: (*After some hesitation.*) I know nothing, Lady Bracknell.

LADY BRACKNELL: I am pleased to hear it. I do not approve of anything that tampers with natural ignorance. Ignorance is like a delicate exotic fruit; touch it and the bloom is gone. The whole theory of modern education is radically unsound. Fortunately in England, at any rate, education produces no effect whatsoever. If it did, it would prove a serious danger to the upper classes, and probably lead to acts of violence in Grosvenor Square. What is your income?

JACK: Between seven and eight thousand a year.

LADY BRACKNELL: (*Makes a note in her book.*) In land, or in investments?

JACK: In investments, chiefly.

LADY BRACKNELL: That is satisfactory. What between the duties expected of one during one's lifetime, and the duties exacted from one after one's death, land has ceased to be either a profit or a pleasure. It gives one position, and prevents one from keeping it up. That's all that can be said about land.

JACK: I have a country house with some land, of course, attached to it, about fifteen hundred acres, I believe; but I don't depend on that for my real income. In fact, as far as I can make out, the poachers are the only people who make anything out of it.

LADY BRACKNELL: A country house! How many bedrooms? Well, that point can be cleared up afterwards. You have a town house, I hope? A girl with a simple, unspoiled nature, like Gwendolen, could hardly be expected to reside in the country.

JACK: Well, I own a house in Belgrave Square, but it is let by the year to Lady Bloxham. Of course, I can get it back whenever I like, at six months' notice.

LADY BRACKNELL: Lady Bloxham? I don't know her.

JACK: Oh, she goes about very little. She is a lady considerably advanced in years.

LADY BRACKNELL: Ah, nowadays that is no guarantee of respectability of character. What number in Belgrave Square?

JACK: 149.

LADY BRACKNELL: (*Shaking her head.*) The unfashionable side. I thought there was something. However, that could easily be altered.

JACK: Do you mean the fashion, or the side?

LADY BRACKNELL: (*Sternly.*) Both, if necessary, I presume. What are your politics?

JACK: Well, I am afraid I really have none. I am a Liberal Unionist.

LADY BRACKNELL: Oh, they count as Tories. They dine with us. Or come in the evening, at any rate. Now to minor matters. Are your parents living?

JACK: I have lost both my parents.

LADY BRACKNELL: To lose one parent, Mr. Worthing, may be regarded as a misfortune; to lose both looks like carelessness. Who was your father? He was evidently a man of some wealth. Was he born in what the Radical papers call the purple of commerce, or did he rise from the ranks of the aristocracy?

JACK: I am afraid I really don't know. The fact is, Lady Bracknell, I said I had lost my parents. It would be nearer the truth to say that my parents seem to have lost me … I don't actually know who I am by birth. I was … well, I was found.

LADY BRACKNELL: Found!

JACK: The late Mr. Thomas Cardew, an old gentleman of a very charitable and kindly disposition, found me, and gave me the name of Worthing, because he happened to have a first-class ticket for Worthing in his pocket at the time. Worthing is a place in Sussex. It is a seaside resort.

LADY BRACKNELL: Where did the charitable gentleman who had a first-class ticket for this seaside resort find you?

JACK: (*Gravely.*) In a handbag.

LADY BRACKNELL: A handbag?

JACK: (*Very seriously.*) Yes, Lady Bracknell. I was in a handbag—a somewhat large, black leather handbag, with handles to it—an ordinary handbag in fact.

LADY BRACKNELL: In what locality did this Mr. James, or Thomas, Cardew come across this ordinary handbag?

JACK: In the cloakroom at Victoria Station. It was given to him in mistake for his own.

LADY BRACKNELL: The cloakroom at Victoria Station?

JACK: Yes. The Brighton line.

LADY BRACKNELL: The line is immaterial. Mr. Worthing, I confess I feel somewhat bewildered by what you have just told me. To be born, or at any rate bred, in a handbag, whether it had handles or not, seems to me to display a contempt for the ordinary decencies of family life that reminds one of the worst excesses of the French Revolution. And I presume you know what that unfortunate movement led to? As for the particular locality in which the handbag was found, a cloakroom at a railway station might serve to conceal a social indiscretion—has probably, indeed, been used for that purpose before now—but it could hardly be regarded as an assured basis for a recognised position in good society.

JACK: May I ask you then what you would advise me to do? I need hardly say I would do anything in the world to ensure Gwendolen's happiness.

LADY BRACKNELL: I would strongly advise you, Mr. Worthing, to try and acquire some relations as soon as possible, and to make a definite effort to produce at any rate one parent, of either sex, before the season is quite over.

JACK: Well, I don't see how I could possibly manage to do that. I can produce the handbag at any moment. It is in my dressing room at home. I really think that should satisfy you, Lady Bracknell.

LADY BRACKNELL: Me, sir! What has it to do with me? You can hardly imagine that I and Lord Bracknell would dream of allowing our only daughter—a girl brought up with the utmost care—to marry into a cloakroom, and form an alliance with a parcel? Good morning, Mr. Worthing!

(LADY BRACKNELL *sweeps out in majestic indignation.*)

JACK: Good morning! (ALGERNON, *from the other room, strikes up the Wedding March.* JACK *looks perfectly furious, and goes to the door.*) For goodness' sake don't play that ghastly tune, Algy. How idiotic you are!

(*The music stops and* ALGERNON *enters cheerily.*)

ALGERNON: Didn't it go off all right, old boy? You don't mean to say Gwendolen refused you? I know it is a way she has. She is always refusing people. I think it is most ill-natured of her.

JACK: Oh, Gwendolen is as right as a trivet. As far as she is concerned, we are engaged. Her mother is perfectly unbearable. Never met such a Gorgon ... I don't really know what a Gorgon is like, but I am quite sure that Lady Bracknell is one. In any case, she is a monster, without being a myth, which is rather unfair ... I beg your pardon, Algy, I suppose I shouldn't talk about your own aunt in that way before you.

ALGERNON: My dear boy, I love hearing my relations abused. It is the only thing that makes me put up with them at all. Relations are simply a tedious pack of people, who haven't got the remotest knowledge of how to live, nor the smallest instinct about when to die.

JACK: Oh, that is nonsense!

ALGERNON: It isn't!

JACK: Well, I won't argue about the matter. You always want to argue about things.

ALGERNON: That is exactly what things were originally made for.

JACK: Upon my word, if I thought that, I'd shoot myself ... (*A pause.*) You don't think there is any chance of Gwendolen becoming like her mother in about a hundred and fifty years, do you, Algy?

ALGERNON: All women become like their mothers. That is their tragedy. No man does. That's his.

JACK: Is that clever?

ALGERNON: It is perfectly phrased! and quite as true as any observation in civilised life should be.

JACK: I am sick to death of cleverness. Everybody is clever nowadays. You can't go anywhere without meeting clever people. The thing has become an absolute public nuisance. I wish to goodness we had a few fools left.

ALGERNON: We have.

JACK: I should extremely like to meet them. What do they talk about?

ALGERNON: The fools? Oh! about the clever people, of course.

JACK: What fools!

ALGERNON: By the way, did you tell Gwendolen the truth about your being Ernest in town, and Jack in the country?

JACK: (*In a very patronising manner.*) My dear fellow, the truth isn't quite the sort of thing one tells to a nice, sweet, refined girl. What extraordinary ideas you have about the way to behave to a woman!

ALGERNON: The only way to behave to a woman is to make love to her, if she is pretty, and to some one else, if she is plain.

JACK: Oh, that is nonsense.

ALGERNON: What about your brother? What about the profligate Ernest?

JACK: Oh, before the end of the week I shall have got rid of him. I'll say he died in Paris of apoplexy. Lots of people die of apoplexy, quite suddenly, don't they?

ALGERNON: Yes, but it's hereditary, my dear fellow. It's a sort of thing that runs in families. You had much better say a severe chill.

JACK: You are sure a severe chill isn't hereditary, or anything of that kind?

ALGERNON: Of course it isn't!

JACK: Very well, then. My poor brother Ernest is carried off suddenly, in Paris, by a severe chill. That gets rid of him.

ALGERNON: But I thought you said that … Miss Cardew was a little too much interested in your poor brother Ernest? Won't she feel his loss a good deal?

JACK: Oh, that is all right. Cecily is not a silly romantic girl, I am glad to say. She has got a capital appetite, goes for long walks, and pays no attention at all to her lessons.

ALGERNON: I would rather like to see Cecily.

JACK: I will take very good care you never do. She is excessively pretty, and she is only just eighteen.

ALGERNON: Have you told Gwendolen yet that you have an excessively pretty ward who is only just eighteen?

JACK: Oh! one doesn't blurt these things out to people. Cecily and Gwendolen are perfectly certain to be extremely great friends. I'll bet you anything you like that half an hour after they have met, they will be calling each other sister.

ALGERNON: Women only do that when they have called each other a lot of other things first. Now, my dear boy, if we want to get a good table at Willis's, we really must go and dress. Do you know it is nearly seven?

JACK: (*Irritably.*) Oh! It always is nearly seven.

ALGERNON: Well, I'm hungry.

JACK: I never knew you when you weren't …

ALGERNON: What shall we do after dinner? Go to a theatre?

JACK: Oh no! I loathe listening.

ALGERNON: Well, let us go to the Club?

JACK: Oh, no! I hate talking.

ALGERNON: Well, we might trot round to the Empire at ten?

JACK: Oh, no! I can't bear looking at things. It is so silly.

ALGERNON: Well, what shall we do?

JACK: Nothing!

ALGERNON: It is awfully hard work doing nothing. However, I don't mind hard work where there is no definite object of any kind.

(*Enter* LANE.)

LANE: Miss Fairfax.

(*Enter* GWENDOLEN. LANE *goes out.*)

ALGERNON: Gwendolen, upon my word!

GWENDOLEN: Algy, kindly turn your back. I have something very particular to say to Mr. Worthing.

ALGERNON: Really, Gwendolen, I don't think I can allow this at all.

GWENDOLEN: Algy, you always adopt a strictly immoral attitude towards life. You are not quite old enough to do that. (ALGERNON *retires to the fireplace.*)

JACK: My own darling!

GWENDOLEN: Ernest, we may never be married. From the expression on mamma's face I fear we never shall. Few parents nowadays pay any regard to what their children say to them. The old-fashioned respect for the young is fast dying out. Whatever influence I ever had over mamma, I lost at the age of three. But although she may prevent us from becoming man and wife, and I may marry some one else, and marry often, nothing that she can possibly do can alter my eternal devotion to you.

JACK: Dear Gwendolen!

GWENDOLEN: The story of your romantic origin, as related to me by mamma, with unpleasing comments, has naturally stirred the deeper fibres of my nature. Your Christian name has an irresistible fascination. The simplicity of your character makes you exquisitely incomprehensible to me. Your town address at the Albany I have. What is your address in the country?

JACK: The Manor House, Woolton, Hertfordshire.

(ALGERNON, *who has been carefully listening, smiles to himself, and writes the address on his shirt-cuff. Then picks up the Railway Guide.*)

GWENDOLEN: There is a good postal service, I suppose? It may be necessary to do something desperate. That of course will require serious consideration. I will communicate with you daily.

JACK: My own one!

GWENDOLEN: How long do you remain in town?

JACK: Till Monday.

GWENDOLEN: Good! Algy, you may turn round now.

ALGERNON: Thanks, I've turned round already.

GWENDOLEN: You may also ring the bell.

JACK: You will let me see you to your carriage, my own darling?

GWENDOLEN: Certainly.

JACK: (*To* LANE, *who now enters.*) I will see Miss Fairfax out.

LANE: Yes, sir. (JACK *and* GWENDOLEN *go off.*)

(LANE *presents several letters on a salver to* ALGERNON. *It is to be surmised that they are bills, as* ALGERNON, *after looking at the envelopes, tears them up.*)

ALGERNON: A glass of sherry, Lane.

LANE: Yes, sir.

ALGERNON: Tomorrow, Lane, I'm going Bunburying.

LANE: Yes, sir.

ALGERNON: I shall probably not be back till Monday. You can put up my dress clothes, my smoking jacket, and all the Bunbury suits …

LANE: Yes, sir. (*Handing sherry.*)

ALGERNON: I hope tomorrow will be a fine day, Lane.

LANE: It never is, sir.

ALGERNON: Lane, you're a perfect pessimist.

LANE: I do my best to give satisfaction, sir.

(*Enter* JACK. LANE *goes off.*)

JACK: There's a sensible, intellectual girl! the only girl I ever cared for in my life. (ALGERNON *is laughing immoderately.*) What on earth are you so amused at?

ALGERNON: Oh, I'm a little anxious about poor Bunbury, that is all.

JACK: If you don't take care, your friend Bunbury will get you into a serious scrape some day.

ALGERNON: I love scrapes. They are the only things that are never serious.

JACK: Oh, that's nonsense, Algy. You never talk anything but nonsense.

ALGERNON: Nobody ever does.

(JACK *looks indignantly at him, and leaves the room.* ALGERNON *lights a cigarette, reads his shirt-cuff, and smiles.*)

ACT 2

Garden at the Manor House. A flight of grey stone steps leads up to the house. The garden, an old-fashioned one, full of roses. Time of year, July. Basket chairs, and a table covered with books, are set under a large yew-tree.

(MISS PRISM *discovered seated at the table.* CECILY *is at the back watering flowers.*)

MISS PRISM: (*Calling.*) Cecily, Cecily! Surely such a utilitarian occupation as the watering of flowers is rather Moulton's duty than yours? Especially at a moment when intellectual pleasures await you. Your German grammar is on the table. Pray open it at page fifteen. We will repeat yesterday's lesson.

CECILY: (*Coming over very slowly.*) But I don't like German. It isn't at all a becoming language. I know perfectly well that I look quite plain after my German lesson.

MISS PRISM: Child, you know how anxious your guardian is that you should improve yourself in every way. He laid particular stress on your German, as he was leaving for town yesterday. Indeed, he always lays stress on your German when he is leaving for town.

CECILY: Dear Uncle Jack is so very serious! Sometimes he is so serious that I think he cannot be quite well

MISS PRISM: (*Drawing herself up.*) Your guardian enjoys the best of health, and his gravity of demeanour is especially to be commended in one so comparatively young as he is. I know no one who has a higher sense of duty and responsibility.

CECILY: I suppose that is why he often looks a little bored when we three are together.

MISS PRISM: Cecily! I am surprised at you. Mr. Worthing has many troubles in his life. Idle merriment and triviality would be out of place in his conversation. You must remember his constant anxiety about that unfortunate young man his brother.

CECILY: I wish Uncle Jack would allow that unfortunate young man, his brother, to come down here sometimes. We might have a good influence over him, Miss Prism. I am sure you certainly would. You know German, and geology, and things of that kind influence a man very much. (CECILY *begins to write in her diary.*)

MISS PRISM: (*Shaking her head.*) I do not think that even I could produce any effect on a character that according to his own brother's admission is irretrievably weak and vacillating. Indeed I am not sure that I would desire to reclaim him. I am not in favour of this modern mania for turning bad people into good people at a moment's notice. As a man sows so let him reap. You must put away your diary, Cecily. I really don't see why you should keep a diary at all.

CECILY: I keep a diary in order to enter the wonderful secrets of my life. If I didn't write them down, I should probably forget all about them.

MISS PRISM: Memory, my dear Cecily, is the diary that we all carry about with us.

CECILY: Yes, but it usually chronicles the things that have never happened, and couldn't possibly have happened. I believe that Memory is responsible for nearly all the three volume novels that Mudie sends us.

MISS PRISM: Do not speak slightingly of the three volume novel, Cecily. I wrote one myself in earlier days.

CECILY: Did you really, Miss Prism? How wonderfully clever you are! I hope it did not end happily? I don't like novels that end happily. They depress me so much.

MISS PRISM: The good ended happily, and the bad unhappily. That is what Fiction means.

CECILY: I suppose so. But it seems very unfair. And was your novel ever published?

MISS PRISM: Alas! no. The manuscript unfortunately was abandoned. (CECILY *starts*.) I use the word in the sense of lost or mislaid. To your work, child, these speculations are profitless.

CECILY: (*Smiling*.) But I see dear Dr. Chasuble coming up through the garden.

MISS PRISM: (*Rising and advancing*.) Dr. Chasuble! This is indeed a pleasure.

(*Enter* CANON CHASUBLE.)

CHASUBLE: And how are we this morning? Miss Prism, you are, I trust, well?

CECILY: Miss Prism has just been complaining of a slight headache. I think it would do her so much good to have a short stroll with you in the Park, Dr. Chasuble.

MISS PRISM: Cecily, I have not mentioned anything about a headache.

CECILY: No, dear Miss Prism, I know that, but I felt instinctively that you had a headache. Indeed I was thinking about that, and not about my German lesson, when the Rector came in.

CHASUBLE: I hope, Cecily, you are not inattentive.

CECILY: Oh, I am afraid I am.

CHASUBLE: That is strange. Were I fortunate enough to be Miss Prism's pupil, I would hang upon her lips. (MISS PRISM *glares*.) I spoke metaphorically. My metaphor was drawn from bees. Ahem! Mr. Worthing, I suppose, has not returned from town yet?

MISS PRISM: We do not expect him till Monday afternoon.

CHASUBLE: Ah yes, he usually likes to spend his Sunday in London. He is not one of those whose sole aim is enjoyment, as, by all accounts, that unfortunate young man his brother seems to be. But I must not disturb Egeria and her pupil any longer.

MISS PRISM: Egeria? My name is Laetitia, Doctor.

CHASUBLE: (*Bowing*.) A classical allusion merely, drawn from the Pagan authors. I shall see you both no doubt at Evensong?

MISS PRISM: I think, dear Doctor, I will have a stroll with you. I find I have a headache after all, and a walk might do it good.

CHASUBLE: With pleasure, Miss Prism, with pleasure. We might go as far as the schools and back.

MISS PRISM: That would be delightful. Cecily, you will read your Political Economy in my absence. The chapter on the Fall of the Rupee you may omit. It is somewhat too sensational. Even these metallic problems have their melodramatic side.

(*Goes down the garden with* DR. CHASUBLE.)

CECILY: (*Picks up books and throws them back on table.*) Horrid Political Economy! Horrid Geography! Horrid, horrid German!

(*Enter* MERRIMAN *with a card on a salver.*)

MERRIMAN: Mr. Ernest Worthing has just driven over from the station. He has brought his luggage with him.

CECILY: (*Takes the card and reads it.*) 'Mr. Ernest Worthing, B. 4, The Albany, W.' Uncle Jack's brother! Did you tell him Mr. Worthing was in town?

MERRIMAN: Yes, Miss. He seemed very much disappointed. I mentioned that you and Miss Prism were in the garden. He said he was anxious to speak to you privately for a moment.

CECILY: Ask Mr. Ernest Worthing to come here. I suppose you had better talk to the housekeeper about a room for him.

MERRIMAN: Yes, Miss.

(MERRIMAN *goes off.*)

CECILY: I have never met any really wicked person before. I feel rather frightened. I am so afraid he will look just like every one else.

(*Enter* ALGERNON, *very gay and debonnair.*) He does!

ALGERNON: (*Raising his hat.*) You are my little cousin Cecily, I'm sure.

CECILY: You are under some strange mistake. I am not little. In fact, I believe I am more than usually tall for my age. (ALGERNON *is rather taken aback.*) But I am your cousin Cecily. You, I see from your card, are Uncle Jack's brother, my cousin Ernest, my wicked cousin Ernest.

ALGERNON: Oh! I am not really wicked at all, cousin Cecily. You mustn't think that I am wicked.

CECILY: If you are not, then you have certainly been deceiving us all in a very inexcusable manner. I hope you have not been leading a double life, pretending to be wicked and being really good all the time. That would be hypocrisy.

ALGERNON: (*Looks at her in amazement.*) Oh! Of course I have been rather reckless.

CECILY: I am glad to hear it.

ALGERNON: In fact, now you mention the subject, I have been very bad in my own small way.

CECILY: I don't think you should be so proud of that, though I am sure it must have been very pleasant.

ALGERNON: It is much pleasanter being here with you.

CECILY: I can't understand how you are here at all. Uncle Jack won't be back till Monday afternoon.

ALGERNON: That is a great disappointment. I am obliged to go up by the first train on Monday morning. I have a business appointment that I am anxious … to miss?

CECILY: Couldn't you miss it anywhere but in London?

ALGERNON: No: the appointment is in London.

CECILY: Well, I know, of course, how important it is not to keep a business engagement, if one wants to retain any sense of the beauty of life, but still I think you had better wait till Uncle Jack arrives. I know he wants to speak to you about your emigrating.

ALGERNON: About my what?

CECILY: Your emigrating. He has gone up to buy your outfit.

ALGERNON: I certainly wouldn't let Jack buy my outfit. He has no taste in neckties at all.

CECILY: I don't think you will require neckties. Uncle Jack is sending you to Australia.

ALGERNON: Australia! I'd sooner die.

CECILY: Well, he said at dinner on Wednesday night, that you would have to choose between this world, the next world, and Australia.

ALGERNON: Oh, well! The accounts I have received of Australia and the next world, are not particularly encouraging. This world is good enough for me, cousin Cecily.

CECILY: Yes, but are you good enough for it?

ALGERNON: I'm afraid I'm not that. That is why I want you to reform me. You might make that your mission, if you don't mind, cousin Cecily.

CECILY: I'm afraid I've no time, this afternoon.

ALGERNON: Well, would you mind my reforming myself this afternoon?

CECILY: It is rather Quixotic of you. But I think you should try.

ALGERNON: I will. I feel better already.

CECILY: You are looking a little worse.

ALGERNON: That is because I am hungry.

CECILY: How thoughtless of me. I should have remembered that when one is going to lead an entirely new life, one requires regular and wholesome meals. Won't you come in?

ALGERNON: Thank you. Might I have a buttonhole first? I never have any appetite unless I have a buttonhole first.

CECILY: A Maréchal Niel? (*Picks up scissors.*)

ALGERNON: No, I'd sooner have a pink rose.

CECILY: Why? (*Cuts a flower.*)

ALGERNON: Because you are like a pink rose, Cousin Cecily.

CECILY: I don't think it can be right for you to talk to me like that. Miss Prism never says such things to me.

ALGERNON: Then Miss Prism is a short sighted old lady. (CECILY *puts the rose in his buttonhole.*) You are the prettiest girl I ever saw.

CECILY: Miss Prism says that all good looks are a snare.

ALGERNON: They are a snare that every sensible man would like to be caught in.

CECILY: Oh, I don't think I would care to catch a sensible man. I shouldn't know what to talk to him about.

(*They pass into the house.* MISS PRISM *and* DR. CHASUBLE *return.*)

MISS PRISM: You are too much alone, dear Dr. Chasuble. You should get married. A misanthrope I can understand—a womanthrope, never!

CHASUBLE: (*With a scholar's shudder.*) Believe me, I do not deserve so neologistic a phrase. The precept as well as the practice of the Primitive Church was distinctly against matrimony.

MISS PRISM: (*Sententiously.*) That is obviously the reason why the Primitive Church has not lasted up to the present day. And you do not seem to realise, dear Doctor, that by persistently remaining single, a man converts himself into a permanent public temptation. Men should be more careful; this very celibacy leads weaker vessels astray.

CHASUBLE: But is a man not equally attractive when married?

MISS PRISM: No married man is ever attractive except to his wife.

CHASUBLE: And often, I've been told, not even to her.

MISS PRISM: That depends on the intellectual sympathies of the woman. Maturity can always be depended on. Ripeness can be trusted. Young women are green. (DR. CHASUBLE *starts.*) I spoke horticulturally. My metaphor was drawn from fruits. But where is Cecily?

CHASUBLE: Perhaps she followed us to the schools.

(*Enter* JACK *slowly from the back of the garden. He is dressed in the deepest mourning, with crepe hatband and black gloves.*)

MISS PRISM: Mr. Worthing!

CHASUBLE: Mr. Worthing?

MISS PRISM: This is indeed a surprise. We did not look for you till Monday afternoon.

JACK: (*Shakes* MISS PRISM'S *hand in a tragic manner.*) I have returned sooner than I expected. Dr. Chasuble, I hope you are well?

CHASUBLE: Dear Mr. Worthing, I trust this garb of woe does not betoken some terrible calamity?

JACK: My brother.

MISS PRISM: More shameful debts and extravagance?

CHASUBLE: Still leading his life of pleasure?

JACK: (*Shaking his head.*) Dead!

CHASUBLE: Your brother Ernest dead?

JACK: Quite dead.

MISS PRISM: What a lesson for him! I trust he will profit by it.

CHASUBLE: Mr. Worthing, I offer you my sincere condolence. You have at least the consolation of knowing that you were always the most generous and forgiving of brothers.

JACK: Poor Ernest! He had many faults, but it is a sad, sad blow.

CHASUBLE: Very sad indeed. Were you with him at the end?

JACK: No. He died abroad; in Paris, in fact. I had a telegram last night from the manager of the Grand Hotel.

CHASUBLE: Was the cause of death mentioned?

JACK: A severe chill, it seems.

MISS PRISM: As a man sows, so shall he reap.

CHASUBLE: (*Raising his hand.*) Charity, dear Miss Prism, charity! None of us are perfect. I myself am peculiarly susceptible to draughts. Will the interment take place here?

JACK: No. He seems to have expressed a desire to be buried in Paris.

CHASUBLE: In Paris! (*Shakes his head.*) I fear that hardly points to any very serious state of mind at the last. You would no doubt wish me to make some slight allusion to this tragic domestic affliction next Sunday. (JACK *presses his hand convulsively.*) My sermon on the meaning of the manna in the wilderness can be adapted to almost any occasion, joyful, or, as in the present case, distressing. (*All sigh.*) I have preached it at harvest celebrations, christenings, confirmations, on days of humiliation and festal days. The last time I delivered it was in the Cathedral, as a charity sermon on behalf of the Society for the Prevention of Discontent among the Upper Orders. The Bishop, who was present, was much struck by some of the analogies I drew.

JACK: Ah! that reminds me, you mentioned christenings I think, Dr. Chasuble? I suppose you know how to christen all right? (DR. CHASUBLE *looks astounded.*) I mean, of course, you are continually christening, aren't you?

MISS PRISM: It is, I regret to say, one of the Rector's most constant duties in this parish. I have often spoken to the poorer classes on the subject. But they don't seem to know what thrift is.

CHASUBLE: But is there any particular infant in whom you are interested, Mr. Worthing? Your brother was, I believe, unmarried, was he not?

JACK: Oh yes.

MISS PRISM: (*Bitterly.*) People who live entirely for pleasure usually are.

JACK: But it is not for any child, dear Doctor. I am very fond of children. No! the fact is, I would like to be christened myself, this afternoon, if you have nothing better to do.

CHASUBLE: But surely, Mr. Worthing, you have been christened already?

JACK: I don't remember anything about it.

CHASUBLE: But have you any grave doubts on the subject?

JACK: I certainly intend to have. Of course I don't know if the thing would bother you in any way, or if you think I am a little too old now.

CHASUBLE: Not at all. The sprinkling, and, indeed, the immersion of adults is a perfectly canonical practice.

JACK: Immersion!

CHASUBLE: You need have no apprehensions. Sprinkling is all that is necessary, or indeed I think advisable. Our weather is so changeable. At what hour would you wish the ceremony performed?

JACK: Oh, I might trot round about five if that would suit you.

CHASUBLE: Perfectly, perfectly! In fact I have two similar ceremonies to perform at that time. A case of twins that occurred recently in one of the outlying cottages on your own estate. Poor Jenkins the carter, a most hard working man.

JACK: Oh! I don't see much fun in being christened along with other babies. It would be childish. Would half past five do?

CHASUBLE: Admirably! Admirably! (*Takes out watch.*) And now, dear Mr. Worthing, I will not intrude any longer into a house of sorrow. I would merely beg you not to be too much bowed down by grief. What seem to us bitter trials are often blessings in disguise.

MISS PRISM: This seems to me a blessing of an extremely obvious kind.

(*Enter* CECILY *from the house.*)

CECILY: Uncle Jack! Oh, I am pleased to see you back. But what horrid clothes you have got on! Do go and change them.

MISS PRISM: Cecily!

CHASUBLE: My child! my child! (CECILY *goes towards* JACK; *he kisses her brow in a melancholy manner.*)

CECILY: What is the matter, Uncle Jack? Do look happy! You look as if you had toothache, and I have got such a surprise for you. Who do you think is in the dining room? Your brother!

JACK: Who?

CECILY: Your brother Ernest. He arrived about half an hour ago.

JACK: What nonsense! I haven't got a brother.

CECILY: Oh, don't say that. However badly he may have behaved to you in the past he is still your brother. You couldn't be so heartless as to disown him. I'll tell him to come out. And you will shake hands with him, won't you, Uncle Jack? (*Runs back into the house.*)

CHASUBLE: These are very joyful tidings.

MISS PRISM: After we had all been resigned to his loss, his sudden return seems to me peculiarly distressing.

JACK: My brother is in the dining room? I don't know what it all means. I think it is perfectly absurd.

(*Enter* ALGERNON *and* CECILY *hand in hand. They come slowly up to* JACK.)

JACK: Good heavens! (*Motions* ALGERNON *away.*)

ALGERNON: Brother John, I have come down from town to tell you that I am very sorry for all the trouble I have given you, and that I intend to lead a better life in the future. (JACK *glares at him and does not take his hand.*)

CECILY: Uncle Jack, you are not going to refuse your own brother's hand?

JACK: Nothing will induce me to take his hand. I think his coming down here disgraceful. He knows perfectly well why.

CECILY: Uncle Jack, do be nice. There is some good in every one. Ernest has just been telling me about his poor invalid friend Mr. Bunbury whom he goes to visit so often. And surely there must be much good in one who is kind to an invalid, and leaves the pleasures of London to sit by a bed of pain.

JACK: Oh! he has been talking about Bunbury, has he?

CECILY: Yes, he has told me all about poor Mr. Bunbury, and his terrible state of health.

JACK: Bunbury! Well, I won't have him talk to you about Bunbury or about anything else. It is enough to drive one perfectly frantic.

ALGERNON: Of course I admit that the faults were all on my side. But I must say that I think that Brother John's coldness to me is peculiarly painful. I expected a more enthusiastic welcome, especially considering it is the first time I have come here.

CECILY: Uncle Jack, if you don't shake hands with Ernest I will never forgive you.

JACK: Never forgive me?

CECILY: Never, never, never!

JACK: Well, this is the last time I shall ever do it. (*Shakes with* ALGERNON *and glares.*)

CHASUBLE: It's pleasant, is it not, to see so perfect a reconciliation? I think we might leave the two brothers together.

MISS PRISM: Cecily, you will come with us.

CECILY: Certainly, Miss Prism. My little task of reconciliation is over.

CHASUBLE: You have done a beautiful action today, dear child.

MISS PRISM: We must not be premature in our judgments.

CECILY: I feel very happy. (*They all go off except* JACK *and* ALGERNON.)

JACK: You young scoundrel, Algy, you must get out of this place as soon as possible. I don't allow any Bunburying here.

(*Enter* MERRIMAN.)

MERRIMAN: I have put Mr. Ernest's things in the room next to yours, sir. I suppose that is all right?

JACK: What?

MERRIMAN: Mr. Ernest's luggage, sir. I have unpacked it and put it in the room next to your own.

JACK: His luggage?

MERRIMAN: Yes, sir. Three portmanteaus, a dressing case, two hat boxes, and a large luncheon basket.

ALGERNON: I am afraid I can't stay more than a week this time.

JACK: Merriman, order the dog cart at once. Mr. Ernest has been suddenly called back to town.

MERRIMAN: Yes, sir. (*Goes back into the house.*)

ALGERNON: What a fearful liar you are, Jack. I have not been called back to town at all.

JACK: Yes, you have.

ALGERNON: I haven't heard any one call me.

JACK: Your duty as a gentleman calls you back.

ALGERNON: My duty as a gentleman has never interfered with my pleasures in the smallest degree.

JACK: I can quite understand that.

ALGERNON: Well, Cecily is a darling.

JACK: You are not to talk of Miss Cardew like that. I don't like it.

ALGERNON: Well, I don't like your clothes. You look perfectly ridiculous in them. Why on earth don't you go up and change? It is perfectly childish to be in deep mourning for a man who is actually staying for a whole week with you in your house as a guest. I call it grotesque.

JACK: You are certainly not staying with me for a whole week as a guest or anything else. You have got to leave … by the four-five train.

ALGERNON: I certainly won't leave you so long as you are in mourning. It would be most unfriendly. If I were in mourning you would stay with me, I suppose. I should think it very unkind if you didn't.

JACK: Well, will you go if I change my clothes?

ALGERNON: Yes, if you are not too long. I never saw anybody take so long to dress, and with such little result.

JACK: Well, at any rate, that is better than being always over dressed as you are.

ALGERNON: If I am occasionally a little over dressed, I make up for it by being always immensely over educated.

JACK: Your vanity is ridiculous, your conduct an outrage, and your presence in my garden utterly absurd. However, you have got to catch the four-five, and I hope you will have a pleasant journey back to town. This Bunburying, as you call it, has not been a great success for you.

(*Goes into the house.*)

ALGERNON: I think it has been a great success. I'm in love with Cecily, and that is everything.

(*Enter* CECILY *at the back of the garden. She picks up the can and begins to water the flowers.*) But I must see her before I go, and make arrangements for another Bunbury. Ah, there she is.

CECILY: Oh, I merely came back to water the roses. I thought you were with Uncle Jack.

ALGERNON: He's gone to order the dog cart for me.

CECILY: Oh, is he going to take you for a nice drive?

ALGERNON: He's going to send me away.

CECILY: Then have we got to part?

ALGERNON: I am afraid so. It's a very painful parting.

CECILY: It is always painful to part from people whom one has known for a very brief space of time. The absence of old friends one can endure with equanimity. But even a momentary separation from anyone to whom one has just been introduced is almost unbearable.

ALGERNON: Thank you.

(*Enter* MERRIMAN.)

MERRIMAN: The dog cart is at the door, sir. (ALGERNON *looks appealingly at* CECILY.)

CECILY: It can wait, Merriman for … five minutes.

MERRIMAN: Yes, Miss. (*Exit* MERRIMAN.)

ALGERNON: I hope, Cecily, I shall not offend you if I state quite frankly and openly that you seem to me to be in every way the visible personification of absolute perfection.

CECILY: I think your frankness does you great credit, Ernest. If you will allow me, I will copy your remarks into my diary. (*Goes over to table and begins writing in diary.*)

ALGERNON: Do you really keep a diary? I'd give anything to look at it. May I?

CECILY: Oh no. (*Puts her hand over it.*) You see, it is simply a very young girl's record of her own thoughts and impressions, and consequently meant for publication. When it appears in volume form I hope you will order a copy. But pray, Ernest, don't stop. I delight in taking down from dictation. I have reached 'absolute perfection'. You can go on. I am quite ready for more.

ALGERNON: (*Somewhat taken aback.*) Ahem! Ahem!

CECILY: Oh, don't cough, Ernest. When one is dictating one should speak fluently and not cough. Besides, I don't know how to spell a cough. (*Writes as* ALGERNON *speaks.*)

ALGERNON: (*Speaking very rapidly.*) Cecily, ever since I first looked upon your wonderful and incomparable beauty, I have dared to love you wildly, passionately, devotedly, hopelessly.

CECILY: I don't think that you should tell me that you love me wildly, passionately, devotedly, hopelessly. Hopelessly doesn't seem to make much sense, does it?

ALGERNON: Cecily!

(*Enter* MERRIMAN.)

MERRIMAN: The dog cart is waiting, sir.

ALGERNON: Tell it to come round next week, at the same hour.

MERRIMAN: (*Looks at* CECILY, *who makes no sign.*) Yes, sir.

(MERRIMAN *retires.*)

CECILY: Uncle Jack would be very much annoyed if he knew you were staying on till next week, at the same hour.

ALGERNON: Oh, I don't care about Jack. I don't care for anybody in the whole world but you. I love you, Cecily. You will marry me, won't you?

CECILY: You silly boy! Of course. Why, we have been engaged for the last three months.

ALGERNON: For the last three months?

CECILY: Yes, it will be exactly three months on Thursday.

ALGERNON: But how did we become engaged?

CECILY: Well, ever since dear Uncle Jack first confessed to us that he had a younger brother who was very wicked and bad, you of course have formed the chief topic of conversation between myself and Miss Prism. And of course a man who is much talked about is always very attractive. One feels there must be something in him, after all. I daresay it was foolish of me, but I fell in love with you, Ernest.

ALGERNON: Darling! And when was the engagement actually settled?

CECILY: On the 14th of February last. Worn out by your entire ignorance of my existence, I determined to end the matter one way or the other, and after a long struggle with myself I accepted you under this dear old tree here. The next day I bought this little ring in your name, and this is the little bangle with the true lover's knot I promised you always to wear.

ALGERNON: Did I give you this? It's very pretty, isn't it?

CECILY: Yes, you've wonderfully good taste, Ernest. It's the excuse I've always given for your leading such a bad life. And this is the box in which I keep all your dear letters. (*Kneels at table, opens box, and produces letters tied up with blue ribbon.*)

ALGERNON: My letters! But, my own sweet Cecily, I have never written you any letters.

CECILY: You need hardly remind me of that, Ernest. I remember only too well that I was forced to write your letters for you. I wrote always three times a week, and sometimes oftener.

ALGERNON: Oh, do let me read them, Cecily?

CECILY: Oh, I couldn't possibly. They would make you far too conceited. (*Replaces box.*) The three you wrote me after I had broken off the engagement are so beautiful, and so badly spelled, that even now I can hardly read them without crying a little.

ALGERNON: But was our engagement ever broken off?

CECILY: Of course it was. On the 22nd of last March. You can see the entry if you like. (*Shows diary.*) 'Today I broke off my engagement with Ernest. I feel it is better to do so. The weather still continues charming.'

ALGERNON: But why on earth did you break it off? What had I done? I had done nothing at all. Cecily, I am very much hurt indeed to hear you broke it off. Particularly when the weather was so charming.

CECILY: It would hardly have been a really serious engagement if it hadn't been broken off at least once. But I forgave you before the week was out.

ALGERNON: (*Crossing to her, and kneeling.*) What a perfect angel you are, Cecily.

CECILY: You dear romantic boy. (*He kisses her, she puts her fingers through his hair.*) I hope your hair curls naturally, does it?

ALGERNON: Yes, darling, with a little help from others.

CECILY: I am so glad.

ALGERNON: You'll never break off our engagement again, Cecily?

CECILY: I don't think I could break it off now that I have actually met you. Besides, of course, there is the question of your name.

ALGERNON: Yes, of course. (*Nervously.*)

CECILY: You must not laugh at me, darling, but it had always been a girlish dream of mine to love some one whose name was Ernest. (ALGERNON *rises,* CECILY *also.*) There is something in that name that seems to inspire absolute confidence. I pity any poor married woman whose husband is not called Ernest.

ALGERNON: But, my dear child, do you mean to say you could not love me if I had some other name?

CECILY: But what name?

ALGERNON: Oh, any name you like—Algernon—for instance …

CECILY: But I don't like the name of Algernon.

ALGERNON: Well, my own dear, sweet, loving little darling, I really can't see why you should object to the name of Algernon. It is not at all a bad name. In fact, it is rather an aristocratic name. Half of the chaps who get into the Bankruptcy Court are called Algernon. But seriously, Cecily … (*Moving to her*) … if my name was Algy, couldn't you love me?

CECILY: (*Rising.*) I might respect you, Ernest, I might admire your character, but I fear that I should not be able to give you my undivided attention.

ALGERNON: Ahem! Cecily! (*Picking up hat.*) Your Rector here is, I suppose, thoroughly experienced in the practice of all the rites and ceremonials of the Church?

CECILY: Oh, yes. Dr. Chasuble is a most learned man. He has never written a single book, so you can imagine how much he knows.

ALGERNON: I must see him at once on a most important christening—I mean on most important business.

CECILY: Oh!

ALGERNON: I shan't be away more than half an hour.

CECILY: Considering that we have been engaged since February the 14th, and that I only met you today for the first time, I think it is rather hard that you should leave me for so long a period as half an hour. Couldn't you make it twenty minutes?

ALGERNON: I'll be back in no time.

(*Kisses her and rushes down the garden.*)

CECILY: What an impetuous boy he is! I like his hair so much. I must enter his proposal in my diary.

(*Enter* MERRIMAN.)

MERRIMAN: A Miss Fairfax has just called to see Mr. Worthing. On very important business, Miss Fairfax states.

CECILY: Isn't Mr. Worthing in his library?

MERRIMAN: Mr. Worthing went over in the direction of the Rectory some time ago.

CECILY: Pray ask the lady to come out here; Mr. Worthing is sure to be back soon. And you can bring tea.

MERRIMAN: Yes, Miss. (*Goes out.*)

CECILY: Miss Fairfax! I suppose one of the many good elderly women who are associated with Uncle Jack in some of his philanthropic work in London. I don't quite like women who are interested in philanthropic work. I think it is so forward of them.

(*Enter* MERRIMAN.)

MERRIMAN: Miss Fairfax.

(*Enter* GWENDOLEN.)

(*Exit* MERRIMAN.)

CECILY: (*Advancing to meet her.*) Pray let me introduce myself to you. My name is Cecily Cardew.

GWENDOLEN: Cecily Cardew? (*Moving to her and shaking hands.*) What a very sweet name! Something tells me that we are going to be great friends. I like you already more than I can say. My first impressions of people are never wrong.

CECILY: How nice of you to like me so much after we have known each other such a comparatively short time. Pray sit down.

GWENDOLEN: (*Still standing up.*) I may call you Cecily, may I not?

CECILY: With pleasure!

GWENDOLEN: And you will always call me Gwendolen, won't you?

CECILY: If you wish.

GWENDOLEN: Then that is all quite settled, is it not?

CECILY: I hope so. (*A pause. They both sit down together.*)

GWENDOLEN: Perhaps this might be a favourable opportunity for my mentioning who I am. My father is Lord Bracknell. You have never heard of papa, I suppose?

CECILY: I don't think so.

GWENDOLEN: Outside the family circle, papa, I am glad to say, is entirely unknown. I think that is quite as it should be. The home seems to me to be the proper sphere for the man. And certainly once a man begins to neglect his domestic duties he becomes painfully effeminate, does he not? And I don't like that. It makes men so very attractive. Cecily, mamma, whose views on education are remarkably strict, has brought me up to be extremely short sighted; it is part of her system; so do you mind my looking at you through my glasses?

CECILY: Oh! not at all, Gwendolen. I am very fond of being looked at.

GWENDOLEN: (*After examining* CECILY *carefully through a lorgnette.*) You are here on a short visit, I suppose.

CECILY: Oh no! I live here.

GWENDOLEN: (*Severely.*) Really? Your mother, no doubt, or some female relative of advanced years, resides here also?

CECILY: Oh no! I have no mother, nor, in fact, any relations.

GWENDOLEN: Indeed?

CECILY: My dear guardian, with the assistance of Miss Prism, has the arduous task of looking after me.

GWENDOLEN: Your guardian?

CECILY: Yes, I am Mr. Worthing's ward.

GWENDOLEN: Oh! It is strange he never mentioned to me that he had a ward. How secretive of him! He grows more interesting hourly. I am not sure, however, that the news inspires me with feelings of unmixed delight. (*Rising and going to her.*) I am very fond of you, Cecily; I have liked you ever since I met you! But I am bound to state that now that I know that you are Mr. Worthing's ward, I cannot help expressing a wish you were—well, just a little older than you seem to be—and not quite so very alluring in appearance. In fact, if I may speak candidly …

CECILY: Pray do! I think that whenever one has anything unpleasant to say, one should always be quite candid.

GWENDOLEN: Well, to speak with perfect candour, Cecily, I wish that you were fully forty-two, and more than usually plain for your age. Ernest has a strong upright nature. He is the very soul of truth and honour. Disloyalty would be as impossible to him as deception. But even men of the noblest possible moral character are extremely susceptible to the influence of the physical charms of others. Modern, no less than Ancient History, supplies us with many most painful examples of what I refer to. If it were not so, indeed, History would be quite unreadable.

CECILY: I beg your pardon, Gwendolen, did you say Ernest?

GWENDOLEN: Yes.

CECILY: Oh, but it is not Mr. Ernest Worthing who is my guardian. It is his brother—his elder brother.

GWENDOLEN: (*Sitting down again.*) Ernest never mentioned to me that he had a brother.

CECILY: I am sorry to say they have not been on good terms for a long time.

GWENDOLEN: Ah! that accounts for it. And now that I think of it I have never heard any man mention his brother. The subject seems distasteful to most men. Cecily, you have lifted a load from my mind. I was growing almost anxious. It would have been terrible if any cloud had come across a friendship like ours, would it not? Of course you are quite, quite sure that it is not Mr. Ernest Worthing who is your guardian?

CECILY Quite sure. (*A pause.*) In fact, I am going to be his.

GWENDOLEN: (*Inquiringly.*) I beg your pardon?

CECILY: (*Rather shy and confidingly.*) Dearest Gwendolen, there is no reason why I should make a secret of it to you. Our little county newspaper is sure to chronicle the fact next week. Mr. Ernest Worthing and I are engaged to be married.

GWENDOLEN: (*Quite politely, rising.*) My darling Cecily, I think there must be some slight error. Mr. Ernest Worthing is engaged to me. The announcement will appear in the MORNING POST on Saturday at the latest.

CECILY: (*Very politely, rising.*) I am afraid you must be under some misconception. Ernest proposed to me exactly ten minutes ago. (*Shows diary.*)

GWENDOLEN: (*Examines diary through her lorgnette carefully.*) It is certainly very curious, for he asked me to be his wife yesterday afternoon at 5.30. If you would care to verify the incident, pray do so. (*Produces diary of her own.*) I never travel without my diary. One should always have something sensational to read in the train. I am so sorry, dear Cecily, if it is any disappointment to you, but I am afraid I have the prior claim.

CECILY: It would distress me more than I can tell you, dear Gwendolen, if it caused you any mental or physical anguish, but I feel bound to point out that since Ernest proposed to you he clearly has changed his mind.

GWENDOLEN: (*Meditatively.*) If the poor fellow has been entrapped into any foolish promise I shall consider it my duty to rescue him at once, and with a firm hand.

CECILY: (*Thoughtfully and sadly.*) Whatever unfortunate entanglement my dear boy may have got into, I will never reproach him with it after we are married.

GWENDOLEN: Do you allude to me, Miss Cardew, as an entanglement? You are presumptuous. On an occasion of this kind it becomes more than a moral duty to speak one's mind. It becomes a pleasure.

CECILY Do you suggest, Miss Fairfax, that I entrapped Ernest into an engagement? How dare you? This is no time for wearing the shallow mask of manners. When I see a spade I call it a spade.

GWENDOLEN: (*Satirically.*) I am glad to say that I have never seen a spade. It is obvious that our social spheres have been widely different.

(*Enter* MERRIMAN, *followed by the footman. He carries a salver, table cloth, and plate stand.* CECILY *is about to retort. The presence of the servants exercises a restraining influence, under which both girls chafe.*)

MERRIMAN: Shall I lay tea here as usual, Miss?

CECILY: (*Sternly, in a calm voice.*) Yes, as usual. (MERRIMAN *begins to clear table and lay cloth. A long pause.* CECILY *and* GWENDOLEN *glare at each other.*)

GWENDOLEN: Are there many interesting walks in the vicinity, Miss Cardew?

CECILY: Oh! yes! a great many. From the top of one of the hills quite close one can see five counties.

GWENDOLEN: Five counties! I don't think I should like that; I hate crowds.

CECILY: (*Sweetly.*) I suppose that is why you live in town? (GWENDOLEN *bites her lip, and beats her foot nervously with her parasol.*)

GWENDOLEN: (*Looking round.*) Quite a well kept garden this is, Miss Cardew.

CECILY: So glad you like it, Miss Fairfax.

GWENDOLEN: I had no idea there were any flowers in the country.

CECILY: Oh, flowers are as common here, Miss Fairfax, as people are in London.

GWENDOLEN: Personally I cannot understand how anybody manages to exist in the country, if anybody who is anybody does. The country always bores me to death.

CECILY: Ah! This is what the newspapers call agricultural depression, is it not? I believe the aristocracy are suffering very much from it just at present. It is almost an epidemic amongst them, I have been told. May I offer you some tea, Miss Fairfax?

GWENDOLEN: (*With elaborate politeness.*) Thank you. (*Aside.*) Detestable girl! But I require tea!

CECILY: (*Sweetly.*) Sugar?

GWENDOLEN: (*Superciliously.*) No, thank you. Sugar is not fashionable any more. (CECILY *looks angrily at her, takes up the tongs and puts four lumps of sugar into the cup.*)

CECILY: (*Severely.*) Cake or bread and butter?

GWENDOLEN: (*In a bored manner.*) Bread and butter, please. Cake is rarely seen at the best houses nowadays.

CECILY: (*Cuts a very large slice of cake, and puts it on the tray.*) Hand that to Miss Fairfax.

(MERRIMAN *does so, and goes out with footman.* GWENDOLEN *drinks the tea and makes a grimace. Puts down cup at once, reaches out her hand to the bread and butter, looks at it, and finds it is cake. Rises in indignation.*)

GWENDOLEN: You have filled my tea with lumps of sugar, and though I asked most distinctly for bread and butter, you have given me cake. I am known for the gentleness of my disposition, and the extraordinary sweetness of my nature, but I warn you, Miss Cardew, you may go too far.

CECILY: (*Rising.*) To save my poor, innocent, trusting boy from the machinations of any other girl there are no lengths to which I would not go.

GWENDOLEN: From the moment I saw you I distrusted you. I felt that you were false and deceitful. I am never deceived in such matters. My first impressions of people are invariably right.

CECILY: It seems to me, Miss Fairfax, that I am trespassing on your valuable time. No doubt you have many other calls of a similar character to make in the neighbourhood.

(*Enter* JACK.)

GWENDOLEN: (*Catching sight of him.*) Ernest! My own Ernest!

JACK: Gwendolen! Darling! (*Offers to kiss her.*)

GWENDOLEN: (*Draws back.*) A moment! May I ask if you are engaged to be married to this young lady? (*Points to* CECILY.)

JACK: (*Laughing.*) To dear little Cecily! Of course not! What could have put such an idea into your pretty little head?

GWENDOLEN: Thank you. You may! (*Offers her cheek.*)

CECILY: (*Very sweetly.*) I knew there must be some misunderstanding, Miss Fairfax. The gentleman whose arm is at present round your waist is my guardian, Mr. John Worthing.

GWENDOLEN: I beg your pardon?

CECILY This is Uncle Jack.

GWENDOLEN: (*Receding.*) Jack! Oh!

(*Enter* ALGERNON.)

CECILY: Here is Ernest.

ALGERNON: (*Goes straight over to* CECILY *without noticing any one else.*) My own love! (*Offers to kiss her.*)

CECILY: (*Drawing back.*) A moment, Ernest! May I ask you—are you engaged to be married to this young lady?

ALGERNON: (*Looking round.*) To what young lady? Good heavens! Gwendolen!

CECILY: Yes, to good heavens, Gwendolen, I mean to Gwendolen.

ALGERNON: (*Laughing.*) Of course not! What could have put such an idea into your pretty little head?

CECILY: Thank you. (*Presenting her cheek to be kissed.*) You may. (ALGERNON *kisses her.*)

GWENDOLEN: I felt there was some slight error, Miss Cardew. The gentleman who is now embracing you is my cousin, Mr. Algernon Moncrieff.

CECILY: (*Breaking away from* ALGERNON.) Algernon Moncrieff! Oh! (*The two girls move towards each other and put their arms round each other's waists protection.*)

CECILY: Are you called Algernon?

ALGERNON: I cannot deny it.

CECILY: Oh!

GWENDOLEN: Is your name really John?

JACK: (*Standing rather proudly.*) I could deny it if I liked. I could deny anything if I liked. But my name certainly is John. It has been John for years.

CECILY: (*To* GWENDOLEN.) A gross deception has been practised on both of us.

GWENDOLEN: My poor wounded Cecily!

CECILY: My sweet wronged Gwendolen!

GWENDOLEN: (*Slowly and seriously.*) You will call me sister, will you not? (*They embrace.* JACK *and* ALGERNON *groan and walk up and down.*)

CECILY: (*Rather brightly.*) There is just one question I would like to be allowed to ask my guardian.

GWENDOLEN: An admirable idea! Mr. Worthing, there is just one question I would like to be permitted to put to you. Where is your brother Ernest? We are both engaged to be married to your brother Ernest, so it is a matter of some importance to us to know where your brother Ernest is at present.

JACK: (*Slowly and hesitatingly.*) Gwendolen—Cecily—it is very painful for me to be forced to speak the truth. It is the first time in my life that I have ever been reduced to such a painful position, and I am really quite inexperienced in doing anything of the kind. However, I will tell you quite frankly that I have no brother Ernest. I have no brother at all. I never had a brother in my life, and I certainly have not the smallest intention of ever having one in the future.

CECILY: (*Surprised.*) No brother at all?

JACK: (*Cheerily.*) None!

GWENDOLEN: (*Severely.*) Had you never a brother of any kind?

JACK: (*Pleasantly.*) Never. Not even of any kind.

GWENDOLEN: I am afraid it is quite clear, Cecily, that neither of us is engaged to be married to any one.

CECILY: It is not a very pleasant position for a young girl suddenly to find herself in. Is it?

GWENDOLEN: Let us go into the house. They will hardly venture to come after us there.

CECILY: No, men are so cowardly, aren't they?

(*They retire into the house with scornful looks.*)

JACK: This ghastly state of things is what you call Bunburying, I suppose?

ALGERNON: Yes, and a perfectly wonderful Bunbury it is. The most wonderful Bunbury I have ever had in my life.

JACK: Well, you've no right whatsoever to Bunbury here.

ALGERNON: That is absurd. One has a right to Bunbury anywhere one chooses. Every serious Bunburyist knows that.

JACK: Serious Bunburyist! Good heavens!

ALGERNON: Well, one must be serious about something, if one wants to have any amusement in life. I happen to be serious about Bunburying. What on earth you are serious about I haven't got the remotest idea. About everything, I should fancy. You have such an absolutely trivial nature.

JACK: Well, the only small satisfaction I have in the whole of this wretched business is that your friend Bunbury is quite exploded. You won't be able to run down to the country quite so often as you used to do, dear Algy. And a very good thing too.

ALGERNON: Your brother is a little off colour, isn't he, dear Jack? You won't be able to disappear to London quite so frequently as your wicked custom was. And not a bad thing either.

JACK: As for your conduct towards Miss Cardew, I must say that your taking in a sweet, simple, innocent girl like that is quite inexcusable. To say nothing of the fact that she is my ward.

ALGERNON: I can see no possible defence at all for your deceiving a brilliant, clever, thoroughly experienced young lady like Miss Fairfax. To say nothing of the fact that she is my cousin.

JACK: I wanted to be engaged to Gwendolen, that is all. I love her.

ALGERNON: Well, I simply wanted to be engaged to Cecily. I adore her.

JACK: There is certainly no chance of your marrying Miss Cardew.

ALGERNON: I don't think there is much likelihood, Jack, of you and Miss Fairfax being united.

JACK: Well, that is no business of yours.

ALGERNON: If it was my business, I wouldn't talk about it. (*Begins to eat muffins.*) It is very vulgar to talk about one's business. Only people like stockbrokers do that, and then merely at dinner parties.

JACK: How can you sit there, calmly eating muffins when we are in this horrible trouble, I can't make out. You seem to me to be perfectly heartless.

ALGERNON: Well, I can't eat muffins in an agitated manner. The butter would probably get on my cuffs. One should always eat muffins quite calmly. It is the only way to eat them.

JACK: I say it's perfectly heartless your eating muffins at all, under the circumstances.

ALGERNON: When I am in trouble, eating is the only thing that consoles me. Indeed, when I am in really great trouble, as any one who knows me intimately will tell you, I refuse everything except food and drink. At the present moment I am eating muffins because I am unhappy. Besides, I am particularly fond of muffins. (*Rising.*)

JACK: (*Rising.*) Well, that is no reason why you should eat them all in that greedy way. (*Takes muffins from* ALGERNON.)

ALGERNON: (*Offering tea cake.*) I wish you would have tea cake instead. I don't like tea cake.

JACK: Good heavens! I suppose a man may eat his own muffins in his own garden.

ALGERNON: But you have just said it was perfectly heartless to eat muffins.

JACK: I said it was perfectly heartless of you, under the circumstances. That is a very different thing.

ALGERNON: That may be. But the muffins are the same. (*He seizes the muffin dish from* JACK.)

JACK: Algy, I wish to goodness you would go.

ALGERNON: You can't possibly ask me to go without having some dinner. It's absurd. I never go without my dinner. No one ever does, except vegetarians and people like that. Besides I have just made arrangements with Dr. Chasuble to be christened at a quarter to six under the name of Ernest.

JACK: My dear fellow, the sooner you give up that nonsense the better. I made arrangements this morning with Dr. Chasuble to be christened myself at 5.30, and I naturally will take the name of Ernest. Gwendolen would wish it. We can't both be christened Ernest. It's absurd. Besides, I have a perfect right to be christened if I like. There is no evidence at all that I have ever been christened by anybody.

I should think it extremely probable I never was, and so does Dr. Chasuble. It is entirely different in your case. You have been christened already.

ALGERNON: Yes, but I have not been christened for years.

JACK: Yes, but you have been christened. That is the important thing.

ALGERNON: Quite so. So I know my constitution can stand it. If you are not quite sure about your ever having been christened, I must say I think it rather dangerous your venturing on it now. It might make you very unwell. You can hardly have forgotten that some one very closely connected with you was very nearly carried off this week in Paris by a severe chill.

JACK: Yes, but you said yourself that a severe chill was not hereditary.

ALGERNON: It usen't to be, I know—but I daresay it is now. Science is always making wonderful improvements in things.

JACK: (*Picking up the muffin dish.*) Oh, that is nonsense; you are always talking nonsense.

ALGERNON: Jack, you are at the muffins again! I wish you wouldn't. There are only two left. (*Takes them.*) I told you I was particularly fond of muffins.

JACK: But I hate tea cake.

ALGERNON: Why on earth then do you allow tea cake to be served up for your guests? What ideas you have of hospitality!

JACK: Algernon! I have already told you to go. I don't want you here. Why don't you go!

ALGERNON: I haven't quite finished my tea yet! and there is still one muffin left. (JACK *groans, and sinks into a chair.* ALGERNON *still continues eating.*)

ACT 3

Morning room at the Manor House.

(GWENDOLEN *and* CECILY *are at the window, looking out into the garden.*)

GWENDOLEN: The fact that they did not follow us at once into the house, as any one else would have done, seems to me to show that they have some sense of shame left.

CECILY: They have been eating muffins. That looks like repentance.

GWENDOLEN: (*After a pause.*) They don't seem to notice us at all. Couldn't you cough?

CECILY: But I haven't got a cough.

GWENDOLEN: They're looking at us. What effrontery!

CECILY: They're approaching. That's very forward of them.

GWENDOLEN: Let us preserve a dignified silence.

CECILY: Certainly. It's the only thing to do now. (*Enter* JACK *followed by* ALGERNON. They whistle some dreadful popular air from a British Opera.*)

GWENDOLEN: This dignified silence seems to produce an unpleasant effect.

CECILY: A most distasteful one.

GWENDOLEN: But we will not be the first to speak.

CECILY: Certainly not.

GWENDOLEN: Mr. Worthing, I have something very particular to ask you. Much depends on your reply.

CECILY: Gwendolen, your common sense is invaluable. Mr. Moncrieff, kindly answer me the following question. Why did you pretend to be my guardian's brother?

ALGERNON: In order that I might have an opportunity of meeting you.

CECILY: (*To* GWENDOLEN.) That certainly seems a satisfactory explanation, does it not?

GWENDOLEN: Yes, dear, if you can believe him.

CECILY: I don't. But that does not affect the wonderful beauty of his answer.

GWENDOLEN: True. In matters of grave importance, style, not sincerity is the vital thing. Mr. Worthing, what explanation can you offer to me for pretending to have a brother? Was it in order that you might have an opportunity of coming up to town to see me as often as possible?

JACK: Can you doubt it, Miss Fairfax?

GWENDOLEN: I have the gravest doubts upon the subject. But I intend to crush them. This is not the moment for German scepticism. (*Moving to* CECILY.) Their explanations appear to be quite satisfactory, especially Mr. Worthing's. That seems to me to have the stamp of truth upon it.

CECILY: I am more than content with what Mr. Moncrieff said. His voice alone inspires one with absolute credulity.

GWENDOLEN: Then you think we should forgive them?

CECILY: Yes. I mean no.

GWENDOLEN: True! I had forgotten. There are principles at stake that one cannot surrender. Which of us should tell them? The task is not a pleasant one.

CECILY: Could we not both speak at the same time?

GWENDOLEN: An excellent idea! I nearly always speak at the same time as other people. Will you take the time from me?

CECILY: Certainly. (GWENDOLEN *beats time with uplifted finger.*)

GWENDOLEN and CECILY: (*Speaking together.*) Your Christian names are still an insuperable barrier. That is all!

JACK and ALGERNON: (*Speaking together.*) Our Christian names! Is that all? But we are going to be christened this afternoon.

GWENDOLEN: (*To* JACK.) For my sake you are prepared to do this terrible thing?

JACK: I am.

CECILY: (*To* ALGERNON.) To please me you are ready to face this fearful ordeal?

ALGERNON: I am!

GWENDOLEN: How absurd to talk of the equality of the sexes! Where questions of self-sacrifice are concerned, men are infinitely beyond us.

JACK: We are. (*Clasps hands with* ALGERNON.)

CECILY: They have moments of physical courage of which we women know absolutely nothing.

GWENDOLEN: (*To* JACK.) Darling!

ALGERNON: (*To* CECILY.) Darling! (*They fall into each other's arms.*)

(*Enter* MERRIMAN. *When he enters he coughs loudly, seeing the situation.*)

MERRIMAN: Ahem! Ahem! Lady Bracknell!

JACK: Good heavens!

(*Enter* LADY BRACKNELL. *The couples separate in alarm. Exit* MERRIMAN.)

LADY BRACKNELL: Gwendolen! What does this mean?

GWENDOLEN: Merely that I am engaged to be married to Mr. Worthing, mamma.

LADY BRACKNELL: Come here. Sit down. Sit down immediately. Hesitation of any kind is a sign of mental decay in the young, of physical weakness in the old. (*Turns to* JACK.) Apprised, sir, of my daughter's sudden flight by her trusty maid, whose confidence I purchased by means of a small coin, I followed her at once by a luggage train. Her unhappy father is, I am glad to say, under the impression that she is attending a more than usually lengthy lecture by the University Extension Scheme on the Influence of a Permanent Income on Thought. I do not propose to undeceive him. Indeed I have never undeceived him on any question. I would consider it wrong. But of course, you will clearly understand that all communication between yourself and my daughter must cease immediately from this moment. On this point, as indeed on all points, I am firm.

JACK: I am engaged to be married to Gwendolen, Lady Bracknell!

LADY BRACKNELL: You are nothing of the kind, sir. And now, as regards Algernon! … Algernon!

ALGERNON: Yes, Aunt Augusta.

LADY BRACKNELL: May I ask if it is in this house that your invalid friend Mr. Bunbury resides?

ALGERNON: (*Stammering.*) Oh! No! Bunbury doesn't live here. Bunbury is somewhere else at present. In fact, Bunbury is dead,

LADY BRACKNELL: Dead! When did Mr. Bunbury die? His death must have been extremely sudden.

ALGERNON: (*Airily.*) Oh! I killed Bunbury this afternoon. I mean poor Bunbury died this afternoon.

LADY BRACKNELL: What did he die of?

ALGERNON: Bunbury? Oh, he was quite exploded.

LADY BRACKNELL: Exploded! Was he the victim of a revolutionary outrage? I was not aware that Mr. Bunbury was interested in social legislation. If so, he is well punished for his morbidity.

ALGERNON: My dear Aunt Augusta, I mean he was found out! The doctors found out that Bunbury could not live, that is what I mean—so Bunbury died.

LADY BRACKNELL: He seems to have had great confidence in the opinion of his physicians. I am glad, however, that he made up his mind at the last to some definite course of action, and acted under proper medical advice. And now that we have finally got rid of this Mr. Bunbury, may I ask, Mr. Worthing, who is that young person whose hand my nephew Algernon is now holding in what seems to me a peculiarly unnecessary manner?

JACK: That lady is Miss Cecily Cardew, my ward. (LADY BRACKNELL *bows coldly to* CECILY.)

ALGERNON: I am engaged to be married to Cecily, Aunt Augusta.

LADY BRACKNELL: I beg your pardon?

CECILY: Mr. Moncrieff and I are engaged to be married, Lady Bracknell.

LADY BRACKNELL: (*With a shiver, crossing to the sofa and sitting down.*) I do not know whether there is anything peculiarly exciting in the air of this particular part of Hertfordshire, but the number of engagements that go on seems to me considerably above the proper average that statistics have laid down for our guidance. I think some preliminary inquiry on my part would not be out of place. Mr. Worthing, is Miss Cardew at all connected with any of the larger railway stations in London? I merely desire information. Until yesterday I had no idea that there were any families or persons whose origin was a Terminus. (JACK *looks perfectly furious, but restrains himself.*)

JACK: (*In a clear, cold voice.*) Miss Cardew is the granddaughter of the late Mr. Thomas Cardew of 149 Belgrave Square, S.W.; Gervase Park, Dorking, Surrey; and the Sporran, Fifeshire, N.B.

LADY BRACKNELL: That sounds not unsatisfactory. Three addresses always inspire confidence, even in tradesmen. But what proof have I of their authenticity?

JACK: I have carefully preserved the Court Guides of the period. They are open to your inspection, Lady Bracknell.

LADY BRACKNELL: (*Grimly.*) I have known strange errors in that publication.

JACK: Miss Cardew's family solicitors are Messrs. Markby, Markby, and Markby.

LADY BRACKNELL: Markby, Markby, and Markby? A firm of the very highest position in their profession. Indeed I am told that one of the Mr. Markby's is occasionally to be seen at dinner parties. So far I am satisfied.

JACK: (*Very irritably.*) How extremely kind of you, Lady Bracknell! I have also in my possession, you will be pleased to hear, certificates of Miss Cardew's birth, baptism, whooping cough, registration, vaccination, confirmation, and the measles; both the German and the English variety.

LADY BRACKNELL: Ah! A life crowded with incident, I see; though perhaps somewhat too exciting for a young girl. I am not myself in favour of premature experiences. (*Rises, looks at her watch.*) Gwendolen! the time approaches for our departure. We have not a moment to lose. As a matter of form, Mr. Worthing, I had better ask you if Miss Cardew has any little fortune?

JACK: Oh, about a hundred and thirty thousand pounds in the Funds. That is all. Goodbye, Lady Bracknell. So pleased to have seen you.

LADY BRACKNELL: (*Sitting down again.*) A moment, Mr. Worthing. A hundred and thirty thousand pounds! And in the Funds! Miss Cardew seems to me a most attractive young lady, now that I look at her. Few girls of the present day have any really solid qualities, any of the qualities that last, and improve with time. We live, I regret to say, in an age of surfaces. (*To* CECILY.) Come over here, dear. (CECILY *goes across.*) Pretty child! your dress is sadly simple, and your hair seems almost as Nature might have left it. But we can soon alter all that. A thoroughly experienced French maid produces a really marvellous result in a very brief space of time. I remember recommending one to young Lady Lancing, and after three months her own husband did not know her.

JACK: And after six months nobody knew her.

LADY BRACKNELL: (*Glares at* JACK *for a few moments. Then bends, with a practised smile, to* CECILY.) Kindly turn round, sweet child. (CECILY *turns completely round.*) No, the side view is what I want. (CECILY *presents her profile.*) Yes, quite as I expected. There are distinct social possibilities in your profile. The two weak points in our age are its want of principle and its want of profile. The chin a little higher, dear. Style largely depends on the way the chin is worn. They are worn very high, just at present. Algernon!

ALGERNON: Yes, Aunt Augusta!

LADY BRACKNELL: There are distinct social possibilities in Miss Cardew's profile.

ALGERNON: Cecily is the sweetest, dearest, prettiest girl in the whole world. And I don't care twopence about social possibilities.

LADY BRACKNELL: Never speak disrespectfully of Society, Algernon. Only people who can't get into it do that. (*To* CECILY.) Dear child, of course you know that Algernon has nothing but his debts to depend upon. But I do not approve of mercenary marriages. When I married Lord Bracknell I had no fortune of any kind. But I never dreamed for a moment of allowing that to stand in my way. Well, I suppose I must give my consent.

ALGERNON: Thank you, Aunt Augusta.

LADY BRACKNELL: Cecily, you may kiss me!

CECILY: (*Kisses her.*) Thank you, Lady Bracknell.

LADY BRACKNELL: You may also address me as Aunt Augusta for the future.

CECILY: Thank you, Aunt Augusta.

LADY BRACKNELL: The marriage, I think, had better take place quite soon.

ALGERNON: Thank you, Aunt Augusta.

CECILY: Thank you, Aunt Augusta.

LADY BRACKNELL: To speak frankly, I am not in favour of long engagements. They give people the opportunity of finding out each other's character before marriage, which I think is never advisable.

JACK: I beg your pardon for interrupting you, Lady Bracknell, but this engagement is quite out of the question. I am Miss Cardew's guardian, and she cannot marry without my consent until she comes of age. That consent I absolutely decline to give.

LADY BRACKNELL: Upon what grounds may I ask? Algernon is an extremely, I may almost say an ostentatiously, eligible young man. He has nothing, but he looks everything. What more can one desire?

JACK: It pains me very much to have to speak frankly to you, Lady Bracknell, about your nephew, but the fact is that I do not approve at all of his moral character. I suspect him of being untruthful. (ALGERNON *and* CECILY *look at him in indignant amazement.*)

LADY BRACKNELL: Untruthful! My nephew Algernon? Impossible! He is an Oxonian.

JACK: I fear there can be no possible doubt about the matter. This afternoon during my temporary absence in London on an important question of romance, he obtained admission to my house by means of the false pretence of being my brother. Under an assumed name he drank, I've just been informed by my butler, an entire pint bottle of my Perrier-Jouet, Brut, '89; wine I was specially reserving for myself. Continuing his disgraceful deception, he succeeded in the course of the afternoon in alienating the affections of my only ward. He subsequently stayed to tea, and devoured every single muffin. And what makes his conduct all the more heartless is, that he was perfectly well aware from the first that I have no brother, that I never had a brother, and that I don't intend to have a brother, not even of any kind. I distinctly told him so myself yesterday afternoon.

LADY BRACKNELL: Ahem! Mr. Worthing, after careful consideration I have decided entirely to overlook my nephew's conduct to you.

JACK: That is very generous of you, Lady Bracknell. My own decision, however, is unalterable. I decline to give my consent.

LADY BRACKNELL: (*To* CECILY.) Come here, sweet child. (CECILY *goes over.*) How old are you, dear?

CECILY: Well, I am really only eighteen, but I always admit to twenty when I go to evening parties.

LADY BRACKNELL: You are perfectly right in making some slight alteration. Indeed, no woman should ever be quite accurate about her age. It looks so calculating ... (*In a meditative manner.*) Eighteen, but admitting to twenty at evening parties. Well, it will not be very long before you are of age and free from the restraints of tutelage. So I don't think your guardian's consent is, after all, a matter of any importance.

JACK: Pray excuse me, Lady Bracknell, for interrupting you again, but it is only fair to tell you that according to the terms of her grandfather's will Miss Cardew does not come legally of age till she is thirty-five.

LADY BRACKNELL: That does not seem to me to be a grave objection. Thirty-five is a very attractive age. London society is full of women of the very highest birth who have, of their own free choice, remained thirty-five for years. Lady Dumbleton is an instance in point. To my own knowledge she has been thirty-five ever since she arrived at the age of forty, which was many years ago now. I see no reason why our dear Cecily should not be even still more attractive at the age you mention than she is at present. There will be a large accumulation of property.

CECILY: Algy, could you wait for me till I was thirty-five?

ALGERNON: Of course I could, Cecily. You know I could.

CECILY: Yes, I felt it instinctively, but I couldn't wait all that time. I hate waiting even five minutes for anybody. It always makes me rather cross. I am not punctual myself, I know, but I do like punctuality in others, and waiting, even to be married, is quite out of the question.

ALGERNON: Then what is to be done, Cecily?

CECILY: I don't know, Mr. Moncrieff.

LADY BRACKNELL: My dear Mr. Worthing, as Miss Cardew states positively that she cannot wait till she is thirty-five—a remark which I am bound to say seems to me to show a somewhat impatient nature—I would beg of you to reconsider your decision.

JACK: But my dear Lady Bracknell, the matter is entirely in your own hands. The moment you consent to my marriage with Gwendolen, I will most gladly allow your nephew to form an alliance with my ward.

LADY BRACKNELL: (*Rising and drawing herself up.*) You must be quite aware that what you propose is out of the question.

JACK: Then a passionate celibacy is all that any of us can look forward to.

LADY BRACKNELL: That is not the destiny I propose for Gwendolen. Algernon, of course, can choose for himself. (*Pulls out her watch.*) Come, dear, (GWENDOLEN *rises*) we have already missed five, if not six, trains. To miss any more might expose us to comment on the platform.

(*Enter* DR. CHASUBLE.)

CHASUBLE: Everything is quite ready for the christenings.

LADY BRACKNELL: The christenings, sir! Is not that somewhat premature?

CHASUBLE: (*Looking rather puzzled, and pointing to* JACK *and* ALGERNON.) Both these gentlemen have expressed a desire for immediate baptism.

LADY BRACKNELL: At their age? The idea is grotesque and irreligious! Algernon, I forbid you to be baptized. I will not hear of such excesses. Lord Bracknell would be highly displeased if he learned that that was the way in which you wasted your time and money.

CHASUBLE: Am I to understand then that there are to he no christenings at all this afternoon?

JACK: I don't think that, as things are now, it would be of much practical value to either of us, Dr. Chasuble.

CHASUBLE: I am grieved to hear such sentiments from you, Mr. Worthing. They savour of the heretical views of the Anabaptists, views that I have completely refuted in four of my unpublished sermons. However, as your present mood seems to be one peculiarly secular, I will return to the church at once. Indeed, I have just been informed by the pew-opener that for the last hour and a half Miss Prism has been waiting for me in the vestry.

LADY BRACKNELL: (*Starting.*) Miss Prism! Did I bear you mention a Miss Prism?

CHASUBLE: Yes, Lady Bracknell. I am on my way to join her.

LADY BRACKNELL: Pray allow me to detain you for a moment. This matter may prove to be one of vital importance to Lord Bracknell and myself. Is this Miss Prism a female of repellent aspect, remotely connected with education?

CHASUBLE: (*Somewhat indignantly.*) She is the most cultivated of ladies, and the very picture of respectability.

LADY BRACKNELL: It is obviously the same person. May I ask what position she holds in your household?

CHASUBLE: (*Severely.*) I am a celibate, madam.

JACK: (*Interposing.*) Miss Prism, Lady Bracknell, has been for the last three years Miss Cardew's esteemed governess and valued companion.

LADY BRACKNELL: In spite of what I hear of her, I must see her at once. Let her be sent for.

CHASUBLE: (*Looking off.*) She approaches; she is nigh.

(*Enter* MISS PRISM *hurriedly.*)

MISS PRISM: I was told you expected me in the vestry, dear Canon. I have been waiting for you there for an hour and three-quarters. (*Catches sight of* LADY BRACKNELL, *who has fixed her with a stony glare.* MISS PRISM *grows pale and quails. She looks anxiously round as if desirous to escape.*)

LADY BRACKNELL: (*In a severe, judicial voice.*) Prism! (MISS PRISM *bows her head in shame.*) Come here, Prism! (MISS PRISM *approaches in a humble manner.*) Prism! Where is that baby? (*General consternation. The* CANON *starts back in horror.* ALGERNON *and* JACK *pretend to be anxious to shield* CECILY *and* GWENDOLEN *from hearing the details of a terrible public scandal.*) Twenty-eight years ago, Prism, you left Lord Bracknell's house, Number 104, Upper Grosvenor Street, in charge of a perambulator that contained a baby of the male sex. You never returned. A few weeks later, through the elaborate investigations of the Metropolitan police, the perambulator was discovered at midnight, standing by itself in a remote corner of Bayswater. It contained the manuscript of a three volume novel of more than usually revolting sentimentality. (MISS PRISM *starts in involuntary indignation.*) But the baby was not there! (*Every one looks at* MISS PRISM.) Prism! Where is that baby? (*A pause.*)

MISS PRISM: Lady Bracknell, I admit with shame that I do not know. I only wish I did. The plain facts of the case are these. On the morning of the day you mention, a day that is for ever branded on my memory, I prepared as usual to take the baby out in its perambulator. I had also with me a somewhat old, but capacious handbag in which I had intended to place the manuscript of a work of fiction that I had written during my few unoccupied hours. In a moment of mental abstraction, for which I never can forgive myself, I deposited the manuscript in the basinette, and placed the baby in the handbag.

JACK: (*Who has been listening attentively.*) But where did you deposit the handbag?

MISS PRISM: Do not ask me, Mr. Worthing.

JACK: Miss Prism, this is a matter of no small importance to me. I insist on knowing where you deposited the handbag that contained that infant.

MISS PRISM: I left it in the cloakroom of one of the larger railway stations in London.

JACK: What railway station?

MISS PRISM: (*Quite crushed.*) Victoria. The Brighton line. (*Sinks into a chair.*)

JACK: I must retire to my room for a moment. Gwendolen, wait here for me.

GWENDOLEN: If you are not too long, I will wait here for you all my life. (*Exit* JACK *in great excitement.*)

CHASUBLE: What do you think this means, Lady Bracknell?

LADY BRACKNELL: I dare not even suspect, Dr. Chasuble. I need hardly tell you that in families of high position strange coincidences are not supposed to occur. They are hardly considered the thing.

(*Noises heard overhead as if some one was throwing trunks about. Every one looks up.*)

CECILY: Uncle Jack seems strangely agitated.

CHASUBLE: Your guardian has a very emotional nature.

LADY BRACKNELL: This noise is extremely unpleasant. It sounds as if he was having an argument. I dislike arguments of any kind. They are always vulgar, and often convincing.

CHASUBLE: (Looking up.) It has stopped now. (*The noise is redoubled.*)

LADY BRACKNELL: I wish he would arrive at some conclusion.

GWENDOLEN: This suspense is terrible. I hope it will last. (*Enter* JACK *with a handbag of black leather in his hand.*)

JACK: (*Rushing over to* MISS PRISM.) Is this the handbag, Miss Prism? Examine it carefully before you speak. The happiness of more than one life depends on your answer.

MISS PRISM: (*Calmly.*) It seems to be mine. Yes, here is the injury it received through the upsetting of a Gower Street omnibus in younger and happier days. Here is the stain on the lining caused by the explosion of a temperance beverage, an incident that occurred at Leamington. And here, on the lock, are my initials. I had forgotten that in an extravagant mood I had had them placed there. The bag is undoubtedly mine. I am delighted to have it so unexpectedly restored to me. It has been a great inconvenience being without it all these years.

JACK: (*In a pathetic voice.*) Miss Prism, more is restored to you than this handbag. I was the baby you placed in it.

MISS PRISM: (*Amazed.*) You?

JACK: (*Embracing her.*) Yes … mother!

MISS PRISM: (*Recoiling in indignant astonishment.*) Mr. Worthing! I am unmarried!

JACK: Unmarried! I do not deny that is a serious blow. But after all, who has the right to cast a stone against one who has suffered? Cannot repentance wipe out an act of folly? Why should there be one law for men, and another for women? Mother, I forgive you. (*Tries to embrace her again.*)

MISS PRISM: (*Still more indignant.*) Mr. Worthing, there is some error. (*Pointing to* LADY BRACKNELL.) There is the lady who can tell you who you really are.

JACK: (*After a pause.*) Lady Bracknell, I hate to seem inquisitive, but would you kindly inform me who I am?

LADY BRACKNELL: I am afraid that the news I have to give you will not altogether please you. You are the son of my poor sister, Mrs. Moncrieff, and consequently Algernon's elder brother.

JACK: Algy's elder brother! Then I have a brother after all. I knew I had a brother! I always said I had a brother! Cecily,—how could you have ever doubted that I had a brother? (*Seizes hold of* ALGERNON.) Dr. Chasuble, my unfortunate brother. Miss Prism, my unfortunate brother. Gwendolen, my unfortunate brother. Algy, you young scoundrel, you will have to treat me with more respect in the future. You have never behaved to me like a brother in all your life.

ALGERNON: Well, not till today, old boy, I admit. I did my best, however, though I was out of practice.

(*Shakes hands.*)

GWENDOLEN: (*To* JACK.) My own! But what own are you? What is your Christian name, now that you have become some one else?

JACK: Good heavens! ... I had quite forgotten that point. Your decision on the subject of my name is irrevocable, I suppose?

GWENDOLEN: I never change, except in my affections.

CECILY: What a noble nature you have, Gwendolen!

JACK: Then the question had better be cleared up at once. Aunt Augusta, a moment. At the time when Miss Prism left me in the handbag, had I been christened already?

LADY BRACKNELL: Every luxury that money could buy, including christening, had been lavished on you by your fond and doting parents.

JACK: Then I was christened! That is settled. Now, what name was I given? Let me know the worst.

LADY BRACKNELL: Being the eldest son you were naturally christened after your father.

JACK: (*Irritably.*) Yes, but what was my father's Christian name?

LADY BRACKNELL: (*Meditatively.*) I cannot at the present moment recall what the General's Christian name was. But I have no doubt he had one. He was eccentric, I admit. But only in later years. And that was the result of the Indian climate, and marriage, and indigestion, and other things of that kind.

JACK: Algy! Can't you recollect what our father's Christian name was?

ALGERNON: My dear boy, we were never even on speaking terms. He died before I was a year old.

JACK: His name would appear in the Army Lists of the period, I suppose, Aunt Augusta?

LADY BRACKNELL: The General was essentially a man of peace, except in his domestic life. But I have no doubt his name would appear in any military directory.

JACK: The Army Lists of the last forty years are here. These delightful records should have been my constant study. (*Rushes to bookcase and tears the books out.*) M. Generals ... Mallam, Maxbohm, Magley, what ghastly names they have—Markby,

Migsby, Mobbs, Moncrieff! Lieutenant 1840, Captain, Lieutenant Colonel, Colonel, General 1869, Christian names, Ernest John. (*Puts book very quietly down and speaks quite calmly.*) I always told you, Gwendolen, my name was Ernest, didn't I? Well, it is Ernest after all. I mean it naturally is Ernest.

LADY BRACKNELL: Yes, I remember now that the General was called Ernest, I knew I had some particular reason for disliking the name.

GWENDOLEN: Ernest! My own Ernest! I felt from the first that you could have no other name!

JACK: Gwendolen, it is a terrible thing for a man to find out suddenly that all his life he has been speaking nothing but the truth. Can you forgive me?

GWENDOLEN: I can. For I feel that you are sure to change.

JACK: My own one!

CHASUBLE: (*To* MISS PRISM.) Laetitia! (*Embraces her*)

MISS PRISM: (*Enthusiastically.*) Frederick! At last!

ALGERNON: Cecily! (*Embraces her.*) At last!

JACK: Gwendolen! (*Embraces her.*) At last!

LADY BRACKNELL: My nephew, you seem to be displaying signs of triviality.

JACK: On the contrary, Aunt Augusta, I've now realised for the first time in my life the vital Importance of Being Earnest.

PYGMALION

A Romance in Five Acts

By George Bernard Shaw

PREFACE

A Professor of Phonetics.

As will be seen later on, Pygmalion needs, not a preface, but a sequel, which I have supplied in its due place. The English have no respect for their language, and will not teach their children to speak it. They spell it so abominably that no man can teach himself what it sounds like. It is impossible for an Englishman to open his mouth without making some other Englishman hate or despise him. German and Spanish are accessible to foreigners: English is not accessible even to Englishmen. The reformer England needs today is an energetic phonetic enthusiast: that is why I have made such a one the hero of a popular play. There have been heroes of that kind crying in the wilderness for many years past. When I became interested in the subject towards the end of the eighteen-seventies, the illustrious Alexander Melville Bell, the inventor of Visible Speech, had emigrated to Canada, where his son invented the telephone; but Alexander J. Ellis was still a London patriarch, with an impressive head always covered by a velvet skull cap, for which he would apologize to public meetings in a very courtly manner. He and Tito Pagliardini, another phonetic veteran, were men whom it was impossible to dislike. Henry Sweet, then a young man, lacked their sweetness of character: he was about as conciliatory to conventional mortals as Ibsen or Samuel Butler. His great ability as a phonetician (he was, I think, the best of them all at his job) would have entitled him to high official recognition, and perhaps enabled him to popularize his subject, but for his Satanic contempt for all academic dignitaries and persons in general who thought more of Greek than of phonetics. Once, in the days when the Imperial

Institute rose in South Kensington, and Joseph Chamberlain was booming the Empire, I induced the editor of a leading monthly review to commission an article from Sweet on the imperial importance of his subject. When it arrived, it contained nothing but a savagely derisive attack on a professor of language and literature whose chair Sweet regarded as proper to a phonetic expert only. The article, being libellous, had to be returned as impossible; and I had to renounce my dream of dragging its author into the limelight. When I met him afterwards, for the first time for many years, I found to my astonishment that he, who had been a quite tolerably presentable young man, had actually managed by sheer scorn to alter his personal appearance until he had become a sort of walking repudiation of Oxford and all its traditions. It must have been largely in his own despite that he was squeezed into something called a Readership of phonetics there. The future of phonetics rests probably with his pupils, who all swore by him; but nothing could bring the man himself into any sort of compliance with the university to which he nevertheless clung by divine right in an intensely Oxonian way. I daresay his papers, if he has left any, include some satires that may be published without too destructive results fifty years hence. He was, I believe, not in the least an ill-natured man: very much the opposite, I should say; but he would not suffer fools gladly.

Those who knew him will recognize in my third act the allusion to the patent shorthand in which he used to write postcards, and which may be acquired from a four and six-penny manual published by the Clarendon Press. The postcards which Mrs Higgins describes are such as I have received from Sweet. I would decipher a sound which a cockney would represent by *zerr*, and a Frenchman by *seu*, and then write demanding with some heat what on earth it meant. Sweet, with boundless contempt for my stupidity, would reply that it not only meant but obviously was the word Result, as no other word containing that sound, and capable of making sense with the context, existed in any language spoken on earth. That less expert mortals should require fuller indications was beyond Sweet's patience. Therefore, though the whole point of his Current Shorthand is that it can express every sound in the language perfectly, vowels as well as consonants, and that your hand has to make no stroke except the easy and current ones with which you write m, n, and u, l, p, and q, scribbling them at whatever angle comes easiest to you, his unfortunate determination to make this remarkable and quite legible script serve also as a shorthand reduced it in his own practice to the most inscrutable of cryptograms. His true objective was the provision of a full, accurate, legible script for our noble but ill-dressed language; but he was led past that by his contempt for the popular Pitman system of shorthand, which he called the Pitfall system. The triumph of Pitman was a triumph of business organization: there was a weekly paper to persuade you to learn Pitman: there were cheap textbooks and exercise books and transcripts of speeches for you to copy, and schools where experienced teachers coached you up to the necessary proficiency. Sweet could not organize his market in that fashion. He might as well have been the Sybil who tore up the leaves of prophecy that nobody would attend to. The four and sixpenny manual, mostly in his lithographed handwriting, that was never vulgarly advertized, may perhaps some day be taken up by a syndicate and pushed upon the public as The Times pushed the Encyclopædia Britannica; but until then it will certainly not prevail against Pitman. I have bought three copies of it during my lifetime; and I am informed by the publishers that its cloistered existence is still a steady and healthy one. I actually learned the system two several times; and yet the shorthand in which I am writing these lines is Pitman's. And the reason is, that my secretary cannot transcribe Sweet, having been perforce taught in the schools of Pitman. Therefore, Sweet railed at Pitman as vainly as Thersites railed at Ajax: his raillery, however it may have eased his soul, gave no popular vogue to Current Shorthand.

Pygmalion Higgins is not a portrait of Sweet, to whom the adventure of Eliza Doolittle would have been impossible; still, as will be seen, there are touches of Sweet in the play. With Higgins's physique and temperament Sweet might have set the Thames on fire. As it was, he impressed himself professionally on Europe to an extent that made his comparative personal obscurity, and the failure of Oxford to do justice to his eminence, a puzzle to foreign specialists in his subject. I do not blame Oxford, because I think Oxford is quite right in demanding a certain social amenity from its nurslings (heaven knows it is not exorbitant in its requirements!); for although I well know how hard it is for a man of genius with a seriously underrated subject to maintain serene and kindly relations with the men who underrate it, and who keep all the best places for less important subjects which they profess without originality and sometimes without much capacity for them, still, if he overwhelms them with wrath and disdain, he cannot expect them to heap honors on him.

Of the later generations of phoneticians I know little. Among them towers the Poet Laureate, to whom perhaps Higgins may owe his Miltonic sympathies, though here again I must disclaim all portraiture. But if the play makes the public aware that there are such people as phoneticians, and that they are among the most important people in England at present, it will serve its turn.

I wish to boast that Pygmalion has been an extremely successful play all over Europe and North America as well as at home. It is so intensely and deliberately didactic, and its subject is esteemed so dry, that I delight in throwing it at the heads of the wiseacres who repeat the parrot cry that art should never be didactic. It goes to prove my contention that art should never be anything else.

Finally, and for the encouragement of people troubled with accents that cut them off from all high employment, I may add that the change wrought by Professor Higgins in the flower-girl is neither impossible nor uncommon. The modern concierge's daughter who fulfils her ambition by playing the Queen of Spain in Ruy Blas at the Théâtre Français is only one of many thousands of men and women who have sloughed off their native dialects and acquired a new tongue. But the thing has to be done scientifically, or the last state of the aspirant may be worse than the first. An honest and natural slum dialect is more tolerable than the attempt of a phonetically untaught person to imitate the vulgar dialect of the golf club; and I am sorry to say that in spite of the efforts of our Royal Academy of Dramatic Art, there is still too much sham golfing English on our stage, and too little of the noble English of Forbes-Robertson.

ACT I

Covent Garden at 11.15 p.m. Torrents of heavy summer rain. Cab whistles blowing frantically in all directions. Pedestrians running for shelter into the market and under the portico of St. Paul's Church, where there are already several people, among them a lady and her daughter in evening dress. They are all peering out gloomily at the rain, except one man with his back turned to the rest, who seems wholly preoccupied with a notebook in which he is writing busily.

The church clock strikes the first quarter.

THE DAUGHTER: [*In the space between the central pillars, close to the one on her left*] I'm getting chilled to the bone. What can Freddy be doing all this time? He's been gone twenty minutes.

THE MOTHER: [*On her daughter's right*] Not so long. But he ought to have got us a cab by this.

A BYSTANDER: [*On the lady's right*] He wont get no cab not until half-past eleven, missus, when they come back after dropping their theatre fares.

THE MOTHER: But we must have a cab. We cant stand here until half-past eleven. It's too bad.

THE BYSTANDER: Well, it aint my fault, missus.

THE DAUGHTER: If Freddy had a bit of gumption, he would have got one at the theatre door.

THE MOTHER: What could he have done, poor boy?

THE DAUGHTER: Other people got cabs. Why couldnt he?

[Freddy *rushes in out of the rain from the Southampton Street side, and comes between them closing a dripping umbrella. He is a young man of twenty, in evening dress, very wet round the ankles*]

THE DAUGHTER: Well, havent you got a cab?

FREDDY: Theres not one to be had for love or money.

THE MOTHER: Oh, Freddy, there must be one. You cant have tried.

THE DAUGHTER: It's too tiresome. Do you expect us to go and get one ourselves?

FREDDY: I tell you theyre all engaged. The rain was so sudden: nobody was prepared; and everybody had to take a cab. Ive been to Charing Cross one way and nearly to Ludgate Circus the other; and they were all engaged.

THE MOTHER: Did you try Trafalgar Square?

THE DAUGHTER: Did you try?

FREDDY: I tried as far as Charing Cross Station. Did you expect me to walk to Hammersmith?

THE DAUGHTER: You havent tried at all.

THE MOTHER: You really are very helpless, Freddy. Go again; and dont come back until you have found a cab.

FREDDY: I shall simply get soaked for nothing.

THE DAUGHTER: And what about us? Are we to stay here all night in this draught, with next to nothing on. You selfish pig —

FREDDY: Oh, very well: I'll go, I'll go. [*He opens his umbrella and dashes off Strandwards, but comes into collision with a flower girl, who is hurrying in for shelter, knocking her basket out of her hands. A blinding flash of lightning, followed instantly by a rattling peal of thunder, orchestrates the incident*]

THE FLOWER GIRL: Nah then, Freddy: look wh' y' gowin, deah.

FREDDY: Sorry. [*He rushes off*]

THE FLOWER GIRL: [*Picking up her scattered flowers and replacing them in the basket*] Theres menners f' yer! Te-oo banches o voylets trod into the mad.

[*She sits down on the plinth of the column, sorting her flowers, on the lady's right. She is not at all an attractive person. She is perhaps eighteen, perhaps twenty, hardly older. She wears a little sailor hat of black straw that has long been exposed to the dust and soot of London and has seldom if ever been brushed. Her hair needs washing rather badly: its mousy color can hardly be natural. She wears a shoddy black coat that reaches nearly to her knees and is shaped to her waist. She has a brown skirt with a coarse apron. Her boots are much the worse for wear. She is no doubt as clean as she can afford to be; but compared to the ladies she is very dirty. Her features are no worse than theirs; but their condition leaves something to be desired; and she needs the services of a dentist*]

THE MOTHER: How do you know that my son's name is Freddy, pray?

THE FLOWER GIRL: Ow, eez ye-ooa san, is e? Wal, fewd dan y' de-ooty bawmz a mather should, eed now bettern to spawl a pore gel's flahrzn than ran away athaht pyin. Will ye-oo py me f'them? [*Here, with apologies, this desperate attempt to represent her dialect without a phonetic alphabet must be abandoned as unintelligible outside London*]

THE DAUGHTER: Do nothing of the sort, mother. The idea!

THE MOTHER: Please allow me, Clara. Have you any pennies?

THE DAUGHTER: No. I've nothing smaller than sixpence.

THE FLOWER GIRL: [*Hopefully*] I can give you change for a tanner, kind lady.

THE MOTHER: [*To* Clara] Give it to me. [Clara *parts reluctantly*] Now [*To the girl*] This is for your flowers.

THE FLOWER GIRL: Thank you kindly, lady.

THE DAUGHTER: Make her give you the change. These things are only a penny a bunch.

THE MOTHER: Do hold your tongue, Clara. [*To the girl*] You can keep the change.

THE FLOWER GIRL: Oh, thank you, lady.

THE MOTHER: Now tell me how you know that young gentleman's name.

THE FLOWER GIRL: I didnt.

THE MOTHER: I heard you call him by it. Dont try to deceive me.

THE FLOWER GIRL: [*Protesting*] Who's trying to deceive you? I called him Freddy or Charlie same as you might yourself if you was talking to a stranger and wished to be pleasant. [*She sits down beside her basket*]

THE DAUGHTER: Sixpence thrown away! Really, mamma, you might have spared Freddy that. [*She retreats in disgust behind the pillar*]

[*An elderly gentleman of the amiable military type rushes into the shelter, and closes a dripping umbrella. He is in the same plight as* Freddy, *very wet about the ankles. He is in evening dress, with a light overcoat. He takes the place left vacant by the daughter's retirement*]

THE GENTLEMAN: Phew!

THE MOTHER: [*To the gentleman*] Oh, sir, is there any sign of its stopping?

THE GENTLEMAN: I'm afraid not. It started worse than ever about two minutes ago. [*He goes to the plinth beside the flower girl; puts up his foot on it; and stoops to turn down his trouser ends*]

THE MOTHER: Oh dear! [*She retires sadly and joins her daughter*]

THE FLOWER GIRL: [*Taking advantage of the military gentleman's proximity to establish friendly relations with him*] If it's worse, it's a sign it's nearly over. So cheer up, Captain; and buy a flower off a poor girl.

THE GENTLEMAN: I'm sorry, I havnt any change.

THE FLOWER GIRL: I can give you change, Captain.

THE GENTLEMAN: For a sovereign? Ive nothing less.

THE FLOWER GIRL: Garn! Oh do buy a flower off me, Captain. I can change half-a-crown. Take this for tuppence.

THE GENTLEMAN: Now dont be troublesome: theres a good girl. [*Trying his pockets*] I really havnt any change—Stop: heres three hapence, if thats any use to you [*He retreats to the other pillar*]

THE FLOWER GIRL: [*Disappointed, but thinking three halfpence better than nothing*] Thank you, sir.

THE BYSTANDER: [*To the girl*] You be careful: give him a flower for it. Theres a bloke here behind taking down every blessed word youre saying.

[*All turn to the man who is taking notes*]

THE FLOWER GIRL: [*Springing up terrified*] I aint done nothing wrong by speaking to the gentleman. Ive a right to sell flowers if I keep off the kerb. [*Hysterically*] I'm a respectable girl: so help me, I never spoke to him except to ask him to buy a flower off me. [*General hubbub, mostly sympathetic to the flower girl, but deprecating her excessive sensibility. Cries of* Dont start hollerin. Who's hurting you? Nobody's going to touch you. Whats the good of fussing? Steady on. Easy, easy, etc., *come from the elderly staid spectators, who pat her comfortingly. Less patient ones bid her shut her head, or ask her roughly what is wrong with her. A remoter group, not knowing what the matter is, crowd in and increase the noise with question and answer:* Whats the row? What she do? Where is he? A tec taking her down. What! him? Yes: him over there: Took money off the gentleman, etc. *The flower girl, distraught and mobbed, breaks through them to the gentleman, crying wildly*] Oh, sir, dont let him charge me. You dunno what it means to me. Theyll take away my character and drive me on the streets for speaking to gentlemen. They—

THE NOTE TAKER: [*Coming forward on her right, the rest crowding after him*] There, there, there, there! who's hurting you, you silly girl? What do you take me for?

THE BYSTANDER: It's all right: he's a gentleman: look at his boots. [*Explaining to the note taker*] She thought you was a copper's nark, sir.

THE NOTE TAKER: [*With quick interest*] Whats a copper's nark?

THE BYSTANDER: [*Inept at definition*] It's a—well, it's a copper's nark, as you might say. What else would you call it? A sort of informer.

THE FLOWER GIRL: [*Still hysterical*] I take my Bible oath I never said a word—

THE NOTE TAKER: [*Overbearing but good-humored*] Oh, shut up, shut up. Do I look like a policeman?

THE FLOWER GIRL: [*Far from reassured*] Then what did you take down my words for? How do I know whether you took me down right? You just shew me what youve wrote about me. [*The note taker opens his book and holds it steadily under her nose, though the pressure of the mob trying to read it over his shoulders would upset a weaker man*] Whats that? That aint proper writing. I cant read that.

THE NOTE TAKER: I can. [*Reads, reproducing her pronunciation exactly*] "Cheer ap, Keptin; n' baw ya flahr orf a pore gel."

THE FLOWER GIRL: [*Much distressed*] It's because I called him Captain. I meant no harm. [*To the gentleman*] Oh, sir, dont let him lay a charge agen me for a word like that. You—

THE GENTLEMAN: Charge! I make no charge. [*To the note taker*] Really, sir, if you are a detective, you need not begin protecting me against molestation by young women until I ask you. Anybody could see that the girl meant no harm.

THE BYSTANDERS GENERALLY: [*Demonstrating against police espionage*] Course they could. What business is it of yours? You mind your own affairs. He wants promotion, he does. Taking down people's words! Girl never said a word to him. What harm if she did? Nice thing a girl cant shelter from the rain without being insulted, etc., etc., etc. [*She is conducted by the more sympathetic demonstrators back to her plinth, where she resumes her seat and struggles with her emotion*]

THE BYSTANDER: He aint a tec. He's a blooming busybody: thats what he is. I tell you, look at his boots.

THE NOTE TAKER: [*Turning on him genially*] And how are all your people down at Selsey?

THE BYSTANDER: [*Suspiciously*] Who told you my people come from Selsey?

THE NOTE TAKER: Never you mind. They did. [*To the girl*] How do you come to be up so far east? You were born in Lisson Grove.

THE FLOWER GIRL: [*Appalled*] Oh, what harm is there in my leaving Lisson Grove? It wasnt fit for a pig to live in; and I had to pay four-and-six a week. [*In tears*] Oh, boo—hoo—oo—

THE NOTE TAKER: Live where you like; but stop that noise.

THE GENTLEMAN: [*To the girl*] Come, come! he cant touch you: you have a right to live where you please.

A SARCASTIC BYSTANDER: [*Thrusting himself between the note taker and the gentleman*] Park Lane, for instance. I'd like to go into the Housing Question with you, I would.

THE FLOWER GIRL: [*Subsiding into a brooding melancholy over her basket, and talking very low-spiritedly to herself*] I'm a good girl, I am.

THE SARCASTIC BYSTANDER: [*Not attending to her*] Do you know where I come from?

THE NOTE TAKER: [*Promptly*] Hoxton.

[*Titterings. Popular interest in the note taker's performance increases*]

THE SARCASTIC ONE: [*Amazed*] Well, who said I didnt? Bly me! You know everything, you do.

THE FLOWER GIRL: [*Still nursing her sense of injury*] Aint no call to meddle with me, he aint.

THE BYSTANDER: [*To her*] Of course he aint. Dont you stand it from him. [*To the note taker*] See here: what call have you to know about people what never offered to meddle with you? Wheres your warrant?

SEVERAL BYSTANDERS: [*Encouraged by this seeming point of law*] Yes: wheres your warrant?

THE FLOWER GIRL: Let him say what he likes. I dont want to have no truck with him.

THE BYSTANDER: You take us for dirt under your feet, dont you? Catch you taking liberties with a gentleman!

THE SARCASTIC BYSTANDER: Yes: tell him where he come from if you want to go fortune-telling.

THE NOTE TAKER: Cheltenham, Harrow, Cambridge, and India.

THE GENTLEMAN: Quite right. [*Great laughter. Reaction in the note taker's favor. Exclamations of* He knows all about it. Told him proper. Hear him tell the toff where he come from? etc] May I ask, sir, do you do this for your living at a music hall?

THE NOTE TAKER: Ive thought of that. Perhaps I shall some day.

[*The rain has stopped; and the persons on the outside of the crowd begin to drop off*]

THE FLOWER GIRL: [*Resenting the reaction*] He's no gentleman, he aint, to interfere with a poor girl.

THE DAUGHTER: [*Out of patience, pushing her way rudely to the front and displacing the gentleman, who politely retires to the other side of the pillar*] What on earth is Freddy doing? I shall get pneumonia if I stay in this draught any longer.

THE NOTE TAKER: [*To himself, hastily making a note of her pronunciation of "monia"*] Earlscourt.

THE DAUGHTER: [*Violently*] Will you please keep your impertinent remarks to yourself?

THE NOTE TAKER: Did I say that out loud? I didnt mean to. I beg your pardon. Your mother's Epsom, unmistakably.

THE MOTHER: [*Advancing between her daughter and the note taker*] How very curious! I was brought up in Largelady Park, near Epsom.

THE NOTE TAKER: [*Uproariously amused*] Ha! ha! What a devil of a name! Excuse me. [*To the daughter*] You want a cab, do you?

THE DAUGHTER: Dont dare speak to me.

THE MOTHER: Oh, please, please Clara. [*Her daughter repudiates her with an angry shrug and retires haughtily*] We should be so grateful to you, sir, if you found us a cab. [*The note taker produces a whistle*] Oh, thank you. [*She joins her daughter*]

[*The note taker blows a piercing blast*]

THE SARCASTIC BYSTANDER: There! I knowed he was a plain-clothes copper.

THE BYSTANDER: That aint a police whistle: thats a sporting whistle.

THE FLOWER GIRL: [*still preoccupied with her wounded feelings*] He's no right to take away my character. My character is the same to me as any lady's.

THE NOTE TAKER: I dont know whether youve noticed it; but the rain stopped about two minutes ago.

THE BYSTANDER: So it has. Why didnt you say so before? and us losing our time listening to your silliness! [*He walks off towards the Strand*]

THE SARCASTIC BYSTANDER: I can tell where y o u come from. You come from Anwell. Go back there.

THE NOTE TAKER: [*Helpfully*] Hanwell.

THE SARCASTIC BYSTANDER: [*Affecting great distinction of speech*] Thenk you, teacher. Haw haw! So long. [*He touches his hat with mock respect and strolls off*]

THE FLOWER GIRL: Frightening people like that! How would he like it himself?

THE MOTHER: It's quite fine now, Clara. We can walk to a motor bus. Come. [*She gathers her skirts above her ankles and hurries off towards the Strand*]

THE DAUGHTER: But the cab—[*Her mother is out of hearing*] Oh, how tiresome! [*She follows angrily*]

[*All the rest have gone except the note taker, the gentleman, and the flower girl, who sits arranging her basket, and still pitying herself in murmurs*]

THE FLOWER GIRL: Poor girl! Hard enough for her to live without being worrited and chivied.

THE GENTLEMAN: [*Returning to his former place on the note taker's left*] How do you do it, if I may ask?

THE NOTE TAKER: Simply phonetics. The science of speech. Thats my profession: also my hobby. Happy is the man who can make a living by his hobby! Y o u can spot an Irishman or a Yorkshireman by his brogue. *I* can place any man within six miles. I can place him within two miles in London. Sometimes within two streets.

THE FLOWER GIRL: Ought to be ashamed of himself, unmanly coward!

THE GENTLEMAN: But is there a living in that?

THE NOTE TAKER: Oh yes. Quite a fat one. This is an age of upstarts. Men begin in Kentish Town with £80 a year, and end in Park Lane with a hundred thousand. They want to drop Kentish Town; but they give themselves away every time they open their mouths. Now I can teach them—

THE FLOWER GIRL: Let him mind his own business and leave a poor girl—

THE NOTE TAKER: [*Explosively*] Woman: cease this detestable boohooing instantly; or else seek the shelter of some other place of worship.

THE FLOWER GIRL: [*With feeble defiance*] Ive a right to be here if I like, same as you.

THE NOTE TAKER: A woman who utters such depressing and disgusting sounds has no right to be anywhere—no right to live. Remember that you are a human being with a soul and the divine gift of articulate speech: that your native language is the language of Shakespear and Milton and The Bible; and dont sit there crooning like a bilious pigeon.

THE FLOWER GIRL: [*Quite overwhelmed, looking up at him in mingled wonder and deprecation without daring to raise her head*] Ah-ah-ah-ow-ow-ow-oo!

THE NOTE TAKER: [*Whipping out his book*] Heavens! what a sound! [*He writes; then holds out the book and reads, reproducing her vowels exactly*] Ah-ah-ah-ow-ow-ow-oo!

THE FLOWER GIRL: [*Tickled by the performance, and laughing in spite of herself*] Garn!

THE NOTE TAKER: You see this creature with her kerbstone English: the English that will keep her in the gutter to the end of her days. Well, sir, in three months I could pass that girl off as a duchess at an ambassador's garden party. I could even get her a place as lady's maid or shop assistant, which requires better English. Thats the sort of thing I do for commercial millionaires. And on the profits of it I do genuine scientific work in phonetics, and a little as a poet on Miltonic lines.

THE GENTLEMAN: I am myself a student of Indian dialects; and—

THE NOTE TAKER: [*Eagerly*] Are you? Do you know Colonel Pickering, the author of Spoken Sanscrit?

THE GENTLEMAN: I am Colonel Pickering. Who are you?

THE NOTE TAKER: Henry Higgins, author of Higgins's Universal Alphabet.

PICKERING: [*With enthusiasm*] I came from India to meet you.

HIGGINS: I was going to India to meet you.

PICKERING: Where do you live?

HIGGINS: 27A Wimpole Street. Come and see me tomorrow.

PICKERING: I'm at the Carlton. Come with me now and lets have a jaw over some supper.

HIGGINS: Right you are.

THE FLOWER GIRL: [*To* Pickering, *as he passes her*] Buy a flower, kind gentleman. I'm short for my lodging.

PICKERING: I really havnt any change. I'm sorry [*He goes away*]

HIGGINS: [*Shocked at the girl's mendacity*] Liar. You said you could change half-a-crown.

THE FLOWER GIRL: [*Rising in desperation*] You ought to be stuffed with nails, you ought. [*Flinging the basket at his feet*] Take the whole blooming basket for sixpence. [*The church clock strikes the second quarter*]

HIGGINS: [*Hearing in it the voice of God, rebuking him for his Pharisaic want of charity to the poor girl*] A reminder. [*He raises his hat solemnly; then throws a handful of money into the basket and follows* Pickering]

THE FLOWER GIRL: [*Picking up a half-crown*] Ah-ow-ooh! [*Picking up a couple of florins*] Aaah-ow-ooh! [*Picking up several coins*] Aaaaaah-ow-ooh! [*Picking up a half-sovereign*] Aaaaaaaaaaaah-ow-ooh!!!

FREDDY: [*Springing out of a taxicab*] Got one at last. Hallo! [*To the girl*] Where are the two ladies that were here?

THE FLOWER GIRL: They walked to the bus when the rain stopped.

FREDDY: And left me with a cab on my hands! Damnation!

THE FLOWER GIRL: [*With grandeur*] Never mind, young man. *I'm* going home in a taxi. [*She sails off to the cab. The driver puts his hand behind him and holds the door firmly shut against her. Quite understanding his mistrust, she shews him her handful of money*] Eightpence aint no object to me, Charlie. [*He grins and opens the door*] Angel Court, Drury Lane, round the corner of Micklejohn's oil shop. Lets see how fast you can make her hop it. [*She gets in and pulls the door to with a slam as the taxicab starts*]

FREDDY: Well, I'm dashed!

ACT II

Next day at 11 a.m. Higgins's *laboratory in Wimpole Street. It is a room on the first floor, looking on the street, and was meant for the drawing-room. The double doors are in the middle of the back wall; and persons entering find in the corner to their right two tall file cabinets at right angles to one another against the walls. In this corner stands a flat writing-table, on which are a phonograph, a laryngoscope, a row of tiny organ pipes with a bellows, a set of lamp chimneys for singing flames with burners attached to a gas plug in the wall by an indiarubber tube, several tuning-forks of different sizes, a life-size image of half a human head, shewing in section the vocal organs, and a box containing a supply of wax cylinders for the phonograph.*

Further down the room, on the same side, is a fireplace, with a comfortable leather-covered easy-chair at the side of the hearth nearest the door, and a coal-scuttle. There is a clock on the mantelpiece. Between the fireplace and the phonograph table is a stand for newspapers.

On the other side of the central door, to the left of the visitor, is a cabinet of shallow drawers. On it is a telephone and the telephone directory. The corner beyond, and most of the side wall, is occupied by a grand piano, with the keyboard at the end furthest from the door, and a bench for the player extending the full length of the keyboard. On the piano is a dessert dish heaped with fruit and sweets, mostly chocolates.

The middle of the room is clear. Besides the easy chair, the piano bench, and two chairs at the phonograph table, there is one stray chair. It stands near the fireplace. On the walls, engravings: mostly Piranesis and mezzotint portraits. No paintings.

Pickering *is seated at the table, putting down some cards and a tuning-fork which he has been using.* Higgins *is standing up near him, closing two or three file drawers which are hanging out. He appears in the morning light as a robust, vital, appetizing sort of man of forty or thereabouts, dressed in a professional-looking black frock-coat with a white linen collar and black silk tie. He is of the energetic, scientific type, heartily, even violently interested in everything that can be studied as a scientific subject, and careless about himself and other people, including their feelings. He is, in fact, but for his years and size, rather like a very impetuous baby "taking notice" eagerly and loudly, and requiring almost as much watching to keep him out of unintended mischief. His manner varies from genial bullying when he is in a good humor to stormy petulance when anything goes wrong; but he is so entirely frank and void of malice that he remains likeable even in his least reasonable moments.*

HIGGINS: [*As he shuts the last drawer*] Well, I think thats the whole show.

PICKERING: It's really amazing. I haven't taken half of it in, you know.

HIGGINS: Would you like to go over any of it again?

PICKERING: [*Rising and coming to the fireplace, where he plants himself with his back to the fire*] No, thank you; not now. I'm quite done up for this morning.

HIGGINS: [*Following him, and standing beside him on his left*] Tired of listening to sounds?

PICKERING: Yes. It's a fearful strain. I rather fancied myself because I can pronounce twenty-four distinct vowel sounds; but your hundred and thirty beat me. I can't hear a bit of difference between most of them.

HIGGINS: [*Chuckling, and going over to the piano to eat sweets*] Oh, that comes with practice. You hear no difference at first; but you keep on listening, and presently you find they're all as different as A from B. [Mrs Pearce *looks in: she is* Higgins's *housekeeper*] What's the matter?

MRS PEARCE: [*Hesitating, evidently perplexed*] A young woman wants to see you, sir.

HIGGINS: A young woman! What does she want?

MRS PEARCE: Well, sir, she says youll be glad to see her when you know what she's come about. She's quite a common girl, sir. Very common indeed. I should have sent her away, only I thought perhaps you wanted her to talk into your machines. I hope Ive not done wrong; but really you see such queer people sometimes— youll excuse me, I'm sure, sir—

HIGGINS: Oh, thats all right, Mrs Pearce. Has she an interesting accent?

MRS PEARCE: Oh, something dreadful, sir, really. I don't know how you can take an interest in it.

HIGGINS: [*To* Pickering] Lets have her up. Shew her up, Mrs Pearce. [*He rushes across to his working table and picks out a cylinder to use on the phonograph*]

MRS PEARCE: [*Only half resigned to it*] Very well, sir. It's for you to say. [*She goes downstairs*]

HIGGINS: This is rather a bit of luck. I'll shew you how I make records. We'll set her talking; and I'll take it down first in Bell's Visible Speech; then in broad Romic;

and then we'll get her on the phonograph so that you can turn her on as often as you like with the written transcript before you.

MRS PEARCE: [*Returning*] This is the young woman, sir.

[*The flower girl enters in state. She has a hat with three ostrich feathers, orange, sky-blue, and red. She has a nearly clean apron, and the shoddy coat has been tidied a little. The pathos of this deplorable figure, with its innocent vanity and consequential air, touches Pickering, who has already straightened himself in the presence of Mrs Pearce. But as to Higgins, the only distinction he makes between men and women is that when he is neither bullying nor exclaiming to the heavens against some featherweight cross, he coaxes women as a child coaxes its nurse when it wants to get anything out of her*]

HIGGINS: [*Brusquely, recognizing her with unconcealed disappointment, and at once, babylike, making an intolerable grievance of it*] Why, this is the girl I jotted down last night. She's no use: Ive got all the records I want of the Lisson Grove lingo; and I'm not going to waste another cylinder on it. [*To the girl*] Be off with you: I dont want you.

THE FLOWER GIRL: Dont you be so saucy. You aint heard what I come for yet. [*To Mrs Pearce, who is waiting at the door for further instruction*] Did you tell him I come in a taxi?

MRS PEARCE: Nonsense, girl! what do you think a gentleman like Mr Higgins cares what you came in?

THE FLOWER GIRL: Oh, we a r e proud! He aint above giving lessons, not him: I heard him say so. Well, I aint come here to ask for any compliment; and if my money's not good enough I can go elsewhere.

HIGGINS: Good enough for what?

THE FLOWER GIRL: Good enough for ye-oo. Now you know, dont you? I'm come to have lessons, I am. And to pay for em too: make no mistake.

HIGGINS: [*Stupent*] Well!!! [*Recovering his breath with a gasp*] What do you expect me to say to you?

THE FLOWER GIRL: Well, if you was a gentleman, you might ask me to sit down, I think. Dont I tell you I'm bringing you business?

HIGGINS: Pickering: shall we ask this baggage to sit down or shall we throw her out of the window?

THE FLOWER GIRL: [*Running away in terror to the piano, where she turns at bay*] Ah-ah-oh-ow-ow-ow-oo! [*Wounded and whimpering*] I wont be called a baggage when Ive offered to pay like any lady.

[*Motionless, the two men stare at her from the other side of the room, amazed*]

PICKERING: [*Gently*] What is it you want, my girl?

THE FLOWER GIRL: I want to be a lady in a flower shop stead of selling at the corner of Tottenham Court Road. But they wont take me unless I can talk more genteel. He said he could teach me. Well, here I am ready to pay him—not asking any favor—and he treats me as if I was dirt.

MRS PEARCE: How can you be such a foolish ignorant girl as to think you could afford to pay Mr Higgins?

THE FLOWER GIRL: Why shouldnt I? I know what lessons cost as well as you do; and I'm ready to pay.

HIGGINS: How much?

THE FLOWER GIRL: [*Coming back to him, triumphant*] Now youre talking! I thought youd come off it when you saw a chance of getting back a bit of what you chucked at me last night. [*Confidentially*] Youd had a drop in, hadnt you?

HIGGINS: [*Peremptorily*] Sit down.

THE FLOWER GIRL: Oh, if youre going to make a compliment of it—

HIGGINS: [*Thundering at her*] Sit down.

MRS PEARCE: [*Severely*] Sit down, girl. Do as youre told. [*She places the stray chair near the hearthrug between* Higgins *and* Pickering, *and stands behind it waiting for the girl to sit down*]

THE FLOWER GIRL: Ah-ah-ah-ow-ow-oo! [*She stands, half rebellious, half bewildered*]

PICKERING: [*Very courteous*] Wont you sit down?

LIZA: [*Coyly*] Dont mind if I do. [*She sits down.*
Pickering *returns to the hearthrug*]

HIGGINS: Whats your name?

THE FLOWER GIRL: Liza Doolittle.

HIGGINS: [*Declaiming gravely*]
Eliza, Elizabeth, Betsy and Bess,
They went to the woods to get a bird's nes':

PICKERING: They found a nest with four eggs in it:

HIGGINS: They took one apiece, and left three in it.
[*They laugh heartily at their own wit*]

LIZA: Oh, dont be silly.

MRS PEARCE: You mustnt speak to the gentleman like that.

LIZA: Well, why wont he speak sensible to me?

HIGGINS: Come back to business. How much do you propose to pay me for the lessons?

LIZA: Oh, I know whats right. A lady friend of mine gets French lessons for eighteen-pence an hour from a real French gentleman. Well, you wouldnt have the face to ask me the same for teaching me my own language as you would for French; so I wont give more than a shilling. Take it or leave it.

HIGGINS: [*Walking up and down the room, rattling his keys and his cash in his pockets*] You know, Pickering, if you consider a shilling, not as a simple shilling, but as a percentage of this girl's income, it works out as fully equivalent to sixty or seventy guineas from a millionaire.

PICKERING: How so?

HIGGINS: Figure it out. A millionaire has about £150 a day. She earns about half-a-crown.

LIZA: [*Haughtily*] Who told you I only—

HIGGINS: [*Continuing*] She offers me two-fifths of her day's income for a lesson. Two-fifths of a millionaire's income for a day would be somewhere about £60. It's handsome. By George, it's enormous! it's the biggest offer I ever had.

LIZA: [*Rising, terrified*] Sixty pounds! What are you talking about? I never offered you sixty pounds. Where would I get—

HIGGINS: Hold your tongue.

LIZA: [*Weeping*] But I aint got sixty pounds. Oh—

MRS PEARCE: Don't cry, you silly girl. Sit down. Nobody is going to touch your money.

HIGGINS: Somebody is going to touch you, with a broomstick, if you don't stop snivelling. Sit down.

LIZA: [*Obeying slowly*] Ah-ah-ah-ow-ee-o! One would think you was my father.

HIGGINS: If I decide to teach you, I'll be worse than two fathers to you. Here! [*He offers her his silk handkerchief*]

LIZA: Whats this for?

HIGGINS: To wipe your eyes. To wipe any part of your face that feels moist. Remember: thats your handkerchief; and thats your sleeve. Dont mistake the one for the other if you wish to become a lady in a shop.

[*Liza, utterly bewildered, stares helplessly at him*]

MRS PEARCE: It's no use talking to her like that, Mr Higgins: she doesnt understand you. Besides, youre quite wrong: she doesnt do it that way at all.

[*She takes the handkerchief*]

LIZA: [*Snatching it*] Here! You give me that handkerchief. He give it to me, not to you.

PICKERING: [*Laughing*] He did. I think it must be regarded as her property, Mrs Pearce.

MRS PEARCE: [*Resigning herself*] Serve you right, Mr Higgins.

PICKERING: Higgins: I'm interested. What about the ambassador's garden party? I'll say youre the greatest teacher alive if you make that good. I'll bet you all the expenses of the experiment you cant do it. And I'll pay for the lessons.

LIZA: Oh, you are real good. Thank you, Captain.

HIGGINS: [*Tempted, looking at her*] It's almost irresistible. She's so deliciously low—so horribly dirty—

LIZA: [*Protesting extremely*] Ah-ah-ah-ah-ow-ow-oo-oo!!! I aint dirty: I washed my face and hands afore I come, I did.

PICKERING: Youre certainly not going to turn her head with flattery, Higgins.

MRS PEARCE: [*Uneasy*] Oh, dont say that, sir: theres more ways than one of turning a girl's head; and nobody can do it better than Mr Higgins, though he may not always mean it. I do hope, sir, you wont encourage him to do anything foolish.

HIGGINS: [*Becoming excited as the idea grows on him*] What is life but a series of inspired follies? The difficulty is to find them to do. Never lose a chance: it doesnt come every day. I shall make a duchess of this draggletailed guttersnipe.

LIZA: [*Strongly deprecating this view of her*] Ah-ah-ah-ow-ow-oo!

HIGGINS: [*Carried away*] Yes: in six months—in three if she has a good ear and a quick tongue—I'll take her anywhere and pass her off as anything. We'll start today: now! this moment! Take her away and clean her, Mrs Pearce. Monkey Brand, if it wont come off any other way. Is there a good fire in the kitchen?

MRS PEARCE: [*Protesting*] Yes; but—

HIGGINS: [*Storming on*] Take all her clothes off and burn them. Ring up Whiteley or somebody for new ones. Wrap her up in brown paper til they come.

LIZA: Youre no gentleman, youre not, to talk of such things. I'm a good girl, I am; and I know what the like of you are, I do.

HIGGINS: We want none of your Lisson Grove prudery here, young woman. Youve got to learn to behave like a duchess. Take her away, Mrs Pearce. If she gives you any trouble, wallop her.

LIZA: [*Springing up and running between* Pickering *and* Mrs Pearce *for protection*] No! I'll call the police, I will.

MRS PEARCE: But Ive no place to put her.

HIGGINS: Put her in the dustbin.

LIZA: Ah-ah-ah-ow-ow-oo!

PICKERING: Oh come, Higgins! be reasonable.

MRS PEARCE: [*Resolutely*] You m u s t be reasonable, Mr Higgins: really you must. You cant walk over everybody like this.

> [Higgins, *thus scolded, subsides. The hurricane is succeeded by a zephyr of amiable surprise*]

HIGGINS: [*With professional exquisiteness of modulation*] I walk over everybody! My dear Mrs Pearce, my dear Pickering, I never had the slightest intention of walking over anyone. All I propose is that we should be kind to this poor girl. We must help her to prepare and fit herself for her new station in life. If I did not express myself clearly it was because I did not wish to hurt her delicacy, or yours.

[*Liza, reassured, steals back to her chair*]

MRS PEARCE: [*To* Pickering] Well, did you ever hear anything like that, sir?

PICKERING: [*Laughing heartily*] Never, Mrs Pearce: never.

HIGGINS: [*Patiently*] Whats the matter?

MRS PEARCE: Well, the matter is, sir, that you cant take a girl up like that as if you were picking up a pebble on the beach.

HIGGINS: Why not?

MRS PEARCE: Why not! But you dont know anything about her. What about her parents? She may be married.

LIZA: Garn!

HIGGINS: There! As the girl very properly says, Garn! Married indeed! Don't you know that a woman of that class looks a worn out drudge of fifty a year after she's married.

LIZA: Whood marry me?

HIGGINS: [*Suddenly resorting to the most thrillingly beautiful low tones in his best elocutionary style*] By George, Eliza, the streets will be strewn with the bodies of men shooting themselves for your sake before Ive done with you.

MRS PEARCE: Nonsense, sir. You mustnt talk like that to her.

LIZA: [*Rising and squaring herself determinedly*] I'm going away. He's off his chump, he is. I dont want no balmies teaching me.

HIGGINS: [*Wounded in his tenderest point by her insensibility to his elocution*] Oh, indeed! I'm mad, am I? Very well, Mrs Pearce: you neednt order the new clothes for her. Throw her out.

LIZA: [*Whimpering*] Nah-ow. You got no right to touch me.

MRS PEARCE: You see now what comes of being saucy. [*Indicating the door*] This way, please.

LIZA: [*Almost in tears*] I didnt want no clothes. I wouldnt have taken them [*She throws away the handkerchief*] I can buy my own clothes.

HIGGINS: [*Deftly retrieving the handkerchief and intercepting her on her reluctant way to the door*] Youre an ungrateful wicked girl. This is my return for offering to take you out of the gutter and dress you beautifully and make a lady of you.

MRS PEARCE: Stop, Mr Higgins. I wont allow it. It's you that are wicked. Go home to your parents, girl; and tell them to take better care of you.

LIZA: I aint got no parents. They told me I was big enough to earn my own living and turned me out.

MRS PEARCE: Wheres your mother?

LIZA: I aint got no mother. Her that turned me out was my sixth stepmother. But I done without them. And I'm a good girl, I am.

HIGGINS: Very well, then, what on earth is all this fuss about? The girl doesnt belong to anybody—is no use to anybody but me. [*He goes to* Mrs Pearce *and begins coaxing*] You can adopt her, Mrs Pearce: I'm sure a daughter would be a great amusement to you. Now dont make any more fuss. Take her downstairs; and—

MRS PEARCE: But whats to become of her? Is she to be paid anything? Do be sensible, sir.

HIGGINS: Oh, pay her whatever is necessary: put it down in the housekeeping book. [*Impatiently*] What on earth will she want with money? She'll have her food and her clothes. She'll only drink if you give her money.

LIZA: [*Turning on him*] Oh you are a brute. It's a lie: nobody ever saw the sign of liquor on me. [*She goes back to her chair and plants herself there defiantly*]

PICKERING: [*In good-humored remonstrance*] Does it occur to you, Higgins, that the girl has some feelings?

HIGGINS: [*Looking critically at her*] Oh no, I dont think so. Not any feelings that we need bother about. [*Cheerily*] Have you, Eliza?

LIZA: I got my feelings same as anyone else.

HIGGINS: [*To* Pickering, *reflectively*] You see the difficulty?

PICKERING: Eh? What difficulty?

HIGGINS: To get her to talk grammar. The mere pronunciation is easy enough.

LIZA: I dont want to talk grammar. I want to talk like a lady.

MRS PEARCE: Will you please keep to the point, Mr Higgins? I want to know on what terms the girl is to be here. Is she to have any wages? And what is to become of her when youve finished your teaching? You must look ahead a little.

HIGGINS: [*Impatiently*] Whats to become of her if I leave her in the gutter? Tell me that, Mrs Pearce.

MRS PEARCE: Thats her own business, not yours, Mr Higgins.

HIGGINS: Well, when Ive done with her, we can throw her back into the gutter; and then it will be her own business again; so thats all right.

LIZA: Oh, youve no feeling heart in you: you dont care for nothing but yourself. [*She rises and takes the floor resolutely*] Here! Ive had enough of this. I'm going. [*Making for the door*] You ought to be ashamed of yourself, you ought.

HIGGINS: [*Snatching a chocolate cream from the piano, his eyes suddenly beginning to twinkle with mischief*] Have some chocolates, Eliza.

LIZA: [*Halting, tempted*] How do I know what might be in them? Ive heard of girls being drugged by the like of you.

> [*Higgins whips out his penknife; cuts a chocolate in two; puts one half into his mouth and bolts it; and offers her the other half*]

HIGGINS: Pledge of good faith, Eliza. I eat one half: you eat the other.

[Liza *opens her mouth to retort: he pops the half chocolate into it*] You shall have boxes of them, barrels of them, every day. You shall live on them. Eh?

LIZA: [*Who has disposed of the chocolate after being nearly choked by it*] I wouldnt have ate it, only I'm too ladylike to take it out of my mouth.

HIGGINS: Listen, Eliza. I think you said you came in a taxi.

LIZA: Well, what if I did? Ive as good a right to take a taxi as anyone else.

HIGGINS: You have, Eliza; and in future you shall have as many taxis as you want. You shall go up and down and round the town in a taxi every day. Think of that, Eliza.

MRS PEARCE: Mr Higgins: youre tempting the girl. It's not right. She should think of the future.

HIGGINS: At her age! Nonsense! Time enough to think of the future when you havnt any future to think of. No, Eliza: do as this lady does: think of other people's futures; but never think of your own. Think of chocolates, and taxis, and gold, and diamonds.

LIZA: No: I dont want no gold and no diamonds. I'm a good girl, I am. [*She sits down again, with an attempt at dignity*]

HIGGINS: You shall remain so, Eliza, under the care of Mrs Pearce. And you shall marry an officer in the Guards, with a beautiful moustache: the son of a marquis, who will disinherit him for marrying you, but will relent when he sees your beauty and goodness—

PICKERING: Excuse me, Higgins; but I really must interfere. Mrs Pearce is quite right. If this girl is to put herself in your hands for six months for an experiment in teaching, she must understand thoroughly what she's doing.

HIGGINS: How can she? She's incapable of understanding anything. Besides, do any of us understand what we are doing? If we did, would we ever do it?

PICKERING: Very clever, Higgins; but not sound sense. [*To* Eliza] Miss Doolittle—

LIZA: [*Overwhelmed*] Ah-ah-ow-oo!

HIGGINS: There! That's all you get out of Eliza. Ah-ah-ow-oo! No use explaining. As a military man you ought to know that. Give her her orders: thats what she wants. Eliza: you are to live here for the next six months, learning how to speak beautifully, like a lady in a florist's shop. If youre good and do whatever youre told, you shall sleep in a proper bedroom, and have lots to eat, and money to buy chocolates and take rides in taxis. If youre naughty and idle you will sleep in the back kitchen among the black beetles, and be walloped by Mrs Pearce with a broomstick. At the end of six months you shall go to Buckingham Palace in a carriage, beautifully dressed. If the King finds out youre not a lady, you will be taken by the police to the Tower of London, where your head will be cut off as a warning to other presumptuous flower girls. If you are not found out, you shall have a present of seven-and-sixpence to start life with as a lady in a shop. If you refuse this offer you will be a most ungrateful and wicked girl; and the angels will weep for you. [*To* Pickering] Now are you satisfied, Pickering? [*To* Mrs Pearce] Can I put it more plainly and fairly, Mrs Pearce?

MRS PEARCE: [*Patiently*] I think youd better let me speak to the girl properly in private. I dont know that I can take charge of her or consent to the arrangement at all. Of course I know you dont mean her any harm; but when you get what you call interested in people's accents, you never think or care what may happen to them or you. Come with me, Eliza.

HIGGINS: Thats all right. Thank you, Mrs Pearce. Bundle her off to the bath-room.

LIZA: [*Rising reluctantly and suspiciously*] Youre a great bully, you are. I wont stay here if I dont like. I wont let nobody wallop me. I never asked to go to Bucknam Palace, I didnt. I was never in trouble with the police, not me. I'm a good girl—

MRS PEARCE: Dont answer back, girl. You dont understand the gentleman. Come with me. [*She leads the way to the door, and holds it open for* Eliza]

LIZA: [*As she goes out*] Well, what I say is right. I wont go near the king, not if I'm going to have my head cut off. If I'd known what I was letting myself in for, I wouldnt have come here. I always been a good girl; and I never offered to say a word to him; and I dont owe him nothing; and I dont care; and I wont be put upon; and I have my feelings the same as anyone else—

> [Mrs Pearce *shuts the door; and* Eliza's *plaints are no longer audible.* Pickering *comes from the hearth to the chair and sits astride it with his arms on the back*]

PICKERING: Excuse the straight question, Higgins. Are you a man of good character where women are concerned?

HIGGINS: [*Moodily*] Have you ever met a man of good character where women are concerned?

PICKERING: Yes: very frequently.

HIGGINS: [*Dogmatically, lifting himself on his hands to the level of the piano, and sitting on it with a bounce*] Well, I havnt. I find that the moment I let a woman make friends with me, she becomes jealous, exacting, suspicious, and a damned nuisance. I find that the moment I let myself make friends with a woman, I become selfish and tyrannical. Women upset everything. When you let them into your life, you find that the woman is driving at one thing and youre driving at another.

PICKERING: At what, for example?

HIGGINS: [*Coming off the piano restlessly*] Oh, Lord knows! I suppose the woman wants to live her own life; and the man wants to live his; and each tries to drag the other on to the wrong track. One wants to go north and the other south; and the result is that both have to go east, though they both hate the east wind. [*He sits down on the bench at the keyboard*] So here I am, a confirmed old bachelor, and likely to remain so.

PICKERING: [*Rising and standing over him gravely*] Come, Higgins! You know what I mean. If I'm to be in this business I shall feel responsible for that girl. I hope it's understood that no advantage is to be taken of her position.

HIGGINS: What! That thing! Sacred, I assure you. [*Rising to explain*] You see, she'll be a pupil; and teaching would be impossible unless pupils were sacred. Ive taught scores of American millionairesses how to speak English: the best looking women in the world. I'm seasoned. They might as well be blocks of wood. *I* might as well be a block of wood. It's—

[Mrs Pearce *opens the door. She has* Eliza's *hat in her hand.* Pickering *retires to the easy-chair at the hearth and sits down*]

HIGGINS: [*Eagerly*] Well, Mrs Pearce: is it all right?

MRS PEARCE: [*At the door*] I just wish to trouble you with a word, if I may, Mr Higgins.

HIGGINS: Yes, certainly. Come in. [*She comes forward*] Dont burn that, Mrs Pearce. I'll keep it as a curiosity. [*He takes the hat*]

MRS PEARCE: Handle it carefully, sir, please. I had to promise her not to burn it; but I had better put it in the oven for a while.

HIGGINS: [*Putting it down hastily on the piano*] Oh! thank you. Well, what have you to say to me?

PICKERING: Am I in the way?

MRS PEARCE: Not at all, sir. Mr Higgins: will you please be very particular what you say before the girl?

HIGGINS: [*Sternly*] Of course. I'm always particular about what I say. Why do you say this to me?

MRS PEARCE: [*Unmoved*] No, sir: youre not at all particular when youve mislaid anything or when you get a little impatient. Now it doesnt matter before me: I'm used to it. But you really must not swear before the girl.

HIGGINS: [*Indignantly*] I swear! [*Most emphatically*] I never swear. I detest the habit. What the devil do you mean?

MRS PEARCE: [*Stolidly*] Thats what I mean, sir. You swear a great deal too much. I dont mind your damning and blasting, and what the devil and where the devil and who the devil—

HIGGINS: Mrs Pearce: this language from your lips! Really!

MRS PEARCE: [*Not to be put off*]—but there is a certain word I must ask you not to use. The girl has just used it herself because the bath was too hot. It begins with the same letter as bath. She knows no better: she learnt it at her mother's knee. But she must not hear it from your lips.

HIGGINS: [*Loftily*] I cannot charge myself with having ever uttered it, Mrs Pearce. [*She looks at him steadfastly. He adds, hiding an uneasy conscience with a judicial air*] Except perhaps in a moment of extreme and justifiable excitement.

MRS PEARCE: Only this morning, sir, you applied it to your boots, to the butter, and to the brown bread.

HIGGINS: Oh, that! Mere alliteration, Mrs Pearce, natural to a poet.

MRS PEARCE: Well, sir, whatever you choose to call it, I beg you not to let the girl hear you repeat it.

HIGGINS: Oh, very well, very well. Is that all?

MRS PEARCE: No, sir. We shall have to be very particular with this girl as to personal cleanliness.

HIGGINS: Certainly. Quite right. Most important.

MRS PEARCE: I mean not to be slovenly about her dress or untidy in leaving things about.

HIGGINS: [*Going to her solemnly*] Just so. I intended to call your attention to that [*He passes on to* Pickering, *who is enjoying the conversation immensely*] It is these little things that matter, Pickering. Take care of the pence and the pounds will take care of themselves is as true of personal habits as of money. [*He comes to anchor on the hearthrug, with the air of a man in an unassailable position*]

MRS PEARCE: Yes, sir. Then might I ask you not to come down to breakfast in your dressing-gown, or at any rate not to use it as a napkin to the extent you do, sir. And if you would be so good as not to eat everything off the same plate, and to remember not to put the porridge saucepan out of your hand on the clean tablecloth, it would be a better example to the girl. You know you nearly choked yourself with a fishbone in the jam only last week.

HIGGINS: [*Routed from the hearthrug and drifting back to the piano*] I may do these things sometimes in absence of mind; but surely I dont do them habitually. [*Angrily*] By the way: my dressing-gown smells most damnably of benzine.

MRS PEARCE: No doubt it does, Mr Higgins. But if you will wipe your fingers—

HIGGINS: [*Yelling*] Oh very well, very well: I'll wipe them in my hair in future.

MRS PEARCE: I hope youre not offended, Mr Higgins.

HIGGINS: [*Shocked at finding himself thought capable of an unamiable sentiment*] Not at all, not at all. Youre quite right, Mrs Pearce: I shall be particularly careful before the girl. Is that all?

MRS PEARCE: No, sir. Might she use some of those Japanese dresses you brought from abroad? I really cant put her back into her old things.

HIGGINS: Certainly. Anything you like. Is that all?

MRS PEARCE: Thank you, sir. Thats all. [*She goes out*]

HIGGINS: You know, Pickering, that woman has the most extraordinary ideas about me. Here I am, a shy, diffident sort of man. Ive never been able to feel really grown-up and tremendous, like other chaps. And yet she's firmly persuaded that I'm an arbitrary overbearing bossing kind of person. I cant account for it.

[Mrs Pearce *returns*]

MRS PEARCE: If you please, sir, the trouble's beginning already. There's a dustman down-stairs, Alfred Doolittle, wants to see you. He says you have his daughter here.

PICKERING: [*Rising*] Phew! I say! [*He retreats to the hearthrug*]

HIGGINS: [*Promptly*] Send the blackguard up.

MRS PEARCE: Oh, very well, sir. [*She goes out*]

PICKERING: He may not be a blackguard, Higgins.

HIGGINS: Nonsense. Of course he's a blackguard.

PICKERING: Whether he is or not, I'm afraid we shall have some trouble with him.

HIGGINS: [*Confidently*] Oh no: I think not. If theres any trouble he shall have it with me, not I with him. And we are sure to get something interesting out of him.

PICKERING: About the girl?

HIGGINS: No. I mean his dialect.

PICKERING: Oh!

MRS PEARCE: [*At the door*] Doolittle, sir. [*She admits Doolittle and retires*]

[Alfred Doolittle *is an elderly but vigorous dustman, clad in the costume of his profession, including a hat with a back brim covering his neck and shoulders. He has well marked and rather interesting features, and seems equally free from fear and conscience. He has a remarkably expressive voice, the result of a habit of giving vent to his feelings without reserve. His present pose is that of wounded honor and stern resolution*]

DOOLITTLE: [*At the door, uncertain which of the two gentlemen is his man*] Professor Higgins?

HIGGINS: Here. Good morning. Sit down.

DOOLITTLE: Morning, Governor. [*He sits down magisterially*] I come about a very serious matter, Governor.

HIGGINS: [*To Pickering*] Brought up in Hounslow. Mother Welsh, I should think. [Doolittle *opens his mouth, amazed.* Higgins *continues*] What do you want, Doolittle?

DOOLITTLE: [*Menacingly*] I want my daughter: thats what I want. See?

HIGGINS: Of course you do. Youre her father, arent you? You dont suppose anyone else wants her, do you? I'm glad to see you have some spark of family feeling left. She's upstairs. Take her away at once.

DOOLITTLE: [*Rising, fearfully taken aback*] What!

HIGGINS: Take her away. Do you suppose I'm going to keep your daughter for you?

DOOLITTLE: [*Remonstrating*] Now, now, look here, Governor. Is this reasonable? Is it fair to take advantage of a man like this? The girl belongs to me. You got her. Where do I come in? [*He sits down again*]

HIGGINS: Your daughter had the audacity to come to my house and ask me to teach her how to speak properly so that she could get a place in a flower-shop. This gentleman and my housekeeper have been here all the time. [*Bullying him*] How dare you come here and attempt to blackmail me? You sent her here on purpose.

DOOLITTLE: [*Protesting*] No, Governor.

HIGGINS: You must have. How else could you possibly know that she is here?

DOOLITTLE: Dont take a man up like that, Governor.

HIGGINS: The police shall take you up. That is a plant—a plot to extort money by threats. I shall telephone for the police [*He goes resolutely to the telephone and opens the directory*]

DOOLITTLE: Have I asked you for a brass farthing? I leave it to the gentleman here: have I said a word about money?

HIGGINS: [*Throwing the book aside and marching down on* Doolittle *with a poser*] What else did you come for?

DOOLITTLE: [*Sweetly*] Well, what would a man come for? Be human, Governor.

HIGGINS: [*Disarmed*] Alfred: did you put her up to it?

DOOLITTLE: So help me, Governor, I never did. I take my Bible oath I aint seen the girl these two months past.

HIGGINS: Then how did you know she was here?

DOOLITTLE: ["*Most musical, most melancholy*"] I'll tell you, Governor, if youll only let me get a word in. I'm willing to tell you. I'm wanting to tell you. I'm waiting to tell you.

HIGGINS: Pickering: this chap has a certain natural gift of rhetoric. Observe the rhythm of his native woodnotes wild. "I'm willing to tell you: I'm wanting to tell you: I'm waiting to tell you." Sentimental rhetoric! Thats the Welsh strain in him. It also accounts for his mendacity and dishonesty.

PICKERING: Oh, please, Higgins: I'm west country myself. [*To* Doolittle] How did you know the girl was here if you didnt send her?

DOOLITTLE: It was like this, Governor. The girl took a boy in the taxi to give him a jaunt. Son of her landlady, he is. He hung about on the chance of her giving him another ride home. Well, she sent him back for her luggage when she heard you was willing for her to stop here. I met the boy at the corner of Long Acre and Endell Street.

HIGGINS: Public house. Yes?

DOOLITTLE: The poor man's club, Governor: why shouldnt I?

PICKERING: Do let him tell his story, Higgins.

DOOLITTLE: He told me what was up. And I ask you, what was my feelings and my duty as a father? I says to the boy, "You bring me the luggage," I says—

PICKERING: Why didnt you go for it yourself?

DOOLITTLE: Landlady wouldnt have trusted me with it, Governor. She's that kind of woman: you know. I had to give the boy a penny afore he trusted me with it, the little swine. I brought it to her just to oblige you like, and make myself agreeable. That's all.

HIGGINS: How much luggage?

DOOLITTLE: Musical instrument, Governor. A few pictures, a trifle of jewelry, and a bird-cage. She said she didnt want no clothes. What was I to think from that, Governor? I ask you as a parent what was I to think?

HIGGINS: So you came to rescue her from worse than death, eh?

DOOLITTLE: [Appreciatively: relieved at being understood] Just so, Governor. Thats right.

PICKERING: But why did you bring her luggage if you intended to take her away?

DOOLITTLE: Have I said a word about taking her away? Have I now?

HIGGINS: [Determinedly] Youre going to take her away, double quick. [He crosses to the hearth and rings the bell]

DOOLITTLE: [Rising] No, Governor. Dont say that. I'm not the man to stand in my girl's light. Heres a career opening for her, as you might say; and—

[Mrs Pearce opens the door and awaits orders]

HIGGINS: Mrs Pearce: this is Eliza's father. He has come to take her away. Give her to him. [He goes back to the piano, with an air of washing his hands of the whole affair]

DOOLITTLE: No. This is a misunderstanding. Listen here—

MRS PEARCE: He cant take her away, Mr Higgins: how can he? You told me to burn her clothes.

DOOLITTLE: Thats right. I cant carry the girl through the streets like a blooming monkey, can I? I put it to you.

HIGGINS: You have put it to me that you want your daughter. Take your daughter. If she has no clothes go out and buy her some.

DOOLITTLE: [Desperate] Wheres the clothes she come in? Did I burn them or did your missus here?

MRS PEARCE: I am the housekeeper, if you please. I have sent for some clothes for your girl. When they come you can take her away. You can wait in the kitchen. This way, please.

[Doolittle, much troubled, accompanies her to the door; then hesitates; finally turns confidentially to Higgins]

DOOLITTLE: Listen here, Governor. You and me is men of the world, aint we?

HIGGINS: Oh! Men of the world, are we? Youd better go, Mrs Pearce.

MRS PEARCE: I think so, indeed, sir. [*She goes, with dignity*]

PICKERING: The floor is yours, Mr Doolittle.

DOOLITTLE: [*To* Pickering] I thank you, Governor. [*To* Higgins, *who takes refuge on the piano bench, a little overwhelmed by the proximity of his visitor; for* Doolittle *has a professional flavor of dust about him*] Well, the truth is, Ive taken a sort of fancy to you, Governor; and if you want the girl, I'm not so set on having her back home again but what I might be open to an arrangement. Regarded in the light of a young woman, she's a fine handsome girl. As a daughter she's not worth her keep; and so I tell you straight. All I ask is my rights as a father; and youre the last man alive to expect me to let her go for nothing; for I can see youre one of the straight sort, Governor. Well, whats a five pound note to you? And whats Eliza to me? [*He returns to his chair and sits down judicially*]

PICKERING: I think you ought to know, Doolittle, that Mr Higgins's intentions are entirely honorable.

DOOLITTLE: Course they are, Governor. If I thought they wasnt, I'd ask fifty.

HIGGINS: [*Revolted*] Do you mean to say, you callous rascal, that you would sell your daughter for £50?

DOOLITTLE: Not in a general way I wouldnt; but to oblige a gentleman like you I'd do a good deal, I do assure you.

PICKERING: Have you no morals, man?

DOOLITTLE: [*Unabashed*] Cant afford them, Governor. Neither could you if you was as poor as me. Not that I mean any harm, you know. But if Liza is going to have a bit out of this, why not me too?

HIGGINS: [*Troubled*] I dont know what to do, Pickering. There can be no question that as a matter of morals it's a positive crime to give this chap a farthing. And yet I feel a sort of rough justice in his claim.

DOOLITTLE: Thats it, Governor. Thats all I say. A father's heart, as it were.

PICKERING: Well, I know the feeling; but really it seems hardly right—

DOOLITTLE: Dont say that, Governor. Dont look at it that way. What am I, Governors both? I ask you, what am I? I'm one of the undeserving poor: thats what I am. Think of what that means to a man. It means that he's up agen middle class morality all the time. If theres anything going, and I put in for a bit of it, it's always the same story: "Youre undeserving; so you cant have it." But my needs is as great as the most deserving widow's that ever got money out of six different charities in one week for the death of the same husband. I don't need less than a deserving man: I need more. I dont eat less hearty than him; and I drink a lot more. I want a bit of amusement, cause I'm a thinking man. I want cheerfulness and a song and a band when I feel low. Well, they charge me just the same for everything as they charge the deserving. What is middle class morality? Just an excuse for never giving me anything. Therefore, I ask you, as two gentlemen, not to play that game on me. I'm playing straight with you. I aint pretending to be deserving. I'm undeserving; and I mean to go on being undeserving. I like it; and that's the truth. Will you take advantage of a man's nature to do him out of the price of his own daughter what he's brought up and fed and clothed by the sweat of his brow until she's growed big enough to be interesting to you two gentlemen? Is five pounds unreasonable? I put it to you; and I leave it to you.

HIGGINS: [*Rising, and going over to* Pickering] Pickering: if we were to take this man in hand for three months, he could choose between a seat in the Cabinet and a popular pulpit in Wales.

PICKERING: What do you say to that, Doolittle?

DOOLITTLE: Not me, Governor, thank you kindly. Ive heard all the preachers and all the prime ministers—for I'm a thinking man and game for politics or religion or social reform same as all the other amusements—and I tell you it's a dog's life anyway you look at it. Undeserving poverty is my line. Taking one station in society with another, it's—it's—well, it's the only one that has any ginger in it, to my taste.

HIGGINS: I suppose we must give him a fiver.

PICKERING: He'll make a bad use of it, I'm afraid.

DOOLITTLE: Not me, Governor, so help me I wont. Dont you be afraid that I'll save it and spare it and live idle on it. There wont be a penny of it left by Monday: I'll have to go to work same as if I'd never had it. It wont pauperize me, you bet. Just one good spree for myself and the missus, giving pleasure to ourselves and employment to others, and satisfaction to you to think it's not been throwed away. You couldn't spend it better.

HIGGINS: [*Taking out his pocket book and coming between* Doolittle *and the piano*] This is irresistible. Let's give him ten. [*He offers two notes to the dustman*]

DOOLITTLE: No, Governor. She wouldnt have the heart to spend ten; and perhaps I shouldnt neither. Ten pounds is a lot of money: it makes a man feel prudent like; and then goodbye to happiness. You give me what I ask you, Governor: not a penny more, and not a penny less.

PICKERING: Why dont you marry that missus of yours? I rather draw the line at encouraging that sort of immorality.

DOOLITTLE: Tell her so, Governor: tell her so. *I'm* willing. It's me that suffers by it. Ive no hold on her. I got to be agreeable to her. I got to give her presents. I got to buy her clothes something sinful. I'm a slave to that woman, Governor, just because I'm not her lawful husband. And she knows it too. Catch her marrying me! Take my advice, Governor: marry Eliza while she's young and dont know no better. If you dont youll be sorry for it after. If you do, she'll be sorry for it after; but better you than her, because you're a man, and she's only a woman and dont know how to be happy anyhow.

HIGGINS: Pickering: if we listen to this man another minute, we shall have no convictions left. [*To* Doolittle] Five pounds I think you said.

DOOLITTLE: Thank you kindly, Governor.

HIGGINS: You're sure you won't take ten?

DOOLITTLE: Not now. Another time, Governor.

HIGGINS: [*Handing him a five-pound note*] Here you are.

DOOLITTLE: Thank you, Governor. Good morning.

[*He hurries to the door, anxious to get away with his booty. When he opens it he is confronted with a dainty and exquisitely clean young Japanese lady in a simple blue cotton kimono printed cunningly with small white jasmine blossoms. Mrs Pearce is with her. He gets out of her way deferentially and apologizes*] Beg pardon, miss.

THE JAPANESE LADY: Garn! Don't you know your own daughter?

DOOLITTLE:	*[exclaiming*	Bly me! it's Eliza!
HIGGINS:	*simul-*	Whats that! This!
PICKERING:	*taneously]*	By Jove!

LIZA: Dont I look silly?

HIGGINS: Silly?

MRS PEARCE: [*At the door*] Now, Mr Higgins, please dont say anything to make the girl conceited about herself.

HIGGINS: [*Conscientiously*] Oh! Quite right, Mrs Pearce. [*To* Eliza] Yes: damned silly.

MRS PEARCE: Please, sir.

HIGGINS: [*Correcting himself*] I mean extremely silly.

LIZA: I should look all right with my hat on. [*She takes up her hat; puts it on; and walks across the room to the fireplace with a fashionable air*]

HIGGINS: A new fashion, by George! And it ought to look horrible!

DOOLITTLE: [*With fatherly pride*] Well, I never thought she'd clean up as good looking as that, Governor. She's a credit to me, aint she?

LIZA: I tell you, it's easy to clean up here. Hot and cold water on tap, just as much as you like, there is. Woolly towels, there is; and a towel horse so hot, it burns your fingers. Soft brushes to scrub yourself, and a wooden bowl of soap smelling like primroses. Now I know why ladies is so clean. Washing's a treat for them. Wish they saw what it is for the like of me!

HIGGINS: I'm glad the bath-room met with your approval.

LIZA: It didnt: not all of it; and I dont care who hears me say it. Mrs Pearce knows.

HIGGINS: What was wrong, Mrs Pearce?

MRS PEARCE: [*Blandly*] Oh, nothing, sir. It doesnt matter.

LIZA: I had a good mind to break it. I didnt know which way to look. But I hung a towel over it, I did.

HIGGINS: Over what?

MRS PEARCE: Over the looking-glass, sir.

HIGGINS: Doolittle: you have brought your daughter up too strictly.

DOOLITTLE: Me! I never brought her up at all, except to give her a lick of a strap now and again. Dont put it on me, Governor. She aint accustomed to it, you see: thats all. But she'll soon pick up your free-and-easy ways.

LIZA: I'm a good girl, I am; and I wont pick up no free-and-easy ways.

HIGGINS: Eliza: if you say again that youre a good girl, your father shall take you home.

LIZA: Not him. You dont know my father. All he come here for was to touch you for some money to get drunk on.

DOOLITTLE: Well, what else would I want money for? To put into the plate in church, I suppose. [*She puts out her tongue at him. He is so incensed by this that* Pickering *presently finds it necessary to step between them*] Dont you give me none of your lip; and dont let me hear you giving this gentleman any of it neither, or youll hear from me about it. See?

HIGGINS: Have you any further advice to give her before you go, Doolittle? Your blessing, for instance.

DOOLITTLE: No, Governor: I aint such a mug as to put up my children to all I know myself. Hard enough to hold them in without that. If you want Eliza's mind improved, Governor, you do it yourself with a strap. So long, gentlemen. [*He turns to go*]

HIGGINS: [*Impressively*] Stop. Youll come regularly to see your daughter. It's your duty, you know. My brother is a clergyman; and he could help you in your talks with her.

DOOLITTLE: [*Evasively*] Certainly. I'll come, Governor. Not just this week, because I have a job at a distance. But later on you may depend on me. Afternoon, gentlemen. Afternoon, maam. [*He takes off his hat to* Mrs Pearce, *who disdains the salutation and goes out. He winks at* Higgins, *thinking him probably a fellow sufferer from* Mrs Pearce's *difficult disposition, and follows her*]

LIZA: Dont you believe the old liar. He'd as soon you set a bull-dog on him as a clergyman. You wont see him again in a hurry.

HIGGINS: I dont want to, Eliza. Do you?

LIZA: Not me. I dont want never to see him again, I dont. He's a disgrace to me, he is, collecting dust, instead of working at his trade.

PICKERING: What is his trade, Eliza?

LIZA: Taking money out of other people's pockets into his own. His proper trade's a navvy; and he works at it sometimes too—for exercise—and earns good money at it. Aint you going to call me Miss Doolittle any more?

PICKERING: I beg your pardon, Miss Doolittle. It was a slip of the tongue.

LIZA: Oh, I dont mind; only it sounded so genteel. I should just like to take a taxi to the corner of Tottenham Court Road and get out there and tell it to wait for me, just to put the girls in their place a bit. I wouldnt speak to them, you know.

PICKERING: Better wait til we get you something really fashionable.

HIGGINS: Besides, you shouldnt cut your old friends now that you have risen in the world. That's what we call snobbery.

LIZA: You dont call the like of them my friends now, I should hope. Theyve took it out of me often enough with their ridicule when they had the chance; and now I mean to get a bit of my own back. But if I'm to have fashionable clothes, I'll wait. I should like to have some. Mrs Pearce says youre going to give me some to wear in bed at night different to what I wear in the daytime; but it do seem a waste of money when you could get something to show. Besides, I never could fancy changing into cold things on a winter night.

MRS PEARCE: [*Coming back*] Now, Eliza. The new things have come for you to try on.

LIZA: Ah-ow-oo-ooh! [*She rushes out*]

MRS. PEARCE: [*Following her*] Oh, dont rush about like that, girl. [*She shuts the door behind her*]

HIGGINS: Pickering: we have taken on a stiff job.

PICKERING: [*With conviction*] Higgins: we have.

ACT III

It is Mrs Higgins's *at-home day. Nobody has yet arrived. Her drawing-room, in a flat on Chelsea embankment, has three windows looking on the river; and the ceiling is not so lofty as it would be in an older house of the same pretension. The windows are open, giving access to a balcony with flowers in pots. If you stand with your face to the windows, you have the fireplace on your left and the door in the right-hand wall close to the corner nearest the windows.*

Mrs Higgins *was brought up on Morris and Burne Jones; and her room, which is very unlike her son's room in Wimpole Street, is not crowded with furniture and little tables and knicknacks. In the middle of the room there is a big ottoman; and this, with the carpet, the Morris wall-papers, and the Morris chintz window curtains and brocade covers of the ottoman and its cushions, supply all the ornament, and are much too handsome to be hidden by odds and ends of useless things. A few good oil-paintings from the exhibitions*

in the Grosvenor Gallery thirty years ago (the Burne Jones, not the Whistler side of them)
are on the walls. The only landscape is a Cecil Lawson on the scale of a Rubens. There is
a portrait of Mrs Higgins as she was when she defied fashion in her youth in one of the
beautiful Rossettian costumes which, when caricatured by people who did not understand,
led to the absurdities of popular estheticism in the eighteen-seventies.

In the corner diagonally opposite the door Mrs Higgins, now over sixty and long past
taking the trouble to dress out of the fashion, sits writing at an elegantly simple writing-
table with a bell button within reach of her hand. There is a Chippendale chair further
back in the room between her and the window nearest her side. At the other side of the
room, further forward, is an Elizabethan chair roughly carved in the taste of Inigo Jones.
On the same side a piano in a decorated case. The corner between the fireplace and the
window is occupied by a divan cushioned in Morris chintz.

It is between four and five in the afternoon.

The door is opened violently; and Higgins *enters with his hat on.*

MRS HIGGINS: [*Dismayed*] Henry! [*Scolding him*] What are you doing here to-day?
It is my at-home day: you promised not to come. [*As he bends to kiss her, she takes*
his hat off, and presents it to him]

HIGGINS: Oh bother! [*He throws the hat down on the table*]

MRS HIGGINS: Go home at once.

HIGGINS: [*Kissing her*] I know, mother. I came on purpose.

MRS HIGGINS: But you mustnt. I'm serious, Henry. You offend all my friends: they
stop coming whenever they meet you.

HIGGINS: Nonsense! I know I have no small talk; but people dont mind. [*He sits on*
the settee]

MRS HIGGINS: Oh! dont they? Small talk indeed! What about your large talk? Really,
dear, you mustnt stay.

HIGGINS: I must. Ive a job for you. A phonetic job.

MRS HIGGINS: No use, dear. I'm sorry; but I cant get round your vowels; and though
I like to get pretty postcards in your patent shorthand, I always have to read the
copies in ordinary writing you so thoughtfully send me.

HIGGINS: Well, this isnt a phonetic job.

MRS HIGGINS: You said it was.

HIGGINS: Not your part of it. Ive picked up a girl.

MRS HIGGINS: Does that mean that some girl has picked you up?

HIGGINS: Not at all. I dont mean a love affair.

MRS HIGGINS: What a pity!

HIGGINS: Why?

MRS HIGGINS: Well, you never fall in love with anyone under forty-five. When will you discover that there are some rather nice-looking young women about?

HIGGINS: Oh, I cant be bothered with young women. My idea of a loveable woman is something as like you as possible. I shall never get into the way of seriously liking young women: some habits lie too deep to be changed. [*Rising abruptly and walking about, jingling his money and his keys in his trouser pockets*] Besides, theyre all idiots.

MRS HIGGINS: Do you know what you would do if you really loved me, Henry?

HIGGINS: Oh bother! What? Marry, I suppose?

MRS HIGGINS: No. Stop fidgeting and take your hands out of your pockets. [*With a gesture of despair, he obeys and sits down again*] Thats a good boy. Now tell me about the girl.

HIGGINS: She's coming to see you.

MRS HIGGINS: I dont remember asking her.

HIGGINS: You didnt. *I* asked her. If youd known her you wouldnt have asked her.

MRS HIGGINS: Indeed! Why?

HIGGINS: Well, it's like this. She's a common flower girl. I picked her off the kerbstone.

MRS HIGGINS: And invited her to my at-home!

HIGGINS: [*Rising and coming to her to coax her*] Oh, thatll be all right. Ive taught her to speak properly; and she has strict orders as to her behavior. She's to keep to two subjects: the weather and everybody's health—Fine day and How do you do, you know—and not to let herself go on things in general. That will be safe.

MRS HIGGINS: Safe! To talk about our health! about our insides! perhaps about our outsides! How could you be so silly, Henry?

HIGGINS: [*Impatiently*] Well, she must talk about something. [*He controls himself and sits down again*] Oh, she'll be all right: dont you fuss. Pickering is in it with me. Ive a sort of bet on that I'll pass her off as a duchess in six months. I started on her some months ago; and she's getting on like a house on fire. I shall win my bet. She has a quick ear; and she's been easier to teach than my middle-class pupils because she's had to learn a complete new language. She talks English almost as you talk French.

MRS HIGGINS: Thats satisfactory, at all events.

HIGGINS: Well, it is and it isnt.

MRS HIGGINS: What does that mean?

HIGGINS: You see, Ive got her pronunciation all right; but you have to consider not only how a girl pronounces, but what she pronounces; and thats where—

[*They are interrupted by the Parlor-Maid, announcing guests*]

THE PARLOR-MAID: Mrs and Miss Eynsford Hill.

> [*She withdraws*]

HIGGINS: Oh Lord! [*He rises; snatches his hat from the table; and makes for the door; but before he reaches it his mother introduces him*]

[Mrs *and* Miss Eynsford Hill *are the mother and daughter who sheltered from the rain in Covent Garden. The mother is well bred, quiet, and has the habitual anxiety of straitened means. The daughter has acquired a gay air of being very much at home in society: the bravado of genteel poverty*]

MRS EYNSFORD HILL: [*To* Mrs. Higgins] How do you do?

> [*They shake hands*]

MRS EYNSFORD HILL: How d'you do? [*She shakes*]

MRS HIGGINS: [*Introducing*] My son Henry.

MRS EYNSFORD HILL: Your celebrated son! I have so longed to meet you, Professor Higgins.

HIGGINS: [*Glumly, making no movement in her direction*] Delighted. [*He backs against the piano and bows brusquely*]

MISS EYNSFORD HILL: [*Going to him with confident familiarity*] How do you do?

HIGGINS: [*Staring at her*] Ive seen you before somewhere. I havent the ghost of a notion where; but Ive heard your voice. [*Drearily*] It doesnt matter. Youd better sit down.

MRS HIGGINS: I'm sorry to say that my celebrated son has no manners. You mustnt mind him.

MISS EYNSFORD HILL: [*Gaily*] I dont. [*She sits in the Elizabethan chair*]

MRS EYNSFORD HILL: [*A little bewildered*] Not at all. [*She sits on the ottoman between her daughter and* Mrs Higgins, *who has turned her chair away from the writing-table*]

HIGGINS: Oh, have I been rude? I didnt mean to be.

[*He goes to the central window, through which, with his back to the company, he contemplates the river and the flowers in Battersea Park on the opposite bank as if they were a frozen desert.*]

[*The* Parlor-Maid *returns, ushering in* Pickering]

THE PARLOR-MAID: Colonel Pickering.

> [*She withdraws*]

PICKERING: How do you do, Mrs Higgins?

MRS HIGGINS: So glad youve come. Do you know Mrs Eynsford Hill—Miss Eynsford Hill?

> [*Exchange of bows. The* Colonel *brings the Chippendale chair a little forward between* Mrs Hill *and* Mrs Higgins, *and sits down*]

PICKERING: Has Henry told you what weve come for?

HIGGINS: [*Over his shoulder*] We were interrupted: damn it!

MRS HIGGINS: Oh Henry, Henry, really!

MRS EYNSFORD HILL: [*Half rising*] Are we in the way?

MRS HIGGINS: [*Rising and making her sit down again*] No, no. You couldnt have come more fortunately: we want you to meet a friend of ours.

HIGGINS: [*Turning hopefully*] Yes, by George! We want two or three people. Youll do as well as anybody else.

[*The* Parlor-Maid *returns, ushering* Freddy]

THE PARLOR-MAID: Mr Eynsford Hill.

HIGGINS: [*Almost audibly, past endurance*] God of Heaven! another of them.

FREDDY: [*Shaking hands with* Mrs Higgins] Ahdedo?

MRS HIGGINS: Very good of you to come. [*Introducing*] Colonel Pickering.

FREDDY: [*Bowing*] Ahdedo?

MRS HIGGINS: I dont think you know my son, Professor Higgins.

FREDDY: [*Going to* Higgins] Ahdedo?

HIGGINS: [*Looking at him much as if he were a pickpocket*] I'll take my oath Ive met you before somewhere. Where was it?

FREDDY: I dont think so.

HIGGINS: [*Resignedly*] It dont matter, anyhow. Sit down.

[*He shakes* Freddy's *hand, and almost slings him on the ottoman with his face to the windows; then comes round to the other side of it*]

HIGGINS: Well, here we are, anyhow! [*He sits down on the ottoman next* Mrs Eynsford Hill, *on her left*] And now, what the devil are we going to talk about until Eliza comes?

MRS HIGGINS: Henry: you are the life and soul of the Royal Society's soirées; but really youre rather trying on more commonplace occasions.

HIGGINS: Am I? Very sorry. [*Beaming suddenly*] I suppose I am, you know. [*Uproariously*] Ha, ha!

MISS EYNSFORD HILL: [*Who considers Higgins quite eligible matrimonially*] I sympathize. I havent any small talk. If people would only be frank and say what they really think!

HIGGINS: [*Relapsing into gloom*] Lord forbid!

MRS EYNSFORD HILL: [*Taking up her daughter's cue*] But why?

HIGGINS: What they think they ought to think is bad enough, Lord knows; but what they really think would break up the whole show. Do you suppose it would be really agreeable if I were to come out now with what I really think?

MISS EYNSFORD HILL: [*Gaily*] Is it so very cynical?

HIGGINS: Cynical! Who the dickens said it was cynical? I mean it wouldnt be decent.

MRS EYNSFORD HILL: [*Seriously*] Oh! I'm sure you dont mean that, Mr Higgins.

HIGGINS: You see, we're all savages, more or less. We're supposed to be civilized and cultured—to know all about poetry and philosophy and art and science, and so on; but how many of us know even the meanings of these names? [*To* Miss Hill] What do you know of poetry? [*To* Mrs Hill] What do you know of science? [*Indicating* Freddy] What does he know of art or science or anything else? What the devil do you imagine I know of philosophy?

MRS HIGGINS: [*Warningly*] Or of manners, Henry?

THE PARLOR-MAID: [*Opening the door*] Miss Doolittle. [*She withdraws*]

HIGGINS: [*Rising hastily and running to* Mrs Higgins] Here she is, mother. [*He stands on tiptoe and makes signs over his mother's head to* Eliza *to indicate to her which lady is her hostess*]

[Eliza, *who is exquisitely dressed, produces an impression of such remarkable distinction and beauty as she enters that they all rise, quite fluttered. Guided by* Higgins's *signals, she comes to* Mrs Higgins *with studied grace*]

LIZA: [*Speaking with pedantic correctness of pronunciation and great beauty of tone*] How do you do, Mrs Higgins? [*She gasps slightly in making sure of the H in* Higgins, *but is quite successful*] Mr Higgins told me I might come.

MRS HIGGINS: [*Cordially*] Quite right: I'm very glad indeed to see you.

PICKERING: How do you do, Miss Doolittle?

LIZA: [*Shaking hands with him*] Colonel Pickering, is it not?

MRS EYNSFORD HILL: I feel sure we have met before, Miss Doolittle. I remember your eyes.

LIZA: How do you do? [*She sits down on the ottoman gracefully in the place just left vacant by* Higgins]

MRS EYNSFORD HILL: [*Introducing*] My daughter Clara.

LIZA: How do you do?

CLARA: [*Impulsively*] How do you do? [*She sits down on the ottoman beside* Eliza, *devouring her with her eyes*]

FREDDY: [*Coming to their side of the ottoman*] Ive certainly had the pleasure.

MRS EYNSFORD HILL: [*Introducing*] My son Freddy.

LIZA: How do you do?

[Freddy *bows and sits down in the Elizabethan chair, infatuated*]

HIGGINS: [*Suddenly*] By George, yes: it all comes back to me! [*They stare at him*] Covent Garden! [*Lamentably*] What a damned thing!

MRS HIGGINS: Henry, please! [*He is about to sit on the edge of the table*] Dont sit on my writing-table: youll break it.

HIGGINS: [*Sulkily*] Sorry.

[*He goes to the divan, stumbling into the fender and over the fire-irons on his way; extricating himself with muttered imprecations; and finishing his disastrous journey by throwing himself so impatiently on the divan that he almost breaks it.* Mrs. Higgins *looks at him, but controls herself and says nothing*]

[*A long and painful pause ensues*]

MRS HIGGINS: [*At last, conversationally*] Will it rain, do you think?

LIZA: The shallow depression in the west of these islands is likely to move slowly in an easterly direction. There are no indications of any great change in the barometrical situation.

FREDDY: Ha! ha! how awfully funny!

LIZA: What is wrong with that, young man? I bet I got it right.

FREDDY: Killing!

MRS EYNSFORD HILL: I'm sure I hope it wont turn cold. Theres so much influenza about. It runs right through our whole family regularly every spring.

LIZA: [*Darkly*] My aunt died of influenza: so they said.

MRS EYNSFORD HILL: [*Clicks her tongue sympathetically*]!!!

LIZA: [*In the same tragic tone*] But it's my belief they done the old woman in.

MRS HIGGINS: [*Puzzled*] Done her in?

LIZA: Y-e-e-e-es, Lord love you! Why should she die of influenza? She come through diphtheria right enough the year before. I saw her with my own eyes. Fairly blue with it, she was. They all thought she was dead; but my father he kept ladling gin down her throat til she came to so sudden that she bit the bowl off the spoon.

MRS EYNSFORD HILL: [*Startled*] Dear me!

LIZA: [*Piling up the indictment*] What call would a woman with that strength in her have to die of influenza? What become of her new straw hat that should have come to me? Somebody pinched it; and what I say is, them as pinched it done her in.

MRS EYNSFORD HILL: What does doing her in mean?

HIGGINS: [*Hastily*] Oh, thats the new small talk. To do a person in means to kill them.

MRS EYNSFORD HILL: [*To* Eliza, *horrified*] You surely dont believe that your aunt was killed?

LIZA: Do I not! Them she lived with would have killed her for a hat-pin, let alone a hat.

MRS EYNSFORD HILL: But it cant have been right for your father to pour spirits down her throat like that. It might have killed her.

LIZA: Not her. Gin was mother's milk to her. Besides, he'd poured so much down his own throat that he knew the good of it.

MRS EYNSFORD HILL: Do you mean that he drank?

LIZA: Drank! My word! Something chronic.

MRS EYNSFORD HILL: How dreadful for you!

LIZA: Not a bit. It never did him no harm what I could see. But then he did not keep it up regular. [*Cheerfully*] On the burst, as you might say, from time to time. And always more agreeable when he had a drop in. When he was out of work, my mother used to give him fourpence and tell him to go out and not come back until he'd drunk himself cheerful and loving-like. Theres lots of women has to make their husbands drunk to make them fit to live with. [*Now quite at her ease*] You see, it's like this. If a man has a bit of a conscience, it always takes him when he's sober; and then it makes him low-spirited. A drop of booze just takes that off and makes him happy. [*To* Freddy, *who is in convulsions of suppressed laughter*] Here! what are you sniggering at?

FREDDY: The new small talk. You do it so awfully well.

LIZA: If I was doing it proper, what was you laughing at? [*To* Higgins] Have I said anything I oughtnt?

MRS HIGGINS: [*Interposing*] Not at all, Miss Doolittle.

LIZA: Well, thats a mercy, anyhow. [*Expansively*] What I always say is—

HIGGINS: [*Rising and looking at his watch*] Ahem!

LIZA: [*Looking round at him; taking the hint; and rising*] Well: I must go. [*They all rise. Freddy goes to the door*] So pleased to have met you. Goodbye. [*She shakes hands with* Mrs Higgins]

MRS HIGGINS: Goodbye.

LIZA: Goodbye, Colonel Pickering.

PICKERING: Goodbye, Miss Doolittle. [*They shake hands*]

LIZA: [*Nodding to the others*] Goodbye, all.

FREDDY: [*Opening the door for her*] Are you walking across the Park, Miss Doolittle? If so—

LIZA: Walk! Not bloody likely. [*Sensation*] I am going in a taxi. [*She goes out*]
[Pickering *gasps and sits down.* Freddy *goes out on the balcony to catch another glimpse of* Eliza]

MRS EYNSFORD HILL: [*Suffering from shock*] Well, I really cant get used to the new ways.

CLARA: [*Throwing herself discontentedly into the Elizabethan chair*] Oh, it's all right, mamma, quite right. People will think we never go anywhere or see anybody if you are so old-fashioned.

MRS EYNSFORD HILL: I daresay I am very old-fashioned; but I do hope you wont begin using that expression, Clara. I have got accustomed to hear you talking about men as rotters, and calling everything filthy and beastly; though I do think it horrible and unladylike. But this last is really too much. Dont you think so, Colonel Pickering?

PICKERING: Dont ask me. Ive been away in India for several years; and manners have changed so much that I sometimes dont know whether I'm at a respectable dinner-table or in a ship's forecastle.

CLARA: It's all a matter of habit. Theres no right or wrong in it. Nobody means anything by it. And it's so quaint, and gives such a smart emphasis to things that are not in themselves very witty. I find the new small talk delightful and quite innocent.

MRS EYNSFORD HILL: [*Rising*] Well, after that, I think it's time for us to go.
                    [Pickering *and* Higgins *rise*]

CLARA: [*Rising*] Oh yes: we have three at-homes to go to still. Goodbye, Mrs Higgins. Goodbye, Colonel Pickering. Goodbye, Professor Higgins.

HIGGINS: [*Coming grimly at her from the divan, and accompanying her to the door*] Goodbye. Be sure you try on that small talk at the three at-homes. Dont be nervous about it. Pitch it in strong.

CLARA: [*All smiles*] I will. Goodbye. Such nonsense, all this early Victorian prudery!

HIGGINS: [*Tempting her*] Such damned nonsense!

CLARA: Such bloody nonsense!

MRS EYNSFORD HILL: [*Convulsively*] Clara!

CLARA: Ha! ha! [*She goes out radiant, conscious of being thoroughly up to date, and is heard descending the stairs in a stream of silvery laughter*]

FREDDY: [*To the heavens at large*] Well, I ask you— [*He gives it up, and comes to* Mrs. Higgins] Goodbye.

MRS HIGGINS: [*Shaking hands*] Goodbye. Would you like to meet Miss Doolittle again?

FREDDY: [*Eagerly*] Yes, I should, most awfully.

MRS HIGGINS: Well, you know my days.

FREDDY: Yes. Thanks awfully. Goodbye. [*He goes out*]

MRS EYNSFORD HILL: Goodbye, Mr Higgins.

HIGGINS: Goodbye. Goodbye.

MRS EYNSFORD HILL: [*To* Pickering] It's no use. I shall never be able to bring myself to use that word.

PICKERING: Dont. It's not compulsory, you know. Youll get on quite well without it.

MRS EYNSFORD HILL: Only, Clara is so down on me if I am not positively reeking with the latest slang. Goodbye.

PICKERING: Goodbye [*They shake hands*]

MRS EYNSFORD HILL: [*To* Mrs Higgins] You mustnt mind Clara. [Pickering, *catching from her lowered tone that this is not meant for him to hear, discreetly joins* Higgins *at the window*] We're so poor! and she gets so few parties, poor child! She doesnt quite know. [Mrs. Higgins, *seeing that her eyes are moist, takes her hand sympathetically and goes with her to the door*] But the boy is nice. Dont you think so?

MRS HIGGINS: Oh, quite nice. I shall always be delighted to see him.

MRS EYNSFORD HILL: Thank you, dear. Goodbye.

[*She goes out*]

HIGGINS: [*Eagerly*] Well? Is Eliza presentable? [*He swoops on his mother and drags her to the ottoman, where she sits down in* Eliza's *place with her son on her left*]

[Pickering *returns to his chair on her right*]

MRS HIGGINS: You silly boy, of course she's not presentable. She's a triumph of your art and of her dressmaker's; but if you suppose for a moment that she doesnt give herself away in every sentence she utters, you must be perfectly cracked about her.

PICKERING: But dont you think something might be done? I mean something to eliminate the sanguinary element from her conversation.

MRS HIGGINS: Not as long as she is in Henry's hands.

HIGGINS: [*Aggrieved*] Do you mean that my language is improper?

MRS HIGGINS: No, dearest: it would be quite proper—say on a canal barge; but it would not be proper for her at a garden party.

HIGGINS: [*Deeply injured*] Well I must say—

PICKERING: [*Interrupting him*] Come, Higgins: you must learn to know yourself. I havnt heard such language as yours since we used to review the volunteers in Hyde Park twenty years ago.

HIGGINS: [*Sulkily*] Oh, well, if you say so, I suppose I dont always talk like a bishop.

MRS HIGGINS: [*Quieting* Henry *with a touch*] Colonel Pickering: will you tell me what is the exact state of things in Wimpole Street?

PICKERING: [*Cheerfully: as if this completely changed the subject*] Well, I have come to live there with Henry. We work together at my Indian Dialects; and we think it more convenient—

MRS HIGGINS: Quite so. I know all about that: it's an excellent arrangement. But where does this girl live?

HIGGINS: With us, of course. Where would she live?

MRS HIGGINS: But on what terms? Is she a servant? If not, what is she?

PICKERING: [*Slowly*] I think I know what you mean, Mrs Higgins.

HIGGINS: Well, dash me if *I* do! Ive had to work at the girl every day for months to get her to her present pitch. Besides, she's useful. She knows where my things are, and remembers my appointments and so forth.

MRS HIGGINS: How does your housekeeper get on with her?

HIGGINS: Mrs Pearce? Oh, she's jolly glad to get so much taken off her hands; for before Eliza came, she used to have to find things and remind me of my appointments. But she's got some silly bee in her bonnet about Eliza. She keeps saying "You dont think, sir": doesnt she, Pick?

PICKERING: Yes: thats the formula. "You dont think, sir." Thats the end of every conversation about Eliza.

HIGGINS: As if I ever stop thinking about the girl and her confounded vowels and consonants. I'm worn out, thinking about her, and watching her lips and her teeth and her tongue, not to mention her soul, which is the quaintest of the lot.

MRS HIGGINS: You certainly are a pretty pair of babies, playing with your live doll.

HIGGINS: Playing! The hardest job I ever tackled: make no mistake about that, mother. But you have no idea how frightfully interesting it is to take a human being and change her into a quite different human being by creating a new speech for her. It's filling up the deepest gulf that separates class from class and soul from soul.

PICKERING: [*Drawing his chair closer to* Mrs Higgins *and bending over to her eagerly*] Yes: it's enormously interesting. I assure you, Mrs Higgins, we take Eliza very seriously. Every week—every day almost—there is some new change. [*Closer again*] We keep records of every stage—dozens of gramophone disks and photographs—

HIGGINS: [*Assailing her at the other ear*] Yes, by George: it's the most absorbing experiment I ever tackled. She regularly fills our lives up; doesnt she, Pick?

PICKERING: We're always talking Eliza.

HIGGINS: Teaching Eliza.

PICKERING: Dressing Eliza.

MRS HIGGINS: What!

HIGGINS: Inventing new Elizas.

HIGGINS:		You know, she has the most extraordinary quickness of ear:
	[*speaking*	
PICKERING:	*together*]	I assure you, my dear Mrs Higgins, that girl
HIGGINS:		just like a parrot. Ive tried her with every
PICKERING:		is a genius. She can play he piano quite beautifully.
HIGGINS:		possible sort of sound that a human being can make—
PICKERING:		We have taken her to classical concerts and to music
HIGGINS:		Continental dialects, African dialects, Hottentot
PICKERING:		halls; and its all the same to her: she plays everything
HIGGINS:		clicks, things it took me years to get hold of; and
PICKERING:		she hears right off when she comes home, whether it's
HIGGINS:		she picks them up like a shot, right away, as if she had
PICKERING:		Beethoven and Brahms or Lehar and Lionel Monckton;
HIGGINS:		been at it all her life.
PICKERING:		though six months ago, she'd never as much as touched a piano—

MRS HIGGINS: [*Putting her fingers in her ears, as they are by this time shouting one another down with an intolerable noise*] Sh-sh-sh—sh! [*They stop*]

PICKERING: I beg your pardon. [*He draws his chair back apologetically*]

HIGGINS: Sorry. When Pickering starts shouting nobody can get a word in edgeways.

MRS HIGGINS: Be quiet, Henry. Colonel Pickering: dont you realize that when Eliza walked into Wimpole Street, something walked in with her?

PICKERING: Her father did. But Henry soon got rid of him.

MRS HIGGINS: It would have been more to the point if her mother had. But as her mother didnt something else did.

PICKERING: But what?

MRS HIGGINS: [*Unconsciously dating herself by the word*] A problem.

PICKERING: Oh, I see. The problem of how to pass her off as a lady.

HIGGINS: I'll solve that problem. Ive half solved it already.

MRS HIGGINS: No, you two infinitely stupid male creatures: the problem of what is to be done with her afterwards.

HIGGINS: I dont see anything in that. She can go her own way, with all the advantages I have given her.

MRS HIGGINS: The advantages of that poor woman who was here just now! The manners and habits that disqualify a fine lady from earning her own living without giving her a fine lady's income! Is that what you mean?

PICKERING: [*Indulgently, being rather bored*] Oh, that will be all right, Mrs. Higgins. [*He rises to go*]

HIGGINS: [*Rising also*] We'll find her some light employment.

PICKERING: She's happy enough. Dont you worry about her. Goodbye. [*He shakes hands as if he were consoling a frightened child, and makes for the door*]

HIGGINS: Anyhow, theres no good bothering now. The thing's done. Goodbye, mother. [*He kisses her, and follows* Pickering]

PICKERING: [*Turning for a final consolation*] There are plenty of openings. We'll do whats right. Goodbye.

HIGGINS: [*To* Pickering *as they go out together*] Let's take her to the Shakespear exhibition at Earls Court.

PICKERING: Yes: lets. Her remarks will be delicious.

HIGGINS: She'll mimic all the people for us when we get home.

PICKERING: Ripping. [*Both are heard laughing as they go downstairs*]

MRS HIGGINS: [*Rises with an impatient bounce, and returns to her work at the writing-table. She sweeps a litter of disarranged papers out of her way; snatches a sheet of paper from her stationery case; and tries resolutely to write. At the third line she gives it up; flings down her pen; grips the table angrily and exclaims*] Oh, men! men!! men!!!

ACT IV

The Wimpole Street laboratory. Midnight. Nobody in the room. The clock on the mantelpiece strikes twelve. The fire is not alight: it is a summer night.

[*Presently* Higgins *and* Pickering *are heard on the stairs*]

HIGGINS: [*Calling down to* Pickering] I say, Pick: lock up, will you? I shant be going out again.

PICKERING: Right. Can Mrs Pearce go to bed? We dont want anything more, do we?

HIGGINS: Lord, no!

[Eliza *opens the door and is seen on the lighted landing in opera cloak, brilliant evening dress, and diamonds, with fan, flowers, and all accessories. She comes to the hearth, and switches on the electric lights there. She is tired: her pallor contrasts strongly with her dark eyes and hair; and her expression is almost tragic. She takes off her cloak; puts her fan and flowers on the piano; and sits down on the bench, brooding and silent.* Higgins, *in evening dress, with overcoat and hat, comes in, carrying a smoking jacket which he has picked up downstairs. He takes off the hat and overcoat; throws them carelessly on the newspaper stand; disposes of his coat in the same way; puts on the smoking jacket; and throws himself wearily into the easy-chair at the hearth.* Pickering, *similarly attired, comes in. He also takes off his hat and overcoat, and is about to throw them on* Higgins's *when he hesitates*]

PICKERING: I say: Mrs Pearce will row if we leave these things lying about in the drawing-room.

HIGGINS: Oh, chuck them over the bannisters into the hall. She'll find them there in the morning and put them away all right. She'll think we were drunk.

PICKERING: We are, slightly. Are there any letters?

HIGGINS: I didnt look. [Pickering *takes the overcoats and hats and goes down stairs.* Higgins *begins half singing half yawning an air from La Fanciulla del Golden West. Suddenly he stops and exclaims*]

I wonder where the devil my slippers are!

[Eliza *looks at him darkly; then rises suddenly and leaves the room*]

[Higgins *yawns again, and resumes his song.* Pickering *returns, with the contents of the letter-box in his hand*]

PICKERING: Only circulars, and this coroneted billet-doux for you. [*He throws the circulars into the fender, and posts himself on the hearthrug, with his back to the grate*]

HIGGINS: [*Glancing at the billet-doux*] Money-lender.

[*He throws the letter after the circulars*]

[Eliza *returns with a pair of large down-at-heel slippers. She places them on the carpet before* Higgins, *and sits as before without a word*]

HIGGINS: [*Yawning again*] Oh Lord! What an evening! What a crew! What a silly tomfoolery! [*He raises his shoe to unlace it, and catches sight of the slippers. He stops unlacing and looks at them as if they had appeared there of their own accord*] Oh! theyre there, are they?

PICKERING: [*Stretching himself*] Well, I feel a bit tired. It's been a long day. The garden party, a dinner party, and the opera! Rather too much of a good thing. But youve won your bet, Higgins. Eliza did the trick, and something to spare, eh?

HIGGINS: [*Fervently*] Thank God it's over!

[Eliza *flinches violently; but they take no notice of her; and she recovers herself and sits stonily as before*]

PICKERING: Were you nervous at the garden party? I was. Eliza didnt seem a bit nervous.

HIGGINS: Oh, she wasnt nervous. I knew she'd be all right. No: it's the strain of putting the job through all these months that has told on me. It was interesting enough at first, while we were at the phonetics; but after that I got deadly sick of it. If I hadnt backed myself to do it I should have chucked the whole thing up two months ago. It was a silly notion: the whole thing has been a bore.

PICKERING: Oh come! the garden party was frightfully exciting. My heart began beating like anything.

HIGGINS: Yes, for the first three minutes. But when I saw we were going to win hands down, I felt like a bear in a cage, hanging about doing nothing. The dinner was worse: sitting gorging there for over an hour, with nobody but a damned fool of a fashionable woman to talk to! I tell you, Pickering, never again for me. No more artificial duchesses. The whole thing has been simple purgatory.

PICKERING: Youve never been broken in properly to the social routine. [*Strolling over to the piano*] I rather enjoy dipping into it occasionally myself: it makes me feel young again. Anyhow, it was a great success: an immense success. I was quite frightened once or twice because Eliza was doing it so well. You see, lots of the real people cant do it at all: theyre such fools that they think style comes by nature to people in their position; and so they never learn. Theres always something professional about doing a thing superlatively well.

HIGGINS: Yes: thats what drives me mad: the silly people dont know their own silly business. [*Rising*] However, it's over and done with; and now I can go to bed at last without dreading tomorrow.

[Eliza's *beauty becomes murderous*]

PICKERING: I think I shall turn in too. Still, it's been a great occasion: a triumph for you. Goodnight. [*He goes*]

HIGGINS: [*Following him*] Goodnight. [*Over his shoulder, at the door*] Put out the lights, Eliza; and tell Mrs Pearce not to make coffee for me in the morning: I'll take tea. [*He goes out*]

    [Eliza *tries to control herself and feel indifferent as she rises and walks across to the hearth to switch off the lights. By the time she gets there she is on the point of screaming. She sits down in* Higgins's *chair and holds on hard to the arms. Finally she gives way and flings herself furiously on the floor, raging*]

HIGGINS: [*In despairing wrath outside*] What the devil have I done with my slippers? [*He appears at the door*]

LIZA: [*Snatching up the slippers, and hurling them at him one after the other with all her force*] There are your slippers. And there. Take your slippers; and may you never have a day's luck with them!

HIGGINS: [*Astounded*] What on earth—! [*He comes to her*] Whats the matter? Get up. [*He pulls her up*] Anything wrong?

LIZA: [*Breathless*] Nothing wrong—with y o u. Ive won your bet for you, havnt I? Thats enough for you. I dont matter, I suppose.

HIGGINS: Y o u won my bet! You! Presumptuous insect! I won it. What did you throw those slippers at me for?

LIZA: Because I wanted to smash your face. I'd like to kill you, you selfish brute. Why didnt you leave me where you picked me out of—in the gutter? You thank God it's all over, and that now you can throw me back again there, do you? [*She crisps her fingers frantically*]

HIGGINS: [*Looking at her in cool wonder*] The creature is nervous, after all.

LIZA: [*Gives a suffocated scream of fury, and instinctively darts her nails at his face*] !!

HIGGINS: [*Catching her wrists*] Ah! would you? Claws in, you cat. How dare you shew your temper to me? Sit down and be quiet. [*He throws her roughly into the easy-chair*]

LIZA: [*Crushed by superior strength and weight*] Whats to become of me? Whats to become of me?

HIGGINS: How the devil do I know whats to become of you? What does it matter what becomes of you?

LIZA: You dont care. I know you dont care. You wouldnt care if I was dead. I'm nothing to you—not so much as them slippers.

HIGGINS: [*Thundering*] T h o s e slippers.

LIZA: [*With bitter submission*] Those slippers. I didnt think it made any difference now.
    [*A pause. Eliza hopeless and crushed. Higgins a little uneasy*]

HIGGINS: [*In his loftiest manner*] Why have you begun going on like this? May I ask whether you complain of your treatment here?

LIZA: No.

HIGGINS: Has anybody behaved badly to you? Colonel Pickering? Mrs Pearce? Any of the servants?

LIZA: No.

HIGGINS: I presume you dont pretend that *I* have treated you badly.

LIZA: No.

HIGGINS: I am glad to hear it. [*He moderates his tone*] Perhaps youre tired after the strain of the day. Will you have a glass of champagne? [*He moves towards the door*]

LIZA: No. [*Recollecting her manners*] Thank you.

HIGGINS: [*Good-humored again*] This has been coming on you for some days. I suppose it was natural for you to be anxious about the garden party. But thats all over now. [*He pats her kindly on the shoulder. She writhes*] Theres nothing more to worry about.

LIZA: No. Nothing more for you to worry about. [*She suddenly rises and gets away from him by going to the piano bench, where she sits and hides her face*] Oh God! I wish I was dead.

HIGGINS: [*Staring after her in sincere surprise*] Why? In heaven's name, why? [*Reasonably, going to her*] Listen to me, Eliza. All this irritation is purely subjective.

LIZA: I dont understand. I'm too ignorant.

HIGGINS: It's only imagination. Low spirits and nothing else. Nobody's hurting you. Nothing's wrong. You go to bed like a good girl and sleep it off. Have a little cry and say your prayers: that will make you comfortable.

LIZA: I heard your prayers. "Thank God it's all over!"

HIGGINS: [*Impatiently*] Well, dont you thank God it's all over? Now you are free and can do what you like.

LIZA: [*Pulling herself together in desperation*] What am I fit for? What have you left me fit for? Where am I to go? What am I to do? Whats to become of me?

HIGGINS: [*Enlightened, but not at all impressed*] Oh, t h a t s whats worrying you, is it? [*He thrusts his hands into his pockets, and walks about in his usual manner, rattling the contents of his pockets, as if condescending to a trivial subject out of pure kindness*] I shouldnt bother about it if I were you. I should imagine you wont have much difficulty in settling yourself somewhere or other, though I hadnt quite realized that you were going away. [*She looks quickly at him: he does not look at her, but examines the dessert stand on the piano and decides that he will eat an apple*] You might marry, you know. [*He bites a large piece out of the apple, and munches it noisily*] You see, Eliza, all men are not confirmed old bachelors like me and the Colonel. Most men are the marrying sort (poor devils!); and youre not bad-looking: it's quite a pleasure to look at you sometimes—not now, of course, because youre crying and looking as ugly as the very devil; but when youre all right and quite yourself, youre what I should call attractive. That is, to the people in the marrying line, you understand. You go to bed and have a good nice rest; and then get up and look at yourself in the glass; and you wont feel so cheap.

    [Eliza *again looks at him, speechless, and does not stir*]

    [*The look is quite lost on him: he eats his apple with a dreamy expression of happiness, as it is quite a good one*]

HIGGINS: [*A genial afterthought occurring to him*] I daresay my mother could find some chap or other who would do very well.

LIZA: We were above that at the corner of Tottenham Court Road.

HIGGINS: [*Waking up*] What do you mean?

LIZA: I sold flowers. I didnt sell myself. Now youve made a lady of me I'm not fit to sell anything else. I wish youd left me where you found me.

HIGGINS: [*Slinging the core of the apple decisively into the grate*] Tosh, Eliza. Dont you insult human relations by dragging all this cant about buying and selling into it. You neednt marry the fellow if you dont like him.

LIZA: What else am I to do?

HIGGINS: Oh, lots of things. What about your old idea of a florist's shop? Pickering could set you up in one: he's lots of money. [*Chuckling*] He'll have to pay for all those togs you have been wearing today; and that, with the hire of the jewellery, will make a big hole in two hundred pounds. Why, six months ago you would have thought it the millennium to have a flower shop of your own. Come! youll be all right. I must clear off to bed: I'm devilish sleepy. By the way, I came down for something: I forget what it was.

LIZA: Your slippers.

HIGGINS: Oh yes, of course. You shied them at me.

    [*He picks them up, and is going out when she rises and speaks to him*]

LIZA: Before you go, sir—

HIGGINS: [*Dropping the slippers in his surprise at her calling him Sir*] Eh?

LIZA: Do my clothes belong to me or to Colonel Pickering?

HIGGINS: [*Coming back into the room as if her question were the very climax of unreason*] What the devil use would they be to Pickering?

LIZA: He might want them for the next girl you pick up to experiment on.

HIGGINS: [*Shocked and hurt*] Is t h a t the way you feel towards us?

LIZA: I dont want to hear anything more about that. All I want to know is whether anything belongs to me. My own clothes were burnt.

HIGGINS: But what does it matter? Why need you start bothering about that in the middle of the night?

LIZA: I want to know what I may take away with me. I dont want to be accused of stealing.

HIGGINS: [*Now deeply wounded*] Stealing! You shouldnt have said that, Eliza. That shews a want of feeling.

LIZA: I'm sorry. I'm only a common ignorant girl; and in my station I have to be careful. There cant be any feelings between the like of you and the like of me. Please will you tell me what belongs to me and what doesnt?

HIGGINS: [*Very sulky*] You may take the whole damned houseful if you like. Except the jewels. Theyre hired. Will that satisfy you? [*He turns on his heel and is about to go in extreme dudgeon*]

LIZA: [*Drinking in his emotion like nectar, and nagging him to provoke a further supply*] Stop, please. [*She takes off her jewels*] Will you take these to your room and keep them safe? I dont want to run the risk of their being missing.

HIGGINS: [*Furious*] Hand them over. [*She puts them into his hands*] If these belonged to me instead of to the jeweler, I'd ram them down your ungrateful throat. [*He perfunctorily thrusts them into his pockets, unconsciously decorating himself with the protruding ends of the chains*]

LIZA: [*Taking a ring off*] This ring isnt the jeweller's: it's the one you bought me in Brighton. I dont want it now. [Higgins *dashes the ring violently into the fireplace, and turns on her so threateningly that she crouches over the piano with her hands over her face, and exclaims*] Dont you hit me.

HIGGINS: Hit you! You infamous creature, how dare you accuse me of such a thing? It is you who have hit me. You have wounded me to the heart.

LIZA: [*Thrilling with hidden joy*] I'm glad. Ive got a little of my own back, anyhow.

HIGGINS: [*With dignity, in his finest professional style*] You have caused me to lose my temper: a thing that has hardly ever happened to me before. I prefer to say nothing more tonight. I am going to bed.

LIZA: [*Pertly*] Youd better leave a note for Mrs Pearce about the coffee; for she wont be told by me.

HIGGINS: [*Formally*] Damn Mrs Pearce; and damn the coffee; and damn you; and damn my own folly in having lavished hard-earned knowledge and the treasure of my regard and intimacy on a heartless guttersnipe. [*He goes out with impressive decorum, and spoils it by slamming the door savagely*]

[Eliza *smiles for the first time; expresses her feelings by a wild pantomime in which an imitation of* Higgins's *exit is confused with her own triumph; and finally goes down on her knees on the hearthrug to look for the ring*]

ACT V

Mrs. Higgins's *drawing-room. She is at her writing-table as before. The* Parlor-Maid *comes in.*

THE PARLOR-MAID: [*At the door*] Mr Henry, maam, is downstairs with Colonel Pickering.

MRS HIGGINS: Well, shew them up.

THE PARLOR-MAID: Theyre using the telephone, maam. Telephoning to the police, I think.

MRS HIGGINS: What!

THE PARLOR-MAID: [*Coming further in and lowering her voice*] Mr Henry's in a state, maam. I thought I'd better tell you.

MRS HIGGINS: If you had told me that Mr Henry was not in a state it would have been more surprising. Tell them to come up when theyve finished with the police. I suppose he's lost something.

THE PARLOR-MAID: Yes, maam. [*Going*]

MRS HIGGINS: Go upstairs and tell Miss Doolittle that Mr Henry and the Colonel are here. Ask her not to come down til I send for her.

THE PARLOR-MAID: Yes, maam.

[Higgins *bursts in. He is, as the* Parlor-Maid *has said, in a state*]

HIGGINS: Look here, mother: heres a confounded thing!

MRS HIGGINS: Yes, dear. Good morning. [*He checks his impatience and kisses her, whilst the* Parlor-Maid *goes out*] What is it?

HIGGINS: Eliza's bolted.

MRS HIGGINS: [*Calmly continuing her writing*] You must have frightened her.

HIGGINS: Frightened her! nonsense! She was left last night, as usual, to turn out the lights and all that; and instead of going to bed she changed her clothes and went right off: her bed wasnt slept in. She came in a cab for her things before seven this morning; and that fool Mrs Pearce let her have them without telling me a word about it. What am I to do?

MRS HIGGINS: Do without, I'm afraid, Henry. The girl has a perfect right to leave if she chooses.

HIGGINS: [*Wandering distractedly across the room*] But I cant find anything. I dont know what appointments Ive got. I'm—

[Pickering *comes in.* Mrs Higgins *puts down her pen and turns away from the writing-table*]

PICKERING: [*Shaking hands*] Good morning, Mrs Higgins. Has Henry told you? [*He sits down on the ottoman*]

HIGGINS: What does that ass of an inspector say? Have you offered a reward?

MRS HIGGINS: [*Rising in indignant amazement*] You dont mean to say you have set the police after Eliza?

HIGGINS: Of course. What are the police for? What else could we do? [*He sits in the Elizabethan chair*]

PICKERING: The inspector made a lot of difficulties. I really think he suspected us of some improper purpose.

MRS HIGGINS: Well, of course he did. What right have you to go to the police and give the girl's name as if she were a thief, or a lost umbrella, or something? Really! [*She sits down again, deeply vexed*]

HIGGINS: But we want to find her.

PICKERING: We cant let her go like this, you know, Mrs Higgins. What were we to do?

MRS HIGGINS: You have no more sense, either of you, than two children. Why—

[*The* Parlor-Maid *comes in and breaks off the conversation*]

THE PARLOR-MAID: Mr Henry: a gentleman wants to see you very particular. He's been sent on from Wimpole Street.

HIGGINS: Oh, bother! I cant see anyone now. Who is it?

THE PARLOR-MAID: A Mr Doolittle, sir.

PICKERING: Doolittle! Do you mean the dustman?

THE PARLOR-MAID: Dustman! Oh no, sir: a gentleman.

HIGGINS: [*Springing up excitedly*] By George, Pick, it's some relative of hers that she's gone to. Somebody we know nothing about. [*To the* Parlor-Maid] Send him up, quick.

THE PARLOR-MAID: Yes, sir.   [*She goes*]

HIGGINS: [*Eagerly, going to his mother*] Genteel relatives! now we shall hear something. [*He sits down in the Chippendale chair*]

MRS HIGGINS: Do you know any of her people?

PICKERING: Only her father: the fellow we told you about.

THE PARLOR-MAID: [*Announcing*] Mr Doolittle.

[*She withdraws*]

[Doolittle *enters. He is brilliantly dressed in a new fashionable frock-coat, with white waistcoat and grey trousers. A flower in his buttonhole, a dazzling silk hat, and patent leather shoes complete the effect. He is too concerned with the business he has come on to notice* Mrs Higgins. *He walks straight to* Higgins, *and accosts him with vehement reproach*]

DOOLITTLE: [*Indicating his own person*] See here! Do you see this? Y o u done this.

HIGGINS: Done what, man?

DOOLITTLE: This, I tell you. Look at it. Look at this hat. Look at this coat.

PICKERING: Has Eliza been buying you clothes?

DOOLITTLE: Eliza! not she. Not half. Why would she buy me clothes?

MRS HIGGINS: Good morning, Mr Doolittle. Wont you sit down?

DOOLITTLE: [*Taken aback as he becomes conscious that he has forgotten his hostess*] Asking your pardon, maam. [*He approaches her and shakes her proffered hand*] Thank you. [*He sits down on the ottoman, on* Pickering's *right*] I am that full of what has happened to me that I cant think of anything else.

HIGGINS: What the dickens has happened to you?

DOOLITTLE: I shouldnt mind if it had only h a p p e n e d to me: anything might happen to anybody and nobody to blame but Providence, as you might say. But this is something that you done to me: yes, you, Henry Higgins.

HIGGINS: Have you found Eliza? Thats the point.

DOOLITTLE: Have you lost her?

HIGGINS: Yes.

DOOLITTLE: You have all the luck, you have. I aint found her; but she'll find me quick enough now after what you done to me.

MRS HIGGINS: But what has my son done to you, Mr Doolittle?

DOOLITTLE: Done to me! Ruined me. Destroyed my happiness. Tied me up and delivered me into the hands of middle class morality.

HIGGINS: [*Rising intolerantly and standing over* Doolittle] Youre raving. Youre drunk. Youre mad. I gave you five pounds. After that I had two conversations with you, at half-a-crown an hour. Ive never seen you since.

DOOLITTLE: Oh! Drunk! am I? Mad! am I? Tell me this. Did you or did you not write a letter to an old blighter in America that was giving five millions to found Moral Reform Societies all over the world, and that wanted you to invent a universal language for him?

HIGGINS: What! Ezra D. Wannafeller! He's dead.

[*He sits down again carelessly*]

DOOLITTLE: Yes: he's dead; and I'm done for. Now did you or did you not write a letter to him to say that the most original moralist at present in England, to the best of your knowledge, was Alfred Doolittle, a common dustman.

HIGGINS: Oh, after your last visit I remember making some silly joke of the kind.

DOOLITTLE: Ah! you may well call it a silly joke. It put the lid on me right enough. Just give him the chance he wanted to shew that Americans is not like us: that they recognize and respect merit in every class of life, however humble. Them words is in his blooming will, in which, Henry Higgins, thanks to your silly joking, he leaves me a share in his Pre-digested Cheese Trust worth three thousand a year on condition that I lecture for his Wannafeller Moral Reform World League as often as they ask me up to six times a year.

HIGGINS: The devil he does! Whew! [*Brightening suddenly*] What a lark!

PICKERING: A safe thing for you, Doolittle. They wont ask you twice.

DOOLITTLE: It aint the lecturing I mind. I'll lecture them blue in the face, I will, and not turn a hair. It's making a gentleman of me that I object to. Who asked him to make a gentleman of me? I was happy. I was free. I touched pretty nigh everybody for money when I wanted it, same as I touched you, Henry Higgins. Now I am worrited; tied neck and heels; and everybody touches me for money. It's a fine thing for you, says my solicitor. Is it? says I. You mean it's a good thing for you, I says. When I was a poor man and had a solicitor once when they found a pram in the dust cart, he got me off, and got shut of me and got me shut of him as quick as he could. Same with the doctors: used to shove me out of the hospital before I could hardly stand on my legs, and nothing to pay. Now they finds out that I'm not a healthy man and cant live unless they looks after me twice a day. In the house I'm not let do a hand's turn for myself: somebody else must do it and touch me for it. A year ago I hadnt a relative in the world except two or three that wouldnt speak to me. Now Ive fifty, and not a decent week's wages among the lot of them. I have to live for others and not for myself: thats middle class morality. Y o u talk of losing Eliza. Dont you be anxious: I bet she's on my doorstep by this: she that could support herself easy by selling flowers if I wasnt respectable. And the next one to touch me will be you, Henry Higgins. I'll have to learn to speak middle class language from you, instead of speaking proper English. Thats where youll come in; and I daresay thats what you done it for.

MRS HIGGINS: But, my dear Mr Doolittle, you need not suffer all this if you are really in earnest. Nobody can force you to accept this bequest. You can repudiate it. Isnt that so, Colonel Pickering?

PICKERING: I believe so.

DOOLITTLE: [*Softening his manner in deference to her sex*] Thats the tragedy of it, maam. It's easy to say chuck it; but I havnt the nerve. Which of us has? We're all intimidated. Intimidated, maam: thats what we are. What is there for me if I chuck it but the workhouse in my old age? I have to dye my hair already to keep my job as a dustman. If I was one of the deserving poor, and had put by a bit, I could chuck it; but then why should I, acause the deserving poor might as well be millionaires for all the happiness they ever has. They dont know what happiness is. But I, as one of the undeserving poor, have nothing between me and the pauper's uniform but this here blasted three thousand a year that shoves me into the middle class. (Excuse the expression, maam: youd use it yourself if you had my provocation). Theyve got you every way you turn: it's a choice between the Skilly of the workhouse and the Char Bydis of the middle class; and I havnt the nerve for the workhouse. Intimidated: thats what I am. Broke. Bought up. Happier men than me will call for my dust, and touch me for their tip; and I'll look on helpless, and envy them. And thats what your son has brought me to. [*He is overcome by emotion*]

MRS HIGGINS: Well, I'm very glad youre not going to do anything foolish, Mr Doolittle. For this solves the problem of Eliza's future. You can provide for her now.

DOOLITTLE: [*With melancholy resignation*] Yes, maam: I'm expected to provide for everyone now, out of three thousand a year.

HIGGINS: [*Jumping up*] Nonsense! he cant provide for her. He shant provide for her. She doesnt belong to him. I paid him five pounds for her. Doolittle: either youre an honest man or a rogue.

DOOLITTLE: [*Tolerantly*] A little of both, Henry, like the rest of us: a little of both.

HIGGINS: Well, you took that money for the girl; and you have no right to take her as well.

MRS HIGGINS: Henry: dont be absurd. If you really want to know where Eliza is, she is upstairs.

HIGGINS: [*Amazed*] Upstairs!!! Then I shall jolly soon fetch her downstairs. [*He makes resolutely for the door*]

MRS HIGGINS: [*Rising and following him*] Be quiet, Henry. Sit down.

HIGGINS: I—

MRS HIGGINS: Sit down, dear; and listen to me.

HIGGINS: Oh very well, very well, very well. [*He throws himself ungraciously on the ottoman, with his face towards the windows*] But I think you might have told me this half an hour ago.

MRS HIGGINS: Eliza came to me this morning. She passed the night partly walking about in a rage, partly trying to throw herself into the river and being afraid to, and partly in the Carlton Hotel. She told me of the brutal way you two treated her.

HIGGINS: [*Bounding up again*] What!

PICKERING: [*Rising also*] My dear Mrs Higgins, she's been telling you stories. We didnt treat her brutally. We hardly said a word to her; and we parted on particularly good terms. [*Turning on* Higgins] Higgins: did you bully her after I went to bed?

HIGGINS: Just the other way about. She threw my slippers in my face. She behaved in the most outrageous way. I never gave her the slightest provocation. The slippers came bang into my face the moment I entered the room—before I had uttered a word. And used perfectly awful language.

PICKERING: [*Astonished*] But why? What did we do to her?

MRS HIGGINS: I think I know pretty well what you did. The girl is naturally rather affectionate, I think. Isnt she, Mr Doolittle?

DOOLITTLE: Very tender-hearted, maam. Takes after me.

MRS HIGGINS: Just so. She had become attached to you both. She worked very hard for you, Henry! I dont think you quite realize what anything in the nature of brain work means to a girl like that. Well, it seems that when the great day of trial came, and she did this wonderful thing for you without making a single mistake, you two sat there and never said a word to her, but talked together of how glad you were that it was all over and how you had been bored with the whole thing. And then you were surprised because she threw your slippers at you! *I* should have thrown the fire-irons at you.

HIGGINS: We said nothing except that we were tired and wanted to go to bed. Did we, Pick?

PICKERING: [*Shrugging his shoulders*] That was all.

MRS HIGGINS: [*Ironically*] Quite sure?

PICKERING: Absolutely. Really, that was all.

MRS HIGGINS: You didnt thank her, or pet her, or admire her, or tell her how splendid she'd been.

HIGGINS: [*Impatiently*] But she knew all about that. We didnt make speeches to her, if thats what you mean.

PICKERING: [*Conscience stricken*] Perhaps we were a little inconsiderate. Is she very angry?

MRS HIGGINS: [*Returning to her place at the writing-table*] Well, I'm afraid she wont go back to Wimpole Street, especially now that Mr Doolittle is able to keep up the position you have thrust on her; but she says she is quite willing to meet you on friendly terms and to let bygones be bygones.

HIGGINS: [*Furious*] Is she, by George? Ho!

MRS HIGGINS: If you promise to behave yourself, Henry, I'll ask her to come down. If not, go home; for you have taken up quite enough of my time.

HIGGINS: Oh, all right. Very well. Pick: you behave yourself. Let us put on our best Sunday manners for this creature that we picked out of the mud. [*He flings himself sulkily into the Elizabethan chair*]

DOOLITTLE: [*Remonstrating*] Now, now, Henry Higgins! have some consideration for my feelings as a middle class man.

MRS HIGGINS: Remember your promise, Henry. [*She presses the bell-button on the writing-table*] Mr Doolittle: will you be so good as to step out on the balcony for a moment. I dont want Eliza to have the shock of your news until she has made it up with these two gentlemen. Would you mind?

DOOLITTLE: As you wish, lady. Anything to help Henry to keep her off my hands. [*He disappears through the window*]

[*The* Parlor-Maid *answers the bell.* Pickering *sits down in* Doolittle's *place*]

MRS HIGGINS: Ask Miss Doolittle to come down, please.

THE PARLOR-MAID: Yes, maam. [*She goes out*]

MRS HIGGINS: Now, Henry: be good.

HIGGINS: I am behaving myself perfectly.

PICKERING: He is doing his best, Mrs Higgins.

[*A pause.* Higgins *throws back his head; stretches out his legs; and begins to whistle*]

MRS HIGGINS: Henry, dearest, you dont look at all nice in that attitude.

HIGGINS: [*Pulling himself together*] I was not trying to look nice, mother.

MRS HIGGINS: It doesnt matter, dear. I only wanted to make you speak.

HIGGINS: Why?

MRS HIGGINS: Because you cant speak and whistle at the same time.

[Higgins *groans. Another very trying pause*]

HIGGINS: [*Springing up, out of patience*] Where the devil is that girl? Are we to wait here all day?

[Eliza *enters, sunny, self-possessed, and giving a staggeringly convincing exhibition of ease of manner. She carries a little work-basket, and is very much at home.* Pickering *is too much taken aback to rise*]

LIZA: How do you do, Professor Higgins? Are you quite well?

HIGGINS: [*Choking*] Am I— [*He can say no more*]

LIZA: But of course you are: you are never ill. So glad to see you again, Colonel Pickering. [*He rises hastily; and they shake hands*] Quite chilly this morning, isnt it? [*She sits down on his left. He sits beside her*]

HIGGINS: Dont you dare try this game on me. I taught it to you; and it doesnt take me in. Get up and come home; and dont be a fool.

[Eliza *takes a piece of needlework from her basket, and begins to stitch at it, without taking the least notice of this outburst*]

MRS HIGGINS: Very nicely put, indeed, Henry. No woman could resist such an invitation.

HIGGINS: You let her alone, mother. Let her speak for herself. You will jolly soon see whether she has an idea that I havnt put into her head or a word that I havnt put into her mouth. I tell you I have created this thing out of the squashed cabbage leaves of Covent Garden; and now she pretends to play the fine lady with me.

MRS HIGGINS: [*Placidly*] Yes, dear; but youll sit down, wont you?

[Higgins *sits down again, savagely*]

LIZA: [*To* Pickering, *taking no apparent notice of* Higgins, *and working away deftly*] Will you drop me altogether now that the experiment is over, Colonel Pickering?

PICKERING: Oh dont. You mustnt think of it as an experiment. It shocks me, somehow.

LIZA: Oh, I'm only a squashed cabbage leaf—

PICKERING: [*Impulsively*] No.

LIZA: [*Continuing quietly*]—but I owe so much to you that I should be very unhappy if you forgot me.

PICKERING: It's very kind of you to say so, Miss Doolittle.

LIZA: It's not because you paid for my dresses. I know you are generous to everybody with money. But it was from you that I learnt really nice manners; and that is what makes one a lady, isnt it? You see it was so very difficult for me with the example of Professor Higgins always before me. I was brought up to be just like him, unable to control myself, and using bad language on the slightest provocation. And I should never have known that ladies and gentlemen didnt behave like that if you hadnt been there.

HIGGINS: Well!!

PICKERING: Oh, thats only his way, you know. He doesnt mean it.

LIZA: Oh, *I* didnt mean it either, when I was a flower girl. It was only my way. But you see I did it; and thats what makes the difference after all.

PICKERING: No doubt. Still, he taught you to speak; and I couldnt have done that, you know.

LIZA: [*Trivially*] Of course: that is his profession.

HIGGINS: Damnation!

LIZA: [*Continuing*] It was just like learning to dance in the fashionable way: there was nothing more than that in it. But do you know what began my real education?

PICKERING: What?

LIZA: [*Stopping her work for a moment*] Your calling me Miss Doolittle that day when I first came to Wimpole Street. That was the beginning of self-respect for me. [*She resumes her stitching*] And there were a hundred little things you never noticed, because they came naturally to you. Things about standing up and taking off your hat and opening doors—

PICKERING: Oh, that was nothing.

LIZA: Yes: things that shewed you thought and felt about me as if I were something better than a scullery-maid; though of course I know you would have been just the same to a scullery-maid if she had been let in the drawing-room. You never took off your boots in the dining room when I was there.

PICKERING: You mustnt mind that. Higgins takes off his boots all over the place.

LIZA: I know. I am not blaming him. It is his way, isnt it? But it made such a difference to me that you didnt do it. You see, really and truly, apart from the things anyone can pick up (the dressing and the proper way of speaking, and so on), the difference between a lady and a flower girl is not how she behaves, but how she's treated. I shall always be a flower girl to Professor Higgins, because he always treats me as a flower girl, and always will; but I know I can be a lady to you, because you always treat me as a lady, and always will.

MRS HIGGINS: Please dont grind your teeth, Henry.

PICKERING: Well, this is really very nice of you, Miss Doolittle.

LIZA: I should like you to call me Eliza, now, if you would.

PICKERING: Thank you. Eliza, of course.

LIZA: And I should like Professor Higgins to call me Miss Doolittle.

HIGGINS: I'll see you damned first.

MRS HIGGINS: Henry! Henry!

PICKERING: [*Laughing*] Why dont you slang back at him? Dont stand it. It would do him a lot of good.

LIZA: I cant. I could have done it once; but now I cant go back to it. Last night, when I was wandering about, a girl spoke to me; and I tried to get back into the old way with her; but it was no use. You told me, you know, that when a child is brought to a foreign country, it picks up the language in a few weeks, and forgets its own. Well, I am a child in your country. I have forgotten my own language, and can speak nothing but yours. Thats the real break-off with the corner of Tottenham Court Road. Leaving Wimpole Street finishes it.

PICKERING: [*Much alarmed*] Oh! but youre coming back to Wimpole Street, arnt you? Youll forgive Higgins?

HIGGINS: [*Rising*] Forgive! Will she, by George! Let her go. Let her find out how she can get on without us. She will relapse into the gutter in three weeks without me at her elbow.

[Doolittle *appears at the centre window. With a look of dignified reproach at* Higgins, *he comes slowly and silently to his daughter, who, with her back to the window, is unconscious of his approach*]

PICKERING: He's incorrigible, Eliza. You wont relapse, will you?

LIZA: No: Not now. Never again. I have learnt my lesson. I dont believe I could utter one of the old sounds if I tried. [Doolittle *touches her on her left shoulder. She drops her work, losing her self-possession utterly at the spectacle of her father's splendor*] A-a-a-a-a-ah-ow-ooh!

HIGGINS: [*With a crow of triumph*] Aha! Just so. A-a-a-a-ahowooh! A-a-a-a-ahowooh! A-a-a-a-ahowooh! Victory! Victory! [*He throws himself on the divan, folding his arms, and spraddling arrogantly*]

DOOLITTLE: Can you blame the girl? Dont look at me like that, Eliza. It aint my fault. Ive come into some money.

LIZA: You must have touched a millionaire this time, dad.

DOOLITTLE: I have. But I'm dressed something special today. I'm going to St. George's, Hanover Square. Your stepmother is going to marry me.

LIZA: [*Angrily*] Youre going to let yourself down to marry that low common woman!

PICKERING: [*Quietly*] He ought to, Eliza. [*To* Doolittle] Why has she changed her mind?

DOOLITTLE: [*Sadly*] Intimidated, Governor. Intimidated. Middle class morality claims its victim. Wont you put on your hat, Liza, and come and see me turned off?

LIZA: If the Colonel says I must, I—I'll [*Almost sobbing*] I'll demean myself. And get insulted for my pains, like enough.

DOOLITTLE: Dont be afraid: she never comes to words with anyone now, poor woman! Respectability has broke all the spirit out of her.

PICKERING: [*Squeezing* Eliza's *elbow gently*] Be kind to them, Eliza. Make the best of it.

LIZA: [*Forcing a little smile for him through her vexation*] Oh well, just to shew theres no ill feeling. I'll be back in a moment. [*She goes out*]

DOOLITTLE: [*Sitting down beside* Pickering] I feel uncommon nervous about the ceremony, Colonel. I wish youd come and see me through it.

PICKERING: But youve been through it before, man. You were married to Eliza's mother.

DOOLITTLE: Who told you that, Colonel?

PICKERING: Well, nobody told me. But I concluded—naturally—

DOOLITTLE: No: that aint the natural way, Colonel: it's only the middle class way. My way was always the undeserving way. But dont say nothing to Eliza. She dont know: I always had a delicacy about telling her.

PICKERING: Quite right. We'll leave it so, if you dont mind.

DOOLITTLE: And youll come to the church, Colonel, and put me through straight?

PICKERING: With pleasure. As far as a bachelor can.

MRS HIGGINS: May I come, Mr Doolittle? I should be very sorry to miss your wedding.

DOOLITTLE: I should indeed be honored by your condescension, maam; and my poor old woman would take it as a tremenjous compliment. She's been very low, thinking of the happy days that are no more.

MRS HIGGINS: [*Rising*] I'll order the carriage and get ready. [*The men rise, except* Higgins] I shant be more than fifteen minutes. [*As she goes to the door* Eliza *comes in, hatted and buttoning her gloves*] I'm going to the church to see your father married, Eliza. You had better come in the brougham with me. Colonel Pickering can go on with the bridegroom.

> [Mrs. Higgins *goes out.* Eliza *comes to the middle of the room between the centre window and the ottoman.* Pickering *joins her*]

DOOLITTLE: Bridegroom! What a word! It makes a man realize his position, somehow. [*He takes up his hat and goes towards the door*]

PICKERING: Before I go, Eliza, do forgive him and come back to us.

LIZA: I dont think papa would allow me. Would you, dad?

DOOLITTLE: [*Sad but magnanimous*] They played you off very cunning, Eliza, them two sportsmen. If it had been only one of them, you could have nailed him. But you see, there was two; and one of them chaperoned the other, as you might say. [*To* Pickering] It was artful of you, Colonel; but I bear no malice: I should have done the same myself. I been the victim of one woman after another all my life; and I dont grudge you two getting the better of Eliza. I shant interfere. It's time for us to go, Colonel. So long, Henry. See you in St. George's, Eliza. [*He goes out*]

PICKERING: [*Coaxing*] Do stay with us, Eliza.

> [*He follows* Doolittle]

> [Eliza *goes out on the balcony to avoid being alone with* Higgins. *He rises and joins her there. She immediately comes back into the room and makes for the door; but he goes along the balcony quickly and gets his back to the door before she reaches it*]

HIGGINS: Well, Eliza, youve had a bit of your own back, as you call it. Have you had enough? and are you going to be reasonable? Or do you want any more?

LIZA: You want me back only to pick up your slippers and put up with your tempers and fetch and carry for you.

HIGGINS: I havnt said I wanted you back at all.

LIZA: Oh, indeed. Then what are we talking about?

HIGGINS: About you, not about me. If you come back I shall treat you just as I have always treated you. I cant change my nature; and I dont intend to change my manners. My manners are exactly the same as Colonel Pickering's.

LIZA: Thats not true. He treats a flower girl as if she was a duchess.

HIGGINS: And I treat a duchess as if she was a flower girl.

LIZA: I see. [*She turns away composedly, and sits on the ottoman, facing the window*] The same to everybody.

HIGGINS: Just so.

LIZA: Like father.

HIGGINS: [*Grinning, a little taken down*] Without accepting the comparison at all points, Eliza, it's quite true that your father is not a snob, and that he will be quite at home in any station of life to which his eccentric destiny may call him. [*Seriously*] The great secret, Eliza, is not having bad manners or good manners or any other particular sort of manners, but having the same manner for all human souls: in short, behaving as if you were in Heaven, where there are no third-class carriages, and one soul is as good as another.

LIZA: Amen. You are a born preacher.

HIGGINS: [*Irritated*] The question is not whether I treat you rudely, but whether you ever heard me treat anyone else better.

LIZA: [*With sudden sincerity*] I dont care how you treat me. I dont mind your swearing at me. I dont mind a black eye: Ive had one before this. But [*Standing up and facing him*] I wont be passed over.

HIGGINS: Then get out of my way; for I wont stop for you. You talk about me as if I were a motor bus.

LIZA: So you are a motor bus: all bounce and go, and no consideration for anyone. But I can do without you: dont think I cant.

HIGGINS: I know you can. I told you you could.

LIZA: [*Wounded, getting away from him to the other side of the ottoman with her face to the hearth*] I know you did, you brute. You wanted to get rid of me.

HIGGINS: Liar.

LIZA: Thank you. [*She sits down with dignity*]

HIGGINS: You never asked yourself, I suppose, whether I could do without you.

LIZA: [*Earnestly*] Dont you try to get round me. Youll have to do without me.

HIGGINS: [*Arrogant*] I can do without anybody. I have my own soul: my own spark of divine fire. But [*With sudden humility*] I shall miss you, Eliza. [*He sits down near her on the ottoman*] I have learnt something from your idiotic notions: I confess that humbly and gratefully. And I have grown accustomed to your voice and appearance. I like them, rather.

LIZA: Well, you have both of them on your gramophone and in your book of photographs. When you feel lonely without me, you can turn the machine on. It's got no feelings to hurt.

HIGGINS: I cant turn your soul on. Leave me those feelings; and you can take away the voice and the face. They are not you.

LIZA: Oh, you are a devil. You can twist the heart in a girl as easy as some could twist her arms to hurt her. Mrs Pearce warned me. Time and again she has wanted to leave you; and you always got round her at the last minute. And you dont care a bit for her. And you dont care a bit for me.

HIGGINS: I care for life, for humanity; and you are a part of it that has come my way and been built into my house. What more can you or anyone ask?

LIZA: I wont care for anybody that doesnt care for me.

HIGGINS: Commercial principles, Eliza. Like [*Reproducing her Covent Garden pronunciation with professional exactness*] s'yollin voylets [*selling violets*], isnt it?

LIZA: Dont sneer at me. It's mean to sneer at me.

HIGGINS: I have never sneered in my life. Sneering doesnt become either the human face or the human soul. I am expressing my righteous contempt for Commercialism. I dont and wont trade in affection. You call me a brute because you couldnt buy a claim on me by fetching my slippers and finding my spectacles. You were a fool: I think a woman fetching a man's slippers is a disgusting sight: did I ever fetch your slippers? I think a good deal more of you for throwing them in my face. No use slaving for me and then saying you want to be cared for: who cares for a slave? If you come back, come back for the sake of good fellowship; for youll get nothing else. Youve had a thousand times as much out of me as I have out of you; and if you dare to set up your little dog's tricks of fetching and carrying slippers against my creation of a Duchess Eliza, I'll slam the door in your silly face.

LIZA: What did you do it for if you didnt care for me?

HIGGINS: [*Heartily*] Why, because it was my job.

LIZA: You never thought of the trouble it would make for me.

HIGGINS: Would the world ever have been made if its maker had been afraid of making trouble? Making life means making trouble. Theres only one way of escaping trouble; and thats killing things. Cowards, you notice, are always shrieking to have troublesome people killed.

LIZA: I'm no preacher: I dont notice things like that. I notice that you dont notice me.

HIGGINS: [*Jumping up and walking about intolerantly*] Eliza: youre an idiot. I waste the treasures of my Miltonic mind by spreading them before you. Once for all, understand that I go my way and do my work without caring twopence what happens to either of us. I am not intimidated, like your father and your stepmother. So you can come back or go to the devil: which you please.

LIZA: What am I to come back for?

HIGGINS: [*Bouncing up on his knees on the ottoman and leaning over it to her*] For the fun of it. Thats why I took you on.

LIZA: [*With averted face*] And you may throw me out tomorrow if I dont do everything you want me to?

HIGGINS: Yes; and you may walk out tomorrow if I dont do everything you want me to.

LIZA: And live with my stepmother?

HIGGINS: Yes, or sell flowers.

LIZA: Oh! if I only could go back to my flower basket! I should be independent of both you and father and all the world! Why did you take my independence from me? Why did I give it up? I'm a slave now, for all my fine clothes.

HIGGINS: Not a bit. I'll adopt you as my daughter and settle money on you if you like. Or would you rather marry Pickering?

LIZA: [*Looking fiercely round at him*] I wouldnt marry you if you asked me; and youre nearer my age than what he is.

HIGGINS: [*Gently*] Than he is: not "than what he is."

LIZA: [*Losing her temper and rising*] I'll talk as I like. Youre not my teacher now.

HIGGINS: [*Reflectively*] I dont suppose Pickering would, though. He's as confirmed an old bachelor as I am.

LIZA: Thats not what I want; and dont you think it. Ive always had chaps enough wanting me that way. Freddy Hill writes to me twice and three times a day, sheets and sheets.

HIGGINS: [*Disagreeably surprised*] Damn his impudence! [*He recoils and finds himself sitting on his heels*]

LIZA: He has a right to if he likes, poor lad. And he does love me.

HIGGINS: [*Getting off the ottoman*] You have no right to encourage him.

LIZA: Every girl has a right to be loved.

HIGGINS: What! By fools like that?

LIZA: Freddy's not a fool. And if he's weak and poor and wants me, may be he'd make me happier than my betters that bully me and dont want me.

HIGGINS: Can he make anything of you? Thats the point.

LIZA: Perhaps I could make something of him. But I never thought of us making anything of one another; and you never think of anything else. I only want to be natural.

HIGGINS: In short, you want me to be as infatuated about you as Freddy? Is that it?

LIZA: No I dont. Thats not the sort of feeling I want from you. And dont you be too sure of yourself or of me. I could have been a bad girl if I'd liked. Ive seen more of some things than you, for all your learning. Girls like me can drag gentlemen down to make love to them easy enough. And they wish each other dead the next minute.

HIGGINS: Of course they do. Then what in thunder are we quarrelling about?

LIZA: [*Much troubled*] I want a little kindness. I know I'm a common ignorant girl, and you a book-learned gentleman; but I'm not dirt under your feet. What I done [*Correcting herself*] what I did was not for the dresses and the taxis: I did it because we were pleasant together and I come—came—to care for you; not to want you to make love to me, and not forgetting the difference between us, but more friendly like.

HIGGINS: Well, of course. Thats just how I feel. And how Pickering feels. Eliza: youre a fool.

LIZA: Thats not a proper answer to give me [*She sinks on the chair at the writing-table in tears*]

HIGGINS: It's all youll get until you stop being a common idiot. If youre going to be a lady, youll have to give up feeling neglected if the men you know dont spend half their time snivelling over you and the other half giving you black eyes. If you cant stand the coldness of my sort of life, and the strain of it, go back to the gutter. Work til you are more a brute than a human being; and then cuddle and squabble and drink til you fall asleep. Oh, it's a fine life, the life of the gutter. It's real: it's warm: it's violent: you can feel it through the thickest skin: you can taste it and smell it without any training or any work. Not like Science and Literature and Classical Music and Philosophy and Art. You find me cold, unfeeling, selfish, dont you? Very well: be off with you to the sort of people you like. Marry some sentimental hog or other with lots of money, and a thick pair of lips to kiss you with and a thick pair of boots to kick you with. If you cant appreciate what youve got, youd better get what you can appreciate.

LIZA: [*Desperate*] Oh, you are a cruel tyrant. I cant talk to you: you turn everything against me: I'm always in the wrong. But you know very well all the time that youre nothing but a bully. You know I cant go back to the gutter, as you call it, and that I have no real friends in the world but you and the Colonel. You know well I couldnt bear to live with a low common man after you two; and it's wicked and cruel of you to insult me by pretending I could. You think I must go back to Wimpole Street because I have nowhere else to go but father's. But dont you be too sure that you have me under your feet to be trampled on and talked down. I'll marry Freddy, I will, as soon as he's able to support me.

HIGGINS: [*Sitting down beside her*] Rubbish! you shall marry an ambassador. You shall marry the Governor-General of India or the Lord-Lieutenant of Ireland, or somebody who wants a deputy-queen. I'm not going to have my masterpiece thrown away on Freddy.

LIZA: You think I like you to say that. But I havnt forgot what you said a minute ago; and I wont be coaxed round as if I was a baby or a puppy. If I cant have kindness, I'll have independence.

HIGGINS: Independence? Thats middle class blasphemy. We are all dependent on one another, every soul of us on earth.

LIZA: [*Rising determinedly*] I'll let you see whether I'm dependent on you. If you can preach, I can teach. I'll go and be a teacher.

HIGGINS: Whatll you teach, in heaven's name?

LIZA: What you taught me. I'll teach phonetics.

HIGGINS: Ha! Ha! Ha!

LIZA: I'll offer myself as an assistant to Professor Nepean.

HIGGINS: [*Rising in a fury*] What! That impostor! that humbug! that toadying igno-
ramus! Teach him my methods! my discoveries! You take one step in his direction
and I'll wring your neck. [*He lays hands on her*] Do you hear?

LIZA: [*Defiantly non-resistant*] Wring away. What do I care? I knew youd strike me
some day. [*He lets her go, stamping with rage at having forgotten himself, and recoils
so hastily that he stumbles back into his seat on the ottoman*] Aha! Now I know how
to deal with you. What a fool I was not to think of it before! You cant take away
the knowledge you gave me. You said I had a finer ear than you. And I can be civil
and kind to people, which is more than you can. Aha! Thats done you, Henry
Higgins, it has. Now I dont care that [*Snapping her fingers*] for your bullying and
your big talk. I'll advertize it in the papers that your duchess is only a flower girl
that you taught, and that she'll teach anybody to be a duchess just the same in six
months for a thousand guineas. Oh, when I think of myself crawling under your
feet and being trampled on and called names, when all the time I had only to lift
up my finger to be as good as you, I could just kick myself.

HIGGINS: [*Wondering at her*] You damned impudent slut, you! But it's better than
snivelling; better than fetching slippers and finding spectacles, isnt it? [*Rising*] By
George, Eliza, I said I'd make a woman of you; and I have. I like you like this.

LIZA: Yes: you turn round and make up to me now that I'm not afraid of you, and
can do without you.

HIGGINS: Of course I do, you little fool. Five minutes ago you were like a millstone
round my neck. Now youre a tower of strength: a consort battleship. You and I
and Pickering will be three old bachelors together instead of only two men and
a silly girl.

[Mrs Higgins *returns, dressed for the wedding.* Eliza *instantly becomes cool and
elegant*]

MRS HIGGINS: The carriage is waiting, Eliza. Are you ready?

LIZA: Quite. Is the Professor coming?

MRS HIGGINS: Certainly not. He cant behave himself in church. He makes remarks
out loud all the time on the clergyman's pronunciation.

LIZA: Then I shall not see you again, Professor. Goodbye. [*She goes to the door*]

MRS HIGGINS: [*Coming to* Higgins] Goodbye, dear.

HIGGINS: Good-bye, mother. [*He is about to kiss her, when he recollects something*]
Oh, by the way, Eliza, order a ham and a Stilton cheese, will you? And buy me a
pair of reindeer gloves, number eights, and a tie to match that new suit of mine,
at Eale & Binman's. You can choose the color. [*His cheerful, careless, vigorous voice
shows that he is incorrigible*]

LIZA: [*Disdainfully*] Buy them yourself. [*She sweeps out*]

MRS HIGGINS: I'm afraid youve spoiled that girl, Henry. But never mind, dear: I'll buy you the tie and gloves.

HIGGINS: [*Sunnily*] Oh, dont bother. She'll buy em all right enough. Goodbye.

[*They kiss. Mrs Higgins runs out. Higgins, left alone, rattles his cash in his pocket; chuckles; and disports himself in a highly self-satisfied manner*]

THE END

SEQUEL

What Happened Afterwards.

The rest of the story need not be shown in action, and indeed, would hardly need telling if our imaginations were not so enfeebled by their lazy dependence on the ready-mades and reach-me-downs of the ragshop in which Romance keeps its stock of "happy endings" to misfit all stories. Now, the history of Eliza Doolittle, though called a romance because of the transfiguration it records seems exceedingly improbable, is common enough. Such transfigurations have been achieved by hundreds of resolutely ambitious young women since Nell Gwynne set them the example by playing queens and fascinating kings in the theatre in which she began by selling oranges. Nevertheless, people in all directions have assumed, for no other reason than that she became the heroine of a romance, that she must have married the hero of it. This is unbearable, not only because her little drama, if acted on such a thoughtless assumption, must be spoiled, but because the true sequel is patent to anyone with a sense of human nature in general, and of feminine instinct in particular.

Eliza, in telling Higgins she would not marry him if he asked her, was not coquetting: she was announcing a well-considered decision. When a bachelor interests, and dominates, and teaches, and becomes important to a spinster, as Higgins with Eliza, she always, if she has character enough to be capable of it, considers very seriously indeed whether she will play for becoming that bachelor's wife, especially if he is so little interested in marriage that a determined and devoted woman might capture him if she set herself resolutely to do it. Her decision will depend a good deal on whether she is really free to choose; and that, again, will depend on her age and income. If she is at the end of her youth, and has no security for her livelihood, she will marry him because she must marry anybody who will provide for her. But at Eliza's age a good-looking girl does not feel that pressure: she feels free to pick and choose. She is therefore guided by her instinct in the matter. Eliza's instinct tells her not to marry Higgins. It does not tell her to give him up. It is not in the slightest doubt as to his remaining one of the strongest personal interests in her life. It would be very sorely strained if there was another woman likely to supplant her with him. But as she feels sure of him on that last point, she has no doubt at all as to her course, and would not have any, even if the difference of twenty years in age, which seems so great to youth, did not exist between them.

As our own instincts are not appealed to by her conclusion, let us see whether we cannot discover some reason in it. When Higgins excused his indifference to young women on the ground that they had an irresistible rival in his mother, he gave the clue to his inveterate old-bachelordom. The case is uncommon only to the extent that remarkable mothers are uncommon. If an imaginative boy has a sufficiently rich mother who has intelligence, personal grace, dignity of character without harshness, and a cultivated sense of the best art of her time to enable her to make her house beautiful, she sets a standard for him against which very few women can struggle, besides effecting for him a disengagement of his affections, his sense of beauty, and his idealism from his specifically sexual impulses. This makes him a standing puzzle to the huge number of uncultivated people who have been brought up in tasteless homes by commonplace or disagreeable parents, and to whom, consequently, litera-ture, painting, sculpture, music, and affectionate personal relations come as modes of sex if they come at all. The word passion means nothing else to them; and that Higgins could have a passion for phonetics and idealize his mother instead of Eliza, would seem to them absurd and unnatural. Nevertheless, when we look round and see that hardly anyone is too ugly or disagreeable to find a wife or a husband if he or she wants one, whilst many old maids and bachelors are above the average in quality and culture, we cannot help suspecting that the disentanglement of sex from the as-sociations with which it is so commonly confused, a disentanglement which persons of genius achieve by sheer intellectual analysis, is sometimes produced or aided by parental fascination.

Now, though Eliza was incapable of thus explaining to herself Higgins's formi-dable powers of resistance to the charm that prostrated Freddy at the first glance, she was instinctively aware that she could never obtain a complete grip of him, or come between him and his mother (the first necessity of the married woman). To put it shortly, she knew that for some mysterious reason he had not the makings of a married man in him, according to her conception of a husband as one to whom she would be his nearest and fondest and warmest interest. Even had there been no mother-rival, she would still have refused to accept an interest in herself that was secondary to philosophic interests. Had Mrs Higgins died, there would still have been Milton and the Universal Alphabet. Landor's remark that to those who have the greatest power of loving, love is a secondary affair, would not have recommended Landor to Eliza. Put that along with her resentment of Higgins's domineering superiority, and her mistrust of his coaxing cleverness in getting round her and evading her wrath when he had gone too far with his impetuous bullying, and you will see that Eliza's instinct had good grounds for warning her not to marry her Pygmalion.

And now, whom did Eliza marry? For if Higgins was a predestinate old bachelor, she was most certainly not a predestinate old maid. Well, that can be told very shortly to those who have not guessed it from the indications she has herself given them.

Almost immediately after Eliza is stung into proclaiming her considered determination not to marry Higgins, she mentions the fact that young Mr Frederick Eynsford Hill is pouring out his love for her daily through the post. Now Freddy is young, practically twenty years younger than Higgins: he is a gentleman (or, as Eliza would qualify him, a toff), and speaks like one; he is nicely dressed, is treated by the Colonel as an equal, loves her unaffectedly, and is not her master, nor ever likely to dominate her in spite of his advantage of social standing. Eliza has no use for the foolish romantic tradition that all women love to be mastered, if not actually bullied and beaten. "When you go to women," says Nietzsche, "take your whip with you." Sensible despots have never confined that precaution to women: they have taken their whips with them when they have dealt with men, and been slavishly idealized by the men over whom they have flourished the whip much more than by women. No doubt there are slavish women as well as slavish men; and women, like men, admire those that are stronger than themselves. But to admire a strong person and to live under that strong person's thumb are two different things. The weak may not be admired and hero-worshipped; but they are by no means disliked or shunned; and they never seem to have the least difficulty in marrying people who are too good for them. They may fail in emergencies; but life is not one long emergency: it is mostly a string of situations for which no exceptional strength is needed, and with which even rather weak people can cope if they have a stronger partner to help them out. Accordingly, it is a truth everywhere in evidence that strong people, masculine or feminine, not only do not marry stronger people, but do not shew any preference for them in selecting their friends. When a lion meets another with a louder roar "the first lion thinks the last a bore." The man or woman who feels strong enough for two, seeks for every other quality in a partner than strength.

The converse is also true. Weak people want to marry strong people who do not frighten them too much; and this often leads them to make the mistake we describe metaphorically as "biting off more than they can chew." They want too much for too little; and when the bargain is unreasonable beyond all bearing, the union becomes impossible: it ends in the weaker party being either discarded or borne as a cross, which is worse. People who are not only weak, but silly or obtuse as well, are often in these difficulties.

This being the state of human affairs, what is Eliza fairly sure to do when she is placed between Freddy and Higgins? Will she look forward to a lifetime of fetching Higgins's slippers or to a lifetime of Freddy fetching hers? There can be no doubt about the answer. Unless Freddy is biologically repulsive to her, and Higgins biologically attractive to a degree that overwhelms all her other instincts, she will, if she marries either of them, marry Freddy.

And that is just what Eliza did.

Complications ensued; but they were economic, not romantic. Freddy had no money and no occupation. His mother's jointure, a last relic of the opulence of Largelady Park, had enabled her to struggle along in Earlscourt with an air of gentility, but not to procure any serious secondary education for her children, much less give the boy a profession. A clerkship at thirty shillings a week was beneath Freddy's dignity, and extremely distasteful to him besides. His prospects consisted of a hope that if he kept up appearances somebody would do something for him. The something appeared vaguely to his imagination as a private secretaryship or a sinecure of some sort. To his mother it perhaps appeared as a marriage to some lady of means who could not resist her boy's niceness. Fancy her feelings when he married a flower girl who had become déclassée under extraordinary circumstances which were now notorious!

It is true that Eliza's situation did not seem wholly ineligible. Her father, though formerly a dustman, and now fantastically disclassed, had become extremely popular in the smartest society by a social talent which triumphed over every prejudice and every disadvantage. Rejected by the middle class, which he loathed, he had shot up at once into the highest circles by his wit, his dustmanship (which he carried like a banner), and his Nietzschean transcendence of good and evil. At intimate ducal dinners he sat on the right hand of the Duchess; and in country houses he smoked in the pantry and was made much of by the butler when he was not feeding in the dining-room and being consulted by cabinet ministers. But he found it almost as hard to do all this on four thousand a year as Mrs Eynsford Hill to live in Earlscourt on an income so pitiably smaller that I have not the heart to disclose its exact figure. He absolutely refused to add the last straw to his burden by contributing to Eliza's support.

Thus Freddy and Eliza, now Mr and Mrs Eynsford Hill, would have spent a penniless honeymoon but for a wedding present of £500 from the Colonel to Eliza. It lasted a long time because Freddy did not know how to spend money, never having had any to spend, and Eliza, socially trained by a pair of old bachelors, wore her clothes as long as they held together and looked pretty, without the least regard to their being many months out of fashion. Still, £500 will not last two young people for ever; and they both knew, and Eliza felt as well, that they must shift for themselves in the end. She could quarter herself on Wimpole Street because it had come to be her home; but she was quite aware that she ought not to quarter Freddy there, and that it would not be good for his character if she did.

Not that the Wimpole Street bachelors objected. When she consulted them, Higgins declined to be bothered about her housing problem when that solution was so simple. Eliza's desire to have Freddy in the house with her seemed of no more importance than if she had wanted an extra piece of bedroom furniture. Pleas as to Freddy's character, and the moral obligation on him to earn his own living, were lost on Higgins. He denied that Freddy had any character, and declared that if he tried to do any useful work some competent person would have the trouble of undoing it: a procedure involving a net loss to the community, and great unhappiness to Freddy himself, who was obviously intended by Nature for such light work as amusing Eliza, which, Higgins declared, was a much more useful and honorable occupation than working in the city. When Eliza referred again to her project of teaching phonetics, Higgins abated not a jot of his violent opposition to it. He said she was not within ten years of being qualified to meddle with his pet subject; and as it was evident that the Colonel agreed with him, she felt she could not go against them in this grave matter, and that she had no right, without Higgins's consent, to exploit the knowledge he had given her; for his knowledge seemed to her as much his private property as his watch: Eliza was no communist. Besides, she was superstitiously devoted to them both, more entirely and frankly after her marriage than before it.

It was the Colonel who finally solved the problem, which had cost him much perplexed cogitation. He one day asked Eliza, rather shyly, whether she had quite given up her notion of keeping a flower shop. She replied that she had thought of it, but had put it out of her head, because the Colonel had said, that day at Mrs. Higgins's, that it would never do. The Colonel confessed that when he said that, he had not quite recovered from the dazzling impression of the day before. They broke the matter to Higgins that evening. The sole comment vouchsafed by him very nearly led to a serious quarrel with Eliza. It was to the effect that she would have in Freddy an ideal errand boy.

Freddy himself was next sounded on the subject. He said he had been thinking of a shop himself; though it had presented itself to his pennilessness as a small place in which Eliza should sell tobacco at one counter whilst he sold newspapers at the opposite one. But he agreed that it would be extraordinarily jolly to go early every morning with Eliza to Covent Garden and buy flowers on the scene of their first meeting: a sentiment which earned him many kisses from his wife. He added that he had always been afraid to propose anything of the sort, because Clara would make an awful row about a step that must damage her matrimonial chances, and his mother could not be expected to like it after clinging for so many years to that step of the social ladder on which retail trade is impossible.

This difficulty was removed by an event highly unexpected by Freddy's mother. Clara, in the course of her incursions into those artistic circles which were the highest within her reach, discovered that her conversational qualifications were expected to include a grounding in the novels of Mr H. G. Wells. She borrowed them in various directions so energetically that she swallowed them all within two months. The result was a conversion of a kind quite common today. A modern Acts of the Apostles would fill fifty whole Bibles if anyone were capable of writing it.

Poor Clara, who appeared to Higgins and his mother as a disagreeable and ridiculous person, and to her own mother as in some inexplicable way a social failure, had never seen herself in either light; for, though to some extent ridiculed and mimicked in West Kensington like everybody else there, she was accepted as a rational and normal—or shall we say inevitable?—sort of human being. At worst they called her The Pusher; but to them no more than to herself had it ever occurred that she was pushing the air, and pushing it in a wrong direction. Still, she was not happy. She was growing desperate. Her one asset, the fact that her mother was what the Epsom greengrocer called a carriage lady had no exchange value, apparently. It had prevented her from getting educated, because the only education she could have afforded was education with the Earlscourt greengrocer's daughter. It had led her to seek the society of her mother's class; and that class simply would not have her, because she was much poorer than the greengrocer, and, far from being able to afford a maid, could not afford even a housemaid, and had to scrape along at home with an illiberally treated general servant. Under such circumstances nothing could give her an air of being a genuine product of Largelady Park. And yet its tradition made her regard a marriage with anyone within her reach as an unbearable humiliation. Commercial people and professional people in a small way were odious to her. She ran after painters and novelists; but she did not charm them; and her bold attempts to pick up and practise artistic and literary talk irritated them. She was, in short, an utter failure, an ignorant, incompetent, pretentious, unwelcome, penniless, useless little snob; and though she did not admit these disqualifications (for nobody ever faces unpleasant truths of this kind until the possibility of a way out dawns on them) she felt their effects too keenly to be satisfied with her position.

Clara had a startling eyeopener when, on being suddenly wakened to enthusiasm by a girl of her own age who dazzled her and produced in her a gushing desire to take her for a model, and gain her friendship, she discovered that this exquisite apparition had graduated from the gutter in a few months' time. It shook her so violently, that when Mr. H. G. Wells lifted her on the point of his puissant pen, and placed her at the angle of view from which the life she was leading and the society to which she clung appeared in its true relation to real human needs and worthy social structure, he effected a conversion and a conviction of sin comparable to the most sensational feats of General Booth or Gypsy Smith. Clara's snobbery went bang. Life suddenly began to move with her. Without knowing how or why, she began to make friends and enemies. Some of the acquaintances to whom she had been a tedious or indifferent or ridiculous affliction, dropped her: others became cordial. To her amazement she found that some "quite nice" people were saturated with Wells, and that this accessibility to ideas was the secret of their niceness. People she had thought deeply religious, and had tried to conciliate on that tack with disastrous results, suddenly took an interest in her, and revealed a hostility to conventional religion which she had never conceived possible except among the most desperate characters. They made her read Galsworthy; and Galsworthy exposed the vanity of Largelady Park and finished her. It exasperated her to think that the dungeon in which she had languished for so many unhappy years had been unlocked all the time, and that the impulses she had so carefully struggled with and stifled for the sake of keeping well with society, were precisely those by which alone she could have come into any sort of sincere human contact. In the radiance of these discoveries, and the tumult of their reaction, she made a fool of herself as freely and conspicuously as when she so rashly adopted Eliza's expletive in Mrs. Higgins's drawing-room; for the new-born Wellsian had to find her bearings almost as ridiculously as a baby; but nobody hates a baby for its ineptitudes, or thinks the worse of it for trying to eat the matches; and Clara lost no friends by her follies. They laughed at her to her face this time; and she had to defend herself and fight it out as best she could.

When Freddy paid a visit to Earlscourt (which he never did when he could possibly help it) to make the desolating announcement that he and his Eliza were thinking of blackening the Largelady scutcheon by opening a shop, he found the little household already convulsed by a prior announcement from Clara that she also was going to work in an old furniture shop in Dover Street, which had been started by a fellow Wellsian. This appointment Clara owed, after all, to her old social accomplishment of Push. She had made up her mind that, cost what it might, she would see Mr. Wells in the flesh; and she had achieved her end at a garden party. She had better luck than so rash an enterprise deserved. Mr. Wells came up to her expectations. Age had not withered him, nor could custom stale his infinite variety in half an hour. His pleasant neatness and compactness, his small hands and feet, his teeming ready brain, his unaffected accessibility, and a certain fine apprehensiveness which stamped him as susceptible from his topmost hair to his tipmost toe, proved irresistible. Clara talked of nothing else for weeks and weeks afterwards. And as she happened to talk to the lady of the furniture shop, and that lady also desired above all things to know Mr.

Wells and sell pretty things to him, she offered Clara a job on the chance of achieving that end through her.

And so it came about that Eliza's luck held, and the expected opposition to the flower shop melted away. The shop is in the arcade of a railway station not very far from the Victoria and Albert Museum; and if you live in that neighborhood you may go there any day and buy a buttonhole from Eliza.

Now here is a last opportunity for romance. Would you not like to be assured that the shop was an immense success, thanks to Eliza's charms and her early business experience in Covent Garden? Alas! the truth is the truth: the shop did not pay for a long time, simply because Eliza and her Freddy did not know how to keep it. True, Eliza had not to begin at the very beginning: she knew the names and prices of the cheaper flowers; and her elation was unbounded when she found that Freddy, like all youths educated at cheap, pretentious, and thoroughly inefficient schools, knew a little Latin. It was very little, but enough to make him appear to her a Porson or Bentley, and to put him at his ease with botanical nomenclature. Unfortunately he knew nothing else; and Eliza, though she could count money up to eighteen shillings or so, and had acquired a certain familiarity with the language of Milton from her struggles to qualify herself for winning Higgins's bet, could not write out a bill without utterly disgracing the establishment. Freddy's power of stating in Latin that Balbus built a wall and that Gaul was divided into three parts did not carry with it the slightest knowledge of accounts or business: Colonel Pickering had to explain to him what a cheque book and a bank account meant. And the pair were by no means easily teachable. Freddy backed up Eliza in her obstinate refusal to believe that they could save money by engaging a bookkeeper with some knowledge of the business. How, they argued, could you possibly save money by going to extra expense when you already could not make both ends meet? But the Colonel, after making the ends meet over and over again, at last gently insisted; and Eliza, humbled to the dust by having to beg from him so often, and stung by the uproarious derision of Higgins, to whom the notion of Freddy succeeding at anything was a joke that never palled, grasped the fact that business, like phonetics, has to be learned.

On the piteous spectacle of the pair spending their evenings in shorthand schools and polytechnic classes, learning bookkeeping and typewriting with incipient junior clerks, male and female, from the elementary schools, let me not dwell. There were even classes at the London School of Economics, and a humble personal appeal to the director of that institution to recommend a course bearing on the flower business. He, being a humorist, explained to them the method of the celebrated Dickensian essay on Chinese Metaphysics by the gentleman who read an article on China and an article on Metaphysics and combined the information. He suggested that they should combine the London School with Kew Gardens. Eliza, to whom the procedure of the Dickensian gentleman seemed perfectly correct (as in fact it was) and not in the least funny (which was only her ignorance) took his advice with entire gravity. But the effort that cost her the deepest humiliation was a request to Higgins, whose pet artistic fancy, next to Milton's verse, was caligraphy, and who himself wrote a most beautiful Italian hand, that he would teach her to write. He declared that she was congenitally incapable of forming a single letter worthy of the least of Milton's words; but she persisted; and again he suddenly threw himself into the task of teaching her with a combination of stormy intensity, concentrated patience, and occasional bursts of interesting disquisition on the beauty and nobility, the august mission and destiny, of human handwriting. Eliza ended by acquiring an extremely uncommercial script which was a positive extension of her personal beauty, and spending three times as much on stationery as anyone else because certain qualities and shapes of paper became indispensable to her. She could not even address an envelope in the usual way because it made the margins all wrong.

Their commercial school days were a period of disgrace and despair for the young couple. They seemed to be learning nothing about flower shops. At last they gave it up as hopeless, and shook the dust of the shorthand schools, and the polytechnics, and the London School of Economics from their feet for ever. Besides, the business was in some mysterious way beginning to take care of itself. They had somehow forgotten their objections to employing other people. They came to the conclusion that their own way was the best, and that they had really a remarkable talent for business. The Colonel, who had been compelled for some years to keep a sufficient sum on current account at his bankers to make up their deficits, found that the provision was unnecessary: the young people were prospering. It is true that there was not quite fair play between them and their competitors in trade. Their week-ends in the country cost them nothing, and saved them the price of their Sunday dinners; for the motor car was the Colonel's; and he and Higgins paid the hotel bills. Mr. F. Hill, florist and greengrocer (they soon discovered that there was money in asparagus; and asparagus led to other vegetables), had an air which stamped the business as classy; and in private life he was still Frederick Eynsford Hill, Esquire. Not that there was any swank about him: nobody but Eliza knew that he had been christened Frederick Challoner. Eliza herself swanked like anything.

That is all. That is how it has turned out. It is astonishing how much Eliza still manages to meddle in the housekeeping at Wimpole Street in spite of the shop and her own family. And it is notable that though she never nags her husband, and frankly loves the Colonel as if she were his favorite daughter, she has never got out of the habit of nagging Higgins that was established on the fatal night when she won his bet for him. She snaps his head off on the faintest provocation, or on none. He no longer dares to tease her by assuming an abysmal inferiority of Freddy's mind to his own. He storms and bullies and derides; but she stands up to him so ruthlessly that the Colonel has to ask her from time to time to be kinder to Higgins; and it is the only request of his that brings a mulish expression into her face. Nothing but some emergency or calamity great enough to break down all likes and dislikes, and throw them both back on their common humanity—and may they be spared any such trial!—will ever alter this. She knows that Higgins does not need her, just as her father did not need her. The very scrupulousness with which he told her that day that he had become used to having her there, and dependent on her for all sorts of little services, and that he should miss her if she went away (it would never have occurred to Freddy or the Colonel to say anything of the sort) deepens her inner certainty that she is "no more to him than them slippers", yet she has a sense, too, that his indifference is deeper than the infatuation of commoner souls. She is immensely interested in him. She has even secret mischievous moments in which she wishes she could get him alone, on a desert island, away from all ties and with nobody else in the world to consider, and just drag him off his pedestal and see him making love like any common man. We all have private imaginations of that sort. But when it comes to business, to the life that she really leads as distinguished from the life of dreams and fancies, she likes Freddy and she likes the Colonel; and she does not like Higgins and Mr. Doolittle. Galatea never does quite like Pygmalion: his relation to her is too godlike to be altogether agreeable.

LOS VENDIDOS

By Luis Valdez and El Teatro Campesino

CHARACTERS

HONEST SANCHO
SECRETARY
FARM WORKER
JOHNNY
REVOLUCIONARIO
MEXICAN-AMERICAN

SCENE: *Honest Sancho's Used Mexican Lot and Mexican Curio Shop. Three models are on display in Honest Sancho's shop: to the right, there is a* REVOLUCIONARIO, *complete with sombrero, carrilleras, and carabina 30–30. At center, on the floor, there is the* FARM WORKER, *under a broad straw sombrero. At stage left is,* JOHNNY, *the Pachuco, filero in hand.*

HONEST SANCHO *is moving among his models, dusting them off and preparing for another day of business.*

SANCHO: Bueno, bueno, mis monos, vamos a ver a quien vendemos ahora, ¿no? *(To audience.)* ¡Quihubo! I'm Honest Sancho and this is my shop. Antes fui contratista pero ahora logré tener mi negocito. All I need now is a customer. (*A bell rings offstage.*) Ay, a customer!
SECRETARY: *(Entering.)* Good morning, I'm Miss Jiménez from—
SANCHO: ¡Ah, una chicana! Welcome, welcome Señorita Jiménez.

Luis Valdez and El Teatro Campesino, "Los Vendidos," *Luis Valdez Early Works: Actos, Bernabe and Pensamiento Serpentino*, pp. 40–52. Copyright 1990 by Arte Publico Press. Reprinted with permission.

SECRETARY: (*Anglo pronunciation.*) JIM-enez.

SANCHO: ¿Qué?

SECRETARY: My name is Miss JIM-enez. Don't you speak English? What's wrong with you?

SANCHO: Oh, nothing, Señorita JIM-enez. I'm here to help you.

SECRETARY: That's better. As I was starting to say, I'm a secretary from Governor Reagan's office, and we're looking for a Mexican type for the administration.

SANCHO: Well, you come to the right place, lady. This is Honest Sancho's Used Mexican lot, and we got all types here. Any particular type you want?

SECRETARY: Yes, we were looking for somebody suave—

SANCHO: Suave.

SECRETARY: Debonair.

SANCHO: De buen aire.

SECRETARY: Dark.

SANCHO: Prieto.

SECRETARY: But of course not too dark.

SANCHO: No muy prieto.

SECRETARY: Perhaps, beige.

SANCHO: Beige, just the tone. Así como cafecito con leche, ¿no?

SECRETARY: One more thing. He must be hard-working.

SANCHO: That could only be one model. Step right over here to the center of the shop, lady. (*They cross to the* FARM WORKER.) This is our standard farm worker model. As you can see, in the words of our beloved Senator George Murphy, he is "built close to the ground." Also take special notice of his four-ply Goodyear huaraches, made from the rain tire. This wide-brimmed sombrero is an extra added feature—keeps off the sun, rain, and dust.

SECRETARY: Yes, it does look durable.

SANCHO: And our farm worker model is friendly. Muy amable. Watch. (*Snaps his fingers.*)

FARM WORKER: (*Lifts up head.*) Buenos días, señorita. (*His head drops.*)

SECRETARY: My, he's friendly.

SANCHO: Didn't I tell you? Loves his patrones! But his most attractive feature is that he's hard-working. Let me show you. (*Snaps fingers.* FARM WORKER *stands.*)

FARM WORKER: ¡El jale! (*He begins to work.*)

SANCHO: As you can see, he is cutting grapes.

SECRETARY: Oh, I wouldn't know.

SANCHO: He also picks cotton. (*Snap.* FARM WORKER *begins to pick cotton.*)

SECRETARY: Versatile isn't he?

SANCHO: He also picks melons. (*Snap.* FARM WORKER *picks melons.*) That's his slow speed for late in the season. Here's his fast speed. (*Snap.* FARM WORKER *picks faster.*)

SECRETARY: ¡Chihuahua! ... I mean, goodness, he sure is a hard worker.

SANCHO: (*Pulls the* FARM WORKER *to his feet.*) And that isn't the half of it. Do you see these little holes on his arms that appear to be pores? During those hot sluggish days in the field, when the vines or the branches get so entangled, it's almost impossible to move; these holes emit a certain grease that allow our model to slip and slide right through the crop with no trouble at all.

SECRETARY: Wonderful. But is he economical?

SANCHO: Economical? Señorita, you are looking at the Volkswagen of Mexicans. Pennies a day is all it takes. One plate of beans and tortillas will keep him going all day. That, and chile. Plenty of chile. Chile jalapenos, chile verde, chile Colorado. But, of course, if you do give him chile (*Snap.* FARM WORKER *turns left face. Snap.* FARM WORKER *bends over.*) then you have to change his oil filter once a week.

SECRETARY: What about storage?

SANCHO: No problem. You know these new farm labor camps our Honorable Governor Reagan has built out by Parlier or Raisin City? They were designed with our model in mind. Five, six, seven, even ten in one of those shacks will give you no trouble at all. You can also put him in old barns, old cars, river banks. You can even leave him out in the field overnight with no worry!

SECRETARY: Remarkable.

SANCHO: And here's an added feature: Every year at the end of the season, this model goes back to Mexico and doesn't return, automatically, until next Spring.

SECRETARY: How about that. But tell me: does he speak English?

SANCHO: Another outstanding feature is that last year this model was programmed to go out on STRIKE! (*Snap.*)

FARM WORKER: ¡HUELGA! ¡HUELGA! Hermanos, sálganse de esos files. (*Snap. He stops.*)

SECRETARY: No! Oh no, we can't strike in the State Capitol.

SANCHO: Well, he also scabs. (*Snap.*)

FARM WORKER: Me vendo barato, ¿y qué? (*Snap.*)

SECRETARY: That's much better, but you didn't answer my question. Does he speak English?

SANCHO: Bueno ... no pero he has other—

SECRETARY: No.

SANCHO: Other features.

SECRETARY: NO! He just won't do!

SANCHO: Okay, okay pues. We have other models.

SECRETARY: I hope so. What we need is something a little more sophisticated.

SANCHO: Sophisti—¿qué?

SECRETARY: An urban model.

SANCHO: Ah, from the city! Step right back. Over here in this corner of the shop is exactly what you're looking for. Introducing our new 1969 JOHNNY PACHUCO model! This is our fast-back model. Streamlined. Built for speed, low-riding, city life. Take a look at some of these features. Mag shoes, dual exhausts, green chartreuse paint-job, dark-tint windshield, a little poof on top. Let me just turn him on. (*Snap.* JOHNNY *walks to stage center with a pachuco bounce.*)

SECRETARY: What was that?

SANCHO: That, señorita, was the Chicano shuffle.

SECRETARY: Okay, what does he do?

SANCHO: Anything and everything necessary for city life. For instance, survival: He knife fights. (*Snap.* JOHNNY *pulls out switch blade and swings at secretary.*)

(SECRETARY *screams.*)

SANCHO: He dances. (*Snap.*)

JOHNNY: (*Singing.*) "Angel Baby, my Angel Baby ..." (*Snap.*)

SANCHO: And here's a feature no city model can be without. He gets arrested, but not without resisting, of course. (*Snap.*)

JOHNNY: ¡En la madre, la placa! I didn't do it! I didn't do it! (JOHNNY *turns and stands up against an imaginary wall, legs spread out, arms behind his back.*)

SECRETARY: Oh no, we can't have arrests! We must maintain law and order.

SANCHO: But he's bilingual!

SECRETARY: Bilingual?

SANCHO: Simón que yes. He speaks English! Johnny, give us some English. (*Snap.*)

JOHNNY: (*Comes downstage.*) Fuck-you!

SECRETARY: (*Gasps.*) Oh! I've never been so insulted in my whole life!

SANCHO: Well, he learned it in your school.

SECRETARY: I don't care where he learned it.

SANCHO: But he's economical!

SECRETARY: Economical?

SANCHO: Nickels and dimes. You can keep JOHNNY running on hamburgers, Taco Bell tacos, Lucky Lager beer, Thunderbird wine, yesca—

SECRETARY: Yesca?

SANCHO: Mota.

SECRETARY: Mota?

SANCHO: Leños ... Marijuana. (*Snap.* JOHNNY *inhales on an imaginary joint.*)

SECRETARY: That's against the law!

JOHNNY: (*Big smile, holding his breath.*) Yeah.

SANCHO: He also sniffs glue. (*Snap.* JOHNNY *inhales glue, big smile.*)

JOHNNY: Tha's too much man, ése.

SECRETARY: No, Mr. Sancho, I don't think this—

SANCHO: Wait a minute, he has other qualities I know you'll love. For example, an inferiority complex. (*Snap.*)

JOHNNY: (*To* SANCHO.) You think you're better than me, huh ése? (*Swings switch blade.*)

SANCHO: He can also be beaten and he bruises, cut him and he bleeds; kick him and he—(*He beats, bruises and kicks* PACHUCO.) Would you like to try it?

SECRETARY: Oh, I couldn't.

SANCHO: Be my guest. He's a great scapegoat.

SECRETARY: No, really.

SANCHO: Please.

SECRETARY: Well, all right. Just once. (*She kicks* PACHUCO.) Oh, he's so soft.

SANCHO: Wasn't that good? Try again.

SECRETARY: (*Kicks* PACHUCO.) Oh, he's so wonderful! (*She kicks him again.*)

SANCHO: Okay, that's enough, lady. You ruin the merchandise. Yes, our Johnny Pachuco model can give you many hours of pleasure. Why, the L.A.P.D. just bought twenty of these to train their rookie cops on. And talk about mainte-nance. Señorita, you are looking at an entirely self-supporting machine. You're never going to find our Johnny Pachuco model on the relief rolls. No, sir, this model knows how to liberate.

SECRETARY: Liberate?

SANCHO: He steals. (*Snap.* JOHNNY *rushes the secretary and steals her purse.*)

JOHNNY: ¡Dame esa bolsa, vieja! (*He grabs the purse and runs. Snap by* SANCHO. *He stops.*)

(SECRETARY *runs after* JOHNNY *and grabs purse away from him, kicking him as she goes.*)

SECRETARY: No, no, no! We can't have any *more* thieves in the State Administration. Put him back.

SANCHO: Okay, we still got other models. Come on, Johnny, we'll sell you to some old lady. (SANCHO *takes* JOHNNY *back to his place.*)

SECRETARY: Mr. Sancho, I don't think you quite understand what we need. What we need is something that will attract the women voters. Something more tradi-tional, more romantic.

SANCHO: Ah, a lover. (*He smiles meaningfully.*) Step right over here, señorita. Introducing our standard Revolucionario and/or Early California Bandit type. As you can see he is well-built, sturdy, durable. This is the International Harvester of Mexicans.

SECRETARY: What does he do?

SANCHO: You name it, he does it. He rides horses, stays in the mountains, crosses deserts, plains, rivers, leads revolutions, follows revolutions, kills, can be killed, serves as a martyr, hero, movie star—did I say movie star? Did you ever see *Viva Zapata? Viva Villa? Villa Rides? Pancho Villa Returns? Pancho Villa Goes Back? Pancho Villa Meets Abbot and Costello*—

SECRETARY: I've never seen any of those.

SANCHO: Well, he was in all of them. Listen to this. (*Snap.*)

REVOLUCIONARIO: (*Scream.*) ¡VIVA VILLAAAAA!

SECRETARY: That's awfully loud.

SANCHO: He has a volume control. (*He adjusts volume. Snap.*)

REVOLUCIONARIO: (*Mousey voice.*) ¡Viva Villa!

SECRETARY: That's better.

SANCHO: And even if you didn't see him in the movies, perhaps you saw him on TV. He makes commercials. (*Snap.*)

REVOLUCIONARIO: Is there a Frito Bandito in your house?

SECRETARY: Oh yes, I've seen that one!

SANCHO: Another feature about this one is that he is economical. He runs on raw horsemeat and tequila!

SECRETARY: Isn't that rather savage?

SANCHO: Al contrario, it makes him a lover. (*Snap.*)

REVOLUCIONARIO: (*To* SECRETARY) ¡Ay, mamasota, cochota, ven pa'ca! (*He grabs* SECRETARY *and folds her back—Latin-lover style.*)

SANCHO: (*Snap.* REVOLUCIONARIO *goes back upright.*) Now wasn't that nice?

SECRETARY: Well, it was rather nice.

SANCHO: And finally, there is one outstanding feature about this model I KNOW the ladies are going to love: He's a GENUINE antique! He was made in Mexico in 1910!

SECRETARY: Made in Mexico?

SANCHO: That's right. Once in Tijuana, twice in Guadalajara, three times in Cuernavaca.

SECRETARY: Mr. Sancho, I thought he was an American product.

SANCHO: No, but—

SECRETARY: No, I'm sorry. We can't buy anything but American-made products. He just won't do.

SANCHO: But he's an antique!

SECRETARY: I don't care. You still don't understand what we need. It's true we need Mexican models such as these, but it's more important that he be *American*.

SANCHO: American?

SECRETARY: That's right, and judging from what you've shown me, I don't think you have what we want. Well, my lunch hour's almost over; I better—

SANCHO: Wait a minute! Mexican but American?

SECRETARY: That's correct.

SANCHO: Mexican but ... (*A sudden flash.*) AMERICAN! Yeah, I think we've got exactly what you want. He just came in today! Give me a minute. (*He exits. Talks from backstage.*) Here he is in the shop. Let me just get some papers off. There. Introducing our new 1970 Mexican-American! Ta-ra-ra-ra-ra-ra-RA-RAAA!

(SANCHO *brings out the* MEXICAN-AMERICAN *model, a clean-shaven middle-class type in business suit, with glasses.*)

SECRETARY: (*Impressed.*) Where have you been hiding this one?

SANCHO: He just came in this morning. Ain't he a beauty? Feast your eyes on him! Sturdy US Steel frame, streamlined, modern. As a matter of fact, he is built exactly like our Anglo models except that he comes in a variety of darker shades: naugahyde, leather, or leatherette.

SECRETARY: Naugahyde.

SANCHO: Well, we'll just write that down. Yes, señorita, this model represents the apex of American engineering! He is bilingual, college educated, ambitious! Say the word "acculturate" and he accelerates. He is intelligent, well-mannered, clean—did I say clean? (*Snap.* MEXICAN-AMERICAN *raises his arm.*) Smell.

SECRETARY: (*Smells.*) Old Sobaco, my favorite.

SANCHO: (*Snap.* MEXICAN-AMERICAN *turns toward* SANCHO) Eric! (*To* SECRETARY.) We call him Eric Garcia. (*To* ERIC.) I want you to meet Miss JIM-enez, Eric.

MEXICAN-AMERICAN: Miss JIM-enez, I am delighted to make your acquaintance. (*He kisses her hand.*)

SECRETARY: Oh, my, how charming!

SANCHO: Did you feel the suction? He has seven especially engineered suction cups right behind his lips. He's a charmer all right!

SECRETARY: How about boards? Does he function on boards?

SANCHO: You name them, he is on them. Parole boards, draft boards, school boards, taco quality control boards, surf boards, two-by-fours.

SECRETARY: Does he function in politics?

SANCHO: Señorita, you are looking at a political MACHINE. Have you ever heard of the OEO, EOC, COD, WAR ON POVERTY? That's our model! Not only that, he makes political speeches.

SECRETARY: May I hear one?

SANCHO: With pleasure. (*Snap.*) Eric, give us a speech.

MEXICAN-AMERICAN: Mr. Congressman, Mr. Chairman, members of the board, honored guests, ladies and gentlemen. (SANCHO *and* SECRETARY *applaud.*) Please, please, I come before you as a Mexican-American to tell you about the problems of the Mexican. The problems of the Mexican stem from one thing and one thing alone: He's stupid. He's uneducated. He needs to stay in school. He needs to be ambitious, forward-looking, harder-working. He needs to think American, American, American, AMERICAN, AMERICAN, AMERICAN. GOD BLESS AMERICA! GOD BLESS AMERICA!! (*He goes out of control.*)

(SANCHO *snaps frantically and the* MEXICAN-AMERICAN *finally slumps forward, bending at the waist.*)

SECRETARY: Oh my, he's patriotic too!

SANCHO: Sí, señorita, he loves his country. Let me just make a little adjustment here. (*Stands* MEXICAN-AMERICAN *up.*)

SECRETARY: What about upkeep? Is he economical?

SANCHO: Well, no, I won't lie to you. The Mexican-American costs a little bit more, but you get what you pay for. He's worth every extra cent. You can keep him running on dry martinis, Langendorf bread.

SECRETARY: Apple pie?

SANCHO: Only Mom's. Of course, he's also programmed to eat Mexican food on ceremonial functions, but I must warn you: an overdose of beans will plug up his exhaust.

SECRETARY: Fine! There's just one more question: How much do you want for him?

SANCHO: Well, I tell you what I'm gonna do. Today and today only, because you've been so sweet, I'm gonna let you steal this model from me! I'm gonna let you drive him off the lot for the simple price of—let's see taxes and license included—$15,000.

SECRETARY: Fifteen thousand DOLLARS? For a MEXICAN!

SANCHO: Mexican? What are you talking, lady? This is a Mexican-AMERICAN! We had to melt down two pachucos, a farm worker and three gabachos to make this model! You want quality, but you gotta pay for it! This is no cheap run-about. He's got class!

SECRETARY: Okay, I'll take him.

SANCHO: You will?

SECRETARY: Here's your money.

SANCHO: You mind if I count it?

SECRETARY: Go right ahead.

SANCHO: Well, you'll get your pink slip in the mail. Oh, do you want me to wrap him up for you? We have a box in the back.

SECRETARY: No, thank you. The Governor is having a luncheon this afternoon, and we need a brown face in the crowd. How do I drive him?

SANCHO: Just snap your fingers. He'll do anything you want.

(SECRETARY *snaps.* MEXICAN-AMERICAN *steps forward.*)

MEXICAN-AMERICAN: RAZA QUERIDA, ¡VAMOS LEVANTANDO ARMAS PARA LIBERARNOS DE ESTOS DESGRACIADOS GABACHOS QUE NOS EXPLOTAN! VAMOS.

SECRETARY: What did he say?

SANCHO: Something about lifting arms, killing white people, etc.

SECRETARY: But he's not supposed to say that!

SANCHO: Look, lady, don't blame me for bugs from the factory. He's your Mexican-American; you bought him, now drive him off the lot!

SECRETARY: But he's broken!

SANCHO: Try snapping another finger.

(SECRETARY *snaps.* MEXICAN-AMERICAN *comes to life again.*)

MEXICAN-AMERICAN: ¡ESTA GRAN HUMANIDAD HA DICHO BASTA! Y SE HA PUESTO EN MARCHA! ¡BASTA! ¡BASTA! ¡VIVA LA RAZA! ¡VIVA LA CAUSA! ¡VIVA LA HUELGA! ¡VIVAN LOS BROWN BERETS! ¡VIVAN LOS ESTUDIANTES! ¡CHICANO POWER!

(*The* MEXICAN-AMERICAN *turns toward the* SECRETARY, *who gasps and backs up. He keeps turning toward the* PACHUCO, FARM WORKER, *and* REVOLUCIONARIO, *snapping his fingers and turning each of them on, one by one.*)

PACHUCO: (*Snap. To* SECRETARY.) I'm going to get you, baby! ¡Viva La Raza!

FARM WORKER: (*Snap. To* SECRETARY.) ¡Viva la huelga! ¡Viva la Huelga! ¡VIVA LA HUELGA!

REVOLUCIONARIO: (*Snap. To* SECRETARY.) ¡Viva la revolución! ¡VIVA LA REVOLUCIÓN!

(*The three models join together and advance toward the* SECRETARY *who backs up and runs out of the shop screaming.* SANCHO *is at the other end of the shop holding his money in his hand. All freeze. After a few seconds of silence, the* PACHUCO *moves and stretches, shaking his arms and loosening up. The* FARM WORKER *and* REVOLUCIONARIO *do the same.* SANCHO *stays where he is, frozen to his spot.*)

JOHNNY: Man, that was a long one, ése. (*Others agree with him.*)

FARM WORKER: How did we do?

JOHNNY: Perty good, look all that lana, man! (*He goes over to* SANCHO *and removes the money from his hand.* SANCHO *stays where he is.*)

REVOLUCIONARIO: En la madre, look at all the money.

JOHNNY: We keep this up, we're going to be rich.

FARM WORKER: They think we're machines.

REVOLUCIONARIO: Burros.

JOHNNY: Puppets.

MEXICAN-AMERICAN: The only thing I don't like is—how come I always got to play the goddamn Mexican-American?

JOHNNY: That's what you get for finishing high school.

FARM WORKER: How about our wages, ése?

JOHNNY: Here it comes right now $3,000 for you, $3,000 for you, $3,000 for you, and $3,000 for me. The rest we put back into the business.

MEXICAN-AMERICAN: Too much, man. Heh, where you vatos going tonight?

FARM WORKER: I'm going over to Concha's. There's a party.

JOHNNY: Wait a minute, vatos. What about our salesman? I think he needs an oil job.

REVOLUCIONARIO: Leave him to me.

(*The* PACHUCO, FARM WORKER, *and* MEXICAN-AMERICAN *exit, talking loudly about their plans for the night. The* MEXICAN-AMERICAN *goes over to* SANCHO, *removes his derby hat and cigar, lifts him up and throws him over his shoulder.* SANCHO *hangs loose, lifeless.*)

REVOLUCIONARIO: (*To audience.*) He's the best model we got! ¡Ajúa! (*Exit.*)

THE CLEAN HOUSE

By Sarah Ruhl

CHARACTERS

LANE: A doctor, a woman in her early fifties. She wears white.

MATILDE: Lane's cleaning lady, a woman in her late twenties. She wears black. She is Brazilian. She has a refined sense of deadpan.

VIRGINIA: Lane's sister, a woman in her late fifties.

CHARLES: Lane's husband, a man in his fifties. A compassionate surgeon. He is child-like underneath his white coat. In Act I, Charles plays Matilde's father.

ANA: An Argentinean woman. She is impossibly charismatic. In Act I, she plays Matilde's mother. She is older than Lane.

Note: Everyone in this play should be able to tell a really good joke.

PLACE

A metaphysical Connecticut. Or, a house that is not far from the sea and not far from the city.

Sarah Ruhl, "The Clean House," *The Clean House and Other Plays*, pp. 1–116. Copyright 2006 by Theatre Communications Group. Reprinted with permission.

SET

A white living room.
White couch, white vase, white lamp, white rug.
A balcony.

Note: The living room needn't be full of living room detail, though it should feel human. The space should transform and surprise. The balcony should feel high but also intimate—a close-up shot.

A NOTE ON PRONUNCIATION

"Matilde" is pronounced by the Americans in the play as "Matilda." It is pronounced by Ana as "Mathilda" at first, until Ana realizes that Matilde is Brazilian. And it is pronounced by Matilde, and the more observant characters in the play, as "Ma-chil-gee," which is the correct Brazilian pronunciation.

Note: See the end of the play for notes on subtitles and jokes.

A NOTE ON DOUBLE CASTING

It is important that Ana and Charles play Matilde's mother and father in Act I. How much can they create, without speaking, a sense of memory and longing, through silence, gesture and dance? Ana's transformation at the very end of the play should create a full circle for Matilde, from the dead to the living and back again.

ACT I

1. Matilde

Matilde tells a long joke in Portuguese to the audience.
We can tell she is telling a joke even though we might not understand the language.
She finishes the joke. She exits.

2. Lane

Lane, to the audience:

LANE

It has been such a hard month.
My cleaning lady—from Brazil—decided that she was depressed one day
and stopped cleaning my house.
I was like: clean my house!
And she wouldn't!
We took her to the hospital and I had her medicated and she
Still Wouldn't Clean.
And—in the meantime—*I've* been cleaning my house!
I'm sorry, but I did not go to medical school to clean my own house.

3. Virginia

Virginia, to the audience:

VIRGINIA

People who give up the *privilege* of cleaning their own houses—they're insane people.

If you do not clean: how do you know if you've made any progress in life? I love dust. The dust always makes progress. Then I remove the dust. That is progress.

If it were not for dust I think I would die. If there were no dust to clean then there would be so much leisure time and so much thinking time and I would have to do something besides thinking and that thing might be to slit my wrists.

Ha ha ha ha ha ha just kidding.

I'm not a morbid person. That just popped out!

My sister is a wonderful person. She's a doctor. At an important hospital. I've always wondered how one hospital can be more important than another hospital. They are places for human waste. Places to put dead bodies.

I'm sorry. I'm being morbid again.

My sister has given up the privilege of cleaning her own house. Something deeply personal—she has given up. She does not know how long it takes the dust to accumulate under her bed. She does not know if her husband is sleeping with a prostitute because she does not smell his dirty underwear. All of these things, she fails to know.

I know when there is dust on the mirror. Don't misunderstand me—I'm an educated woman. But if I were to die at any moment during the day, no one would have to clean my kitchen.

4. Matilde

Matilde, to the audience:

MATILDE

The story of my parents is this. It was said that my father was the funniest man in his village. He did not marry until he was sixty-three because he did not want to marry a woman who was not funny. He said he would wait until he met his match in wit.

And then one day he met my mother. He used to say: your mother—and he would take a long pause—(*Matilde takes a long pause*)—is funnier than I am. We have never been apart since the day we met, because I always wanted to know the next joke.

My mother and father did not look into each other's eyes. They laughed like hyenas. Even when they made love they laughed like hyenas. My mother was old for a mother. She refused many proposals. It would kill her, she said, to have to spend her days laughing at jokes that were not funny.

Pause.

I wear black because I am in mourning. My mother died last year. Have you ever heard the expression: "I almost died laughing"? Well that's what she did. The doctors couldn't explain it. They argued. They said she choked on her own spit, but they don't really know. She was laughing at one of my father's jokes. A joke he took one year to make up, for the anniversary of their marriage. When my mother died laughing, my father shot himself. And so I came here, to clean this house.

5. Lane and Matilde

Lane enters.
Matilde is looking out the window.

LANE

Are you all right?

MATILDE

Yes.

LANE

Would you please clean the bathroom when you get a chance?

MATILDE

Yes.

LANE

Soon?

MATILDE

Yes.

Matilde looks at Lane.

LANE

The house is very dirty.

Matilde is silent.

This is difficult for me. I don't like to order people around. I've never had a live-in maid.

Matilde is silent.

Matilde—what did you do in your country before you came to the United States?

MATILDE

I was a student. I studied humor. You know—jokes.

LANE

I'm being serious.

MATILDE

I'm being serious too. My parents were the funniest people in Brazil. And then they died.

LANE

I'm sorry.
That must be very difficult.

MATILDE

I was the third funniest person in my family. Then my parents died, making me the first funniest. There was no one left to laugh at my jokes, so I left.

LANE

That's very interesting. I don't—always—understand the arts. Listen. Matilde. I understand that you have a life, an emotional life—and that you are also my cleaning lady. If I met you at—say—a party—and you said, I am from a small village in Brazil, and my parents were comedians, I would say, that's very interesting. You sound like a very interesting woman.

But life is about context.

And I have met you in the context of my house, where I have hired you to clean. And I don't want an interesting person to clean my house. I just want my house—cleaned.

Lane is on the verge of tears.

MATILDE

(*With compassion*) Is something wrong?

No, it's just that—I don't like giving orders in my own home. It makes me—uncomfortable. I want you to do all the things I want you to do without my having to tell you.

MATILDE

Do you tell the nurses at the hospital what to do?

LANE

Yes.

MATILDE

Then pretend I am your nurse.

LANE

Okay.
Nurse—would you polish the silver, please?

MATILDE

A doctor does not say: Nurse—would you polish the silver, please? A doctor says: Nurse—polish the silver!

LANE

You're right. Nurse—polish the silver!

MATILDE

Yes, Doctor.
Matilde gets out silver polish and begins polishing.
Lane watches her for a moment, then exits.

6. Matilde

Matilde stops cleaning.

MATILDE

This is how I imagine my parents.

Music.
A dashing couple appears.

They are dancing.

They are not the best dancers in the world.
They laugh until laughing makes them kiss.
They kiss until kissing makes them laugh.

> *They dance.*
> *They laugh until laughing makes them kiss.*
> *They kiss until kissing makes them laugh.*
> *Matilde watches.*
> *Matilde longs for them.*

7. Virginia and Matilde

The doorbell rings.
The music stops. Matilde's parents exit.
They blow kisses to Matilde
Matilde waves back.
The doorbell rings again.
Matilde answers the door.
Virginia is there.

MATILDE

Hello.

VIRGINIA

Hello. You are the maid?

MATILDE

Yes.
You are the sister?

VIRGINIA

Yes.
How did you know?

MATILDE

I dusted your photograph.
My boss said: this is my sister. We don't look alike.

I thought: you don't look like my boss. You must be her sister.
My name is Matilde. (*Brazilian pronunciation of Matilde: Ma-chil-gee*)

VIRGINIA

I thought your name was Matilde. (*American pronunciation of Matilde: Matilda*)

MATILDE

Kind of.

VIRGINIA

Nice to meet you.

MATILDE

Nice to meet you. I don't know your name.

VIRGINIA

Oh! My name is Virginia.

MATILDE

Like the state?

VIRGINIA

Yes.

MATILDE

I've never been to Virginia.

VIRGINIA

Maybe I should go.

MATILDE

To Virginia?

VIRGINIA

No. I mean, am I interrupting you?

MATILDE

No. I was just—cleaning. Your sister is at work.

VIRGINIA

She's always at work.

MATILDE

Would you like to come in?

VIRGINIA

Yes. Actually—I came to see you.

They enter the living room.

Lane tells me that you've been feeling a little blue.

MATILDE

Blue?

VIRGINIA

Sad.

MATILDE

Oh. She told you that?

VIRGINIA

Come, sit on the couch with me.

MATILDE

Okay.

Virginia goes to sit on the couch.
She pats the couch.
Matilde sits down next to her.

VIRGINIA

Do you miss home?

MATILDE

Of course I do. Doesn't everyone?

VIRGINIA

Is that why you've been sad?

MATILDE

No. I don't think so. It's just that—I don't like to clean houses. I think it makes me sad.

VIRGINIA

You don't like to clean houses.

MATILDE

No.

VIRGINIA

But that's so simple!

MATILDE

Yes.

VIRGINIA

Why don't you like to clean?

MATILDE

I've never liked to clean. When I was a child I thought: if the floor is dirty, look at the ceiling. It is always clean.

VIRGINIA

I like cleaning.

MATILDE

You do? Why?

VIRGINIA

It clears my head.

MATILDE

So it is, for you, a religious practice?

VIRGINIA

No. It's just that: cleaning my house—makes me feel clean.

MATILDE

But you don't clean other people's houses. For money.

VIRGINIA

No—I clean my own house.

MATILDE

I think that is different.

VIRGINIA

Do you feel sad *while* you are cleaning? Or before? Or after?

MATILDE

I am sad when I think about cleaning. But I try not to think about cleaning while I am cleaning. I try to think of jokes. But sometimes the cleaning makes me mad. And then I'm not in a funny mood. And *that* makes me sad. Would you like a coffee?

VIRGINIA

I would *love* some coffee.

Matilde goes to get a cup of coffee from the kitchen.
Virginia takes stock of her sister's dust.
Virginia puts her finger on the tabletops to test the dust.
Then she wipes her dirty finger on her skirt.
Then she tries to clean her skirt but she has nothing to clean it with.
Matilde comes back and gives her the coffee.

Thank you.

MATILDE

You're welcome.

Virginia drinks the coffee.

VIRGINIA

This is good coffee.

MATILDE

We make good coffee in Brazil.

VIRGINIA

Oh—that's right. You do!

MATILDE

Does that help you to place me in my cultural context?

VIRGINIA

Lane didn't describe you accurately.
How old are you?

MATILDE

Young enough that my skin is still good.
Old enough that I am starting to think: is my skin still good?
Does that answer your question?

VIRGINIA

Yes. You're twenty-seven.

MATILDE

You're good.

VIRGINIA

Thank you.
Listen. Matilde. (*American pronunciation*)

MATILDE

Matilde. (*Brazilian pronunciation*)

VIRGINIA

Yes.
I have a proposition for you.

A proposition?

A deal.
I like to clean. You do not like to clean. Why don't I clean for you?

You're joking.

No.

I don't get it. What do you want from me?

Nothing.

Then—why?

I have my house cleaned by approximately 3:12 every afternoon. I have folded the corner of every sheet. The house is quiet. The gold draperies are singing a little lullaby to the ottoman. The silverware is gently sleeping in its box. I tuck in the forks, the spoons, the knives. I do not have children.

I'm sorry.

(*With increasing velocity*) Don't be sorry. My husband is barren. Is that the right word for a man? I never thought that the world was quite good enough for children anyway. I didn't trust myself to cope with how sick and ugly the world is and how beautiful children are, and the idea of watching them grow into the dirt and mess of the world—someone might kidnap them or rape them or otherwise trample on their innocence, leaving them in the middle of the road, naked, in some perverse sexual position, to die, while strangers rode past on bicycles and

---

tried not to look. I've thought about doing some volunteer work, but I don't know who to volunteer for.

A pause. She looks at Matilde.

Since I was twenty-two, my life has gone downhill, and not only have I not done what I wanted to do, but I have lost the qualities and temperament that would help me reverse the downward spiral—and now I am a completely different person. I don't know why I am telling you all of this, Mathalina.

Matilde thinks about correcting Virginia. She doesn't.

MATILDE

Go on.

VIRGINIA

I used to study Greek literature. One summer my husband and I went to Europe. It was supposed to be relaxing but I have trouble relaxing on vacations. We were going to see ruins and I was going to write about ruins but I found that I had nothing to say about them. I thought: why doesn't someone just sweep them up! Get a very large broom!

I'm sorry. I was trying to say …

MATILDE

You were telling me how your life has gone downhill since you were twenty-two.

VIRGINIA

Yes. The point is: every day my house is cleaned by three o'clock. I have a lot of—time.

I'd be very happy to come here and clean Lane's house before Lane gets home from work. That is what I'm telling you. Only don't tell her. She wouldn't like it.

MATILDE

I will let you clean the house if it will make you feel better.

Let's start in the bathroom. I love cleaning the toilet. It's so dirty, and then it's so clean!

8. Lane and Matilde

Matilde is reading the funny papers.
Lane enters.

LANE

It's so clean!

MATILDE

Yes.

LANE

The medication is helping?

MATILDE

I'm feeling much better.

LANE

Well—that's terrific.

Lane exits.
Matilde takes out her medication.
She undoes the bottle,
takes one pill out,
looks at it,
and throws it in the garbage can.

9. Matilde

Matilde, to the audience:

MATILDE

The perfect joke makes you forget about your life. The perfect joke makes you remember about your life. The perfect joke is stupid when you write it down. The perfect joke was not made up by one person. It passed through the air and you caught it. A perfect joke is somewhere between an angel and a fart.

This is how I imagine my parents:

Music.
Matilde's mother and father appear.
They sit at a café.

My mother and father are at a café.
My mother is telling my father a joke.
It is a dirty joke.
My father is laughing so hard that he is banging his knee on the underside of the table.
My mother is laughing so hard that she spits out her coffee.
I am with them at the café. I am eight years old.
I say: what's so funny?
(I *hate* not understanding a joke.)
My mother says: ask me again when you're thirty.
Now I'm almost thirty. And I'll never know the joke.

Matilde's mother and father look at her.
They exit.

10. Virginia and Matilde

The next day.
Virginia folds laundry.
Matilde watches.
Virginia is happy to be cleaning.

MATILDE

You're good at that.

VIRGINIA

Thank you.

MATILDE

You want to hear a joke?

VIRGINIA

Not really.

MATILDE

Why?

VIRGINIA

I don't like to laugh out loud.

MATILDE

Why?

VIRGINIA

I don't like my laugh. It's like a wheeze. Someone once told me that. Who was it—my husband? Do you have a husband?

MATILDE

No.

VIRGINIA

That's good.

MATILDE

Do you like your husband?

VIRGINIA

My husband is like a well-placed couch. He takes up the right amount of space. A man should not be too beautiful. Or too good in bed. A man should be—functional. And well chosen. Otherwise you're in trouble.

MATILDE

Does he make you laugh?

VIRGINIA

Oh no. Something uncontrollable would come out of my mouth when he wanted it to. I wouldn't like that.

MATILDE

A good joke cleans your insides out. If I don't laugh for a week, I feel dirty. I feel dirty now, like my insides are rotting.

VIRGINIA

Someone should make you laugh. I'm not the person to do it.

MATILDE

Virginia. My mother once said to me: Matilde, in order to tell a good joke, you have to believe that your problems are very small, and that the world is very big. She said: if more women knew more jokes, there would be more justice in this world.

Virginia thinks about that.
Virginia comes across a white pair of women's underwear.
Matilde watches.

VIRGINIA

I've never seen my sister's underwear before.

MATILDE

Her underwear is practical. And white.

Virginia continues to fold underwear.

VIRGINIA

I wonder if Lane has gone through menopause yet. Her underwear is very white. Some women throw out underwear when they get a bloodstain. Other women keep washing the stain.

MATILDE

I can't afford to throw away underwear. If I could, believe me, I would. I would buy new underwear every day: purple, red, gold, orange, silver …

Virginia folds a pair of men's underwear.

VIRGINIA

It's a little weird to be touching my brother-in-law's underwear. He's a very handsome man.

When he and Lane first met, I thought: Lane gets the best of everything. A surgeon. With a specialty. He's—charismatic.

Virginia touches her brother-in-law's underwear as she folds.

Then I thought: it's better to have a husband who is not *too* handsome. Then you don't worry about him.

Virginia comes across a pair of women's black underwear.

These don't look like Lane.

MATILDE

No.

VIRGINIA

Too shiny.

MATILDE

Too sexy.

Matilde and Virginia look at each other.

11. Lane and Virginia Have Coffee

Lane and Virginia have coffee in the living room.

VIRGINIA

The house is so clean!

LANE

Thanks.

VIRGINIA

It's working out—with your maid? What's her name?

LANE

(*American pronunciation*) Matilde.

VIRGINIA

That's right: Matilde. (*American pronunciation*)
Don't they say Matilde (*Brazilian pronunciation*) in Brazil?

LANE

I don't know.

VIRGINIA

I think they do.

LANE

How would you know?

Virginia shrugs.

VIRGINIA

Mmm …

LANE

Well, I'm sure she would tell me if I were saying her name wrong. Anyway. She seems much better. How are you?

VIRGINIA

Oh, fine.
How's Charles?

LANE

Why do you ask?

VIRGINIA

No reason.

LANE

He's fine.

VIRGINIA

That's good. The last time I saw Charles was Christmas. You both work so hard.

LANE

He's been doing nine surgeries a day—we hardly see each other. I mean, of course we see each other, but, you know how it is. More coffee?

VIRGINIA

No, thanks.

LANE

Matilde! Could you clear these, please?

Matilde enters.

MATILDE

(*To Virginia*) Your cup, miss?

VIRGINIA

Oh, I'll get it—

Matilde winks at Virginia.
Matilde clears the plates.

Thanks.

MATILDE

Did everyone like their coffee?

LANE AND VIRGINIA

Yes.

MATILDE

Good.

Matilde exits.

LANE

Oh. That's Matilde. Sorry. That was rude. I should have introduced you. Or is it rude? Do you introduce the maid to the company?

Virginia

I'm not the company. I'm your sister.

Lane

You're right.
I should have introduced you. I can't get used to having another person in the house.

Virginia

Mmm. Yes. It must make you uncomfortable to—I don't know—read a magazine while someone cleans up after you.

Lane

I don't read magazines, Virginia. I go to work exhausted and I come home exhausted. That is how most of the people in this country function. At least people who have jobs.

A pause.
For a moment,
Lane and Virginia experience
a primal moment during which they
are seven and nine years old,
inside the mind, respectively.
They are mad.
Then they return quite naturally
to language, as adults do.

Sorry—I didn't mean—

Virginia

I know.

At the same time:

Virginia	Lane
Are you—?	I keep meaning to—

VIRGINIA

What?

LANE

Oh—it's just—I keep meaning to have you two over for dinner. It's ridiculous—living so close and never seeing each other.

VIRGINIA

You're right. Maybe next week?

LANE

Next week is crazy. But soon.

Virginia nods.

12. Lane and Matilde

Night.
Matilde tries to think up the perfect joke.
Matilde looks straight ahead,
in the dark, in the living room.
She thinks.
Lane comes home from work.
She turns a light on.

LANE

Oh! You startled me.

MATILDE

You startled me, too.

LANE

What are you doing in the dark?

MATILDE

I was trying to think up a joke.
Almost had one.
Now it's gone.

Oh—well—can you get it back again?

I doubt it.

Oh.
Is Charles home?

No.

Did he call?

(*With compassion*) No.

Oh, well, he's probably just sleeping at the hospital.

Matilde is silent.

Sometimes there's no time to call home from the hospital. You're going from patient to patient, and it's—you know—crazy. When we were younger—Charles and I—we would page each other, we had this signal—two for good night—and three for—well, I don't know why I'm thinking about this right now. The point is—when you get older, you just know that a person is thinking of you, and working hard, and thinking of you, and you don't need them to call anymore. Since Charles and I are both doctors we both—understand—how it is.

Mmm.

Well, good night.

MATILDE

Good night.

LANE

Are you going to—just—sit here in the dark?

MATILDE

I might stay up a little longer to—what's the word?—tidy up.

LANE

Oh. Great. Just shut the light off when you—

Matilde turns the light off.

Oh. Good night.

MATILDE

Good night.

> *Lane exits.*
> *Matilde tries to think up the perfect joke.*
> *She closes her eyes.*
> *The lights around her go from night to day*
> *as she composes.*

13. Virginia and Matilde. Then Lane.

Virginia enters.
Matilde opens her eyes.
Virginia irons.
Matilde watches.

MATILDE

I have a really good joke coming.

VIRGINIA

That's good.

MATILDE

You know how most jokes go in threes? Like this: Da da DA. I'm making up one that goes in sixes: Da da Da, da da DA.

VIRGINIA

I didn't know jokes had time signatures.

MATILDE

Oh, they do. Ask me what my profession is then ask me what my greatest problem is.

VIRGINIA

What's your profession?

MATILDE

I'm a comedian.

VIRGINIA

What's your—

MATILDE

Timing.

VIRGINIA

That's good.

MATILDE

But you're not laughing.

VIRGINIA

I'm laughing on the inside.

MATILDE

Oh. I like it better when people laugh on the outside.
I'm looking for the perfect joke, but I'm afraid if I found it, it would kill me.

Virginia comes upon a pair of women's red underwear.

VIRGINIA

My God!

MATILDE

Oh ...
No— (*As in—he wouldn't dare*)

VIRGINIA

No.

MATILDE

But— (*As in—he might dare*)

VIRGINIA

Do you think—here—in the house?

MATILDE

Maybe a park. I bet he puts them in his pocket, afterwards, and forgets, because he's so happy. And then she's walking around for the day, with no underwear, and you know what? She probably likes it.

VIRGINIA

I hope it's not a nurse. It's such a cliché.

MATILDE

If she's a nurse, they would pass each other in the hospital, and she would say: hello, Doctor. And she knows, and he knows: no underwear.

VIRGINIA

No underwear in a *hospital?* It's unsanitary.

MATILDE

Or—maybe he just *likes* women's underwear. He might try them on.

VIRGINIA

Charles? No!

MATILDE

It's possible. You don't like to think about it, because he's your brother-in-law, but these things happen, Virginia. They do.

> *Lane enters.*
> *Virginia quickly puts down the iron and sits.*
> *Matilde stands and begins to iron badly.*
> *Virginia hides the red underwear.*

LANE

(*To Virginia*) What are you doing here?

VIRGINIA

Nothing.
How was work?

> *Lane moves to the kitchen.*

Where are you going?

LANE

I'm going in the other room to shoot myself.

VIRGINIA

You're joking, right?

LANE

(*From the kitchen*) Right.

> *Matilde and Virginia look at each other.*
> *Matilde folds underwear.*
> *Virginia sits.*
> *Virginia stands.*
> *Virginia sits.*
> *Virginia stands.*
> *Virginia has a deep impulse to order the universe.*
> *Virginia arranges objects on the coffee table.*

Lane enters.
Her left hand is bleeding.
She holds it with a dish towel.

VIRGINIA

Lane—what—are you—?

LANE

I'm disguising myself as a patient.

VIRGINIA

That's not funny.

LANE

I cut myself.

They look at her, alarmed.

Don't worry. Even my wounds are superficial.

VIRGINIA

Lane?

LANE

Can opener. I was making a martini.

VIRGINIA

Why do you need a can opener to make a martini?

LANE

I didn't have the right kind of fucking olives, okay? I only have black olives! In a fucking can.

VIRGINIA

Lane?

LANE

He's gone off with a patient.

VIRGINIA

What?

LANE

His patient.

MATILDE

Oh …

LANE

Yes.

Virginia and Matilde glance toward the red underwear and look away.

VIRGINIA

Was it a—?

LANE

Mastectomy. Yes.

VIRGINIA

Wow. That's very—

LANE

Generous of him?

MATILDE

(*To Virginia*) A mastectomy?

Virginia gestures toward her breast.
Matilde nods.

VIRGINIA

How old is she?

LANE

Sixty-seven.

Oh!

LANE

What?

VIRGINIA

Not what I expected.

LANE

A young nurse? The maid? No. He's in love.

VIRGINIA

But—with an older woman?

LANE

Yes.

VIRGINIA

I'm almost—impressed. She must have substance.

LANE

She's not a doctor.

VIRGINIA

Well, most men in his position … he's still—so—good-looking …

LANE

Virginia!

VIRGINIA

Sorry.

LANE

I've never been jealous, I've never been suspicious. I've never thought any other woman was my equal. I'm the best doctor. I'm the smartest, the most well-loved by my patients. I'm athletic. I have poise. I've aged well. I can talk to *anyone* and be on equal footing. How, I thought, could he even *look* at anyone else. It would be absurd.

VIRGINIA

Wow. You really are—confident.

LANE

I was blind. He didn't want a doctor. He wanted a housewife.

A pause.
Lane looks around the house.
She sees the objects on the coffee table—
a vase, some magazines, forcefully arranged.
She sees Matilde folding laundry, badly.

(*To Virginia*) Have you been cleaning my house?

Virginia and Matilde look at each other.
Matilde stops folding laundry.

VIRGINIA

No, I haven't been cleaning your house.

LANE

Those objects on the coffee table—that is how you arrange objects.

Virginia looks at the coffee table.

VIRGINIA

I don't know what you mean.

LANE

Matilde—has Virginia been cleaning the house?

VIRGINIA

I said no.

LANE

I asked Matilde.
Has Virginia been cleaning the house?

Yes.

For how long?

Two weeks.

You're fired.

A pause.

You're both fired.

You can't do that.
This is my fault.

I'm *paying* her to clean my house!

And your house is clean!

This has nothing to do with you, Virginia.

This has *everything* to do with me.

Matilde—do you have enough money saved for a plane ticket back home?

No.

LANE

You can stay one more week. I will buy you a plane ticket.

VIRGINIA

Lane. Your husband left you today.

LANE

I'm aware of that.

VIRGINIA

You're not capable of making a rational decision.

LANE

I'm always capable of making a rational decision!

MATILDE

You don't need to buy me a plane ticket. I'm moving to New York to become a comedian. I only need a bus ticket.

VIRGINIA

(*To Lane*) You can't do this!

LANE

I will not have you cleaning my house, just because the maid is depressed—

VIRGINIA

She's not depressed. She doesn't like to clean! It makes her sad.

Lane looks at Matilde.

LANE

Is that true?

MATILDE

Yes.

LANE

So—
then—
(*To Virginia*) why?

VIRGINIA

I don't know.

LANE

You looked through my things.

VIRGINIA

Not really.

LANE

I find this—incomprehensible.

VIRGINIA

Can't I do a nice thing for you without having a *motive*?

LANE

No.

VIRGINIA

That's—

LANE

You have better things to do than clean my house.

VIRGINIA

Like what?

LANE

I—

VIRGINIA

Like what?

LANE

I don't know.

VIRGINIA

No, you don't know.
I wake up in the morning, and I wish that I could sleep through the whole day, but there I am, I'm awake.

So I get out of bed. I make eggs for my husband. I throw the eggshells in the disposal. I listen to the sound of delicate eggshells being ground by an indelicate machine. I clean the sink. I sweep the floor. I wipe coffee grounds from the counter.

I might have done something different with my life. I might have been a scholar. I might have described one particular ruin with the cold-blooded poetry of which only a first-rate scholar is capable. Why didn't I?

LANE

I don't know.

VIRGINIA

I wanted something—big. I didn't know how to ask for it. Don't blame Matilde. Blame me. I wanted—a task.

LANE

I'm sorry.
I don't know what to say.
Except:
(*To Matilde*) you're fired.

VIRGINIA

It's not her fault! You can't do this.

LANE

(*To Virginia*) What would you like me to do?

VIRGINIA

Let me ... take care of you.

I don't need to be taken care of.

VIRGINIA

Everybody needs to be taken care of.

LANE

Virginia. I'm all grown-up.
I DO NOT WANT TO BE TAKEN CARE OF.

VIRGINIA

WHY NOT?

LANE

I don't want my sister to clean my house. I want a stranger to clean my house.

Virginia and Lane look at Matilde.

MATILDE

It's all right. I'll go.
I'll pack my things.
Good-bye, Virginia.
Good luck finding a task.

She embraces Virginia.

Good-bye, Doctor.
Good luck finding your husband.

She exits.
Lane and Virginia look at each other.

14. Lane. Then Matilde. Then Virginia.

Lane, to the audience:

LANE

This is how I imagine my ex-husband and his new wife.

Charles and Ana appear.
He undoes her gown.
Is it a hospital gown or a ball gown?

My husband undoes her gown.
He is very gentle.
He kisses her right breast.

Charles kisses Ana's right breast.

He kisses the side of it.
He kisses the shadow.
He kisses her left torso.

He kisses her left torso.

He kisses the scar,

He kisses the scar.

the one he made.
It's a good scar.
He's a good surgeon.
He kisses her mouth.
He kisses her forehead.
It's a sacred ritual, and
I hate him.

Matilde enters with her suitcase.
The lovers remain.
They continue to kiss one another
on different body parts, a ritual.

MATILDE

Is there anything else before I go?

LANE

No. Thank you.

                          MATILDE

Who are they?

                          LANE

My husband and the woman he loves. Don't worry. It's only my imagination.

                          MATILDE

They look happy.

                          LANE

Yes.

                          MATILDE

People imagine that people who are in love are happy.

                          LANE

Yes.

                          MATILDE

That is why, in your country, people kill themselves on Valentine's Day.

                          LANE

Yes.

                          MATILDE

Love isn't clean like that. It's dirty. Like a good joke. Do you want to hear a joke?

                          LANE

Sure.

   Matilde tells a joke in Portuguese.

Is that the end?

                          MATILDE

Yes.

                          LANE

Was it funny?

MATILDE

Yes. It's not funny in translation.

LANE

I suppose I should laugh then.

MATILDE

Yes.

Lane tries to laugh.
She cries.

You're crying.

LANE

No, I'm not.

MATILDE

I think that you're crying.

LANE

Well—yes. I think I am.

Lane cries.
She laughs.
She cries.
She laughs.
And this goes on for some time.
Virginia enters.

VIRGINIA

Charles is at the door.

LANE

What?

VIRGINIA

Charles. In the hall.

MATILDE

Oh …

LANE

You let him in?

VIRGINIA

What could I do?
And—there's a woman with him.

LANE

In the *house*?

VIRGINIA

Yes.

LANE

What does she look like? Is she pretty?

VIRGINIA

No.
(*With a sense of apology*) She's beautiful.

LANE

Oh.

From offstage:

CHARLES

Lane?

The women look at each other.
Blackout.
Intermission.

ACT 2

The white living room has become a hospital.
Or the idea of a hospital.
There is a balcony above the white living room.

1. Charles Performs Surgery on the Woman He Loves

Ana lies under a sheet.
Beautiful music.
A subtitle projects: Charles Performs Surgery on the Woman He Loves.
Charles takes out surgical equipment.
He does surgery on Ana.
It is an act of love.
If the actor who plays Charles is a good singer,
it would be nice if he could sing
an ethereal medieval love song in Latin
about being medically cured by love
as he does the surgery.

If the actress who plays Ana is a good singer,
it would be nice if she recovered from the surgery
and slowly sat up and sang a contrapuntal melody.
When the surgery is over,
Charles takes off Ana's sheet.
Underneath the sheet,
she is dressed in a lovely dress.
They kiss.

2. Ana

Ana, to the audience:

ANA

I have avoided doctors my whole life.
I don't like how they smell. I don't like how they talk. I don't admire their emotional lives. 1 don't like how they walk. They walk very fast to get somewhere—tac tac tac—I am walking somewhere important. I don't like that. I like a man who saunters. Like this.

Ana saunters across the stage like a man.

But with Charles, it was like—BLAM!
My mind was going: you're a doctor, I hate you.
But the rest of me was gone, walking out the door, with him.
When he performed surgery on me,
we were already in love.
I was under general anesthetic but I could sense him there.
I think he put something extra in—during the surgery.
Into the missing place.
There are stories of surgeons who leave things inside the body by mistake:
rubber gloves, sponges, clamps—
But—you know—I think Charles left his soul inside me.
Into the missing place.

She touches her left breast.

3. Charles

Charles, to the audience:

CHARLES

There are jokes about breast surgeons.
You know—something like—I've seen more breasts in this city
than—
I don't know the punch line.
There must be a punch line.

I'm not a man who falls in love easily. I've been faithful to my wife. We fell in love when we were twenty-two. We had plans. There was justice in the world. There was justice in love. If a person was good enough, an equally good person would fall in love with that person. And then I met—Ana. Justice had nothing to do with it.

There once was a very great American surgeon named Halsted. He was married to a nurse. He loved her—immeasurably. One day Halsted noticed that his wife's hands were chapped and red when she came back from surgery. And so he invented rubber gloves. For her. It is one of the great love stories in medicine. The difference between inspired medicine and uninspired medicine is love.

When I met Ana, I knew:
I loved her to the point of invention.

4. Charles and Ana

CHARLES

I'm afraid that you have breast cancer.

ANA

If you think I'm going to cry, I'm not going to cry.

CHARLES

It's normal to cry—

ANA

I don't cry when I'm supposed to cry. Are you going to cut it off?

CHARLES

You must need some time—to digest—

ANA

No. I don't need time. Tell me everything.

CHARLES

You have a variety of options. Many women don't opt for a mastectomy. A lumpectomy and radiation can be just as effective as—

ANA

I want you to cut it off.

CHARLES

You might want to talk with family members—with a husband—are you married?—or with—

ANA

Tomorrow.

Tomorrow?

ANA

Tomorrow.

CHARLES

I'm not sure I have any appointments open tomorrow—

ANA

I'd like you to do it tomorrow.

CHARLES

Then we'll do it tomorrow.

They look at each other.
They fall in love.

ANA

Then I'll see you tomorrow, at the surgery.

CHARLES

Good-bye, Ana.

ANA

Good-bye.

They look at each other.
They fall in love some more.

Am I going to die?

CHARLES

No. You're not going to die.
I won't let you die.

They fall in love completely.
They kiss wildly.

What's happening?

ANA

I don't know.

CHARLES

This doesn't happen to me.

ANA

Me neither.

CHARLES

Ana, Ana, Ana, Ana ... your name goes backwards and forwards ... I love you ...

ANA

And I love you.
Take off your white coat.

They kiss.

5. Lane, Virginia, Matilde, Charles and Ana

We are back in the white living room.
We are deposited at the end of the last scene of the first act.
Charles is at the door, with Ana.

CHARLES

Lane?

LANE

Charles.

CHARLES

Lane. I want us all to know each other. I want to do things right, from the beginning. Lane: this is Ana. Ana: this is my wife, Lane.

ANA

Nice to meet you. I've heard wonderful things about you. I've heard that you are a wonderful doctor.

LANE

Thank you.

Ana holds out her hand to Lane.
Lane looks around in disbelief
Then Lane shakes Ana's hand.

CHARLES

This is my sister-in-law, Virginia.

ANA

Hello.

VIRGINIA

How do you do.

MATILDE

(*To Ana*) You look like my mother.

ANA

Ah!

LANE

(*To Ana*) This is the maid, Matilde.
(*To Charles*) I fired her this morning.

ANA

Encantada, Matilde.
(*Nice to meet you, Matilde.*)

MATILDE

Encantada. Sou do Brasil.
(*Nice to meet you. I'm from Brazil.*)

ANA

Ah! Eu falo um pouco de portugues, mas falo mal.
(*I know a little bit of Portuguese, but it's bad.*)

MATILDE

Eh! boa tentativa! 'ta chegando la!
Es usted de Argentina?
(*Ah! Good try! Not bad!*
You're from Argentina?)

ANA

(*In Spanish*) ¿Cómo lo sabe?
(*How did you know?*)

MATILDE

(*Imitating Ana's accent*) ¿Cómo lo sabe?
(*How did you know?*)

> *They laugh.*

LANE

We've all met. You can leave now, Charles.

CHARLES

What happened to your wrist?

LANE

Can opener.

CHARLES

Oh.
> *Charles examines the bandage on Lane's wrist.*
> *She pulls her hand away.*

MATILDE

¿Ha usted estado alguna vez en Brasil?
(*Have you ever been to Brazil?*)

ANA

Una vez, para estudiar rocas.
(*Once to study rocks.*)

MATILDE

(*For a moment not understanding the Spanish pronunciation*) Rocas?
Ah, *rochas!*
(*Ah, rocks! In Brazil it is pronounced "hochas."*)

ANA

Sí! *rochas!* (*Pronounces it "hochas."*)

They laugh.

VIRGINIA

Should we sit down?

LANE

Virginia!

They all sit down.

(*To Virginia*) Could you get us something to drink.

VIRGINIA

What would you like?

MATILDE

I would like a coffee.

ANA

That sounds nice. I'll have coffee, too.

VIRGINIA

Charles?

CHARLES

Nothing for me, thanks.

VIRGINIA

Lane?

LANE

I would like some hard alcohol in a glass with ice. Thank you.

Virginia exits.

So.

CHARLES

Lane. I know this is unorthodox. But I want us to know each other.

ANA

You are very generous to have me in your home.

LANE

Not at all.

ANA

Yes, you are very generous. I wanted to meet you. I am not a home-wrecker. The last time I fell in love it was with my husband, a long time ago. He was a geologist and a very wild man, an alcoholic. But so fun! So crazy! He peed on lawns and did everything bad and I loved it. But I did not want to have children with him because he was too wild, too crazy. I said you have to stop drinking and then he did stop drinking and then he died of cancer when he was thirty-one.

Matilde murmurs with sympathy.

My heart was broken and I said to myself: I will never love again. And I didn't. I thought I was going to meet my husband in some land of afterlife with fabulous rocks. Blue and green rocks. And then I met Charles. When Charles said he was married I said Charles we should stop but then Charles referred to Jewish law and I had to say that I agreed and that was that. I wanted you to understand.

LANE

Well, I don't understand. What about Jewish law.

CHARLES

In Jewish law you are legally *obligated* to break off relations with your wife or husband if you find what is called your *bashert*.

ANA

Your soul mate.

CHARLES

You are *obligated* to do this. Legally bound. There's something—metaphysically—objective about it.

LANE

You're not Jewish.

CHARLES

I know. But I heard about the *bashert*—on a radio program. And it always stuck with me. When I saw Ana I knew that was it. I knew she was my *bashert*.

ANA

There is a *midrash* that says when a baby is forty days old, inside the mother's stomach, God picks out its soul mate, and people have to spend the rest of their lives running around to find each other.

LANE

So you are Jewish?

ANA

Yes.

LANE

And your husband was a geologist.

ANA

Yes.

LANE

And you're from Argentina.

ANA

Yes.

LANE

Well. It's all making sense.

CHARLES

Lane. Something very objective happened to me. It's as though I suddenly tested positive for a genetic disease that I've had all along. *Ana has been in my genetic code.*

ANA

Yes. It is strange. We didn't feel guilty because it was so *objective*.

CHARLES

Lane. Something very objective happened to me. It's as though I suddenly tested positive for a genetic disease that I've had all along. *Ana has been in my genetic code.*

ANA

Yes. It is strange. We didn't feel guilty because it was so *objective*. And yet both of us are moral people. I don't know Charles very well but I think he is moral but to tell you the truth even if he were immoral I would love him because the love I feel for your husband is so overpowering.

LANE

And this is what you've come to tell me. That you're both innocent according to Jewish law.

ANA AND CHARLES

Yes.

Virginia enters with the drinks.

MATILDE

Thank you.

ANA

Thank you.

Lane takes a glass from Virginia.

LANE

(*To Virginia*) Charles has come to tell me that according to Jewish law, he has found his soul mate, and so our marriage is dissolved. He doesn't even need to feel guilty. How about that.

VIRGINIA

You have found your *bashert*.

LANE

How the hell do you know about a *bashert*?

VIRGINIA

I heard it on public radio.

CHARLES

I'm sorry that it happened to you, Lane. It could just as well have happened the other way. You might have met your *bashert*, and I would have been forced to make way. There are things—big invisible things—that come unannounced—they walk in, and we have to give way. I would even congratulate you. Because I have always loved you.

LANE

Well. Congratulations.

A silence. A cold one.

MATILDE

Would anyone like to hear a joke?

ANA

I would.

Matilde tells a short joke in Portuguese.
Ana laughs. No one else laughs.

¡Qué bueno! ¡Qué chiste más bueno!
(*What a good joke!*)
(*To Lane*) You are firing Matilde?

LANE

Yes.

ANA

Then we'll hire her to clean our house. I hate to clean. And Charles likes things to be clean. At least I think he does. Charles? Do you like things to be clean?

CHARLES

Sure, I like things to be clean.

ANA

Matilde? Would you like to work for us?

MATILDE

There is something you should know. I don't like to clean so much.

ANA

Of course you don't. Do you have any other skills?

MATILDE

I can tell jokes.

ANA

Perfect. She's coming to live with us.

LANE

My God! You can't just walk into my home and take everything away from me.

ANA

I thought you fired this young woman.

LANE

Yes. I did.

ANA

Have you changed your mind?

LANE

I don't know. Maybe.

ANA

Matilde, do you have a place to live?

MATILDE

No.

ANA

So she'll come live with us.

VIRGINIA

Matilde is like family.

MATILDE

What?

VIRGINIA

Matilde is like a sister to me.

ANA

Is this true?

MATILDE

I don't know. I never had a sister.

VIRGINIA

We clean together. We talk, and fold laundry, as women used to do. They would gather at the public fountains and wash their clothes and tell stories. Now we are alone in our separate houses and it is terrible.

ANA

So it is Virginia who wants you to stay. Not Lane.

LANE

We both want her to stay. We love (*An attempt at the Brazilian pronunciation*) Matilde.

ANA

Matilde?

MATILDE

I am confused.

LANE

I depend on Matilde. I couldn't stand to replace her. Matilde—are you unhappy here with us?

MATILDE

I—

LANE

Is it the money? You could have a raise.

ANA

Matilde—you should do as you wish. My house is easy to clean. I own hardly anything. I own one table, two chairs, a bed, one painting and I have a little fish whose water needs to be changed. I don't have rugs so there is no vacuuming. But you would have to do Charles' laundry. I will not be his washerwoman.

VIRGINIA

Excuse me. But I think that people who are in love—really in love—would like to clean up after each other. If I were in love with Charles I would enjoy folding his laundry.

Virginia looks at Charles.
Lane looks at Virginia.
Virginia looks at Lane.

ANA

Matilde—what do you think? If you stay with us, there is only one condition: you will have to tell one joke a day. I like to laugh.

VIRGINIA

Please don't leave us, Matilde.

MATILDE

I will split my time. Half with Lane and Virginia, half with Ana and Charles. How is that?

                              ANA

Lane?

                              LANE

Matilde is a free agent.

                              ANA

Of course she is.

                              CHARLES

Well.
That's settled.

                              LANE

Are you leaving now?

                              CHARLES

Do you want me to leave?

                              LANE

Yes.

                              CHARLES

Okay. Then we'll leave.
Ana and I are going apple picking this afternoon.
She's never been apple picking.
Would anyone like to join us?

                              MATILDE

I've never been apple picking.

                              CHARLES

So Matilde will come. Virginia?

                              VIRGINIA

I love apple picking.

                              LANE

Virginia!

CHARLES

Lane?

LANE

You must be insane! Apple picking! My god! I'M SORRY! But—apple picking? This is not a foreign film! We don't have an *arrangement*! You don't even *like* foreign films! Maybe you'll pretend to like foreign films, for *Ana*, but I can tell you now, Ana, he doesn't like them! He doesn't like reading the subtitles! It gives him a headache!

CHARLES

Lane. I don't expect you to—understand this—immediately. But since this thing—has happened to me—I want to live life to the fullest. I know—what it must sound like. But it's different. I want to go apple picking. I want to go to Machu Picchu. You can be part of that. I want to share my happiness with you.

LANE

I don't want your happiness.

MATILDE

(To Ana) Es cómo una telenovela.
(It's like a soap opera.)

CHARLES

Lane—I—

LANE

What.

CHARLES

I hope that you'll forgive me one day.

LANE

Go pick some apples. Good-bye.

CHARLES

Good-bye.

ANA

Good-bye.

MATILDE

Good-bye.

VIRGINIA

I'll stay.

Ana, Matilde and Charles exit.

LANE

I want to be alone.

VIRGINIA

No, you don't.

LANE

Yes, I do.

VIRGINIA

No, you don't.
Do you want—I don't know—a hot water bottle?

LANE

No, I don't want a hot water bottle, Virginia.

VIRGINIA

I just thought—

LANE

—That I'm nine years old with a cold?

VIRGINIA

I don't know what else to do.

A pause.

You know, actually, I think I'd like one. It sounds nice.

6. Ana's Balcony

Ana and Matilde are up on Ana's balcony.
It is high above the white living room.
It is a small perch, overlooking the sea,
with two chairs, and a fish bowl.
Through French doors,
one can enter or exit the balcony.
A room leading to the balcony is suggested but unseen.
Ana and Matilde are surrounded by apples.
The following dialogue may be spoken
in a combination of Portuguese and Spanish
and subtitled in English.
Underneath the balcony,
Lane is in her living room.
She lies down with a hot water bottle.
Ana polishes an apple.
Ana and Matilde look around at all of the apples.

ANA

We're never going to eat all of these damn apples.

MATILDE

But it's nice to have so many.
So many that it's *crazy* to have so many.
Because you can never eat them all.

ANA

Yes.

Ana picks out an apple and eats it.

MATILDE

I like the green ones. Which ones do you like?

The yellow ones. They're sweeter.

MATILDE

We could take one bite of each, and if it's not a really, really good apple we can throw it into the sea.

ANA

Now you're talking like a North American.

MATILDE

It will be fun.

ANA

Okay.

They start taking bites of each apple
and if they don't think it's a perfect apple they throw it into the sea.
The sea is also Lane's living room.
Lane sees the apples fall into her living room.
She looks at them.

MATILDE

I made up eighty-four new jokes since I started working for you. I only made up one at the other house. It was a good one though. Sometimes you have to *suffer* for the really good ones.

ANA

Why don't you tell jokes for a job?

MATILDE

Someday.

Matilde throws an apple core into the living room.

ANA

Why someday? Why not now?

MATILDE

I'm looking for the perfect joke. But I am afraid if I found it, it would kill me.

ANA

Why?

MATILDE

My mother died laughing.

ANA

I'm sorry.

MATILDE

Thank you.
She was laughing at one of my father's jokes.

ANA

What was the joke?

MATILDE

I'll never know.
Let's not talk about sad things.

CHARLES

(From offstage) Ana!

ANA

We're on the balcony!

Matilde bites an apple.

MATILDE

Try this one.

ANA

Mmmm. Perfecta.

Charles rushes in wearing scrubs.
He goes to Ana and kisses her all over

and continues to kiss her all over.

We were just eating apples.

CHARLES

Aren't they delicious?

ANA

Here is the very best one.

Charles takes a bite of the best apple.

CHARLES

Divine!
Excuse me, Matilde.
I need to borrow this woman.

He kisses Ana.
He picks up Ana and carries her off into the bedroom.

MATILDE

Have fun.

ANA AND CHARLES

Thank you! We will!

They exit.
Matilde, to the audience:

MATILDE

The perfect joke happens by accident. Like a boil on your backside that you pop. The perfect joke is the perfect music. You want to hear it only once in your life, and then, never again.

A subtitle projects: Matilde Tries to Think Up the Perfect Joke.
She looks out at the sea.
She thinks.

7. Matilde, Virginia and Lane

Virginia is cleaning. She is happy.
Lane, in pajamas, shuffles cards.
Lane shouts to Matilde who is on the balcony:

LANE

Matilde! Your deal.

Matilde leaves the balcony.

VIRGINIA

Lane—your couch is filthy. Wouldn't it be nice to have a fresh, clean slip-cover? I could sew you one.

LANE

That would be nice. It would give you a project.

Matilde enters.

Your deal.

Matilde sits.
Above them, on the balcony,
Ana and Charles dance a slow dance.

So.
Are you happy there? At the other house?

MATILDE

Yes.

LANE

What's her house like?

MATILDE

It's little. She has a balcony that overlooks the sea.

LANE

What's her furniture like?

A table from one place—a chair from another place. It doesn't go together. But it's nice.

What does she cook?

I'm not a spy!

I'm sorry.

They play cards.
On the balcony,
Charles and Ana finish their dance.
They exit, into the bedroom.
Lane puts down a card.

Do they seem like they are very much in love?

Yes.

How can you tell?

They stay in bed half the day. Charles doesn't go to work. He cancels half his patients. He wants to spend all his time with Ana.

Oh.

A pause.

Because Ana is dying again.

VIRGINIA

What?

MATILDE

Her disease came back.
She says she won't take any medicine.
She says it's poison.
He says: you have to go to the hospital!
And she says: I won't go to the hospital!
Then they really fight,
It's like a soap opera.
Charles yells and throws things at the wall.

LANE

Charles never yells.

MATILDE

Oh, he yells.
They broke all the condiments and spices yesterday.
There was this one yellow spice—
it got in their hair and on their faces
until they were all yellow.

A spice jar goes flying from the balcony.
A cloud of yellow spice lands in Lane's living room.

LANE

She won't go to the hospital?

MATILDE

No.
I might have to spend more time at the other house.
To help.

VIRGINIA

Poor Charles.

LANE

Poor Charles? Poor Ana. Poor me!

Poor sounds funny if you say it lots of times in a row: poor, poor, poor, poor, poor, poor, poor. Poor. Poor. Poor. Doesn't it sound funny?

VIRGINIA

Lane? Are you all right?

LANE

Oh, me? I'm fine.

8. Ana and Charles Try to Read One Another's Mind

Ana and Charles on the balcony.
Ana is dressed in a bathrobe.

CHARLES

Eight.

ANA

No, seven. You were very close.

CHARLES

I'll go again.

ANA

Okay.

CHARLES

Four.

ANA

Yes!

CHARLES

I knew it! I could see four apples. Now: colors.

ANA

Okay.

I'll start.

Red.

No.

Blue.

No.

I give up.

Purple. We have to concentrate harder. Like this. Ready? You go.

I'm tired.

Sorry. I'll stop.

Why all these guessing games?

You know Houdini?

The magician?

Yes. Houdini and his wife practiced reading each other's minds. So that—if one of them died—they'd be able to talk to each other—you know, after.

ANA

Did it work?

CHARLES

No.

ANA

Oh.

CHARLES

But I love you more than Houdini loved his wife. He was distracted—by his magic. I'm not distracted. Ana. Let's go to the hospital.

ANA

I told you. No hospitals!

Charles is sad.

Charles, don't be sad.

CHARLES

Don't be sad! My God!

ANA

I can't take this.
I'm going for a swim.
Matilde!
Come look after Charles.
I'm going swimming.

Ana exits.
Charles looks out over the balcony,
watching Ana run out to the water.

CHARLES

Ana! Think of a country under the water! I'll guess it from the balcony!

MATILDE

She can't hear you.

Charles disrobes to his underwear.
He throws his clothes off the balcony.
They land in Lane's living room.

CHARLES

Excuse me, Matilde. I'm going for a swim.

MATILDE

I thought you can't swim.

CHARLES

I'll learn to swim.

Underneath the balcony, in Lane's living room,
Lane comes across Charles's sweater.
She breathes it in.
Charles leans over the balcony.

Ana! What's the country? I think it's a very small country! Is it Luxembourg? Ana!

He runs off.
Matilde looks out over the water.
A pause.
Matilde is startled.
Suddenly, with great clarity,
Matilde thinks up the perfect joke.

MATILDE

My God.
Oh no.
My God.
It's the perfect joke.
Am I dead?
No.

9. Lane and Virginia. Then Matilde.

Lane sits with Charles's sweater in her hands.
Virginia enters, vacuuming.

LANE

Stop it!

VIRGINIA

What?

LANE

Stop cleaning!

VIRGINIA

Why?

LANE

I DON'T WANT ANYTHING IN MY HOUSE TO BE CLEAN EVER AGAIN!
I WANT THERE TO BE DIRT AND PIGS IN THE CORNER. MAYBE SOME
COW MANURE SOME BIG DIRTY SHITTY COWS AND SOME SHITTY
COW SHIT LOTS OF IT AND LOTS OF DIRTY FUCKING SOCKS—AND
NONE OF THEM MATCH—NONE OF THEM—BECAUSE YOU KNOW
WHAT—THAT IS HOW I FEEL.

Lane unplugs the vacuum.

VIRGINIA

Wow. I'm sorry.

LANE

And you know what? I will not let my house be a breeding ground for your weird
obsessive dirt fetish. I will not permit you to feel like a better person just because
you push dirt around all day on my behalf.

VIRGINIA

I was just trying to help.

LANE

Well, it's not helping.

VIRGINIA

I wonder—when it was—that you became—such a bitch? Oh, yes, I remember. Since the day you were born, you thought that anyone with a *problem* had a defect of the will. You're wrong about that. Some people have problems, real problems—

LANE

Yes. I see people with *real problems* all day long. At the hospital.

VIRGINIA

I think—there's a small part of me that's enjoyed watching your life fall apart. To see you lose your composure—for once! I thought: we can be real sisters who tell each other real things. But I was wrong. Well, fine. I'm not picking up your dry cleaning anymore. I'm going to get a job.

LANE

What job?

VIRGINIA

Any job!

LANE

What are you qualified to do at this point?

VIRGINIA

No wonder Charles left. You have no compassion.

LANE	VIRGINIA
I do so have compassion. I do so have compassion!	Ana is a woman with compassion.

VIRGINIA

Really. How so.

LANE

I traded my whole life to help people who are sick! What do you do?

Virginia and Lane breathe.
Virginia and Lane are in a state of silent animal warfare,
a brand of warfare particular to sisters.

I'm going to splash some water on my face.

VIRGINIA

Good.

Lane exits.
Virginia, alone.
On the balcony Ana puts on a record—
an aria, most likely Italian.
Ana listens to opera on the balcony, looking out over the sea.
Virginia dumps a plant on the ground and the dirt spills onto the floor.
She realizes with some surprise that she enjoys this.
Virginia makes a giant operatic mess in the living room.
Matilde enters.

MATILDE

What are you doing? Virginia?

VIRGINIA

I'M MAKING A MESS!

Virginia finishes making her operatic mess.
The aria ends.
Ana leaves the balcony.

MATILDE

You are okay?

VIRGINIA

Actually. I feel fabulous.

Matilde sits down.
Matilde puts her head in her arms.
Lane enters.

LANE

What the hell happened here?

VIRGINIA

I was mad. Sorry.

Virginia flicks a speck of dirt.
Lane looks at Matilde.

LANE

(To Virginia) What's wrong with her?

Virginia shrugs.

MATILDE

It's a mess.

VIRGINIA

I'll clean it up.

MATILDE

Not this—Ana, Charles—it's a mess.

LANE

Have they—fallen out of love?

MATILDE

No.

VIRGINIA

Is she very sick?

MATILDE

Yes.

LANE

Oh.

How terrible.

MATILDE

Yes.
And now Charles has gone away.

LANE

What?

MATILDE

(To Lane) To Alaska.

VIRGINIA

What?

MATILDE

(To Virginia) To Alaska.

LANE

But—why?

MATILDE

He says he's going to chop down a tree for Ana.

VIRGINIA

What?

MATILDE

A "you" tree.
He called it a you tree.

Matilde points: you.

VIRGINIA

A you tree?

MATILDE

A you tree. He says he's going to invent a new "you medicine."

VIRGINIA

My God. He's gone crazy with love!

LANE

He's not crazy. It's a yew tree. (*Spelling it out*) Y-E-W. A Pacific yew tree. The bark was made into Taxol in 1967. It makes cancer cells clog up with microtubules so they're slower to grow and divide.

MATILDE

He said it was a special tree.

LANE

Yes. It is a special tree.

MATILDE

He wants to plant the tree in Ana's courtyard so she can smell the tree from her balcony.
She won't go to the hospital. So he said he would bring the hospital to her.

VIRGINIA

That's beautiful.

LANE

It's not beautiful, Virginia. There is a woman dying, alone, while Charles chops down a fucking tree. How heroic.

VIRGINIA

Does she need a doctor?

MATILDE

Yes. But she won't go to the hospital. So I thought I would ask.
Do you know any doctors who go to the house?

VIRGINIA

You mean house calls?

MATILDE

Yes, house calls.

Virginia and Matilde look at Lane.

> LANE

Why are you looking at me?

They continue to look at Lane.

You want me to take care of my husband's soul mate.

> VIRGINIA

Look at her as a patient. Not a person. You can do that.

> LANE

If she wanted to see a doctor, she'd go to the hospital. I am *not* going to her house. It would be totally inappropriate.

They look at Lane.
In the distance, Charles walks slowly across the stage dressed in a parka, looking for his tree.
A great freezing wind.

10. Lane Makes a House Call to Her Husband's Soul Mate

On Ana's balcony.
Lane listens to Ana's heart with a stethoscope.

> LANE

Breathe in. Breathe in again.

Lane takes off her stethoscope.

Are you having any trouble breathing?

> ANA

No. But sometimes it hurts when I breathe.

> LANE

Where?

ANA

Here.

LANE

Do you have pain when you're at rest?

ANA

Yes.

LANE

Where?

ANA

In my spine.

LANE

Is the pain sharp, or dull?

ANA

Sharp.

LANE

Does it radiate?

ANA

Like light?

LANE

I mean—does it move from one place to another?

ANA

Yes. From here to there.

LANE

How's your appetite?

ANA

Not great.
You must hate me.

LANE

Look—I'm being a doctor right now. That's all.

Lane palpates Ana's spine.

Does that hurt?

ANA

It hurts already.

LANE

I can't know anything without doing tests.

ANA

I know.

LANE

And you won't go to the hospital.

ANA

No.

LANE

All right.

ANA

Do you think I'm crazy?

LANE

No.

A small pause.

ANA

Well. Can I get you anything to drink? I have some iced tea.

LANE

Sure. Thank you.

Ana exits.
Lane looks out over the balcony at the water.
Lane starts to weep.
Ana enters with iced tea.

ANA

Lane?

LANE

Oh God! I'm *not* going to cry in front of you.

ANA

It's okay. You can cry. You must hate me.

LANE

I don't hate you.

ANA

Why are you crying?

LANE

Okay! I hate you!
You—glow—with some kind of—thing—I can't *acquire* that—this—thing—sort of—glows off you—like a veil—in reverse—you're like *anyone's* soul mate—because you have that—thing—you have a balcony—I don't have a balcony—Charles looks at you—he glows, too—you're like two glowworms—he never looked at me like that.

ANA

Lane.

LANE

I looked at our wedding pictures to see—maybe—he looked at me that way—back then—and no—he didn't—he looked at me with *admiration*—I didn't know there was another way to be looked at—how could I know—I didn't know his face was capable of *doing that*—the way he looked at you—in my living room.

ANA

I'm sorry.

No you're not. If you were really sorry, you wouldn't have done it. We do as we please, and then we say we're sorry. But we're not sorry. We're just—uncomfortable—watching other people in pain.

Ana hands Lane an iced tea.

Thank you.

Lane drinks her iced tea.
They both look at the fish in the bowl.

What kind of fish is that?

ANA

A fighting fish.

LANE

How old is it?

ANA

Twelve.

LANE

That's old for a fish.

ANA

I keep expecting it to die. But it doesn't.

Lane taps on the bowl.
The fish wriggles.

How did you and Charles fall in love?

LANE

He didn't tell you?

ANA

No.

Oh. Well, we were in medical school together. We were anatomy partners. We fell in love over a dead body.

They look at each other.
Lane forgives Ana.

ANA

Want an apple?

LANE

Sure.

Ana gives Lane an apple.
Lane takes a bite and stops.

Did Charles pick this apple?

ANA

I don't know who picked it.

Lane eats the apple.

LANE

It's good.

In the distance,
Charles walks across the stage in a heavy parka.
He carries a pick axe.
On the balcony, it is snowing.

11. Lane Calls Virginia

Lane and Virginia on the telephone.

LANE

I saw Ana.

VIRGINIA

And?

LANE

She's coming to live with me.

VIRGINIA

What?

LANE

She can't be alone. She's too sick. I invited her.

VIRGINIA

That's generous. I'm impressed.

LANE

So will you be around—during the day—to help Matilde look after her?

VIRGINIA

Oh, me? No. I got a job.

LANE

What?

VIRGINIA

I got a job.

LANE

Doing what?

VIRGINIA

I'm a checkout girl. At the grocery store.

LANE

You're not.

VIRGINIA

I am. I had my first day. I liked it. I liked using the cash register. I liked watching the vegetables go by on the conveyer belt. Purple, orange, red, green, yellow. My colleagues were nice. They helped me if my receipts got stuck in the machine. There was fellow feeling among the workers. Solidarity. And I liked it.

                              LANE

Wow.

                              VIRGINIA

So, I'm sorry. But I'll be too busy to help you.

   Pause.

                              LANE

You made that story up.

                              VIRGINIA

Fine.

                              LANE

So you'll help me.

                              VIRGINIA

You want my help?

                              LANE

Yes.

                              VIRGINIA

Are you sure?

                              LANE

Yes.

                              VIRGINIA

Say: I want your help.

   A small pause.

                              LANE

I want your help.

Then I'll help you.

12. Ana and Virginia. Then Matilde. Then Lane.

All of Ana's possessions have been moved into Lane's living room.
Ana's fish is in a bowl on the coffee table.
There are bags of apples on the carpet.
And luggage. With clothes spilling out of a bag.
Virginia is preparing a special tray of food for Ana.
Virginia listens to Ana.

ANA

People talk about *cancer* like it's this special thing you have a *relationship* with. And it becomes blood count, biopsy, chemotherapy, radiation, bone marrow, blah blah blah blah blah. As long as I live I want to retain my own language.

Mientras tengo vida, quiero procurar mantener mi proprio idioma.

No extra hospital words. I don't want a relationship with a disease. I want to have a relationship with death. That's important. But to have a relationship with a *disease*—that's some kind of bourgeois invention. And I hate it.

Virginia gives Ana the tray.

Thank you.

Ana eats a bite.

VIRGINIA

Do you like it?

ANA

It's delicious. What is it?

VIRGINIA

A casserole. No one makes casserole anymore. I thought it might be comforting.

ANA

What's in it?

VIRGINIA

Things you wouldn't want to know about.

ANA

Well, it's good.
Thank you for taking care of me, Virginia.

Virginia is moved.

What's wrong?

VIRGINIA

I'm not used to people thanking me.

Matilde enters, holding a telegram.
She hands it to Ana.

MATILDE

There is a telegram. From Charles.

In the distance, Charles appears
wearing a heavy parka.
Inside the living room, it snows.

CHARLES

Dear Ana. Stop.
Have cut down tree. Stop.
Cannot get on plane with tree. Stop.
Must learn to fly plane. Stop.
Wait for me. Stop.
Your beloved, Charles.

ANA

I want him to be a nurse and he wants to be an explorer.
Asi es la vida.
(That's life.)

Charles exits.
Lane enters.

LANE

Hi.

ANA

Hello!

An awkward moment.

VIRGINIA

Would anyone like ice cream? I made some ice cream.

MATILDE

You *made* it?

VIRGINIA

It was no trouble.

ANA

I love ice cream.

VIRGINIA

Do you like chocolate?

ANA

Who doesn't like chocolate. Crazy people.

VIRGINIA

I'll get spoons.

MATILDE

I'll help you.

Matilde and Virginia exit.
Lane sees Ana's fish.

LANE

He made it all right.

ANA

He's a strong fish.

Lane taps the fish bowl.
The fish wriggles.
Matilde and Virginia come back with spoons and ice cream.
After a moment of hesitation, Lane takes a spoon from Virginia.
They all eat ice cream out of the same container.

Mmmm! Amazing!

MATILDE

It must be what God eats when he is tired.

ANA

So soft!

MATILDE

Sometimes ice cream in this country is so hard.

ANA

Sí.

LANE

I like ice cream.

They all eat ice cream.

ANA

Can you imagine a time before ice cream? When they couldn't keep things frozen? There was once a ship filled with ice—it sailed from Europe to South America. The ice melted by the time it got to South America. And the captain of the ship was bankrupt. All he had to sell when he got there was water.

VIRGINIA

A ship full of water.

MATILDE

A ship full of water.

They finish the ice cream.
No one cleans up.

VIRGINIA

(To Ana) You look feverish. Are you warm?

ANA

I'm cold.

VIRGINIA

I'll get a thermometer.

ANA

No thermometers!

LANE

How about a blanket?

ANA

Okay. I'd like a blanket.

LANE

(To Virginia) Where do I keep blankets?

VIRGINIA

I'll show you.

Lane and Virginia exit.

ANA

Matilde. My bones hurt.

MATILDE

I know they do.

Do you know what it feels like when your bones hurt?

MATILDE

No.

ANA

I hope you never know.
Matilde. You once told me that your father killed your mother with a joke.

MATILDE

Yes.

ANA

I would like you to kill me with a joke.

MATILDE

I don't want to kill you. I like you.

ANA

If you like me, help me.

MATILDE

What about Charles? Will you wait for him?

ANA

No.

MATILDE

Why?

ANA

I'd lose all my bravery.

MATILDE

I understand.

ANA

You'll do it then?

A pause.

MATILDE

Okay.

ANA

When?

MATILDE

When you want me to.

ANA

You don't need time to make up a joke?

MATILDE

I made it up on your balcony.

ANA

Tomorrow, then.

MATILDE

Tomorrow.

Lane enters with a blanket.
She hands it to Ana.

LANE

I hope it's warm enough.

ANA

Thank you.
(To Matilde) Good night.

MATILDE

(To Ana) Good night.

Ana puts her head on the pillow, closing her eyes.

(Whispering to Lane) Are you coming?

LANE

In a minute.

Matilde exits.
Lane sits on the floor and watches Ana sleep.
She guards her the way a dog would guard a rival dog,
if her rival were sick.

13. Matilde Tells Ana a Joke

The light turns from night to day.
The next day.
Lane, Virginia and Matilde are gathered around Ana.

ANA

I want to say good-bye to everyone before Matilde tells me a joke.

LANE

Can't I give you anything for the pain?

ANA

No.

LANE

You're sure?

ANA

Yes. Good-bye, Lane.

LANE

Good-bye, Ana.

They embrace.

ANA

Take care of Charles.

LANE

You think I'll be taking care of him?

ANA

Of course.

LANE

Why?

ANA

You love him. Good-bye Virginia.

Virginia weeps.

Don't cry. Thank you for taking care of me.

Virginia weeps.

Oh—see? That makes it worse. Oh, Virginia. I can't take it. Matilde. Let's have the joke.

MATILDE

Are you ready?

ANA

Yes.
Everyone's always dying lying down. I want to die standing up.

Ana stands.

(*To Lane and Virginia*) The two of you had better leave the room. I don't want you dying before your time.

They nod.
They leave.

Matilde.
Deseo el chiste ahora.
(*I want the joke now.*)

The lights change.
Music.

Matilde whispers a joke in Ana's ear.
We don't hear it.
We hear sublime music instead.
A subtitle projects: The Funniest Joke in the World.
Ana laughs and laughs.
Ana collapses.
Matilde kneels beside her.
Matilde wails.

MATILDE

Ohhh …

Lane and Virginia rush in.
Lane checks Ana's pulse.
The women look at one another.

VIRGINIA

What do we do?

LANE

I don't know.

VIRGINIA

You're the doctor!

LANE

I've never seen someone die in a house before.
Only in a hospital.
Where they clean everything up.

VIRGINIA

What do the nurses do?

MATILDE

They close the eyes.

LANE

That's right.

Matilde closes Ana's eyes.

                           MATILDE

And they wash the body.

                            LANE

I'll wash her.

   Lane goes to get a towel and a bowl of water.

                          VIRGINIA

Should we say a prayer?

                           MATILDE

You say a prayer, Virginia.
A prayer cleans the air the way water cleans the dirt.

                          VIRGINIA

Ana. I hope you are apple picking.

   Lane enters with a bowl of water.
   She washes Ana's body.
   Time slows down.

                           CHARLES

(From offstage) Ana!

   Charles pounds on the door.

Ana! Ana!

   The women look at one another.
   Lane goes to Charles.
   Charles walks in carrying an enormous tree.
   He is sweating and breathing heavily.
   He has carried his tree great distances.

I brought back this tree. The bark—

                    LANE

I know.

                    CHARLES

It won't help?

                    LANE

No.

                    CHARLES

Why?

                    LANE

Charles.

                    CHARLES

You were here?

                    LANE

Yes.

                    CHARLES

Can I see her?

    Lane nods.

                    LANE

Charles?

    Lane kisses Charles on the forehead.

                    CHARLES

Thank you. Will you hold my tree?

    Lane nods.
    Lane holds the tree.
    Charles moves toward Ana's body.
    He collapses over her body
    as the lights come up on Matilde.

14. Matilde

Matilde, to the audience:

MATILDE

This is how I imagine my parents.

Ana and Charles transform into Matilde's mother and father.
Under Charles's parka he is dressed as Matilde's father.
Under Ana's bathrobe, she is dressed as Matilde's mother.

My mother is about to give birth to me. The hospital is too far away.
My mother runs up a hill in December and says: now!
My mother is lying down under a tree.
My father is telling her a joke to try and keep her calm.

Matilde's father whispers a joke in Portuguese to Matilde's mother.

My mother laughed.
She laughed so hard that I popped out.
My mother said I was the only baby who laughed
when I came into the world.
She said I was laughing at my father's joke.
I laughed to take in the air.
I took in some air, and then I cried.

Matilde looks at her parents.
A moment of completion between them.
Matilde looks at the audience.

I think maybe heaven is a sea of untranslatable jokes. Only everyone is laughing.

THE END

A NOTE ON SUBTITLES

The director might consider projecting subtitles in the play for some scene titles and some stage directions. I suggest these:

A woman tells a joke in Portuguese. (page 445)

Lane. (445)

Virginia. (445)

Matilde. (446)

Virginia takes stock of her sister's dust. (454)

Lane and Virginia experience a primal moment during which they are seven and nine years old. (465)

Matilde tries to think up the perfect joke. (466)

Matilde tries to think up the perfect joke. (468)

Virginia has a deep impulse to order the universe. (471)

Charles performs surgery on the woman he loves. (485)

Ana. (485)

Charles. (486)

They fall in love. (488)

They fall in love some more. (488)

They fall in love completely. (489)

Ana's balcony. (503)

Matilde tries to think up the perfect joke. (506)

Ana and Charles try to read one another's mind. (510)

Lane makes a house call to her husband's soul mate. (520)

Lane forgives Ana. (525)

Lane calls Virginia. (525)

The funniest joke in the world. (537)

A NOTE ON JOKES

Thanks is due to all the people who helped me with jokes and translations in *The Clean House*: Caridad Svich, Fernando Oliveira, Anna Fluck, Giovanna Sardelli, Claudine Barros.

I want the choice of jokes to be somewhat open, allowing for the possibility that different productions may come up with different and more perfect Brazilian jokes. So please use these jokes as you will.

Joke #1, to be told in Act 1, Scene 1:

Um homem tava a ponto de casar e ele tava muito nervosa ao preparar-se pra noite de nupias porque ele nunca tuvo sexo en la vida de ele. Enton ele vai pra médico e pergunta: "O que que eu devo fazor?" O medico fala: "Não se preocupa. Voce coloca uma nota de dez dolares na bolso direito y voce practica: '10, 10, 10, 10.'" Enton el homen vai pra casa y practica todo semana: "10,10,10." Aí ele volta pra médico y lhe fala: "Muito bem! Agora você coloca uma nota de, 10 no bolso direito e uma nota do 20 (vinte) no bolso esquerdo e practica: '10, 20, 10, 20, 10, 20; **10, 20.'"**

Ele foi pra casa praticoli toda semana: "10, 20; 10, 20; 10, 20." Ele volta pra medico y ele falou: "É isso aí! Agora voce coloca uma nota de 10 no bolso direito, uma de 20 no bolso esquerdo e uma de 100 (cem) na frente. Aí você practica: '10, 20, 100; 10, 20, 100; 10, 20, 100.'" Aí ele casou. A noite de núpcias chegou. Ele tava con sua mulher todo bonita e gustosa e ele comencou a fazer amor: "10, 20, 100; 10, 20, 100; 10, 20, 100. Ai, que se foda o trocado: 100, 100, 100!!!"

translation:

A man is getting married. He's never had sex and he's very nervous about his wedding night. So, he goes to a doctor and he says, "I'm really nervous, what should I do?" The doctor says, "Don't worry about it. Go home and put a ten-dollar bill in your right pocket and you practice: '10! 10! 10!,' moving your hips to the left." So, he goes home and after a week of practice, he returns to the doctor who says, "Very good. Now, go back home and put a ten-dollar bill in your right-hand pocket, a twenty-dollar bill in your left-hand pocket and go: '10! 20! 10! 20!'" (The joke teller moves hips from side to side) So, he practices, does very well, returns to the doctor who says, "Perfect! Now you're going to put a ten-dollar bill in your left-hand pocket, a twenty-dollar bill in your right-hand pocket and a hundred-dollar dollar bill in front, where you will go like this, '10! 20! 100!, 10! 20!, 100!'"

The man practices as he is told, goes back to the doctor who says, "Perfect! You're ready to go!"

The big day arrives and the man is very excited about his night with his wife. The time comes and he is in bed and he starts with his wife: "10! 20! 100!, 10! 20! 100!, 10! 20! 100! Oh, fuck the change: 100! 100! 100!"

Joke #2, to be told in Act 1, Scene 14:

Por que os homens na cama são como comida de microondas. Estão prontos em trinta segundos.

translation:

Why are men in bed like microwave food? They're done in thirty seconds.

Joke #3, to be told in Act 2, Scene 5:

O melhor investimento que existe é comprar um argentino pelo valor que ele vale e depois vendê-lo pelo valor que ele acha que vale.

translation:

The best investment ever is to buy an Argentinean for what he is really worth and later sell him for what he thinks he is worth.

A NOTE ON ACT 2, SCENE 6

If the actors playing Ana and Matilde can speak a combination of Spanish and Portuguese, I suggest using this combination of Spanish, Portuguese and English (subtitled where necessary) for this section of the scene.

ANA

Nunca podremos comer todas estas malditas manzanas.
(We're never going to eat all of these damn apples.)

MATILDE

Mas é muito bom ter muitas ...
E uma loucura ter tantas
Porque nos nunca vamos poder comer todas.
(But it's nice to have so many ...
So many that it's crazy to have so many
Because you can never eat them all.)

ANA

Es así!
(Yes!)

Ana picks out an apple and eats it.

MATILDE

Eu gosto das maçãs verdes.
De qual que você gosta?
(I like the green ones.
Which ones do you like?)

ANA

Las amarillas, son las mas dulces.

(The yellow ones. They're sweeter.)

MATILDE

A gente pode dar uma mordida em cada uma e se a maca não for realmente divina a gente joga no mar.
(We could take a bite of each apple and if it's not a really, really good apple we can throw it into the sea.)

ANA

Ché! Hablás como Norte Americana.
(Now you're talking like a North American.)

MATILDE

Sería bem divertido.
(It will be fun.)

ANA

Okay.

They start taking bites of each apple
and if they don't think it's a perfect apple
they throw it into the sea.
The sea is also Lane's living room.
Lane sees the apples fall into her living room.
She looks at them.

MATILDE

I made up eighty-four new jokes since I started working for you. I only made up one at the other house. It was a good one though. Sometimes you have to *suffer* for the really good ones.

ANA

Why don't you tell jokes for a job?

MATILDE

Someday.

Matilde throws an apple core into the living room.

ANA

Why someday? Why not now?

MATILDE

I'm looking for the perfect joke. But I am afraid if I found it, it would kill me.

ANA

Por que?
(Why?)

MATILDE

Minha mãe morreu dando risada.
(My mother died laughing.)

ANA

Lo siento.
(I'm sorry.)

MATILDE

Obrigada.
Ela estava rindo de uma das piadas do meu pai.
(Thank you.
She was laughing at one of my father's jokes.)

ANA

Cuál era el chiste?
(What was the joke?)

MATILDE

Eu nunca saberei. Mas não vamos falar de coisas tristes.
(I'll never know.
Let's not talk about sad things.)

CHARLES

(From offstage) Ana!

Matilde bites an apple.

Try this one.

ANA

Mmmm. Perfecta!

The scene continues as is ...

THE GOD OF CARNAGE

By Yasmina Reza
Translated by Christopher Hampton

CHARACTERS
Véronique Vallon
Michel Vallon
Annette Reille
Alain Reille

All are in their forties

A living room. No realism.
Nothing superfluous.

The Vallons and the Reilles, sitting down, facing one another. We need to sense right away
that the place belongs to the Vallons and that the two couples have just met.
    In the centre, a coffee table, covered with art books.
Two big bunches of tulips in vases.
    The prevailing mood is serious, friendly and tolerant.

VÉRONIQUE: So, this is our statement—you'll be doing your own, of course … 'At
    5.30 p.m. on the 3rd November, in Aspirant Dunant Gardens, following a verbal
    altercation, Ferdinand Reille, eleven, armed with a stick, struck our son, Bruno
    Vallon, in the face. This action resulted in, apart from a swelling of the upper lip,
    the breaking of two incisors, including injury to the nerve in the right incisor.'
ALAIN: Armed?

VÉRONIQUE: Armed? You don't like 'armed'—what shall we say, Michel, furnished, equipped, furnished with a stick, is that all right?

ALAIN: Furnished, yes.

MICHEL: 'Furnished with a stick'.

VÉRONIQUE: (*making the correction*) Furnished. The irony is, we've always regarded Aspirant Dunant Gardens as a haven of security, unlike the Montsouris Park.

MICHEL: She's right. We've always said the Montsouris Park no, Aspirant Dunant Gardens yes.

VÉRONIQUE: Absolutely. Anyway, thank you for coming. There's nothing to be gained from getting stuck down some emotional cul-de-sac.

ANNETTE: We should be thanking you. We should.

VÉRONIQUE: I don't see that any thanks are necessary. Fortunately, there is still such a thing as the art of co-existence, is there not?

ALAIN: Which the children don't appear to have mastered. At least, not ours!

ANNETTE: Yes, not ours! … What's going to happen to the tooth with the affected nerve? …

VÉRONIQUE: We don't know yet. They're being cautious about the prognosis. Apparently the nerve hasn't been totally exposed.

MICHEL: Only a bit of it's been exposed.

VÉRONIQUE: Yes. Some of it's been exposed and some of it's still covered. That's why they've decided not to kill the nerve just yet.

MICHEL: They're trying to give the tooth a chance.

VÉRONIQUE: Obviously it would be best to avoid endodontic surgery.

ANNETTE: Well, yes …

VÉRONIQUE: So there'll be an interim period while they give the nerve a chance to recover.

MICHEL: In the meantime, they'll be giving him ceramic crowns.

VÉRONIQUE: Whatever happens, you can't have an implant before you're eighteen.

MICHEL: No.

VÉRONIQUE: Permanent implants can't be fitted until you finish growing.

ANNETTE: Of course. I hope … I do hope it all works out.

VÉRONIQUE: Let's hope so.

Slight hiatus.

ANNETTE: Those tulips are gorgeous.

VÉRONIQUE: It's that little florist's in the Mouton-Duvernet Market. You know, the one right up the top.

ANNETTE: Oh, yes.

VÉRONIQUE: They come every morning direct from Holland, ten euros for a bunch of fifty.

ANNETTE: Oh, really!

VÉRONIQUE: You know, the one right up the top.

ANNETTE: Yes, yes.

VÉRONIQUE: You know he didn't want to identify Ferdinand.

MICHEL: No, he didn't.

VÉRONIQUE: Impressive sight, that child, face bashed in, teeth missing, still refusing to talk.

ANNETTE: I can imagine.

MICHEL: He also didn't want to identify him for fear of looking like a sneak in front of his friends; we have to be honest, Véronique, it was nothing more than bravado.

VÉRONIQUE: Of course, but bravado is a kind of courage, isn't it?

ANNETTE: That's right ... So how ...? What I mean is, how did you find out Ferdinand's name? ...

VÉRONIQUE: Well, we explained to Bruno he wasn't helping this child by shielding him.

MICHEL: We said to him if this child thinks he can go on hitting people with impunity, why should he stop?

VÉRONIQUE: We said to him, if we were this boy's parents, we would definitely want to be told.

ANNETTE: Absolutely.

ALAIN: Yes ...

His mobile vibrates.

Excuse me ...

He moves away from the group; as he talks, he pulls a newspaper out of his pocket.

... Yes, Maurice, thanks for calling back. Right, in today's *Le Monde,* let me read it to you ... 'According to a paper published in the *Lancet* and taken up yesterday in the *FT,* two Australian researchers have revealed the neurological side-effects of Antril, a hypertensive beta-blocker, manufactured at the Verenz-Pharma laboratories. These side-effects range from hearing loss to ataxia ...' So who the hell is your media watchdog? ... Yes, it's very bloody inconvenient ... No, what's most inconvenient about it as far as I'm concerned is the AGM's in two weeks. Do you have an insurance contingency to cover litigation? … OK … Oh, and Maurice, Maurice, ask your DOC to find out if this story shows up anywhere else … Call me back.

He hangs up.

… Excuse me.

MICHEL: So you're …

ALAIN: A lawyer.

ANNETTE: What about you?

MICHEL: Me, I have a wholesale company, household goods, and Véronique's a writer and works part-time in an art-history bookshop.

ANNETTE: A writer?

VÉRONIQUE: I contributed to a collection on the civilisation of Sheba, based on the excavations that were restarted at the end of the Ethiopian-Eritrean war. And I have a book coming out in January on the Darfur tragedy.

ANNETTE: So you specialise in Africa.

VÉRONIQUE: I'm very interested in that part of the world.

ANNETTE: Do you have any other children?

VÉRONIQUE: Bruno has a nine-year-old sister, Camille. Who's furious with her father because last night her father got rid of the hamster.

ANNETTE: You got rid of the hamster?

MICHEL: Yes. That hamster made the most appalling racket all night. Then it spent the whole day fast asleep. Bruno was in a very bad way, he was driven crazy by the noise that hamster made. As for me, to tell you the truth, I've been wanting to get rid of it for ages, so I said to myself, right, that's it. I took it and put it out in the street. I thought they loved drains and gutters and so on, but not a bit of it, it just sat there paralysed on the pavement. Well, they're not domestic animals, they're not wild animals, I don't know where their natural habitat is. Dump them in the woods, they're probably just as unhappy. I don't know where you're meant to put them.

ANNETTE: You left it outside?

VÉRONIQUE: He left it there and tried to convince Camille it had run away. But she wasn't having it.

ALAIN: And had the hamster vanished this morning?

MICHEL: Vanished.

VÉRONIQUE: And you, what field are you in?

ANNETTE: I'm in wealth-management.

VÉRONIQUE: Is it at all possible—forgive me for putting the question so bluntly— that Ferdinand might apologise to Bruno?

ALAIN: It'd be good if they talked.

ANNETTE: He has to apologise, Alain. He has to tell him he's sorry.

ALAIN: Yes, yes. Of course.

VÉRONIQUE: But is he sorry?

ALAIN: He realises what he's done. He just doesn't understand the implications. He's eleven.

VÉRONIQUE: If you're eleven, you're not a baby any more.

MICHEL: You're not an adult either! We haven't offered you anything—coffee, tea, is there any of that *clafoutis* left, Ronnie? It's an extraordinary *clafoutis*!

ALAIN: I wouldn't mind an espresso.

ANNETTE: Just some water.

MICHEL: (*to Véronique, on her way out*) Espresso for me too, darling, and bring the *clafoutis* anyway. (*After a hiatus.*) What I always say is, we're a lump of potter's clay and it's up to us to fashion something out of it. Perhaps it won't take shape till the very end. Who knows?

ANNETTE: Mm.

MICHEL: You have to taste the *clafoutis*. Good *clafoutis* is an endangered species.

ANNETTE: You're right.

ALAIN: What is it you sell?

MICHEL: Domestic hardware. Locks, doorknobs, soldering irons, all sorts of household goods, saucepans, frying pans …

ALAIN: Money in that, is there?

MICHEL: Well, you know, it's never exactly been a bonanza, it was pretty hard when we started. But provided I'm out there every day pushing my product, it rubs along. At least it's not seasonal, like textiles. Although we do sell a lot of *foie gras* pots in the run-up to Christmas!

ALAIN: I'm sure …

ANNETTE: When you saw the hamster sitting there, paralysed, why didn't you bring it back home?

MICHEL: Because I couldn't pick it up.

ANNETTE: You put it on the pavement.

MICHEL: I took it out in its cage and sort of tipped it out. I just can't touch rodents.

Véronique comes back with a tray. Drinks and the clafoutis.

VÉRONIQUE: I don't know who put the *clafoutis* in the fridge. Monica puts everything in the fridge, she won't be told. What's Ferdinand said to you? Sugar?

ALAIN: No, thanks. What's in the *clafoutis*?
VÉRONIQUE: Apples and pears.
ANNETTE: Apples and pears?
VÉRONIQUE: My own little recipe.

She cuts the clafoutis and distributes slices.

It's going to be too cold, shame.
ANNETTE: Apples and pears, this is a first.
VÉRONIQUE: Apples and pears, it's pretty textbook, but there's a trick to it.
ANNETTE: There is?
VÉRONIQUE: Pears need to be cut thicker than apples. Because pears cook faster than apples.
ANNETTE: Ah, of course.
MICHEL: But she's not telling you the real secret.
VÉRONIQUE: Let them try it.
ALAIN: Very good. It's very good.
ANNETTE: Tasty.
VÉRONIQUE: ... Gingerbread crumbs!
ANNETTE: Brilliant!
VÉRONIQUE: It's a version of the way they make *clafoutis* in Picardy. To be quite honest, I got it from his mother.
ALAIN: Gingerbread, delicious ... Well, at least all this has given us a new recipe.
VÉRONIQUE: I'd have preferred it if it hadn't cost my son two teeth.
ALAIN: Of course, that's what I meant.
ANNETTE: Strange way of expressing it.
ALAIN: Not at all, I ...

His mobile vibrates, he looks at the screen.

I have to take this ... Yes, Maurice ... No, no, don't ask for right of reply, you'll only feed the controversy ... Are you insured? ... Mm, mm ... What are these symptoms, what is ataxia? ... What about on a standard dose? ... How long have you known about this? ... And all that time you never recalled it? ... What's the turnover? ... Ah, yes. I see ... Right.

He hangs up and immediately dials another number, scoffing clafoutis all the while.

ANNETTE: Alain, do you mind joining us?

ALAIN: Yes, yes, I'm coming ... (*To the mobile.*) Serge? ... They've known about the risks for two years ... An internal report, but it didn't formally identify any undesirable side-effects ... No, they took no precautions, they didn't insure, not a word about it in the annual report ... Impaired motor skills, stability problems, in short you look permanently pissed ... (*He laughs along with his colleague.*) ... Turnover, a hundred and fifty million dollars ... Blanket denial ... Idiot wanted to demand a right of reply. We certainly don't want a right of reply—on the other hand if the story spreads we could put out a press release, say it's disinformation put about two weeks before the AGM. ... He's going to call me back ... OK.

He hangs up.

Actually I hardly had any lunch.

MICHEL: Help yourself, help yourself.

ALAIN: Thanks. I'm incorrigible. What were we saying?

VÉRONIQUE: That it would have been nicer to meet under different circumstances.

ALAIN: Oh, yes, right.

So the *clafoutis*, it's your mother's?

MICHEL: The recipe is my mother's, but Ronnie made this one.

VÉRONIQUE: Your mother doesn't mix pears and apples!

MICHEL: No.

VÉRONIQUE: Poor thing has to have an operation.

ANNETTE: Really? What for?

VÉRONIQUE: Her knee.

MICHEL: They're going to insert a rotatable prosthesis made of metal and polyethylene. She's wondering what's going to be left of it when she's cremated,

VÉRONIQUE: Don't be horrible.

MICHEL: She refuses to be buried next to my father. She wants to be cremated and put next to her mother who's all on her own down south. Two urns, looking out to sea, trying to get a word in edgeways. Ha, ha! ...

Smiles all round. Hiatus.

ANNETTE: We're very touched by your generosity. We appreciate the fact you're trying to calm the situation down rather than exacerbate it.

VÉRONIQUE: Frankly, it's the least we can do.

MICHEL: Yes!

ANNETTE: Not at all. How many parents standing up for their children become infantile themselves? If Bruno had broken two of Ferdinand's teeth, I'm afraid Alain and I would have been a good deal more thin-skinned about it. I'm not certain we'd have been so broad-minded.

MICHEL: Course you would!

ALAIN: She's right. By no means certain.

MICHEL: Oh, yes. Because we all know very well it might easily have been the other way round.

Hiatus.

VÉRONIQUE: So what does Ferdinand have to say about it? How does he view the situation?

ANNETTE: He's not saying much. I think he's still slightly in shock.

VÉRONIQUE: He understands that he's disfigured his playmate?

ALAIN: No. No, he does not understand that he's disfigured his playmate.

ANNETTE: Why are you saying that? Ferdinand understands very well!

ALAIN: He understands he's behaved like a thug, he does not understand that he's disfigured his playmate.

VÉRONIQUE: You don't care for the word, but the word is unfortunately accurate.

ALAIN: My son has not disfigured your son.

VÉRONIQUE: Your son has disfigured my son. Come back at five and have a look at his mouth and teeth.

MICHEL: Temporarily disfigured.

ALAIN: The swelling on his lip will go down, and as for his teeth, take him to the best dentist—I'm prepared to chip in …

MICHEL: That's what the insurance is for. What we'd like is for the boys to make up so that this sort of thing never happens again.

ANNETTE: Let's arrange a meeting.

MICHEL: Yes. That's the answer.

VÉRONIQUE: Should we be there?

ALAIN: They don't need to be coached. Just let them do it man to man.

ANNETTE: Man to man? Alain, don't be ridiculous. Having said that, we don't necessarily have to be there. It'd probably be better if we weren't, wouldn't it?

VÉRONIQUE: The question isn't whether we should be there or not. The question is, do they want to talk to one another, do they want to have a reckoning?

MICHEL: Bruno wants to.

VÉRONIQUE: What about Ferdinand?

ANNETTE: It's no use asking his opinion.

VÉRONIQUE: But it has to come from him.

ANNETTE: Ferdinand has behaved like a hooligan, we're not interested in what mood he's in.

VÉRONIQUE: If Ferdinand is forced to meet Bruno in a punitive context, I can't see the results would be very positive.

ALAIN: Madame, our son is a savage. To hope for any kind of spontaneous repentance would be fanciful. Right, I'm sorry, I have to get back to the office. You stay, Annette, you'll tell me what you've decided, I'm no use whichever way you cut it. Women always think you need a man, you need a father, as if they'd be the slightest use. Men are a dead weight, they're clumsy and maladjusted—oh, you can see a stretch of the overground metro, that's great!

ANNETTE: I'm really embarrassed, but I can't stay either … My husband has never exactly been a pushchair father!

VÉRONIQUE: What a pity. It's lovely, taking the baby for a walk. And it lasts such a short time. You always enjoyed taking care of the children, didn't you, Michel? You loved pushing the pushchair.

MICHEL: Yes, I did.

VÉRONIQUE: So what have we decided?

ANNETTE: Could you come by the house with Bruno about seven-thirty?

VÉRONIQUE: Seven-thirty? … What do you think, Michel?

MICHEL: Well … If I may …

ANNETTE: Go on.

MICHEL: I rather think Ferdinand ought to come here.

VÉRONIQUE: Yes, I agree.

MICHEL: I don't think it's for the victim to go traipsing around.

VÉRONIQUE: That's right.

ALAIN: Personally, I can't be anywhere at seven-thirty.

ANNETTE: Since you're no use, we won't be needing you.

VÉRONIQUE: All the same, it would be better if his father were here.

Alain's mobile vibrates.

ALAIN: All right, but then it can't be this evening. Hello? … There's no mention of this in the executive report. And no risk has been formally established. There's no evidence …

He hangs up.

VÉRONIQUE: Tomorrow?

ALAIN: I'm in The Hague tomorrow.

VÉRONIQUE: You're working in The Hague?

ALAIN: I have a case at the International Criminal Court.

ANNETTE: The main thing is that the children speak to one another. I'll bring Ferdinand here at seven-thirty and we can leave them to have their reckoning. No? You don't look very convinced.

VÉRONIQUE: If Ferdinand is not made aware of his responsibilities, they'll just look at each other like a pair of china dogs, it'll be a catastrophe.

ALAIN: What do you mean, madame? What do you mean, 'made aware of his responsibilities'?

VÉRONIQUE: I'm sure your son is not a savage.

ANNETTE: Of course Ferdinand isn't a savage.

ALAIN: Yes, he is.

ANNETTE: Alain, this is absurd, why say something like that?

ALAIN: He's a savage.

MICHEL: How does he explain his behaviour?

ANNETTE: He doesn't want to discuss it.

VÉRONIQUE: But he ought to discuss it.

ALAIN: He ought to do any number of things, madame. He ought to come here, he ought to discuss it, he ought to be sorry for it, clearly you have parenting skills that put us to shame, we hope to improve, but in the meantime, please bear with us.

MICHEL: Now, now! This is idiotic. Don't let's end up like this!

VÉRONIQUE: I'm only thinking of him, I'm only thinking of Ferdinand.

ALAIN: I got the message.

ANNETTE: Let's just sit down for another couple of minutes.

MICHEL: Another drop of coffee?

ALAIN: A coffee, OK.

ANNETTE: Then I'll have one too. Thanks.

MICHEL: That's all right, Ronnie, I'll do it.

Hiatus. Annette delicately shuffles some of the numerous art books dispersed around the coffee table.

ANNETTE: I see you're a great art-lover.

VÉRONIQUE: Art. Photographs. To some extent it's my job.

ANNETTE: I adore Bacon.

VÉRONIQUE: Ah, yes. Bacon.

ANNETTE: (*turning the pages*) … Cruelty. Majesty.

VÉRONIQUE: Chaos. Balance.

ANNETTE: That's right …

VÉRONIQUE: Is Ferdinand interested in art?

ANNETTE: Not as much as he should be … What about your children?

VÉRONIQUE: We try. We try to fill the gaps in the educational system.

ANNETTE: Yes …

VÉRONIQUE: We try to make them read. To take them to concerts and exhibitions. We're eccentric enough to believe in the pacifying abilities of culture!

ANNETTE: And you're right …

Michel comes back with the coffee.

MICHEL: *Clafoutis*, is it a cake or a tart? Serious question. I was just thinking in the kitchen—*Linzertorte*, for example, is that a tart? Come on, come on, you can't leave that one little slice.

VÉRONIQUE: *Clafoutis* is a cake. The pastry's not rolled out, it's mixed in with the fruit.

ALAIN: You really are a cook.

VÉRONIQUE: I love it. The thing about cooking is you have to love it. In my view, it's only the classic tart, that's to say on a pastry base, that deserves to be called a tart.

MICHEL: What about you, do you have other children?

ALAIN: A son from my first marriage.

MICHEL: I was wondering, not that it's at all important, what started the quarrel. Bruno won't say a blind word about it.

ANNETTE: Bruno refused to let Ferdinand join his gang.

VÉRONIQUE: Bruno has a gang?

ALAIN: He also called Ferdinand a grass.

VÉRONIQUE: Did you know Bruno had a gang?

MICHEL: No. Fantastic!

VÉRONIQUE: Why is it fantastic?

MICHEL: Because I had my own gang.

ALAIN: Me too.

VÉRONIQUE: And what does that entail?

MICHEL: There are five or six kids devoted to you and ready to sacrifice themselves. Like in *Spartacus*.

ALAIN: Absolutely, like in *Spartacus*!

VÉRONIQUE: Who knows about Spartacus these days?

ALAIN: They use a different model. Spiderman.

VÉRONIQUE: Anyway, clearly you know more than we do. Ferdinand hasn't been as silent as you led us to believe. And do we know why Bruno called him a grass? No, sorry, stupid, that's a stupid question. First of all, I couldn't care less, also it's beside the point.

ANNETTE: We can't get involved in children's quarrels.

VÉRONIQUE: And it's none of our business.

ANNETTE: No.

VÉRONIQUE: On the other hand, what is our business is what unfortunately happened. Violence is always our business.

MICHEL: When I was leader of my gang, when I was twelve, I fought Didier Leglu, who was bigger than me, in single combat.

VÉRONIQUE: What are you talking about, Michel? What's that got to do with it?

MICHEL: No, you're right, it's got nothing to do with it.

VÉRONIQUE: We're not discussing single combat. The children weren't fighting.

MICHEL: I know, I know. I just suddenly had this memory.

ALAIN: There's not that big a difference.

VÉRONIQUE: Oh, yes, there is. Excuse me, monsieur, there's a very big difference.

MICHEL: There's a very big difference.

ALAIN: What?

MICHEL: With Didier Leghu, we'd agreed to have a fight.

ALAIN: Did you beat the shit out of him?

MICHEL: Up to a point.

VÉRONIQUE: Right, shall we forget Didier Leglu? Would you allow me to speak to Ferdinand?

ANNETTE: By all means!

VÉRONIQUE: I wouldn't want to do it without your permission.

ANNETTE: Speak to him. What could be more natural?

ALAIN: Good luck.

ANNETTE: Stop it, Alain. I don't understand you.

ALAIN: Madame thinks …

VÉRONIQUE: Véronique. This will work out better if we stop calling each other 'madame' and 'monsieur'.

ALAIN: Véronique, you're motivated by an educational impulse, which is very sympathetic …

VÉRONIQUE: If you don't want me to speak to him, I won't speak to him.

ALAIN: No, speak to him, read him the riot act, do what you like.

VÉRONIQUE: I don't understand why you don't seem to care about this.

ALAIN: Madame …

MICHEL: Véronique.

ALAIN: Of course I care, Véronique, enormously. My son has injured another child …

VÉRONIQUE: On purpose.

ALAIN: See, that's the kind of remark that puts my back up. Obviously, on purpose.

VÉRONIQUE: But that makes all the difference.

ALAIN: The difference between what and what? That's what we're talking about. Our son picked up a stick and hit your son. That's why we're here, isn't it?

ANNETTE: This is pointless.

MICHEL: Yes, she's right, this kind of argument is pointless.

ALAIN: Why do you feel the need to slip in 'on purpose'? What kind of message is that supposed to be sending me?

ANNETTE: Listen, we're on a slippery slope, my husband is desperate about all sorts of other things. I'll come back this evening with Ferdinand and we'll let things sort themselves out naturally.

ALAIN: I'm not in the least desperate.

ANNETTE: Well, I am.

MICHEL: There's nothing to be desperate about.

ANNETTE: Yes, there is.

Alain's mobile vibrates.

ALAIN: Don't make any statement … No comment … No, of course you mustn't take it off the market! If you take it off the market, you become responsible … The minute you take Antril off the market, you're admitting liability! There's nothing in the annual accounts. If you want to be sued for falsifying the executive report and given the elbow in two weeks' time, take it off the market …

VÉRONIQUE: Last year, on Open Day, wasn't it Ferdinand who played Monsieur de … ?

ANNETTE: Monsieur de Pourceaugnac.

VÉRONIQUE: Monsieur de Pourceaugnac.

ALAIN: We'll think about the victims later, Maurice … Let's see what the shares do after the AGM …

VÉRONIQUE: He was extraordinary.

ANNETTE: Yes …

ALAIN: We are not going to take the medicine off the market just because two or three people are bumping into the furniture! … Don't make any statements for the time being … Yes. I'll call you back …

He cuts him off and phones his colleague.

VÉRONIQUE: I remember him very clearly in *Monsieur de Pourceaugnac*. Do you remember him, Michel?

MICHEL: Yes, yes …

VÉRONIQUE: He was hilarious when he was in drag.

ANNETTE: Yes …

ALAIN: (*to his colleague*) … They're panicking, they've got the media up their arse, you have to prepare a press release, not something defensive, not at all, on the contrary, go out all guns blazing, you insist that Verenz-Pharma is the victim of a destabilisation attempt two weeks before its Annual General Meeting, where does this paper come from, why should it have fallen out of the sky just now, etcetera and so on … Don't say anything about health problems, just ask one question: who's behind this report? … Right.

He hangs up. Brief hiatus.

MICHEL: They're terrible, these pharmaceutical companies. Profit, profit, profit.

ALAIN: You're not supposed to be listening to my conversation.

MICHEL: You're not obliged to have it in front of me.

ALAIN: Yes, I am. I'm absolutely obliged to have it here. Not my choice, I can assure you.

MICHEL: They dump any old crap on you without giving it a second thought.

ALAIN: In the therapeutic field, every advance brings with it risk as well as benefit.

MICHEL: Yes, I understand that. All the same. Funny job you've got.

ALAIN: Meaning?

VÉRONIQUE: Michel, this is nothing to do with us.

MICHEL: Funny job.

ALAIN: And what is it you do?

MICHEL: I have an ordinary job.

ALAIN: What is an ordinary job?

MICHEL: I told you, I sell saucepans.

ALAIN: And doorknobs.

MICHEL: And toilet fittings. Loads of other things.

ALAIN: Ah, toilet fittings. Now we're talking. That's really interesting.

ANNETTE: Alain.

ALAIN: It's really interesting. I'm interested in toilet fittings.

MICHEL: Why shouldn't you be?

ALAIN: How many types are there?

MICHEL: Two different systems. Push-button or overhead flush.

ALAIN: I see.

MICHEL: Depending on the feed.

ALAIN: Well, yes.

MICHEL: Either the water comes down from above or up from under.

ALAIN: Yes.

MICHEL: I could introduce you to one of my warehousemen who specialises in this kind of thing, if you like. You'd have to leg it out to Saint-Denis la Plaine.

ALAIN: You seem to be very much on top of the subject.

VÉRONIQUE: Are you intending to punish Ferdinand in any way? You can carry on with the plumbing in some more appropriate setting.

ANNETTE: I'm not feeling well.

VÉRONIQUE: What's the matter?

ALAIN: Yes, you're very pale, sweetheart.

MICHEL: Palish, certainly.

ANNETTE: I feel sick.

VÉRONIQUE: Sick? … I have some Moxalon …

ANNETTE: No, no … It'll be all right …

VÉRONIQUE: What could we … ? Coke. Coke's very good.

She immediately sets off in search of it.

ANNETTE: It'll be all right …

MICHEL: Walk around a bit. Take a few steps.

She takes a few steps. Véronique comes back with the Coca-Cola.

ANNETTE: Really? You think so? …

VÉRONIQUE: Yes, yes. Small sips.

ANNETTE: Thank you …

Alain has discreetly called his office.

ALAIN: … Give me Serge, will you, please? … Oh, right … Ask him to call me back, ask him to call me back right away …

He hangs up.

It's good, is it, Coca-Cola? I thought it was just supposed to be for diarrhoea.

VÉRONIQUE: Not only for that. (*To Annette.*) All right?

ANNETTE: All right … Véronique, if we want to reprimand our child, we'll do it in our own way and without having to account to anybody.

MICHEL: Absolutely.

VÉRONIQUE: What do you mean, 'absolutely', Michel?

MICHEL: They can do whatever they like with their son, it's their prerogative.

VÉRONIQUE: I don't think so.

MICHEL: What do you mean, you don't think so, Ronnie?

VÉRONIQUE: I don't think it is their prerogative.

ALAIN: Really? Explain.

His mobile vibrates.

I'm sorry … (*To his colleague.*) Excellent … But don't forget, nothing's been proved, there's nothing definite … Get this straight, if anyone fucks up, Maurice is a dead man in two weeks, and us with him.

ANNETTE: That's enough, Alain! That's enough now with the mobile! Will you pay attention to what's going on here, shit!

ALAIN: Yes … Call me back and read it to me.

He hangs up.

What's the matter with you, have you gone mad, shouting like that? Serge heard everything.

ANNETTE: Good! Drives me mad, that mobile, endlessly!

ALAIN: Listen, Annette, I'm already doing you a big favour being here in the first place …

VÉRONIQUE: Extraordinary thing to say.

ANNETTE: I'm going to throw up.

ALAIN: No, you're not, you are not going to throw up.

ANNETTE: Yes, I am …

MICHEL: Do you want to go to the lavatory?

ANNETTE: (*to Alain*) No one's forcing you to stay.

VÉRONIQUE: No, no one's forcing him to stay.

ANNETTE: I'm feeling dizzy …

ALAIN: Stare at a fixed point. Stare at a fixed point, Woof-woof.

ANNETTE: Go away, leave me alone.

VÉRONIQUE: She would be better off in the lavatory.

ALAIN: Go to the lavatory. Go to the lavatory if you want to throw up.

MICHEL: Give her some Moxalon.

ALAIN: You don't suppose it could be the *clafoutis*?

VÉRONIQUE: It was made yesterday!

ANNETTE: (*to Alain*) Don't touch me! …

ALAIN: Calm down, Woof-woof.

MICHEL: Please, why get worked up about nothing?

ANNETTE: According to my husband, everything to do with house, school or garden is my department.

ALAIN: No, it's not!

ANNETTE: Yes, it is. And I understand why. It's deathly, all that. It's deathly.

VÉRONIQUE: If it's so deathly, why have children in the first place?

MICHEL: Maybe Ferdinand senses your lack of interest.

ANNETTE: What lack of interest?

MICHEL: You just said …

Annette vomits violently. A brutal and catastrophic spray, part of which goes over Alain. The art books on the coffee table are likewise deluged.

Go and fetch a bowl, go and fetch a bowl!

Véronique runs out to look for a bowl and Michel hands her the coffee tray, just in case. Annette retches again, but nothing comes out.

ALAIN: You should have gone to the lavatory, Woof-woof, this is ridiculous!

MICHEL: Your suit's definitely copped it!

Very soon, Véronique is back with a basin and a cloth. The basin is given to Annette.

VÉRONIQUE: Well, it's certainly not the *clafoutis*, it couldn't possibly be.

MICHEL: It's not the *clafoutis,* it's nerves. This is pure nerves.

VÉRONIQUE: (*to Alain*) Would you like to clean up in the bathroom? Oh, no, the Kokoschka! Oh, my God!

Annette vomits bile into the basin.

MICHEL: Give her some Moxalon.

VÉRONIQUE: Not now, she can't keep anything down.

ALAIN: Where's the bathroom?

VÉRONIQUE: I'll show you.

Véronique and Alain leave.

MICHEL: It's nerves. It's a panic attack. You're a mum, Annette. Whether you want to be or not. I understand why you feel desperate.

ANNETTE: Mmm.

MICHEL: What I always say is, you can't control the things that control you.

ANNETTE: Mmm …

MICHEL: With me, it's the cervical vertebrae. The vertebrae seize up.

ANNETTE: Mmm …

She brings up a little more bile. Véronique returns with another basin, containing a sponge.

VÉRONIQUE: What are we going to do about the Kokoschka?

MICHEL: Well, I would spray it with Mr Clean … The problem is how to dry it … Or else you could sponge it down and put a bit of perfume on it.

VÉRONIQUE: Perfume?

MICHEL: Use my Kouros, I never wear it.

VÉRONIQUE: It'll warp.

MICHEL: We could run the hair-dryer over it and flatten it out under a pile of other books. Or iron it like they do with banknotes.

VÉRONIQUE: Oh, my God …

ANNETTE: I'll buy you another one.

VÉRONIQUE: You can't find it! It went out of print years ago!

ANNETTE: I'm terribly sorry …

MICHEL: We'll salvage it. Let me do it, Ronnie.

She hands him the basin of water and the sponge, disgusted. Michel gets started on cleaning up the book.

VÉRONIQUE: It's a reprint of the catalogue from the '53 London exhibition, more than twenty years old! …

MICHEL: Go and get the hair-dryer. And the Kouros. In the towel cupboard.

VÉRONIQUE: Her husband's in the bathroom.

MICHEL: Well, he's not stark naked, is he?

She goes out as he continues to clean up.

... There, that's the worst of it. *The People of the Tundra* needs a bit of a wipe … I'll be back.

He goes out with the used basin. Véronique and Michel return more or less simultaneously. She has the bottle of perfume, he has the basin containing fresh water. Michel finishes cleaning up.

VÉRONIQUE: (*to Annette*) Feeling better?
ANNETTE: Yes …
VÉRONIQUE: Shall I spray?
MICHEL: Where's the hair-dryer?
VÉRONIQUE: He's bringing it when he's finished with it.
MICHEL: We'll wait for him. We'll put the Kouros on last thing.
ANNETTE: Can I use the bathroom as well?
VÉRONIQUE: Yes. Yes, yes. Of course.
ANNETTE: I can't tell you how sorry I am …

Véronique takes her out and returns immediately.

VÉRONIQUE: What a nightmare! Horrible!
MICHEL: Tell you what, he'd better not push me much further.
VÉRONIQUE: She's dreadful as well.
MICHEL: Not as bad.
VÉRONIQUE: She's a phoney.
MICHEL: Less irritating.
VÉRONIQUE: They're both dreadful! Why do you keep siding with them?

She sprays the tulips.

MICHEL: I don't keep siding with them, what are you talking about?
VÉRONIQUE: You keep vacillating, trying to play both ends against the middle.
MICHEL: Not at all!
VÉRONIQUE: Yes, you do. Going on about your triumphs as a gang leader, telling them they're free to do whatever they like with their son when the child is a public menace—when a child's a public menace, it's everybody's concern, I can't believe she puked all over my books!

She sprays the Kokoschka.

MICHEL: (*pointing*) Put some on *The People of the Tundra*.

VÉRONIQUE: If you think you're about to spew, you go to the proper place.

MICHEL: … And the Foujita.

VÉRONIQUE: (*spraying everything*) This is disgusting.

MICHEL: I was pushing it a bit with the shithouse systems.

VÉRONIQUE: You were brilliant.

MICHEL: Good answers, don't you think?

VÉRONIQUE: Brilliant. The warehouseman was brilliant.

MICHEL: What an arsehole. And what did he call her?! …

VÉRONIQUE: Woof-woof.

MICHEL: That's right, 'Woof-woof!'

VÉRONIQUE: Woof-woof!

They both laugh. Alain returns, hair-dryer in hand.

ALAIN: That's right, I call her Woof-woof.

VÉRONIQUE: Oh … I'm sorry, I didn't mean to be rude … It's so easy to make fun of other people's nicknames! What about us, what do we call each other, Michel? Far worse, isn't it?

ALAIN: Were you wanting the hair-dryer?

VÉRONIQUE: Thank you.

MICHEL: Thank you.

He takes the hair-dryer.

We call each other 'darjeeling', like the tea. Far more ridiculous, if you ask me!

Michel switches on the machine and starts drying the hooks. Véronique flattens out the damp pages.

Smooth them out, smooth them out.

VÉRONIQUE: (*as she smooths out the pages, raising her voice above the noise*) How's the poor thing feeling, better?

ALAIN: Better.

VÉRONIQUE: I reacted very badly, I'm ashamed of myself.

ALAIN: Not at all.

VÉRONIQUE: I just steamrollered her about my catalogue, I can't believe I did that.

MICHEL: Turn the page. Stretch it out, stretch it out properly.

ALAIN: You're going to tear it.

VÉRONIQUE: You're right … That's enough, Michel, it's dry. Objects can become ridiculously important, half the time you can't even remember why.

Michel shuts the catalogue and they both cover it with a little cairn of heavy books. Michel finishes drying the Foujita, The People of the Tundra, *etc. …*

MICHEL: There we are! Good as new. Where does 'Woof-woof' come from?
ALAIN: 'How much is that doggie in the window?'
MICHEL: I know it! (*He sings.*) 'The one with the waggly tail.'
ALAIN: 'Woof-woof.'
MICHEL: Ha, ha! … Ours comes from our honeymoon in India. Idiotic, really!
VÉRONIQUE: Shouldn't I go and see how she is?
MICHEL: Off you go, darjeeling.
VÉRONIQUE: Shall I? …

Annette returns.

… Ah, Annette! I was worried about you … Are you feeling better?
ANNETTE: I think so.
ALAIN: If you're not sure, stay away from the coffee table.
ANNETTE: I left the towel in the bathtub, I wasn't sure where to put it.
VÉRONIQUE: Perfect.
ANNETTE: You've cleaned it all up. I'm so sorry.
MICHEL: Everything's great. Everything's in order.
VÉRONIQUE: Annette, forgive me, I've taken hardly any notice of you. I've been obsessed with my Kokoschka.
ANNETTE: Don't worry about it.
VÉRONIQUE: The way I reacted, very bad of me.
ANNETTE: Not at all … (*After an embarrassed hiatus.*) Something occurred to me in the bathroom …
VÉRONIQUE: Yes?
ANNETTE: Perhaps we skated too hastily over …
I mean, what I mean is …
MICHEL: Say it, Annette, say it.
ANNETTE: An insult is also a kind of assault.
MICHEL: Of course it is.
VÉRONIQUE: Well, that depends, Michel.
MICHEL: Yes, it depends.

ANNETTE: Ferdinand's never shown any signs of violence. He wouldn't have done that without a reason.

ALAIN: He got called a grass!

His mobile vibrates.

I'm sorry! …

He moves to one side, making elaborately apologetic signs to Annette.

… Yes … As long as there aren't any statements from victims. We don't want any victims. I don't want you being quoted alongside victims! … A blanket denial and if necessary attack the newspaper … They'll fax you a draft of the press release, Maurice.

He bangs up.

If anyone calls me a grass, I'm liable to get annoyed.

MICHEL: Unless it's true.

ALAIN: What did you say?

MICHEL: I mean, suppose it's justified?

ANNETTE: My son is a grass?

MICHEL: Course not, I was joking.

ANNETTE: Yours is as well, if that's to be the way of it.

MICHEL: What do you mean, ours is as well?

ANNETTE: Well, he did identify Ferdinand.

MICHEL: Because we insisted!

VÉRONIQUE: Michel, this is completely beside the point.

ANNETTE: What's the difference? Whether you insisted or not, he gave you the name.

ALAIN: Annette.

ANNETTE: Annette what? (*To Michel.*) You think my son is a grass?

MICHEL: I don't think anything.

ANNETTE: Well, if you don't think anything, don't say anything. Stop making these insinuations.

VÉRONIQUE: Let's stay calm, Annette. Michel and I are making an effort to be reasonable and moderate …

ANNETTE: Not that moderate.

VÉRONIQUE: Oh, really? What do you mean?

ANNETTE: Moderate on the surface.

ALAIN: I really have to go. Woof-woof …

ANNETTE: All right, go on, be a coward.

ALAIN: Annette, right now I'm risking my most important client, so this responsible parent routine …

VÉRONIQUE: My son has lost two teeth. Two incisors.

ALAIN: Yes, yes, I think we all got that.

VÉRONIQUE: One of them for good.

ALAIN: He'll have new ones, we'll give him new ones! Better ones! It's not as if he's burst an eardrum!

ANNETTE: We're making a mistake not to take into account the origin of the problem.

VÉRONIQUE: There's no origin. There's just an eleven-year-old child hitting someone. With a stick.

ALAIN: Armed with a stick.

MICHEL: We withdrew that word.

ALAIN: You withdrew it because we objected to it.

MICHEL: We withdrew it without any protest.

ALAIN: A word deliberately designed to rule out error or clumsiness, to rule out childhood.

VÉRONIQUE: I'm not sure I'm able to take much more of this tone of voice.

ALAIN: You and I have had trouble seeing eye to eye right from the start.

VÉRONIQUE: There's nothing more detestable than to be attacked for something you yourself consider a mistake. The word 'armed' was inappropriate, so we changed it. Although, if you stick to the strict definition of the word, its use is far from inaccurate.

ANNETTE: Ferdinand was insulted and he reacted. If I'm attacked, I defend myself, especially if I find myself alone, confronted by a gang.

MICHEL: Puking seems to have perked you up.

ANNETTE: Are you aware how crude that sounds?

MICHEL: We're people of good will. All four of us, I'm sure. Why let these irritants, these pointless aggravations push us over the edge? …

VÉRONIQUE: Oh, Michel, that's enough! Let's stop beating about the bush. If all we are is moderate on the surface, let's forget it, shall we!

MICHEL: No, no, I refuse to allow myself to slide down that slope.

ALAIN: What slope?

MICHEL: The deplorable slope those two little bastards have perched us on! There, I've said it!

ALAIN: I'm not sure Ronnie has quite the same outlook.

VÉRONIQUE: Véronique!

ALAIN: Sorry.

VÉRONIQUE: So Bruno's a little bastard now, is he, poor child. That's the last straw!

ALAIN: Right, well, I really do have to leave you.

ANNETTE: Me too.

VÉRONIQUE: Go on, go, I give up.

The Vallon telephone rings.

MICHEL: Hello? … Oh, Mum … No, no, we're with some friends, but tell me about it … Yes, do whatever the doctor wants you to do … They've given you Antril?! Wait a minute, Mum, wait a minute, don't go away … (*To Alain.*) Antril's your crap, isn't it? My mother's taking it!

ALAIN: Thousands of people take it.

MICHEL: You stop taking that stuff right now. Do you hear what I'm saying, Mum? Immediately … Don't argue, I'll explain later … Tell Dr Perolo I'm forbidding you to take it … Why luminous? … So that you can be seen? … That's completely ridiculous … All right, we'll talk about it later. Lots of love, Mum. I'll call you back.

He hangs up.

She's hired luminous crutches, so she doesn't get knocked down by a truck. As if someone in her condition would be strolling down the motorway in the middle of the night. They've given her Antril for her blood pressure.

ALAIN: If she takes it and stays normal, I'll have her called as a witness. Didn't I have a scarf? Ah, there it is.

MICHEL: I do not appreciate your cynicism. If my mother displays the most minor symptom, I'll be initiating a class action.

ALAIN: Oh, that'll happen anyway.

MICHEL: So I should hope.

ANNETTE: Goodbye, madame …

VÉRONIQUE: Behaving well gets you nowhere. Courtesy is a waste of time, it weakens you and undermines you …

ALAIN: Right, come on, Annette, let's go, enough preaching and sermons for today.

MICHEL: Go on, go. But can I just say one thing: having met you two, it's pretty clear that for what's-his-name, Ferdinand, there are mitigating circumstances.

ANNETTE: When you murdered that hamster …

MICHEL: Murdered?!

ANNETTE: Yes.

MICHEL: I murdered the hamster?!

ANNETTE: Yes. You've done your best to make us feel guilty, but your virtue went straight out the window once you decided to be a killer.

MICHEL: I absolutely did not murder that hamster!

ANNETTE: Worse. You left it, shivering with terror, in a hostile environment. That poor hamster is bound to have been eaten by a dog or a rat.

VÉRONIQUE: It's true! That is true!

MICHEL: What do you mean, 'that is true'?

VÉRONIQUE: It's true. What do you expect me to say? It's appalling what must have happened to that creature.

MICHEL: I thought the hamster would be happy to be liberated. I thought it was going to run off down the gutter jumping for joy!

VÉRONIQUE: Well, it didn't.

ANNETTE: And you abandoned it.

MICHEL: I can't touch those things! For fuck's sake, Ronnie, you know very well, I'm incapable of touching that whole species!

VÉRONIQUE: He has a phobia about rodents.

MICHEL: That's right, I'm frightened of rodents, I'm terrified of snakes, anything close to the ground, I have absolutely no rapport with! So that's the end of it!

ALAIN: (*to Véronique*) And you, why didn't you go out and look for it?

VÉRONIQUE: Because I had no idea what had happened! Michel didn't tell us, me and the children, that the hamster had escaped till the following morning. I went out immediately, immediately, I walked round the block, I even went down to the cellar.

MICHEL: Véronique, I find it intolerable to be in the dock all of a sudden for this hamster saga that you've seen fit to reveal. It's a personal matter which is nobody else's business but ours and which has nothing to do with the present situation! And I find it incomprehensible to be called a killer! In my own home!

VÉRONIQUE: What's your home got to do with it?

MICHEL: My home, the doors of which I have opened, the doors of which I have opened wide in a spirit of reconciliation, to people who ought to be grateful to me for it!

ALAIN: It's wonderful the way you keep patting yourself on the back.

ANNETTE: Don't you feel any guilt?

MICHEL: I feel no guilt whatsoever. I've always found that creature repulsive. I'm ecstatic that it's gone.

VÉRONIQUE: Michel, that is ridiculous.

MICHEL: What's ridiculous? Have you gone crazy as well? Their son bashes up Bruno, and I get shat on because of a hamster?

VÉRONIQUE: You behaved very badly with that hamster, you can't deny it.

MICHEL: Fuck the hamster!

VÉRONIQUE: You won't be able to say that to your daughter this evening.

MICHEL: Bring her on! I'm not going to let myself be told how to behave by some nine-year-old bruiser.

ALAIN: Hundred per cent behind you there.

VÉRONIQUE: Pathetic.

MICHEL: Careful, Véronique, you be careful, I've been extremely restrained up to now, but I'm two inches away from crossing that line.

ANNETTE: And what about Bruno?

MICHEL: What about Bruno?

ANNETTE: Isn't he upset?

MICHEL: If you ask me, Bruno has other problems.

VÉRONIQUE: Bruno was less attached to Nibbles.

MICHEL: Grotesque name as well!

ANNETTE: If you feel no guilt, why do you expect our son to feel any?

MICHEL: Let me tell you this, I'm up to here with these idiotic discussions. We tried to be nice, we bought tulips, my wife passed me off as a lefty, but the truth is, I can't keep this up any more, I'm fundamentally uncouth.

ALAIN: Aren't we all?

VÉRONIQUE: No. No. I'm sorry, we are not all fundamentally uncouth.

ALAIN: Well, not you, obviously.

VÉRONIQUE: No, not me, thank the Lord.

MICHEL: Not you, darjee, not you, you're a fully evolved woman, you're skid-resistant.

VÉRONIQUE: Why are you attacking me?

MICHEL: I'm not attacking you. Quite the opposite.

VÉRONIQUE: Yes, you're attacking me, you know you are.

MICHEL: You organised this little get-together, I just let myself be recruited …

VÉRONIQUE: You let yourself be recruited?

MICHEL: Yes.

VÉRONIQUE: That's detestable.

MICHEL: Not at all. You stand up for civilisation, that's completely to your credit.

VÉRONIQUE: Exactly, I'm standing up for civilisation! And it's lucky there are people prepared to do that! (*She's on the brink of tears.*) You think being fundamentally uncouth's a better idea?

ALAIN: Come on now, come on …

VÉRONIQUE: (*as above*) Is it normal to criticise someone for not being fundamentally uncouth? ...

ANNETTE: No one's saying that. No one's criticising you.

VÉRONIQUE: Yes, they are! ...

She bursts into tears.

ALAIN: No, they're not!

VÉRONIQUE: What were we supposed to do? Sue you? Not speak to one another and try to slaughter each other with insurance claims?

MICHEL: Stop it, Ronnie ...

VÉRONIQUE: Stop what?! ...

MICHEL: You've got things out of proportion ...

VÉRONIQUE: I don't give a shit! You force yourself to rise above petty-mindedness ... and you finish up humiliated and completely on your own ...

Alain's mobile has vibrated.

ALAIN: ... Yes ... 'Let them prove it!' ... 'Prove it' ... but if you ask me, best not to answer at all ...

MICHEL: We're always on our own! Everywhere! Who'd like a drop of rum?

ALAIN: ... Maurice, I'm in a meeting, I'll call you back from the office ...

He cuts the line.

VÉRONIQUE: So there we are! I'm living with someone who's totally negative.

ALAIN: Who's negative?

MICHEL: I am.

VÉRONIQUE: This was the worst idea! We should never have arranged this meeting!

MICHEL: I told you.

VÉRONIQUE: You told me?

MICHEL: Yes.

VÉRONIQUE: You told me you didn't want to have this meeting?!

MICHEL: I didn't think it was a good idea.

ANNETTE: It was a good idea ...

MICHEL: Oh, please! ...

He raises the bottle of rum.

Anybody?

VÉRONIQUE: You told me it wasn't a good idea, Michel?!

MICHEL: Think so.

VÉRONIQUE: You think so!

ALAIN: Wouldn't mind a little drop.

ANNETTE: Didn't you have to go?

ALAIN: I could manage a small glass, now we've got this far.

Michel pours a glass for Alain.

VÉRONIQUE: You look me in the eye and tell me we weren't in complete agreement about this!

ANNETTE: Calm down, Véronique, calm down, this is pointless …

VÉRONIQUE: Who stopped anyone touching the *clafoutis* this morning? Who said, 'Let's keep the rest of the *clafoutis* for the Reilles'?! Who said it?!

ALAIN: That was nice.

MICHEL: What's that got to do with it?

VÉRONIQUE: What do you mean, 'what's that got to do with it'?

MICHEL: If you invite people, you invite people.

VÉRONIQUE: You're a liar, you're a liar! He's a liar!

ALAIN: You know, speaking personally, my wife had to drag me here. When you're brought up with a kind of John Wayne-ish idea of virility, you don't want to settle this kind of problem with a lot of yakking.

Michel laughs.

ANNETTE: I thought your model was Spartacus.

ALAIN: Same family.

MICHEL: Analogous.

VÉRONIQUE: Analogous! Are there no lengths you won't go to humiliate yourself, Michel?

ANNETTE: Obviously it was pointless dragging you here.

ALAIN: What were you hoping for, Woof-woof? It's true, it's a ludicrous nickname— were you hoping for a glimpse of universal harmony? This rum is terrific.

MICHEL: It is, isn't it? *Coeur de Chauffe*, fifteen years old, direct from Santa Rosa.

VÉRONIQUE: And the tulips, whose idea was that? I said it's a shame the tulips are finished, I didn't say rush down to Mouton-Duvernet at the crack of dawn.

ANNETTE: Don't work yourself up into this state, Véronique, it's crazy.

VÉRONIQUE: The tulips were his idea! Entirely his idea! Aren't we allowed a drink?

ANNETTE: Yes, Véronique, and I would like one too. By the way, it's quite amusing, someone descended from Spartacus and John Wayne who can't even pick up a mouse.

MICHEL: Will you shut up about that hamster! Shut up! ...

He gives Annette a glass of rum.

VÉRONIQUE: Ha, ha! You're right, it's laughable!

ANNETTE: What about her?

MICHEL: I don't think she needs any.

VÉRONIQUE: Give me a drink, Michel.

MICHEL: No.

VÉRONIQUE: Michel!

MICHEL: No.

Véronique tries to snatch the bottle out of his hands. Michel resists.

ANNETTE: What's the matter with you, Michel?!

MICHEL: All right, there you are, take it. Drink, drink, who cares?

ANNETTE: Is alcohol bad for you?

VÉRONIQUE: It's wonderful.

She slumps.

ALAIN: Right ... Well, I don't know ...

VÉRONIQUE: (*to Alain*) ... Listen, monsieur ...

ANNETTE: Alain.

VÉRONIQUE: Alain, we're not exactly soul-mates, you and me, but, you see, I live with a man who's decided, once and for all, that life is second rate. It's very difficult living with a man who comforts himself with that thought, who doesn't want anything to change, who can't work up any enthusiasm about anything ...

MICHEL: He doesn't give a fuck. He doesn't give a fuck about any of that.

VÉRONIQUE: You have to believe ... you have to believe in the possibility of improvement, don't you?

MICHEL: He's the last person you should be telling all this.

VÉRONIQUE: I'll talk to who I like, for fuck's sake!

The telephone rings.

MICHEL: Who the fuck's this now? … Yes, Mum … He's fine. I say he's fine, he's lost his teeth, but he's fine … Yes, he's in pain. He's in pain, but it'll pass. Mum, I'm busy, I'll call you back.

ANNETTE: He's still in pain?

VÉRONIQUE: No.

ANNETTE: Then why worry your mother?

VÉRONIQUE: He can't help himself. He always has to worry her.

MICHEL: Right, that's enough, Véronique! What is this psychodrama?

ALAIN: Véronique, are we ever interested in anything but ourselves? Of course we'd all like to believe in the possibility of improvement. Of which we could be the architect and which would be in no way self-serving. Does such a thing exist? Some people drag their feet, it's their strategy, others refuse to acknowledge the passing of time, and drive themselves demented—what difference does it make? People struggle until they're dead. Education, the miseries of the world … You're writing a book about Darfur, fine, I can understand you saying to yourself, right, I'm going to choose a massacre, what else does history consist of, and I'm going to write about it. You do what you can to save yourself.

VÉRONIQUE: I'm not writing the book to save myself. You haven't read it, you don't know what it's about.

ALAIN: It makes no difference.

Hiatus.

VÉRONIQUE: Terrible stink of Kouros! …

MICHEL: Ghastly.

ALAIN: You certainly laid it on.

ANNETTE: I'm sorry.

VÉRONIQUE: Not your fault. I was the one spraying like a lunatic … Anyway, why can't we take things more lightly, why does everything always have to be so exhausting? …

ALAIN: You think too much. Women think too much.

ANNETTE: There's an original remark, I bet that's thrown you for a loop.

VÉRONIQUE: 'Think too much', I don't know what that means. And I don't see the point of existence without some kind of moral conception of the world.

MICHEL: See what I have to live with?

VÉRONIQUE: Shut up! Will you shut up?! I detest this pathetic complicity! You disgust me.

MICHEL: Come on, have a sense of humour.

VÉRONIQUE: I don't have a sense of humour. And I have no intention of acquiring one.

MICHEL: What I always say is, marriage: the most terrible ordeal God can inflict on you.

ANNETTE: Great.

MICHEL: Marriage and children.

ANNETTE: There's no call for you to share your views with us, Michel. As a matter of fact, I find it slightly indecent.

VÉRONIQUE: That's not going to worry him.

MICHEL: You mean you don't agree?

ANNETTE: These observations are irrelevant. Alain, say something.

ALAIN: He's entitled to his opinions.

ANNETTE: Yes, but he doesn't have to broadcast them.

ALAIN: Well, yes, perhaps …

ANNETTE: We don't give a damn about their marriage. We're here to settle a problem to do with our children, we don't give a damn about their marriage.

ALAIN: Yes, but …

ANNETTE: But what? What do you mean?

ALAIN: There's a connection.

MICHEL: There's a connection! Of course there's a connection.

VÉRONIQUE: There's a connection between Bruno having his teeth broken and our marriage?!

MICHEL: Obviously.

ANNETTE: We're not with you.

MICHEL: Children consume and fracture our lives. Children drag us towards disaster, it's unavoidable. When you see those laughing couples casting off into the sea of matrimony, you say to yourself, they have no idea, poor things, they just have no idea, they're happy. No one tells you anything when you start out. I have an old school pal who's just about to have a child with his new girlfriend. I said to him, 'A child, at our age, are you insane?' The ten or a dozen good years left to us before we get cancer or a stroke, and you're going to bugger yourself up with some brat?

ANNETTE: You don't really believe what you're saying.

VÉRONIQUE: He does.

MICHEL: Of course I believe it. Worse, even.

VÉRONIQUE: Yes.

ANNETTE: You're demeaning yourself, Michel.

MICHEL: Is that right? Ha, ha!

ANNETTE: Stop crying, Véronique, you can see it only encourages him.

MICHEL: (*to Alain, who's refilling his empty glass*) Help yourself, help yourself—exceptional, isn't it?

ALAIN: Exceptional.

MICHEL: Could I offer you a cigar? …

VÉRONIQUE: No, no cigars!

ALAIN: Pity.

ANNETTE: You're not proposing to smoke a cigar, Alain!

ALAIN: I shall do what I like, Annette, if I feel like accepting a cigar, I shall accept a cigar. If I'm not smoking, it's because I don't want to upset Véronique, who's already completely lost it. She's right, stop snivelling, when a woman cries, a man is immediately provoked to the worst excesses. Added to which, Michel's point of view is, I'm sorry to say, entirely sound.

His mobile vibrates.

… Yes, Serge … Go ahead … Put Paris, the date … and the exact time …

ANNETTE: This is hideous!

ALAIN: (*moving aside and muffling his voice to escape her fury*) … Whatever time you send it. It has to look piping hot straight out of the oven … No, not 'We're surprised'. 'We condemn'. 'Surprised' is feeble …

ANNETTE: This goes on from morning to night, from morning to night he's glued to that mobile! That mobile makes mincemeat of our lives!

ALAIN: Er … just a minute …

He covers the mobile.

Annette, this is very important! …

ANNETTE: It's always very important. Anything happening somewhere else is always more important.

ALAIN: (*resuming*) Go ahead … Yes … Not 'procedure', 'manoeuvre'. 'A manoeuvre, timed for two weeks before the annual accounts,' etc. …

ANNETTE: In the street, at dinner, he doesn't care where …

ALAIN: A 'paper' in inverted commas! Put the word 'paper' in inverted commas …

ANNETTE: I'm not saying another word. Total surrender. I want to be sick again.

MICHEL: Where's the basin?

VÉRONIQUE: I don't know.

ALAIN: … You just have to quote me: 'This is simply a disgraceful attempt to manipulate share prices … '

VÉRONIQUE: Here it is. Go on, off you go.

MICHEL: Ronnie …

VÉRONIQUE: Everything's all right. We're fully equipped.

ALAIN: '… share prices and to undermine my client,' confirms Maître Reille, counsel for the Verenz-Pharma company' … AP, Reuters, general press, specialised press, Uncle Tom Cobley and all …

He hangs up.

VÉRONIQUE: She wants to throw up again.

ALAIN: What's the matter with you?

ANNETTE: I'm touched by your concern.

ALAIN: It's upsetting me!

ANNETTE: I am sorry. I must have misunderstood.

ALAIN: Oh, Annette, please! Don't let us start now! Just because they're quarrelling, just because their marriage is fucked, doesn't mean we have to compete!

VÉRONIQUE: What right do you have to say our marriage is fucked? Who gave you permission?

Alain's mobile vibrates.

ALAIN: … They just read it to me. We're sending it to you, Maurice … 'Manipulation', 'manipulate share prices.' It's on its way.

He hangs up.

… Wasn't me who said it, it was François.

VÉRONIQUE: Michel.

ALAIN: Michel, sorry.

VÉRONIQUE: I forbid you to stand in any kind of judgement over our relationship.

ALAIN: Then don't stand in judgement over my son.

VÉRONIQUE: That's got nothing to do with it! Your son injured ours!

ALAIN: They're young, they're kids, kids have always given each other a good drubbing during break. It's a law of life.

VÉRONIQUE: No, no, it isn't!

ALAIN: Course it is. You have to go through a kind of apprenticeship before violence gives way to what's right. Originally, let me remind you, might was right.

VÉRONIQUE: Possibly in prehistoric times. Not in our society.

ALAIN: Our society? Explain 'society'.

VÉRONIQUE: You're exhausting me, these conversations are exhausting.

ALAIN: You see, Véronique, I believe in the god of carnage. He has ruled, uninterruptedly, since the dawn of time. You're interested in Africa, aren't you? ... (*To Annette, who retches.*) ... Feeling bad?

ANNETTE: Don't worry about me.

ALAIN: I am worried.

ANNETTE: Everything's fine.

ALAIN: As a matter of fact, I just came back from the Congo. Over there, little boys are taught to kill when they're eight years old. During their childhood, they may kill hundreds of people, with a machete, with a 12.7, with a Kalashnikov, with a grenade launcher, so you'll understand that when my son picks up a bamboo rod, hits his playmate and breaks a tooth, or even two, in Aspirant Dunant Gardens, I'm likely to be less disposed than you to horror and indignation.

VÉRONIQUE: You're wrong.

ANNETTE: (*mocking*) 12.7! ...

ALAIN: Yes, that's what they're called.

Annette spits in the basin.

MICHEL: Are you all right?

ANNETTE: ... Perfectly.

ALAIN: What's the matter with you? What's the matter with her?

ANNETTE: It's just bile! It's nothing!

VÉRONIQUE: Don't lecture me about Africa. I know all about Africa's martyrdom, I've been steeped in it for months ...

ALAIN: I don't doubt it. Anyway, the Prosecutor of the International Criminal Court has opened an inquiry on Darfur ...

VÉRONIQUE: You think I don't know about that?

MICHEL: Don't get her started on that! For God's sake!

Véronique throws herself at her husband and hits him several times, with an uncontrolled and irrational desperation. Alain pulls her off him.

ALAIN: You know what, I'm starting to like you!

VÉRONIQUE: Well, I don't like you!

MICHEL: She's a supporter of peace and stability in the world.

VÉRONIQUE: Shut up!

Annette retches. She picks up her glass of rum and lifts it to her mouth.

MICHEL: Are you sure about that?

ANNETTE: Yes, yes, it'll do me good.

Véronique follows suit.

VÉRONIQUE: We're living in France. We're not living in Kinshasa! We're living in France according to the principles of Western society. What goes on in Aspirant Dunant Gardens reflects the values of Western society! Of which, if it's all the same to you, I am happy to be a member.

MICHEL: Beating up your husband is one of those principles, is it?

VÉRONIQUE: Michel, this is going to end badly.

ALAIN: She threw herself on you in such a frenzy. If I were you, I'd be rather touched.

VÉRONIQUE: I'll do it again in a minute.

ANNETTE: He's making fun of you, you do realise?

VÉRONIQUE: I don't give a shit.

ALAIN: I'm not making fun, on the contrary. Morality decrees we should control our impulses, but sometimes it's good not to control them. You don't want to be singing 'Ave Maria' when you're fucking. Where can you find this rum?

MICHEL: That vintage, I doubt you can.

ANNETTE: 12.7! Ha, ha!

VÉRONIQUE: (*same tone*) 12.7, you're right!

ALAIN: That's right. 12.7.

ANNETTE: Why can't you just say gun?

ALAIN: Because 12.7 is correct. You don't just say gun.

ANNETTE: Who's this 'you'?

ALAIN: That's enough, Annette. That's enough.

ANNETTE: The great warriors, like my husband, you have to give them some leeway, they have trouble working up an interest in local events.

ALAIN: It's true.

VÉRONIQUE: I don't see why. I don't see why. We're citizens of the world. I don't see why we should give up the struggle just because it's on our doorstep.

MICHEL: Oh, Ronnie! Do stop shoving these thoughts for the day down our throat.

VÉRONIQUE: I'm going to kill him.

Alain's mobile has vibrated.

ALAIN: … Yes, all right, take out 'regrettable' … 'Crude'. 'A crude attempt to …' That's it …

VÉRONIQUE: She's right, this is becoming unbearable!

ALAIN: ... Otherwise he approves the rest? ... Fine, fine. Very good.

He hangs up.

What were we saying? ... 12.7 millimetre? ...

VÉRONIQUE: I was saying, whether my husband likes it or not, that no one place is more important than another when it comes to exercising vigilance.

ALAIN: Vigilance ... well ... Annette, it's ridiculous to drink, the state you're in.

ANNETTE: What state? On the contrary.

ALAIN: Vigilance, it's an interesting idea ...

His mobile. It's Serge.

... Yes, no, no interviews before the circulation of the press release.

VÉRONIQUE: That's it. I insist you break off this horrendous conversation!

ALAIN: ... Absolutely not ... The shareholders won't give a fuck ... Remind him, the shareholder is king ...

Annette launches herself at Alain, snatches the mobile and, after a brief look-round to see where she can put it, shoves it into the vase of tulips.

Annette, what the ...!

ANNETTE: So there.

VÉRONIQUE: Ha, ha! Well done!

MICHEL: (*horrified*) Oh, my God!

ALAIN: Are you completely insane? Fuck!!

He rushes towards the vase, but Michel, who has got in ahead of him, fishes out the dripping object.

MICHEL: The hair-dryer! Where's the hair-dryer?

He finds it and turns it on at once, directing it towards the mobile.

ALAIN: You need locking up, poor love! This is incomprehensible! ... I had everything in there! ... It's brand new, it took me hours to set up!

MICHEL: (*to Annette, above the infernal din of the hair-dryer*) Really, I don't understand you. That was completely irresponsible.

ALAIN: Everything's on there, my whole life ...

ANNETTE: His whole life! …

MICHEL: (*still fighting the noise*) Hang on, we might be able to fix it …

ALAIN: No chance! It's fucked! …

MICHEL: We'll take out the battery and the SIM-card. Can you open it?

Alain tries to open it with no conviction.

ALAIN: I haven't a clue, I've only just got it.

MICHEL: Let's have a look.

ALAIN: It's fucked … And they think it's funny, they think it's funny!

MICHEL: (*opening it easily*) There we are.

He goes back on the offensive with the hair-dryer, having laid out the various parts.

You, Véronique, you at least could have the manners not to laugh at this!

VÉRONIQUE: (*laughing heartily*) My husband will have spent his entire afternoon blow-drying!

ANNETTE: Ha, ha, ha!

Annette makes no bones about helping herself to more rum. Michel, immune to finding any of this amusing, keeps busy, concentrating intently.

For a moment, there's only the sound of the hairdryer. Alain has slumped.

ALAIN: Leave it, mate. Leave it. There's nothing to be done …

Michel finally switches off the hair-dryer.

MICHEL: We'll have to wait a minute … (*Hiatus.*) You want to use our phone?

Alain gestures that he doesn't and that he couldn't care less.

I have to say …

ANNETTE: Yes, what is it you have to say, Michel?

MICHEL: No … I really can't think what to say.

ANNETTE: Well, if you ask me, everyone's feeling fine. If you ask me, everyone's feeling better. (*Hiatus.*) … Everyone's much calmer, don't you think? … Men are so wedded to their gadgets … It belittles them … It takes away all their authority … A man needs to keep his hands free … If you ask me. Even an attaché case is enough to put me off. There was a man, once, I found really attractive, then I saw him with a square shoulder-bag, a man's shoulder-bag, but that was it. There's nothing worse than a shoulder-bag. Although there's also nothing worse than a mobile phone. A man ought to give the impression that he's alone … If you ask me. I mean, that he's capable of being alone … ! I also have a John Wayne-ish idea of virility. And what was it he had? A Colt .45. A device for creating a vacuum … A man who can't give the impression that he's a loner has no texture … So, Michel, are you happy? It is somewhat fractured, our little … What was it you said? … I've forgotten the word … but in the end … everyone's feeling more or less all right … If you ask me.

MICHEL: I should probably warn you, rum drives you crazy.

ANNETTE: I've never felt more normal.

MICHEL: Right.

ANNETTE: I'm starting to feel rather pleasantly serene.

VÉRONIQUE: Ha, ha! That's wonderful! … 'Rather pleasantly serene'.

MICHEL: As for you, darjeeling, I fail to see what's to be gained by getting publicly pissed.

VÉRONIQUE: Get stuffed.

Michel goes to fetch the cigar box.

MICHEL: Choose one, Alain. Relax.

VÉRONIQUE: Cigars are not smoked in this house!

MICHEL: Those are Hoyo, those are Monte Cristo Number 3 and Number 4.

VÉRONIQUE: You don't smoke in a house with an asthmatic child!

ANNETTE: Who's asthmatic?

VÉRONIQUE: Our son.

MICHEL: Didn't stop you buying a fucking hamster.

ANNETTE: It's true, if somebody has asthma, keeping animals isn't recommended.

MICHEL: Totally unrecommended!

ANNETTE: Even a goldfish can prove counter-productive.

VÉRONIQUE: Do I have to listen to this fatuous nonsense?

She snatches the cigar box out of Michel's hands and slams it shut brutally.

I'm sorry, no doubt I'm the only one of us not feeling rather pleasantly serene. In fact, I've never been so unhappy. I think this is the unhappiest day of my life.

MICHEL: Drinking always makes you unhappy.

VÉRONIQUE: Michel, every word that comes out of your mouth is destroying me. I don't drink. I drank a mouthful of this shitty rum you're waving about as if you were showing the congregation the Turin Shroud. I don't drink and I bitterly regret it, it'd be a relief to be able to take refuge in a little drop at every minor setback.

ANNETTE: My husband's unhappy as well. Look at him. Slumped. He looks as if someone's left him by the side of the road. I think it's the unhappiest day of his life too.

ALAIN: Yes.

ANNETTE: I'm so sorry, Woof-woof.

Michel starts up the hair-dryer again, directing it at the various parts of the mobile.

VÉRONIQUE: Will you turn off the hair-dryer?! The thing is buggered.

The telephone rings.

MICHEL: Yes! … Mum, I told you we were busy … Because it could kill you! That medication is poison! Someone's going to explain it to you …

He hands the receiver to Alain.

Tell her.

ALAIN: Tell her what? …

MICHEL: Everything you know about that crap you're peddling.

ALAIN: … How are you, madame? …

ANNETTE: What can he tell her? He doesn't know the first thing about it!

ALAIN: Yes … And does it hurt? … Of course. Well, the operation will fix that … And the other leg, I see. No, no I'm not an orthopaedist … (*Aside.*) She keeps calling me 'doctor' …

ANNETTE: Doctor, this is grotesque—hang up!

ALAIN: But you … I mean to say, you're not having any problems with your balance? … Oh, no. Not at all. Not at all, Don't listen to any of that. All the same, it'd probably be just as well to stop taking it for the moment. Until … until you've had a chance to get quietly through your operation … Yes, you sound as if you're on very good form …

Michel snatches the receiver from him.

MICHEL: All right, Mum, is that clear, stop taking the medication, why do you always have to argue, stop taking it, do what you're told, I'll call you back ... Lots of love, love from us all.

He hangs up.

She's killing me. One pain in the arse after another!

ANNETTE: Right then, what have we decided? Shall I come back this evening with Ferdinand? No one seems to give a toss any more. All the same, I should point out, that's what we're here for.

VÉRONIQUE: Now I'm starting to feel sick. Where's the bowl?

Michel takes the bottle of rum out of Annette's reach.

MICHEL: That'll do.

ANNETTE: To my mind, there are wrongs on both sides. That's it. Wrongs on both sides.

VÉRONIQUE: Are you serious?

ANNETTE: What?

VÉRONIQUE: Are you aware of what you're saying?

ANNETTE: I am. Yes.

VÉRONIQUE: Our son Bruno, to whom I was obliged to give two Extra Strength Nurofen last night, is in the wrong?

ANNETTE: He's not necessarily innocent.

VÉRONIQUE: Fuck off! I've had quite enough of you.

She grabs Annette's handbag and hurls it towards the door.

Fuck off!

ANNETTE: My handbag! ... (*Like a little girl.*) Alain! ...

MICHEL: What's going on? They've slipped their trolley.

ANNETTE: (*gathering up her scattered possessions*) Alain, help! ...

VÉRONIQUE: 'Alain, help!'

ANNETTE: Shut up! ... She's broken my compact! And my atomiser! (*To Alain.*) Defend me, why aren't you defending me? ...

ALAIN: We're going.

He prepares to gather up the parts of his mobile.

VÉRONIQUE: It's not as if I'm strangling her!

ANNETTE: What have I done to you?

VÉRONIQUE: There are not wrongs on both sides! Don't mix up the victims and the executioners!

ANNETTE: Executioners!

MICHEL: You're so full of shit, Véronique, all this simplistic claptrap, we're up to here with it!

VÉRONIQUE: I stand by everything I've said.

MICHEL: Yes, yes, you stand by what you've said, you stand by what you've said, your infatuation for a bunch of Sudanese coons is bleeding into everything now.

VÉRONIQUE: I'm appalled. Why are you choosing to show yourself in this horrible light?

MICHEL: Because I feel like it. I feel like showing myself in a horrible light.

VÉRONIQUE: One day you may understand the extreme gravity of what's going on in that part of the world and you'll be ashamed of this inertia and your repulsive nihilism.

MICHEL: You're just wonderful, darjeeling, you're the best of us all!

VÉRONIQUE: I am. Yes.

ANNETTE: Let's get out of here, Alain, these people are monsters!

She drains her glass and goes to pick up the bottle.

ALAIN: (*preventing her*) … Stop it, Annette.

ANNETTE: No, I want to drink some more, I want to get pissed out of my head, this bitch hurls my handbag across the room and no one bats an eyelid, I want to get drunk!

ALAIN: You already are.

ANNETTE: Why are you letting them call my son an executioner? You come to their house to settle things and you get insulted and bullied and lectured on how to be a good citizen of the planet—our son did well to clout yours, and I wipe my arse with your charter of human rights!

MICHEL: A mouthful of grog and, bam, the real face appears.

VÉRONIQUE: I told you! Didn't I tell you?

ALAIN: What did you tell him?

VÉRONIQUE: That she was a phoney. This woman is a phoney. I'm sorry.

ANNETTE: (*upset*) Ha, ha, ha! …

ALAIN: When did you tell him?

VÉRONIQUE: When you were in the bathroom.

ALAIN: You'd known her for fifteen minutes but you could tell she was a phoney.

VÉRONIQUE: It's the kind of thing I pick up on right away.

MICHEL: It's true.

VÉRONIQUE: I have an instinct for that kind of thing.

ALAIN: And 'phoney', what does that mean?

ANNETTE: I don't want to hear any more! Why are you putting me through this, Alain?

ALAIN: Calm down, Woof-woof.

VÉRONIQUE: She's someone who tries to round off corners. Full stop. She's all front. She doesn't care any more than you do.

MICHEL: It's true.

ALAIN: It's true.

VÉRONIQUE: 'It's true'! Are you saying it's true?

MICHEL: They don't give a fuck! They haven't given a fuck since the start, it's obvious! Her too, you're right!

ALAIN: And you do, I suppose? (*To Annette.*) Let me say something, love. (*To Michel.*) Explain to me in what way you care, Michel. What does the word mean in the first place? You're far more authentic when you're showing yourself in a horrible light. To tell the truth, no one in this room cares, except for Véronique, whose integrity, it has to be said, must be acknowledged.

VÉRONIQUE: Don't acknowledge me! Don't acknowledge me!

ANNETTE: I care. I absolutely care.

ALAIN: We only care about our own feelings, Annette, we're not social crusaders, (*To Véronique.*) I saw your friend Jane Fonda on TV the other day, I was inches away from buying a Ku Klux Klan poster …

VÉRONIQUE: What do you mean, 'my friend'? What's Jane Fonda got to do with all this? …

ALAIN: You're the same breed. You're part of the same category of woman—committed, problem-solving. That's not what we like about women, what we like about women is sensuality, wildness, hormones. Women who make a song and dance about their intuition, women who are custodians of the world depress us—even him, poor Michel, your husband, he's depressed …

MICHEL: Don't speak for me!

VÉRONIQUE: Who gives a flying fuck what you like about women? Where does this lecture come from? A man like you, who could begin to give a fuck for your opinion?

ALAIN: She's yelling. She's a regimental sergeant major

VÉRONIQUE: What about her, doesn't she yell?! When she said that little bastard had done well to clout our son?

ANNETTE: Yes, he did do well! At least he's not a snivelling little poof!

VÉRONIQUE: Yours is a grass, is that any better?

ANNETTE: Alain, let's go! What are we doing, staying in this dump?

She makes to leave, then returns towards the tulips which she lashes out at violently. Flowers fly, disintegrate and scatter all over the place.

There, there, that's what I think of your pathetic flowers, your hideous tulips! … Ha, ha, ha! (She bursts into tears.) … It's the worst day of my life as well.

Silence.
   A long stunned pause.
   Michel picks something up off the floor.

MICHEL: (*to Annette*) This yours?

Annette takes a spectacle case, opens it and takes out a pair of glasses.

ANNETTE: Thanks …

MICHEL: Not broken? …

ANNETTE: No …

Hiatus.

MICHEL: What I always say is …

Alain starts gathering up the stems and petals.

Leave it.

ALAIN: No …

The telephone rings. After some hesitation, Véronique picks up the receiver.

VÉRONIQUE: Yes, darling … Oh, good … Will you be able to do your homework at Annabelle's? … No, no, darling, we haven't found her … Yes, I went all the way to the supermarket. But you know, my love, Nibbles is very resourceful, I think you have to have faith in her. You think she was happy in a cage? … Daddy's very sad, he didn't mean to upset you … Of course you will. Yes, of course you'll speak to him again. Listen, darling, we're worried enough already about your brother … She'll eat … she'll eat leaves … acorns, conkers … she'll find things, she knows what food she needs … Worms, snails, stuff that drops out of rubbish bins, she's like us, she's omnivorous … See you soon, sweetheart.

Hiatus.

MICHEL: I dare say that creature's stuffing its face as we speak.
VÉRONIQUE: No.

Silence.

MICHEL: What do we know?

JOKES AND THE COMIC

By Sigmund Freud

Translated by James Strachey

I
T IS ONLY WITH misgivings that I venture to approach the problem of the comic itself. It would be presumptuous to expect that my efforts would be able to make any decisive contribution to its solution when the works of a great number of eminent thinkers have failed to produce a wholly satisfactory explanation. My intention is in fact no more than to pursue the lines of thought that have proved valuable with jokes a short distance further into the sphere of the comic.

The comic arises in the first instance as an unintended discovery derived from human social relations. It is found in people—in their movements, forms, actions and traits of character, originally in all probability only in their physical characteristics but later in their mental ones as well or, as the case may be, in the expression of those characteristics. By means of a very common sort of personification, animals become comic too, and inanimate objects. At the same time, the comic is capable of being detached from people, in so far as we recognize the conditions under which a person seems comic. In this way the comic of situation comes about, and this recognition affords the possibility of making a person comic at one's will by putting him in situations in which his actions are subject to these comic conditions. The discovery that one has it in one's power to make someone else comic opens the way to an undreamt-of yield of comic pleasure and is the origin of a highly developed technique. One can make *oneself* comic, too, as easily as other people. The methods that serve to make people comic are: putting them in a comic situation, mimicry, disguise, unmasking, caricature, parody, travesty, and so on. It is obvious that these techniques can be used to serve hostile and aggressive purposes. One can make a person comic in order to make him become contemptible, to deprive him of his claim to dignity and authority.

But even if such an intention habitually underlies making people comic, this need not be the meaning of what is comic spontaneously.

This irregular survey of the occurrences of the comic will already show us that a very extensive field of origin is to be ascribed to it and that such specialized conditions as we found, for instance, in the naive are not to be expected in it. In order to get on the track of the determining condition that is valid for the comic, the most important thing is the choice of an introductory case. We shall choose the comic of movement, because we recollect that the most primitive kind of stage performance—the pantomime—uses that method for making us laugh. The answer to the question of why we laugh at the clown's movements is that they seem to us extravagant and inexpedient. We are laughing at an expenditure that is too large. Let us look now for the determining condition outside the comic that is artificially constructed—where it can be found unintended. A child's movements do not seem to us comic, although he kicks and jumps about. On the other hand, it *is* comic when a child who is learning to write follows the movements of his pen with his tongue stuck out; in these associated motions we see an unnecessary expenditure of movement which we should spare ourselves if we were carrying out the same activity. Similarly, other such associated motions, or merely exaggerated expressive movements, seem to us comic in adults too. Pure examples of this species of the comic are to be seen, for instance, in the movements of someone playing skittles who, after he has released the ball, follows its course as though he could still continue to direct it. Thus, too, all grimaces are comic which exaggerate the normal expression of the emotions, even if they are produced involuntarily as in sufferers from St. Vitus's dance (chorea). And in the same way, the passionate movements of a modern conductor seem comic to any unmusical person who cannot understand their necessity. Indeed, it is from this comic of movement that the comic of bodily shapes and facial features branches off; for these are regarded as though they were the outcome of an exaggerated or pointless movement. Staring eyes, a hooked nose hanging down to the mouth, ears sticking out, a hump-back—all such things probably only produce a comic effect in so far as movements are imagined which would be necessary to bring about these features; and here the nose, the ears and other parts of the body are imagined as more movable than they are in reality. There is no doubt that it is comic if someone can "waggle his ears", and it would certainly be still more comic if he could move his nose up and down. A good deal of the comic effect produced on us by animals comes from our perceiving in them movements such as these which we cannot imitate ourselves.

But how is it that we laugh when we have recognized that some other person's movements are exaggerated and inexpedient? By making a comparison, I believe, between the movement I observe in the other person and the one that I should have carried out myself in his place. The two things compared must of course be judged by the same standard, and this standard is my expenditure of innervation, which is linked to my idea of the movement in both of the two cases. ...

Thus a uniform explanation is provided of the fact that a person appears comic to us if, in comparison with ourselves, he makes too great an expenditure on his bodily functions and too little on his mental ones; and it cannot be denied that in both these cases our laughter expresses a pleasurable sense of the superiority which we feel in relation to him. If the relation in the two cases is reversed—if the other person's physical expenditure is found to be less than ours or his mental expenditure greater— then we no longer laugh, we are filled with astonishment and admiration.[1]...

Mankind have not been content to enjoy the comic where they have come upon it in their experience; they have also sought to bring it about intentionally, and we can learn more about the nature of the comic if we study the means which serve to *make* things comic. First and foremost, it is possible to produce the comic in relation to oneself in order to amuse other people—for instance, by making oneself out clumsy or stupid. In that way one produces a comic effect exactly as though one really were these things, by fulfilling the condition of the comparison which leads to the difference in expenditure. But one does not in this way make oneself ridiculous or contemptible, but may in some circumstances even achieve admiration. The feeling of superiority does not arise in the other person if he knows that one has only been pretending; and this affords fresh evidence of the fundamental independence of the comic from the feeling of superiority.

As regards making *other people* comic, the principal means is to put them in situations in which a person becomes comic as a result of human dependence on external events, particularly on social factors, without regard to the personal characteristics of the individual concerned—that is to say, by employing the comic of situation. This putting of someone in a comic situation may be a *real* one (a practical joke)—by sticking out a leg so that someone trips over it as though he were clumsy, by making him seem stupid by exploiting his credulity, or trying to convince him of something nonsensical, and so on—or it may be simulated by speech or play. The aggressiveness, to which making a person comic usually ministers, is much assisted by the fact that the comic pleasure is independent of the reality of the comic situation, so that everyone is in fact exposed, without any defence, to being made comic.

But there are yet other means of making things comic which deserve special consideration and also indicate in part fresh sources of comic pleasure. Among these, for instance, is *mimicry*, which gives quite extraordinary pleasure to the hearer and makes its object comic even if it is still far from the exaggeration of a caricature. It is much easier to find a reason for the comic effect of *caricature* than for that of mere mimicry. Caricature, parody and travesty (as well as their practical counterpart, unmasking) are directed against people and objects which lay claim to authority and respect, which are in some sense 'sublime'.[2] They are procedures for *Herabsetzung,* as the apt German expression has it. What is sublime is something large in the figurative, psychical sense; and I should like to suggest, or rather to repeat my suggestion, that, like what is somatically large, it is represented by an increased expenditure. It requires little observation to establish that when I speak of something sublime I innervate my speech in a different way, I make different facial expressions, and I try to bring the whole way in which I hold myself into harmony with the dignity of what I am having an idea of. I impose a solemn restraint upon myself—not very different from what I should adopt if I were to enter the presence of an exalted personality, a monarch, or a prince of science. I shall hardly be wrong in assuming that this different innervation in my ideational mimetics corresponds to an increased expenditure. The third instance of an increased expenditure of this kind is no doubt to be found when I proceed in abstract trains of thought instead of in the habitual concrete and plastic ones. When, therefore, the procedures that I have discussed for the degradation of the sublime allow me to have an idea of it as though it were something commonplace, in whose presence I need not pull myself together but may, to use the military formula, 'stand easy', I am being spared the increased expenditure of the solemn restraint; and the comparison between this new ideational method (instigated by empathy) and the previously habitual one, which is simultaneously trying to establish itself—this comparison once again creates the difference in expenditure which can be discharged by laughter.

Caricature, as is well known, brings about degradation by emphasizing in the general impression given by the exalted object a single trait which is comic in itself but was bound to be overlooked so long as it was only perceivable in the general picture. By isolating this, a comic effect can be attained which extends in our memory over the whole object. This is subject to the condition that the actual presence of the exalted object himself does not keep us in a reverential attitude. If a comic trait of this kind that has been overlooked is lacking in reality, a caricature will unhesitatingly create it by exaggerating one that is not comic in itself; and the fact that the effect of the caricature is not essentially diminished by this falsification of reality is once again an indication of the origin of comic pleasure.

Parody and *travesty* achieve the degradation of something exalted in another way: by destroying the unity that exists between people's characters as we know them and their speeches and actions, by replacing either the exalted figures or their utterances by inferior ones. They are distinguished from caricature in this, but not in the mechanism of their production of comic pleasure. The same mechanism is also used for *unmasking,* which only applies where someone has seized dignity and authority by a deception and these have to be taken from him in reality. We have already met with a few examples of the comic effect of unmasking in jokes—for instance, in the story of the aristocratic lady who, at the first onset of her labour-pains, exclaimed 'Ah!

mon Dieu!' but whom the doctor would not assist till she cried out 'Aa-ee, aa-ee!' Having come to know the characteristics of the comic, we can no longer dispute that this anecdote is in fact an example of comic unmasking and has no justifiable claim to be called a joke, it only recalls jokes by its setting and by the technical method of 'representation by something very small' [loc.cit.]—in this case the patient's cry, which is found sufficient to establish the indication for treatment. It nevertheless remains true that our linguistic sense, if we call on it for a decision, raises no objection to our calling a story like this a joke. We may explain his by reflecting that linguistic usage is not based on the scientific insight into the nature of jokes that we have arrived at in this laborious investigation. Since one of the functions of jokes is to make hidden sources of comic pleasure accessible once more, any device that brings to light something that is not manifestly comic may, by loose analogy, be termed a joke. This applies preferably, however, to unmasking as well as to other methods of making people comic.[3]

Under the heading of 'unmasking' we may also include a procedure for making things comic with which we are already acquainted—the method of degrading the dignity of individuals by directing attention to the frailties which they share with all humanity, but in particular the dependence of their mental functions on bodily needs. The unmasking is equivalent here to an admonition: such and such a person, who is admired as a demigod, is after all only human like you and me. Here, too, are to be placed the efforts at laying bare the monotonous psychical automatism that lies behind the wealth and apparent freedom of psychical functions. We came across examples of 'unmasking' of this kind in the marriage-broker jokes, and felt a doubt at the time whether these anecdotes have a right to be counted as jokes. We are now able to decide with greater certainty that the anecdote of the echo who reinforced all the assertions of the marriage-broker and finally confirmed his admission that the bride had a hump with the exclamation 'And *what* a hump!'—that this anecdote is essentially a *comic* story, an example of the unmasking of a psychical automatism. Here, however, the comic story is only serving as a façade. For anyone who will attend to the hidden meaning of the marriage-broker anecdotes, the whole thing remains an admirably staged joke; anyone who does not penetrate so far is left with a comic story. The same thing applies to the other joke, about the marriage-broker who, in order to answer an objection, ended by confessing the truth with a cry of "But I ask you, who would lend such people anything?" Here again we have a comic unmasking as the façade for a joke, though in this instance the characteristic of a joke is much more unmistakable, since the marriage-broker's remark is at the same time a representation by the opposite. In trying to prove that the people are rich he at the same time proves that they are *not* rich, but very poor. Here a joke and the comic are combined, and teach us till the same remark can be both things at once. ...

Every theory of the comic is objected to by its critics on the score that its definition overlooks what is essential to the comic: 'The comic is based on a contrast between ideas.' 'Yes, in so far as the contrast has a comic and not some other effect.' 'The feeling of the comic arises from the disappointment of an expectation.' 'Yes, unless the disappointment, is in fact a distressing one.' No doubt the objections are justified; but we shall be over-estimating them if we conclude from them that the essential feature of the comic has hitherto escaped detection. What impairs the universal validity of these definitions are conditions which are indispensable for the generating of comic pleasure; but we do not need to look for the essence of the comic in them. In any case, it will only become easy for us to dismiss the objections and throw light on the contradictions to the definitions of the comic if we suppose that the origin of comic pleasure lies in a comparison of the difference between two expenditures. Comic pleasure and the effect by which it is known—laughter—can only come about if this difference is unutilizable and capable of discharge. We obtain no pleasurable effect but at most a transient sense of pleasure in which the characteristic of being comic does not emerge, if the difference is put to another use as soon as it is recognized. Just as special contrivances have to be adopted in the case of jokes in order to prevent the use elsewhere of the expenditure that is recognized as superfluous, so, too, comic pleasure can only appear in circumstances that guarantee this same condition. For this reason occasions on which these differences in expenditure occur in our ideational life are uncommonly numerous, but the occasions on which the comic emerges from those differences are relatively quite rare.

Two observations force themselves on anyone who studies even cursorily the conditions for the generation of the comic from difference in expenditure. First, there are cases in which the comic appears habitually and as though by force of necessity, and on the contrary others in which it seems entirely dependent on the circumstances and on the standpoint of the observer. But secondly, unusually large differences very often break through unfavourable conditions, so that the comic feeling emerges in spite of them. In connection with the first of these points it would be possible to set up two classes—the inevitably comic and the occasionally comic—though one must be prepared from the first to renounce the notion of finding the inevitability of the comic in the first class free from exceptions. It would be tempting to enquire into the determining conditions for the two classes.

The conditions, some of which have been brought together as the 'isolation' of the comic situation, apply essentially to the second class. A closer analysis elicits the following facts:

(*a*) The most favourable condition for the production of comic pleasure is a generally cheerful mood in which one is 'inclined to laugh'. In a toxic mood of cheerfulness almost everything seems comic, probably by comparison with the expenditure in a normal state. Indeed, jokes, the comic and all similar methods of getting pleasure from mental activity are no more than ways of regaining this cheerful mood—this euphoria—from a single point of approach, when it is not present as a general disposition of the psyche.

(*b*) A similarly favourable effect is produced by an *expectation* of the comic, by being attuned to comic pleasure. For this reason, if an intention, to make something comic is communicated to one by someone else, differences of such a low degree are sufficient that they would probably be overlooked if they occurred in one's experience unintentionally. Anyone who starts out to read a comic book or goes to the theatre to see a farce owes to this intention his ability to laugh at things which would scarcely have provided him with a case of the comic in his ordinary life. In the last resort it is in the recollection of having laughed and in the expectation of laughing that he laughs when he sees the comic actor come on to the stage, before the latter can have made any attempt at making him laugh. For that reason, too, one admits feeling ashamed afterwards over what one has been able to laugh at at the play.

(*c*) Unfavourable conditions for the comic arise from the kind of mental activity with which a particular person is occupied at the moment. Imaginative or intellectual work that pursues serious aims interferes with the capacity of the cathexes for discharge—cathexes which the work requires for its displacements—so that only unexpectedly large differences in expenditure are able to break through to comic pleasure. What are quite specially unfavourable for the comic are all kinds of intellectual processes which are sufficiently remote from what is perceptual to bring ideational mimetics to a stop. There is no place whatever left for the comic in abstract reflection except when that mode of thought is suddenly interrupted.

(*d*) The opportunity for the release of comic pleasure disappears, too, if the attention is focused precisely on the comparison from which the comic may emerge. In such circumstances what would otherwise have the most certain comic effect loses its comic force. A movement or a function cannot be comic for a person whose interest is directed to comparing it with a standard which he has clearly before his mind. Thus the examiner does not find the nonsense comic which the candidate produces in his ignorance; he is annoyed by it, while the candidate's fellow students, who are far more interested in what luck he will have than in how much he knows, laugh heartily at the same nonsense. A gymnastic or dancing instructor seldom has an eye for the comic in his pupils' movements; and a clergyman entirely overlooks the comic in the human weaknesses which the writer of comedies can bring to light so effectively. The comic process will not bear being hypercathected by attention; it must be able to take its course quite unobserved—in this respect, incidentally, just like jokes. It would, however, contradict the nomenclature of the 'processes of consciousness' of which I made use, with good reason, in my *Interpretation of Dreams* if one sought to speak of the comic process as a necessarily unconscious one. It forms part, rather, of the preconscious; and such processes, which run their course in the preconscious but lack the cathexis of attention with which consciousness is linked, may aptly be given the name of 'automatic'. The process of comparing expenditures must remain automatic if it is to produce comic pleasure.

(*e*) The comic is greatly interfered with if the situation from which it ought to develop gives rise at the same time to a release of strong affect. A discharge of the operative difference is as a rule out of the question in such a case. The affects, disposition and attitude of the individual in each particular case make it understandable that the comic emerges and vanishes according to the standpoint of each particular person, and that an absolute comic exists only in exceptional instances. The contingency or relativity of the comic is therefore far greater than that of a joke, which never happens of its own accord but is invariably *made*, and in which the conditions under which it can find acceptance can be observed at the time at which it is constructed. The generation of affect is the most intense of all the conditions that interfere with the comic and its importance in this respect has been nowhere overlooked.[4] For this reason it has been said that the comic feeling comes easiest in more or less indifferent cases where the feelings and interests are not strongly involved. Yet precisely in cases where there is a release of affect one can observe a particularly strong difference in expenditure bring about the automatism of release. When Colonel Butler[5] answers Octavio's warnings by exclaiming 'with a bitter laugh': '*Thanks* from the House of Austria!' his embitterment does not prevent his laughing. The laugh applies to his memory of the disappointment he believes he has suffered; and on the other hand the magnitude of the disappointment cannot be portrayed more impressively by the dramatist than by his showing it capable of forcing a laugh in the midst of the storm of feelings that have been released. I am inclined to think that this explanation would apply to every case in which laughter occurs in circumstances other than pleasurable ones and accompanied by intensely distressing or strained emotions.

(*f*) If we add to this that the generating of comic pleasure can be encouraged by any other pleasurable accompanying circumstance as though by some sort of contagious effect (working in the same kind of way as the fore-pleasure principle with tendentious jokes), we shall have mentioned enough of the conditions governing comic pleasure for our purposes, though certainly not all of them. We can then see that these conditions, as well as the inconstancy and contingency of the comic effect, cannot be explained so easily by any other hypothesis than that of the derivation of comic pleasure from the discharge of a difference which, under the most varying circumstances, is liable to be used in ways other than discharge.

NOTES

1. The contradictoriness with which the determining conditions of the comic are pervaded—the fact that sometimes an excess and sometimes an insufficiency seems to be the source of comic pleasure—has contributed no little to the confusion of the problem. Cf. Lipps (1898, 47).

2. 'Degradation' [in English in the original]. Bain (1865, 248) writes: 'The occasion of the Ludicrous is the Degradation of some person or interest, possessing dignity, in circumstances that excite no other strong emotion.' [The English word 'degradation' has accordingly been used in all that follows as a translation of '*Herabsetzung*'.]

3. 'Thus every conscious and ingenious evocation of the comic (whether the comic of contemplation or of situation) is in general described as a joke. We, of course, cannot here make use of this concept of the joke either.' (Lipps, 1898, 78.)

4. 'It is easy for you to laugh; it means nothing more to you.'

5. [In Schiller's tragedy *Wallensteins Tod* (II, 6). Colonel Butler, a veteran Irish soldier in the Imperial army during the Thirty Years War, believes that he has been snubbed by the Emperor and is preparing to desert to his enemies. Octavio Piccolomini, his superior officer, begs him to reconsider the position and reminds him of the thanks which Austria owes him for his forty years' loyalty, and to this Butler replies in the words quoted above.]

LAUGHTER

By Henri Bergson
Translated by Fred Rothwell

THE COMIC IN GENERAL—THE COMIC ELEMENT IN FORMS AND MOVEMENTS—EXPANSIVE FORCE OF THE COMIC

WHAT DOES LAUGHTER mean? What is the basal element in the laughable? What common ground can we find between the grimace of a merry-andrew, a play upon words, an equivocal situation in a burlesque and a scene of high comedy? What method of distillation will yield us invariably the same essence from which so many different products borrow either their obtrusive odour or their delicate perfume? The greatest of thinkers, from Aristotle downwards, have tackled this little problem, which has a knack of baffling every effort, of slipping away and escaping only to bob up again, a pert challenge flung at philosophic speculation.

Our excuse for attacking the problem in our turn must lie in the fact that we shall not aim at imprisoning the comic spirit within a definition. We regard it, above all, as a living thing. However trivial it may be, we shall treat it with the respect due to life. We shall confine ourselves to watching it grow and expand. Passing by imperceptible gradations from one form to another, it will be seen to achieve the strangest metamorphoses. We shall disdain nothing we have seen. Maybe we may gain from this prolonged contact, for the matter of that, something more flexible than an abstract definition,—a practical, intimate acquaintance, such as springs from a long companionship. And maybe we may also find that, unintentionally, we have made an acquaintance that is useful. For the comic spirit has a logic of its own, even in its wildest eccentricities. It has a method in its madness. It dreams, I admit, but it conjures up in its dreams visions that are at once accepted and understood by the whole of a social group. Can it then fail to throw light for us on the way that human imagination works, and more particularly social, collective, and popular imagination? Begotten of real life and akin to art, should it not also have something of its own to tell us about art and life?

At the outset we shall put forward three observations which we look upon as fundamental. They have less bearing on the actually comic than on the field within which it must be sought.

The first point to which attention should be called is that the comic does not exist outside the pale of what is strictly *human*. A landscape may be beautiful, charming and sublime, or insignificant and ugly; it will never be laughable. You may laugh at an animal, but only because you have detected in it some human attitude or expression. You may laugh at a hat, but what you are making fun of, in this case, is not the piece of felt or straw, but the shape that men have given it,—the human caprice whose mould it has assumed. It is strange that so important a fact, and such a simple one too, has not attracted to a greater degree the attention of philosophers. Several have defined man as "an animal which laughs." They might equally well have defined him as an animal which is laughed at; for if any other animal, or some lifeless object, produces the same effect, it is always because of some resemblance to man, of the stamp he gives it or the use he puts it to.

Here I would point out, as a symptom equally worthy of notice, the *absence of feeling* which usually accompanies laughter. It seems as though the comic could not produce its disturbing effect unless it fell, so to say, on the surface of a soul that is thoroughly calm and unruffled. Indifference is its natural environment, for laughter has no greater foe than emotion. I do not mean that we could not laugh at a person who inspires us with pity, for instance, or even with affection, but in such a case we must, for the moment, put our affection out of court and impose silence upon our pity. In a society composed of pure intelligences there would probably be no more tears, though perhaps there would still be laughter; whereas highly emotional souls, in tune and unison with life, in whom every event would be sentimentally prolonged and re-echoed, would neither know nor understand laughter. Try, for a moment, to become interested in everything that is being said and done; act, in imagination, with those who act, and feel with those who feel; in a word, give your sympathy its widest expansion: as though at the touch of a fairy wand you will see the flimsiest of objects assume importance, and a gloomy hue spread over everything. Now step aside, look upon life as a disinterested spectator: many a drama will turn into a comedy. It is enough for us to stop our ears to the sound of music in a room, where dancing is going on, for the dancers at once to appear ridiculous. How many human actions would stand a similar test? Should we not see many of them suddenly pass from grave to gay, on isolating them from the accompanying music of sentiment? To produce the whole of its effect, then, the comic demands something like a momentary anesthesia of the heart. Its appeal is to intelligence, pure and simple.

This intelligence, however, must always remain in touch with other intelligences. And here is the third fact to which attention should be drawn. You would hardly appreciate the comic if you felt yourself isolated from others. Laughter appears to stand in need of an echo. Listen to it carefully: it is not an articulate, clear, well-defined sound; it is something which would fain be prolonged by reverberating from one to another, something beginning with a crash, to continue in successive rumblings, like thunder in a mountain. Still, this reverberation cannot go on for ever. It can travel within as wide a circle as you please: the circle remains, none the less, a closed one. Our laughter is always the laughter of a group. It may, perchance, have happened to you, when seated in a railway carriage or at *table d'hôte,* to hear travellers relating to one another stories which must have been comic to them, for they laughed heartily. Had you been one of their company, you would have laughed like them, but, as you were not, you had no desire whatever to do so. A man who was once asked why he did not weep at a sermon when everybody else was shedding tears replied: "I don't belong to the parish!" What that man thought of tears would be still more true of laughter. However spontaneous it seems, laughter always implies a kind of secret freemasonry, or even complicity, with other laughers, real or imaginary. How often has it been said that the fuller the theatre, the more uncontrolled the laughter of the audience! On the other hand, how often has the remark been made that many comic effects are incapable of translation from one language to another, because they refer to the customs and ideas of a particular social group! It is through not understanding the importance of this double fact that the comic has been looked upon as a mere curiosity in which the mind finds amusement, and laughter itself as a strange, isolated phenomenon, without any bearing on the rest of human activity. Hence those definitions which tend to make the comic into an abstract relation between ideas: "an intellectual contrast," "a patent absurdity," etc., definitions which, even were they really suitable to every form of the comic, would not in the least explain why the comic makes us laugh. How, indeed, should it come about that this particular logical relation, as soon as it is perceived, contracts, expands and shakes our limbs, whilst all other relations leave the body unaffected? It is not from this point of view that we shall approach the problem. To understand laughter, we must put it back into its natural environment, which is society, and above all must we determine the utility of its function, which is a social one. Such, let us say at once, will be the leading idea of all our investigations. Laughter must answer to certain requirements of life in common. It must have a *social* signification.

Let us clearly mark the point towards which our three preliminary observations are converging. The comic will come into being, it appears, whenever a group of men concentrate their attention on one of their number, imposing silence on their emotions and calling into play nothing but their intelligence. …

Before going further, let us halt a moment and glance around. As we hinted at the outset of this study, it would be idle to attempt to derive every comic effect from one simple formula. The formula exists well enough in a certain sense, but its development does not follow a straightforward course. What I mean is that the process of deduction ought from time to time to stop and study certain culminating effects, and that these effects each, appear as models round which new effects resembling them take their places in a circle. These latter are not deductions from the formula, but are comic through their relationship with those that are. To quote Pascal again, I see no objection, at this stage, to defining the process by the curve which that geometrician studied under the name of *roulette* or cycloid—the curve traced by a point in the circumference of a wheel when the carriage is advancing in a straight line: this point turns like the wheel, though it advances like the carriage. Or else we might think of an immense avenue such as are to be seen in the forest of Fontainebleau, with *crosses* at intervals to indicate the crossways: at each of these we shall walk round the cross, explore for a while the paths that open out before us, and then return to our original course. Now, we have just reached one of these mental crossways. *Something mechanical encrusted on the living* will represent a cross at which we must halt, a central image from which the imagination branches off in different directions. What are these directions? There appear to be three main ones. We will follow them one after the other, and then continue our onward course.

1. In the first place, this view of the mechanical and the living dovetailed into each other makes us incline towards the vaguer image of *some rigidity or other* applied to the mobility of life, in an awkward attempt to follow its lines and counterfeit its suppleness. Here we perceive how easy it is for a garment to become ridiculous. It might almost be said that every fashion is laughable in some respect. Only, when we are dealing with the fashion of the day, we are so accustomed to it that the garment seems, in our mind, to form one with the individual wearing it. We do not separate them in imagination. The idea no longer occurs to us to contrast the inert rigidity of the covering with the living suppleness of the object covered: consequently, the comic here remains in a latent condition. It will only succeed in emerging when the natural incompatibility is so deep-seated between the covering and the covered that even an immemorial association fails to cement this union: a case in point is our head and top hat. Suppose, however, some eccentric individual dresses himself in the fashion of former times our attention is immediately drawn to the clothes themselves; we

absolutely distinguish them from the individual, we say that the latter *is disguising himself,*—as though every article of clothing were not a disguise!—and the laughable aspect of fashion comes out of the shadow into the light.

Here we are beginning to catch a faint glimpse of the highly intricate difficulties raised by this problem of the comic. One of the reasons that must have given rise to many erroneous or unsatisfactory theories of laughter is that many things are comic *de jure* without being comic *de facto,* the continuity of custom having deadened within them the comic quality. A sudden dissolution of continuity is needed, a break with fashion, for this quality to revive. Hence the impression that this dissolution of continuity is the parent of the comic, whereas all it does is to bring it to our notice. Hence, again, the explanation of laughter by *surprise, contrast,* etc., definitions which would equally apply to a host of cases in which we have no inclination whatever to laugh. The truth of the matter is far from being so simple. ...

2. Our starting-point is again "something mechanical encrusted upon the living." Where did the comic come from in this case? It came from the fact that the living body became rigid, like a machine. Accordingly, it seemed to us that the living body ought to be the perfection of suppleness, the ever-alert activity of a principle always at work. But this activity would really belong to the soul rather than to the body. It would be the very flame of life, kindled within us by a higher principle and perceived through the body, as though through a glass. When we see only graceful-ness and suppleness in the living body, it is because we disregard in it the elements of weight, of resistance, and, in a word, of matter; we forget its materiality and think only of its vitality, a vitality which we regard as derived from the very principle of intellectual and moral life. Let us suppose, however, that our attention is drawn to this material side of the body; that, so far from sharing in the lightness and subtlety of the principle with which it is animated, the body is no more in our eyes than a heavy and cumbersome vesture, a kind of irksome ballast which holds down to earth a soul eager to rise aloft. Then the body will become to the soul what, as we have just seen, the garment was to the body itself—inert matter dumped down upon living energy. The impression of the comic will be produced as soon as we have a clear apprehension of this putting the one on the other. And we shall experience it most strongly when we are shown the soul *tantalised* by the needs of the body: on the one hand, the moral personality with its intelligently varied energy, and, on the other, the stupidly monotonous body, perpetually obstructing everything with its machine-like obstinacy. The more paltry and uniformly repeated these claims of the body, the more striking will be the result. But that is only a matter of degree, and the general law of these phenomena may be formulated as follows: *Any incident is comic that calls our attention to the physical in a person, when it is the moral side that is concerned.* ...

3. Let us then return, for the last time, to our central image—something mechanical encrusted on something living. Here, the living being under discussion was a human being, a person. A mechanical arrangement, on the other hand, is a thing. What, therefore, incited laughter, was the momentary transformation of a person into a thing, if one considers the image from this standpoint. Let us then pass from the exact idea of a machine to the vaguer one of a thing in general. We shall have a fresh series of laughable images which will be obtained by taking a blurred impression, so to speak, of the outlines of the former and will bring us to this new law: *We laugh every time a person gives us the impression of being a thing.* ... The comic is that side of a person which reveals his likeness to a thing, that aspect of human events which, through its peculiar inelasticity, conveys the impression of pure mechanism, of automatism, of movement without life. Consequently it expresses an individual or collective imperfection which calls for an immediate corrective. This corrective is laughter, a social gesture that singles out and represses a special kind of absent-mindedness in men and in events. ...

Hence the equivocal nature of the comic. It belongs neither altogether to art nor altogether to life. On the one hand, characters in real life would never make us laugh were we not capable of watching their vagaries in the same way as we look down at a play from our seat in a box; they are only comic in our eyes because they perform a kind of comedy before us. But, on the other hand, the pleasure caused by laughter, even on the stage, is not an unadulterated enjoyment; it is not a pleasure that is exclusively esthetic or altogether disinterested. It always implies a secret or unconscious intent, if not of each one of us, at all events of society as a whole. In laughter we always find an unavowed intention to humiliate, and consequently to correct our neighbour, if not in his will, at least in his deed. This is the reason a comedy is far more like real life than a drama is. The more sublime the drama, the more profound the analysis to which the poet has had to subject the raw materials of daily life in order to obtain the tragic element in its unadulterated form. On the contrary, it is only in its lower aspects, in light comedy and farce, that comedy is in striking contrast to reality: the higher it rises, the more it approximates to life; in fact, there are scenes in real life so closely bordering on high-class comedy that the stage might adopt them without changing a single word.